T-LEVELS
THE NEXT LEVEL QUALIFICATION

New Collaborative Learning Trust

This book is due for return on or before the last date shown below.

- 7 OCT 2024

Tassoni

Louise Burnham

Janet King

HODDER EDUCATION
AN HACHETTE UK COMPANY

This edition follows Version 4 of the T Level Technical Qualification in Education and Childcare, first teaching from September 2023.

This resource has been endorsed by national awarding organisation, NCFE. This means that NCFE has reviewed them and agreed that they meet the necessary endorsement criteria.

Whilst NCFE has exercised reasonable care and skill in endorsing this resource, we make no representation, express or implied, with regard to the continued accuracy of the information contained in this resource. NCFE does not accept any legal responsibility or liability for any errors or omissions from the resource or the consequences thereof.

'T-LEVELS' is a registered trade mark of the Department for Education.

'T Level' is a registered trade mark of the Institute for Apprenticeships and Technical Education. The T Level Technical Qualification is a qualification approved and managed by the Institute for Apprenticeships and Technical Education.

Every effort has been made to trace all copyright holders, but if any have been inadvertently overlooked, the Publishers will be pleased to make the necessary arrangements at the first opportunity.

Although every effort has been made to ensure that website addresses are correct at time of going to press, Hodder Education cannot be held responsible for the content of any website mentioned in this book. It is sometimes possible to find a relocated web page by typing in the address of the home page for a website in the URL window of your browser.

Hachette UK's policy is to use papers that are natural, renewable and recyclable products and made from wood grown in well-managed forests and other controlled sources. The logging and manufacturing processes are expected to conform to the environmental regulations of the country of origin.

Orders: please contact Hachette UK Distribution, Hely Hutchinson Centre, Milton Road, Didcot, Oxfordshire, OX11 7HH. Telephone: +44 (0)1235 827827. Email education@hachette.co.uk Lines are open from 9 a.m. to 5 p.m., Monday to Friday. You can also order through our website: www.hoddereducation.co.uk

ISBN: 978 1 0360 0509 2

© Penny Tassoni, Louise Burnham and Janet King 2023

First published in 2021
This edition published in 2023 by
Hodder Education,
An Hachette UK Company
Carmelite House
50 Victoria Embankment
London EC4Y 0DZ

www.hoddereducation.co.uk

Impression number   10 9 8 7 6 5 4 3 2

Year   2027 2026 2025 2024

All rights reserved. Apart from any use permitted under UK copyright law, no part of this publication may be reproduced or transmitted in any form or by any means, electronic or mechanical, including photocopying and recording, or held within any information storage and retrieval system, without permission in writing from the publisher or under licence from the Copyright Licensing Agency Limited. Further details of such licences (for reprographic reproduction) may be obtained from the Copyright Licensing Agency Limited, www.cla.co.uk

Cover photo © Jules Selmes Photography

Illustrations by Integra Software Services Pvt. Ltd., Pondicherry, India.

Typeset in India by Integra Software Services Pvt. Ltd., Pondicherry, India.

Printed by CPI Group UK

A catalogue record for this title is available from the British Library.

Contents

Acknowledgements and photo credits iv

Guide to the book vi

THE CORE

Core Chapter 1	Wider Context	1
Core Chapter 2	Supporting Education	15
Core Chapter 3	Safeguarding, Health and Safety and Wellbeing	42
Core Chapter 4	Behaviour	58
Core Chapter 5	Parents, Families and Carers	81
Core Chapter 6	Working with Others	92
Core Chapter 7	Child Development	103
Core Chapter 8	Observation and Assessment	136
Core Chapter 9	Reflective Practice	152
Core Chapter 10	Equality and Diversity	162
Core Chapter 11	Special Educational Needs and Disability	172
Core Chapter 12	English as an Additional Language	193
Core Skill 1	Communicate information clearly to engage children and young people	203
Core Skill 2	Work with others to plan and provide activities to meet children's and young people's needs	205
Core Skill 3	Use formative and summative assessment to monitor children's and students' progress to plan and shape educational opportunities	206
Core Skill 4	How to assess and manage risks to your own and others' safety when planning activities	207

EARLY YEARS EDUCATOR

PO1	Support and Promote Children's Play, Development and Early Education	211
PO2	Develop Relationships with Children to Facilitate their Development	253
PO3	Plan, Provide and Review Care, Play and Educational Opportunities to Enable Children to Progress	264
PO4	Safeguard and Promote the Health, Safety and Wellbeing of Children	281
PO5	Work in Partnership with Colleagues, Parents, Carers and Other Professionals to Support Children's Development	332
Assessment		340

Glossary 348

Index 352

Acknowledgements

We would like to thank all the teachers who have given their feedback to us during the development of this textbook, including: Fiona Craig, Grimsby Institute, TEC Partnership; Dawn Hiscox, Peter Symonds College; Penny Muka, Uxbridge College; Bernadette Turner, Dudley College of Technology; and Jill Clausen, Havant & South Downs College.

Penny Tassoni

I would like to thank my great friend and co-author, Louise Burnham, for her support during this project. I would also like to thank my other co-author, as well as Rachel Edge, Ruth Murphy and Emma Coopshon for their work. My thanks also go to the numerous practitioners and teachers whose dedication to children has inspired me. Finally, I need to thank my family, and especially Sofia and Olivia, who are helping me to maintain a 'hands on' approach to my writing.

Louise Burnham

I would like to thank Gemma Kirby, Nadeem Qureshi and Paul Showell for their advice around secondary assessments, Heather Rouse for information on the EYFS to Year 1 transfer, and Luke Burnham for information about iGCSEs.

I would also like to thank Rachel Edge and Ruth Murphy at Hodder Education and my co–authors, Penny Tassoni and Janet King, for all their support during this process.

Janet King

With thanks to Hodder Education and my co-authors for their positive encouragement and support. To all the wonderful colleagues and students, both past and present, that I have had the pleasure and privilege to work with, and to all education and childcare students and staff for the difference that they make to babies, children, and young people every single day. With love to my family.

Photo credits

The Publishers would like to thank the following for permission to reproduce copyright material.

Page 1 © Jules Selmes/Hodder Education; page 4 © JulesSelmes/Hodder Education; page 8 © fizkes - stock.adobe.com; page 10 © Jules Selmes/Hodder Education; page 11 © JulesSelmes2014; page 12 © Getty Images/iStockphoto/Thinkstock; page 14 © Monkey Business / stock.adobe.com; page 15 © Robert Read / Alamy Stock Photo; page 17 © Jules Selmes/Hodder Education; page 20 © Monkey Business/stock.adobe.com; page 24 © Jacob Crees Cockayne/Hodder Education; page 27 © Penny Tassoni; page 36 © Blend Images / Alamy Stock Photo; page 38 © Monkey Business/stock.adobe.com; page 42 © Monkey Business - stock.adobe.com; page 47 © Shutterstock / Monkey Business Images; page 56 © ilona75/123RF.com; page 58 © Jules Selmes/Hodder Education; page 63 © Jules Selmes/Hodder Education; page 66 © Monkey Business – stock.adobe.com; page 74 © Jacob Crees Cockayne/Hodder Education; page 75 © Jules Selmes/Hodder Education; page 81 © Africa Studio – stock.adobe.com; page 86 © Africa Studio – stock.adobe.com; page 89 © Ben/stock.adobe.com; page 90 *l* © PicsArt – stock.adobe.com, *r* © Maryna – stock.adobe.com; page 92 © Jules Selmes/Hodder Education; page 99 © Jules Selmes/Hodder Education; page 103 © Jacob Crees Cockayne/Hodder Education; page 105 © Jacob Crees Cockayne/Hodder Education; page 106 © Jacob Crees Cockayne/Hodder Education; page 111 © Jacob Crees Cockayne/Hodder Education; page 114 © Uschi Hering – stock.adobe.com; page 117 © Jules Selmes/Hodder

Photo credits

Education; page 123 © Jules Selmes/Hodder Education; page 124 © Jacob Crees Cockayne/Hodder Education; page 130 © Jules Selmes/Hodder Education; page 133 *l* © Jules Selmes/Hodder Education, *r* © Picture Partners / Alamy Stock Photo; page 136 © Monkey Business – stock.adobe.com; page 139 © Jacob Crees Cockayne/Hodder Education; page 141 © lordn/stock.adobe.com; page 146 © Image Source / Alamy Stock Photo; page 148 © Jules Selmes/Hodder Education; page 150 © Jules Selmes/Hodder Education; page 152 © contrastwerkstatt/stock.adobe.com; page 157 © WavebreakmediaMicro / stock.adobe.com; page 162 © Rawpixel.com / Shutterstock.com; page 168 © Jacob Crees Cockayne/Hodder Education; page 171 © Wavebreak Media Ltd / 123RF; page 172 © Stella – stock.adobe.com; page 174 © Jules Selmes/Hodder Education; page 176 © Hammersmith and Fulham Council; page 187 © BSIP SA / Alamy Stock Photo; page 191 © mjowra. –123RF; page 193 © Angela Hampton Picture Library / Alamy Stock Photo; page 198 © stockphoto mania – stock.adobe.com; page 199 © Jules Selmes/Hodder Education; page 202 © Jacob Crees Cockayne/Hodder Education; page 204 © zinkevych – stock.adobe.com; page 208 © felix – Fotolia; page 210 Reproduced by kind permission of HSE. HSE would like to make it clear it has not reviewed this product and does not endorse the business activity of Hodder Education.; page 212 © Tomorrow's Child UK Ltd ; page 218 © digitalskillet1 – stock.adobe.com; page 220 © Jules Selmes/Hodder Education; page 223 © tan4ikk – stock.adobe.com; page 225 © Crown Copyright, covered by the Open Government Licence; page 226 © JulesSelmes2014; page 238 © Jacob Crees Cockayne/Hodder Education; page 243 © Picture This Images / Alamy Stock Photo; page 244 © Matej – stock.adobe.com; page 253 © Andrew Callaghan/Hodder Education; page 254 © mavoimages – stock.adobe.com; page 256 © Impact Photography – stock.adobe.com; page 261 © Jules Selmes/Hodder Education; page 263 © Jules Selmes/Hodder Education; page 264 © Jules Selmes/Hodder Education; page 266 © Cavan–Images – Shutterstock.com; page 272 © Penny Tassoni; page 281 © Jules Selmes/Hodder Education; page 284 © Andrew Callaghan/Hodder Education; page 286 © Lost_in_the_Midwest – stock.adobe.com; page 287 © Kawee – stock.adobe.com; page 290 © Digital Mammoth – stock.adobe.com; page 292 © Andrey Kuzmin – stock.adobe.com; page 296 © Kzenon – stock.adobe.com; page 300 © Jules Selmes/Hodder Education; page 306 © Natalia Lisovskaya/stock.adobe.com; page 308 © Sherry Young – stock.adobe.com; page 311 © stopabox – stock.adobe.com; page 318 © Md Saddam Hossin / Alamy Stock Vector; page 324 © 24K-Production - stock.adobe.com; page 331 © subhanbaghirov – stock.adobe.com; page 332 © JackF – stock.adobe.com; page 337 © Robert Kneschke - stock.adobe.com

Contains public sector information licensed under the Open Government Licence v3.0.

Contains public sector information published by the Health and Safety Executive and licensed under the Open Government Licence.

Education and Early Years T Level: Early Years Educator

Guide to the book

When starting your T Level Technical Qualification in Education and Early Years course, you should check on the NCFE QualHub website to find out which version of the specification you should be following. This textbook follows Version 4, which is first teaching from September 2023. If you are following a later version, ensure you know how your version has been updated.

The following features can be found in this book.

Learning outcomes

Core knowledge outcomes that you must understand and learn.

Key term

Understand important terms.

Reflect

Tasks and questions providing an opportunity to reflect on the knowledge learned.

In practice

Tasks and questions designed to apply knowledge in workshops and simulated working environments.

Test yourself

A knowledge consolidation feature containing questions and tasks to aid understanding and guide you to think about a topic in detail.

Research

Research-based activities – either stretch and challenge activities, enabling you to go beyond the course, or industry placement-based activities encouraging you to discover more about your placement.

Practice points

Helpful tips and guidelines to help develop professional skills during the industry placement.

Good to know

Highlights knowledge content that will be useful when completing your OS synoptic assessments.

Case study

Placing knowledge into a fictionalised, real-life context. Useful to introduce problem solving and dilemmas.

CORE Chapter 1:
Wider Context

In this chapter, we will be looking at the scope of provision in education and childcare, the features and functions of the services available for babies, children and young people and their families, and how these support them.

As well as exploring this vast and diverse range of service provision, you will be introduced to the different occupational roles that exist across the education and childcare sector, and learn about the responsibilities that staff working in these roles hold.

Learning outcomes

This chapter covers the following knowledge outcomes for Core Element 1:
- **1.1** Understand the differences between a range of early years and education provision, from 0–19 years
- **1.2** Understand the different responsibilities of a range of roles, the entry requirements and possible career progression routes in the sector

1.1 Early years and education provision from birth to 19 years

As you learn about the service provision and the diverse roles and responsibilities held by staff, you will also increase your own knowledge and understanding of the diverse employment opportunities open to you. Before we start to explore the different types of setting it will be useful to introduce some terms.

Types of setting

- **Voluntary:** This means provision that has been set up and funded by donations and voluntary contributions. It may, for example, be run by a charity or church group in the local community, and parents may have to pay a donation to help cover costs. In some cases, parents or carers may stay and supervise their children so that they can socialise with others, but the ways in which these settings operate vary. If children are left with staff, the setting will need to be registered with and inspected by **Ofsted**.
- **Private:** This means that parents need to pay for the provision as it is run privately. This may include settings such as a crèche, a workplace nursery, private day nursery or a childminder's home. These settings will need to be registered with and inspected by Ofsted if they are providing regular care and education for children. For example, a childminder will need to be registered and inspected, but a crèche that may just provide care from time to time does not.
- **Statutory/maintained:** This term is used for settings that are government-funded as they have to be available by law, such as schools. They will be registered and inspected by Ofsted. They may also be known as 'maintained' settings.
- **Independent:** This term is usually used for independent schools that are not paid for by government or state funding, so in most cases, parents will be charged for them (some free or subsidised places are offered in line with schools' charitable status, and certain children may be placed in an independent school by local authorities – see page 7.). Independent schools will still have to follow the Early Years Foundation Stage (EYFS) Framework and are also inspected by Ofsted.
- **Homeschooling:** Parents have the right to educate their children at home (Education Act 1996). See page 6 for more information.

> **Key term**
>
> ***Ofsted:*** stands for the Office for Standards in Education, Children's Services and Skills. Ofsted inspects and regulates services providing education and skills for learners of all ages, including those who care for babies, children and young people.

Early years provision

Let's begin by considering the range of early years and education provision that may be accessed by babies, children and young people, their features and how they operate so that similarities and differences can be identified.

In their early years, children may be cared for by a range of different services across early years provision, including:
- childminders
- nannies
- nurseries
- pre-schools.

Childminders

Childminders work in their own homes and look after other people's children, often combining this with caring for their own children. Lone working can be demanding and challenging as there will be no one else to lend a hand. However, childminders can choose the hours they work and the services they provide.

Childminders will care for children's welfare, learning and development, and develop trusting professional relationships with parents, carers and others as required. Childminders are professionals providing **holistic** care and educational learning experiences. They need to plan for and resource diverse play provision for babies and children, often across a range of ages, provide food and drinks (or prepare them if they are provided by parents/carers), and promote physical care routines such as nappy changing and toileting, rest and sleep provision, and outdoor experiences.

> **Key term**
>
> ***Holistic:*** overall or all round; the idea that the parts of something are interconnected so looking at the whole rather than each individual part. Here, it means all-round care needs, with an appreciation of the contribution of each care need to overall wellbeing.

CORE Chapter 1: Wider Context

> **Good to know**
>
> 'Anyone who looks after one or more children under the age of eight years in England or under the age of 12 years in Wales, to whom they are not related, on domestic premises, for reward, and for a total of more than two hours in any day must register as a childminder.'
>
> (Source: Professional Association for Childcare and Early Years (PACEY))
>
> www.pacey.org.uk
>
> Childminders who do not register may receive a fine or even a prison sentence if they do not register with Ofsted.

Registered childminders are typically self-employed and run their own business from home, or they may register through a childminding agency. It is not unusual for childminders to employ childminding assistants as their business grows, and this allows them to care for more children at any given time.

In England, the **childminder ratios** identifying the number of children that a childminder can care for, and the safeguarding and welfare requirements that must be in place, are included within the **Early Years Statutory Framework**.

You will learn more about the areas of learning and how the Early Years Statutory Framework is arranged in other chapters, specifically on pages 16–18. If you take the Early Years occupational specialism you will spend more time exploring its requirements.

There is pre-registration training and guidance that childminders need to undertake, and continuing professional development (CPD) is always recommended.

A childminder may apply for different types of registration:
- The **Early Years Register** is for those caring for children from birth to the 31 August after their fifth birthday. All registered childminders in England on the Early Years Register are inspected against the requirements of the Early Years Statutory Framework.
- The **Childcare Register**, which has two parts: compulsory registration for childminders that are caring for children aged from five up to eight years, and voluntary registration for childminders caring for children aged eight and over.

Many childminders are on both registers to enable them to care for a wide age range of children, but the appropriate ratios must be maintained for the age group (see Good to know).

> **Good to know**
>
> Childminders must be aware of ratios. The ratios will inform them how many children, and their age ranges, they can care for at any time. The Early Years Statutory Framework will guide childminders with regard to their role, including up-to-date information about ratios.

What do nannies do?

Nannies usually care for babies and children belonging to one family in the parents'/carers' own home. Sometimes, a nanny will be 'live in', but they can also live outside the home and travel to work. Nannies typically work alone to meet the needs of the babies and young children they care for. They may also be employed to work overseas. A professional nanny will carry out similar roles to a childminder, but typically for the children of one family in the family's home.

Nanny agencies may be able to support both the nanny and the family, and will be able to offer advice on important issues such as:
- **placement** – bringing the nanny and family together, and supporting both parties to maintain a positive relationship
- **contract** – nanny contracts can be essential in ensuring the nanny has a valid and reasonable job description and terms of employment
- **suitability checks** – the nanny agency may undertake recruitment safety checks such as a Disclosure and Barring Service (**DBS**) check, paediatric first aid, training and qualifications, as well as employment history; some nanny agencies may be able to support nannies with any training requirements
- **legal obligations** – the agency may be able to offer advice around contracts, pensions and taxation.

> **Key term**
>
> **DBS:** stands for Disclosure and Barring Service, part of the suitability checks that must be made on individuals in the UK involved in the care of children and young people under 18 years of age. These specifically look at any criminal convictions recorded against an individual and are an important feature of safeguarding. You will find out more about DBS processes as you prepare for placement, as it is likely you will be required to undertake a DBS check yourself.

For more on safeguarding, see Core Chapter 3.

The nanny agency may also be able to promote social networks for the nanny, which is very important, especially if he or she is living away from home.

> **Research**
>
> Visit https://nationalcareers.service.gov.uk/job-profiles/nanny to find out more about what it is like to work as a professional nanny.

Nursery provision

▲ Can you think of different types of early years settings?

There are two main types of nursery provision: day nursery and statutory/maintained nursery school or class. The latter is usually attached to a primary school. Independent nursery settings are also available.

Day nursery provision caring for children from birth to five years of age

This is usually a private provision and parents/carers will pay for their child to have a place at the nursery. There are, however, government-funded free childcare places that certain children are entitled to if they meet particular criteria. The day nursery is usually open all year round and for most of the day, from early morning to early evening. The day nursery will be registered with and inspected by Ofsted. The day nursery must meet the requirements set within the Early Years Statutory Framework.

Staff working in a day nursery work in ratio according to their training and qualifications, and meet the holistic care needs of children, including physical, cognitive, speech, language and communication, social and emotional.

Qualifications that staff hold will vary from Level 2 to Level 7 (master's level), and the roles are equally diverse, but everyone is likely to be involved in observing children and planning for their next steps in line with the statutory framework. Day nurseries are often accessed by students for practical work placements following an early years specialism.

Statutory/maintained nursery schools or classes are local authority funded schools, with a head teacher and qualified teachers leading a team of specialist early years staff, providing education and care for three to four year olds (and increasingly for two year olds).

A **nursery class** is usually part of a primary school and will typically be led by a nursery teacher. Parents do not pay for their child/children to attend. Children are typically aged three to four when they attend, but some may be younger. The nursery will be open in term time only. Children will usually move on to the primary school and the head of the primary is the head teacher for the nursery class too. The nursery will be inspected by Ofsted and follow the requirements of the Early Years Statutory Framework.

A **nursery school** will function in the same way as a nursery class but statutory maintained nursery schools are not typically part of a primary school and will have their own head teacher. Nursery schools can be statutory/maintained or independent. Examples of independent nursery schools include Montessori nursery schools.

> **Research**
>
> ▶ Look up independent Montessori nursery schools and statutory/maintained nursery schools to find out more about them.
> ▶ Summarise information regarding their approaches, and any similarities and differences in the services they offer.
> ▶ Present your findings as a chart or table.

Pre-schools

Pre-schools are classed as voluntary settings. This implies that there is no cost. In practice, though, costs usually do apply, however, these costs are low. Pre-schools often provide three hours of sessional care for children. Children attend pre-schools at around the age of two years, and provision is similar to the staffing and regulatory requirements of day care. Parents are often actively involved in pre-school settings.

CORE Chapter 1: Wider Context

> **Good to know**
>
> '[In England] Children must start full-time education once they reach compulsory school age. This is on 31 December, 31 March or 31 August following their fifth birthday – whichever comes first.'
>
> (Source: www.gov.uk/schools-admissions/school-starting-age)

> **Reflect**
>
> To help you to consolidate your knowledge and understanding:
> - Compare and contrast the forms of early years sector provision listed above.
> - What similarities can you find?
> - What are the differences between the types of sector provision?

Read the following case study and reflect on the discussion points.

> **Case study**
>
> Anita is the mother of two children under five years of age: Shelley is 18 months and Lola is four. Anita is planning to return to full-time work in the next two months and is considering the childcare options available to her.
> - Work in small groups to identify the range of provision Anita and her children could use.
> - Compare and contrast the provision identified.
> - In your group, discuss any advantages or disadvantages to different types of childcare available and share your thoughts with your peers.

School provision

There are many different types of school in the UK, educating children from age five up to age sixteen. Ofsted inspects services providing education and skills for pupils of all ages.

Maintained schools

Maintained schools, providing both primary and secondary education, are a common category. They include:
- community schools
- voluntary controlled schools
- voluntary aided schools (usually church or faith schools)
- foundation schools
- trust schools
- special schools.

> **Good to know**
>
> Children may formally leave school on the last Friday in June if they are 16 by the end of the summer holidays. They must then do one of the following until the age of 18:
> - stay in full-time education, for example, at a college
> - start an apprenticeship or traineeship
> - spend 20 hours or more a week working or volunteering, while in part-time education or training.

As mentioned earlier in this chapter, statutory maintained schools are those funded by the local authority. Parents/carers do not need to pay for their child/children to attend. As you can see from the list below, there are different types of schools that fall into the maintained category.

- **Maintained community schools** are state funded, are not influenced by business or religious groups, and must follow the National Curriculum. Teaching and learning will be led by head teachers, teaching staff and teaching assistants/learning support mentors. The school staffing structure will include non-teaching staff and an active governing body.
- **Voluntary controlled schools** usually have foundation or trust status, for instance, connected to a Christian denomination, that has some influence in the running of the school but makes no financial contribution. The teaching and learning, as well as the regulatory body, remain the same as for community schools.
- **Voluntary aided schools** – as with voluntary controlled schools, there is influence from the foundation or the trust. However, in a voluntary aided school the foundation or trust will contribute financially to the upkeep of the school.
- **Foundation schools** function in the same way as a maintained school, with greater responsibility placed on the governing body, which is sometimes supported by representatives from religious groups in the running of the school.
- **Trust schools** function as foundation schools, supported by a charitable foundation (the charitable foundation is known as a trust).

- **Special schools** are attended by children who have an **education, health and care plan (EHCP)**. The admission of children with an EHCP to schools is a decision made by the local authority, which has statutory responsibility for arranging appropriate provision via the Statutory Special Educational Needs Panel. The admissions process for a special school admission involves either an EHCP or information and evidence gathered at an annual review meeting. Special schools with pupils aged 11 and older can specialise in one of the four areas of special educational needs:
- communication and interaction
- cognition and learning
- social, emotional and mental health
- sensory and physical needs.

  Schools can further specialise within these categories to reflect the special needs they help with, for example autistic spectrum disorders, visual impairment or speech, language and communication needs (SLCN).

> **Key term**
>
> *Education, health and care plan (EHCP):* an EHCP is for children and young people aged up to 25 who need more support than is available through special educational needs support; it is drawn up to outline provision for a child or young person following an assessment of special educational needs. EHCPs identify educational, health and social needs, and set out the additional support to meet those needs. Find out more here: www.gov.uk/children-with-special-educational-needs/extra-SEN-help
>
> For more on assessment of special educational needs, see Core Chapter 11, page 179.

> **Good to know**
>
> Maintained schools in England must follow the National Curriculum. They may focus on specific subjects (such as RE in a church school) but the curriculum must be followed appropriately at each key stage. Maintained schools must also follow the SEN Code of Practice.

Non-maintained schools

Just because maintained schools are funded by the local authority, this does not mean that all non-maintained schools are not (i.e. charge fees to attend). Non-maintained schools are divided into:
- academies
- free schools
- private schools (including independent special schools).

Academies

Academies are run by an academy trust and receive their funding directly from the government. They have more control over how they do things than community schools. Academies do not charge school fees. Academies are inspected by Ofsted and follow the same rules on admissions, special educational needs and exclusions as other state schools. They can decide upon the length of school terms and the school day and whether or not to follow the National Curriculum. Students attending academies sit the same exams as other state schools. If a school funded by the local authority is judged 'inadequate' by Ofsted then it *must* become an academy.

Free schools

Free schools are funded by the government but are not run by the local authority and therefore have more control over how they do things. Free schools are 'all-ability' schools and do not use academic selection processes like a grammar school. As with academies, free schools can decide upon the length of school terms and the school day and whether or not to follow the National Curriculum. They can also set their own pay and conditions for staff.

Private schools

Private schools (also known as independent schools) charge fees to attend and do not receive general government funding. Similar to academies and free schools, pupils do not have to follow the National Curriculum. All private schools must be registered with the government and are inspected regularly.

Under the Children and Families Act 2014, an **independent special school** is an independent school that is organised to make **special educational provision (SEP)** for pupils with special educational needs. There may be circumstances when the local authority must pay a pupil's fees – for example, if the independent school is named in the pupil's education, health and care plan (EHCP), which means the local authority then has a financial responsibility.

> For more on pupils with special educational needs, see Core Chapter 11.

Home schooling

As mentioned on page 2, parents have the right to educate their children at home. In this case, children must have access to a full-time curriculum. They do not need to follow the National Curriculum, however, learning will be monitored by the local authority. Children with SEND or a school attendance order must be given consent from the local authority for home schooling.

> **Research**
>
> Find out more about independent special schools on the government website: **www.gov.uk/government/publications/independent-special-schools-and-colleges**
> Find out more about alternative provision for children and young people.

> **Good to know**
>
> Students aged 16–25 can request a SEND assessment themselves. For example, an individual may request a diagnosis for dyslexia. Find more information here: **www.gov.uk/children-with-special-educational-needs/extra-SEN-help**

> **Test yourself**
>
> Produce a table including the maintained and non-maintained school provision talked about in this section. In the table, identify as many features and functions for each provision as you can. Next, highlight the similarities and summarise any differences.

Post-16 provision

Of course, educational opportunities continue after the age of 16 and there is a diverse range of provision available for students in England once they have turned 16 years of age. There are different categories of qualifications and courses of study. This includes a more 'academic' path, studying for A-levels, Applied General Qualifications or the International Baccalaureate, or a wide range of more 'vocational' courses, including apprenticeships and traineeships for competence-based, work-related employment training, and technical education that allows students to prepare for specific occupational roles, as well as support with progression to higher education.

Let's take a look at the different settings where students can undertake the variety of training options open to them:

- school sixth forms
- sixth-form colleges
- general further education and **tertiary colleges**
- private, independent and voluntary providers (publicly funded)
- employers
- special colleges (including agriculture and horticulture colleges)
- art, design and performing arts colleges
- higher education institutions (HEIs).

School sixth forms

School sixth forms are based in schools and cater for students aged 16–19. This period of study is also referred to as Key Stage 5, or Years 12 and 13. While studying in sixth form, students typically prepare for A-level, International Baccalaureate or technical qualifications. A student can be in sixth form in a maintained school or in a private school.

Sixth-form colleges

Sixth-form colleges are generally larger than a school sixth form, but smaller than a further education college. The range of courses offered is, therefore, likely to be more diverse than that of the school sixth form.

Further education colleges

Further education (FE) colleges generally offer a wider provision than sixth form. For example, as well as A-level, International Baccalaureate or technical qualifications at Key Stage 5, the student will be able to find a course that is set at various levels, often beginning at Level 1 and stretching to Level 5, including higher-level apprenticeships and foundation degrees. Some colleges work in partnership with HEIs (universities) to deliver degree programmes too. FE colleges prepare students for the world of work as well as for study at higher level. Students accessing FE colleges are diverse, including adult students and students with special educational needs.

> **Key terms**
>
> *Tertiary college:* an institution that provides general and vocational FE for students aged 16–19. Such colleges provide the next stage of education, after primary and secondary. They are distinct from general FE colleges in that they cater for a specific age group, and offer a less extensive and varied curriculum.
>
> *Further education colleges:* include general FE and tertiary colleges, sixth-form colleges and specialist colleges, as well as adult education provision. You can find out more on the government's website.

Private, independent and voluntary providers (publicly funded)

Students may train and work within the private, independent and voluntary sector. For example, you may complete your study with a private training company rather than in a school or college. Apprentices may complete their training under the supervision of private, independent and voluntary provision – for example, a private day nursery, an independent school, or within a charitable or not-for-profit organisation.

Employers

Certain employers have worked with the Institute for Apprenticeships and Technical Education in the production of apprenticeship standards. Employers have significantly influenced the standards for education and training due to their leadership in their sectors.

Special colleges (including agriculture and horticulture colleges)

Special colleges sometimes offer residential facilities and usually focus on a particular specialist area, such as music. They have a wealth of expertise to meet the needs of children and young people with special educational needs and disabilities from secondary age and beyond.

Art, design and performing arts colleges

Art, design and performing arts are specialist areas of study where students can develop the skills needed to work in a range of roles relating to this sector.

Higher education institutions

These institutions (HEIs) offer university-level programmes. At university, students can study undergraduate and then postgraduate programmes after taking most Level 3 general or technical qualifications (such as this one). As an undergraduate, you will study towards a foundation or full degree (Level 5–6 qualification); as a postgraduate, you may study towards a master's (Level 7) or even a doctorate (Level 8).

▲ Can you think of any learning benefits from collaborating with peers?

Research

- Find out about three universities offering undergraduate programmes in education and early years provision. What entry requirements do they ask for? What sorts of study programmes are included?
- Find out more about traineeships and apprenticeships in education and early years provision by looking at the Institute for Apprenticeships and Technical Education website: **www.instituteforapprenticeships.org**
- Identify the knowledge, skills and behaviours relevant to roles within early years education and teaching assistant roles.

Reflect

Andreas is 16 years of age. He would like to be a primary school teacher. What options does Andreas have to reach his career goal?

Olivia is 16 years of age and would like to work as an early years educator for two years and then train to be a nursery teacher. What options does Olivia have to reach her career goal?

How and when education became compulsory in England and how this has changed over time

Educating children has not always been a legal requirement or open to all, and the law in England has evolved regarding at what age children must start and finish their schooling. The table below shows the most significant dates in this process.

CORE Chapter 1: Wider Context

Year	Change in education law	
1870	Introduction of compulsory education	For the first time, the government mandates the provision of elementary education for children aged 5–13 years of age under the Elementary Education Act 1870. Attendance is compulsory for boys and girls aged 5–10 years of age until attainment of the 'educational standard'.
1893–1921	School leaving age raised	The school leaving age is raised to 11 in 1893, 12 in 1899 and to 14 in 1921.
1944	The Education Act 1944	State education is now free for all children. The act created separate primary schools (for children aged 5–11) and secondary schools (11–15). Local education authorities (LEAs) also had to ensure nursery provision, disability provision and boarding. The compulsory school age was raised to 15, then 16 in 1972.
1972	Compulsory education raised to age 16	Preparation for raising the school leaving age started in 1964 and was established in 1972 in preparation for school leavers the following June.
1988	The Education Reform Act 1988	This act introduced a compulsory National Curriculum consisting of 14 subjects. Teachers were no longer in charge of the curriculum but were accountable for it through the introduction of compulsory standardised assessments at ages 7, 11, 14 (SATs) and 16 (GCSE).
2008	The Education and Skills Act 2008	Government statistics showed that 11% of 16 to 18 year olds were neither continuing their education after completion of their GCSEs, nor in full-time employment or an apprenticeship. This led to increased unemployment rates. A child may leave school on the last Friday in June if they will be 16 by the end of the summer holidays. They must then do one of the following until they are 18: • stay in full-time education, for example, at an FE college • start an apprenticeship or traineeship • spend 20 hours or more a week working or volunteering, while in part-time education or training.

▲ How the law in England has evolved regarding the age at which children must start and finish schooling

Regulation

In this section, we are going to find out a little bit more about regulation and how regulation contributes to education and childcare specifically, including:
▶ Department for Education (DfE)
▶ Office for Standards in Education, Children's Services and Skills (Ofsted)
▶ Office of Qualifications and Examinations Regulation (Ofqual).

Department for Education (DfE)

The **Department for Education** is the part of government responsible, in England, for Children's Services and education, including early years, schools, higher and further education policy, apprenticeships and wider skills.

The DfE has key responsibilities for teaching and learning in education. It also produces statutory guidance around legislation to influence how we work within education and childcare. This guidance is produced through the development of policies and procedures intended to keep babies, children and young people safe, healthy and well.

Many key publications, such as *The Early Years Statutory Framework* and *The National Curriculum*, are published by the Department for Education.

Office for Standards in Education, Children's Services and Skills (Ofsted)

We have already discussed **Ofsted** in this chapter (page 2), including a key term and examples of the role of Ofsted. Ofsted works to keep babies, children and young people safe, and to promote high standards in education and childcare.

Ofsted inspects and regulates registered settings in education and childcare to raise standards, and ensure that babies, children, young people and adults who are accessing education receive the best possible teaching and learning. Inspections are carried out regularly to maintain standards, set action plans and support quality in practice (www.gov.uk/government/organisations/ofsted).

Office of Qualifications and Examinations Regulation (Ofqual)

The **Office of Qualifications and Examinations Regulation (Ofqual)** regulates qualifications, examinations and assessments in England.

Regulated qualifications include general education, such as GCSEs and A-levels, Technical qualifications and others that have been submitted by awarding organisations (exam boards) for regulation. This means that Ofqual has a responsibility to check that the qualifications meet appropriate standards, that they prepare the students taking them for work or further study, and that teachers and students have all the information they need to deliver the qualification successfully. Ofqual will also consider how well the qualifications prepare students for the next stage; this is sometimes referred to as how 'fit for purpose' the qualifications are. Regulation by Ofqual reassures everyone involved that qualifications have been thoroughly considered for validity and reliability (www.gov.uk/government/organisations/ofqual).

1.2 Occupational roles in education and childcare

This section looks in more detail at the different responsibilities of the diverse roles that exist in education and childcare, to help you consider the specific entry requirements for particular occupations and understand possible career progression routes in the sector.

To help us to categorise the occupational roles, let's consider them as general roles and specialist roles. Bear in mind, however, that it is possible that an individual identified as working in a general role will also be responsible for a specialist role – for example, a teacher may also be a designated safeguarding officer/lead person.

General roles in education and childcare

These can be categorised as follows:
- early years practitioner
- early years educator
- room leader
- teaching assistant
- teacher/lecturer
- head teacher.

Early years practitioner

This is a designated occupational role within the early years workforce. The **early years practitioner** will be qualified at Level 2 in early years care and education, and will work alongside the Level 3 early years educator.

The qualification that the early years practitioner holds means they meet the criteria required to work within this occupational role. The responsibilities they hold are diverse, and they will be involved in all aspects of caring for babies and young children from birth to five, as identified in the Early Years Statutory Framework.

Their daily routine is likely to include most or all of the following duties:
- meeting the individual physical care routines of children
- observing and planning
- working with others, including parents/carers, colleagues and other professionals
- record keeping and reporting
- promoting effective playful interactions with babies and young children.

▲ How is this adult enhancing the children's experiences?

Early years educator

The **early years educator** is a designated occupational role within the early years workforce. They will be qualified at Level 3 and will work within the ratios specified in the Early Years Statutory Framework. A Level 3 early years educator, once qualified, will be able to progress within the early years workforce to take a position such as room leader, and may also take up leadership, deputy management and management roles. The early years educator will undertake all the duties of the early years practitioner, but will hold greater responsibility and accountability for intervention and quality, as appropriate. The early years educator will take an active role as a key person, observing and planning for next steps effectively, liaising with parents/carers and other professionals to ensure the best outcome for children in their care, while maintaining the requirements of the Early Years Statutory Framework to keep children safe, healthy and well.

Room leader

The **room leader** will be an experienced early years educator and, as such, all of those responsibilities will apply to this occupational role too. The room leader will be responsible for the running of a room – for example, a pre-school room with children aged three to four, or a baby room with children under two years. Although each setting will decide on the age ranges of its different rooms, children usually tend to be cared for in age ranges with time to come together as larger groups, particularly at quieter times of the day or at mealtimes. The room leader's responsibility may extend to managing budgets and ordering resources/equipment, as well as making sure that child ratios and other legislative requirements within the Early Years Statutory Framework are met. The room leader may have responsibility for undertaking peer observations, appraisals and performance management of colleagues, such as early years practitioners or students.

▲ Some teaching assistants may work one-to-one with pupils

> **Reflect**
>
> Nannies and childminders make a valuable contribution to the early years workforce; there is information about these significant roles earlier in this section. Take the opportunity to look back at the role of the professional nanny and childminder to give you a broader insight into the occupational roles that exist within the early years workforce.

> **Good to know**
>
> Occupational maps can be found on the NCFE website. The link below leads to a career progression map, which will give you the opportunity to think about different career pathways in education and childcare. The NCFE website also has case studies to read through that may inspire your own career aspirations.
>
> www.ncfe.org.uk/media/lhgf14ie/children-and-young-people-progression-map.pdf

Teaching assistant

The **teaching assistant** will support teaching and learning for individuals or for groups of pupils, working closely with the class teacher. The teaching assistant may work one-to-one with a single pupil or with a small group of children with special educational needs and disabilities (SEND) to carry out the teacher's lessons in a **differentiated** way to meet their needs (see Core Chapter 2).

> For more about SEND, see Core Chapter 11.

Teaching assistants will also update, record and monitor progress, and undertake activities such as guided reading. They will be expected to support planning and attend meetings as appropriate. There are opportunities for the teaching assistant to progress to higher level teaching assistant (HLTA) status, and in this role they will be able to undertake more responsibilities working with pupils, such as leading some lessons. A teaching assistant may also choose to undertake a graduate programme to train as a teacher.

> **Good to know**
>
> More information about the role of the teaching assistant and the qualifications that can support this pathway can be found on the NCFE website:
> www.ncfe.org.uk/sector-specialisms/education-and-training/
>
> You can find out more about higher level teaching assistant standards at the HLTA website:
> www.hlta.org.uk

Education and Early Years T Level: Early Years Educator

▲ What does this photo tell you about the level of engagement between the teacher and the children?

> **Good to know**
>
> Various pathways to head teaching are outlined on the National Careers website: https://nationalcareers.service.gov.uk/job-profiles/headteacher

Teacher/lecturer

Teachers and lecturers usually have similar responsibilities. For example, both are involved in advancing teaching and learning through planning, team collaboration and significantly raising students' knowledge, understanding and skills through effective strategies. The qualifications and the journey the teacher and lecturer may take may vary, however.

- The **teacher** is likely to work in school environments and will be a qualified teacher (QTS). Their training will have included study at higher education level in order to achieve QTS.
- The **lecturer** is likely to work in further or higher education and, as well as academic qualifications, may also have significant industry experience. For example, a lecturer in early years may have worked extensively in the early years workforce. To teach in higher education, universities often require postgraduate qualifications and a commitment to ongoing research.

Head teacher

The head teacher will be responsible for the day-to-day running of the school. Being a head teacher is a challenging and responsible position. Some of the responsibilities required of this role are:
- liaise with the governing body
- engage with the school ethos and values/mission in partnership with pupils, staff, parents and carers
- lead teaching and learning
- staff recruitment, appraisal and disciplinary procedures.

Specialist roles

Some of the specialist roles that exist within education and childcare include:
- special educational needs and disabilities coordinator (SENDCo)
- designated safeguarding lead (DSL)
- mental health lead
- mentor/pastoral support
- physical activity and nutrition coordinator (PANCo)
- counsellor
- careers advisor.

Individuals holding a general role within education and childcare may also be responsible for some of the specialist roles that are listed here.

Special educational needs and disabilities coordinator (SENDCo)

Each setting, whether an early years setting or a school, will have a **SENDCo** in place. The SENDCo will be responsible for liaising with parents/carers, colleagues and other professionals to ensure that individual children's needs are met, and resources and equipment provided in line with organisational policy and procedures, and in adherence with the Special Educational Needs Code of Practice.

In an early years setting, an experienced early years educator usually takes this role. There are qualifications that can be taken at Level 2, Level 3 and Level 4 to support the SENDCo to manage their responsibilities efficiently. In a school, a class teacher will undertake the role of SENDCo and formal training will be required to hold this responsibility.

Designated safeguarding lead (DSL)

Safeguarding babies, children and young people is everyone's responsibility. However, in education and childcare, a named member of staff will hold the position of **designated safeguarding officer** or **designated safeguarding lead**, in line with the Children Act 2004. Having a named member of staff holding responsibility for safeguarding means there can be clear leadership, guidance and professional partnerships.

The designated safeguarding lead will undergo relevant training to be able to support staff in recognising signs and symptoms of need in babies, children and young people, and will advise staff, ensuring that processes for raising concerns are clear and straightforward. The designated safeguarding lead will take a role in recording and reporting to ensure best practice.

> **Research**
>
> Statutory guidance is updated regularly to ensure the best possible outcomes for babies, children and young people.
>
> Visit **www.gov.uk** to see the latest information and guidance around the role of the designated safeguarding officer/lead and summarise your findings.

Mental health lead

The emotional health and mental wellbeing of children and young people is significant to holistic health, development and learning. Working in education and childcare, mental health lead practitioners will support children, young people and their families, as well as supporting staff with appropriate strategies and approaches to promote positive wellbeing.

> **Research**
>
> The Mental Health Foundation Association has produced useful documents to support an understanding of the importance of recognising mental health in children and young people, and the significance of intervention for a child's holistic health and wellbeing.
>
> Find out more about the important specialist role of the mental health first aider in education and childcare here: **https://mhfaengland.org**

Mentor/pastoral support

Mentoring supports staff to develop confidence and competence in education and childcare. A mentor is more experienced or more knowledgeable in a particular aspect of the occupational role and helps by guiding and supporting a less experienced or less knowledgeable person. This is often seen at the beginning of someone's career, where an experienced colleague mentors a new member of staff.

On placement, you may be mentored by an experienced colleague. Their specialist knowledge and skills can be invaluable in helping you to develop the knowledge, understanding and skills that are required in this type of work.

Pastoral support for children and young people in education and childcare is concerned with the child's or young person's overall health, welfare and wellbeing. This is a whole-school approach that is concerned with how children and young people are settling in to their environment. Mentoring programmes, such as 'buddy systems' that connect younger and more experienced pupils/students with one another, can make a positive difference during transition or when learning new skills.

Physical activity and nutrition coordinator (PANCo)

Many early years settings are striving to have a member of staff responsible for promoting physical exercise and nutrition in the setting. The **physical activity and nutrition coordinator (PANCo)** will have undertaken specific training at Level 4 in order to lead in this specialist role. They will advise staff and liaise with parents to improve the setting's approach in this area.

Counsellor

If staff in education and childcare are concerned about the welfare and wellbeing of children and young people they may consider specialist intervention. There are different professionals that can support in times of need – for example, an **educational psychologist** can carry out assessments to support individuals with possible learning difficulties, and may also support children with emotional problems that may impact self-esteem and behaviour. **Children and Young People's Mental Health Services (CYPMHS)** offers specialist support, including counselling. A **social worker** may be able to provide counselling services, especially where safeguarding and welfare concerns have been raised.

Careers advisor

Careers advisors in education are able to inform students about a diverse range of occupational roles, training and qualifications, study programmes and career journeys, such as opportunities for promotion.

Careers advisors will also be able to support with administration issues such as writing a CV, applying for a job or for further study, and are skilled in using assessment tools such as psychometric testing.

▲ It is important for young people to be included in discussions involving them to help them reach informed decisions about their futures

Case study

Jayden is three years of age. He lives with his mum and younger sister, who is aged 14 months. Nursery staff are concerned about Jayden's emotional wellbeing. During their observations, they have noticed how Jayden, usually a friendly and sociable young boy, has become withdrawn, even shying away from interaction with his **key person**. Jayden's key person met with his mum at nursery. Jayden's mum became very upset as she explained that Jayden's dad was seriously ill and being cared for in a hospice.
- ▶ Summarise the situation and the potential impact on Jayden, his sister and their mum.
- ▶ How could the setting support Jayden and his family?
- ▶ What other professionals may be able to offer support to Jayden and his family at this very sad time?

Key term

Key person: a member of staff in an early years setting who works closely with a designated group of children and their parents, carers and family.

See Core Chapter 5 for more information.

Assessment practice

1. Identify **two** features of maintained schools.
2. List **one** similarity and **one** difference between academy schools and maintained schools.
3. List **three** responsibilities held by an early years educator.
4. Summarise the role of Ofqual in education and childcare.
5. A local authority primary school is an example of:
   a) a private service
   b) a statutory service
   c) a voluntary service.
6. Which of the following do **not** need to follow the National Curriculum?
   a) academy schools
   b) voluntary aided schools
   c) state primary schools
   d) state secondary schools
7. Describe the role of the designated safeguarding lead in education and childcare.
8. Explain the role of Ofsted in education and childcare.
9. Compare the role of the childminder with that of the professional nanny.
10. Analyse the role of the physical activity and nutrition coordinator for children's holistic health and wellbeing.

CORE Chapter 2:
Supporting Education

Supporting children's and young people's education is complex. In this chapter, we look at the education frameworks in England and also the skills that adults need to work effectively with children and young people, which include providing feedback. We consider different theories of how children and young people learn and also the factors that might affect their development, including the role of metacognition skills. This chapter looks at the role of technology in learning, and we also consider why some children and young people may find literacy and mathematics challenging.

Learning outcomes

This chapter covers the following knowledge outcomes for Core Element 2:

2.1　The origin and purpose of the Early Years Foundation Stage and the National Curriculum from Key Stage 1 to Key Stage 4

2.2　The skills and attributes that support children's and young people's education

2.3　Current theoretical and pedagogical approaches applied in education and the evidence that underpins them

2.4　How metacognition supports children and young people to manage their own learning

2.5　How practitioners provide effective feedback and why it is important in supporting children's and young people's educational development

2.6　Why up-to-date and appropriate technology is important to effectively support children's and young people's educational development

2.7　How personal, educational and environmental factors may affect engagement and development in reading, literacy and mathematics

2.1 The origin and purpose of the Early Years Foundation Stage and the National Curriculum from Key Stage 1 to Key Stage 4

The Early Years Foundation Stage

The Statutory Framework for the Early Years Foundation Stage is usually referred to as the EYFS. It was introduced in 2008 to improve opportunities for children aged from birth to five years (including the reception year) and also to ensure minimum safety and welfare standards were in place. There were revisions to it in 2012 and 2017, and most recently in 2021. The EYFS built upon previous governments' curricula and requirements dating back to 1996, when funding for free or subsidised nursery places for specific age groups was first introduced for parents.

Early Learning Goals and Assessment

The EYFS has **Early Learning Goals**, which are outcomes that most children are expected to achieve by the end of their reception year. These outcomes are measured by teachers carrying out observations and then assessing children's progress. This measurement is known as the **Early Years Foundation Stage Profile (EYFSP)**. Results of the profile are passed on to the government via local authorities. At the time of writing, children will also have a communication and language assessment from 2021 when they first start in the reception class. This measurement is known as the **Reception Baseline Assessment (RBA)**.

Schools providing EYFS and National Curriculum

Some primary schools have a nursery as well as a reception class. When this is the case, they will be working with both curricula. They are required to provide the EYFS for nursery and reception, but then the National Curriculum for children once they start in Year 1.

Inspection of education settings

The inspection of most education settings, including childminders' and early years settings in England, is carried out by Ofsted. In private or independent schools, this work is done by a separate inspection body called the Independent Schools Inspectorate, whose work is monitored by Ofsted. Ofsted reports its findings to the Department for Education. It also publishes reports each year about overall trends in standards in education.

> See Core Chapter 1 for more on the inspection of education settings.

The scope of the Early Years Foundation Stage (EYFS)

The EYFS does not just look at early education, but also sets legal requirements for the safeguarding and wellbeing of children aged from birth to five years in early years settings and in the reception year. These requirements cover staffing ratios, outings and the administration of medicines. Inspections of early years settings look at both the quality of education and whether settings are meeting safeguarding and welfare requirements.

> **Research**
>
> Download the latest copy of the Statutory Early Years Foundation Stage Framework from the **gov.uk** website.
>
> Work out how many adults are needed to work in a day care setting without a qualified teacher for each of the following:
> ▶ eight babies aged from birth to ten months
> ▶ seven children aged two years
> ▶ 12 children aged three to four years.

Learning and development requirements

There are seven areas of learning and development set out in the EYFS. Since 2012, they have been split into two sections: prime and specific. The prime areas of the EYFS are seen as the foundation for later learning and so are the focus for working with babies and toddlers.

There are three prime areas, as shown in the diagram and described opposite.

CORE Chapter 2: Supporting Education

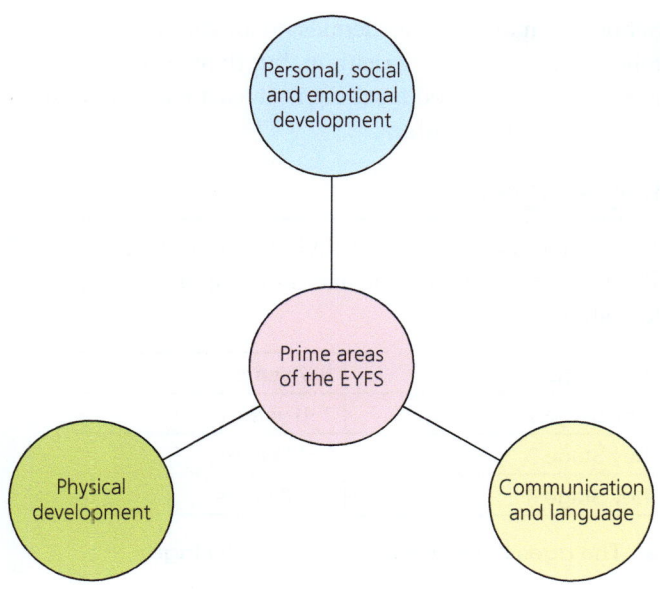

▲ The prime areas of the EYFS

1. **Personal, social and emotional development (PSED):** this area of learning and development is about children's emotional and social skills as well as their behaviour and attitudes.
2. **Physical development:** this area of learning and development is about children's physical skills. At the time of writing, it also includes learning about being healthy, but this may change with the revisions proposed for 2021.
3. **Communication and language:** this is about developing children's ability to talk, listen and understand. Learning new vocabulary is part of this.

The progress check at age two

When children are two years old, early years settings are required to do a check that looks at the progress children are making in the prime areas. This is often referred to by practitioners as the **progress check** or the 'two-year-old check'. This check was introduced in 2012 and the aim was that it would link to a health check of two year olds carried out by health visitors.

> For more on the role of health visitors, see Core Chapter 6.

Specific areas of learning and development

In addition to the prime areas, there are four specific areas of learning and development. These link to later curriculum areas within the National Curriculum.

1. **Mathematics:** this area of learning and development looks at several aspects of mathematics including number, shape, size and measurement.

> **Research**
> ▶ Look at a copy of the EYFS and read the section that outlines mathematics as an area of learning and development.
> ▶ Read the Early Learning Goals for mathematics.
> ▶ To what extent do the Early Learning Goals assess the entirety of the area of learning and development?

2. **Literacy:** this area of learning and development looks at children learning to read, write and understand texts. In the early years, this includes helping children to develop a love of books, poems and rhymes.

▲ How might sharing books with young children encourage a love of books later?

3. **Understanding of the world:** this area of learning and development focuses on children learning about their local community, nature, and also their personal history and that of others. In the current EYFS, this area also includes technology.
4. **Expressive arts and design:** this is a wide-ranging area that includes music, painting and modelling, but also role play and drama.

Characteristics of effective teaching and learning

To help early years settings understand how best to provide activities and opportunities for the areas of learning development, the EYFS gives three characteristics of how babies and young children learn:
1. Playing and exploring
2. Active learning
3. Creating and thinking.

These are known as the characteristics of effective teaching and learning, and Ofsted looks at them as part of its inspections.

> **Research**
>
> Find out more about the characteristics of effective teaching and learning by downloading and reading a recent copy of the EYFS and also *Development Matters*, the guidance published to support the EYFS.
>
> For each characteristic of effective teaching and learning, can you explain how children might show it through how they approach play and experiences?

The National Curriculum

The **National Curriculum** was introduced in England in 1988. Its aim was to make sure that all pupils were having the same opportunities to learn key subjects and also that there was a way of measuring standards. Before the National Curriculum was introduced, it was the responsibility of individual schools to decide what and how much to teach of any subject. As part of the National Curriculum, tests known as SATs (Statutory Assessment Tests) were also introduced at the end of each key stage.

Schools that are now academies no longer have to follow the National Curriculum, but they must ensure that their content and teaching is at least equivalent to the National Curriculum.

Key stages

The National Curriculum is divided into four stages. The table below shows the ages associated with each **key stage**.

Key Stage 1	5–7 years
Key Stage 2	7–11 years
Key Stage 3	11–14 years
Key Stage 4	14–16 years

▲ The ages associated with each key stage

The content of the National Curriculum is decided by the Department for Education. By law, the Department for Education is required to publish programmes of study for each National Curriculum subject. Schools can, however, organise how they teach the content provided that it is taught to all pupils. Subjects in the National Curriculum are split into **core subjects**, which are English, mathematics and science, and **foundation subjects**.

The table below lists the core and foundation subjects that are required at different key stages.

Key stages	1	2	3	4
Age	5–7	7–11	11–14	14–16
Year groups	1–2	3–6	7–9	10–11
Core subjects				
English	✔	✔	✔	✔
Mathematics	✔	✔	✔	✔
Science	✔	✔	✔	✔
Foundation subjects				
Art and design	✔	✔	✔	
Citizenship			✔	✔
Computing	✔	✔	✔	✔
Design and technology	✔	✔	✔	
Languages		✔	✔	
Geography	✔	✔	✔	
History	✔	✔	✔	
Music	✔	✔	✔	
Physical education	✔	✔	✔	✔

▲ The core and foundation subjects required at different key stages

Key Stage 4

Pupils in Key Stage 4 are preparing for GCSEs or other Level 2 qualifications, and so there is more flexibility since they have some choice over what they study. All pupils must still study English, mathematics and science; these are known as 'core' subjects. In addition, they must continue with computer science, physical education and citizenship, although they may not need to be assessed in these; these are known as foundation subjects. Pupils also have to take at least one subject from the following:
▶ arts (art and design, music, dance, drama and media arts)
▶ design and technology
▶ humanities (geography, history, religious education)
▶ modern foreign languages.

The EBacc (English Baccalaureate)

To encourage schools to offer pupils a spread of GCSEs that will give them a broad base of study, the government has introduced the **English Baccalaureate (EBacc)**. The EBacc is not a qualification in itself, but a performance indicator. Schools are measured on the number of pupils that take GCSEs in these subjects.

The EBacc is composed of:
▶ English language and literature
▶ maths
▶ the sciences (either two GCSEs that cover physics, chemistry and biology, or three single-science GCSEs, which might include computer science)
▶ geography or history
▶ a modern or ancient language.

Alternative options to GCSEs

Some schools will offer vocational qualifications alongside GCSEs. These may include technical qualifications in health and social care, business studies or travel and tourism.

> **Reflect**
>
> What subjects did you study at Key Stage 4?
>
> Which subjects did you take a GCSE or Level 2 vocational equivalent in?

Other requirements for schools

In addition to the National Curriculum, schools also have other teaching requirements, as described.

Worship and religious education

All state schools have to make provision for a daily act of collective worship – many schools will hold an assembly, for example. Schools must teach religious education to pupils at every key stage.

Relationships and sex education (RSE)

Primary schools are required to provide relationships education in Key Stages 1 and 2. Sex education is not compulsory in Key Stages 1 and 2, although primary schools will cover reproduction as part of the science curriculum. Where a primary school provides sex education, parents can choose to withdraw their child.

In Key Stages 3 and 4, schools must provide sex and relationships education. However, if they choose, parents can ask that their child be excused for all or some of the lessons.

Post-16 education: 16–19 years (A-levels and technical)

After pupils have finished Key Stage 4, they have the following choices.
▶ Find a job.
▶ Begin an apprenticeship. Apprentices take a qualification while working for an employer. The apprentices are paid an apprentice wage, which is set by the government. Apprenticeships last between one and four years depending on the level of the qualification that is being taken.
▶ Take a traineeship. These are often short-term jobs with an employer that may later lead to an apprenticeship. The amount of training that takes place will depend on the employer.
▶ Study for a technical qualification such as a T Level.
▶ Study for A-levels.

They may also combine work or volunteering (20 hours or more) with part-time education or training.

All young people must continue to study maths and English if they have not achieved Grade 4 in their GCSEs (or equivalent) as part of their post-16 education. They can either resit these GCSEs or take equivalents, e.g. in functional skills.

> **Reflect**
>
> ▶ Why did you choose to study a technical qualification?
> ▶ Did you consider any other post-16 routes?
> ▶ Do you know anyone who chose another route? How has this gone for them?

2.2 The skills and attributes that support children's and young people's education

There are many ways in which adults support children and young people with their education.

Involving children in planning their own learning

One of the ways that adults use to support children and young people is to involve them in planning for their own learning. This might mean asking pre-school children which resources and activities they might like. In a school setting, it might mean asking children or young people to choose projects to work on or decide on ways to present information. Involving children and young people is more likely to motivate them. This usually results in them concentrating harder, which means they are more likely to learn.

> **Reflect**
>
> In your placement, look at the ways in which adults give children and/or young people opportunities to plan their own learning.
>
> What are the benefits of this approach?

Communicating clearly, using positive and appropriate language for the age and stage of development

Being able to communicate well with children and young people is perhaps one of the most important skills to master. To communicate well, you need to adapt what you are saying or how you are saying it to the individual child or young person. This means that the way an adult might communicate to a nervous three year old will be different to the communication style used with a confident fourteen year old. To communicate well you need to focus on the following elements.

Language level

You need to think about the language level of the child or young person. This is linked to their age and stage of development. It is worth remembering that some children and young people may be new to English. Some children and young people may have disabilities such as hearing loss, language delay or special educational needs that affect how easily they can understand spoken language.

> See Core Chapter 12 for more on English as an additional language.

Facial expression and body language

Our faces and our bodies are important in communication. Positive communication such as smiling, using our hands or nodding when listening works well when providing information. On the other hand, when reprimanding or trying to prevent unwanted behaviour, adults may look sterner!

▲ Why is positive communication important in teaching young people?

Posture

Whether we stand, sit, kneel or squat makes a difference to communication. Positive communication is more likely when we are at the same level as the child or young person. This is particularly important to remember with young children. With older children and young people, there may be times when by standing rather than sitting you convey that you have authority. Standing over a child or young person is not, however, helpful when encouraging, coaching or supporting is our aim.

Proximity

Proximity refers to how close we are to the child or young person. Being at a distance can make it harder for a child or young person to pay attention. Ideally, for encouraging, supporting and coaching, you should aim to be fairly close, but not so close for it to feel threatening.

> **Reflect**
>
> Watch how adults in your placement setting communicate with children/young people.
> - How do they hold their attention?
> - How do they adapt their language and communication style to suit the situation or the individual they are working with?

Giving effective feedback and facilitating children's and young people's self-assessment

As part of being able to communicate with children and young people, we need to be able to provide them with feedback. We also need to help them analyse their own work and progress. This is called **self-assessment**. We look at feedback and self-assessment later in this chapter.

Managing your own and others' time

To work well with children and young people, you need to be organised. This includes time management: your own and other people's.

Managing your time

You need to be punctual, but also learn how long tasks take to do – for example, how long it takes to put up a display or set up a role-play area. Knowing how long things take means you can plan your time carefully. There are consequences when you do not manage your time. Children and young people who are waiting for things to be ready are more likely to show unwanted behaviour because they become bored. Colleagues and parents may also become frustrated with you and, over a period of time, may lose confidence in you.

Managing others' time

During lessons and activities, you need to keep an eye on the time and also judge how long it will take children and young people to do things. If adults do not do this well, there is a danger that children and young people will not have time to finish tasks and activities or tidy away. This can lead to children and young people feeling rushed or frustrated because they can never finish things. In some cases, the opposite can be true. Some children or young people may finish quickly and then become bored waiting. This is one reason why careful planning and differentiating activities is so important. Differentiating activities is about making sure that children and young people are given tasks that are matched to their level of skills and knowledge.

> **Practice points**
>
> Take the following steps to help you with time management.
> - Wear a watch or keep a clock near you.
> - Time how long it takes children and young people to do things such as collecting resources or tidying away.
> - Allow more time when you are doing things for the first time.
> - When planning activities and lessons always allow a little extra time.
> - Watch how other adults manage their time.

Understanding a child's behaviour

There are many factors that might affect how a child responds and behaves. We look at these factors in more detail in Unit 4. One of the factors that affects children is their ability to regulate their emotions and actions. Adults help children develop this skill in a range of ways. One of these is called 'co-regulation'. Co-regulation means actively supporting children at moments when they are feeling overwhelmed, for example, taking an older child to a quiet place or cuddling a baby who is upset.

> We look at ways of managing behaviour in Core Chapter 4.

Observing and assessing individuals

One of the ways we support education is to recognise the skills and knowledge that have been acquired by children and young people. This is done through observation and assessment, which are covered in Core Chapter 8.

As part of observing and assessing, we also need to identify where children or young people would benefit from having more support or teaching. **Early identification** is very important – the earlier we identify children and young people who need additional support, the better. This is because, otherwise, children may begin to believe that they are not capable and so lose motivation. The term **tailored intervention** is used to describe when we provide support that is designed to help children and young people develop a specific skill or piece of knowledge.

> **Key terms**
>
> **Early identification:** quickly recognising that a child or young person may need additional support.
>
> **Tailored intervention:** designing support to help a child or young person pick up a specific skill or piece of knowledge.

Engaging disengaged children and young people by involving them in their own learning and assessment

Some children and young people can lose interest or motivation. As we saw a little earlier in this section, encouraging them to be involved in their learning and also assessment can be a good strategy.

Attributes that inform teachers'/practitioners' professional behaviour and why they are important to effectively support children's and young people's education

What makes a good teacher or practitioner? As well as using various skills, there are certain professional behaviours that are needed. The table below shows these professional behaviours and the reasons why they support children's and young people's education.

Approachability	When a child or young person needs more support or reassurance when they have a problem, they need an adult who looks friendly and kind.
Confidence	Children and young people need to feel secure. Adults who look and sound confident can help them feel safe.
Empathy	Adults need to understand how a child or young person might be feeling and then to show empathy.
Knowledge	Children and young people need adults who know about what they are teaching. For young children, it is important that adults also use accurate language.
Passion	Adults who work best with children and young people and love helping them, will love their work and want to be in the setting.
Patience	Children and young people learn things at different speeds. They may also work harder sometimes than others. Being patient is, therefore, essential.
Positivity	Adults who work well with children and young people manage to remain enthusiastic even when things are not going smoothly. They are positive with children and young people, but also with their colleagues and other adults.
Reflection	The ability to step back and think about a situation or a child's or young person's needs is essential. Being able to reflect can allow us to change how we are doing things, to make it easier for children and young people to learn.
Resourcefulness	Being able to think creatively and also think quickly is important for adults working with children and young people. It may be that a piece of equipment that was key to an activity is broken and we quickly have to come up with a new activity.
Respect for others	Adults who work well in education and childcare settings have respect for others. This shows in their relationships with colleagues, parents and also with children and young people. By showing respect for children and young people, we are also acting as role models for them in their relationships with others.

▲ Professional behaviours and how they support children's and young people's education

> **Case study**
>
> Chris is a Key Stage 2 teacher. He specialises in science teaching and takes different year groups across the school. The children respond well to him. He has a sense of humour, but can also be firm where necessary. He is kind and warm and goes out of his way to support children who need a little more time for their learning. One of the reasons why the children enjoy his teaching is that he surprises them with new experiments. He also follows children's interests and encourages them to be active in their learning. He looks at the outcomes that need to be taught and thinks about the best way to make them interesting for children. When it is his turn to teach a class, he arrives on time and has with him the resources he needs. His colleagues respect and like him because he is reliable, friendly and always ready to help out.
> ▶ What attributes does Chris show?
> ▶ How do these attributes help him to be an effective teacher?
> ▶ What impact might Chris have on children's education?

2.3 Current theoretical and pedagogical approaches applied in education and the evidence that underpins them

Education is an area where new ideas frequently emerge about how best to support children and young people to learn. Theories and ideas about teaching and learning are often influenced by developments in other areas including psychology, philosophy, computer science and neuroscience. In some cases, ideas about teaching and learning emerge that are relevant only to certain age groups. An example of this, as we will see, is the use of online courses which by their nature cannot be used with children in early years settings.

For the purposes of this qualification, five theoretical and pedagogical approaches are given:
1. behaviourism
2. cognitive constructivism
3. social constructivism
4. connectivism
5. humanism.

The way these approaches have been interpreted and the evidence given to support them may not be recognised in other contexts.

Behaviourism

Behaviourism is an approach that has its roots in psychology and zoology. Some principles of behaviourism are now associated with explaining and shaping children's and young people's behaviour. In this specification, behaviourism is looked at in the context of helping children and young people remember information.

An example of behaviourism is when children learn their multiplication tables by rote in order to receive praise or a reward.

In psychology, the term **conditioning** is an important feature in behaviourism. It refers to the way that responses are shaped as a result of what happens to the child or young person. The term **stimuli** (singular: **stimulus**) is used to describe the 'triggers' or the 'what happens' part of the process. Two types of conditioning emerged in the field of psychology: classical conditioning and operant conditioning.

Classical conditioning

Classical conditioning occurs when the stimuli is presented first. Two experiments showed how classical conditioning worked. (These are given in the specification as examples of underpinning evidence, although they would not be considered as relevant in education in other contexts.)
▶ Ivan Pavlov did a study where a bell rang before dogs were fed. After a while, the dogs learned that the bell signalled food, and started to salivate when they heard a bell, even when eventually no food was given.
▶ John Watson showed that classical conditioning could create a phobia in a child. The child, named 'Little Albert', became afraid of a rat because a loud noise was made whenever he saw the rat.

Operant conditioning

Operant conditioning is associated with B.F. Skinner's work. The specification for this T Level lists his work as underpinning evidence for behaviourism. He suggested that humans and animals learn through exploring the environment and then drawing conclusions based on the consequences of their behaviour. His work acknowledged the role of being active in the learning process. This is an important difference from classical conditioning.

Skinner used the term 'reinforcers'. A **reinforcer** strengthens or weakens the response following an action. Skinner divided reinforcers into three groups:
1. positive reinforcers
2. negative reinforcers
3. punishments.

A **positive reinforcer** is something that is likely to increase the likelihood of the action being repeated. Skinner suggested that using positive reinforcement was the most effective way of encouraging new learning. Positive reinforcers for children include gaining adults' attention, praise, sweets and treats. Positive reinforcement is the most commonly used method of shaping children's and young people's responses in education. In the classroom, positive reinforcers include stickers, attention or even a smile from the teacher.

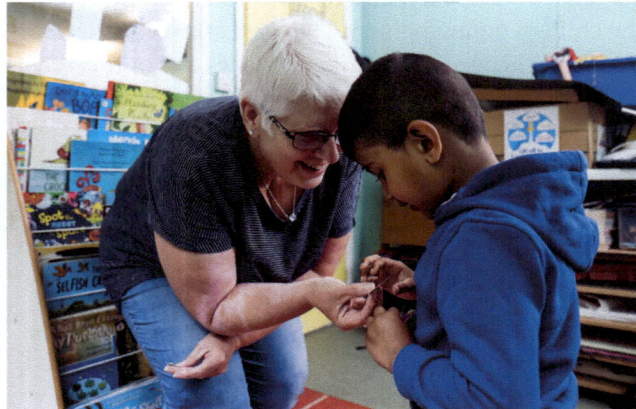

▲ How might being awarded this sticker affect how this child behaves in the future?

Negative reinforcers are likely to make us repeat behaviour as well, but this is usually to stop something from occurring. If a parent continually nags a child to tidy up and the child gets tired of being nagged, they might tidy up in order to stop the nagging.

Punishers (things to be avoided) are likely to stop us from repeating behaviour. For example, we may learn to stay away from an electric fence after receiving a shock.

Skinner found during his experiments that it was often hard to predict what would act as a reinforcer, and that it was sometimes only after the event that this became clear. An example of this is when children sometimes deliberately behave badly in order to attract an adult's attention. If they manage to attract the attention, they are more likely to show the behaviour again, despite being told off. Gaining the adult's attention in this case is the positive reinforcer even if they are being told off.

Sometimes the action of the child or young person will be in itself the positive reinforcer. For example, a toddler might repeatedly climb onto a table because they have learned that they like the sensation of climbing.

Using behaviourism as an approach in education is complex, for two reasons:
1. Continuity: behaviourism can be used to support learning and shape behaviour, but information may not be retained if it is not practised for a while.
2. Motivation: the learner is motivated by the reinforcement that the teacher provides, such as receiving a sticker or praise from the teacher. If positive reinforcement stops, learners may not continue with the activity.

Behaviourism is therefore rarely used as a single approach when teaching. This is because it is thought that when a child or young person wants to learn something, they retain and understand the information better.

The specification gives an outline of the theory, which is shown in this table. (This is a simplified model and it may not be recognised in other contexts.)

Element of the theory	Explanation of the element
Antecedents	A stimuli that signals expected behaviour/responses.
Consequences	A stimuli that encourages or reduces the occurrence of the behaviour.
Positive and negative reinforcement	Reinforcement can modify behaviour and learning (operant conditioning).
Continuity of reinforcements	Continuity is essential for making long-term associations in learning. Using reinforcements becomes habit/response-forming.
Association of experience (positive/negative reinforcement) with behavioural response	The student's motivation for learning is dependent on the teacher's response.

▲ Elements of behaviourism theory

Pedagogical approach

Three ways are given in the specification as to how behaviourism might be used when teaching.

1. Questioning:

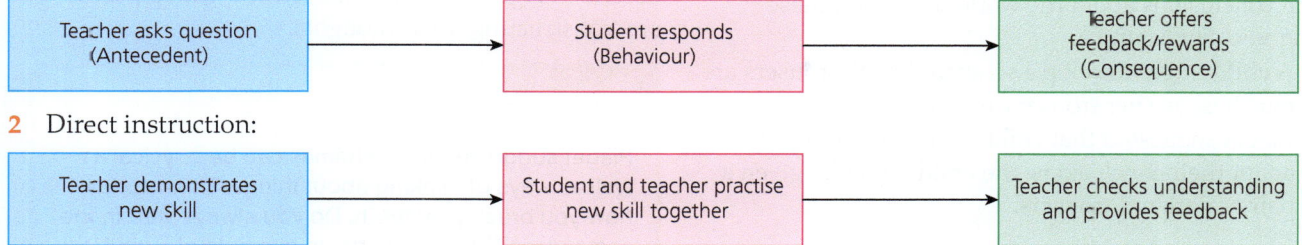

2. Direct instruction:

3. Mastery learning: this is a new approach to teaching mathematics. It involves:
   - the **key instant recall facts (KIRF)** approach, which supports a solid grasp of key facts
   - a blend of direct instruction and practice
   - feedback provided by both teacher and peers.

Underpinning evidence

The examples in this table are used in the specification to suggest that they are linked to the behaviourist approach. However, some of them will not necessarily be recognised as relevant by others.

Behaviourist studies	Explanation
Bloom's taxonomy	Bloom helped to classify educational objectives such as 'identify' or 'evaluate' into different levels and the skills associated with them. Teachers can use this system to help them design programmes that support learners to make progress.
Pavlov's dogs study	This study showed that dogs could be trained to salivate in response to a bell rather than food (see page 23).
Watson's 'Little Albert' experiment	Watson showed that phobias can be created if punishers are associated with an object or animal (see page 23).
Skinner's study of operant conditioning (Skinner box)	Skinner showed that using reinforcers (especially rewards) could shape the behaviour of rats and also pigeons. Rats had to find their way out of a maze-type box, and were given food when they succeeded. Skinner showed that, over time, the rats became faster at navigating the maze.

▲ Underpinning evidence for behaviourism

Constructivism

While behaviourism focuses on the importance of learning as the result of stimuli and rewards, constructivism takes the approach that there are active processes taking place for the child or young person. They are not passive in the learning. Two types of constructivism are given in the specification: **cognitive constructivism** and **social constructivism**. Both approaches agree that children are active learners and construct their thinking as a result of experiences.

Cognitive constructivism

This approach focuses on the cognitive processes that take place when learning occurs. It focuses on how a child's or young person's thinking changes as a result of new information.

A key influence in this approach is Jean Piaget. His work is given in the specification as underpinning evidence for this approach.

Jean Piaget

Jean Piaget was originally a zoologist but became involved in testing children's intelligence. He soon became fascinated by the way that young children seemed to have their own logic, and that groups of children at the same age often gave the same incorrect answers. Having observed his own children closely and also carried out experiments with children of different ages, he created a theory that explains how children learn and also how their cognitive development changes over time.

Education and Early Years T Level: Early Years Educator

Children's thinking

Piaget came to the conclusion that children develop patterns of actions and thinking that provide them with conclusions about the world. He called these **schemas**. For example:

▶ A child might develop a schema that all trousers are blue because her trousers are blue.
▶ Piaget suggested that children are later forced to adapt their conclusions: the child might be given a pair of dark red trousers.

Piaget used specific terms to describe how young children develop or adapt new schemas. The terms **assimilation** and **accommodation** are used in the specification.

> **Key term**
>
> *Schema:* a pattern of thought or behaviour.

The process of absorbing new information and then developing new schemas to accommodate the new information is why the term **constructivist** is used to describe Piaget's theory. Children and young people are 'constructing' their thoughts.

> **Reflect**
>
> Piaget suggested that schemas can be physical as well as ways of thinking about things. Think about how you brush your teeth. Do you always start in the same place? This would be an example of a physical schema.
>
> What other physical schemas are part of your daily routine?

> **Research**
>
> The concept of the child as an active learner is reflected in the EYFS. Download a copy of the EYFS by visiting www.education.gov.uk
> ▶ Read the section relating to the characteristics of learning.
> ▶ How does this relate to Piaget's view that children learn using their experiences?

Piaget's stages of cognitive development

Piaget also suggested that as children develop and have more experiences, these are reflected in their thinking. He grouped children's cognitive development into four broad stages. Each stage has certain features. The table below outlines these four stages.

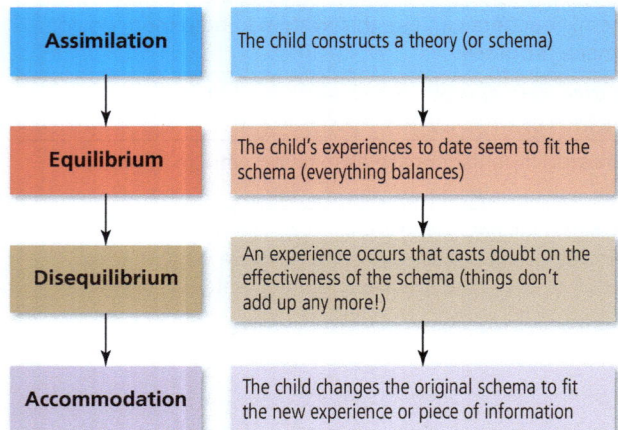

▲ Piaget's theory of how children develop or change existing schemas

Stage	Features	Development
Sensorimotor 0–2 years	Development of object permanence Child begins to use symbols, e.g. language	Babies' first schemas are physical ones. They learn to repeat movements and control them. By 8–9 months, babies gain the concept of **object permanence**. They search for objects that have been hidden rather than accept that they have 'disappeared'. Babies start to understand that words have meanings – thus they are starting to use symbols.
Preoperational (2–7 years)	Child uses symbols in play and thought Egocentrism Animism Inability to conserve	Children become active users of symbols, especially in their play; e.g. a cardboard box is used as an oven. Children assume that their experiences and preferences are shared by everyone else. Piaget called this **egocentrism**. They talk or draw objects as if they had feelings too; e.g. a sun with a happy face. Piaget called this **animism**. Children have not understood conservation (see below).

CORE Chapter 2: Supporting Education

Stage	Features	Development
Concrete operations (7–11 years)	Ability to conserve Children begin to solve mental problems using practical supports such as counters and objects	Children understand that just because objects may have been reordered, the quantity remains the same: 10 counters in a circle is the same as 10 counters in a straight line. Piaget called this **conservation**. Children understand the importance of rules and enjoy games that have rules. They also impose rules on others; e.g. 'You can't put that there!' They use everyday objects and their own experiences to help them solve and think about problems; e.g. a child makes a bridge that looks like one that she has seen.
Formal operations (11–15 years)	Solving abstract problems without props Ability to analyse and hypothesise	Young people are now able to manipulate thoughts and ideas to solve problems without needing practical props; e.g. reading a map. They are also able to hypothesise about situations in a realistic way; e.g. 'What would you do if someone gave you £1000 to do badly in an exam?' Interestingly, later in life, Piaget suggested that formal operations did not develop automatically, and that experience and training may be needed in some areas.

▲ Piaget's stages of cognitive development

▲ How is the child showing animism in this drawing?

Research

It is interesting to repeat one of Piaget's tests with children. Ask your placement supervisor if you can observe a child in your setting aged four years.
▶ Set out eight buttons in a row.
▶ Count the buttons with the child.
▶ Agree that there are eight buttons there.
▶ Move the buttons around to form a close group.
▶ Ask the child if there are still the same number. What do they say?

Pedagogical approach

The specification gives three ways in which the cognitivist approach may be used in different types of settings (these links may not be recognised in other contexts).

1 HighScope: this is an early childhood programme that began in the USA. Teachers provide challenging experiences and resources matched to students' stage of development.

Research

Some settings in the UK have been influenced by the HighScope approach. Find out more about HighScope by visiting https://highscope.org/our-practice/preschool-curriculum/

2 Project-based learning: students engage in real-life problems, such as designing a product, and are responsible for their choices, decisions and solutions.
3 Virtual reality: using digital technology, learning takes place within a simulated real-world environment. Here the student directly interacts with objects, tests out their ideas and instantly experiences the result of their actions

Underpinning evidence

Four sources are given as underpinning evidence for the cognitivist approach, including Piaget's four stages of development, which we have already considered.

Jerome Bruner's three modes of representation

Jerome Bruner's work has several aspects. In the specification, he is listed as underpinning evidence for both cognitive constructivism and also social constructivism.

In terms of cognitive constructivism, he suggested that there are different modes of thinking. Adults can access all of them, but children acquire them over time.

Mode of thinking	Explanation
Enactive 0–1 years	Learning and thought take place because of physical movements.
Iconic 1–6 years	Thoughts are developed as mental images; e.g. a child thinks about milk and sees in their mind a picture of it.
Symbolic 7 years+	Thinking can be encoded using symbols such as language or numbers; e.g. a child can write down their thoughts.

▲ Bruner's modes of thinking

Kolb's experiential learning cycle

David Kolb presents a learning theory which is based on the principles of active learning and the processing of information. His learning theory is still influential and has affected practice in many education settings.

He outlines four stages in the learning process. Each stage needs to be completed for learning to take place, but where the learner starts in the circle would depend on their learning style. (See the diagram depicting Kolb's experiential learning cycle, on page 153.)

- Concrete experience: the learner tries out something themselves.
- Reflective observation: the learner considers how well they did.
- Abstract conceptualisation: the learner thinks about how to improve on their attempt, which might be seeking advice or reading information.
- Planning active experimentation: the learner considers their experience of doing the activity alongside their new insights, and thinks about how they will approach the task or activity next time.

Kolb's learning theory is discussed again on page 153.

> **Research**
>
> Visit the Institute for Experiential learning's website to look at a video explaining Kolb's learning theory:
>
> https://experientiallearninginstitute.org/resources/what-is-experiential-learning/

Bloom's taxonomy

Bloom's taxonomy is included as underpinning evidence for cognitive constructivism in the specification although this might not be included in other contexts. Bloom's taxonomy is a list of verbs that is used by educationalists to help them structure objectives and learning outcomes.

Social constructivism

Social constructivism has many similarities with cognitive constructivism, but it emphasises the importance of social interaction in the learning process.

One of the enduring names associated with this approach is Lev Vygotsky, who showed that children's thinking and understanding could be developed further through interactions with adults and older peers (see underpinning evidence, page 30).

Three key elements behind the theories of social constructivism are given in the specification. This description of the theory of social constructivism may not be recognised in all contexts.

- Active: learning is a social process between teachers and peers.
- Interactions: students' understanding and knowledge of the world are based on the quality of their interactions with others.
- Environment: the learning environment, home environment, culture and society can influence the quality of interactions.

Pedagogical approach

The specification outlines six ways in which social constructivism may be applied in different settings (these may not be accepted in other contexts).

1. Enquiry-based learning: the teacher plans activities to provoke curiosity and interaction between peers.
2. Modelling: the teacher models how to complete a task and the student observes, before practising the task for themselves.
3. Flipped learning: the teacher provides material that students can access independently (for example, through a virtual learning environment, or VLE).
   – The teacher observes and **scaffolds** activities during group learning.
   – The teacher differentiates content to make it accessible for all.
   – Formative assessments help the teacher to plan future teaching and learning.
4. Commentary:
   – To develop students' vocabulary, the teacher talks through what they are doing.
   – The teacher demonstrates thinking skills, such as problem solving.
5. Sustained shared thinking:
   – The teacher and student share a genuine interest in an activity, conversation or discovery.
   – This can occur between individuals or in a group setting.

CORE Chapter 2: Supporting Education

6   Reflection: the teacher talks about what went well and encourages the student to develop their own thinking.

> **Key term**
>
> *Scaffolding:* the way an adult supports children's and young people's learning through questions and comments.

Underpinning evidence

The following examples are given by the specification as underpinning evidence (these may not be accepted in other contexts).

Bergmann and Sams – flipping the classroom

Aaron Sams and Jonathan Bergmann were teaching chemistry at a secondary school in 2006. While searching for ways to make teaching more effective, they started to prepare materials for students to look at before they came to class. In their book *Flip Your Classroom*, they outline their project and explain how as a result of blended learning, students' interest and understanding of chemistry improved. This approach is outlined in the previous section, 'Pedagogical approach'.

Bruner's discovery learning

Bruner's work is also considered by the specification to be an example of cognitive constructivism, and we looked at his three modes of representation on pages 27–28. In the specification for this qualification, his work is also considered in relation to social constructivism. This is because he also highlighted the role of the adult in supporting children's learning.

The adult's role in children's learning

Bruner believed that adults play a vital role in children's development. He suggested that children could learn anything provided that the information was sufficiently simplified and presented to them in a way that they could access.

He proposed that a **spiral curriculum** would be an effective way of teaching children. Children would learn something at a simplified level, then it could be repeatedly covered in increasing depth.

While Bruner suggested that information had to be presented at the right level, he felt that children learned best when they were able to discover things for themselves. This has been dubbed **discovery learning**. He was opposed to rote learning, and saw the role of the adult as that of a facilitator of learning, rather than a provider.

> **Key term**
>
> *Spiral curriculum:* the concept that a subject may be repeatedly taught but in increasing depth.

> **Reflect**
>
> Are there topics that children or young people will be taught more than once in your placement setting?

Bruner also valued play as a tool for children's learning, but suggested through his research that adults are able to enrich and develop children's learning if they join children in play. Through observing children in a range of different play settings, he showed that when children played without any adult input, their play and ideas were less sophisticated than when adults were involved.

> **Research**
>
> Chris Athey's work on play schemas has been very influential in the early years sector. Find out more about play schemas by visiting www.pacey.org.uk/working-in-childcare/spotlight-on/schemas or by typing the term 'play schemas' into a search engine.

Vygotsky's zone of proximal development

Lev Vygotsky, a Russian psychologist working at around the same time as Piaget, also thought that children were more active in their learning. However, he suggested that the role of interaction between adults (or older children) and the child was of great significance. Young children were in effect apprentices, and learned from watching, interacting with and being coached by adults or older children.

His theory is therefore sometimes referred to as a **social constructivist** model. Value is placed on the social dimension of learning. According to Vygotsky, children developed more sophisticated thinking and reasoning through interactions, which he referred to as higher-level thinking.

One of the most influential parts of his theory is the **zone of proximal development (ZPD)**. Vygotsky used this term to describe the way in which, through adult interaction, children's cognition develops. The ZPD describes the potential difference between a child's current abilities and what they might be able to achieve given adult encouragement and interaction. The diagram shows what this means in practice.

1) The adult observes that the child is able to count objects one by one.

2) The adult shows the child how to count in pairs.

3) Eventually, the child learns how to do this alone.

▲ The zone of proximal development in practice

In this example, the child could count, but had not seen or discovered how to count in pairs. With the adult's help, the child's development has been extended.

> **Reflect**
>
> Does your setting identify children's or young people's current stage of development and then plan activities?

Connectivism

The connectivist approach is based on the premise that we do not need to rely on a teacher. Instead, we can gain information from a range of sources including social networks and also through technology, especially the internet. Using technology, children and young people can connect with others and also find a range of sources to gain information.

Theory

The theory of connectivism is particularly associated with George Siemens. The features given in the specification come from his paper 'Learning theory for the digital age'.

1. Technology: according to connectivist thought, technology supports many of the learning sequences identified by earlier theories. Students in today's education and childcare settings have greater access to online information, ideas and communities of learning.
2. Nodes and links:
   – **Nodes** are objects (a person, a book, a webpage) that can be connected as part of a learning network.
   – In this approach, a diversity of opinions and sources is key.

– Learning occurs when students make links between nodes, and they continue to make and maintain connections to form knowledge.
– In this way, 'know how' and 'know what' is replaced for learners by 'know where to find knowledge'.

3. Currency of knowledge: in today's world, knowledge quickly becomes obsolete, and learning is thus a continual process. Learning is therefore more important than knowing.
4. Informal: formal learning no longer makes up the main way knowledge is acquired. Informal learning can happen anywhere, and does not only take place in the classroom or the childcare setting.

Pedagogical approach

The specification lists four ways in which the connectivist approach might be used in settings (these may not be accepted in other contexts).

1. **Massive open online courses (MOOCs)**: these are online courses that can feature a mix of traditional course materials, user forums and communities of practice to connect and support learners.

> **Research**
>
> There are many online courses available which are free or low cost, such as the Khan academy (www.khanacademy.org).
>
> If you have the opportunity, talk to a range of people aged 18–65 (at least 20 individuals).
> ▶ Find out whether or not they have used online courses.
> ▶ Ask them about their experience and whether they would do other courses like these.
>
> Collate this information mathematically as a series of graphs to show which age groups:
> ▶ are most likely to use online courses
> ▶ have the highest satisfaction rates.

2. Social networking: this facilitates the informal exchange of information between learners. Interactions can take place between students at any time of the day or night.
3. Gamification: this approach turns tasks and assignments into competitive, interactive games, such as Duolingo for language learning.
4. Immersive learning: students are immersed in a task, working together to find, assess and make connections between information located in the digital world and the natural environment.

Underpinning evidence

Three sources of evidence are given in the specification.

George Siemens

We have explored Siemens' theory of learning in the digital age above. The skill for children and young people is to know where to find and share accurate and relevant information, who to connect with, how to connect, and how to analyse the information gained.

Downes' modernised learning delivery strategies

Stephen Downes and Siemens collaborated on the connectivist approach as well as working independently. Downes developed modernised learning delivery strategies in 2018 while working with the Canada School of Public Service to review and improve its online delivery. He looked at mobile devices, collaborative working and virtual libraries to include links to videos and podcasts.

Lave and Wenger's community of practice

Jean Lave and Etienne Wenger developed the 'community of practice' as a theory in its own right, separate from Siemens' and Downes' work. It focuses on the social ways in which groups of people come together in order to learn, exchange ideas and explore information about something they are interested in. A key way in which this theory differs from Siemens' and Downes' work is that groups may come together in person, such as at a book club.

Humanism

Humanism is a type of philosophy that views people as essentially good and capable. The humanist approach to education focuses on the feelings, attitudes and welfare of the child or young person. There is a belief that humans have a thirst for knowledge and learning, and the role of the adult is to provide the right conditions for children and young people, who should be trusted with their own learning.

Theory

The specification sets out the following key features of holistic learning (these may not be accepted in other contexts).

▶ Holistic learning: individuals construct knowledge in the context of their own unique feelings, values and experience. Feelings are as important as knowledge in the learning process.

- Student-centred: the teacher's role is to facilitate rather than deliver learning. Learning should be personalised to each individual student.
- Self-actualisation: a student's potential can be fulfilled only when their physical and affective needs have been met.
- Agency: humans are intentional and seek meaning, value and creativity.

Pedagogical approach

The specification outlines ways in which this theory may influence a range of education settings:

Aspects of theory	Influence in the education setting
Student-initiated learning	The student is given freedom to select learning materials and manage their own progress. Learning decisions rest with the student, not the teacher.
Holistic	The teacher considers the student's whole being, including home environment and other factors which could impact on learning. The teacher acts as a coach, helping students to achieve their goals.
Safe and nurturing environment	The teacher creates an environment in which students feel physically and emotionally safe, and can focus on learning.

▲ Influence of humanism on education settings

Underpinning evidence

Several sources of underpinning evidence are given in the specification. Their relevance to the humanist approach to education may not be accepted in all contexts.

Bronfenbrenner's ecological system

Urie Bronfenbrenner is known for his ecological systems theory, later retitled bioecological system. He argued that children's and young people's development is influenced by a wide range of environmental factors: their parents and teachers, but also their community and in turn the wider society and culture in which they live.

His theory is often presented in a diagram like the one below. His work has helped teachers and practitioners to think about how wider issues such as poverty and attitudes in the community may affect children's and young people's learning and development.

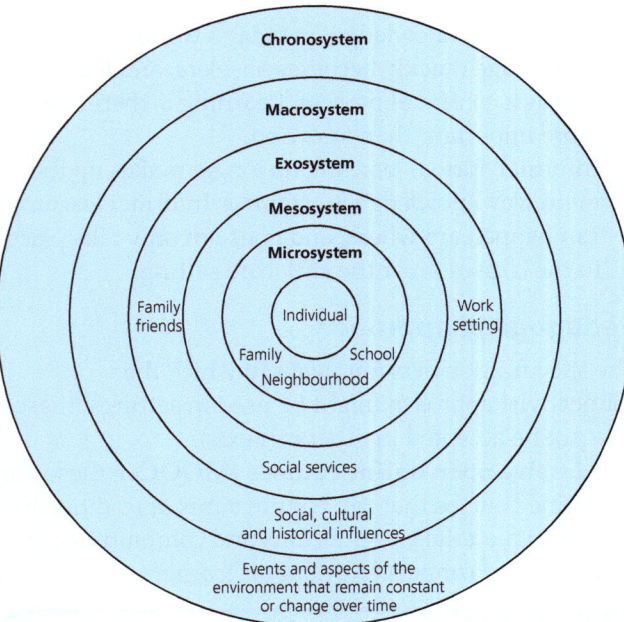

▲ Bronfenbrenner's ecological systems theory

- **Microsystem**: the child's immediate environment, such as parents, siblings, teachers and friends.
- **Mesosystem**: this looks at the relationship between different elements of the microsystem. For example, if a parent disagrees with another family member, both in the child's microsystem, their conflict may negatively affect the child's learning and development. On the other hand, when a teacher and a parent have a good relationship and share information, this is likely to positively affect the child's learning and development.
- **Exosystem**: this looks at how events, people and places that the child is not directly connected to can still influence their learning and development. For example, the closure of a local job centre may affect how easily a child's parent can look for work. This in turn affects the stress levels of the parent and their interactions with the child.

- **Macrosystem**: the wider environment and context in which the child or young person lives. It includes the culture, religious values, economy and politics of the country in which the child or young person lives. A child who grows up in a prosperous country may have free education for longer and may have access to better health services.
- **Chronosystem**: the events that occur during children's and young people's lives which may have an effect on their development, such as growing up in a time of war. For example, children and young people have lived through the COVID-19 pandemic. Their lives and those of their families will have been changed as a result.

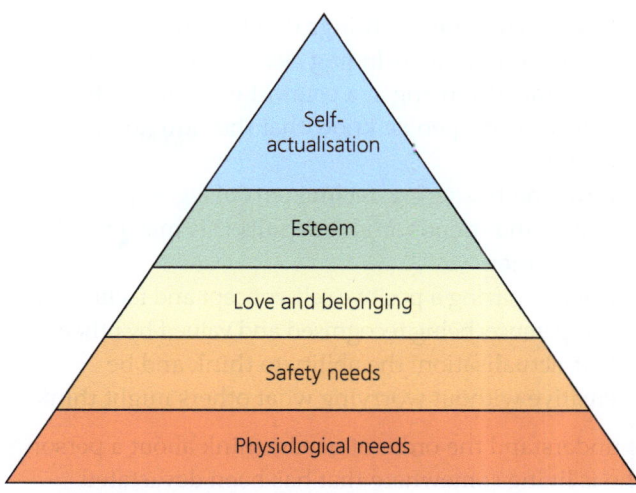

▲ Maslow's hierarchy of needs

Case study

Rufus lives with his parents and older sister in a comfortable neighbourhood. They have a garden and his grandparents live close by. Rufus' parents are both employed and have good jobs. Rufus is looked after by a local childminder who is a friend of the family, and also by his grandparents.

Since his older sister's birth, Rufus' parents have been part of a parenting network. The parents in the group often message one another, share photographs and give one another advice. They often all meet up for social occasions. Recently Rufus' mother has been offered the chance to study for a degree by her employer. The scheme for employers was set up by the government, which is keen to improve education for adults in the workforce. The government believes that a more educated workforce will help the economy out of recession. Rufus' mother is enjoying studying, but it has meant that she has less time to spend with Rufus and sometimes she becomes quite stressed.

1. Using Bronfenbrenner's model, think about the direct influences on Rufus.
2. Again using Bronfenbrenner's model, identify some of the indirect influences on Rufus.
3. Why is it important for adults working with children to think about the context in which children live?

United Nations Convention on the Rights of the Child 1989

The UNCR is a list of 45 rights that all children and young people should have, regardless of where they live or their personal circumstances. Some of the articles are relevant to the humanist pedagogy.

- Article 12 states: 'Every child has the right to express their views, feelings and wishes in all matters affecting them, and to have their views considered and taken seriously.'
- Article 29 relates to education and states that this 'must develop every child's personality, talents and abilities to the full. It must encourage the child's respect for human rights, as well as respect for their parents, their own and other cultures, and the environment.'

Maslow's hierarchy of needs

Abraham Maslow was a humanist, and is particularly well known for suggesting that humans have a hierarchy of needs. Each need has to be met in order for humans to be able to realise their potential.

The hierarchy of needs was a theory of motivation and has been widely adopted by industry as well as education. His original work was in text format but a diagram has since been developed that helps to explain his theory:

- Physiological needs: things that the human body needs to survive, including clean water, shelter, food and also being at a comfortable temperature.
- Safety needs: people know that they are not in danger.
- Love and belonging: feeling part of a group, having family and friends, and for adults this may include a life partner.
- Esteem: having a positive self-concept and feelings of competence; being recognised and valued by others.
- Self-actualisation: the ability to think and be creative without worrying what others might think.

To understand the order of needs, think about a person who is living somewhere that has been devastated by war. There is no running water or anywhere to live. Is that person likely to paint a masterpiece (self-actualisation) or go to get water, food and look for shelter (meeting physiological and security needs)?

Rogers' experiential learning

In his 1969 book *Freedom to Learn*, psychologist Carl Rogers outlined the importance of meaningful learning for children and young people. This is often referred to as **experiential learning**, where the needs and wants of the learner are the focus. As part of this theory, Carl Rogers stresses the importance of a positive climate in which learning takes place.

While Carl Rogers did have views on education and teaching, he is best known for influencing modern approaches to counselling.

2.4 How metacognition supports children and young people to manage their own learning

Have you ever been in a lesson when your mind has drifted and then you have made yourself concentrate more? The skill that you used is known as metacognition. Metacognition is the ability to understand, be aware and then try to control one's own mental processes.

The importance of metacognition

Metacognition is a broad term and includes the wide range of strategies that we can use to improve our concentration, learning and memory. Here are some of the ways that children and young people could use metacognition to manage their learning:

- **Identifying the strengths and areas for development in their own learning:** Metacognition skills can help children and young people to think about what they find easy and difficult. This is important in learning because to make progress in areas where you are weak, you first need to work out what they are. While adults can do this for children and young people, it is always more effective when children and young people can do this for themselves.
- **Using cognitive strategies to 'construct' knowledge:** One of the ways that we learn is to connect different pieces of knowledge. We may, for example, know that clouds are needed for rain; we may also know that there can be clouds without any rain. A metacognition skill would be to find out what colour clouds are associated with large amounts of rain. By doing this, new knowledge could be developed.
- **Using metacognitive strategies to regulate and evaluate their own learning:** Children and young people can use their metacognition skills to 'make' themselves try hard, practise again or seek help. They can use metacognition skills to recognise what they have found easy or difficult, and what they need to do next.

How metacognition positively impacts on children's and young people's education and achievement

Children and young people who have developed good metacognition skills have significant advantages when it comes to education and achievement. It is worth recognising first that these skills develop over time. Metacognition is linked to the development of memory and the ability to analyse and use information, so young children have less developed metacognition skills. Metacognition skills develop over time, with older children and young people being able to access some of them.

Adults can help with metacognition skills by sharing some of the strategies they use. These might include highlighting text that needs to be memorised, testing yourself to check what you know or thinking about the last place you used something that you have lost. Adults can also encourage metacognition skills by asking children and young people what they think – for example, 'What are you happy with? What do you need to concentrate on next?'

Ways in which metacognition skills can positively impact on education achievement

▶ **Building up a set of transferable strategies and skills that they can apply to new subjects and situations:** Children and young people with strong metacognition skills are able to consciously think about strategies and skills that they have experienced in the past and use them in new situations. This can help them solve new problems.
▶ **Better preparation for assessments:** Many assessments require that children and young people spend time revising knowledge or practising skills. Those who have strong metacognition skills do better in assessments. This is because they are able to analyse where they need to put in more effort and they are also able to develop strategies to help them remember things, such as thinking about a professor who has lost a finger to remember that there is only one 'f' in 'professor'.
▶ **Monitoring their own understanding:** If children and young people have good metacognition skills they are able to ask themselves about whether or not they have understood a specific piece of information, task or skill. They should also be able to analyse the best way of doing something about it – for example, finding a new resource, asking a friend/adult for help, or rereading or repeating the task.
▶ **Identifying barriers to their own learning and actively minimising them:** Children and young people can use their metacognition skills to work out how they learn and remember information best, and also what affects their learning. This might include recognising that they find it hard to concentrate when it is noisy or when they are tired. Using this analysis, they can actively look for ways to improve their learning.
▶ **Learning from mistakes in order to avoid them in the future:** Children and young people who have good metacognition skills can accurately analyse information from their mistakes in order to improve their performance.
▶ **Adapting their learning strategies as appropriate to the task:** When children and young people have strong metacognition skills they can think about how best they learn and choose strategies that are suited to both them and the task.

> **Case study**
>
> Shona and Rahima are both in Year 6. Each week they have a spelling test. Each week, Shona does badly while Rahima normally does very well. Shona looks at the words the night before. Rahima looks at the words on the day they are given by the teacher. She works out which ones she already can spell. She then divides the rest of the words into three groups. Each night, she writes out one group of words and plays games with them. She also writes out the hardest words and displays them on her wardrobe door. The day before the test, she asks her parent to call out the words so she can practise spelling them. She has learned these strategies because her mother used to do them with her when she was younger.
>
> When asked about their test results, Shona says that she has looked at the words, but she has been unlucky.
> ▶ Who has the most developed metacognition skills?
> ▶ How do these skills affect the result of the test?
> ▶ What has been the role of the adult in developing metacognition skills?

2.5 How practitioners provide effective feedback and why it is important in supporting children's and young people's educational development

In the past, adults often looked at schoolchildren's work and just said 'well done' or 'good'. This did not really help children know what they needed to do more of or how to improve. Today, we know that by providing feedback to children and young people we can help them reflect on their work, guide them and so support them to make progress in their learning.

The term 'formative feedback' is sometimes used to describe this process.

> As well as learning, feedback can also be used to support children's and young people's behaviour (see Core Chapter 4).

Here are some key points in relation to feedback. It should be:

- ▶ **Timely:** Having a conversation with an adult or written feedback works better during or soon after the task or activity. This is because the child or young person is more likely to retain the information. It also matters because during or soon after an activity or task, a child or young person is more likely to be interested and motivated.
- ▶ **Clear and detailed:** Effective feedback helps children and young people know exactly what they have done well, but also what they need to do to improve.
- ▶ **Relevant to criteria:** While young children need simply to enjoy their learning and experiences, later on, children and young people will be preparing for assessments or qualifications. These might include swimming certificates and music exams, but also qualifications. When this is the case, adults need to help children and young people understand what they need to do to achieve the assessment or qualification. They need to know how they are doing and also what they need to do to meet the requirements. This might mean giving young people the qualification syllabus and encouraging them to check their own work against it.
- ▶ **Action-orientated:** Effective feedback helps children and young people know what they need to do next and provides them with goals for the future. This helps them to plan their next tasks or approaches. **Action-orientated feedback** might focus a child on checking punctuation or a young person on researching the meaning of a word. It might also help children and young people prioritise what they need to do first. This might help prevent them becoming overwhelmed. As well as helping children and young people understand what actions they need to take next, action-orientated feedback may also help them to understand what they need to continue to do.

▲ These young people are learning about catering. Why is it important that they are given action-orientated feedback?

- ▶ **Ongoing:** Effective feedback is continuous. This can help children and young people to be guided towards outcomes and also to avoid learning skills or knowledge incorrectly. Continuous feedback can also be motivating as children and young people know that their work and effort is being valued. As we have already seen, children and young people need to be involved in their feedback. If this process is continuous, they can develop the skills they need in order to learn self-evaluation and reflection.
- ▶ **Interactive:** Effective feedback is interactive. We might ask questions to find out what the child or young person thinks, or to help them see something from a different perspective – for example, 'What would happen if …?' If we make sure that effective feedback is interactive, children and young people are more likely to feel positive and motivated.

2.6 Why up-to-date and appropriate technology is important to effectively support children's and young people's educational development

These days, it is rare to find an educational setting that does not use technology in some way to support children's and young people's learning. In early years settings, the use of technology with babies and young children is usually kept to a minimum, as first-hand experiences and physically playing with objects are thought to offer the best way for this age group to learn. Early years practitioners, on the other hand, will use technology to share information with parents and professionals, and also to help them record progress.

As they develop, technology is increasingly introduced as a way for children and young people not only to find knowledge, but also to develop their skills and understanding of technology. The National Curriculum now includes learning how to use code for programming.

Here are some of the ways in which you may find technology being used:

- **Monitoring children's and young people's progress:** Many settings have software that tracks progress or adults input information into systems that can be accessed by colleagues.
- **Ease of sharing information:** Many settings use technology to share information. They may do so with the local authority about national assessments, for example. Most settings will also communicate and share information with parents. A setting may have its own website, for example. In early years, parents can often access their child's 'learning journey' online.
- **Using a variety of media to introduce and explore a topic:** Many settings will use technology to gain children's and young people's interest. They may show a photo, play a film clip or music, or a podcast. In addition, many settings will encourage children and young people to follow up on something that they have seen or done by going online.
- **Planning and designing suitable online and offline learning materials and assessments:** In schools, many adults use technology to find and also create offline and online activities and materials to use with children and young people. Some materials can also be used for assessment purposes. One of the advantages of some online resources is that they have already been mapped to the National Curriculum. A disadvantage of online resources is that they may not link to children's and young people's interests or level of development.

Research

Choose a National Curriculum subject and key stage or an area of learning and development from the EYFS.

Using one of these websites, evaluate the quality of resources on offer:
- www.bbc.co.uk/bitesize
- www.twinkl.co.uk
- www.hamilton-trust.org.uk

- **Equipping children and young people to navigate a vast amount of information and evaluate the validity of sources:** We have seen from the early approach to learning known as connectivism (page 30) that children and young people must learn how to navigate information that is online. Using technology alongside children and young people can help them develop the skills to recognise when information may be inaccurate or biased.

Case study

Sofia is four years old. She is with her childminder. It is first thing in the morning and the other children are not due to arrive for a while. They go into the garden to water the seeds they have planted. Sofia spots a 'lizard' on a plant. The childminder takes a photograph of it. They spend some time looking at it. The childminder suggests that they can go inside and find out more about what they have seen. Using the photograph, they compare it to similar images online. The childminder prints out the photograph and together they write a caption. Sofia tells her mother later in the day that they have seen a newt.

- Explain why this is a good example of how technology can build on first-hand experiences.
- How is technology supporting Sofia's literacy skills?
- Why is it important Sofia learns that technology can be used to find out things?

- **Making learning accessible for children and young people with special educational needs and disabilities (SEND):** Some aspects of technology, such as voice-activated typing, can make a significant difference to children and young people with SEND. Here are some simple ways in which technology can make a difference:
  - using a screen and changing the size of the font to help children and young people with visual impairment
  - using touchscreen technology to help children and young people to access activities such as drawing if they have difficulty with motor skills (see page 60)
  - using audio books to help children and young people who find reading difficult
  - using online programs that allow children and young people to learn at their own pace and repeat lessons.
- **Communicating and collaborating safely with children and young people online:** Online technology means that children and young people can meet other children and young people online. This can be an exciting learning opportunity, especially where they connect with other children and young people from different countries and cultures. They can talk about their lives, schooling and also share aspects of their lives that are important to them. The role of the adult is to help children and young people learn how to do this safely. Also, as children and young people are increasingly connected to one another via social media, adults also have to teach them how people tend to show only 'their best selves' online.

▲ Why is it important for adults to guide young people to ensure their safety online?

- **Modelling legal, ethical and secure methods of accessing/using online data and media:** By using technology and guiding children and young people, we can show them how to use the internet and associated technology safely. With young people, this includes ethical and legal aspects such as illegal streaming of films, sporting activities and music. It is also important for children and young people to be taught the importance of privacy and protecting their personal information.
- **Helping to prepare children and young people for future careers and digital citizenship:** Technology is now an everyday part of life and is likely to remain so. For children and young people, it is now an essential part of an educational programme to know how to use and benefit from it.

> **Research**
> - Talk to two young people aged between 11 and 16 years.
> - Find out what forms of technology they use (e.g. tablets, phones, laptops).
> - What websites or apps do they use the most?
> - Do they use social media and, if so, how often?
> - How many hours a day are they using some form of technology?

> **Research**
> Talk to the adults in your placement setting.
> - How do they use technology to support the education of children and young people?
> - Are there any drawbacks to using technology with children and young people? What are they?
> - Do they use technology to support assessment?

2.7 How personal, educational and environmental factors may affect engagement and development in reading, literacy and mathematics

Reading, writing and mathematics are considered to be essential for children and young people to master. Unfortunately, some children and young people can lose motivation or find learning literacy and mathematics difficult. There are many factors that can affect children's and young people's engagement and development in these areas. For the purposes of this qualification, we are dividing them into three broad areas: personal factors, educational factors and environmental factors.

Personal factors

Some of the personal factors that may affect engagement and development in reading, literacy and mathematics are described in the table below.

Level of cognitive and language development	In order for young children to learn to read and begin to write, they must have fluent language. Later, children and young people who have good vocabulary levels are likely to find reading more enjoyable and produce higher levels of writing. Language is also needed for mathematics and problem solving. Children and young people need to analyse and retrieve information, and this is linked to both cognitive development and language development.
Physical health and wellbeing	Children and young people who are in good health are more likely to have higher attendance in early years settings and schools. This means they do not miss out on experiences and teaching.
Special educational needs and disabilities (SEND)	Some types of SEND may cause children and young people to have delays in development. This might be because they have learning difficulties and need longer to learn concepts. It may also be because their disability causes them to have absences.

Motivation and interest	How much a child or young person wants to learn can affect their progress in literacy and mathematics. As we will see, motivation is also linked to how things are taught and the encouragement available.
Confidence to try without fear of failure	Mistakes are part of learning. When children and young people are fearful of making a mistake, they may miss out on opportunities to learn.
Socio-economic circumstances	Children and young people from poorer families may sometimes be at a disadvantage. They may not have time or space to do their homework. They may also not have had the same opportunities to see and apply literacy and mathematical concepts (e.g. a trip to the zoo may involve reading the signs, being aware of space and size, and paying for an entrance ticket).
Bilingualism: English as an additional language (EAL)	Children and young people who have more than one language may not always have the vocabulary needed to talk and use concepts in mathematics. If they are new to English, they may also need more support to help them learn how print works in English (see Core Chapter 12).
Previous experiences or support	How much a child or young person has enjoyed looking at books, reading, writing and doing mathematics will influence their attitude towards it. Positive experiences will help children and young people to persevere.

▲ Personal factors that may affect engagement and development in reading, literacy and mathematics

Educational factors

Educational factors are those factors that relate to what happens when children and young people are in education settings. Early years settings and schools can differ widely. A child or young person who thrives in one may not do so well in another. Some children and young people also attend private education, where the adult–pupil ratio may be more favourable. Here are some educational factors that might make a difference to children's and young people's learning and engagement in literacy and mathematics.

The quality of teaching and support at varying stages of development

Children and young people can benefit from adults who enjoy teaching and supporting learning. Being with an adult who is skilful and with whom they have a good relationship really matters to children's and young people's life chances. Here are some examples of ways in which high-quality teaching can make a difference at varying stages of development.

Early years settings
▶ **Reading:** Adults take time to share books with individual children. They choose books that they know are right for the child's language level and that will be enjoyable. They encourage children to talk about the story and, when children are developmentally ready, they draw their attention to print. Young children associate books with pleasure and are keen to learn to read when they start school.
▶ **Writing:** Adults provide interesting activities that will encourage young children to make marks using paint, crayons and sensory materials. Adults often write in front of children and so act as role models. They show those children who are ready how to make letter shapes. By the time the children start school, they are motivated and confident to make letter shapes and marks.
▶ **Mathematics:** Adults talk to children as they play, and draw their attention to concepts such as size and shape. Adults look for opportunities during daily routines to count objects and actions with children. Children start school already having words to describe size, shape, time and measure. They also enjoy counting with adults and may recognise a few numbers.

School settings
▶ **Reading:** When children are learning to read, adults are supportive and encouraging when mistakes are made. They also teach methodically so that children acquire knowledge about reading systematically. At all ages, they choose a wide range of books and texts to help pupils become confident readers. Later they help young people to analyse stories, poems and texts, and to discuss them.
▶ **Writing:** When children are learning to write, adults make them feel confident so that they are not afraid of making mistakes. As children develop their writing skills, adults may show them spelling strategies, and provide information about

punctuation and grammar. They encourage children to enjoy writing and look for ways of building their confidence. With young people, adults encourage them to reflect on their writing.
- **Mathematics:** Adults look for activities that will build children's and young people's confidence and skills in mathematics. They try different approaches when a child or young person does not understand a concept. Adults use assessment to make sure that a child or young person has acquired a concept before building on it. They try to make mathematics relevant, and encourage children and young people to ask questions and to seek support.

> **Reflect**
>
> As a child or young person, did you experience some good teaching that helped you with literacy and mathematics? What was it?

Age- and stage-appropriate materials

Resources can play a part in children's and young people's engagement in literacy and mathematics. A well-resourced setting can provide children and young people with plenty of opportunities to inspire their learning and can also help them apply their learning. At all ages, a wide range of books that are of interest to children and young people can make a difference to engagement in reading. Resources and materials are effective only when they are age appropriate and when they are combined with good teaching.

Use of aids and adaptations

Some children and young people with a disability or learning needs may need physical resources that help them with their learning in literacy and mathematics. An example of this might be audio books for children and young people who cannot see print or who struggle with reading.

Use of synthetic phonics (reading and literacy)

Synthetic phonics is an approach to learning to read and write. The idea is that sounds in words are broken down to their smallest component (e.g. c-a-t). Synthetic phonics is currently the approach used in English schools, although it is worth noting that there are other approaches. It is a systematic approach, meaning teachers follow a highly structured programme. This means, for example, that all children begin by learning the same six sounds: S-A-T-P-I-N. In theory, children are not meant to move on to other letter sounds until they have mastered these. This structured approach is thought to help many children learn to read.

> **Research**
>
> If you have a placement in a primary or infant school, find out whether it uses synthetic phonics with its reception and Year 1 children.
>
> If so, does it also use other methods alongside synthetic phonics?

Environmental factors

Where children and young people grow up and what they experience can make a difference to their learning generally, but also to their interest in literacy and mathematics. Here are some examples of environmental factors:

- **Exposure to a stimulating, language-rich environment and resources:** In the early years of a child's life, interaction with parents and family members makes a significant difference to their later literacy and mathematical skills. The term 'language-rich environment' is used to describe opportunities to talk, listen and engage with others. For older children and young people, a language-rich environment can still make a difference. Some families seem naturally to discuss and debate topics. This, in turn, can help children and young people learn how to argue, negotiate and use language for thinking.
- **Opportunities to practise and apply knowledge:** Children and young people are often given homework. Homework helps them to practise and consolidate knowledge and skills. Not all children and young people have quiet spaces where they can do their homework, however, and so can miss out on time to learn and practise skills. In addition, some children and young people have more opportunities than others to apply their knowledge. A young person may, for example, help out in a family's business and so learn about accounts or handling money. This, in turn, can support their mathematical skills.
- **Support and involvement from parents or carers, peers and other professionals:** We have seen that good teaching makes a significant difference to children and young people. So, too, do the other people in their lives. Children and young people not only need encouragement, but also sometimes advice. This can come from their family members, friends or a neighbour, or from other professionals such as counsellors.

Assessment practice

1. Outline the positive effects on learning if a humanist approach is taken.
2. Explain what is meant by modelling in the context of social learning theory.
3. Identify **two** criticisms of operant conditioning when used in relation to teaching children and young people.
4. Why might having a closed mind-set affect a young person's progress in mathematics?
5. Explain what is meant by a connectivist approach to learning.
6. Give **one** example of a metacognition skill that would help a young person to learn.
7. Explain why feedback needs to be clear and detailed when working with young people.
8. Why do children who are in language-rich home environments have an advantage in literacy activities?

CORE Chapter 3: Safeguarding, Health and Safety and Wellbeing

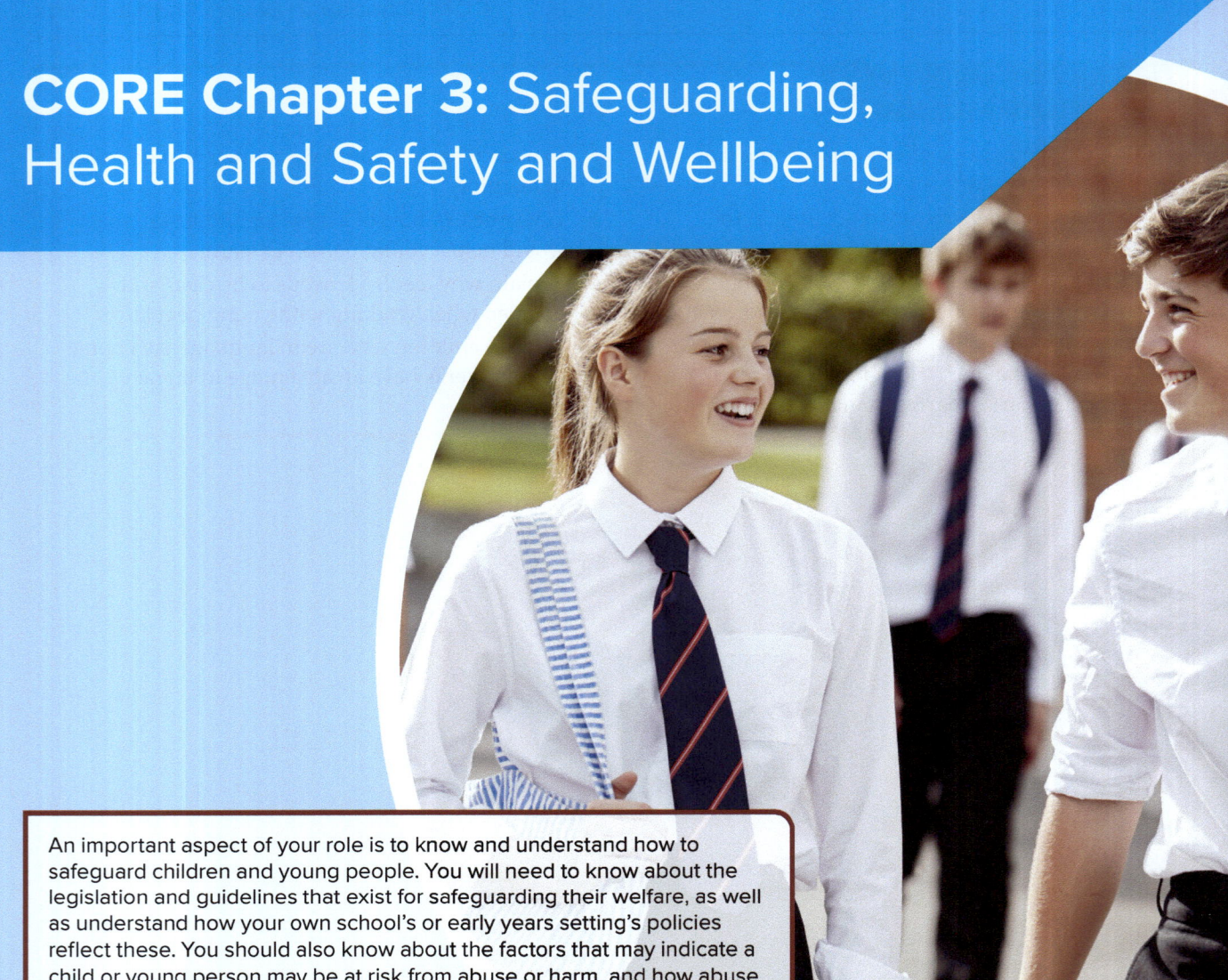

An important aspect of your role is to know and understand how to safeguard children and young people. You will need to know about the legislation and guidelines that exist for safeguarding their welfare, as well as understand how your own school's or early years setting's policies reflect these. You should also know about the factors that may indicate a child or young person may be at risk from abuse or harm, and how abuse may affect their development and behaviour. Finally, you should know what action to take if you have concerns about a child's or young person's wellbeing.

Learning outcomes

This chapter covers the following knowledge outcomes for Core Element 3:

- **3.1** The requirements and purpose of legislation in relation to educational settings
- **3.2** How statutory guidance informs policies and procedures in educational settings
- **3.3** The importance of children's and young people's emotional health and its impact on their overall wellbeing
- **3.4** The difference between a child or young person 'at risk' and a child or young person 'in need'
- **3.5** The factors that may indicate that a child or young person is in danger or at risk of abuse
- **3.6** The legal definition of a position of trust, as defined by the Sexual Offences Act 2003, and how power and influence can be used and abused when working with children and young people
- **3.7** Grooming when defined as an individual developing a relationship of trust to manipulate, exploit and abuse a child or young person
- **3.8** The range of indicators that an adult in the setting may have inappropriate relationships with children and young people, and how to deal with this
- **3.9** How abuse, neglect, bullying, persecution and violence may impact on children's and young people's development and behaviour

CORE Chapter 3: Safeguarding, Health and Safety and Wellbeing

3.1 The requirements and purpose of legislation in relation to educational settings

Legislation	Purpose	Requirements
Health and Safety at Work etc. Act 1974	This act defines: • employers' responsibilities to protect the health, safety and welfare at work of employees and members of the public, • employees' duties to protect themselves and each other.	Under this act, all those who work in schools or colleges will have responsibility for health and safety, which includes: • reporting hazards • following the policies and procedures of the setting for health and safety • using safety equipment and PPE (personal protective equipment) where needed • ensuring all materials, equipment and resources are safe • not harming themselves or others by their actions.
Female Genital Mutilation Act 2003	This act provides legal protection and safeguarding for victims of, or those at risk of, Female Genital Mutilation (FGM).	The act makes it an offence to carry out or assist a girl in performing FGM, whether or not this takes place in or outside the UK. FGM is a form of abuse and can cause long-term mental health and physical problems for the victim. Under this act, it is also an offence to fail to protect a girl from risk. All those working with children and young people have a responsibility to be vigilant. They should know the signs to look out for, which include: • excitement about going to a 'special' holiday home • extended school absence, which is repeated • withdrawn behaviour or anxiety • having difficulty walking, sitting or moving around. Girls who live in the UK whose families are from a community that practises FGM are at greater risk. Any professional working with children and/or young people should follow their setting's procedures for reporting any suspected or potential cases of FGM. Where potential cases are suspected, protection orders can be put in place. Both the NSPCC and NHS websites have more information on FGM. See www.nspcc.org.uk and www.nhs.uk
Children Act 2004	This act introduced measures to support multi-agency working to keep children safe.	The Children Act 1989 was amended in 2004 and 2006 to reinforce the message that all organisations and professionals that work with children and young people have a duty to help safeguard and promote the welfare of children. The act outlines the responsibilities of parents and all those who work with children and young people. It includes two specific sections that focus on **safeguarding**: 1 Section 17 – this states that services must be put in place by local authorities to 'safeguard and promote the welfare of children within their area who are in need'. 2 Section 47 – this states that the local authority has a duty to investigate instances where it has 'reasonable cause to suspect that a child is suffering, or likely to suffer, significant harm'. The 2004 Act also created the posts of separate Children's Commissioners for England, Northern Ireland, Scotland and Wales, and new Local Safeguarding Children Boards (now Local Safeguarding Partnerships) to allow the function to investigate and review all children's deaths in a local area.

> **Key term**
>
> **Safeguarding:** action taken to promote the welfare of children and protect them from harm (as defined by the NSPCC, 2018).

Legislation	Purpose	Requirements
Safeguarding Vulnerable Groups Act 2006	This act places a statutory duty on organisations to undertake suitability checks on all individuals working with children and vulnerable adults.	The DBS (Disclosure and Barring Service) check is now a legal requirement for working with children and young people. It applies to the health and social care sectors as well as those working in education and early years.
Children and Families Act 2014 (Part 3: Children and young people with special educational needs (SEN) and disabilities)	This act introduced new provisions to ensure the welfare of children and young people with SEND, including education, health and care plans (EHCPs).	When working in schools and early years settings, you need to know about the SEND Code of Practice, which is about the law for children and young people who have SEND from birth to 25 years. The Code of Practice: • gives families and their children more control over welfare and decision-making • establishes the requirement for an EHCP which sets out the SEN assessment and provision for children and young people under 25. For more on the SEND Code of Practice 2015, see Core Chapter 11.
Counter-Terrorism and Security Act 2015	This act places a duty on specified authorities to consider the need to prevent people from being drawn into terrorism.	You will need to know about and understand the Prevent Duty Guidance 2021 which is based on this legislation. This will influence your responsibilities under your organisation's safeguarding policy.
Data Protection Act 2018	This act defines responsibilities for using personal data fairly, lawfully and responsibly.	The Data Protection Act incorporates the UK GDPR – the UK's version of the General Data Protection (GDPR), which is an EU regulation. It affects the way in which schools and colleges record, store and share personal information such as: • names, addresses, dates of birth • photographs • National Insurance numbers and bank details of staff • information about medical conditions, needs or allergies • progress reports on pupils/exam results • information on pupils' needs and welfare, including SEN assessments • information on the safeguarding of pupils • staff development reviews.

▲ The legal requirements and purpose of various pieces of legislation in relation to educational settings

Test yourself

1. Which act places a statutory duty on organisations to carry out suitability checks on all staff?
2. What is the difference between the Data Protection Act 2018 and GDPR?
3. What are your responsibilities under the Health and Safety at Work etc. Act 1974?

Research

Find out more about any three of the pieces of legislation listed on the previous pages.
▶ How do they affect what you or others in your setting do in the workplace?
▶ Why is it important for schools and early years settings to be up to date with their policies and procedures?

3.2 How statutory guidance informs policies and procedures

By law, all organisations working with children and young people up to the age of 18 need to have guidelines, policies and procedures to make sure they are protected and kept safe from harm. The following statutory guidance should support and inform policies and procedures in your school or early years setting.

Health and safety

Health and safety: responsibilities and duties for schools 2021

If you are working in a school, the guidelines for health and safety are outlined in this document on the www.gov.uk website. It sets out the requirements and responsibilities regarding health and safety which all staff need to know when working with children and young people. This includes the steps staff must take to keep children and young people safe, secure and well both on school or college premises or when off-site, for example on school trips. The guidelines also state what needs to be included in a school health and safety policy and schools' responsibilities for assessing risk.

EYFS Safeguarding and Welfare Requirements

The EYFS Safeguarding and Welfare Requirements are one of the three sections in the EYFS Statutory Framework. This means that they are a legal requirement for all early years settings. In Core Chapter 2, we looked at this document in relation to the learning and development requirements and assessment, which are the first two sections of the document. The third section of this document relates to safeguarding and welfare requirements. These must therefore influence the policies and procedures in early years settings.

The EYFS Safeguarding and Welfare Requirements relate to a wide range of topics which affect policies and procedures, such as:

- Child protection: staff must look out for any areas of concern regarding a child, and must have policies and procedures to safeguard children.
- Suitable people: settings must make sure that all those who look after children are suitable to carry out their role. For example, they must have a DBS check. Settings need to have procedures for checking these requirements.
- Staff qualifications, training, support and skills: all settings need to ensure that staff have appropriate qualifications and training, and are supported in keeping up to date with any additional requirements. At least one person on site or on a trip is required to have a full and current paediatric first aid certificate.
- Key person: each child in the setting must have a key person who will get to know them and their needs, and build a relationship with their parents and carers. This will support their individual needs and welfare.
- Staff to child ratios: these are set out in detail in the document and are a legal requirement. They are set out separately for childminders and early years providers.
- Health and accidents: this relates to the promotion of health, including oral health, and the requirement for providers to have procedures in place for responding to illness and administering medicines. They must also ensure that a written record is kept of any accidents or injuries, and the first aid treatment which has been given. In the case of serious accidents, injuries or the death of any child while on the premises, Ofsted and local child protection agencies must be informed.
- Managing children's behaviour: this relates to corporal punishment, which must not be given or threatened by anyone caring for children under any circumstances. Physical intervention may be used only to prevent immediate danger of injury and a record of any physical intervention must be kept by the setting.
- Safety and suitability of premises, environment and equipment: all settings must ensure that their premises are fit for purpose and that they have appropriate fire detection and control equipment, such as fire extinguishers and smoke detectors. The environment should also comply with the requirements of health and safety legislation, including hygiene.
- Risk assessment: all settings must carry out regular risk assessments, both in the environment and before going on outings. These must identify potential risks or hazards and what can be done to minimise them.
- Special educational needs: all settings are required to have the appropriate arrangements for supporting children who have SEND. For more on this, see Core Chapter 11.
- Information and records: all settings must be aware of and follow the requirements of the Data Protection Act, GDPR and the Freedom of Information Act 2000.

You should read through this section of the EYFS Statutory Framework if you are working with babies and young children, to ensure that you are fully aware of your legal responsibilities with regard to their welfare.

In practice

Choose one area from Section 3 of the EYFS Statutory Framework. Find out more about it and how it affects what you do in your role.

Security

Prevent Duty Guidance : for England and Wales 2023

This guidance outlines all key areas that staff should be aware of in the context of safeguarding. It refers to the Counter-Terrorism and Security Act 2015, which states that 'all specified authorities', including schools and registered childcare providers, should have 'due regard to the need to prevent people from being drawn into terrorism. All those who work with children and young people should understand and be aware of the guidance'. The setting's safeguarding policy should outline the level of risk, which will vary considerably between organisations and locality.

Confidentiality of information

The following two pieces of statutory guidance are closely linked, and settings will need to meet statutory requirements to guarantee confidentiality of information. Although there are some differences in the small print (such as possible criminal sanctions), the principles are very similar. This is necessary so that information which is shared with the European Union is managed in a similar way and the two broadly comply with each other.

Data Protection Act 2018

This act replaces the Data Protection Act 1998, as it is linked to the EU's GDPR. It informs the policies and procedures which organisations must have around recording, storing and sharing information and keeping it safe (see also Section 3.1). All those who use personal data must follow a set of rules which are called 'Data protection principles'. The six principles of the Data Protection Act directly relate to the first seven principles of the GDPR (see below).

The Data Protection Act 2018 also gives individuals the right to find out what information organisations store about them and how this information is used.

UK General Data Protection Regulation (UK GDPR)

Under the UK GDPR, all those who keep and use personal data on individuals must follow seven principles. The information must be:
1 used fairly, lawfully and transparently
2 used only for the specified purpose
3 used in a way which is limited to what is necessary
4 used in a way that is accurate and kept up to date where needed
5 not kept for longer than is necessary
6 handled securely and protected against unauthorised access
7 kept within the principles of GDPR.

Safeguarding and promoting the welfare of children and young people

Supporting Pupils at School with Medical Conditions 2015

This guidance is specifically for schools; early years settings should refer to the EYFS guidance in Section 3.

Although its main purpose is to ensure that pupils with medical conditions are properly supported and cared for alongside their education, it also points out that these pupils may be vulnerable due to their conditions, and highlights that there may be social and emotional implications for them, particularly if their needs are complex.

The school's safeguarding policy should highlight staff responsibilities and procedures for implementing and reviewing healthcare plans.

Working Together to Safeguard Children 2023

This guidance informs safeguarding policies. It sets out how different agencies such as healthcare professionals, adult social care and educational practitioners should work together in order to protect children and young people, and promote their welfare. It puts the child or young person at the centre of all decisions that are made and highlights the importance of early help.

Multi-agency Statutory Guidance on Female Genital Mutilation 2020

This statutory guidance document provides information, guidance and support for all those who have a responsibility to safeguard girls from FGM. It sets out the requirements of the legislation, which places a mandatory duty on all healthcare, education and medical professionals to report concerns immediately to the police.

Keeping Children Safe in Education 2023

This statutory guidance was first introduced in 2014 to promote the safeguarding and welfare of children and young people, and has been regularly updated since; its most recent update was in September 2022.

The guidance applies to all schools and colleges in England, and to maintained nursery schools. The latest version should be referred to when writing safeguarding policies, as it provides details about managing important issues such as peer-on-peer abuse, as well as CSE (child sexual exploitation) and CCE (child criminal exploitation). This document should be read alongside the statutory guidance 'Working Together to Safeguard Children' and the advice 'What to do if you are worried a child is being abused' (both available on the www.gov.uk website).

> **Test yourself**
>
> 1 Why is it important for schools and early years settings to know about this legislation and guidance?
> 2 How will staff know about it?
> 3 How will it influence what happens in the workplace?

> **In practice**
>
> ▶ Look at three of the following policies within your organisation:
>   – record-keeping policy
>   – assessment policy
>   – confidentiality policy
>   – special educational needs policy
>   – safeguarding policy.
> ▶ What do these policies say about recording, storing and sharing information?
> ▶ How does this relate to the legislation above?

3.3 The importance of children's and young people's emotional health and its impact on their overall wellbeing

The emotional health of children and young people has been recognised by mental health organisations as having a direct influence on their overall wellbeing and also their ability to learn. In 2017, the government published a Green paper 'Transforming children and young people's mental health provision' to set out schools' and colleges' responsibilities around mental health. In addition to this, statistics released by the Mental Health Foundation in 2018 showed that 1 in 9 children aged 5 to 15 had a diagnosed mental health disorder, a rise from 1 in 10 in 2004 (source: www.mentalhealth.org.uk/blog/what-new-statistics-show-about-childrens-mental-health). For these reasons, it is important that all those who work with children and young people are aware of how emotional health impacts on children's later resilience and outcomes as adults.

Importance of children's personal circumstances in relation to their holistic wellbeing

Children's personal circumstances and environment and their holistic wellbeing are closely related. A child who is safe and secure, well-loved and surrounded by supportive family and who is able to have a range of experiences, is more likely to have a positive outcome in later life. In 2015, Public Health England published a list of eight principles for schools and colleges which contribute to a child's wellbeing and emotional health. It also listed the types of positive personal factors which will give children and young people better outcomes with regard to their wellbeing:

▶ feeling loved, valued and protected
▶ being part of a family and having a sense of belonging at home, in school and within their community
▶ being in good health, and having a balanced diet and exercise
▶ having the freedom to play and enjoy themselves
▶ being hopeful and optimistic
▶ going to a school that looks after pupil wellbeing
▶ having a voice and a sense of control over their own life
▶ having resilience and the ability to problem solve.

▲ Why is it important for young children to be able to play together?

> **Reflect**
>
> Consider each of these factors and give a reason why each one is important. Can you think of any more factors which might influence a child or young person's emotional wellbeing?
> ▶ For more on how environmental factors affect children's development, see Core Chapter 7, K1.2.

Significance of emotional health for positive relationships

Our emotional health is about how we think and feel; it determines how we deal with emotions and experiences, or how we **self-regulate**. It also affects how we deal with the emotions of others. We therefore need to have a healthy relationship with ourselves (positive self-esteem) and understand our own emotions so that we can have positive relationships with others. According to the NHS Every Mind Matters, healthy relationships are vital to our mental wellbeing.

> Self-regulation is discussed further in Chapter 2, K2.6.

> **Case study**
>
> Rio is in Year 6 and has low self-esteem. This affects his behaviour and also his relationships with his friends as he becomes angry with himself when he feels that he cannot do something, and lashes out. You have been asked to work with the SENDCo to help Rio to understand his emotions and think of strategies to help him to deal with them when he is upset. The SENDCo has provided you with some resources and also wants to send you on some ELSA training.
> ▶ How will spending some time talking about his emotions support Rio?
> ▶ What other strategies might you use with him to support his emotional health?

> **Key term**
>
> **Self-regulation:** an individual's ability to control their own emotions, thoughts and behaviour and to adapt to changing situations and cope with unexpected stress.

For children and young people who find their emotional health hard to manage, early years settings, schools and colleges will need to have appropriate support in place. Strategies such as playing games and sports, encouraging turn taking and supporting children and young people's social skills will all help them to develop positive relationships with others. In some cases schools will have an emotional literacy support assistant (ELSA) who is specially trained in supporting pupils with issues such as managing emotions, bereavement, self-esteem, problem solving and managing friendships.

> For more on strategies to develop self-regulation, see Core Chapter 4.

> **Research**
>
> Find out about Leah Kuyper's Zones of Regulation.
>
> How might this be a useful way of supporting children and young people to manage their emotional health?
> ▶ For more on attachment theory and how early attachments influence adult relationships see Core Chapter 7.
> ▶ For more about self-regulation and how it supports children's development see Performance Outcome 2.6.

CORE Chapter 3: Safeguarding, Health and Safety and Wellbeing

3.4 The difference between a child or young person 'at risk' and a child or young person 'in need'

It is important that you know the difference between these two terms. A child or young person **at risk** is one who is in a position of vulnerability to abuse or harm. This means that the abuse or harm may be happening (but may also not be), or is at risk of happening; this might be due to a range of factors, such as those discussed in Section 3.5.

A child or young person **in need** is defined by law as a person under 18 who needs extra support to improve their opportunities through the services of the local authority, whether this is due to their personal circumstances or a medical or physical need. This means that they may be in social care, such as **looked after children**, children with disabilities, or those with other safeguarding and welfare needs.

> **Key term**
>
> **Looked after child (LAC):** a child who has been in the care of their local authority for more than 24 hours, sometimes also referred to as children in care. This can include children living with foster parents, in a residential children's home, hostel or secure accommodation.

> **Reflect**
>
> Anna is six and lives with her mum and stepdad. She is in school every day and her parents are always involved in school-based events. Staff have noticed that recently Anna is very quiet and has become quite withdrawn. Lunchtime staff have also said that she is not eating. They have mentioned this to her mum but have been told that she is upset because they have had to cancel their holiday.
>
> Roman is 15 and lives with his mum. He is her carer as she has multiple sclerosis and limited independence, as well as depression. The family have a designated social worker, but Roman is regularly absent from school.
>
> ▶ Which of these children might be considered at risk and which in need?
> ▶ Would you do anything in either situation?

The mandatory reporting requirements to escalate concerns that a child or young person is in need or at risk

> See Sections 3.1 and 3.2, and also Early Years Educator K4.1.

In order to comply with legislation, policies and procedures, it is a responsibility of all those who work with children and young people to keep them safe and free from harm. As educators we are also responsible for ensuring that we support children and young people to achieve the best possible outcomes. This means that we as professionals must, by law, report any concerns that a child or young person is in need or at risk.

The document 'Keeping Children Safe in Education' (September 2020) signposts more detailed information. It states that all staff in a setting must be aware of and understand their part in upholding their responsibilities under the local early help process.

It also mentions that staff should know that under the Children Act 1989 there is a process for making referrals to children's social care and also for statutory assessments. It highlights in particular two sections of this act: section 17 (children in need) and section 47 (a child suffering, or likely to suffer, significant harm) and the fact that staff may be involved in these assessments.

If you suspect that a child or young person in your school or early years setting is in need or at risk, you must follow the correct policies and procedures that are in place in your organisation as soon as possible. You should receive training in your organisation's safeguarding or child protection policy at induction or through ongoing staff continuing professional development (CPD). This will outline the indicators of concern or abuse and set out in a clear way the steps you should follow.

In most cases, you would be obliged to share your concerns immediately with your **designated safeguarding lead (DSL)**, outlining why and what has happened or been said; they would then take your concerns further. The procedures the organisation has put in place should be clear and easy to follow. In some cases, organisations may have a flowchart that details what to do at each stage, and how to proceed if you are not happy with the response or action that is taken.

If a child or young person has confided in you, safeguarding is one of the cases in which you have to tell them that you cannot keep the information to yourself, as you need to protect their safety. All information shared with the DSL should be confidential – they will decide if the concerns should be referred on to other professionals on a 'need to know' basis.

> **Key term**
>
> **Designated safeguarding lead (DSL):** person in a school or early years setting who is responsible for all safeguarding issues.

> **Research**
>
> Using a copy of your school's or early years setting's safeguarding policy, outline in chronological order the steps you would need to take if you had concerns about a child or young person in your setting.
> ▶ Why is it important to follow the policy correctly?
> ▶ What does the policy say about confidentiality, and why?

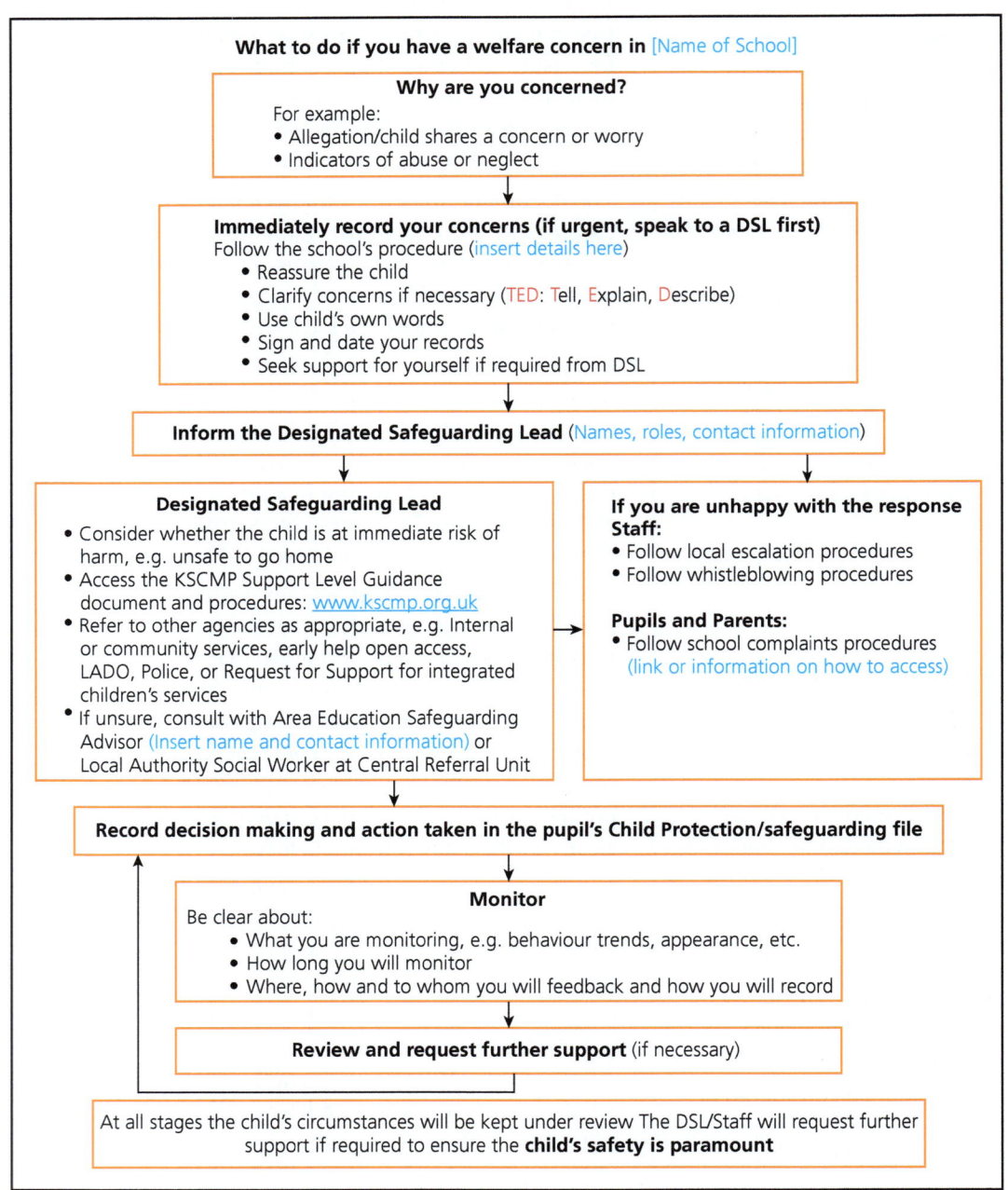

▲ Example of a safeguarding/child protection policy for a school
Source: KELSI www.kelsi.org.uk/__data/assets/pdf_file/0020/66008/Child-Protection-Exemplar-Policy-for-schools.pdf

CORE Chapter 3: Safeguarding, Health and Safety and Wellbeing

3.5 The factors that may indicate that a child or young person is in danger or at risk of abuse

You should know about the different kinds of abuse that children and young people may be vulnerable to. This is very important, as you will be responsible for reporting any concerns you might have, as discussed in Section 3.6.

Abuse is normally categorised as follows:
- physical abuse – when someone is physically hurt or harmed
- emotional abuse – when someone is continually emotionally mistreated
- sexual abuse – when sexual activity is forced upon someone, including child sexual exploitation (CSE)
- neglect – when a baby's or child's basic needs are persistently not met
- domestic abuse – when there is violent behaviour within a relationship
- bullying and cyber bullying – when a child is bullied by their peers
- child criminal exploitation (CCE) – when a child is trafficked or exploited and made to commit crimes, for example, as part of a gang.

(Note that an individual may be subject to more than one type of abuse.)

> For more on the different types of abuse, how to recognise them and who to report to, see also Early Years Educator K4.2.

You should also know about factors that may indicate that a child or young person is more in danger or at risk of abuse. According to the World Health Organization (WHO), research has shown that there is often a link between abuse and certain characteristics of the child and their environment. Some of these are outlined briefly in the following table.

Individual factors	Reasons
Physical or developmental disability	Children and young people who have a physical or developmental disability may be more vulnerable to abuse for a number of reasons: • they may be unable to stop the abuser • they may have less of an understanding of what is happening • they may be less likely to tell others about the abuse.
Child or young person has been impacted by an abusive relationship	If abuse is already in the child's or young person's home, they will be more likely to suffer abuse themselves.
Lack of secure attachment with parent/carer	If a child or young person does not have a secure and loving attachment with a parent or carer, this may increase the likelihood of abuse.
Parental factors	**Reasons**
Parent has already abused a child or young person/been abused	Parents who have been abused themselves or who are already known to have abused a child or young person may be more likely to abuse a child or young person.
Unrealistic expectations of parents/lack of skills	Parents who are uninformed, or who do not know about child development or may not have appropriate parenting skills may be more likely to abuse. They may not know how to manage conflict situations or understand ways in which they can support their children more effectively.
Parental isolation	Parents who are more socially isolated or who have limited support from family and friends or the local community may be more likely to abuse children and young people.
Parental mental illness	According to the WHO research, the children of parents who have mental health issues, poor self-esteem or self-control are more at risk from abuse.
Parent is suffering with drug or alcohol addiction	Parents who are using drugs or alcohol are also more likely to abuse their children.
Environmental factors	**Reasons**
Overcrowding in the home, poverty or lack of opportunity to improve	High rates of poverty or overcrowding are more likely to increase stress levels in the home, which can lead to abuse.
Domestic abuse	Where there is already abuse in the home, children and young people are likely to be subject to it themselves. In addition, children witnessing domestic abuse is also a form of abuse.

▲ Factors that may indicate more risk of abuse

> **Case study**
>
> You are working in a Year 3 class in a school that is in a deprived area. You have noticed that a new child in your class, Jack, rarely speaks to anyone and is unable to stay focused on any activity. He is brought to school by his grandmother and you know that he is a child who receives free school meals and has a social worker. He is also regularly without the appropriate clothing for the weather and is the last to respond to any communications the school sends home.
> - Outline any concerns you might have about Jack.
> - Do you think these factors mean that Jack is being abused?
> - What would you do in this situation?

3.6 The legal definition of a position of trust, as defined by the Sexual Offences Act 2003

This act states that it is an offence for someone over the age of 18 to engage in sexual activity with someone under that age where they are in a position of trust. It gives specific conditions in which an adult is said to be in a position of trust in relation to a younger person. These are limited to circumstances in which a child or young person is particularly vulnerable, or the relationship of trust is strong, and these circumstances include the child or young person:

- being in a care home, or in residential care or fostered
- being in full-time education in which the older person is involved in caring for them
- being in a hospital, children's home or residential establishment that cares for children with physical or learning disabilities, mental illness or behavioural problems.

It is important that all adults working with children and young people are aware of the fact that they are in a position of trust, and that they should not abuse it in any way.

How power and influence can be used and abused when working with children and young people

Adults who are in a position of trust are role models for children and young people, as well as people who have authority and influence over them. Children and young people may aspire to be like them and want to please them. It is important for this influence to be used in a positive way to support children and young people and build their confidence and self-esteem, and that adults show integrity through what they do and how they behave, as well as in their relationships with others. However, all of these things also mean that it is easier for an adult to do the things listed in the following table.

What they might do	How they might do it
Take advantage of an individual	Those in a position of trust may use their influence to exploit a child or young person for their own benefit.
Gain unauthorised access to private or sensitive information for their own or others' advantage	Adults may look at sensitive information, which they are not entitled to do, in order to find out more about the child or young person for their own advantage.
Manipulate an individual	Those in a position of power may try to manipulate a child or young person by controlling them and using their position to get what they want.
Use a position of trust to bully, humiliate or undermine	Adults may use their position to use verbal abuse in ways that make the child or young person feel humiliated or bullied.
Threaten punishment for non-compliance with unreasonable demands	Adults may threaten a child or young person by telling them that they will punish them if they do not do what they have asked them to.

▲ How adults may use power and influence to abuse children and young people

3.7 Grooming as defined as an individual developing a relationship, trust and emotional connection with a child or young person so that they can manipulate, exploit and abuse them

Unfortunately, babies, children or young people may be groomed or exploited by those they trust. This means that adults may develop a relationship with them specifically to manipulate or abuse them.

Grooming can take place online or in person, although it is more likely to be in person with very young children. Sadly, abuse may take place by adults who are members of the child's or young person's family; there have also been cases where staff members in early years settings have abused children and young people in their care. This is part of the reason that all staff and volunteers need to have a DBS certificate before working with children and young people.

Method of grooming	How this may occur
By adults in a position of trust	This may happen if adults have developed a relationship with children and young people, and then abuse the trust which is placed in them.
	These could be adults either in the home, who work with the child or know them through the wider community.
	If you have any concerns about an adult in a position of trust in your setting, you should follow the setting's whistleblowing policy (see below).
By interfamilial abuse	Interfamilial grooming is abuse carried out by a close family member or friend. A young child will trust those closest to them, and so is unlikely to talk about it as they will not know that it is wrong.
Through the use of inappropriate games	Young children will not know that they are being groomed. Groomers may abuse them by saying that they are going to play a game, which may then be inappropriate.
Through online materials and communication	Groomers may target older children online and send them materials or messages. They may flatter them and build relationships through finding out more about them.
Through observing sexual behaviour of others/being exposed to pornographic content	Children and young people may be forced to watch pornographic content or other people's sexual behaviour.
Through threats of harm to the individual or family	Groomers sometimes use blackmail to control or intimidate children and young people, and to prevent them from telling others.
Through county lines	Groomers will target vulnerable children and young people by befriending them and giving them gifts or money to gain their trust. They will then recruit them into taking illegal drugs into a different area through the use of criminal networks and are likely to exploit and intimidate them to do this. County lines refers to the mobile phone lines which are used to order the drugs. County lines is a form of child criminal exploitation.

▲ How different methods of grooming occur

Research

Find out what is meant by the term 'whistleblowing'.

What procedures does your setting have in place for raising concerns in this area? What are your responsibilities?

A range of signs of grooming or exploitation

The signs of grooming will be similar to other types of abuse.

For more on types of abuse and how to recognise it, see Performance Outcome 4.2.

Education and Early Years T Level: Early Years Educator

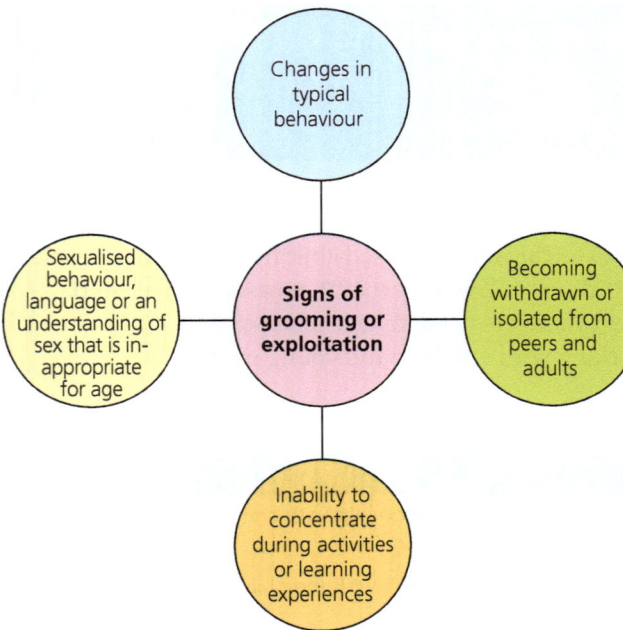

▲ Do you know how to look for signs of grooming or exploitation?

Appropriate action to take when grooming or abuse is suspected

Following the safeguarding policies and procedures of the setting

If you suspect grooming or abuse for any reason, you should always ensure that you follow your setting's procedures.

For more on this, see Performance Outcome 4.2.

Reporting immediately to the setting's DSL

Your setting must by law have a DSL, and this person should be known to all staff.

Liaising with local authority designated officer (LADO)

If grooming or abuse is suspected and has been reported to the designated safeguarding lead (DSL), it is likely that they will then report this to the LADO. Each local authority will have a LADO who is responsible for managing responses to and coordinating any safeguarding allegations.

Remaining calm and professional if disclosures are made

It is very important to stay calm and reassure the child or young person if they make any disclosures to you. It is unlikely that they will understand what has happened, particularly if they are very young, but it may still be very upsetting for them and they will be seeking help.

If an adult discloses suspected abuse, or if you have been made aware of something that suggests this, you should speak to your DSL before doing anything else.

Maintaining accurate and coherent records and reports

Make sure you follow your setting's confidentiality policy and tell only the DSL. You should ensure that anything which is written down is passed immediately to them or stored safely.

Sharing information only when required and maintaining confidentiality

All information concerning safeguarding should be shared only on a need-to-know basis.

> **Practice points**
> - Be clear on your legal and day-to-day safeguarding responsibilities under your setting's safeguarding policy.
> - Be alert, particularly if you have vulnerable children or young people in your setting.
> - Know how to report your concerns, and who you should tell.
> - Make sure information is kept confidential.
> - Use appropriate recording and reporting methods.

3.8 The range of indicators that an adult in a setting may have inappropriate relationships with children and young people

Although fortunately very rare, it is possible that an adult in your setting may develop an inappropriate relationship with a child or young person. You should be aware of the kinds of indicators that might suggest they are doing this, and act on this if necessary.

▶ **Being overly affectionate, giving gifts, or showing favouritism with a child or young person:** You may notice that an adult spends more time with or shows a preference for a particular child or young person, or seems keen to be with them.

▶ **Spending time alone with a child or young person:** You may notice that the adult is finding ways of spending time alone with the child or young person. This is never advisable, as both the child and the adult are vulnerable to allegations.

▶ **Making friends with a child's or young person's parents and/or visiting them at home:** Although it is important to have good relationships with parents, particularly when children are very young, it is important for practitioners to maintain professional boundaries. This means that they should not be friends outside the setting or on social media.

▶ **Using private texts or social media to communicate with a child/young person:** This is always inappropriate and most schools and early years settings will state it in their safeguarding policy.

How practitioners deal with suspected abuse in line with the educational setting's codes of conduct

In all cases, safeguarding concerns should be acted on immediately. Appropriate actions include those listed in the table below.

What practitioners should do	Explanation
Observing and recording as appropriate	Practitioners should immediately note down their concerns or what they have seen. They should include the date, where they were and what they were doing, and exactly what was observed or was said to them by the child or young person. This will help them to remember for reporting purposes. They should store this information confidentially – for example, in a password-protected file.
Following organisational policies and procedures for child protection	Within the organisation, it is important to make sure that practitioners use the safeguarding or child protection policy to ensure that each step has been followed correctly.
Following procedures set out by the local safeguarding partnership	The local safeguarding partnership will outline the steps to take if a school or early years setting has concerns about a child or young person. This will include what to do outside office hours.
Following accurate lines of reporting in a timely manner	Practitioners should always act on any safeguarding concerns at the earliest possible opportunity, by reporting to their DSL.
Maintaining professional boundaries	At all times, and especially when dealing with suspected or alleged abuse, practitioners will need to ensure that they remain professional.
Contacting the police if a child or young person is in immediate danger	In an emergency, or if they know a child or young person is in danger, adults should always call 999.

▲ Appropriate actions to take where there are safeguarding concerns

> **Case study**
>
> You are working in a secondary school as a language assistant and have noticed that a pupil is spending a lot of time in the department and is regularly hanging around waiting to speak to a particular teacher. You ask the pupil if you can help her but she is insistent on speaking to the teacher.
> ▶ Should you have any concerns in this instance?
> ▶ Would you do anything and, if so, what?

3.9 How abuse, neglect, bullying, persecution and violence may impact on children's and young people's development and behaviour

▲ How might a pupil be affected by bullying or abuse?

Research by a number of organisations has shown that these types of abuse will have an impact on a child's or young person's development if they are not addressed, particularly if they take place in infancy or early childhood. Depending on the type of abuse and how long it goes on, it can potentially affect all areas of development, and have long-lasting effects throughout an individual's life. In addition, those who suffer abuse and maltreatment may also be more likely to be exposed to other negative experiences such as parental substance abuse or poverty, which will also affect their development.

Area of impact	Effect
Educational attainment	If a child or young person is suffering some form of abuse or persecution, their brain development may be affected, which may cause low self-esteem and affect their cognitive development; this will have a direct impact on educational attainment. It is also likely to affect how much they are able to focus on what they are doing in the setting. They are likely to be distracted, unable to complete their work and may lack interest in what they are doing in school. They may also have more absences or lateness than others in the school or early years setting, which will again affect their attainment.
Attachments and relationships	In cases where children and young people have spent time in care and suffered abuse or maltreatment, they may suffer from attachment disorders. Those suffering abuse are likely to be anxious and upset, and may withdraw from their relationships with others, not wanting to talk to or spend time with them. They may distrust others and become isolated, which will affect their social and emotional development.
SEN	Children and young people who have special educational needs are likely to find it more difficult to make progress due to distractions and anxieties. They may be unwilling or unable to talk about what has happened, or, depending on their level of need, be unaware that they are suffering abuse.
Physical health	Children's and young people's physical health can be affected, particularly if they are physically abused or suffer from neglect. They may also lose their appetite, which may affect their growth and physical development. They are also at greater risk of developing health conditions such as type 2 diabetes, malnutrition, poor lung function, and vision and oral health problems.
Mental health	Abuse such as bullying or violence is likely to cause extreme anxiety, and loss of confidence and self-esteem for the victim. This will mean that, without support, the child or young person may have long-term psychological effects.
Inappropriate behaviour: • self-harm, suicide • alcohol and/or drug misuse • aggression • risky or sexualised behaviour/promiscuity • criminality	The effects of abuse may cause different types of inappropriate behaviour in children and young people, as listed here. This is because they are more likely to try to find ways of forgetting about what is happening to them, or try to get attention in another way, even if this is not positive attention. In some cases, they may carry out the abuse that has happened to them on someone else. In young children, an indicator of sexual abuse can be that they are using words or acting out situations that are not age appropriate. In extreme cases, a child or young person may self-harm, for example, by cutting themselves, or through bulimia, or have suicidal thoughts. These types of behaviour may be difficult to spot but the pupil may be withdrawn and lack energy.
Socio-economic status	Abuse, neglect and persecution may have long-term effects on a child's or young person's socio-economic status in the future. A study by the Public Health Research Consortium (PHRC) entitled 'Child Maltreatment and Adult Living Standards at 50 Years', using British data, found that of the 8,076 people studied, the level of maltreatment had a direct association with outcomes, and that this rose if there was more than one type of maltreatment.

▲ How a child or young person might be affected by abuse

CORE Chapter 3: Safeguarding, Health and Safety and Wellbeing

Assessment practice

1. How does legislation influence what happens in schools and early years settings?
2. Name **three** pieces of legislation that have an impact on safeguarding practice.
3. What is the UK GDPR?
4. Give **two** examples of how schools and early years settings can support children's and young people's health and wellbeing.
5. Explain the difference between a child or young person defined as 'in need' and a child or young person considered 'at risk'.
6. Name **four** types of abuse.
7. Explain the steps you would take if you had cause for concern about a child or young person.
8. Define what is meant by an adult being in a position of trust.
9. Explain the purpose of the local safeguarding partnership.
10. How might abuse impact on a child's or young person's physical and mental health?

CORE Chapter 4:
Behaviour

One of the roles of adults when working with children and young people is to guide their behaviour. This is important so that they can not only learn to be with others and feel comfortable in a variety of different situations, but also attain and achieve well. This chapter looks at the many factors affecting behaviour, including a child's stage of development and their self-concept. We also look at the role of adults in supporting children and young people.

Learning outcomes

This chapter covers the following knowledge outcomes for Core Element 4:

- **4.1** How the stages of children's and young people's social, emotional and physical development may inform their behaviour, and how practitioners can use this information to meet children's and young people's needs
- **4.2** How a range of individual, environmental and educational factors can positively or negatively influence children's and young people's behaviour
- **4.3** The link between self-esteem, identity and inappropriate behaviour
- **4.4** The development of self-concept and its impact on children's and young people's behaviour, cognition and social development
- **4.5** Why children and young people must know how to adapt their behaviour to different social contexts
- **4.6** Why it is important to set and follow behaviour management policy and processes
- **4.7** How home, family circumstances and care history can affect children's and young people's behaviour
- **4.8** How children and young people may respond to both positive and negative verbal and non-verbal communication from adults
- **4.9** How and why practitioners provide positive approaches to motivate children's and young people's behaviour, attainment and achievement
- **4.10** Why practitioners use a range of strategies for setting clear expectations of behaviour
- **4.11** How and why practitioners use a range of strategies to support children and young people to develop self-regulation and resilience
- **4.12** Why practitioners use a range of strategies to deal with behaviour
- **4.13** How and why practitioners use a range of strategies to motivate children and young people to test and stretch their skills and abilities
- **4.14** How practitioners assess risks to their own and others' safety when dealing with challenging behaviour

This chapter also includes three knowledge outcomes from Early Years Educator Performance Outcome 2. Text relating to Early Years Educator is highlighted. Note that this content will not form part of the core assessments.
- **K2.4** Typical behaviours for age and stage of development
- **K2.5** Implications of a range of behavioural signs and approaches to their management
- **K2.7** Factors affecting children's behaviour

CORE Chapter 4: Behaviour

4.1 How the stages of children's and young people's social, emotional and physical development may inform their behaviour, and how practitioners can use this information to meet children's and young people's needs

In Core Chapter 7, we look at the stages of social, emotional and physical development. Understanding and recognising the stages of development is important for practitioners because they often link to children's behaviour and overall needs.

By understanding children's and young people's development, practitioners are able to make sure that what they are expecting of children and young people is fair. A good example of this is taking turns. Developmentally, most three year olds can take turns, but two year olds will struggle with this. If a practitioner knows that a couple of children find it hard to share equipment, they may either provide additional equipment or guide the children so that they can develop the skill. In this section, we will look at the links between behaviour and stages of development.

> You should read this section alongside Core Chapter 7, pages 103–11.

How stages of social development inform behaviour

Social development is about the ability to be with others and to understand them.

> As you can see from Core Chapter 7, social development takes time.

Here are some links between behaviour and social development.

Understanding of social norms

Social norms are the invisible rules of behaviour that allow us to fit in with others. Most children from three years old will start to copy group behaviours. If they see that all the children around them are tidying up, they may start to do the same. Social norms can particularly affect older children's and young people's behaviour. This is because, developmentally, they have a strong need to fit in and be part of a group.

> **Case study**
>
> Patrick is 14 years old and loves music and singing. He would like to be a singer one day. When the music teacher announces that there will be a new choir, Patrick feels excited, but many of his classmates groan loudly. Patrick starts to join in with the groaning.
> ▶ What is the social norm in Patrick's class in relation to the choir?
> ▶ Why did Patrick join in with the groaning even though he likes singing?
> ▶ How might the social norms of his class affect Patrick's attainment?

Ability to relate to others and levels of empathy

Relating to others requires many skills. The ability to do this is linked to stage of development. While babies and toddlers have some ability to recognise the emotions of others, the ability to understand others' intentions takes longer. While most children have some level of this at around seven years, it continues to develop. In addition, to develop friendships with others, children and young people need to develop **empathy** – this is the ability to recognise and respond to the feelings of others. When there are problems with the ability to relate to others, children and young people may react to situations inappropriately.

Special educational needs and disabilities

Some children's and young people's social development and, therefore, behaviour can be affected by their special needs or disabilities. For example, a child who has social communication difficulties may want to play with a group of children, but not have the social skills to do so. The child may then become angry and hit one of them.

Stages of emotional development that may inform behaviour

Children's and young people's emotional development is linked to their behaviour. Here are some examples of how.

Ability to name and regulate own emotions

The ability to manage emotions affects children's and young people's behaviour. This is known as self-regulation (see page 74). While, developmentally, young children find it hard to regulate their emotions, typically, most older children and young people can control their impulses and emotions. This is partly because they learn to recognise how they are feeling and have the language to name emotions. This, in turn, can help them to use language to express how they are feeling rather than doing this through actions. Where children and young people find this difficult, we might see tantrums, anger and other outbursts.

Levels of maturity

In Core Chapter 7 we look at the typical ages and stages of social and emotional development. These can only be used as a guide as individual children and young people may show different levels of maturity.

Special educational needs and disabilities

Some children with special educational needs and disabilities (SEND) may not show typical emotional development. This might be because their special educational need or disability is causing them to be frustrated or affecting how easily they can manage their emotions. Some types of disability, such as hearing or sight loss, may also impact on children and young people's social and emotional development. They may be frustrated because they cannot communicate as easily as their peers because they cannot fully understand or see them.

Stages of physical development that may inform behaviour

Throughout childhood and into adolescence children's bodies grow and develop. Physical development and growth can affect how some children and young people behave. Here are some examples of how physical development may affect behaviour.

Development of gross and fine motor skills

As discussed in Core Chapter 7, babies and young children develop skills that will help them to do more. These include gross motor skills that allow them to throw and kick, but also fine motor skills that allow them to feed themselves, pick things up and manipulate them. As fine and gross motor skills develop, children are able to explore more. They may, for example, start to climb on furniture or touch things that may not be safe. Sometimes, children may also want to touch, hold or do things, but have not yet mastered the necessary skills. This can sometimes lead to frustration.

Body changes as a result of puberty

During adolescence, young people's bodies change because of increased hormonal activity. Some types of hormonal activity are associated with moodiness as well as impulsiveness. In addition, sleep patterns can be disturbed, which can exacerbate swings in mood. A range of behaviours are associated with puberty, including anger, tearfulness, frustration and withdrawal.

EY **K2.4** Typical behaviours for age and stage of development, to inform practice when developing relationships with children

It is very helpful for practitioners to understand typical development and how this affects young children's behaviour. If we understand development, it becomes easier to have fair expectations. The table on the next page lists some overall stages and associated behaviours, although it is worth remembering that these can only be used as a broad guide.

Age	Stage	Typical behaviour	Goals for behaviour
0–1	<ul><li>Inquisitive and starting to explore their environment</li><li>Developing bonds and trusting relationships with those around them</li></ul>	<ul><li>Prone to clinginess with primary carers (see attachment, page 113)</li><li>Puts objects to mouth to explore</li></ul>	<ul><li>Not applicable</li></ul>
1–2	<ul><li>Becoming more self-aware</li><li>Becoming more independent from primary carers</li><li>Exploring the wider environment, including new objects or people</li><li>Imitating the behaviour of others around them</li><li>Can be soothed when unhappy or upset by parents and familiar people</li></ul>	<ul><li>Beginning to show resistant behaviour, particularly when encouraged to do something that they do not want to do</li><li>Throws objects to floor when frustrated</li><li>May attempt to climb on furniture</li><li>Wants adults' attention</li></ul>	<ul><li>To play alongside other children</li><li>To carry out simple instructions such as 'get your shoes'</li></ul>
2–3	<ul><li>Little understanding of safety and so requiring supervision</li><li>High levels of activity and independence at times</li><li>Ability to self-soothe when unhappy or upset</li><li>Beginning to control own feelings and impulses</li><li>Plays alone but interested in others</li></ul>	<ul><li>Pushing more boundaries</li><li>No understanding of the need to share toys</li><li>Dislikes others sharing adults' attention</li><li>Struggling to self-regulate</li><li>More prone to a range of mood changes as they explore feelings</li><li>Often frustrated when unable to achieve desired goals</li></ul>	<ul><li>To wait for needs to be met</li><li>To share toys or food with another child with the support of an adult</li><li>To play alongside another child</li><li>To say 'thank you' with a reminder from adults</li><li>To follow simple instructions with help, such as 'tidy up now'</li></ul>
3–5	<ul><li>Able to play with other children for short periods</li><li>Growing in independence</li><li>Growing in ability to recognise own feelings and emotions</li><li>Better able to regulate/control own feelings and emotions from four years</li><li>Asking questions to learn more about their environment</li><li>Showing affection and forming bonds with individuals outside of the family</li><li>From four years, starting to recognise need for rules and boundaries</li></ul>	<ul><li>Able to share and take turns when not tired or hungry</li><li>May copy inappropriate language from other children or adults without understanding</li><li>May have aggressive outbursts when tired or hungry</li></ul>	Three to four years:<ul><li>To follow rules in games when supported by an adult</li><li>To say 'please' and 'thank you' without reminders</li><li>To take turns and share equipment</li></ul>Four to five years:<ul><li>To ask permission to use others' toys or resources</li><li>To tidy up after activities</li><li>To follow instructions most of the time</li></ul>
5–7	<ul><li>Ability to express their thoughts, feelings and desires clearly and with meaning, e.g. foods they like, activities they do not like</li><li>Developing wider social networks during school and outside activities</li><li>Increasing independence from family members</li><li>Enjoying forming friendships and being accepted by others</li><li>Increasingly able to understand own emotions and aware of the feelings of others around them</li><li>Enjoying achievements and the sense of pride they bring</li><li>Enjoying and using rules</li><li>Knowing when they are not keeping to the rules</li><li>Having many self-help skills</li></ul>	<ul><li>May say what rules are, but may not always follow them</li><li>Sometimes, prone to being self-critical, particularly if they get something wrong, such as losing in a group activity</li></ul>	<ul><li>To follow instructions from adults</li><li>To apologise to others</li><li>To listen to others</li><li>To take some appropriate responsibility</li><li>To be helpful and thoughtful</li></ul>

▲ Some overall stages and their associated behaviour

4.2 How a range of individual, environmental and educational factors can positively or negatively influence children's and young people's behaviour

There are many factors that influence children's and young people's behaviour. Some aspects of their behaviour relate heavily to their actual needs. By understanding some of the factors and, therefore, needs of children and young people, we can support their behaviour more easily.

Individual factors

Children and young people can show very different behaviours. This is because there are individual factors at work. Here are a few examples of individual factors.

Self-esteem

Self-esteem is about how you value yourself. How children and young people value themselves can make a difference to how they behave. We look at this further later in this chapter (Section 4.3).

Special educational needs and disabilities (SEND)

> We saw in Section 4.1 how some children and young people with SEND may, because of their stage of development, show some behaviours.

Age

> We look at how stages of development affect children's and young people's behaviour in Section 4.1 and also in Core Chapter 7.

Typically, children and young people find it easier to manage their impulses and behaviour as they become older. This is partly because they may have more advanced language skills as well as experience of how to manage their stress. Children and young people who have good language skills may find it easier to manage their impulses and behaviour. This is because they can use words to express how they are feeling.

Environmental factors

Where and how children and young people grow up can affect their behaviour.

Culture and religious beliefs

Culture, including religious beliefs, can affect children's and young people's behaviour. This is because it can affect the expectations that adults have of children and young people.

> There is more on this in Section 4.7.

Care history

Some children and young people do not live with their biological parents. They may be fostered or adopted. While this can be a positive experience, for some children and young people their care history may affect their emotional security and, therefore, their behaviour.

> We look at this in Section 4.7.

Family circumstances

Every family is different and so are their circumstances. Children and young people may live with many siblings or none. Their families may be wealthy or poor. Some may live in the countryside, others in the city. Some family circumstances can affect behaviour. Events such as bereavement, relationship breakdown or unexpected money worries can put pressures and stresses on parents or carers. As a result, they may not be able to provide emotional security, resources or time for their children. This in turn can lead children and young people to show negative behaviours.

Educational factors

In education settings, there are a number of factors that can affect behaviour.

CORE Chapter 4: Behaviour

Bullying and discrimination

Sadly, some children and young people experience bullying and/or discrimination. This can change their behaviour. They may withdraw, or they may become aggressive or uncooperative.

Peer relationships

When children and young people are with others who are supportive and friendly, we may see more positive behaviour. On the other hand, where a child or young person does not have friends or is not accepted by others, we may see a range of negative behaviours, including frustration and aggression.

Relationships between children and young people and practitioners

How well children and young people get on with adults can make a huge difference to behaviour. Where relationships are strong, children and young people are more likely to be cooperative and show positive behaviours. On the other hand, if relationships are poor, negative behaviours such as uncooperativeness, anger and lack of concentration are likely.

▲ How can you tell that this child has a good relationship with this practitioner?

EY K2.7 Factors affecting children's behaviour

We have seen that there are various factors that can affect children's behaviour. For this outcome we will look at some additional factors.

Tiredness and hunger

Tiredness and hunger are the commonest reasons why, during a session or day, children will show inappropriate behaviours. When young children are tired, they often become restless, hyperactive, and have more tantrums and outbursts. The same is true when young children become hungry. This is because tiredness and hunger make it harder for them to self-regulate and manage their emotions. As self-regulation (see page 74 of this chapter) is already limited in children under four years, adults need to notice early on when young children are starting to look tired and/or hungry.

Stress

Most young children will become stressed when they are separated from their parents, unless they have a key person. In addition, some environments can prove to be very stressful for some young children, such as when there is a lot of noise and movement and/or when adults are very loud. This is why calm early years settings where young children have plenty of time with their key person tend to have fewer incidents of inappropriate behaviours.

Changes to routine

Knowing what to expect and having routines can give young children a sense of security. It also helps them with their self-regulation, as they know what to expect. Most young children find it very hard to cope when routines have to change, which can cause them to become overexcited or anxious. This means that wherever possible we should try to avoid making significant changes to routines. Young children may also find it hard to fall asleep when they are out of routine, causing tiredness.

> **Case study**
>
> Kris is working for the first time in the toddler room. She is keen to make sure that the children have fun. She thinks that the routines are boring and unnecessary so she decides it is time to shake things up. She puts on very loud music and dances around. When her colleague says that it will soon be snack time, Kris says that it doesn't really matter. Some of the children are looking very anxious. One or two children are bouncing around and climbing on furniture. When her supervisor comes in to see why it is so noisy, she sees three children who are crying, one having a tantrum and one throwing bricks at the door.
> - Explain why routines are necessary for children.
> - Why are some of the children showing signs of anxiety?
> - Explain the behaviours of the children having tantrums and throwing bricks.

Attachment and emotional security

On pages 113–16 we look at how attachments are made and their importance. We also look at this in Performance Outcome 2. You should read these sections alongside this to understand the importance of attachments and also what is meant by a secure attachment. Where babies' and young children's parents or main attachments are not present, we will see separation anxiety unless the children are with a key person with whom they have a strong attachment. When young children do not have a secure attachment within a setting, they are more likely to show a range of behaviours that include aggression and attention-seeking, but also withdrawal.

Babies and children may not have a strong attachment to their parents for a range of reasons. When this is the case, we are more likely to see behaviours that are not typical for their age. These may include aggression and withdrawal, but also indifference towards others and their feelings.

Planned or unplanned transition

Where there are significant changes in young children's lives, such as family breakdown or bereavement, we may see a range of behaviours that are linked to anxiety.

> In Core Chapter 7, we look at how we can support young children during planned or unplanned transitions (see page 134).

Safeguarding needs

Some behaviours that young children show may be linked to safeguarding needs.

> We look at behaviours that may indicate that children have safeguarding needs in Core Chapter 3.

4.3 The link between self-esteem, identity and inappropriate behaviour

The term **self-esteem** is often used to describe how we value ourselves overall. It is linked to our own identity or **self-concept** (how we see ourselves). Self-esteem can affect how we behave, how hard we try and also how we expect to be treated by others. Children and young people who have experienced bullying, for example, may develop low self-esteem. This, in turn, can affect their outlook on others. They may expect others to treat them badly and so may find it hard to trust others in the future. Self-esteem is not fixed. It develops over childhood and can change according to our life experiences.

Children's and young people's self-esteem can affect whether or not they show inappropriate behaviours. Sadly, some children and young people come to the conclusion that they are not able to show expected behaviours. They may think that they are simply not capable of changing their behaviour. This, in turn, means they may continue to show inappropriate behaviours and this, in turn, confirms their idea of themselves. Changing a child's or young person's self-esteem requires patience.

In the same way that children and young people can develop low self-esteem, some children and young people can develop feelings of superiority and overconfidence. This can lead to risk-taking behaviours and also a lack of empathy towards others. When children and young people are overconfident, they can sometimes become frustrated or angry when there is a gap between what they think they should achieve and reality. In some cases overconfidence can also mean that children and young people expect to be treated differently to their peers and, again, when this does not occur they may withdraw, show anger or be moody.

4.4 The three elements that impact the development of children's and young people's self-concept

There are three elements to forming a self-concept:
1. self-image – how you see yourself
2. self-esteem – how you value yourself
3. ideal self – how you would like to be.

How self-esteem is influenced by the ideal self and self-image

It is thought that where an older child's or young person's ideal self nearly matches up to their **self-image**, they will have high self-esteem. On the other hand, if a child's or young person's ideal self differs a great deal from how they see themselves, they will have lower self-esteem.

> **Case study**
>
> Jantine is 14 years old. He has a few close friends and is doing well at school, although he is not top in any subject. He loves playing football although has not played in the first team, unlike his best friend. He is a little overweight and shorter than some of the other boys in his class. He thinks of himself as being 'sort of average'. His teachers and his parents think that he could do much better if he put in more effort. When asked who he admires most and why, he chooses a professional footballer. Jantine says that he thinks that this man is cool, good looking, clever, rich and has lots of friends. When asked if one day he could be like that, Jantine shakes his head and says 'no way'.
> ▶ How does Jantine see himself?
> ▶ What does Jantine's choice of the footballer tell you about his ideal self?
> ▶ How might Jantine's self-esteem affect how hard he works and tries to improve his school work and his football?

How children and young people develop self-concept

Self-concept develops over time. There are distinct stages in its development:
- ▶ **The existential self:** Very early on, babies become aware of themselves. They realise that they are separate to their parents or carers. They see that if they touch something, it might move. If they smile at an adult or another child, the other person may smile back. Babies also start to respond to their name, knowing that it is 'theirs'. We also see in early childhood that children often do things and then look to see what the reactions of others are. The development of self-awareness is thought to explain some classic toddler behaviours such as not wanting to share toys and saying things such as 'mine'.
- ▶ **The categorical self:** This is sometimes referred to as **self-definition**. It is about how children and young people define themselves. In early childhood, we will see that children often talk with certainty about their age, what they can do and their gender. Interestingly, as children and young people develop and compare themselves to others, the way they define themselves changes. They are often less certain in their statements and add in more qualifiers. They may say things such as 'I am quite good at …'.

The possible impact of positive and negative self-concept

It is useful to understand how self-concept can affect aspects of children's and young people's development.

Behaviour

Self-concept can influence how hard children and young people try to fit in to social norms. When children and young people identify themselves as being 'good' or 'sensible', they are more likely to show expected behaviour as they view themselves as being capable of it. On the other hand, when a child or young person categorises themselves as being 'difficult' or 'naughty', they will often display behaviours that reinforce this position. This can become a vicious cycle.

Cognition

We know that effort and practice can affect our learning. Where children and young people have a low self-concept in relation to their learning, they are less likely to concentrate and try. They may use strategies to avoid learning, such as attention seeking or disrupting others. On the other hand, children who have a positive self-concept may see themselves as capable and able, with practice and support, to learn.

Social and emotional development

Self-concept also affects our ability to regulate our emotions and our relationships with others. Children and young people who feel that they are good with other people are more likely to be warm and empathetic. This in turn means that they are more likely to attract more friends. On the other hand, children and young people who have low self-concept may withdraw, or show aggressive or frustrated behaviours. This in turn may limit the number and the quality of their friendships.

4.5 Why children and young people must know how to adapt behaviour to different social contexts

When we look at behaviour, it is important to recognise that how we need to behave depends on who we are with and also where we are. We may joke and fool around when we are at a party with friends, but it would not be appropriate at a serious or sad event such as a funeral. This learning is part of our social development, although it is worth noting that children and young people who have social communication difficulties may not automatically be able to adapt their behaviour. This is why recognising children and young people who may need additional support is so important. Let's look at some of the key reasons why children and young people need to be able to adapt their behaviour.

Learning in educational settings

In order to learn, children and young people need to manage their behaviour. This is important for their own learning, but also so as not to disrupt others. Children and young people may need to be patient and persevere, but also to work cooperatively with others as part of their learning.

Developing impulse control

Impulse control is linked to the ability to self-regulate. It is important that children and young people can manage their immediate impulses as this can affect their learning. It may mean not giving up when frustrated or waiting one's turn to answer a question.

Conforming to social norms

In every situation, there are expectations and ways of behaving. These are called **social norms**. Recognising the social norms and adapting our behaviour helps us to fit in and be accepted by others. Children and young people sometimes need help to know what to do and how to behave in some situations.

▲ What are the social norms in this classroom?

Making friends and maintaining relationships

Children and young people who can adapt their behaviour are more likely to have friends and to have good relationships with others. This is because relationships require us to pick up cues about how to behave based on others' actions, gestures and mood, and then to adjust our own behaviour. It is not a good idea to play a practical joke, for example, on someone when they are very stressed, or laugh when they are very upset. Children and young people also need to impulse-control in order to listen to others, take turns and not blurt out something that might offend someone.

4.6 The importance of setting and following behaviour management policy and processes

We know that children and young people find it easier to manage their own behaviour when they know what is expected of them. We also know that they can find it hard when adults are not consistent in these expectations. This means that all settings will have a behaviour policy. The policy will also include processes or procedures for adults to follow. When you start on placement or in employment in a new setting it is essential for you to find out about and follow the behaviour policy. Here are some benefits of having a behaviour policy:

▶ **Clarifying the expected standard of behaviour:** A behaviour policy helps not only adults, children and young people, but also parents, to understand the values and expected behaviours of a setting.

> As we will see in Core Chapter 5, children and young people benefit when parents and adults work closely together.

▶ **Giving children and young people a chance to have input, resulting in more ownership and buy-in:** A behaviour policy will include ways of involving children and young people in expected behaviour. This might include encouraging adults to explain the reasons for rules and also taking on board the comments of children and young people. Some school settings may have school councils or class representatives who can put forward their ideas for changes to aspects of behaviour policy.

▶ **Setting realistic expectations for behaviour:** We have seen that children's and young people's behaviour changes according to their development. A behaviour policy should set out expectations that are fair and realistic, and based upon age and stage of development. Stage of development is important when working with children who have special educational needs.

▶ **Safety for all children and young people:** One of the reasons why a behaviour policy is needed is to ensure safety. There may be rules, for example, about how many young children can be on the climbing frame at once, or rules for young people about how they move around school corridors or during a PE class. As well as physical safety, behaviour policies will also cover bullying and other aspects that might affect emotional wellbeing.

▶ **Consistent approach to behaviour management:** Where children and young people will spend time with more than one adult, it is important that all adults' expectations are the same. If children and young people find that different adults expect different things, they may become unsettled, and this may lead to some children and young people spending their time testing the system.

▶ **Fairness in how children or young people are rewarded and sanctioned:** It is essential that children and young people feel that they are being treated fairly. A behaviour policy that looks at both rewards and sanctions or consequences of inappropriate behaviour can ensure that children and young people are treated fairly. Adults working in settings must make sure that they follow rewards and sanctions as set out in the behaviour policy, even if they do not always agree with it, as consistency is essential.

▶ **Opportunities to celebrate success:** Some behaviour policies, especially those in schools, also include ways to reward or celebrate the actions or efforts of either groups of children and young people or individuals. Examples of this include receiving a sticker in the classroom or a certificate in assembly.

> **Research**
>
> Find out your placement's behaviour policy.
>
> What should happen if one young child bites another? Describe the steps staff should take in this situation.

4.7 How home, family circumstances and care history affect children's and young people's behaviour

Parental expectations

Parents play a significant part in shaping children's and young people's behaviours.

> In Core Chapter 5, we discuss how parents may have different styles of bringing up their children.

Some parents may expect their children to show obedience, while others may focus on helping others. Some parents may not impose any boundaries or expectations of behaviour. Understanding parenting style can help us to understand how we can support children's and young people's behaviour.

History and consistency of care

Stability is important in children's and young people's development, particularly in terms of key adult relationships. Where family breakdown occurs and key people in children's lives are no longer present or available, this can cause emotional difficulties. These in turn can cause children to show inappropriate behaviours such as aggression.

> You can read more about attachment in Core Chapter 7.

Culture and community

How we behave is also linked to our family's culture and the community in which we live. In some cultures and communities, for example, children and young people are expected to show respect for adults by not questioning them or answering back. In some cultures and communities, boys are treated differently to girls and expectations of boys' behaviour may be lower. This can mean that some boys may find it hard to follow instructions, take turns or be patient.

Adult and child or young person's relationships and interactions

The warmth of relationships and interactions between adults, especially parents, can impact on behaviour. Where children and young people have been exposed to aggression, hostility or negativity, they may develop low self-esteem, and also model this behaviour. On the other hand, where there has been warmth and support, children and young people may feel more settled and emotionally secure. This can result in them showing more care and empathy for others.

How practitioners can use information about individuals' home, family and care circumstances to anticipate and deal effectively with unwanted behaviour

When it comes to supporting children and young people, this is essential. We need to find out from parents and carers the story of their children's lives and any changes to their circumstances. Information that is shared must always be kept confidential, but as professionals, we can use it in a variety of ways.

> In Core Chapter 5, we will look at the importance of working in partnership with parents.

Working with parents/carers to help them find support and advice

Sometimes, parents may let us know that their family circumstances are about to change or have changed. They may also tell us about their child's behaviour at home. It is not uncommon for children and young people to show appropriate behaviour in settings, but to be very challenging at home. If we work with parents in ways that mean they feel they can tell us when they are struggling with behaviour, we can help them gain information and advice from a variety of sources. This might include parenting courses, bereavement and relationship counselling, or financial services.

Sharing information with relevant colleagues to support multi-agency work and early interventions

With permission from parents, unless there is a safeguarding issue, information can be shared with other professionals to support the child or young person.

> In Core Chapter 5 we look at the range of colleagues in multi-agency roles that work with the family or the child/young person.
>
> For more on safeguarding, see Core Chapter 3, page 43.

CORE Chapter 4: Behaviour

Supporting individuals through planned and unplanned transitions

The term **transition** is used to describe changes in children's and young people's lives. Some changes may be quite small and have few effects, but others, such as a bereavement or family breakdown, can be significant and may affect development, including behaviour. Knowing what is happening or about to happen in a child's or young person's life can help us to make the transition easier.

> See Core Chapter 7 for more about different types of transition and how to support children and young people in connection with these.

Informing a behaviour management plan

When children or young people show unwanted behaviour, we may draw up a plan to support them. This is sometimes referred to as a behaviour management plan or a behaviour support plan. In order for the plan to work, we need to know what might be causing the behaviour. Information about the child's or young person's family circumstances will help to influence it.

In some cases, children's and young people's behaviour is linked to a special educational need and it may not always be possible for them to modify their behaviour. A good example of this might be a child who has autism who may not cope with sudden changes and may react by throwing an object or hiding away. If adults recognise when a child has special educational needs, they can adapt the environment and their interactions and so prevent behaviours that may cause problems for others. We look at special educational needs in Unit 11.

Setting and monitoring individual behaviour targets

In some settings, such as schools, the behaviour management plan will also have some targets. These are likely to be shared with everyone involved but also with the older child or young person. To make these targets achievable, it is important to know as much as possible about what is happening in the child's or young person's life.

> **Case study**
>
> Andrew is 11 years old. He has been in foster care for the past three years. Last week, his foster carer told his teacher that Andrew has been having nightmares about starting at secondary school. The foster carer also said that Andrew was due to meet his birth parents for a contact visit at the weekend. Previously, after contact visits Andrew has been upset and angry. At a staff meeting, Andrew's teacher passes on this information so that if Andrew's behaviour changes, they will understand why. Andrew's teacher also plans some activities that may help Andrew to talk about his feelings.
> ▶ Why was it important for Andrew's teacher to know about the changes in Andrew's life?
> ▶ How might this information affect how his behaviour may be managed?
> ▶ Why is it important to share information with colleagues?

4.8 How children and young people may respond to both positive and negative verbal and non-verbal communication

The way we communicate with children and young people makes a significant difference not only to their behaviour, but also to their learning. We have seen that the development of self-concept is significantly linked to how adults talk and respond to children and young people. Tone of voice and body language are often just as important as the words that people use. You may remember a time when someone said 'have a good day' while not looking at you and using a flat, bored voice!

How we communicate both **verbally** and **non-verbally** has significant impact on how children and young people respond.

> **Key terms**
>
> **Verbal:** the use of words as well as how the words are said.
>
> **Non-verbal:** communication that takes place without words being said.

Verbal communication

Talking to children and young people is a key way in which we can support behaviour and also learning. For verbal communication to be effective, it is important we think about the following factors.

Level of language

The length of our sentences and the words we use must be at the right language level for the child or young person. We need them to understand what is being said. If a message is very important, shorter sentences or even single words work best: 'Stop now!', 'Good work' or 'No!' Too much talking can stop children and young people from understanding the key messages.

Clarity

Some adults are not always very clear. They say things like 'Shall we put these away now?' when they really mean 'These are going away now.' They can then become cross when children or young people do not put the items away. Make sure you say what you mean.

Pause and response time

It is helpful to remember that there is a gap between something being said and the other person understanding what is meant. For babies, young children and young people with language needs, this gap can be quite long. It is helpful for all ages to leave pauses as this allows time for understanding. This is very important when explaining concepts or ideas. When using verbal communication for teaching, check children's or young people's understanding, and encourage them to ask questions or to comment.

> **Practice points**
>
> **Giving instructions**
> - Make sure you have the child's or young person's attention first, e.g. say their name.
> - Be clear whether you are giving an instruction or whether there is a choice.
> - Keep instructions short but be positive in your body language and tone.
> - For young children or young people with language needs, give one instruction at a time.
> - Give praise or acknowledgement after each instruction has been carried out.

Non-verbal communication

Eye contact

Looking directly at the child or young person is useful as we can check that we have their full attention. Having a child's or young person's attention is not only important in learning, but also in supporting behaviour. We can also use eye contact and watch reactions to check that there has been understanding. Staring at a child or young person and holding their gaze is a good 'warning' strategy. On the other hand, during ordinary conversation, this can cause fear and be intimidating, making children and young people feel stressed.

Tone

The tone of our voice sends a message to children and young people. Enthusiastic tones are encouraging and can be persuasive. On the other hand, negative and sharp, angry tones can backfire. They can make children and young people feel stressed and increase aggression or fear. The volume of our voices can also influence the tone. Quiet, slow and calm speech can make children and young people stay or become calm because they can see that the adult is in control. Shouting, on the other hand, is ineffective in many situations. It creates stress and so can trigger angry or fearful responses in children or young people.

Proximity

How far away we are (our **proximity**) during communication can matter. Being close with warm tone and words can be encouraging and positive. Being very close when angry words and body language are being used can be intimidating, especially if the adult is higher than the child or young person. Occasionally, this can be useful to show a child or young person that we are not pleased or we mean what we say, but it is not a strategy to use frequently.

> **Key term**
>
> **Proximity:** the distance between the child or young person and the adult.

CORE Chapter 4: Behaviour

Gesture

The most common **gestures** are those we make with our hands and our heads. There are positive gestures like nodding, clapping or a thumbs-up; combined with a smile and warm words, they send positive messages. This in turn can encourage children or young people to show wanted behaviour or, when learning, to concentrate and persevere. Some gestures such as a 'no' with a head movement can be useful when combined with eye contact as a non-verbal signal to show a child or young person that they need to stop what they are doing.

> **Key term**
>
> **Gestures:** actions involving fingers, hands or feet, used when communicating.

Pointing

Pointing is a gesture, but it has a special purpose in non-verbal communication. It draws a child's or young person's attention to a specific object or item. With babies, we use pointing and eye contact to show them something that will be the focus of our talk. This helps them link objects with words. With a young person, we may point to a chair where they are meant to sit or to a sign to remind them of the rules. How children and young people respond to pointing will be linked to eye contact, body language and also to how any words are said. 'Get here!' said as a command while pointing is very different to 'Look, it's over there', said with a smile to help a child find something.

Body language

Body language refers to how we use our bodies to communicate, and can also include facial expressions. Where adults are trying to be positive, they may use open body language. In open body language, the adult is relaxed, they smile and their arms are relaxed. When communication is negative or the adult is tense, we may see closed body language: arms might be folded and there is no smiling. Open body language is useful to send out relaxed, encouraging messages. This can help children and young people to feel good about what they are doing. Closed body language, sharp tone of voice, staring and stern words send out warning signals.

> **Practice points**
>
> **Positive communication**
> - Positive communication strategies tend to work best with children and young people.
> - Make sure that your non-verbal and verbal communication send out the same messages, e.g. do not smile if you are telling a toddler to stop hitting another child.
> - Make sure that your voice has enthusiasm and is positive when encouraging children and young people.

4.9 Why practitioners provide positive approaches to motivate children's and young people's behaviour, attainment and achievement

We know that the amount of effort that we put in to anything can improve how well we do. To encourage children's learning, but also desired behaviour, practitioners use positive approaches. Many strategies work for both behaviour and supporting learning.

Incentive and recognition systems

Many different types of incentive and recognition system are used in settings. The simplest one, which is often used with young children, is to give a sticker at the time the behaviour is being shown. Other systems work by children or young people collecting tokens, points or stickers, with the view that doing so will lead to a reward. These systems include:

- **Star charts:** Star charts are often used for individuals, usually to tackle specific behaviours. Children and young people put a star or sticker on a chart when they show the wanted behaviour. When they have an agreed number of stickers, they then get a reward.

- **Marbles in a jar:** This approach is often used for groups of children or young people. They are given a marble that they put in a jar. Marbles are counted at the end of the week and rewards are decided. Incentives may include extra playtime or a game.
- **House points:** Children or young people are divided into groups, teams or houses. When they show wanted behaviour or have worked or achieved well, they are given points that are recorded. At the end of a half term or term, the house with the greatest number of points is given a certificate, trophy or extra treats.

> **Practice points**
>
> ### Using incentive and recognition systems
> - Children and young people know what they must do to get the reward.
> - Expectations for behaviour or achievement must be realistic, otherwise, children and young people will quickly lose interest.
> - Make sure that the incentive is something of interest to the child or young person.
> - Make sure that children and young people understand the reasons behind the expected behaviour or achievement goal.
> - Review the system regularly to check that it is effective.

Tidying up star chart				
Name	Week 1	Week 2	Week 3	Week 4
Ayse	★★			
Sofia	★			
Ben	★★★★			
Max	★★			
Rufus	★★			

▲ How might having a tidy up chart change children's behaviour?

Establishing positive relationships and using appropriate praise

One of the greatest needs for children and young people is adult attention, respect and warmth. Sadly, where children and young people are not getting sufficient attention, they often show attention-seeking behaviours. By making sure that positive attention is given along with praise, we can often change behaviour. We can motivate children and young people and change their behaviour over time through getting to know them and showing that we care about and value them. It is worth finding out about children's and young people's interests – for example, their favourite programme or toy – so that we can have conversations about something other than their work or behaviour.

> **Practice points**
>
> **Positive attention and praise**
> - Avoid giving attention when children and young people are showing unwanted behaviour to get attention. Instead, try distraction for younger children, or ignoring them.
> - When wanted behaviour is being shown, give immediate positive attention and praise.
> - Link the praise and attention to the wanted behaviour – for example, 'Well done! You are working hard.'
> - Be sincere in your praise – for example, don't say 'That's amazing!' when the work is not. Children and young people know when adults are doing this and it loses its impact.
> - Praise and positive attention will take time to work with children and young people who have low self-esteem or whose self-concept is based on being 'naughty'.

Formative feedback to help children and young people improve

Formative feedback is a way of giving children and young people information and guidance in order that they can improve their behaviour or attainment. For behaviour, this might mean talking through what a child or young person is doing well and what their next steps might be. This approach can also be used to improve attainment in schools, and may be done either in conversation or through written comments on work.

> **Key term**
>
> **Formative feedback:** verbal or written information that helps children or young people to work out how they can improve.

4.10 How practitioners use a range of strategies to set clear expectations of behaviour

Children and young people find it easier when adults are clear about what they can and can't do. This is particularly important when they move setting or are in new situations such as going on an outing. A range of strategies can be used, as described below.

Establishing a structured approach

A structured approach is often about having routines. This means that children and young people get into habits of what to do and how to behave at certain times. A structured approach may include the start of the day, lunchtime and home time. Having a clear approach helps children and young people feel secure.

Setting age- and stage-appropriate ground rules and boundaries

Expectations for behaviour only work if children and young people can actually manage them. We saw earlier in the chapter how the age and stage of children and young people can affect their behaviour. Our starting point is always to think about what is fair before we set boundaries and ground rules. One of the changes as children and young people develop is that we should increasingly set the rules and boundaries with them. This allows them to understand the rationale of these and they are then more likely to respect them.

Alongside boundary setting, older children and young people need to know what the consequences of breaking boundaries might be. We might, for example, say to a group of seven year olds that they can play with a ball, but if they kick it towards the windows, the ball will be removed.

Acting fairly and consistently

We have seen several times in this chapter the importance of consistency. Children and young people find it hard when rules or expectations keep changing. This is why a behaviour policy is used in settings. Having said that, sometimes in order to act fairly, adults need to show a little flexibility. If this is the case, they need to tell children and young people why the rules have been changed or a child is being treated differently.

Modelling appropriate behaviour

One of the key ways in which adults help children and young people is by modelling the behaviour that is expected. If we want children and young people to talk quietly, we need to be quiet ourselves. We can encourage young children to tidy up by doing it alongside them or encourage young people to pick up litter or items from the floor by modelling this. Modelling behaviour combined with positive reinforcement (see below) can be highly effective.

Positive reinforcement

We have seen how by using positive reinforcement strategies such as praise or even rewards we can encourage expected behaviour as well as improve attainment. In new situations, when we see children or young people are doing something for the first time, we need to be quick to praise and acknowledge. This helps establish wanted behaviours quickly.

4.11 The range of strategies to develop self-regulation and resilience

Self-regulation is the ability to control our impulses and emotions. It is an important skill because it affects children's and young people's ability to cope when things are stressful, to concentrate and persevere, and also to maintain relationships. Children who have developed high levels of self-regulation are more likely to cope with new challenges in their lives and so develop resilience.

> Self-regulation is discussed further in Chapter 2, K2.6.

There are a number of ways in which we can help children and young people to develop self-regulation skills. When planning strategies, we need to consider a child's current level of self-regulation and tailor any strategies accordingly.

Playing games/interactive sessions that encourage turn-taking and impulse control

Many games, including those using technology, require children and young people to cope with strong emotions such as losing or winning. Adults can work with them to role-model and talk through ways of managing these strong emotions. It may be that children and young people learn to 'step back' when things are going badly, to calm down. Games and interactive sessions can be adapted to add to or reduce the amount of excitement/stress involved. Quick, short games that do not have prizes, for example, are easier to cope with than longer games with higher stakes.

▲ Why do games offer a way to help children and young people learn to control their emotions?

Sharing stories that encourage reflection on own and others' emotions

The ability to use words to express complex feelings is important in the development of self-regulation. When children or young people are unable to express their feelings, they are more likely to show aggressive, frustrated and impatient behaviours. Working on language levels and vocabulary is, therefore, a key strategy. There are many ways of doing this, but using stories and books to discuss the feelings and motives of characters can make a difference. We can also use stories to help children and young people find connections between the characters' feelings and their own.

Modelling coping skills

Some children and young people are lucky. Their parents and the adults around them deal with stress well. This in turn allows them to copy the strategies that adults are using. When working with children and young people we need to show how to cope when things are stressful. Modelling coping skills as a strategy works best when adults explain what they are doing as well – for example, an adult might say 'I am counting to ten and taking deep breaths.'

Encouraging physical exercise

Physical exercise can reduce the hormones that are linked to stress. Routine physical exercise is especially important when children's and young people's lives are stressful. In addition, during moments of stress, we can encourage children and young people to manage their emotions by doing things such as jumping up and down on the spot or going for a fast run around a playground until they feel a little calmer.

▲ How can physical exercise support these children's ability to self-regulate?

Supporting socialisation

Some children and young people may need adults to help them socialise, as their self-regulation skills are still developing. This is particularly important with young children, who may benefit from having an adult to guide them while they are still learning to manage their emotions. Older children and young people who, for a variety of reasons, find social skills such as turn-taking and sharing difficult may also need this support.

Encouraging problem solving and supporting reframing challenges in a positive light

Being able to reflect on why we are stressed and how to deal with it positively is a useful strategy for children and young people. It works better with children and young people who have developed good language and thinking skills. This approach requires adults at first to guide children and young people through it. A series of questions can be helpful. They can teach problem solving, and help children and young people to focus on next steps in a positive way.

> ### Practice points
>
> Here are examples of the types of question that might be used to encourage problem solving:
> - What is happening that is making you feel stressed?
> - What emotions are you feeling?
> - Is the source of the stress very short term, temporary or longer term?
> - Is the cause of the stress within your control? For example, 'I am behind with my work because I am watching too many films.'
> - What can you do to eliminate or reduce the cause of the stress?
> - If the stress is outside your control, what can you do to distance yourself from it or lower it? For example, use distraction techniques, exercise.
> - Have you coped and survived similar stress before and, if so, what worked for you?
> - What support might you need or use to help you cope with this stress?

Encouraging mindfulness

Mindfulness has been shown to be useful as a way of helping children and young people to reduce stress. There are several techniques, but they all work on the principle of encouraging children to 'step back', accept and focus on their feelings. To learn mindfulness, children and young people need to be guided but, over time, some older children and young adults will adopt it as a strategy without prompting.

> ### Key term
>
> *Mindfulness:* a technique of reducing stress that involves acknowledging emotions and sensations.

Creating opportunities for children and young people to take supported risks

Fear of failing or not doing well at something can hold back children and young people. They can develop resilience by trying out new things and challenging themselves. By overcoming challenges, children and young people can build resilience. The first step is often to encourage those children and young people who are low in resilience to 'have a go'. Ideally, we need to choose opportunities for children and young people that are challenging but not insurmountable, especially if we guide or support them.

4.12 A range of strategies to respond to behaviour

Adults can respond to with behaviour in children in various ways. Some of these strategies are actually about preventing inappropriate behaviours by understanding the needs of children and young people. A good example of this is attention-seeking behaviours. Attention-seeking tells us that children and young people need more attention. The trick is not to respond to the behaviour itself at the time, but to increase the amount of attention given at other times.

Being fair and consistent

Throughout this chapter, we have looked at the importance of having fair expectations and also consistency. When dealing with inappropriate behaviour, it is important that it is dealt with consistently. This sometimes includes consistently ignoring it, as we have seen in the case of attention-seeking, as we need children and young people to learn that they do not gain attention through these behaviours.

Focusing on the behaviour, rather than the individual

We know that self-concept plays a part in behaviour. It is, therefore, good practice to talk about specific behaviours that need changing rather than about overall characteristics of a child or young person. For example, 'stop being silly' is a general statement. A child or young person may start to believe that they are simply silly. It would be better to say, 'You are making too much noise.' With older children and young people, it is also helpful to add in an explanation of how their behaviour is affecting others – for example, 'When you are noisy, it makes it hard for other people to concentrate.'

Referring to and following the behaviour policy and student code of practice

Earlier in the chapter, we saw that adults must follow the behaviour policy of a setting. This provides consistency and also gives them a clear idea of how to handle different situations. With older children and young people, it can also be helpful to refer to the student code of conduct so that they understand that it is not you suddenly changing the rules – for example, 'You know you are not allowed to run in the corridors while you are in school. It is in the student code.'

Encouraging co-regulation

Children and young people often need an adult to help them calm down and cope in a situation. This process is often referred to as co-regulation. The advantage of working in this way is that over time children and young people can develop some of the skills of self-regulatory behaviour for themselves. An example of this is when we might distract a child from a situation that is difficult for them. Over time, children may start to use this technique for themselves when they are feeling overwhelmed.

Using language that clarifies expectations

We can help children and young people move away from showing unwanted behaviour by clearly stating what they need to do instead: 'If you want to play with the large ball, you need to go outside.'

Providing a calm, safe environment

Children and young people are less likely to become overwhelmed and show responses associated with stress if they are in a calm environment and feel safe. As part of creating a calm, safe environment, routines are important. Routines provide a level of predictability which can be helpful for those children and young people who are easily overwhelmed and show unwanted responses as a result. As part of a calm environment, it is also important to think about noise, visual distractions and movements. Keeping these to a minimum can reduce anxiety and stress responses. It is also important that adults stay calm and show calm responses, by for example lowering their voice tone, moving more slowly and showing open body language.

CORE Chapter 4: Behaviour

EY K2.5 The implications of the behavioural signs a child may display

Sometimes, young children's behaviour may give us clues that they have unmet needs that we need to address. This might mean talking to parents to establish if there are any home circumstances that may be affecting their behaviour. Some types of behaviour may also be linked to safeguarding issues. If you have safeguarding concerns, you should always follow them up in line with the safeguarding policy of your setting.

Regression

There are many reasons why babies and young children might regress. Sometimes, it is simply because they are tired, hungry or poorly. This might mean that a child who can normally feed her- or himself asks to be helped. Regression is also linked to transitions or changes in family life, such as the arrival of a new baby. However, it is also a recognised behavioural sign of abuse.

Withdrawal

Young children are likely to become distressed and withdrawn when their key adults are not available.

> This is linked to separation anxiety (see Core Chapter 7).

Other reasons for withdrawal may include changes to home life. It is also a behavioural sign of abuse.

Attention-seeking

Many young children will show attention-seeking behaviours, especially those under four or five years old. This is because, developmentally, they actually need a lot of time with their key adults. When children are showing attention-seeking behaviours, it is important to recognise that this is usually a sign that they are not getting sufficient attention either at home and/or in the setting. Attention-seeking behaviours usually increase when there are changes in the home, such as the arrival of a new baby.

> **Practice points**
> - Think about the cause of the attention-seeking behaviour, e.g. boredom, insecurity, changes in the home.
> - Avoid making eye contact during attention-seeking behaviour.
> - If it is safe to do so, ignore the behaviour at the time.
> - Significantly increase the amount of positive one-to-one attention at other times.

Antisocial behaviour

Few young children show behaviours that could be categorised as deliberately antisocial. Developmentally, all young children are learning how to be with others. Having said that, you should always notice highly unusual behaviours that are not age-typical, such as a five year old who is biting.

Self-damaging behaviour

The self-damaging behaviours we may see in older children and young people are rare in babies and young children. Signs that a baby or child is emotionally showing extreme stress include refusal to eat, or self-soothing behaviours that are intense and extreme such as banging their head against a surface. Any behaviours that seem extreme or unusual should always be followed up. It may be that there are safeguarding issues or that the child needs additional support.

Distress

Babies and young children do cry. The difference between crying and distress is that in the latter case the crying is very intense and it is hard to reassure or comfort the baby or child. Distress can mean that a baby or young child is in pain and needs medical attention – for example, they may have meningitis (see page 314).

Acting out of character

Any change to how babies and young children behave needs to be noticed if it persists for more than a week or so. There could be many reasons for this, including changes to home life such as family breakdown. It is also a potential sign of abuse.

Depression

Babies and young children can become depressed. Signs of depression in this age group include not eating, regression, withdrawal and difficulty relating to others. The cause of depression in babies and young children is usually related to separation anxiety and a disruption in attachment. It is always important to notice signs of depression, and to consider what emotional support babies and children may need.

> For more on separation anxiety and disruptions to attachment, see Core Chapter 7.

Anxiety

Many babies and young children will show signs of anxiety when they are away from their parents. This is linked to separation anxiety. Signs of anxiety include self-soothing when it is not nap time, such as thumb sucking and rocking. Anxiety may also include young children not talking to adults or not responding to activities. It is important to take these signs of anxiety seriously because if we cannot relax and settle children there is a danger of depression and longer-term emotional difficulties.

Approaches to the management of inappropriate behaviour

We have already looked at the following approaches to the management of inappropriate behaviours:

- applying rules fairly and consistently in line with the setting's policies (page 76)
- modelling and reinforcing positive behaviour (page 74)
- praise, encouragement and use of incentives (pages 71–2 and 73)
- building positive relationships (page 73)
- encouraging self-regulation and co-regulation (page 74).

In addition, here are some other approaches to consider.

Establishing the cause of the behaviours

While it is possible to deal with unwanted behaviours at the time, it is always better to work out their cause. By doing this, it may be possible to prevent further behaviours from occurring.

Involving children in setting rules and boundaries

From around two or three years, it may be possible to involve children in the setting of simple rules, although there is no guarantee they will follow them consistently. Depending on children's level of cognition and language, we can also set some simple boundaries with them.

> **Reflect**
>
> Have you seen how adults in your work placement try to involve children in setting boundaries and rules?

Collaborative problem solving

Some negative behaviours can be managed by supporting children to find solutions for themselves. Young children from around three years can often do this. They may, for example, come up with a system for sharing resources such as tricycles, although to do this they may need to be supported by adults.

Clarifying expectations on an ongoing basis

Young children often find it hard to remember what they should be doing and how they should be behaving. It is not enough just to tell them once. It is also important to realise that young children cannot always generalise so if you say that they should not climb up on a table, they may not realise that this also applies to climbing up on a window sill.

Encouraging self-regulation

In addition to the self-regulation strategies that we considered on pages 74–6, adults can help young children develop self-regulation by maintaining routines, being calm and also being consistent in their approach.

4.13 How practitioners use a range of strategies to motivate children and young people to test and stretch their skills and abilities, including setting high, realistic expectations

Many children and young people are capable of a lot more than they realise. One of the challenges when working with children and especially young people is to help them realise this. There are several strategies that can work well and can help not just behaviour, but also academic progress and wellbeing.

Using age- and stage-appropriate praise and encouragement

We have seen that praise can be a positive reinforcement for behaviour. It can be powerful as a tool to help children and young people stretch themselves. To do this, practitioners need to praise children and young people when they are putting in effort or are showing high levels of perseverance and resilience. If praise is given when children and young people have not made much of an effort, there is a danger that they learn that even if they hardly try they can still get attention. For praise and encouragement to work, the expectations have to be fair while still challenging.

Involving parents/carers as part of a whole-setting approach

Parents and carers play an important role in helping children and young people to work and try hard. They need to know what their child's next steps might be in order to encourage them. This is why reports, parent–practitioner meetings and information sessions are important. Parents and carers can also share information about how their child is doing at home.

> See Core Chapter 5 (page 82) for further information about parent–practitioner partnerships.

Giving individuals a role/responsibility

Being given responsibility, even at a young age, can help with self-concept and confidence. When giving responsibility it is important that it is age- and stage-appropriate, with a very high likelihood that the child or young person can manage it. If the responsibility is too much, it may backfire and they may learn that they are not capable. Responsibility for an eight year old might mean taking the register or a message to the office.

Encouraging self-reflection

While a key strategy with young children is to praise them, ideally, we need children and young people to do things for themselves rather than just to get praise from others. The transition to this requires that adults start asking questions such as, 'How did that feel?' or 'Are you pleased with yourself?' This can help children and young people learn to motivate themselves.

Rewarding effort and success

Rewarding success is linked to positive reinforcement. There have, however, been some studies showing that adults should focus on rewarding effort rather than just achievement. While rewarding success can be useful in the short term and with young children, rewarding effort helps children and young people to learn the skills of perseverance.

Celebrating mistakes as learning opportunities

It is not possible to get everything right in life. For children and young people, this applies to both behaviour and learning. This means that if things do not work out for children and young people, we need to help them learn from their mistakes. For children with sufficient language and thinking skills, we should encourage them to think about what they could have done differently and how they would approach a similar situation in the future. In terms of supporting behaviour, we might also ask why they think the behaviour occurred and the feelings behind it. By using mistakes as learning opportunities, children and young people can not only learn to modify their behaviour, but also to develop skills that are important to making progress in learning.

Encouraging children and young people to recognise one another's positive behaviour

Children and young people often find it easier to manage their behaviour when their peers are encouraging. This requires practitioners to create a culture where children and young people work together as a team. Practitioners can do this by praising children and young people who show care and support for others, and also by discouraging children from telling tales (snitching) on other children.

4.14 How practitioners assess risks to their own and others' safety when dealing with challenging behaviour

Sometimes, children and young people can show behaviour that might cause injury to themselves or others. A toddler, for example, might try to throw wooden bricks during a tantrum, or a 14 year old may throw a chair across a classroom. It is important that practitioners are able to quickly assess risks and find ways to deal safely with this type of behaviour.

Following the setting's policies and procedures

An important starting point is to know and follow the setting's behaviour policy and procedures. These should help you know when, how and if you should use physical restraint. The behaviour policy and procedures will also outline when, how and if you should move other children and young people away, and how and when to summon help.

Being aware of individuals' prior history

Knowing a child's or young person's prior history of challenging behaviour is useful. It means that we can plan ahead to prevent the behaviour from occurring in the first place. We can also think about how we might manage the behaviour if it occurs. While knowing about a child's or young person's history is useful, it is important for adults to always stay positive. Expectations of negative behaviour can actually provoke incidents.

Recognising triggers and early warning signs

Most challenging behaviours are caused by stress, boredom or frustration. Tiredness and hunger can also play a part. By recognising the triggers of challenging behaviour, we can also prevent incidents. This may mean giving additional attention and support to a pupil who you know will find a task difficult so that they do not have a chance to become frustrated. With a toddler, it might mean reading a story just before lunch. As well as recognising triggers, we also have to pick up on the early warning signs that an incident is about to happen. A few examples of early warning signs include:
- raised, angry voices
- excited, uncontrolled behaviour
- withdrawn, sulky behaviours.

Assessing the likelihood of harm to self and others

At the start of an incident, it is essential to stay calm and quickly assess what the potential risks are. If there is a lot of anger and frustration being shown, it is best to talk quietly and move slowly. This can help to calm down the situation. A risk assessment should be done to work out what may be the immediate dangers.

Removing hazards and reducing risk

As part of risk assessment, the behaviour policy and procedures should be followed to remove or reduce risk. This might involve instructing others to leave the area or removing objects that may cause injury. The focus is always on reducing the risk of harm both to the child or young person and to others.

> **Assessment practice**
>
> 1. Give **two** reasons why children and young people need to adapt their behaviour to different social contexts.
> 2. Give **three** examples of factors that might influence a child's or young person's behaviour.
> 3. Explain how a positive self-concept may impact on a child's or young person's behaviour.
> 4. Why is it important that everyone in a setting follows the behaviour policy?
> 5. Give **one** example of a positive non-verbal communication, and explain how it might influence a child's or young person's behaviour.
> 6. Explain the role of praise in supporting children's and young people's positive behaviour.
> 7. Explain why self-regulation is important in children's and young people's ability to manage their behaviour.
> 8. Give **two** positive approaches to motivate children and young people.

CORE Chapter 5:
Parents, Families and Carers

When working within education and childcare, professional relationships with primary carers contribute to best practice and improved outcomes. In this chapter, we will consider the important role of parents, families and carers in the lives of babies, children and young people. We will explore strategies to build professional relationships with parents, the challenges and barriers to effective partnership working that may exist, and ways that these may be overcome. As a professional in education and childcare, parents may approach you for advice and guidance, and this chapter will consider where to find a range of reliable resources to support parents, carers and families.

Learning outcomes

This chapter covers the following knowledge outcomes for Core Element 5:
- **5.1** The advantages of working with parents, carers and wider families to support children and young people
- **5.2** The different contexts in which children may grow up and the importance of being sensitive to this
- **5.3** How to overcome possible barriers to effective partnerships with parents, carers and wider families
- **5.4** Where to find a range of reliable resources to support parents and carers and the wider family

5.1 The advantages of working with parents, carers and wider families to support children and young people

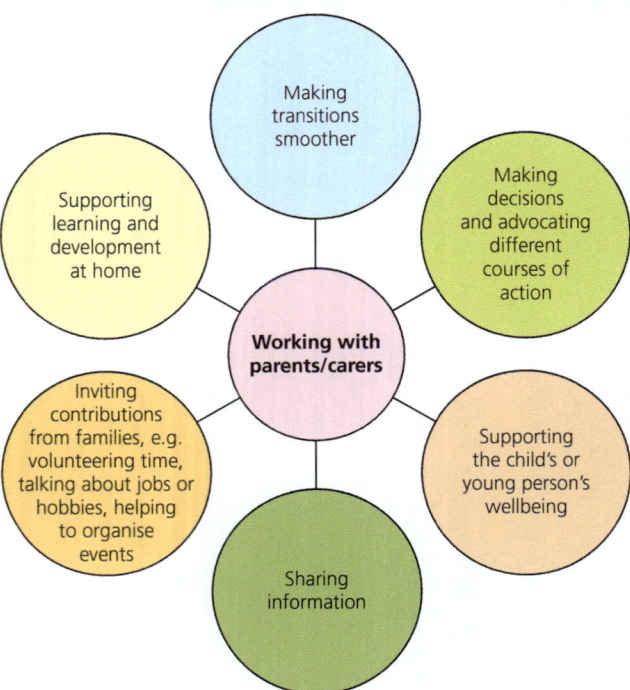

▲ There are several reasons why it is good to work in partnership with parents and carers

Parents, carers and families are sometimes referred to as the **primary carers** for their child/children. This means that they typically provide for their needs, have responsibility to ensure these are met and decide what is best for their child/children. Working collaboratively with professionals in education and childcare to develop professional partnerships with parents, carers and families can contribute significantly to the quality of the experience for all involved.

A shared level of expectation

Working in partnership with parents, carers and families creates a shared level of expectation. For example, exchanging information about the setting with the parent could be particularly useful. Parents and carers will need to be made aware of expectations for teaching and learning – for example, the approach to home learning, school uniform, code of conduct, and opportunities for parents and carers to be actively engaged. For babies and young children, this will include discussions around care needs, what to provide for children and what is provided at the setting. Policies also help parents and carers to understand the level of expectation – for example, sharing expectations for behaviour may be helpful.

As we know, parents, carers and families want what is best for their children. There is a shared expectation that children will benefit from their experiences in education and care, both through educational attainment, but also, and significantly, that children will benefit holistically. Positive outcomes for children are, therefore, an acknowledged shared level of expectation. Parents and carers should expect high-quality education and care, provided by professional staff who are qualified, experienced and skilled to meet the children's individual needs within the legislative framework as required.

Making transitions smoother

Partnerships with parents, carers and families can be of particular benefit during transition.

> You will consider how transition may influence development in Core Chapter 7 (Section 7.6, page 131), which has useful information about the different types of transitions that typically exist in education and childcare.

There are many transitions that children will experience, such as changes to the family dynamic, and some of these will be unplanned. In this section, however, we will consider typical planned transitions in education and childcare. These include:
- starting nursery (or other early years setting)
- moving between carers in the early years setting (for example, from baby room to toddler room)
- starting primary school
- moving through classes and key stages in primary school
- starting secondary school
- moving through classes and key stages in secondary school
- starting at college (or sixth form)
- starting employment (apprenticeship).

Parents, carers and families know their child the best; they are very valuable sources of information for education and childcare staff, and education and childcare staff provide the same in return, offering advice and guidance, discussing any concerns and signposting to services as appropriate. Professional partnerships rely on effective communication and trust. Building and maintaining effective professional partnerships supports smooth transition through effective communication, discussing any concerns and working collaboratively to prepare and support children before and during transition.

Let's consider how transition may impact children and young people, and how educational settings can support children and young people at these times.

- **Starting nursery (or other early years setting):** For babies, the stage of attachment and the role of the key person is fundamental in establishing a safe and secure transition. Preparation for starting nursery with young children should wherever possible not be rushed but a relaxed, gradual transition. Some young children may be very excited about starting nursery, but this does not detract from their emotional needs and the importance of the key person for building and maintaining secure relationships with children and their families.
- **Moving between carers in the early years setting (for example, from baby room to toddler room):** We often underestimate how moving from one room to another can be a huge transition for young children. The familiarity of a physical space offers emotional security and a level of independence to babies and young children. Moving between rooms gradually, mixing with children and staff from another room, can be helpful. Some early years settings will come together at specific times of the day, such as early morning and late afternoon as well as being able to enjoy mealtimes together. This social experience supports holistic development and wellbeing during this type of transition.
- **Starting primary school:** This is a huge milestone in a young child's life. The child is likely to feel a mixture of strong, powerful emotions, such as excitement, anxiety or fear. It is important to reassure children and for staff to prepare them. There are several approaches staff can take to support this transition. Staff from both settings can meet to allow for an exchange of relevant information. Visits and settling-in days are popular and prepare the child through gradual introductions. Making friendships is an important feature of this transition and when children feel secure in their personal and physical environment, they will be more likely to develop healthy dispositions for learning.
- **Moving through classes and key stages in primary school:** Again, the move between classrooms can bring strong feelings. Children may feel a little excited but are likely to have some concerns, too. As children get older and move through school, they are usually reassured by their strong friendship groups that they have established and moving class together with a friend can be far less scary. Children also begin to understand what the transition is, and it becomes an expected event that they can talk about more easily. This does not make the transition any less significant and staff should monitor how children are settling in and be mindful of their individual needs.
- **Starting secondary school:** This can, for some, be one of the biggest transitions in education. It brings together groups of children from different primary schools, so settling can be a difficult time. Children are also likely to be experiencing sensitive periods of time in their physical development and with the onset of puberty there are many changes that children may experience. The changes in routine, the walk to school or the need to travel further, the different classroom layouts and the changes in teaching staff as well as lessons, expectations and even a change in uniform can all add to transition challenges for children. Settling-in days, taster days and activities to encourage friendship groups, through tutor classes and group activities for example, support this transition for children.
- **Moving through classes and key stages in secondary school:** As children progress through secondary school they often do so with strong friendship groups, but this is not always the case and staff should be mindful of interruptions to friendship groups and support a sense of belonging for all children. Expectations change as children progress through secondary school, exams, career choices and next steps planning in education.
- **Starting at college (or sixth form):** This can be another significant transition for young people. There may be a change in social groups as young people consider their career choices and options for further study. Making new friends, adjusting to new routines and new teaching and learning content can be challenging. Some areas of study, like education and childcare, require placement experience in a real work environment and this too brings its own challenges for students as they enter the world of work for the first time. Taster days, induction and the skills of a mentor or personal tutor can really

help students to settle into new routines and feel comfortable in their environment.

- **Starting employment:** Starting a job is very exciting but there will be feelings of apprehension, too. Students will be exposed to a world of work for potentially the first time and will very quickly be expected to meet expectations, follow new routines and work with colleagues. Induction, mentors and supervision opportunities will support a new member of staff, such as an apprentice, to feel confident in their new environment.

Transitions are not always planned and, even for planned transitions, children's holistic development and wellbeing may be impacted. Children with special educational needs or who are experiencing additional personal circumstances will need to be professionally supported through transitions to ensure consistency of education and care. Parents and carers should also be encouraged to be actively involved in transition. Unplanned transitions such as a sudden unexpected change in family dynamic may further impact on holistic health, development and wellbeing as well as potentially further impacting planned transitions and how well they may cope with challenging situations.

Supporting learning and development at home

Influences from the home environment are of tremendous importance for babies, children and young people. Home experiences also offer a great opportunity for learning to take place. Through positive partnership working with parents, carers and families, staff in education and childcare will be able to support this. There are many examples of learning in the home environment – for example, younger children can learn a great deal from everyday routines. Children experience matching, sorting and counting quite incidentally when getting dressed, setting the table or going shopping, for example. Young children enjoy stories; being read to and sharing books together not only provides opportunities for early literacy and a love of books, but can also just be the pleasure that children and parents/carers find in spending time together. Many early years settings will be able to share books for home reading, sometimes with props and activities that can be enjoyed together. Visits to the local library can also extend home school learning; there are often events for children and parents/carers to nurture a love of books and storytelling.

For older children, home learning may extend to topics and projects that they can work through at home. The key to supporting learning and development at home lies in communication and positive relationships between staff in education and childcare and parents, carers and families.

A child's love for music is often nurtured in the home environment. Musical instruments are very expensive and so some schools will lend children instruments to enable them to continue their learning in their home environment.

Developing a partnership with parents, carers and families that is strong enough to actively encourage learning and development at home is an important role for all staff across education and childcare.

> **Case study**
>
> Ella is four years of age. She loves spending time being creative, and enjoys mixing colours and painting at nursery. Ella spends a lot of time with her grandparents and her grandfather has asked staff if Ella could spend less time painting and more time preparing for school.
> - How could staff support Ella's grandfather to understand the benefits of creativity for learning?
> - Can you think of ways that the staff at the nursery could support Ella's grandparents by providing some creative home learning experiences that they could enjoy with her?

> **Research**
>
> Find out more about guided reading and how parents can be involved in supporting children with independent reading strategies at home.

Involving parents, carers and families in the setting

Actively involving parents, carers and families in a child's education and care is important. Settings can involve parents, carers and families in many ways, including:

- **Volunteering time in the setting:** Parents, carers and families may volunteer time in the setting, working alongside staff in education and childcare. This may include supporting off-site visits or listening to children read, or even specialist talks with older children around hobbies and interests – for example, cooking or sewing with the children. Such experiences strengthen the professional relationship between staff and parents, promoting a welcoming environment, as well as raising confidence in children while widening their experiences too.

▶ **Helping with events:** There are often opportunities when staff numbers need to be boosted, such as when taking children on organised events and celebrations. Parents, carers and families play a vital role here, often supporting planning stages as well as helping during an event. Parents, carers and families can be actively involved in their children's education, giving their time to support in any parent groups or organisations, for example. In some settings across education and childcare, there are parent teacher associations (PTAs). Regardless of the setting, parents, carers and families are much valued as key partners in education and childcare, and will often be called upon to support at events, open days and fundraising activities.

Sharing information and supporting the child's or young person's wellbeing

When parents, carers and families work in partnership with settings, trust develops between them. This encourages sharing important information about their children with staff, which means staff have a greater insight into the needs and personal circumstances of children. In the same way, parents can share photos of activities or events at home so staff can encourage some children to contribute during circle time, for example. It is not uncommon for early years settings and schools to use protected, secure online arrangements in line with policy and procedure, for sharing photographs and feedback which might share the child's achievements or participation as it happens.

When there is a trusting relationship between staff and parents, carers and families this helps the staff in all aspects of education and welfare. For example, parents and carers are much more likely to approach staff to share sensitive information about their child/children if there is a feeling of trust. When parents and carers do share important information about their child it can support staff to ensure that the child/children receive the best possible care. When staff are aware of a child's personal circumstances, such as a family bereavement, ill health, mental health issue or a change in the family dynamic, they are much more able to support that child and monitor their progress.

Making decisions and advocating different courses of action

Advocacy involves listening to others, and providing accurate and relevant information and options to support an individual to make informed decisions. An effective advocate will always listen and never judge. When staff feel that they need to share information with parents, carers and families in the best interests of the child, they are advocating on behalf of the child. Parents, carers and families will also advocate on behalf of their child – for example, by discussing their child's needs and any specific provision that their child may need.

There are specific roles for parents and carers to get involved in decision making within education and childcare, such as parent governor or member of the PTA.

> **Research**
>
> Find out more about the role of parent governors and summarise the role they play in education and childcare. Contribute to a group discussion to share your findings. It may be useful to work in groups and look at the role of the governor in different types of settings, from early years to post-compulsory education.

5.2 The different contexts in which children may grow up

In order to work effectively with parents, carers and families, staff working in education and childcare must understand the characteristics of different family structures. In this section, we will look at some different types of family structure, including:

▶ **Nuclear families:** A nuclear family unit typically consists of two parents raising a child/children. This includes families where one or both parents may identify as lesbian, gay, bisexual or transgender (LGBT).
▶ **Single-parent families:** A single-parent family unit consists of a lone parent raising a child/children.
▶ **Extended families:** An extended family unit consists of multiple members of the same family living in the same home and possibly co-raising the child/children.

- **Foster families:** A foster family unit will consist of foster parents who care for children, typically, in the short term, who are not their own.
- **Adoptive families:** An adoptive family unit will consist of adoptive parents, and at least one child who has been adopted and lives with the adoptive family as part of the permanent family unit.
- **Blended/stepfamilies:** A blended or stepfamily unit consists of a combination of two separate families, with one or both parents having children from previous relationships.

▲ An extended family

The characteristics of parenting styles

The influence of parents, carers and families is significant for children's holistic development. There are different types of parenting style. To help us to understand the characteristics of parenting styles, let's consider some of them:

- **Authoritarian:** An authoritarian parenting style will place an emphasis on obedience and control. This style of parenting leaves little room for negotiation or compromise, and reasons for rules are not necessarily explained to children and young people.
- **Permissive:** A permissive parenting style will typically have few rules or expectations. There may be a relaxed approach to behaviour, and children tend to have more choice and responsibility.
- **Authoritative:** An authoritative parenting style will set rules and expectations with clear boundaries. Parents will take time to explain these to their children, and to listen to and consider their views.
- **Instinctive:** An instinctive parenting style is, as its name suggests, strongly influenced by instinct. The style will be highly reactive to the parents' own upbringing.
- **Uninvolved:** An uninvolved parenting style is typically characterised by a lack of responsiveness, leaving children alone, and this may in extreme circumstances lead to neglect.
- **Helicopter:** A helicopter parenting style may mean that parents are heavily involved in every aspect of their children's lives, which may limit their independence and lead to frustration.

Why it is important to be sensitive to different parenting styles and different family contexts

Most parents, carers and families want what is best for their children. It is important to be sensitive to different parenting styles, and mindful of the important role parents, carers and families play as their child's first educators. This helps staff in education and childcare to:

- **Value and respect families:** This is critical to effective communication, making connections, and establishing and maintaining positive professional relationships based on trust. It also ensures fair and **inclusive practice**, with nobody shown preference or discrimination. This will also support the effective exchange of information between staff in the setting and parents, carers and families, which leads to better outcomes for children.

> **Key term**
>
> *Inclusive practice:* Developing an approach that recognises the diversity of children and young people, and promotes positive attitudes, differentiation and respect.

- **Contribute to inclusion in planning and provision:** Listening to parents, carers and families helps with planning effectively for children's needs and stage of development, and shows an appreciation of their individual circumstances.
- **Inform understanding of behavioural context:** Professional relationships with staff will support development of trust with parents, carers and families. This helps to promote ways of working together and modelling the same things, giving a consistency of expectation in relation to behaviour.

- **Inform understanding of developmental delay:** Parents and carers must be appreciated and valued as the child's first or primary educator. As such the parent or carer is often the first to notice any concerns about their child's development. It is essential that staff in education and childcare settings listen attentively and sensitively to any concerns raised by parents and carers and act accordingly. Sometimes, staff in education and childcare will need to have conversations with parents and carers that are sensitive, such as discussing their child's development, raising any developmental concerns. All conversations are most effective when staff and parents, carers and families are aware of and sensitive to the individual family context and parenting approach, and are supportive rather than judgemental.

5.3 Understand the possible barriers to effective partnerships with parents, carers and wider families

When establishing effective partnerships with parents, carers and families there are many possible barriers that may exist. Some of these are as follows:

- **Time constraints:** Parents, carers and families will have commitments, including employment and responsibilities for other siblings or dependants. Finding time to hold a discussion beyond a few minutes can be challenging for some parents.
- **Work commitments:** Parents, carers and families will have a commitment to their employer or be self-employed. Some may also work irregular hours or shift patterns, so their availability may vary more than that of someone who works part-time or consistent weekday hours.
- **Limited resources:** Some settings will find it difficult to resource meetings. For example, there may be limited private areas for discussions to be held where parents, carers and families feel able to speak openly to staff, or if a meeting is planned at a time that requires additional travel, this puts an extra burden on the parent, carer or family, who may find the cost of travel a challenge.
- **Mistrust from families:** When professional relationships between staff in education and childcare and parents, carers and families have not been established it may be difficult to establish trust, making it less likely that parents, carers and families will approach staff and exchange information with them. Parents, carers and families may also find it difficult to build a relationship with staff in education and childcare. This can be for many reasons. They may feel that by admitting they need support or by sharing personal circumstances they may be judged as parents and carers. Where barriers exist, it is the responsibility of staff in education and childcare to use strategies to actively engage them and break down any barriers in the best interests of the child or young person.
- **English as an additional language:** If English is not their first language or they have little or no ability to speak it, there may be a language barrier that exists between parents, carers and families and the staff in a setting. This brings challenges for all aspects of communication and working together.
- **Special educational needs or disabilities (SEND):** Parents, carers and families may have special educational needs themselves or care for an individual with SEND. Remember that not all SEND conditions are visible and it is important to be sensitive to the needs of all families.
- **Family members' own negative educational experiences:** Parents, carers and families may have had negative experiences themselves in their own education – for example, racism and/or bullying. Because of this, they may feel reluctant to engage with staff and may choose to hold back from information sharing.

How to overcome possible barriers

Staff in education and childcare settings should work in ways that overcome such barriers. Examples of useful strategies include:

- **The key person:** A key person is a member of staff who works in an early years setting; one of their main responsibilities will be to develop positive partnership working with the parents, carers and families of specific children. Older children and young people will benefit from the pastoral support of a class teacher or personal tutor, who will monitor and review the emotional welfare of the children and young people that they are involved with.
- **Offering an open-door policy:** Many settings across education and childcare will allow parents/carers to drop in and meet with staff at any time without requiring an appointment, with the aim of accommodating parents' varied lifestyles and commitments.

- **Encouraging home communication:** Settings will share information through a range of different media to enable consultation and improve communication, including secure family forums and apps, parent/carer questionnaires, and regular telephone or email contact. This must always be secure and access restricted only to those who are entitled to receive this information.
- **Ensuring the building is accessible:** Settings need to be accessible and inclusive for the benefit of all staff, families, children and visitors, who may have a variety of access needs – for example, adaptations in the physical environment to include hearing aid loops, Braille signs, wheelchair lifts, ramps and accessible toilets/changing rooms.
- **Organising open days/evenings:** Many settings will organise open days or evening events to reach out to as many people as possible at a time that is convenient. This gives parents, carers and families time to exchange information and discuss their child/young person.
- **Using translators or child advocates:** Staff in education and childcare may use the specialist support of a translator or sign language interpreter, or they may work with other children and young people to support communication with parents, carers and family members. Newsletters should be presented in a way that all parents and carers can understand. The home language used by the child's or young person's parents and carers should always be valued; there is always a way of communicating effectively and staff must find an approach that works.
- **Offering home visits:** Staff in education and childcare may offer home visits at certain stages. This is a strategy that is often used during transition in the early years when young children are starting nursery for the first time, for example. Parents and carers will often feel more comfortable in their own home and this can remove any barriers that may exist for the parent or carer regarding time, access and travel costs. Home visits can also be beneficial for the teacher as they can begin to appreciate the holistic needs of the family. Staff working across education and early years are able to maximise the use of technology to maintain communication and exchange information. This may include updates and information about open days, trips and events, as well as virtual meetings that may replace face-to-face meetings with parents/carers.

Case studies

Read through the following case studies before responding to the questions. You may choose to work independently or with others.

Jayita is a single parent with two children, aged seven and ten years old. A childminder brings the children to school and collects them each day as Jayita has to work during this time.
- How can staff ensure that they communicate effectively with Jayita?
- Why is establishing that communication with Jayita so important?

Stefan is three years old and uses English as a second language. His parents do not speak English and manage to communicate with the support of Marianne, Stefan's older sister, who is aged eight.
- Why do you think it is important that staff are able to communicate with Stefan's parents?
- What might happen if Stefan's parents feel they are not included in conversations about their son's education and care?

Darren is a single parent. He cares for his daughter, Jo, aged 18 months. Staff at the early years setting that Jo attends each day are finding it difficult to communicate effectively with Darren as he always appears in a rush, and seems nervous and anxious when approached by staff.
- How can staff in the early years setting promote effective communication with Darren?

5.4 Where to find a range of reliable resources to support parents, carers and wider families

From time to time, parents, carers and families may face challenges that will benefit from support from outside of the education and childcare setting – for example, an unexpected change to family circumstances that impacts on health, employment, income or housing.

CORE Chapter 5: Parents, Families and Carers

There are a range of reliable resources provided by services to support parents, carers and families, including:
- charities
- the NHS and healthcare centres
- community centres
- Citizens Advice
- Children's Services
- the Special Educational Needs and Disabilities Information Advice and Support Services (SENDIASS).

▲ Citizens Advice

Resource	What it is and where to find it
Charities	A wide range of charities exist to help parents, carers and families navigate challenging situations, such as: • National Childbirth Trust (NCT) • Gingerbread for single parents • Disability Rights UK • Anxiety UK • Crisis for homeless people • Turn2us for financial support. These charities provide information online about how to access their services, through websites and phone numbers.
NHS	The NHS provides a range of support services for parents, carers and families for both physical and mental health. These will support children, young people and their parents with physical health conditions and mental health issues, and can be accessed through GP surgeries, hospitals and healthcare centres.
Healthcare centres	Larger healthcare centres exist to provide a wider range of NHS services for the community. They support parents and carers, particularly those who have children with health needs, through access to community nurses and pharmacies.
Community centres	Community centres provide a neighbourhood space or hub for local residents to meet. This could be a purpose-built community centre or an organisation run through a town, village or church hall. Weekly events might take place such as a youth club, sports events, Guides and Brownies, Scouts and Cubs, community groups (e.g. faith groups) or recreational activities.
Citizens Advice	Citizens Advice is available to provide advice and support to parents, carers and families on a wide range of issues. It has premises in most towns and can usually be accessed through telephone appointments or online.
Children's Services	Children's Services exist to support vulnerable people, including children, young people and their parents, and to protect their wellbeing. They are usually based in the home setting. Children, young people and their parents may be referred to Children's Services through another service such as a doctor, school or health visitor. They may also refer themselves.
SENDIASS	This is a locally based service which provides information, support and advice for parents and carers of children and young people who have SEND, and also provides direct support for 16 to 25 year olds. It is accessed online through a local page, and helps all those who need advice and additional resources.

▲ Resources to support parents, carers and wider families

For more on this, see Core Chapter 1.

Reflect

Work in groups to explore the different services identified above. Find examples from across the services listed and produce a factsheet to summarise the support available for parents, carers and families. This information could be collated as a resource file, or the information could be shared through a group discussion or peer group presentation with a question-and-answer session.

Assessment practice

1. Identify **three** benefits of parental engagement in education and childcare.
2. Suggest **two** ways in which parental engagement can be promoted in education and childcare.
3. Identify **one** barrier to effective partnership working with parents and explain how it may be overcome.
4. List **three** different parenting styles and explain each one.
5. Define the term blended/stepfamily unit.
6. Which type of family unit describes a family living with or close to relatives?
    a) nuclear
    b) extended
    c) adoptive
    d) stepfamily
7. Starting nursery is an example of a transition. Analyse the role of effective partnerships with parents, carers and families during a transition.
8. A parent at your setting has confided in you that his family is struggling with large financial debt, and due to recent unemployment is feeling unable to cope. What support would it be appropriate to give?

Project practice

Read through the newsletter from a childminder to parents/carers below, then complete the tasks that follow.

Welcome to my summer newsletter, to keep parents informed about my childminding services and plans for the future, changes, holiday dates and general reminders. I would welcome your input! Should you have any ideas for subjects for my winter newsletter that you might find interesting, or any activities you want to share with me that I can do with your children, please let me know.

It has been lovely welcoming all the children back after a somewhat unusual time with the pandemic.

We missed all the children during lockdown, and they have all certainly missed each other! It has been lovely seeing them all restart their friendships with their buddies, and to watch the wonderful ideas and creative play they are getting involved in.

We have been spending more time in the garden for wellbeing, lots of fresh air and physical activity, and have been washing hands very frequently throughout the day.

The vegetables some of the children helped sow in mid-May and at the beginning of June are growing beautifully. We have harvested some carrots and spring onions, which the children delighted in pulling out of the ground and eating!

Our watermelons are starting to form. It is amazing to see the two small mini-watermelons forming behind the flower!

CORE Chapter 5: Parents, Families and Carers

All the children are involved in caring for the various fruits and vegetables, and have been watering them and watching them change almost on a daily basis.

We have been discussing how the watermelon flowers are pollinated by bees, wasps and other nectar-seeking insects who hop from flower to flower to distribute the pollen.

Since the children have shown a lot of interest in the plants, our summer project is called 'Plants that grow underground and plants that grow above ground'.

The children have created some lovely art work of sunflowers, pumpkins and watermelons. We also did an activity on healthy eating. Due to current restrictions, I will share the playroom enquiry wall with you by WhatsApp!

We have been sharing books on healthy foods and growing vegetables, as well as nursery songs to support learning.

This week, we harvested our potatoes from the vegetable patch.

After collecting the potatoes, the children individually peeled and mixed their own ingredients to make tuna, potato and sweetcorn fishcakes using these freshly harvested potatoes. This brought the learning to life and children ate their fishcakes with lots of enthusiasm!

The sweetcorn is growing so fast. Although it is not ripe yet, the children have been watching the stalks grow. We will be measuring their length every day using a tape measure and recording the growth twice a week. The sunflowers are being measured too! I have been encouraging new words and more complex vocabulary around the activity where these can be introduced.

I hope you enjoyed seeing the pictures of your child harvesting from the veg patch and the cooking of the fishcakes on WhatsApp, along with other photos of your children engaged in activities this term!

General reminders

Plenty of wet weather changes of clothes – lots of water play is planned!

My holidays dates are:

Friday 14–21 Aug (incl.)

Thurs 24 Dec–1 Jan (incl.)

Task 1
- Identify the different ways the childminder is involving the parents/carers.
- Think about children in different settings across education and childcare, and how staff at these settings involve parents/carers and families. Make a list of as many different ways you can think of, and discuss with your peers the benefits to staff, parents, carers and families.

Task 2
Devise a leaflet for parents/carers that suggests a range of different ways to become involved in their children's education. You should identify the benefits of working in partnership with parents and carers.

Task 3
Describe how staff in education and childcare encourage home school learning.

CORE Chapter 6:
Working with Others

In this chapter, we will consider the range of diverse services that can be accessed by parents/carers, families, children and young people to offer support and guidance. When considering the range of services available we will take the opportunity to explore the roles of other professionals, and the significance of professional relationships and boundaries for effective partnership working. Collaborative ways of working for improved outcomes in the care and education of children and young people will be at the core of this chapter.

Learning outcomes

This chapter covers the following knowledge outcomes for Core Element 6:

- 6.1 How agencies and services support children, parents/carers and wider families
- 6.2 The roles of other professionals in supporting children, parents/carers and families
- 6.3 How to work collaboratively with other agencies and professionals
- 6.4 Why practitioners establish and maintain professional boundaries and relationships with children and young people, families and other professionals

This chapter also includes one knowledge outcome from Early Years Educator Performance Outcome 5. Text relating to Early Years Educator is highlighted. Note that this content will not form part of the core assessments.
- K5.3 The roles and responsibilities of external agencies involved in early years settings

6.1 How agencies and services support children, parents/carers and wider families

Charities and voluntary organisations

There are a range of charitable, voluntary or not-for-profit organisations that provide services for children, young people and their families. These are not-for-profit organisations that may also receive some funding from a local authority that values and requires the services that the organisation is able to provide within its region. Charitable organisations rely on donations to some extent, but are also able to provide services for children and young people as part of local authority provision. This involves a service-level agreement (a kind of contract) between a local authority and a charitable organisation, which allows the local authority to fund the voluntary setting in order that children and young people can benefit from the specialist support offered by the voluntary service.

There are many examples of such charitable and voluntary organisations and it may be useful to think about any such organisations that operate in your local area.

> **Good to know**
>
> Registered charities are part of the voluntary sector. Not all voluntary organisations are registered as charities (e.g. some community groups).

Some key organisations in this sector are:
- Family Action
- Family Rights Group
- Action for Children
- NSPCC
- Save the Children.

Some information is provided below on each of these organisations. As a member of staff it is useful to know about organisations that can support children, young people and families in particular circumstances. Staff in education and childcare may work as part of a professional team with staff from other organisations, including those listed above, in order to share information about the child, young person or family and work towards improved outcomes.

- **Family Action** aims to provide 'practical, emotional and financial support to families and to individuals who are experiencing poverty, disadvantage and social isolation'. www.family-action.org.uk
- **Family Rights Group** aims to support parents, carers and families by providing advice, guidance and advocacy, particularly regarding at-risk children and the care system. Family Rights Group will offer advice to individuals requiring support about their rights and any potential options that may be available to them in particular circumstances – for example, when social workers or courts make decisions about their child's or children's welfare. www.frg.org.uk
- **Action for Children** exists to provide support to children and young people through practical and emotional care, including advocacy services to ensure children's and young people's voices are heard, when they feel unable to do so themselves or if they find themselves in situations requiring specialist support. Action for Children will support children, young people and families in crisis – for example, children and families living in abusive situations, homelessness or in danger of eviction – and offers advice and practical help. www.actionforchildren.org.uk
- The **NSPCC** is a charity working to safeguard and protect children and young people from abuse. It provides many services, including national helplines, advice for children and families, therapeutic services, research and insight, as well as offering advice and training in schools and colleges. www.nspcc.org.uk
- **Save the Children** works in the UK and across the world to provide services to children, young people and their families, keeping them safe and healthy. The charity works with schools to support families with children's learning and literacy, helps low-income families with skills and resources to support their children in learning and development, and campaigns for fairer outcomes for children and young people. www.savethechildren.org.uk

> **Research**
>
> List as many charitable and voluntary organisations that work with children, young people and families as you can. Find out what services they provide and for whom. Create a resource file of the organisations that you find. Include information on which organisations operate within your own local area.

Public services

Public services can be broken down into two categories: **statutory** and **non-statutory** public services. Statutory public services are required to be provided by law, i.e. local or national government must ensure they exist and are funded. Statutory public services include the National Health Service (NHS), education and social services, local education authority service provision and Children's Services.

Non-statutory public services are not required by law, but are still needed by the public in practical situations and these services still provide crucial help. Examples include electricity, gas and water supplies. These are available but may not be publicly managed, but instead be provided by private companies, as is the case in the UK.

The National Health Service

The NHS was set up in 1948 to provide healthcare in the UK that is free at the point of use. This includes some mental health provision as well as services related to all aspects of physical health. Some services, such as prescription charges in England, ophthalmic services and dental services, are now charged for. However, they remain free of charge for children from birth to 16 years of age (or in full-time education), for those who are pregnant or with a baby under 12 months of age, as well as for families who are in receipt of certain benefits. Other exemptions may also apply. In Scotland, Northern Ireland and Wales no charges are made for prescriptions.

> **Good to know**
>
> In the same way that local authorities may develop service-level agreements with voluntary services to provide services for children, young people and families, the NHS also has links with private organisations. An example of this may be an individual accessing counselling through the NHS, where the counselling service may be provided by a private service.
>
> Clinical commissioning groups (CCGs) are responsible for decision making involving the types of services that their local authorities will allocate funding to. This can lead to different levels of service provision and access in different local authorities. An example of this would be speech and language therapy.

> **Research**
>
> Work with your peers in a small group to list as many different types of services that are provided by the NHS as you can, and the type of support they offer for children, young people and their families.

Child and Young People's Mental Health Services (CYPMHS)

Mental health services provided by the NHS include dedicated services for children and young people. Specialist CYPMHS are NHS mental health services that focus on the needs of children and young people. The term Children and Adolescent Mental Health Services (CAMHS) is an older term for the main specialist NHS community service within the wider CYPMHS that may be available locally.

Multidisciplinary teams that work within children's and young people's mental health services include one or more of the following specialist occupational roles:
- psychiatrist
- psychologist
- social worker
- nurse
- support worker
- occupational therapist
- psychological therapist (this may include child psychotherapists, family psychotherapists, play therapists and creative art therapists)
- primary mental health link workers
- specialist substance misuse workers.

> **Key term**
>
> *Multidisciplinary team:* a team that consists of professionals working together from across the sector who have different roles. For example, a health visitor and a social worker may work together with an early years practitioner to bring together their specialist expertise in order to support a child and their family at a particular time.

> **Research**
>
> Work together with your peers to explore the specialist roles listed above. Find out what each role involves when supporting children, young people and their families, and make notes.

Children's Services (education and social services for children)

Children's Services are provided by each local authority. The services offered within Children's Services include education and social services. Children's social services will provide specialist staff to support families with babies, children and young people in need of additional help, guidance and intervention as appropriate. The types of circumstances when social services may be accessed include:
- when there is a risk of harm or abuse to a baby, child or young person
- when a family is caring for a baby, child or young person with a disability
- when caring for **looked after children** and where fostering and adoption services are required.

> **Key term**
>
> **Looked after child (LAC):** a child who has been in the care of their local authority for more than 24 hours, sometimes also referred to as children in care. This can include children living with foster parents, in a residential children's home, hostel or secure accommodation.

Local education authorities

Children's education services are provided through local education authorities (LEAs, part of local government) and will include schools and colleges and their special educational needs provision. As you know, there are many different types of education and childcare provision. Education, health and care plans (EHCPs) are put in place by the local authority. The head teacher/manager will work with the SENDCo to make sure that these plans are reviewed as appropriate to ensure the strategies shared are being effective.

> For more on the different types of education and childcare provision, see Core Chapter 1.

Special educational needs review team

The EHC review team is responsible for statutory education, health and care needs assessments for children and young people aged from birth to 25 years, in line with the SEND Code of Practice.

When a child or young person has been identified as having a special educational need or disability, settings should make plans to:
- remove barriers to learning
- put in place effective special educational provision.

> See Core Chapter 11 for more on EHC and SEND in general.

SEND support is offered as part of the **graduated approach**. This is a four-part approach that works in a cycle. The four stages are:
1. Assess
2. Plan
3. Do
4. Review.

> **Research**
>
> Education, health and care plans (EHCPs) are developed, monitored and reviewed in line with the graduated approach. Find out more about the graduated approach as it applies to the role of staff in education and childcare.

6.2 The roles of other professionals in supporting children, parents/carers and families

Children, young people and families may benefit from support from professionals who can offer specialist advice, guidance and intervention strategies as appropriate. Some of these specialist roles include:
- **Educational psychologist:** Educational psychologists are applied psychologists who work across the educational system and also in the community. They may also work with individuals and families.
- **Education mental health practitioner:** An education mental health practitioner (EMHP) will be employed through a healthcare organisation. As well as working in healthcare centres or settings they will also work in education, for example in schools, colleges or special schools. They are trained to support children and young people with a range of mental health difficulties such as anxiety and depression and to provide strategies to manage their needs as well as liaise with parents and carers.
- **General practitioner (GP):** GPs are qualified medical doctors working in health centres/surgeries within the local community. They work with others as part of multidisciplinary teams to support the **holistic** care needs of individuals. GPs work in health promotion and lifestyle change to prevent

poor health across the lifespan. They also have a vital role in safeguarding and protection, working with other professionals to keep children, young people and families safe.

> **Key term**
>
> *Holistic:* overall or all round; the idea that the parts of something are interconnected so looking at the whole rather than each individual part. Here it means all-round care needs, with an appreciation of the contribution of each care need to overall wellbeing.

Other professionals working with the GP as part of a multidisciplinary team include nurses, midwives, health visitors (see below), physiotherapists and occupational therapists.

- **School nurse:** School nurses are typically responsible for an individual school or group of schools. The school nurse works with children, young people and families to promote holistic health, including the mental health and wellbeing of children and young people from five to nineteen years of age.
- **Health visitor:** A health visitor is a qualified nurse or midwife who has undertaken additional relevant training for this specialist role. The health visitor will work within the community and will support babies, young children and their families. Health visitors often hold clinics in a GP surgery or health centre but will also make home visits.
- **Social worker:** Social workers provide support for children, young people and families who need additional support. This additional support can be required to safeguard and protect babies, children and young people at times of need. They will also work with families and other professionals to ensure best outcomes for children and young people with disabilities, as well as those who are looked after children.
- **SENDCo:** The special educational needs and disabilities coordinator works with the nursery, school or college to ensure that the individual SEND needs of children and young people are met. They contribute to meetings and advocate in the best interests of the children. SENDCos will produce an EHCP for children and young people aged up to 25 years of age. The SENDCo will offer advice, and work collaboratively with other professionals and families to ensure best practice is consistently applied. SENDCos in school settings will be qualified teachers. They will need to undertake further study to maintain their role.

> See Core Chapter 11 for more on SEND.

- **SENDCo/Area SENDCos:** These are experienced teachers working with young children with special educational needs and/or disabilities (SEND) and their families. They work for the local authority and are able to offer advice as well as signpost to additional services and support.
- **Local Authority Designated Officer (LADO):** All information regarding potential or actual harm to children and young people must be reported in accordance with policy and procedures that are in line with statutory guidelines identified through Keeping Children Safe in Education 2022. In the event of a concern/allegation about the headteacher, where the headteacher is also the sole proprietor of an independent school, or a situation where there is a conflict of interest in reporting the matter to the headteacher, this should be reported directly to the LADO. The local LADO should be accessible on the local authority's website.
- **Youth worker:** Youth workers work directly with children and young people, and typically work within the community. One important role of the youth worker is to develop healthy relationships with children and young people, often in the role of advocate, to make sure that children and young people are involved in decision making that affects them.
- **Counsellor:** Counselling is often available on the NHS and is accessed at a GP surgery. Counselling services may also be accessible via school or college. Counselling can help support children and young people to manage and cope with personal circumstances that impact their mental wellbeing.

> **Good to know**
>
> Mental health and wellbeing are a priority when working with children and young people. Guidance from the NHS on supporting children and young people can be found at:
>
> www.nhs.uk/oneyou/every-mind-matters/childrens-mental-health

- **Occupational therapist (OT):** Occupational therapists develop care routines, and identify strengths and difficulties that children and young people experience in everyday life. For instance, a child with an identified need in fine and gross motor skills would see an OT; they work in education and childcare settings to support staff, other professionals, parents and carers in understanding these. Working together will allow for consistent practice that supports children and young people. Professional OTs have been trained in mental and physical health. They work to maximise children's development in all skills needed for play, learning and self-care activities (these are children's 'occupations'). An OT will consider personal, social and emotional, physical and environmental factors when working to promote participation and independence.

- **Speech and language therapist:** Speech and language therapists work to support the development of children's speech or language when speech and language needs have been identified. This may include working alongside professionals to assess and offer supportive strategies for children experiencing swallowing difficulties. For example, the speech and language therapist may work with children with mild, moderate or severe learning difficulties, language delay and/or specific difficulties in producing sounds. The speech and language therapist may visit the nursery or school and support the staff working at different settings, providing strategies that have been developed to support children's speech and language, as well as person-centred strategies and approaches.

> **Research**
>
> Find out about integrated services for children, young people and their families in your local area, and the provision in place to support babies, children and young people and their families. A good place to start is by looking up Sure Start, Children's Centres and Family Hubs.

EY K5.3 The roles and responsibilities of external agencies involved in early years settings

There are many different external agencies that work alongside early years staff to support children in their early years. In this chapter, you have been introduced to many professionals that may work with babies and young children and their families. They offer different types of services and support to parents/carers and practitioners in the best interests of the child.

- **Children's Services** provide social services, advice and guidance around child protection, including the action to take if a child discloses information or if harm or abuse is suspected. A child protection agency will support local early years settings with procedures that must be followed if children are at risk of harm or actually experiencing harm. Your setting will have a policy with procedures that must be followed if a child requires protection. Ensuring that services are coordinated around a child is absolutely essential.
- **Family Hubs** offer coordinated support for families within the local area to provide different services. Here professionals work collaboratively to achieve improved outcomes for children, young people and their families. At Family Hubs, families with children aged from birth to 19 years can receive coordinated support and well-informed advice about any aspect of parenting. **Children's Centres** also offer this type of holistic coordinated approach to care for the child and family.
- **Team Around the Child (TAC)/Team Around the Family (TAF)** meetings bring together a team of specialised practitioners to meet identified needs of the child and family. These meetings will be held when professionals need to share advice and guidance in the best interests of the child. For example, if a young person is experiencing mental health problems, a TAC meeting may be arranged. In this situation, the TAC may include a class teacher, GP and psychologist.

> **Research**
>
> When in your work placement with children, make time to talk to your placement mentor about the different professionals that may be involved in the setting.

Healthcare services may work with early years settings. For example, if a practitioner is concerned with the developmental progress of a child, the early years setting may work in partnership with one of the occupational roles listed in the table below, which explains the role of key healthcare service professionals. A child may be following an EHCP, which may have been contributed to by several specialists, including the early years special educational needs and disabilities coordinator (SENDCo).

Healthcare service professional	How they support children
Speech and language therapist	Focused and consistent approaches to support children with speech, language and communication needs
Physiotherapist/occupational therapist	Supporting children with a physical disability or who require ongoing support and routine care considerations
Counselling and therapeutic agencies such as Children and Young People's Mental Health Services (CYPMHS)	Supporting children in relation to emotional behavioural wellbeing, often associated with trauma
Educational/child psychologist	Providing support as a result of assessment for children
Nurse specialist or school nurse	Monitoring children's health, carrying out health assessments and immunisations, supporting families where children have specific health needs, and advising families on making lifestyle choices; in some settings, there may also be access to a community or school nurse who can further support and advise
Health visitor	Offering health education; may become a key partner within early years settings as they will often have a relationship with the family having been involved in the care and developmental progress of babies and very young children
	May offer advice on development, nutrition and generic care requirements

▲ Key healthcare service professionals and their roles

The benefits of working collaboratively with other agencies and professionals for improved outcomes for children/young people

When professionals work together towards shared goals, they promote a consistent approach towards best practice and improved outcomes for children and young people. For example, a child or young person with mental health concerns will benefit most from the advice of specialist professionals that is shared with all of those involved in their education and care.

It is much easier for children and young people and their families and professionals involved to access advice and support when there is good communication and collaboration between professionals involved. Communication should be clear, straightforward and value the contribution of all involved. The needs of children and young people should be reviewed regularly to make sure that any strategies and advice being followed remain effective. This is best achieved through regular communication and collaboration.

Collaborative working also enables the sharing of skills, knowledge and expertise to ensure best practice remains accurate and up to date.

Through collaboration, professionals will find referrals for expert intervention much more straightforward, accurate and appropriate to meet the needs of children and young people. Staff in education and childcare will be skilled in child development and educational curricula and will be able to identify need in children and young people, simplifying the referral process. For example, with a child not reaching expected developmental stages, they will know that they may benefit from the intervention of a healthcare specialist.

CORE Chapter 6: Working with Others

6.3 Work collaboratively with other agencies and professionals

▲ What sorts of information may be exchanged between the teacher and the parent/carer?

In this section, we will consider some key features involved in collaborative partnership working in education and childcare, which are important considerations when working with other agencies and professionals.

It is of course essential to build professional relationships with others in order to work collaboratively. For example, it is important to listen, to communicate effectively and to be reliable. Professional relationships are built on trust and respect: value one another's specialist expertise, and work towards shared goals in the best interests of the child, young person and their family.

Maintaining confidentiality and protecting sensitive data

Always remember the importance of confidentiality. Take this opportunity now to remind yourself of legislation relevant to confidentiality, data protection and how to store sensitive data securely. It is important to understand what we mean by sensitive data – for example, the personal information of children and young people, including their date of birth, home address, any personal circumstances and medical requirements as appropriate, will be protected through the Equality Act 2010. The General Data Protection Regulation (GDPR) 2018 is relevant to the data held about children, and the additional protection and safeguarding practices that must be followed. For example, children and young people may be less aware of the risks, consequences and safeguards involved in the processing of their personal data. There are policies and procedures that staff legally must follow when working in education and childcare to ensure the confidentiality and storage of sensitive data is consistently upheld. Sensitive data includes any personal data that staff hold about babies, children, young people and families.

> For more discussion of legislation and policies surrounding confidentiality and sensitive data, see Core Chapter 10.

> **Research**
> ▶ Look at the Department for Education's website to learn more about its publication *Keeping Children Safe in Education*.
> ▶ Look at the Early Years Alliance website to find out more about how sensitive data must be protected: www.eyalliance.org.uk/preparing-your-early-years-setting-gdpr
> ▶ Health and safety policies now include guidance around online security. Look at school, college and nursery policies to summarise how sensitive data is stored securely online. You may want to share your findings with your peers.

Gaining parental consent when appropriate

As discussed in Core Chapter 5 (page 81), it is essential to work closely with parents, carers and families. Staff working in education and childcare should always ensure they have gained parental consent as appropriate. For example, consent from those with parental responsibility for a child to go on trips and outings must be obtained before taking the child off the premises. Details about consent arrangements are usually discussed during registration periods when settling in to a setting. For example, parents/carers and families may give or refuse consent for photographs of their children to be used in newsletters or publicity, or for children to take part in short off-site visits that would enrich their experiences.

Reporting concerns and referrals

It is important that staff working in education and childcare are able, first of all, to recognise when intervention and collaborative partnership working is required and, second, that they are then able to identify the most appropriate service for intervention. Early intervention and referral to a specialist – for example, to a speech and language therapist if a speech, communication or language need is identified – can make a tremendous difference to the outcomes for the child's or young person's progress. Working closely with the child's or young person's family is often important during referrals, but be aware that child protection emergency situations may be an exception to this rule.

Following relevant policies/procedures

Policies and procedures are in place in education and childcare to keep everyone safe, to ensure legislation is being followed, and so that there is guidance and advice for staff as they follow any required action in any given situation. Unless there is a sound reason not to, staff should always discuss their concerns with their line manager or the most suitable person. For example, if there is a concern around a child's or young person's development, the special educational needs coordinator will need to be involved, and they will liaise with the head teacher/manager as appropriate.

6.4 Understand why practitioners establish and maintain professional boundaries and relationships with children/young people, families and other professionals

In Core Chapter 5 (page 81), we looked at the significance of establishing and maintaining professional partnerships with children, young people, parents, carers and their wider families. At the same time, professional boundaries are essential when working in education and childcare. When employed in this sector, the purposes of these boundaries are as follows.

Facilitating partnership working

Staff in education and childcare are responsible for collaborating with others in the best interests of the child, young person and their family. It is important that staff are able to identify needs accurately and recognise the benefits of working with relevant professionals when supporting children's and young people's needs. The setting within education and childcare may bring all of the professionals together, lead meetings and ensure everyone involved is kept up to date with outcomes, including reporting on the child's or young person's progress.

Protecting emotional wellbeing

Staff in education and childcare are educators in a holistic sense, and must be attentive to a child's or young person's all-round health, development and learning. Keeping children safe and responding to their emotional health will ultimately promote learning and their disposition to learning.

Respecting children's and young people's privacy

Children's and young people's rights must be valued at all times. Practice in education and childcare must ensure that children and young people are treated with dignity and that their right to privacy is maintained. For example, a child that requires support with personal care routines should be treated with respect, valuing their personal needs and respecting their privacy and dignity throughout.

Avoiding distraction from the practitioner's role

Staff in education and childcare must be aware of their job role, their responsibilities, and the boundaries and limits of their role. It is important to always understand what is expected and what action to take in different situations. It is also important to make sure that job descriptions are fully understood and followed by staff.

Providing structure and expectations

It is always important to set expectations clearly and ensure that everyone involved is aware of what is likely to happen, what their role is and what is expected of them.

Reducing conflict

Working in partnership with others can be complex. Everyone will have a view that is important to them. When working with others, effective communication is a key principle. It is important to listen to the views of everyone involved and always work towards shared goals that are in the best interests of the child or young person and their family.

Promoting safeguarding and preventing the misuse of power

Listening to others, respecting and valuing individuals, and making sure the voice of the child, young person and their family is heard is key to this. To do otherwise is to take advantage of trust and potentially allow the child's or young person's voice to be lost. Always remember that child-centred education and care is essential for best practice.

> It may be useful to reflect on the role of advocacy here (see Core Chapter 5, page 85).

Maintaining confidentiality

Staff working in education and childcare must always follow policy and procedures that are in place around confidentiality. As we have seen earlier in this chapter, maintaining confidentiality is essential in education and childcare.

> See also Core Chapter 10, page 165.

Practitioners' use of social media

In each childcare or educational setting, there will be policies around the use of social media, both in terms of staff's personal accounts and any official accounts for the setting. Misuse of social media is serious and can be detrimental to:
- professional boundaries
- effective partnership working
- confidentiality
- safeguarding.

Staff working in education and childcare must make themselves aware of all policies and procedures, including those involving social media, what is acceptable and what is not. These will set expectations for all staff and the use of social media. Having an appreciation of the seriousness of neglecting online policies and procedures is essential. For example, when working in education and childcare, staff may receive requests from children, young people and parents/carers who would like to connect with their personal accounts on online social media sites. It is important never to accept such requests. Being connected to children, young people and their families through social media is not only unprofessional, but also places that member of staff at risk. These kinds of relationships with children and young people outside of the setting are inappropriate and unprofessional, and leave staff vulnerable to accusations of misuse of power in relation to safeguarding and protection.

Case study

Megan is a new member of staff at a school. She is keen to develop positive relationships with her students. At the end of Megan's first week, one of the students that she has been teaching finds her contact details on social media and sends her a friend request.
- ▶ What action should Megan take in this situation?
- ▶ Explain the importance of following a setting's policy.

Research

When working in partnership, professionals may collaborate together, developing a Team Around the Child or Family (TAC or TAF).

Find out about TACs and TAFs. Summarise the features of this collaborative partnership working, and the benefits to the child, young person and family of working in this way.

Case study

Hana lives with her two young children, Marianna aged six and Alfie aged three months. She has recently become a single parent, and has moved to a new area and is missing the additional support she had received from members of her extended family. The class teacher at the school Marianna recently started to attend has met with the head teacher to share their concerns about Marianna's emotional wellbeing. They have noticed that Marianna is not participating in class and is reluctant to communicate, even with adults. Hana is concerned about how she is coping with both of her children. During a visit to the GP surgery to register her family, the health visitor noticed Hana was upset in the waiting area. The health visitor made an appointment for a home visit to introduce herself to the family.
- ▶ Summarise the issue.
- ▶ Which professionals are already involved?
- ▶ Can you think of any other professional services that could become involved to support Hana and her children?
- ▶ Identify the support that you feel Hana and her family may benefit from, and give reasons for your response.

Education and Early Years T Level: Early Years Educator

Case study

Grace is four years of age and has Down's syndrome. She has been receiving speech, language and communication support, which has improved her ability to communicate and has helped her progress in her learning. Grace understands language and can follow simple instructions (**receptive language**), but finds it difficult to express herself through communication (expressive language). She has been benefiting from regular support from a speech and language therapist. Grace is preparing to move on to primary school and her parents are concerned that the hard work achieved by the early years staff and the speech and language therapist may be lost.

- ▶ Identify the professionals involved in Grace's education and care.
- ▶ Describe the role of the professionals involved and how collaboration could benefit Grace and support her through this transition.
- ▶ How could early years staff and the primary school teacher work together to reassure Grace's parents?

Key term

Receptive language: the ability to understand what is being said through language.

Assessment practice

1. Describe the role of the speech and language therapist.
2. Identify **two** benefits of working with other professionals in education and childcare.
3. Explain the importance of confidentiality when working in education and childcare.
4. A job description helps staff in education and childcare to know what is expected of them within the boundaries and limits of their occupational role. Is this (a) true or (b) false?
5. Describe what is understood by multidisciplinary working.
6. Name **four** professional roles that work with children and young people.
7. Explain why there are policies and procedures in place regarding the use of social media in education and childcare.
8. Using an example, analyse the benefits of early intervention for a child's or young person's speech, communication and language development.

CORE Chapter 7: Child Development

All adults working with children and young people need to know how they grow and develop. This is needed in order to know how best to work with and plan for them. It is also needed in order to carry out observations and assessments, which we look at in Core Chapter 8. In this chapter, we look at the stages and patterns of expected development from infancy to adolescence. We look at attachment theories and how they affect healthy social and emotional development, as well as the development and importance of friendships. We also focus on the process by which babies and children acquire language and how adults can support language at all ages. We finish the chapter by thinking about how to support children and young people when there are changes in their lives. These are known as transitions.

Learning outcomes

This chapter covers the following knowledge outcomes for Core Element 7:

- 7.1 The expected patterns of children's and young people's development in infancy, early childhood, middle childhood and adolescence
- 7.2 Theories of attachment and their application to practice
- 7.3 How children and young people develop receptive and expressive language, and ways of supporting children
- 7.4 The role of adults in promoting language development at different ages
- 7.5 How children and young people develop friendships and the impact of these on wellbeing
- 7.6 How practitioners use a range of strategies to support children and young people through expected and unexpected transitions

This chapter also includes five knowledge outcomes from Early Years Educator Performance Outcomes 1 and 2. Text relating to Early Years Educator is highlighted. Note that this content will not form part of the core assessments.

- K1.2 How a range of biological and environmental factors may impact on children's learning and development
- K1.3 How specific areas of development can impact on children's holistic development within play and early education
- K1.5 The expected stages of language acquisition and how a range of biological and environmental factors can affect the speed of acquisition
- K2.1 Different forms of attachment that children develop, and key aspects of attachment theories related to current practice and the key person
- K2.2 The features of secure attachment and how it impacts positively on children's development and behaviour
- K2.3 The potential positive and negative effects of transitions and significant events on children's relationships and holistic development

K1.3 How specific areas of children's development can impact on holistic development within play and early education

The way that children grow and develop is often divided into areas. We can follow children's progress in each of these areas as there is usually a pattern to how they develop. We look at these patterns of development later in this chapter. Interestingly, the areas are interlinked. One area of development helps another or, where there is a difficulty, may impact on others. The term **holistic development** is often used to describe the way that areas of development are interlinked.

Speech, language and communication

Being able to communicate with others, talk and understand them makes a significant difference to other developmental skills. Here are some examples of how it does so:

- **Forming bonds and building relationships with others:** Being able to communicate and talk is important in making friends with other children and also in building relationships with parents and other adults. Very early on, babies learn to smile, make eye contact and vocalise in order to form relationships.
- **Expressing their needs and interests, and having them met:** When children can communicate well, they are able to express their needs and have them met. They can also talk about things that interest them and ask questions. When children cannot express their needs, they are more likely to become frustrated or they may withdraw. There is a significant link between children's language development and their behaviour, which is why supporting children's language is considered to be so important.
- **Supporting children's early writing skills:** It is easy to forget but writing is about putting down words. When children have low levels of language for their age and stage, they often find it harder to cope not only with learning to read, but also to write.

> **Reflect**
>
> Do you sometimes find that you are talking as you are writing?
>
> Explain the link between being able to talk and learning to write.

Personal, social and emotional development

Personal, social and emotional development is about expressing and controlling emotions as well as making relationships and understanding others. It is important for a number of reasons. Here are a few examples:

- **Managing own emotions and behaviour to adapt effectively to settings' rules and routines:** Children's behaviour is linked to their emotional and social development. Children who have strong relationships with others and are emotionally secure are more likely to understand others and also to respond to them appropriately. They are also more likely to show behaviours that are age appropriate, and so cope with rules, routines and boundaries.

> We look at the links between children's behaviour and their emotional and social development in Core Chapter 4.

- **Children's confidence and self-esteem to cooperate and play with others:** Children who are confident and have positive self-esteem are more likely to build strong relationships with others. This in turn can support their self-esteem and confidence as having friends and playing with others is important, especially from three years.

> For more on confidence and self-esteem, see Core Chapter 4.

- **Social and emotional skills impact on children's school readiness:** In order for children to be ready and to cope with the demands of school and more formal learning, they need a range of skills and experiences, known as **school readiness**. These include the ability to separate from parents, play with others, but also to adapt their behaviour. Children also need to be able to take turns, share and not interrupt adults who are speaking. These are all skills linked to social and emotional development. Where children have not gained these skills, they may find it harder to listen, learn and cope with the demands of a busy classroom.

CORE Chapter 7: Child Development

▲ What is the impact of these children's social skills on their confidence and self-esteem?

Physical development

Physical development is about how we use our bodies to walk and balance, but also to write, open a book and feed ourselves. Physical development can impact widely on children's development, including the following:

- **Increased motivation in children's play, learning and development:** Being able to move and make small hand movements opens the door to children's learning. As they start to be able to do more, children are increasingly motivated to try out new things, but also to persevere.
- **Fine and gross motor skills impact on children's ability to access the environment and activities, and support natural curiosity:** Once children can move and coordinate their hand movements, they are able to explore and this in turn helps them to learn. They may find out about steps as they climb them, or toddlers might scribble and so develop an interest in reading and writing.
- **Self-efficacy in dressing and feeding supports children's confidence and self-esteem through personal achievement:** Children's self-esteem and confidence is linked to how capable they feel. The term *self-efficacy* is used to describe how capable children feel. By being able to dress and feed themselves, children can feel more competent. Dressing and feeding require balance, hand–eye coordination and strength in the hands.

> **Key terms**
>
> **School readiness:** a collection of skills and experiences that help children to be ready for school.
> **Self-efficacy:** the feeling of being a capable person.

Cognitive development

Cognitive development is about being able to think, learn and understand concepts such as time or number. It is also about memory, problem solving and reasoning. Cognitive development in children is linked to their language development. As children develop language, they can use it to help them store and so remember experiences, objects and ideas.

How cognitive abilities can impact on mastery and competence in speech, language and communication

Learning to use a language is linked to children's level of cognition. This is because language is abstract. For example, when we use the word 'up', the sounds represent the concept of 'up'. Children have to remember these sounds and link them to the concept of 'up'. The link between cognition and language means that some children who have learning difficulties may need additional time to understand and use language.

How problem solving skills support children in developing physical self-care skills

Dressing requires quite a lot of practice, but also calls for problem solving. Children have to work out which way a garment goes on or, in the case of shoes, on which foot. They also have to use problem solving to work out how to put things on.

> **Reflect**
>
> Observe a child who is still learning to dress put on a coat, shoes or a jumper.
> 1. How are they using problem solving to manage this task?
> 2. What physical skills are they using?
> 3. How is this task developing their sense of being a capable child?

> **How understanding concepts enables children to establish and maintain emotional intelligence**
>
> The ability to recognise emotions and the intentions of others, and to respond appropriately, is sometimes known as **emotional intelligence**. As children's cognitive development increases, they begin to understand abstract concepts such as jealousy, disappointment and also fairness. This helps in their understanding of their own emotions, but also those of others. This in turn helps them to develop emotional intelligence.
>
> > **Key term**
> >
> > **Emotional intelligence:** the ability to recognise emotions and the intentions of others, and to respond appropriately.

7.1 The expected patterns of children's and young people's development

Everyone working with children and young people needs to know what to expect in terms of their development. This information can then be used to identify children and young people who may need additional support, but also as a starting point to plan activities and manage behaviour. In this section, we look at cognitive development, physical development, and social and emotional development. Later in this chapter, we will look at expected development in relation to language.

Cognitive development

Cognitive development is about how we think, learn, remember and use information. It is sometimes known as intellectual development. There are many skills within cognitive development, such as the ability to problem solve, put things into categories and think about things such as number. Cognitive development also encompasses the way that we use our five senses. Sight, sound, smell, taste and touch all provide information to the brain that in turn helps us to coordinate our bodies and so adjust our responses to any given situation. The term **sensory perception** is sometimes used to describe the way the senses provide constant feedback to the brain.

A good example of a skill involving many aspects of cognitive development is doing a jigsaw puzzle. It requires thinking about the shape of the pieces and also being logical. When pieces do not fit, the eyes and hands provide information back to the brain which may prompt us to turn a piece slightly.

Cognitive development is closely linked to language development. This is because language plays an important role in how we process information and then retrieve it. The ability to look at things, name and categorise them seems to help us link pieces of information together. A good example of how language and cognition work together is the way in which, when you are stressed, you might say things out loud in order to organise yourself. The link between language and cognition is thought to be the reason why, although babies do have memories, we cannot retrieve our memories of being a baby.

▲ Why is memory important in this matching game?

Interestingly, cognitive development is one area in which we will find significant differences between individuals. These differences become very apparent during late childhood and adolescence. The reasons for the differences between children and young people are complex. They include the amount of time spent studying and reading, but also whether adults provide opportunities and support to do more challenging tasks requiring cognition.

Age	Cognitive skills
0–1 year	From 3 months: • Recognises familiar faces and voices From 8 months: • Looks for an object that has been removed • Places an object in a container when asked • Finds an object that has been seen and then hidden
1–2 years	• Understands simple instructions, such as 'come' • Points to parts of the body • Points to a named picture
2–3 years	• Completes a three-piece puzzle • Copies a circle • Matches textures • Is able to point to little and big (e.g. 'Which is the big spoon?') • Matches three colours • Stacks beakers in order • Can find the odd one out in a group of objects (e.g. a large bead in a group of shells)
3–4 years	• Tells if an object is light or heavy • Is able to repeat a simple story • Matches objects one-to-one (e.g. putting one plate on each placemat on the table) • Points to long and short objects • Is able to sort objects by shape and size • Knows the name of the primary colours • Names three shapes • Counts ten objects with support
4–5 years	• Recognises and writes own name • Picks up a number of objects (e.g. 'Find me four large beads') • Names eight or more colours • Is able to decide which object is the heavier by comparing objects • Is able to complete a 20-piece jigsaw
5–6 years	• Counts accurately to 20 or more • Can manage simple calculations using objects • Can play a board game involving simple rules • Can point to half and whole objects • Enjoys simple jokes • Is able to make connections between different experiences and articulate these easily
6–7 years	• Can read and write • Can play a board game that requires some logic • Can manage simple calculations without the use of concrete objects • Can predict what might happen next in a story • Understands and can make simple jokes • Can argue using some logic
7–11 years	• Able to read and write and, from around 9 years, able to do so quite easily • Able to play board games and understands the need for rules • Learning how to tell the time and use money, and able to do so from 9 years old • Can talk about hypothetical events (e.g. 'What would you do if you were given £50?') • Able to calculate without using objects (e.g. adding two numbers together) • Can make connections between what they already know and new information
11–16 years	• Ability in some situations to be systematic in order to solve problems (e.g. searching for a lost object carefully) • Developing ability to predict and speculate about complex abstract issues, e.g. 'Should everyone earn the same?' • Speed is increasing on some tasks as memory and processing skills develop (e.g. quicker to spot matching cards in a game) • Logic is developing and so games requiring strategy, such as chess and Monopoly, are enjoyed by some young people • Growing ability to analyse texts and abstract problems (e.g. 'How do you know that this character is lying?')
16+ years	• Significant differences between individuals at this age, partly dependent on their level of education and interests • Ability to think ahead in the short term, but not yet able to imagine the consequences of actions and decisions in the very long term; this is because the part of the brain that deals with decision making is still developing

▲ Cognitive skills at different ages

Physical development

Physical development is the range of movements and skills we use in everyday life, such as the ability to walk or to put on clothes. Physical development is important to overall development because being able to move, balance and use hands is linked to being independent, and to opportunities to learn and develop further skills. As you can see from the information in the table, the first four or five years are significant as many skills are gained in this time. Babies move from having survival reflexes to being able to consciously control some of their movements. After early childhood changes are less rapid, although as you will see there are some changes during puberty.

One of the key differences between the skill levels of older children and young people is the opportunity to develop and practise skills. This means that a young person who is interested in gymnastics will develop strength and balance, whereas a young person who enjoys running will develop increased levels of stamina.

Physical development is often divided into two broad areas: fine motor movements and gross motor movements (see table).

Fine motor movements are small, precise movements of the hand or sometimes the foot. They include movements such as turning a page in a book. **Gross motor movements** are larger movements that require whole-limb or whole-body movements, such as lifting a box or walking.

> **Reflect**
>
> Observe for 5 minutes a child or young person engaged in an activity.
> ▶ Record how they are using their fine and/or gross motor movements.
> ▶ How easily could they manage the activity without these skills?

Age	Fine motor movements	Gross motor movements
Birth	• Babies are born with a range of survival reflexes, such as the palmar reflex, where they grasp anything that touches their palm • Reflexes are not conscious movements • Over time, many reflexes are lost and replaced by controlled movements	
3 months	• Clasps and unclasps hands	• Moves head to watch things
6 months	• Can pass a toy from one hand to the other • Can reach and grasp toys	• Can sit up with support • Can roll from front to back
9 months	• Can hold and bite bread crust • Can put hand around cup or bottle • Can use rattle or shaker • Can play with simple toys (e.g. rattles, cups)	• Can sit up without help • May be crawling or attempting to move • Stands while holding on to something
12 months	• Points to objects using index finger • Can pass a toy to an adult and release it	• Stands and can walk holding on to furniture
1–2 years	• Picks up objects between thumb and finger (**pincer grasp**) • Can use spoon to feed • Can hold a cup and drink from it • Can build a tower of three bricks	• From 18 months is walking well • Enjoys climbing into low chairs • Pushes or pulls toys on floor • Walks down steps one at a time, using two feet to each step • Towards 2 years, can run and stop without knocking into objects
2–3 years	• Can use a spoon to feed independently • Develops a preferred hand for holding pencils and other objects • Can build a tower of seven or more cubes • Can make circular marks and also horizontal and vertical lines with pencil or paints	• Walks upstairs one foot joining the other • Climbs climbing frame • Can throw ball • Can ride a tricycle and steer it • Can kick a ball gently • At 3 years, can stand and walk on tiptoe
3–4 years	• Can build a tower of nine cubes • Threads large wooden beads • Holds pencil in preferred hand • Can cut with scissors	• Jumps from low step two feet together • Walks up and down stairs using alternate feet for each stair • Can steer tricycle and manage corners • Can balance briefly on one foot at 4 years

Age	Fine motor movements	Gross motor movements
4–5 years	• Can use a spoon and fork well to eat • Can dress and undress, but can't do laces, button or zips • Can cut along a line with scissors • Can thread small beads • Can use jigsaws and toys with small parts • Can copy name	• Can sit with knees crossed • Can stand and run on tiptoe • Can bounce and catch a large ball • Can kick a ball with some accuracy
5–7 years	• Can thread a large needle and sew large stitches • Can colour within the lines of a picture or shape • Forms letters correctly and, from 6 years, finds handwriting easier • Can colour in shapes and, from 6 years, with increased accuracy • Can use scissors to cut along line and, from 6 years, can cut out circles	• Can walk on a narrow line • Can stand on one foot and hop easily • Can skip and move rhythmically to music • Can hop on each foot • Can throw, catch and kick well • Uses coordinated movements for climbing, swimming and riding a bike • Can walk backwards quickly
7–11 years	• Increased skill and accuracy across all fine motor movements • Drawings increasingly detailed and skilled • Handwriting may be joined-up • Easily making fine movements required to use technology	• Increased coordination allowing for skill in sports (e.g. football, gymnastics, swimming) • The level of mastery is time dependent
11–16 years	• Puberty may temporarily affect fluency of movements after a growth spurt; changes in body shape may affect spatial awareness • During adolescence, some young people may become short-sighted; this may affect their ability to see clearly, which might in turn affect their movements • During puberty, the heart and lungs grow and there is potential for increased stamina • Changes during puberty also increase overall strength – especially in boys, whose muscles increase	
16+	• High level of skill in both fine and gross motor development, but skill level on any task is dependent on how much time is spent on the activity; this in turn links to interest levels	

▲ Fine and gross motor movements

Social and emotional development

Social and emotional development encompasses two areas of development that are closely linked, which is why they are often grouped together. Social development is about the relationships we have with others and also how we adjust our behaviour to fit in with others. Emotional development is about our feelings and also our identity.

The diagram shows how social and emotional development is made up of many different elements.

> In Core Chapter 4, we looked at self-concept and also self-regulation. You may wish to revisit these sections as they cover elements of emotional development.

Social and emotional development is closely linked to the relationships that children and young people have with adults, especially their close family.

▲ Social and emotional development

Age	Social development	Emotional development
0–3 months	• Watches parent's face • Smiles and coos	• Cries to show distress • Will calm down when hears voice of parent
6 months	• Responds to faces and tones of voice	• Screams with annoyance • Enjoys being with parents and family members • May self-soothe by sucking fingers
9 months	• Laughs and enjoys being played with	• Is unsure about strangers • Shows preference to be with parents or main caregivers
12 months	• Enjoys playing simple games such as peek-a-boo	• Cries if cannot see parent or main caregiver
15 months	• Enjoys playing simple games with adult (e.g. building up and knocking down stacking beakers)	• Confident to explore environment if parent or main caregiver is present • Shows affection to familiar family members and friends
18 months–2 years	• Will bring toys and objects to share and show adults • Interested in other children of same age but cannot play with them cooperatively • May try to make adults laugh (e.g. put cup on head)	• Shows strong emotions including anger as well as pleasure • Can be determined • Tantrums when frustrated • May show jealousy if attention given to another child • Changes emotions quickly • Will become distressed if cannot see parent or familiar adult • Beginning to empathise with another person's distress by showing own distress
2–3 years	• Interested in being with other children • **Parallel play** is seen • Shows concern when others are crying • Is not yet sharing or turn-taking unless supported by an adult • Shows kindness and compassion spontaneously towards others	• Begins to be aware of their gender • Has quickly changing emotions • Likelihood of tantrums when frustrated • Has feelings of jealousy and anger towards other children • Will want to be close to a parent or a familiar adult • Will become distressed if cannot see parent or familiar adult • Shows increasing independence (self-care skills and play)
3–5 years	• Will enjoy playing with other children • Can play cooperatively and take turns, unless tired • Enjoys pretend play and will take on different roles (play becomes more complex from 4 years)	• Will find it easier to separate from parents, especially if with familiar adults or friends • Will still show strong emotions but will cope with upsets more easily • Can explain their feelings • Express likes and dislikes
5–7 years	• Preferred friendships often same gender • Can cooperate in deciding rules for games • Ability to communicate with others freely and without prompting from adults	• Starting to be more self-conscious and embarrassed; also reflecting on how they are doing in comparison to others (e.g. noticing when others get a sticker) • May occasionally have tantrums but mainly showing cooperative behaviour
7–11 years	• Friendships are stable and important, and usually same gender • Some girls' friendships can be intense • Understand rules and consequences • Play may become elaborate, with turn-taking	• Increasingly aware of their achievements in comparison to others • Able to manage their immediate impulses and so rarely have outbursts • Still need reassurance and support from parents and family members • Have a sense of right and wrong, which can be quite black and white • Self-esteem is usually positive during this period

Age	Social development	Emotional development
11–16 years	• Increasing amount of time spent with friends rather than family members • Friendship groups become larger • Influence of friends and peers becomes stronger	• Increasing levels of insecurity as a result of changes to body shape, peer pressure and developing sense of the ideal self For more on this, see Core Chapter 4. • Behaviours associated with self-esteem may occur (e.g. eating disorders, self-harming) • Hormonal swings, which can result in tantrums, outbursts and lack of cooperation • Exploration of own identity and a potential distancing from family • Higher levels of risk taking and experimentation that peak at around 16
16+	• Friendships are more selective and not necessarily same gender • Romantic relationships may be forming	• Risk-taking behaviours and experimentation starting to reduce • Increased levels of independence and also, in some people, confidence

▲ How social and emotional development links to children's and young people's relationships with adults

▲ At what age can children share resources?

Key term

Parallel play: two or more children engaged in their own individual play but in close proximity to each other.

Test yourself

1 Give two features of social and emotional development for children aged two to three years.
2 Give two features of social and emotional development for children aged seven to eleven years.
3 At what age would you expect a child to be able to thread some large beads?
4 At what age might you expect a baby to be sitting up alone?
5 At what age might you expect children to start to play board games?

K1.2 How a range of biological and environmental factors may impact on children's learning and development

Two children of the same age may not show the same levels of development. This is because there are a range of factors that can promote or hinder development. We can divide these into two broad types: biological and environmental.

It is now understood that both biological and environmental factors can work together to influence children's learning and development.

Biological factors

These are linked to things that occur before or during birth. They include factors that are directly linked to a child's genetic inheritance, or changes to the genes as a result of a faulty egg or sperm. In some cases, biological factors will be immediately apparent, such as where a child is born with a heart condition. In other cases, something in the environment may be a trigger. A good example of this is asthma. A child may be born predisposed to asthma, but as a result of living in an area with high levels of pollution, the asthma may be triggered. The table below shows some examples of biological factors.

Physical traits Some physical traits are linked to genetic inheritance	Height, physical strength, face shape, eye colour	Adults often give taller children more responsibility and so more opportunities Children who are not happy with the way they look may not feel as confident
Physical health Some medical conditions are more likely as a result of genetic inheritance	Diabetes, asthma, sickle cell anaemia	Illness may stop children from joining in activities They may feel different from other children They may fall behind with their schoolwork if they need time off school
Special educational needs Some special educational needs are more likely as a result of chromosomal abnormalities such as Down's syndrome Some special educational needs may occur as a result of pregnancy and birth	Autism spectrum conditions, dyslexia Foetal alcohol syndrome Lack of oxygen at birth	Children may need more support to master some skills Some children with social and communication difficulties may find it harder to make friends
Disabilities Some disabilities are linked to genetic inheritance; others may occur during pregnancy and birth It is also possible for disabilities to occur as a result of accidents, illness or trauma	Deafness, sight problems, cerebral palsy, spina bifida	Children with a disability may need additional support or equipment to join in activities They may feel different to other children Some children may also have more absences from early years settings or schools as a result of medical or other appointments
Personality and temperament	Shyness, curiosity, outgoingness	Children who are more outgoing may be more interested in making friends; this will help their social development Children who are curious are more likely to try out new experiences and explore more; this will support their intellectual development

▲ Examples of biological factors

CORE Chapter 7: Child Development

Environmental factors

These factors happen around and to us. Where we live, the size of our family and all of our early experiences – including our relationships with parents/carers – all combine to shape our development.

Early attachment and care status

The early attachments made between parents and babies are significant. Later in this chapter, we look at the importance of these and also what might happen if children do not form these bonds. We also consider the impact on children who have been separated from their attachments, which may occur when a child is taken into foster care, for example (see page 116).

Children who are lucky in that they have strong and continued attachments to parents are more likely to have stronger language, as attachment and interaction tend to go hand in hand. In addition, we are likely to see later that children with strong attachments find it easier to show the social and emotional skills needed to make friendships.

Parental/guardian/family support

How much support children receive from their parents/guardians can make a difference to their learning and development. This is one reason why the Early Years Foundation Stage (EYFS) requires early years settings to involve/guardians parents by, for example, sharing observations or giving parents/guardians suggestions of things they can do. Parental/guardian support may include sharing books at home, providing opportunities for practising mathematics, but also helping children to regulate their behaviour.

In addition, it is now recognised that parents/guardians who have access to support and advice may find it easier to make early attachments. They may also find it easier to cope with some of the demands of parenting. The stress levels of parents/guardians who feel supported are lower and this in turn reduces stress in children, which is known to affect brain development as well as health.

Financial

Sadly, there is a link between growing up in a poor family and children's learning and development. This is because having money gives families more options. They may live in safer and larger homes. Families with more income tend to be able to buy healthier food, which can improve health, but also development. Families who are wealthier also have more opportunities to do things that will provide stimulation as well as enjoyment for their children – for example, going on holidays, music and swimming lessons.

> **Research**
>
> Find out about the effects of poverty on children's development and later outcomes.
> Visit www.suttontrust.com and download the report titled 'Low income and early cognitive development', published by the Sutton Trust.

Access to play spaces and the outdoor environment

Children can learn from playing and being outdoors. The importance of children being outdoors is recognised by the EYFS and it is a requirement for all early years settings to spend time outside each day. While some families have gardens or live close to parks, this is not the case for all children. This means that some children have limited chances to explore nature and to develop physical skills through playing outdoors.

Interpersonal relationships

The quality of the relationships children have with their wider family, early years practitioners and, as they become older, friends can affect their learning and development. This is because relationships make a difference to children's confidence and self-esteem. We also know that where children do not have strong relationships with others, this can make them feel stressed, especially when they are not with their parents (see the section on separation anxiety, below).

7.2 Attachment theory and how early attachments influence adult relationships

Children's and young people's development is significantly influenced by the quality of the relationships they have, particularly with their parents and other key people in their lives. These special relationships are called **attachments** or **bonds**. For this outcome, we look at the theories behind attachment and their importance.

There are several theories of attachment it is worth knowing about. They tend to build on one another rather than compete.

Bowlby

The importance of attachment to children's and young people's later lives was studied by John Bowlby. His work has been very influential and has been used as a starting point for other theorists.

Innate attachment to one figure

Bowlby suggested that babies were born primed to develop an attachment to one key person in their lives. He focused particularly on that attachment being the mother. He suggested that this was a survival instinct for a baby because by attaching to one person, the baby could be protected and have its needs met.

Maternal deprivation

In his research, Bowlby looked at the family circumstances of young people who were in an offenders' institution. He found that nearly all of them had had a separation from their mothers. He concluded that being deprived of a mother in the early years of a child's life would affect their later social and emotional development. He called this maternal **deprivation**. In his work, he found that even a short separation of just a week in the first two years of life could affect later behaviour and the quality of the mother–child relationship.

Separation anxiety

As part of his work on maternal deprivation, Bowlby also noted that young children became very distressed when they were separated from their mothers. He looked at what happened when mothers and children were separated because of hospital admission. He noted that, when this occurred, there were clear stages:
- **Protest:** In the early stages of not being with their mothers, young children cry, scream and are very distressed.
- **Despair:** Children become withdrawn and very quiet, as if they have given up hope.
- **Detachment:** After a period of separation, children 'give up' on their attachment and, when reunited, will avoid contact with their parent.

Internal working model

Bowlby was one of the first to recognise that the quality of the first bond or attachment a child makes will be a template for later relationships, and also for the child's or young person's view of others. Bowlby called this an 'internal working model'. In Core Chapter 4, we looked at how attachment can impact on behaviour. We saw that where attachment is not secure, children and young people may show more aggression or have a lower self-concept.

> Revisit Core Chapter 4 if you need to remind yourself of this.

▲ What is this baby learning about relationships?

The importance of Bowlby's work

There have been some criticisms of Bowlby's work, some of which he accepted. First, he focused only on mothers providing the attachment and having caring responsibilities, rather than any other caregivers. He also suggested that babies would make a bond only with one person. He called this **monotropy**. Subsequent research has shown that babies can make strong attachments to more than one person, including fathers. Bowlby was also criticised for suggesting that mothers should stay with their babies for the first two years of their lives. This has now been challenged by other researchers (e.g. Schaffer and Emerson).

Here are some of the ways that Bowlby's work has changed many practices.
- **Policies in hospitals and early years settings:** The understanding of separation anxiety means that when children are in hospital, parents can stay with and/or visit them. It also means that early years settings have settling-in policies to ensure that babies and children do not become distressed due to missing their parent(s). Later work from a married couple called the Robertsons showed that the impact of separation can be reduced if children have become attached to another adult before separation takes place. This work is the basis for the **key person system** that is used in early years settings (see page 118).

▶ **Continued contact for absent parents:** Bowlby's work also shows the importance of children having continued contact with absent parents – for example, in the case of family breakdown. It also explains why, when contact between the absent parent and the child breaks down, children are reluctant to spend time with the absent parent because of detachment.

Ainsworth

Mary Ainsworth worked with John Bowlby and developed his work further. While Bowlby focused on the physical presence of the mother, Ainsworth looked at the quality of the attachment to the mother. She considered how sensitive mothers were to their babies' and toddlers' needs. She then came up with an experiment to test the quality of attachment that babies and toddlers had with their mothers. The experiment is known as the 'Strange Situation'.

Strange Situation experiment

The experiment took place with babies and toddlers aged between nine and eighteen months. It took around 20 minutes and is in two parts.

Part 1:
▶ Child and mother are put in a room. Mother is asked not to participate as the baby or toddler explores.
▶ A stranger enters and talks to the parent. The parent then leaves the room.
▶ The stranger engages with the child, following their cues.
▶ The parent comes back in and the stranger leaves.

Part 2:
▶ Parent leaves the room and the child is alone.
▶ Stranger comes in and engages with the child, following their cues.
▶ Parent enters and the stranger leaves.

Mary Ainsworth looked at many aspects of the child's reactions during this experiment, including the reaction of the child when the parent left and then came in again. Ainsworth also considered how much the child explored and interacted with the stranger. Based on the reactions of the babies and toddlers, three types of attachment style were noted, as described below, although a fourth has since been added following research by Mary Main and Judith Solomon in 1986.

1 **Secure attachment:** Babies and toddlers who have parents who are sensitive to their needs are more likely to be securely attached. Secure attachment behaviours mean that babies and toddlers are able to explore when their parent is present as they use them as a safe base. They are relaxed when the stranger is present alongside the parent, but show distress when the parent leaves. They are pleased to see their parent return and are quick to calm down and recover.

2 **Insecure avoidant attachment:** Babies and toddlers who show this style of attachment tend to ignore the parent and do not react when the parent leaves. They do not explore very much and show no fear of the stranger. Their reactions to the mother and the stranger are similar. It is thought that children with insecure avoidant attachment have parents who routinely ignore the needs of their child.

3 **Insecure ambivalent/resistant attachment:** Babies and toddlers who showed this attachment style were clingy to the parent even before the experiment started. They were intensely fearful of the stranger. When the parent was reunited with the baby or child, they were hard to comfort and settle down. Babies and toddlers showed anger or helplessness. It is thought that this type of attachment style is linked to inconsistent parenting, where the child's needs are met at some times but not at others.

4 **Disorganised-disoriented attachment:** This fourth attachment style was added after it was noted that some children did not fit neatly into the other three categories. While babies and toddlers in the other categories followed a pattern in how they behaved, babies and toddlers with this style showed a range of emotions, including fear and freezing. While some wanted to be close to the parent, others did not.

Influence

This piece of work has helped influence advice to parents. It is now understood that tuning in to children and being sensitive to their needs can affect later development. Classes such as baby massage are often used to increase the amount of responsiveness between parent and child. The research also identified that parents who had experienced trauma, including bereavement and depression, were more likely to have children with disorganised-disoriented attachment styles. The link between attachment and depression is now increasingly recognised and more support is provided to parents.

Criticisms

There are some criticisms of the experiment. First, it is thought that babies' and toddlers' experiences of being left with others may affect their responses. There is also some thought that parents are responding to their babies' temperament. We know, for example, that some babies at birth are easier to settle than others.

Rutter

As with Mary Ainsworth, Michael Rutter used Bowlby's work as a starting point for his own research. He concluded that Bowlby had failed to see the difference between a baby who has never formed a relationship with a mother and one who did have a relationship and then experienced separation. He used the term **privation** for babies who had never formed an attachment, and **deprivation** for those babies and toddlers who had been separated from their mothers.

The different effects of privation and deprivation

Rutter looked at case histories of children who had experienced either privation or deprivation. He saw that children who had never formed an attachment fared worse than those who had started off with an attachment. They were more likely in childhood to show attention-seeking behaviours and to be dependent, as well as being ready to form relationships and friendships with anyone. The effects in later life included antisocial behaviour and lack of empathy.

> **Case study**
>
> Amy is four years old. She was taken into foster care when she was six months old because social workers were concerned about her health and wellbeing. Her mother was unable to care for or bond with her due to an alcohol addiction. After her mother started a rehabilitation programme, Amy was briefly placed with her, but her mother began drinking again. The social workers were concerned and she was placed in care once more but with a new foster carer. After a few months, the foster carer was taken seriously ill and the placement ended. Amy has since been in five other short-term placements. At school, her teachers find her behaviour challenging. She has lower levels of language than the other children, and finds it hard to share and care for others.
> ▶ Using Rutter's theory of attachment, explain whether Amy is likely to have experienced privation or deprivation.
> ▶ How might Amy's behaviour and development be linked to her early life?

Cognitive and language development

Rutter also noted that there was a link between attachment and cognitive and language development. He saw that, as well as providing an emotional template, attachment has a role in supporting cognition and language.

Influence

Rutter's work has helped early years settings to recognise the role of attachment in children's education, and in emotional and social development. This work has helped professionals focus on the quality of attachment.

Recognition of the different outcomes for children stemming from privation and deprivation has also meant that young babies who are removed into care are usually put with a foster family so that they can develop an attachment. This is because the experience of having an attachment is recognised as being protective.

Criticisms

There are some criticisms of Rutter's work based on his choice of case histories, as the numbers involved are relatively small.

Schaffer and Emerson's work

Rudolf Schaffer and Peggy Emerson looked at babies for the first 18 months of their lives. They visited them monthly in their homes and asked parents to keep a diary. When visiting the parents, the researchers noted the adults' sensitivity to the children as well as their interactions.

Babies attach to adults who are responsive

By noting how adults responded to their babies and looking at the babies' reactions, they observed that the quality of responses mattered more than the length of time that an adult spent with them.

Development of attachments

Schaffer and Emerson's work also established that there was a sequence by which babies developed attachments (see table).

CORE Chapter 7: Child Development

Stage	Age	Features
Asocial stage	0–6 weeks	Babies are happy to be with anyone. They stare at human faces or representations of faces (e.g. a smiling sun).
Indiscriminate attachment	6 weeks–7 months	Babies are happy to be with anyone but from around 3 months smile more at familiar faces and are likely to be soothed more easily by a familiar adult. They have no fear of strangers and can be left without showing separation anxiety.
Specific attachment	7 months onwards	Babies will develop one 'special person' for whom they have a clear preference. They show separation anxiety when this adult is not available. They also show stranger anxiety.
Multiple attachments	10 months	Where babies regularly see other adults, including grandparents, childminders or early years practitioners, they can develop attachments to them. The quality of these attachments will depend on the responsiveness of the adult, not the amount of time spent with them.

▲ Schaffer and Emerson's sequence of attachments

Schaffer and Emerson also picked out some particular features of this development:
- **Stranger anxiety** – when babies start to be fearful or wary of unfamiliar adults, even when they are with their parents.
- **Separation anxiety** – when babies start to cry when their parent leaves the room.
- **Social referencing** – when babies look at their parents to help them respond, e.g. they hear a loud bang and if the parent does not seem bothered, they do not cry.

> **Key term**
>
> **Social referencing:** how babies and young children look at adults' responses as a guide to how they should themselves react.

Influence of Schaffer's and Emerson's work

Schaffer and Emerson were able to show that Bowlby's theory that babies attach to just one caregiver was not accurate. They were also able to show that the quality of adult response matters more than time. This has proved reassuring for working parents, who now know that, provided they spend 'quality time' with their baby, an attachment can still be formed.

The work of Schaffer and Emerson about the sequence of attachment has been used by some settings to influence their settling-in policies.

Criticisms

Concerns have been raised that Schaffer and Emerson's sample size was too small and reliant on parent observation. In addition, the study was not carried out in several different geographical areas, so there may be cultural bias.

▲ From what age can children form multiple attachments?

EY K2.1 Understand the different forms of attachment

Here, we have looked at Schaffer and Emerson's theory of multiple attachments. Their work has been widely recognised by researchers in the field. We can see that babies and young children have **primary attachments**. These are usually the first and strongest bonds that are made with parents and are very significant in terms of later development. We can also see that babies from around 12 months go on to have further **significant attachments**. These are with people such as siblings and family friends, but also the person in the early years setting known as the **key person**.

Ways of reducing separation anxiety

Bowlby's and Ainsworth's work showed that when babies or young children were separated from their parents, they exhibited a pattern of distress known as separation anxiety. The effects of separation anxiety, even when this is relatively short term, are now known to have a negative effect on young children's later abilities to cope with change. This means that when babies and young children transition into early years settings and school, care has to be taken to prevent them from becoming distressed. A strategy to prevent separation anxiety was first put forward by two researchers, the Robertsons. They showed that if children who were due to be separated from their primary carer had formed another attachment before separation took place, the effects of separation were significantly reduced. In current practice, this means that a key person is now allocated to every child, with the view that they develop a special relationship that will allow the child to cope without their primary carer. The key person role is a legal requirement in England within the EYFS.

The role of the key person

The key person role is significant in the EYFS. There are four key elements to the role.

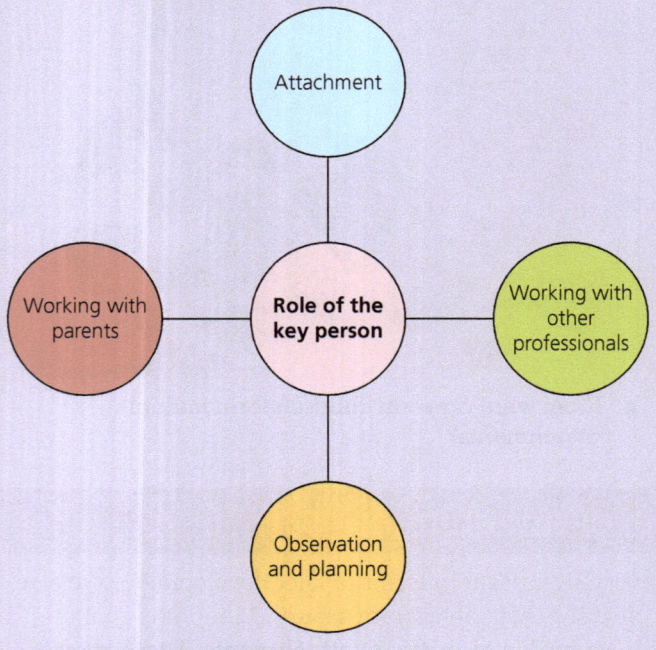

▲ Role of the key person

1. **Attachment:** Babies and young children need to have an attachment or special relationship with an adult if their parents are not with them. This prevents them from becoming stressed and developing separation anxiety (see page 114). Before children start at an early years setting, they should have developed a relationship with their key person. This should develop further so that children become attached to the key person. Having an attachment with a key person supports children's development, particularly their emotional and social development.

2. **Working with parents:** The key person also works closely with parents. They may share information about what the child has been doing and find out about the child at home. The key person will also find out about the wishes of parents in relation to food, skincare and clothing. The key person will share information about how the child's development is progressing and will work with parents to write a written assessment summarising the child's development. The key person will be on hand to advise parents where appropriate about how to support their child's development. When it is time for children to go to school or move to another setting, the key person will also work with parents to make this transition as smooth as possible.

3. **Observation and planning:** As the key person will spend time with children and get to know them, in most settings the key person will write observations and assessments. They will also plan activities and opportunities for children based on their interests, what parents tell them and also the children's stages of development.

4. **Working with other professionals:** There may be times when the key person will work alongside other professionals to provide information or to support the child. This is because the key person will know the child well and also be able to comment on their levels of development. A good example of this is where a speech and language therapist may want to find out more about the child's communication in an early years setting, or may ask a key person to implement a programme of therapy.

EY K2.2 The features of secure attachment in children

It is useful to be able to recognise the signs that a child has developed a secure attachment.

Ability to settle

When children have a secure relationship with their key person, they quickly settle down when they first arrive in a setting. They may also show joy when they see their key person.

Express anxiety when away from primary caregiver

Showing anxiety when parents are not available and there is no familiar adult is a sign of a secure attachment. When children are in early years settings, they will show the same anxiety if they cannot see their key person because of a lunch break or because of shift patterns. To prevent separation anxiety, it is good practice for early years settings to make sure that there is a second person available who also has a strong relationship with the child.

Returns to primary caregiver for comfort and safety

Securely attached children will often go to their parent if they fall over or if they are scared. When a child has a secure attachment with a key person, they will also do this.

Seeking behaviours

A feature of secure attachments is the way that children often seek out their parent or key person in order to play with them or to show them something. A child may want their key person or parent to watch as they do something they are proud of.

Ability to show and receive affection

When children have secure attachments, they are quick to hug and want a cuddle with adults they have an attachment with. They are also happy to receive physical affection. Interestingly, a sign of insecure attachment or sometimes abuse is that children will seek affection from strangers.

Trust in others

While babies and young children will be wary of strangers, we can see that they trust their parents and key person. This in turn allows for later development of trust.

How secure attachment can have a positive impact on children's development and behaviour

In Core Chapter 4, we looked at behaviour. We also saw that, when children have insecure attachments or have had a series of separations, this might affect their behaviour.

> Revisit Core Chapter 4 if you need to remind yourself of this.

On the other hand, children who have secure attachments are more likely to show concern towards others and also exhibit behaviour that is typical for their age and stage of development. There are many other benefits when children have secure attachments. This is partly linked to Bowlby's theory of children developing a template for future relationships based on the quality of love and affection they have received.

The diagram shows the positive effects of a secure attachment.

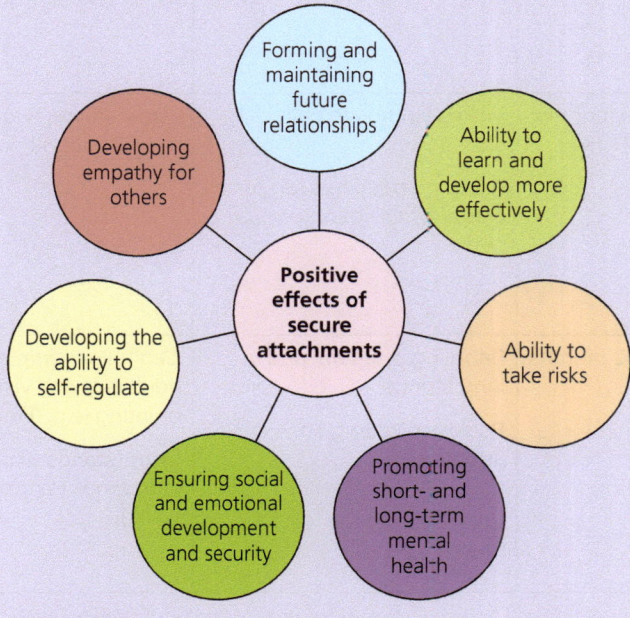

▲ Positive effects of secure attachments

7.3 How children develop receptive and expressive language

Language development is linked to many areas of development. Language helps us to understand and communicate with others. This means that it is closely linked to children's and young people's social and emotional development, including their ability to show appropriate behaviour. Once children are talking fairly well at around three years, we can see that the way they play with others changes. They are likely to take turns and be more cooperative. Language development is also linked to children's and young people's ability to learn and think in complex ways. Language is usually divided into two broad areas:

1. **Receptive language:** Receptive language is about listening to and understanding what is said. This is an important component of communication. For babies, and later on for children and young people, learning a new language, this tends to be the first step.

> For more on children and young people learning a new language, see Core Chapter 12.

2. **Expressive language:** Expressive language is about using vocabulary or words and sentences to express meaning. In babies and toddlers, expressive language may consist of just single words combined with gesture or facial expression.

It is useful to know how babies and young children develop language. It is also interesting to see how over time children and young people use language. The table below describes expected development of language.

Age	Expressive language	Receptive language	Ways to support development
6 weeks	Coos	Recognises parent's voice and calms down if crying Turns to look at speaker's face	Responding to baby during vocalisations, smiling and making eye contact Plenty of cuddles and smiles
3 months	Makes happy sounds when spoken to	Can be soothed quickly when adult talks and holds baby	Talking to the baby and responding immediately to vocalisations
6 months	Babbles with repeated sounds (dah-dah) Laughs and chuckles when happy	Turns to look at parent if hears voice across the room	Using routines with repeated phrases and words Talking to the baby but leaving pauses so baby can respond Using exaggerated facial expressions that mimic what the baby is feeling (e.g. smiling)
9 months	Makes sounds to gain attention Babbling becomes longer and baby will babble when alone	Understands two or three phrases used frequently by adults (e.g. 'no', 'bye-bye')	Continuing to talk during routines using repeated phrases and words Gaining baby's attention, pointing to objects and naming them Waiting for baby to respond and showing pleasure when baby vocalises
12 months	Babbling is tuneful and in long strings Raises voice to gain attention	Can follow simple instructions when adult is giving visual cues such as pointing (e.g. 'Find your shoes') Understands words used frequently in routines (e.g. 'cup', 'spoon', 'go for a walk')	Talking about what the baby is doing using a commentary style (e.g. 'You are banging the bricks!') Continued use of talk during routines Allowing time for baby to respond Pointing to objects that baby is interested in and naming them

CORE Chapter 7: Child Development

Age	Expressive language	Receptive language	Ways to support development
15 months	Continues to babble Uses two to six words	Understands many words Can follow a simple instruction of three or four words (e.g. 'Give me the ball')	Talking in the 'here and now' about what the toddler is doing Sharing books and following the toddler's interest Giving one simple instruction at a time Allowing time for toddlers to respond to questions or instructions
18 months	Talks using babbling and different sounds when alone Uses 6–20 words When adults talk, toddlers will often echo back last word	Enjoys looking at books and pointing to pictures Understands instructions and simple conversations Enjoys hearing and tries to join in nursery rhymes	
2 years	Uses 50 or more words Puts two words together to make simple sentences Refers to self by name Talks to self Echoes back words when adults are talking	Carries out a simple instruction, which may have many words (e.g. 'Tell Mandy that lunch is ready') Can point to several parts of the body Understands a wide range of words Speech may be difficult to understand	Modelling simple sentences (e.g. 'You have eaten everything up!') Avoiding asking too many questions Making eye contact and getting down to children's height Making sure you have their attention before talking, even if this means waiting for them to finish what they are doing Listening carefully to what children are trying to say, even when speech is unclear
2.5 years	Uses 200-plus words Knows full name Constantly asking simple questions such as 'what' and 'where' May stammer if in a rush or when trying to say a complex sentence Says and knows a few rhymes	Enjoys simple books Knows and recognises a few rhymes Understands most of what adults say to them Is starting to follow an instruction with two parts (e.g. 'Get your toothbrush and bring it here') Speech is becoming clearer	Avoiding asking series of questions and always allowing plenty of time for children to respond Not telling children who are stammering to slow down – instead slow down your own speech Showing children that you are listening to them by getting down to their level
3 years	Asks many questions beginning with 'what', 'why' and 'who' Speech is tuneful and children can whisper, for example Large vocabulary Uses 'I', 'me', 'he' and 'him' Most of what is said can be understood by others	Listens to stories and enjoys sharing books Can follow instructions in two parts (e.g. 'Find Teddy's hat and put it on him') Speech can usually be understood by adults	Talking about what children are doing and following their lead in what they want to talk about Keeping background noise down so as to be able to hear what children are saying when their speech is unclear Not correcting children's speech, but instead repeating back to them what they are trying to say, using correct pronunciation and grammar
4 years	Can be understood easily by others Most of what they say is grammatically correct Loves asking questions Enjoys telling stories	Enjoys hearing jokes, especially ones with sounds Knows several nursery rhymes Can pick out rhymes Loves hearing stories and sharing books	Encouraging children to tell you about events that have happened or to retell a story in a book Using questions to help children think and explain (e.g. 'I wonder why you like those shoes') Using opportunities to model new vocabulary (e.g. 'That is a lovely shade of blue. It's called royal blue')

Age	Expressive language	Receptive language	Ways to support development
5–7 years	Often asks the meanings of words or the word for an object Loves using words accurately and will correct others (e.g. 'That's not a shoe, that's a boot!') Argues and squabbles using language	Loves hearing and making up jokes Can pick out individual sounds in words (important for learning to read) Can listen to instructions or a story as part of a group without interruption	Encouraging children to settle disputes using language Planning experiences and activities to introduce new vocabulary (e.g. hatching chicks, cooking) When reading to children, explaining the meaning of unfamiliar phrases or words
7–11 years	Can use language to help solve problems and to organise their thoughts Uses language to express their feelings to others Can use language to explain their thinking to others	Can follow a complex story or instructions Vocabulary continues to develop as a result of reading, experiences and conversations with adults	Encouraging the use of language for explanation and problem solving by making comments or questions (e.g. 'I wonder why that won't stay in place') Modelling and encouraging children to use language to help them learn and remember (e.g. 'How do you think you can remember that?')
11–16 years	Can use language to present an argument or to talk hypothetically Can use language to rationalise their concerns or anxieties Able to consciously moderate their language according to who they are with	Able to listen to others and retain information	Modelling and talking to young people about how language changes according to who you are with (e.g. formal and informal) Encouraging young people to debate and question, and supporting them in this Using newspapers and media to help them analyse how words and phrases can have impact
16+ years	May be skilled communicators depending on their self-esteem and experiences	As above	As above

▲ The development of receptive and expressive language

Test yourself

1. At what age is a child likely to be able to use 200 words?
2. From what age do children enjoy hearing and using jokes?
3. Explain the difference between a seven year old's use of language and that of a sixteen year old.

Theories relating to children's/young people's language development

Over a number of years, several theories looking at the development of language have been put forward.

> Some of these link back to the learning theories we looked at in Core Chapter 2.

Noam Chomsky

Chomsky suggested that babies were born with the potential to learn language. He proposed that this was innate or instinctive. He looked at the way in which babies and young children appear to follow a pattern in terms of how they learn language and are able to detect grammar. He used the term **language acquisition device (LAD)** to talk about the structures in the brain that made this possible.

Since Chomsky's work in the 1960s, further knowledge about how babies and children develop language has been acquired. It is now thought that Chomsky's belief that learning language is instinctive is correct, but also that there might be a critical period in which this needs to take place.

Jean Piaget

> In Core Chapter 2, we looked at Piaget's work in relation to how children and young people think. You will need to review this in order to look at the four stages of the development of thinking that he outlined.

Piaget suggested that there were four stages in the development of children's and young people's thinking. His view of language was that it is a tool to support thinking, and so reflects their level of understanding at the time. He used the term **egocentric** speech to describe when talk is not aimed at anyone else. Young children will often talk out loud to themselves when they play. The other form of language use is **socialised**. This is when children use language as a tool for communication.

Piaget's work focused on children being active in their learning and using their experiences as a basis for their thinking. It has been criticised for underestimating children's thinking and language.

Stage of cognitive development	Use of language at this stage
Sensorimotor	Language use is egocentric
	Crying is to meet babies' own needs
Preoperational	Children continue to use egocentric language (e.g. talk as they play)
	One feature of this stage is animism and their use of language reflects this (e.g. giving a cuddly toy a voice or drawing a smile on a moon)
	In this period, children start to use language symbolically and talk about things that are not present
Concrete operations	Children's language changes in line with their ability to think logically
Formal operations	In this period, they use 'socialised' language that reflects their ability to 'decentre', recognising that others may have different perspectives

▲ Use of language at each stage of cognitive development

> **Key term**
>
> *Animism:* ascribing feelings and personality to inanimate objects, e.g. 'my car is happy'.

Jerome Bruner

While Chomsky recognised that babies and young children come primed to learn language, he did not particularly focus on the role of the adult. Bruner's work suggests that adults also have a role in helping babies and children develop language. He used the term **language acquisition support system (LASS)**, suggesting that adults have the ability to, step by step, support babies' and children's language through, for example, everyday routines. An adult might say 'all gone' when a baby finishes a feed, but then later on, when the child has more language, add complexity by saying 'Look, it's all gone.' In this way, Bruner suggested that adults were scaffolding babies' and young children's language. Interestingly, research that looks at how adults, especially parents, interact with babies and young children appears to confirm this. Bruner's theory explains why there can be significant differences between the language learning of children of the same age – some may be better supported by adults than others.

▲ Explain how sharing a book with an adult may develop this child's language

Lev Vygotsky

> We have already looked at Vygotsky's theory of learning in Core Chapter 2. It would be helpful for you to reread this section.

In terms of language, Vygotsky viewed it as central to learning. The interactions that children have with their parents, family members and others help to develop their cognition. Unlike Piaget, Vygotsky believed that it was language that drove thought.

Vygotsky suggested that thought and language begin by being two different activities – for example, when a baby babbles it is not using babbling as a way of thinking. At around the age of two or three years, the activities merge and at this point the child uses language to help them think.

Vygotsky also differentiated between two types of speech: inner speech, which helps us to think, and external speech, which we use to communicate with others. An example of inner speech would be when we say either aloud or inwardly, 'Then, I am going to …' as a way of directing ourselves. Vygotsky believed that until children are about seven, they are not able to use these types of speech in distinct ways, which means their speech is often a blend of the two, with young children often providing a running commentary on themselves as they play.

▲ How is the adult helping to develop this child's language?

Vygotsky's approach is significant because it suggests that, without interactions, children's ability to think will be limited. His approach is why adults may pose questions to children and young people as a way of extending their learning. The role of interaction in learning also means that the quality of the relationships we have with children and young people is significant.

B.F. Skinner

> In Core Chapter 2, we looked at the theory of operant conditioning (page 23) so refer back to that now.

Skinner applied his theory to how children develop language. He thought that the responses of adults following vocalisations such as babbling were responsible for the development of language. While it is true that babies and young children do need adults to respond to them, operant conditioning theory does not explain the steps behind how children learn language. If children were learning only through imitation and praise, they would not make grammatical mistakes such as 'me swimmed' as adults are unlikely to have said that. Overall, Skinner's theory of language development is not seen as being helpful.

> **Test yourself**
>
> 1 What do the terms 'LAD' and 'LASS' refer to?
> 2 Which theorists suggested them?
> 3 Outline why Vygotsky's approach to language differed from that of Piaget.

K1.5 The expected stages of language acquisition between birth and three years

Earlier in this chapter, we looked at the broad stages of language development. If you are working in early years, it is important to have a more detailed understanding of language acquisition in the first three years. This is important because we know that early identification of children who may not be following typical stages of development is essential so that they can be referred or given additional support.

There are two phases of language learning in the first two years:
1 pre-linguistic
2 linguistic.

Pre-linguistic phase

In this phase, babies are tuning in to faces and voices. They are learning to detect sounds and connect them with routines, actions or objects. In this phase, babies are also learning to communicate using sounds, and exploring the sounds that they can make.

Linguistic phase

This phase is when babies and toddlers start to use words or sounds in a consistent way. In this phase, they start to use increasing numbers of words and are learning new words.

CORE Chapter 7: Child Development

Age	Features	Details
0–3 months	Eye contact Recognising voices	Has different cries to express hunger, tiredness or needing company – parents have to learn to recognise these cries
		A baby starts to soothe when they hear the voice of parents or familiar carers
		Smiles in response to others
		Stares and makes eye contact
3–6 months	Cooing	Babies coo around three months as a sign of pleasure
		Sensitive to the facial expressions of others, including smiles or anxiety
		In this period, babies laugh and chuckle when happy or amused
		Early signs of babbling begin – sounds are usually short (e.g. 'ba', 'da')
6–9 months	Babies blend vowels and consonants together to make tuneful sounds (e.g. 'ba', 'ma', 'da')	Babbling has been described as learning the tune before the words – the baby seems to be practising its sounds
		Babies increase the number of sounds or phonemes – this is sometimes called phonemic expansion
		All babies, even deaf babies, produce a wide range of sounds during this period
		Babies are now skilled communicators – they quickly pick up on the emotions of others, use eye contact and may try to make others laugh
9–10 months	Babies babble but the range of sounds is limited	The range of sounds or phonemes that babies produce becomes more limited and reflects the phonemes used in the language they are hearing
		At this stage, it would in theory be possible to distinguish between babies who are in different language environments
		At 10 months babies are also understanding 17 or more words
		Babies' communication skills have also developed further and they can understand a lot of what is being said to them, either through word recognition or by reading faces
11–12 months	Babies seem to repeat the same sounds in long strings (e.g. 'bababab')	Long strings of babbling, which are tuneful, come before first words; it can sound as if babies are actually talking
		They now know how to attract adults' attention by pointing and raising their voices
Around 12 months	Babies repeatedly use one or more sounds that have meaning for them	The first words are often unclear and so gradually emerge; they are often one sound, but are used regularly in similar situations (e.g. 'baga' to mean drink and cuddle)
		Babbling continues
12–18 months	Toddlers start to use one word in a variety of ways	Toddlers use **holophrases** to make their limited vocabulary more useful for them; this means that one word is used in several situations, but the tone of voice and the context help the adult understand what the toddler means
		Most toddlers have between 10 and 15 words by 18 months
		By this time, toddlers have often learned how to get adults' attention and how to make them laugh
18–24 months	Two words are put together to make a mini-sentence	Toddlers begin to combine words to make sentences
		They seem to have grasped which are the key words in a sentence (e.g. 'dada gone', 'dada come')
24–36 months	A large increase in children's vocabulary combined with increasing use of sentences	This is a period in which children's language seems to evolve rapidly – they learn words so rapidly that it becomes hard for parents to count them!
		At the same time, the child uses more complicated structures in their speech
		Plurals and negatives begin to be used (e.g. 'no dogs here!')

▲ Features of the linguistic phase

How a range of biological and environmental factors can affect the speed of acquisition

Two children of the same age may show differences in how quickly they learn language. We can divide these factors into two broad areas: biological and environmental.

Biological factors

Some common biological factors are described in the table below.

Biological factors	Effects on speed of language acquisition
Hearing/speech or language impairment	Some children may have a permanent hearing loss, which can affect their ability to use spoken language
	Other children may have a language impairment (e.g. a processing difficulty that makes it harder for them to consistently use the speech sounds)
Age and stage	See earlier in the chapter (page 110) for how the age and developmental stage of children affects how much language they are using
Cognitive abilities and difficulties	Some children may have learning difficulties that affect how easily they can pick up and use language; their progress may be slower than that of others
	Spoken language is abstract, making it hard for some children to use; using signs such as Makaton and pictures is often a strategy to make it easier
The child's temperament and personality	Some children are more sociable than others; this means that they seek out the company of adults and other children, and so have more opportunities to hear and use language
Ear, nose and throat infections	Some infections can affect children's hearing or ability to talk clearly (e.g. after a cold, a child may have a build-up of fluid in the ear); this type of hearing loss is not permanent, but needs to be identified as, in some cases, medical intervention is needed

▲ Common biological factors that affect speed of language acquisition

Environmental factors

Use of dummies

The advice regarding using dummies is complex. Some research has shown that the risk of cot death can be reduced if a dummy is used in the first six months when a baby is put down to sleep. It is recommended that dummy use is stopped after 12 months because it can cause problems with speech and language. It affects speech because when toddlers talk with a dummy in their mouth, it restricts the movement of the tongue and its ability to make certain speech sounds. It can also affect language because toddlers may not talk as much. It is also harder to communicate with a child who has a dummy because facial expressions are reduced.

> **Research**
>
> Find out more about the advantages and disadvantages of using dummies in infancy. Visit the following organisation's websites to help you with your research:
> ▶ NHS
> ▶ Lullaby Trust
> ▶ Royal College of Speech and Language Therapists.

Parental influence/role modelling

Parents have an important role to play in language development. As a result of knowing and loving their children, they can often understand what a baby's cry or a toddler's facial expression means. They can also understand what their children are trying to say, even when others can't. This means that most parents are children's first teachers when it comes to language learning. This links to Vygotsky's and Bruner's theories of language. Parents are also able to build receptive language in young children by pointing to objects and also by talking to them. As a result of hearing and watching parents, babies and children often copy actions and, later, words. This means that parents are actually role-modelling language.

Bonding/attachment and relationships with others

The strength of the relationship that babies and children have with their parents and others can affect their language. Quite simply, babies and children talk more to the people they like being with. When babies and children do not have a strong relationship, they reduce their eye contact and communication, even if adults are trying to talk to them.

Early stimulation and engagement in talking

In the first couple of years, it is essential that babies are talked to and their early babbles and vocalisations responded to. This stimulates those parts of the brain that are associated with language. Sadly, not all parents know that this is an essential first step and those babies and toddlers who do not have early opportunities for interaction may be delayed in language.

Language-rich environment/stimulation

Babies, children and also adults are more likely to talk if they have something worth talking about. In the first couple of years, books and toys are resources that create a focus for talk. As children become older, as well as books, activities become important too, such as doing some cooking or painting. This means that the environment we create, including toys, activities and routine, has to be considered as a way of promoting language.

Home life and support

At home, some children have more opportunities for interaction than others. This may be due to the amount of time that parents have available and the number of siblings, but also the knowledge of parents. Screen time with digital devices, for example, may be used a lot in some homes, but unless parents and children are watching together, this can reduce opportunities for language. On the other hand, some parents may eat with their children, share books at bedtime, and chat to them during routines such as bath or shower time. Small amounts of frequent interaction like this at home can add up and so make quite a difference to children's language.

Older siblings speaking for the child

In some families, older siblings get into the habit of 'helping out' the younger one by getting them things or talking on their behalf. While this is quite sweet, it can mean that toddlers and young children lose the motivation to talk as there is no need for them to do so. This can result in a mismatch where children's spoken language is poor, but their understanding or receptive language is good.

Bilingualism

Some babies and young children will be learning two or sometimes three languages at the same time.

> As discussed in Core Chapter 12, this type of bilingualism is known as simultaneous.

As languages are essentially codes, this means that children have to learn more than one code at once. While children will show typical patterns of language development, a few children may have fewer words than average at two years. A delay should always be followed up in case there are other difficulties (e.g. a hearing loss). In some cases, parents may be advised to use their languages differently to make it easier for children to detect which code is being used.

7.4 How adults can promote language development at different ages

It takes four years for children to develop fluent language. At all ages, children and young people need adults to carefully listen and tune into what they are saying. While children may be fluent at four years, older children and young adults need to learn to use their language to solve problems, express their feelings and to interact with others. The role of the adult in this period is to develop further vocabulary and thinking skills. There are many strategies and activities that can be used to support the development of language, as outlined in the table below.

Age	Strategies and activities	Notes
0–2 years	Sharing nursery rhymes	Nursery rhymes help babies and toddlers to bond with adults and also to hear the sounds of the language
	Using repetitive language	Babies and toddlers need simplified and repetitive language
	Giving simple instructions	Toddlers are able to follow a single instruction, but adults can help them by pointing or showing what needs to happen
	Maintaining appropriate eye contact	Gaining babies' and toddlers' attention with eye contact helps them to focus and learn language
	Using visual aids (toys and puppets) Using simple picture books Using gesture Talking about what is happening ('the here and now')	Babies and toddlers need to link the words that we are saying to actions and objects – adults can do this by using gesture, but also by talking about things as they are happening Visual aids and story books can be helpful

Age	Strategies and activities	Notes
	Listening and tuning into children's communication	Babies and toddlers need adults who carefully listen and pay attention to them. This means tuning in and responding to their body language as well as their vocalisations
	Enjoying turn taking in conversation when interacting with babies	Babies and toddlers learn to talk and turn take by having adults who respond positively to their vocalisations and body language
2–4 years	Sharing books (story sacks and props)	Looking at books can encourage children to talk and develop vocabulary
	Engaging in child-initiated conversation	Listening and responding to what children want to talk about is a key way in which we can develop language
	Facilitating circle time	Circle time, if it is fun and carried out in small groups, can help 3 year olds take turns; it is not advised for 2 year olds
	Providing a range of role-play activities	Older 2 and 3 year olds enjoy role play; the props can provide opportunities for children to use new vocabulary Role play also encourages children to talk to one another
	Listening and tuning into children's communication	Children need adults who take time to listen to them and give them time to respond. Children's speech sounds may be unclear and so adults have to tune into what children are saying
4–7 years	Modelling correct use of language, tone and expression	Throughout childhood, modelling language is important; this means using accurate vocabulary and being grammatically correct
	Engaging in paired reading activity	Paired reading is a strategy used in Key Stages 1 and 2; it can help improve confidence and fluency
	Encouraging descriptive language	We can promote vocabulary by modelling words used for description
	Planning literacy activities and word games	As children's language develops, they enjoy playing word games such as 'I spy' and, for older children, Scrabble and word search games
	Listening and tuning into children's communication	Children will talk more and be able to express more complex ideas when adults take time to listen to them and show interest in what children are saying
7–11 years	Introducing a wide range of texts	Children's vocabulary and understanding of grammatical structures is helped when they read widely, but also when they are read to; this means that a variety of stories, books and poems are important
	Providing opportunities for creative writing	Creative writing can help children use the vocabulary that they are developing
	Facilitating group discussion	Group discussions can help children learn to express themselves, although they may need adults to role-model turn-taking and also to give them confidence
	Introducing new vocabulary through spelling and definitions	Children enjoy learning new words; some words can later be remembered more easily if children understand the roots of them
	Listening and tuning into children's communication	As children move towards puberty, they need adults who listen to them and show interest in what they are saying, but also to pick up on any of the underlying worries and issues that children may have
11–19 years	Involving children and young people in discussions and debates	In small and large groups, we can help children and young people learn to use language to present arguments and debate; this use of language means listening carefully to others and using language as a tool to analyse

Age	Strategies and activities	Notes
	Facilitating individual and group presentations	Presenting information to others can help young people to develop skills involved in explanation
		It can also build confidence provided that support is given to those young people who find it hard to talk in front of others
	Encouraging sophisticated vocabulary through wider research and reading	Reading a wide range of texts, including poetry, can increase vocabulary and knowledge
		By encouraging research on topics of interest, we can support young people to develop high-level as well as specialist vocabulary, such as professional vocabulary that is used in particular career pathways
	Listening and tuning into children's and young people's communication	Children and young people will need adults who listen and engage with their ideas and emotions. Adults need also to be able to pick up on any worries and issues that they may have

▲ Strategies and activities that can be used to support the development of language

> **Reflect**
>
> Create a leaflet for parents of children aged from birth to five years that will give them practical tips and strategies to support their child's language development.

> **Reflect**
>
> Ask children and young people of different ages about their friendships:
> 1. Ask whether they have friends and why they are friends.
> 2. Find out what they think makes a good friend.
> 3. Compare their answers to Robert Selman's framework of friendships.
> 4. To what extent do you feel that Selman's framework of friendships relates to your own conversations with children and young people of different ages?

7.5 How children and young people develop friendships and their impact on wellbeing

In the 1930s, Mildred Parten looked at how babies and young children play together. She suggested there were stages in social play, with toddlers playing next to each other and three year olds being able to play cooperatively.

In the 1980s, Robert Selman proposed a framework that outlined the different developmental stages of friendship. His work was based on interviews with children and young people. He noted that there are significant differences between children's and young people's understanding of friendship. This is reflected in the wide and overlapping age bands. The table below describes Selman's five stages of friendship.

Henri Tajfel's and John Turner's social identity theory

In-group vs. out-group

At break time in schools, we will often see distinct groups of older children and young people. In secondary schools, for example, it is common to find a 'sporty' group, a 'popular' group and a 'brainy' group. Each group has a clear identity. We see the division of people into groups in all walks of life, such as football fans and supporters of political parties. Sometimes, these divisions cause conflict and violence. Tajfel's and Turner's social identity theory looks at why and also how people do this.

Level	Stage	Age	Features
Level 0	Momentary physical interaction	3–6 years	Children will play with others according to circumstance and convenience rather than because of deeper feelings
Level 1	One-way assistance	5–9 years	An understanding that a friend does nice things for you but not understanding that friendship works two ways
			The desire to have friends at this age can mean that some children will stay friends with another child who is not particularly kind to them

Level	Stage	Age	Features
Level 2	Two-way fair-weather cooperation	7–12 years	Expectation that friends will repay a favour, gift or action
			Friendship may end if one child feels that they are not getting anything in return
Level 3	Intimate mutual sharing	8–15 years	Acts of kindness and generosity occur without an expectation of a reciprocal action
			High levels of trust and loyalty, but may feel that another is betraying them if they have separate friendships or take part in activities in which they are not included
Level 4	Mature friendship (autonomous interdependence)	12+ years	Ability to accept others and be accepted
			Ability to recognise the differences between their friends
			Understanding that their friends will have other friends they do not have in common

▲ Robert Selman's five-level framework of friendships

Tajfel and Turner suggest that being part of a group (the **in-group**) and feeling in some way superior to another group (the **out-group**) raises an individual's self-esteem. Being part of the in-group can provide a sense of purpose and belonging, and so can become part of someone's identity.

The three stages of social identity

Tajfel and Turner suggest that the three stages in the development of a social identity are as follows.

1. **Categorisation:** Very early on in childhood, we learn to put things into categories. A Labrador is a dog. Dogs have fur. Dogs are animals. Categorising is a normal part of cognitive development. It allows for short cuts in our thinking. As well as objects and other things such as animals, we also categorise people. We categorise by size and age, but also by the jobs people do. The process of categorisation also helps us to understand our own identity by recognising what we are like in comparison to others. A three year old out of nappies may say, 'I am not a baby' as a result of recognising that babies wear nappies and cannot walk like they can.

2. **Social identification:** Once a child or young person has identified with a group, their reactions and behaviours increasingly reflect those of a group. A young person who is part of a highly competitive swimming team might train more often or buy a certain brand of swimming goggles. It is worth noting at this point that children and young people, as well as adults, will identify with and be a member of several groups.

3. **Social comparison:** Once children or young people have identified themselves with a group, they need to draw favourable comparisons with other groups. This is how they maintain high self-esteem. An individual in the 'brainy' group at school will notice the test scores of other children and be pleased that their group has higher grades.

How friendships can positively impact on children and young people

Friendships often help children and young people to feel valued. They can provide many benefits, including the following.

Mental health

Humans are social beings. This is one reason why, by the time a child reaches six or seven, having friends becomes so important. When children or young people have difficulties in making friends or have friendship

▲ What effect might their friendship have on these boys' resilience?

CORE Chapter 7: Child Development

groups that are not supportive, this can affect their mental health negatively.

Resilience

The ability to cope with setbacks and problems is partly linked to how much support a child and young person has available to them. Friends, especially in adolescence, can provide understanding and support. They may also be able to help a young person reflect or seek further help.

Social skills

Throughout childhood and adolescence, children and young people learn social skills and also boundaries through friendships and being with others.

Self-concept

We have seen that Tajfel's and Turner's theory of social identity says that being part of a friendship group is linked to identity. A positive self-concept is more likely if a friendship is supportive. It is worth noting that sometimes children and young people may have friendships that are not supportive, and this may be harmful in terms of self-concept.

Self-esteem/confidence

As we saw in Core Chapter 4, there is a link between self-esteem, confidence and self-concept.

> Revisit Core Chapter 4 if you need to remind yourself of this.

Where children and young people have friendships that are supportive, they are more likely to have higher levels of self-esteem. On the other hand, where a child or young person does not have friends, their self-esteem may be lower.

Children and young people with special educational needs and disabilities

For children and young people with special educational needs and disabilities, friendships are particularly important. They provide the benefits that we have seen, but they may also in some cases provide mutual support if the other child or young person has similar needs.

7.6 The difference between expected and unexpected transitions, and how practitioners use a range of strategies to support children and young people through them

A transition is an interruption or change to a child's or young person's life. Some transitions are small and have little impact on children and young people, but others can affect their learning, behaviour and development. Some transitions are expected and so can be planned for. Others can occur suddenly, so there is no time to prepare children and young people.

Expected transitions

Expected transitions are often easier because adults and parents can prepare children and young people in advance. The table below gives some examples of transitions that can be planned for. We also looked at transitions in Core Chapter 5 (page 82).

Unexpected transitions

These are changes in children's and young people's lives that were not planned. They can be stressful because adults and parents may not have had the time to prepare children and young people. The table below gives some examples of unexpected transitions.

> **Key term**
>
> **Gender transition:** when a child or young person wants to change from their biological gender to the one that they identify with.

Transition	Description
Transition from home to childcare	For babies and young children, being with new carers is an important transition; this might mean starting at a childminder, nursery or pre-school
	Some children may also move from one early years setting to another
Movement between school years or between school and FE or HE	Starting school, moving school years or changing establishments are significant transitions because children and young people have to adapt to new routines, new adults and a new peer group
Adolescent transition and body changes	While growing up is normal, the physical changes in moving from being a child to an adult can provoke anxiety
	As well as physical changes, there are also emotional and social changes that take place

Education and Early Years T Level: Early Years Educator

Transition	Description
Gender transition	Sometimes, children and young people feel that their biological gender does not match with how they feel about themselves; under medical and psychological supervision, they may start the process of changing gender
Changes in relationships	Changes in relationships, such as a parent's boyfriend moving in, can be planned for
	Changes in relationships may also include a friend who is moving away or a change of teacher
Post-school decisions	When young people leave school, they need to make a decision about their next steps; moving to a job, apprenticeship or further study can feel daunting

▲ Examples of expected transitions

Transition	Description
Moving house or location	Some children and young people live in rental accommodation and may change home every six months or year
	Parents may not know whether or not they can stay in their home
Illness	The illness of a parent or of a child or young person can cause significant disruption – a child or young person may need time off school and in some cases may need to go to hospital
	Where a parent or family member is ill, a child or young person may find that their home life is disrupted; they may even need to become a carer
Change of employment	Any changes in family life can be disruptive – a change of employment might mean that a parent needs to work at night or may not be as available to help with homework or to play
Change to family structure	Changes to family structure may include family breakdown where one parent leaves, but also the formation of a new stepfamily
	A change of family structure may also occur if a grandparent or other family member moves in
	The arrival of a new baby can also change a family's usual routines and structure
Pregnancy	An unplanned pregnancy is a significant life change for a young person – they may need to make decisions about continuing the pregnancy or how they will manage with a baby
Bereavement	The death of a parent, family member or friend is likely to have a significant impact on a child or young person, especially where it is sudden or unexpected

▲ Examples of unexpected transitions

How practitioners use a range of strategies to prepare and support children and young people through transitions

We have seen that there are a number of circumstances where children or young people will face a transition. Sensitive adults can reduce the emotional and social impact of these transitions. There are a number of ways in which we can support children and young people.

Providing accurate and current information to the child or young person

Knowing what is happening or what is going to happen can reduce anxiety in children and young people. It is important that any information shared with children and young people is accurate and also links to what parents or colleagues have said. If there are differences or inaccuracies, children and young people may become confused or find it hard to trust in future. As part of giving information, adults must also be careful to be realistic and honest, to avoid false hopes or raised expectations.

Giving opportunities to discuss feelings and ask questions

As well as having information, children and young people need time to talk about the transition. Older children and young people may need to think through and talk about their feelings. All ages of children are likely to have questions. Sometimes, these questions may seem trivial, such as 'Will my hamster be able to come?', but they should all be taken seriously. Sometimes, children and young people will ask one question to see whether they can trust the adult before asking another question.

Interestingly, some children and young people may need time to discuss their feelings or ask questions.

This is because they may need time to process the information, especially if they have had a shock. It is, therefore, important to expect that children and young people may raise questions or want to talk about the changes in their lives several times. Young children may also ask the same question repeatedly.

Involving individuals in their own transition planning

One of the ways that we can reduce stress during and after transition is to give children and young people some control and help them make some decisions. It is important, though, that any transition planning that we involve them in is age and stage appropriate. A good example of this might be the way that an older child might choose a piece of work to show to their next teacher or a young child has a box into which they pack their favourite toys when they move home.

Using school-readiness strategies

For young children about to start reception class, it is important that we help them to prepare. School readiness is the collection of skills that children need to make this transition. These include language, self-care skills and their ability to self-regulate. Children also have to be able to do some self-care tasks, such as being able to dress and feed themselves.

▲ How can self-care skills help children to feel more confident when starting school?

Following settling-in policies and procedures

Early years settings and reception classes usually have policies and procedures in place to help babies and children make the transition from home. These **settling-in policies** can reduce separation anxiety for babies and children, especially those who have never been cared for by anyone but their parents. The aim of settling-in policies and procedures is to make sure that babies and young children have developed a relationship with an adult from the setting or school so that they can cope when their parents are not there. Good settling-in policies and procedures also involve parents as they need to feel confident that their children will be happy and can cope.

Implementing support through a buddy system, counsellor, mentor or learning support assistant

In school settings, children and young people can be supported through a buddy system. This is a system where children or young people can talk to another child or young person. This works very well when a pupil is new to a school or class. In cases where a child or young person has experienced family breakdown or bereavement, the other child or young person may have had a similar experience. As well as a buddy system, trained adults can also support children. This might include a counsellor, mentor or a learning support assistant. Adults can provide support to individual children and young people or to small groups where appropriate. As well as discussion, they may also use resources such as books and stories or provide play opportunities that will allow children to express their emotions.

Liaising with parents/carers and other professionals

When preparing for transition and supporting children and young people, we need to talk to others involved, including parents and any professionals who work with the child or young person. This is because we need to agree strategies and also make sure that the messages children and young people receive from adults are the same. This can prevent confusion and also anxiety.

▲ How can sharing information with parents help with transitions?

Referring individuals for specialist support as appropriate

Some transitions, such as a parent with a diagnosis of terminal illness, are so significant that specialist support needs to be sought. Referrals to specialist services and organisations, including bereavement charities and child psychiatrists, can happen only with parental consent. In some cases, it may be appropriate to signpost organisations to parents. In addition, many organisations that deal with family breakdown, mental health issues and bereavement have online pages or packs that are designed for early years practitioners and school staff.

K2.3 The potential positive and negative effects of a range of transitions and significant events that children may experience

We have seen that children and young people may experience both planned and unexpected transitions. We have already looked at the following transitions in this chapter:
- moving home
- loss of significant people/bereavement
- illness.

It is also worth looking at some other transitions that it is common for young children to experience.

Some common transitions

Here we look at a few examples of common transitions.

Moving to school

The start of school can be a big step for young children. They may move to a larger building with more adults and children who are older than them. They may also be in a class with more children and fewer adults than they are used to.

Moving between settings and carers

Some children will, during the week, spend time at different settings and with different carers. A child may start their day with a grandparent or childminder before going on to a pre-school. In some cases, children may also move from a pre-school into a school nursery. They have to build a relationship with a new carer, but also to learn what they can and cannot do.

Starting and moving through day care

Starting in day care, and moving from one room to another, is a significant transition: babies and toddlers become very attached to their key person and so leaving them to go to a new room can be tricky. In the same way, starting in day care and leaving parents for the first time can cause separation anxiety unless time is spent helping children to settle in.

> **Practice points**
>
> **Day care transitions**
>
> It is important to build a relationship with the child before they separate from their parent or move room. Here are some tips:
> - Try playing with the child while they are with their parent or existing key person.
> - When the child is relaxed with you, see if they can play for a few minutes alone with you.
> - Avoid putting the child under pressure by asking them questions or making intense eye contact.
> - Let the child get to know you at their own speed.

Birth of a sibling

The arrival of a new baby in the family can cause a range of emotions in young children. This is an emotional transition, but sometimes a physical one as children may have to move or share a room. In addition, a new baby may also change the existing routines in a family.

Living outside of the home

There may be circumstances when children are not living at home. This might be because there are child protection issues and they have been moved to foster care. Where children are moved to live with people they do not know, they may show a range of behaviours and emotions.

Family breakdown

It is not uncommon for parents to separate during the first few years of a young child's life. Family breakdown can be very difficult for children. They may need to navigate going from one parent's home to another, or not seeing an absent parent very often. In addition, some children may also have the challenge of developing new relationships with their parents' new partners.

Potential positive and negative effects of transitions

How children respond to transitions depends on a number of factors, including how much support they have had and whether the transition was planned or unplanned. Earlier in this chapter, we looked at ways of supporting children and young people through transition.

Here are some ways in which children may respond both positively and negatively to a change in their lives.

Being anxious, insecure or clingy

Where a transition involves relationships and separation, it is likely that children will show separation anxiety or other signs of anxiety, including clinginess. This can be prevented where children have already built a relationship and so are familiar with the person who will be taking care of them.

Being motivated or confident

Not all transitions are negative. Some children may be moving from one home to a better one. In the same way, some children may look forward to having a new baby and be keen to show responsibility. Changing room in day care, if the child already knows the adults, can feel exciting for some children as there may be new play opportunities and activities.

Regression and atypical behaviour

Some children cope with anxiety and uncertainty by regressing. Children who were able to dress and feed themselves may start to want adults to help them. They may also show a range of behaviours that are not age and stage typical. A four year old may have tantrums or start hitting other children. While regression and unwanted behaviours are common after some transitions, if they persist the child may need additional help.

Excited about a new experience or challenge

Change for some children can be something they see as exciting, especially when adults have been positively preparing them for it. This is often the case for children who are about to start school or join a sibling at a pre-school. Usually children who are excited about the new experience or challenge have already built relationships with the adults in the situation or setting.

Not wanting to engage in education or activities

Some young children who are experiencing stress because of a transition may not be interested in joining in with other children or trying out new activities. When children are reluctant to join in, it may be that they have not developed a sufficiently strong relationship with an adult in the setting. If children are withdrawing and not joining in after two weeks, it is important to seek additional advice.

> **Case study**
>
> Martha is two years old. She has moved from the baby room into the toddler room. She has always been very settled and happy. Due to recent staff changes, Martha does not know either of the adults in the toddler room. Her mother is worried because for the first time since she joined the nursery, Martha has cried during drop-off. Neither of the adults in the toddler room can persuade her to play with them. Martha is also not talking to them. She has spent today sucking her thumb and keeping away from the adults.
> ▶ Using attachment theory, explain why Martha is unsettled.
> ▶ Explain how this transition is affecting Martha's learning.
> ▶ How could this transition have been handled differently?

> **Assessment practice**
>
> 1 Give **one** example of a gross motor skill that would be expected in a child aged four years.
> 2 At what age might you expect a child to be able to thread large beads?
> 3 Outline the main criticisms of Bowlby's work in relation to attachment.
> 4 Explain what is meant by the term 'attachment'.
> 5 What are the signs of separation anxiety?
> 6 At what age might you expect a child to have around 200 words?
> 7 Give **one** example of an unexpected transition and describe how it might affect a child aged eight years.
> 8 Give **one** strategy that can be used to support the transition of a four year old into school.

CORE Chapter 8:
Observation and Assessment

Whatever type of educational setting you are going to work in, you will need to know about and use observation and assessment. This is because as educators we need to be able to look at what children and young people know so that we can plan for them and take forward their learning and development. Because assessment is an ongoing process, schools and early years settings will use different types of observation and assessment in different situations, and it will serve a range of purposes.

Learning outcomes

This chapter covers the following knowledge outcomes for Core Element 8:

- **8.1** The purpose of national assessments and benchmarks
- **8.2** The different purposes of formative and summative assessment
- **8.3** The purpose of accurately observing, recording and reporting on children's and young people's participation, conceptual understanding and progress
- **8.4** The different roles that practitioners play in assessment processes and requirements

This chapter also includes two knowledge outcomes from Early Years Educator Outcome 3. Text relating to Early Years Educator is highlighted. Note that this content will not form part of the core assessments.
- **K3.2** The purpose of observation, assessment and planning, and different approaches towards the assessment of children and planning
- **K3.4** Different types of assessment and their purpose

The knowledge from this chapter also corresponds with Core Skill 3: Use formative and summative assessment to monitor children's and students' progress to plan and shape educational opportunities.

CORE Chapter 8: Observation and Assessment

8.1 The purpose of national assessments and benchmarks

National assessments and **benchmarks** are one of the ways in which schools and early years settings monitor children's and young people's progress. All registered early years and educational settings have a **statutory** obligation to do this and to report their results. Standardised assessment, where results are checked against a standard, also provides a consistent way of reporting to parents and local authorities about how children and young people are progressing at specific ages and stages. This process is **regulated** by Ofqual, which states in the Apprenticeship, Skills, Children and Learning Act 2009 that its objectives are to ensure that national assessments are reliable, consistent and comparable, and that the public can have confidence in this.

For more information on Ofqual, see Core Chapter 1.

Key terms

Benchmark: a point of reference for checking standards.

Statutory: something that is required by law.

Regulation: control of a process by a set of rules.

Monitoring and recording children's and young people's achievement

The key purpose of national assessments and benchmarks is to monitor and record children's and young people's achievement against that of others of the same age and stage. It also helps us to look at individuals over time. This is helpful in several ways:
- It builds a national picture of how children and young people are progressing in different areas and across different subjects.
- It informs professionals and helps them to plan for children's and young people's individual needs.
- It informs parents about their child's progress.

Depending on your role and the age group with which you work, you will need to know about and support this type of formal assessment at different stages as prescribed by national guidelines. You may also be asked to record pupils' progress in different formats.

Differentiating between individuals' performance

National assessments also give us an opportunity to look at how children and young people vary in their achievements at different stages. It is important to remember that all children and young people are unique and will learn and develop at their own rates as well as having strengths and weaknesses in different areas. It is helpful to look at individuals' performances and to see how they are progressing over time. Early years managers and head teachers will also look regularly at pupils' assessment data to see how individuals are moving forward, and to notice if progress is not being made so that steps can be put in place to support them.

Promoting standards and confidence in the National Curriculum, and supporting the regulation of state-funded provision

Where the government, and therefore the taxpayer, funds educational settings (known as **state-funded** provision) – for example, in the case of state schools and some elements of early years provision – they need to be seen to give value for money. Because of this, it is important that they are **accountable** for the way in which they work. They will also need to be registered and inspected by Ofsted to ensure that they are working to a high standard. Along with checks on pupil progress through assessment, these measures ensure that there is regulation in the way in which educational settings work. This is then fed back to parents and local authorities.

Key terms

State funded: money that the government provides for something.

Accountable: required or expected to justify actions or decisions.

National assessment is also a way of promoting standards and confidence in the National Curriculum. This means that it is a way of ensuring that children and young people are working towards a similar level of achievement nationally in key areas, particularly literacy, numeracy and science. Formal assessment will take place at specific times during a child's or young person's progression through the education system, starting with the Early Years Foundation Stage (EYFS).

> For more on types of national assessment see Section 8.2, and for more on formal assessment throughout the education system, see Core Chapter 1.

8.2 The different purposes of formative and summative assessment

K3.4 Different types of assessment and their purpose

- **Formative assessment** (assessment for learning): carried out via observations and used to review progress in the short term, such as at the end of a day.
- **Summative assessment** (assessment of learning): carried out via the EYFS Profile and used to sum up a child's development at the end of the EYFS.

> **Key terms**
>
> *Formative assessment:* frequent, often informal, assessment that is designed to generate ongoing evidence of children's and young people's progress and attainment, and is used to inform the next steps.
>
> *Summative assessment:* a final assessment, usually occurring at the end of a period of study, which is used to sum up children's and young people's overall level of attainment, and to provide data for stakeholders.

We will use different types of assessment for different purposes during a child's or young person's educational journey. Some of these will be written down and formal, while others may simply involve looking at how a child or young person approaches a task or interacts with others, and forming a picture of them. Each approach is valuable and all give us information about pupils' levels of understanding and achievement, while formal assessments enable managers to monitor children's and young people's progress over time by providing data.

Assessments can also highlight if a child or young person needs extra help in a specific area of development or learning. However, it should be remembered that assessment is only one aspect of the educational process and it is also about practitioners knowing the whole child or young person, and what they know and are able to do. Educators should ensure that they are always assessing for a reason and be clear on what this is.

Formative assessment

Formative assessment is sometimes called **assessment for learning (AfL)**. It is ongoing, which means it takes place on a day-to-day basis when teachers, teaching assistants and early years practitioners are talking to children and young people, observing them and listening to the ways in which they respond to learning activities. We also use it to consolidate or go over pupil's previous learning and check how much they can remember. It can be used at the end of the day and assessment will then feed in to planning so that teachers and early years practitioners can use it to inform the next steps of children's learning. Formative assessment helps us to set specific targets for children and young people as it gives an up-to-date indication of what they know and how they are learning.

Examples of formative assessment are shown in the accompanying diagram.

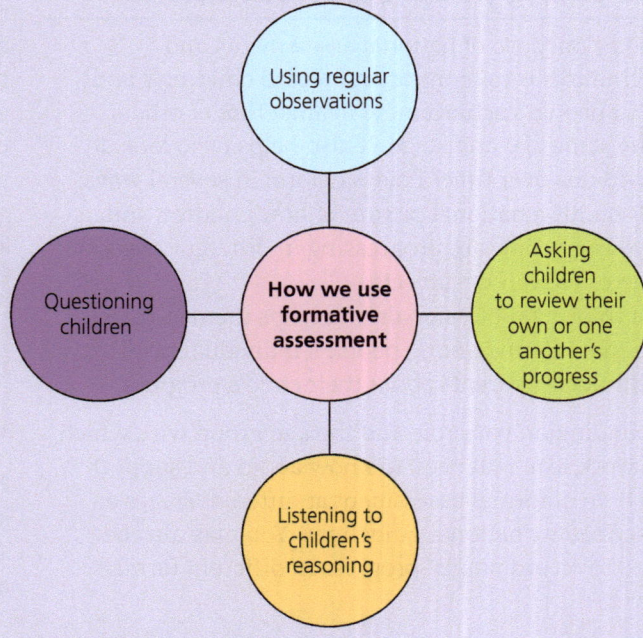

▲ Examples of formative assessment

Using regular observations of children and young people

We may use **formal** or **informal observations** of children so that we can look more closely at what they are doing and plan for their individual needs. In the EYFS, practitioners carry out observations and note down aspects of children's learning and development as an integral part of the curriculum. This helps them to monitor children's knowledge, skills and development towards the Early Learning Goals. Anything that is significant is recorded in a child's individual profile or **learning journal**. In schools, formal observations will follow a set format and you may be given a template to use when carrying them out so that you can note down particular points – for example, how long the child is able to stay focused on a task.

> For more on the EYFS, see Core Chapter 1, page 2, and for more on the Early Learning Goals, see Core Chapter 2, page 16.

Key terms

Formal observations: structured observations taking place within a set time in which the observer has specific criteria to look for.

Informal observations: simple observations that take place during the course of the day, which may look at behaviour, relationships or confidence.

Learning journal: in the EYFS, individual learning journals may be used as a record of a child's progress and achievements during the year. They may include observations, photos and quotes from the child.

They may also be used when working with children and young people who have special educational needs, to help us to look at specific areas (see Sections 8.3 and 8.4). Observations may also include quotes or photographs of children and young people, which can also be used as evidence of their achievement.

> For more detail on the purpose of observations see Section 8.3, page 144.

Sometimes, you also might make observations of children and young people that assess behaviour, wellbeing or relationships with others, or look at how they approach a task. You may also note down observations during breaks or extracurricular activities, which may still be relevant to the child or young person as a whole, and their progress or development. For example, it may be that you become aware of something that is not related to a learning activity, such as a safeguarding or wellbeing issue, or an incidence of bullying. You should make a note of this and feed back to colleagues later, so that they are aware of it.

Case study

Sophie is on playground duty with Years 1 and 2. She notices that two Year 2 pupils, Amira and Della, have been walking round the playground deep in conversation for a long time. When they pass her, she asks if they are OK and Amira starts to cry. Della tells her that Amira's parents have split up and that she is upset about it.
▶ What would you do first?
▶ Why is it important for staff working with Amira to know about this?

▲ How do you make a note of children's and young people's learning when you are working with them?

Questioning children and young people to check their knowledge and understanding of a particular topic or concept

When working with small or large groups, or with individuals, careful questioning enables us to find out exactly what they know and assess their learning. We can target our questions in a way that encourages children or young people to expand on their answers and tell us more. We call this **open questioning**. A closed question, on the other hand, will usually require only a one-word answer and will not give us much information about what children and young people know.

Key term

Open question: a question that cannot be answered with a yes or no response.

> **Reflect**
>
> ▸ Reflect on these two versions of a question that might be asked at the start of a topic:
>   1. Adult: Today we are going to be looking at producers and predators. Is a bird a predator, Sophie?
>   2. Adult: Today we are going to be looking at producers and predators. What can you tell me about what this means?
> ▸ Looking at the questions above, which would you say is an example of an open question?
> ▸ How will the pupil's answer give us more information about what they know?

☹	I don't understand this yet
😐	I think I understand but I need more practice
🙂	I understand this well and can do it on my own

▲ What type of self-assessment have you seen used in classrooms and early years settings?

Listening to pupils' reasoning when they are talking about their learning

When we are working with pupils, it can be a helpful method of formative assessment to talk to them about what they are doing and why they are doing it. In this way we can build a picture of their thought processes. It also gives us an opportunity to guide them in their learning if this is needed.

Asking pupils to review their own or one another's progress

Another method of formative assessment is known as **self-assessment** or **peer-assessment**. This involves asking children and young people about how close they think they are to meeting learning objectives at the end of a session. It helps them to evaluate their own learning and think about what they need to do next.

With younger children, thumbs-up or traffic light systems may be used at the end of a lesson or activity so that teaching staff can gain a quick snapshot of their level of understanding.

With older children, teachers may ask them to write their own assessment under their work in exercise books, or ask them to show how they feel about their learning at the end of the session by talking about specific success criteria.

Peer-assessment, or assessing one another's work, is also often used with older children and young people. They will need to develop experience over time so that they can use this approach effectively; this will also help them to learn to assess their own work and to self-reflect on their learning.

The kinds of questions they could ask might be:
▸ Have they met the learning objective? How can you tell?
▸ Can you find a place where they have done well and explain why they have done well?
▸ Can you find an area in which they can improve and explain how they could do this?

Core Chapter 2 has more on how to review children's and young people's learning, and how to give feedback to them during learning activities.

> **Practice points**
>
> ▸ Make sure you know the learning objective of each session when working with children and young people so that you know what you are assessing them against.
> ▸ Use mainly open questioning to help assess children's learning.
> ▸ Check on learning towards the objective by talking to children about what they are doing.
> ▸ Ask children and young people to regularly self- and peer-review their own and one another's work.

CORE Chapter 8: Observation and Assessment

Summative assessment

Summative assessment, or assessment of learning, will take place at the end of a scheme of work, stage or academic year. This is so that teaching staff are able to report to parents and senior managers about the progress of children and young people in their class or year group. In early years settings and primary schools, this will include the more formal assessments prescribed by the Department for Education that provide data to schools and, at a national level, to Ofsted. In secondary schools up to GCSE, teachers will assess pupils regularly and set their own tests and exams, although this may vary between schools.

The kinds of summative assessment that will take place include the following.

Reception Baseline Assessment (RBA)

This takes place during the autumn term in reception classes. It is carried out within the first six weeks of a child starting school and will be overseen by the class teacher or early years coordinator, and looks at what children know and are able to do when they come in to school. It is an oral (spoken) assessment in which children will be given a series of simple tasks to do while working one-to-one with an adult, such as describing pictures or counting objects. This assessment then gives schools a starting point from which to measure pupils' progress while they are in primary school. It had been due to start in September 2020 but at time of writing this has been postponed to September 2021. RBA only covers children's starting point in language, communication and literacy, and mathematics.

Early Years Foundation Stage Profile

The EYFS Profile is an assessment that is carried out at the end of the summer term in reception, before children move in to Year 1. It is a report for parents and teachers about children's development and learning at the end of the EYFS. This form of summative assessment requires teachers to report children as Expected or Emerging against each of the 17 Early Learning Goals.

The EYFS Profile also helps to support transition to Year 1 and helps teachers plan for children's needs at the start of Key Stage 1.

End of Key Stage 1 teacher assessments

Teachers must report pupil levels in English reading, English writing, mathematics and science at the end of Key Stage 1, or when children are seven. Teacher assessment means that teachers must make their own professional judgements using a range of evidence from their observations and knowledge of pupils across the curriculum. They must also manage formal assessments to support their judgement: National Curriculum assessments in reading and mathematics are sent to schools and carried out by teaching staff in order to support teacher assessment. In addition, teachers may choose to carry out an optional English grammar, punctuation and spelling test to support their teacher assessment. At the time of writing in 2020, these are due to be discontinued from 2022/23 and Reception Baseline Assessment will be used as a starting point for measuring progress in primary schools.

▲ Do you think it is important to have a baseline assessment when children start school?

Key Stage 2 Statutory Assessment Tests (SATs)

These externally marked tests are carried out in the summer term of Year 6, before pupils move to secondary school. They are in English reading and grammar, punctuation and spelling, and maths. In addition, every two years a sample of pupils from around 1,900 schools also take a science test, which is marked externally. These results will then be passed to secondary schools so that they have an up-to-date picture of each child's academic achievement. However, in many cases, they will also carry out their own assessments, and base GCSE predictions on these. Key Stage 2 SATs are also used to form part of school league tables, which are published nationally.

Key Stage 3

From Key Stage 3 onwards, schools are no longer required to carry out national assessments. However, teachers are expected to assess pupils' progress in key areas on a regular basis and feed back to head teachers so that they can monitor pupils and add this to their data. It is a statutory requirement that they report end of key stage results to local authorities and the DfE as well as to parents. Assessment will usually take the form of end-of-year exams, but schools may vary in their approaches. Secondary schools will usually carry out diagnostic assessments at the start of the September term in Year 7 (sometimes known as **CATs** or **Cognitive Abilities Tests**) as this will give them a snapshot of pupils' ability and understanding in key areas and demonstrate how they learn best. These results may then be used to group pupils by ability and in some cases they are used to predict GCSE outcomes.

The following qualifications, which are provided by recognised awarding bodies and organisations, are not part of national assessment as they are designed and carried out differently, but are still national benchmarks and still regulated by Ofqual.

Key Stage 4: GCSEs/International GCSEs

GCSEs or International GCSEs (sometimes known as iGCSEs) in a range of subjects are taken by pupils in secondary schools in England, Wales and Northern Ireland (or for International GCSEs, abroad) at the age of 16. The results of these assessments give pupils a stepping stone to the next stage in their education, and provide schools with data on pupils' level of achievement, when they may go on to take A-levels or T Levels, or consider an apprenticeship. It is a requirement that schools publish their Key Stage 4 results.

Diagnostic assessment

This form of assessment gives us a picture of a child's or young person's level of achievement at any stage. This can be a useful means of assessing their existing knowledge at the beginning of a new topic or scheme of work. It is also helpful to carry out a diagnostic assessment if a new pupil starts at a setting before their records arrive from a previous school or setting. Diagnostic assessments are also used by other professionals, such as speech and language therapists and educational psychologists, when looking at children's and young people's development in a specific area, so that they can make recommendations for support.

> **In practice**
>
> In early years settings, children will also have a progress check at age two. Parents, healthcare workers, early years staff and any other professionals working with the child are invited to contribute. Find out more about it and how it is put together.
> ▶ Why do you think this check is carried out at such a young age?
> ▶ How does the progress check at age two help professionals to plan for next steps?

K3.2 The purpose of observation, assessment and planning, and different approaches towards the assessment of children and planning

Observation, assessment and planning are all key aspects of our work in early years. It is important to be clear on what each of them means and of their purpose so that you will be able to support children's learning and development effectively.
- ▶ Observation means watching, gathering and recording information about children in order to build a clear picture of their needs.
- ▶ Assessment is a process through which we identify and record a child's needs, interests and current stage of learning and development.
- ▶ Planning is the way in which we make use of information collected during observation and assessment to plan appropriate provision and to support developmental progress for individual children.

CORE Chapter 8: Observation and Assessment

Understand the different approaches towards the assessment of children

> For **observations**: See Sections 8.2 and 8.3.

- **Questions and answers:** Questioning children is a key part of assessment. Careful questioning and talking to children allows us to find out what they know, and allows us to take their learning forward. It is important to remember that we should use questioning in a way that allows them to talk about what they are doing and give them opportunities to discover things for themselves.

> There is more on questioning in Section 8.2.

- **Group activities:** Carrying out group activities with children allows us to look at their social skills and how they work with others. It is a helpful way of assessing the personal, social and emotional aspects of children's learning, and their communication and language skills.
- **Partnerships with parents, carers and other professionals:** Developing partnerships with parents, carers and other professionals is important for assessment as it is a way of finding out more about children and what they are able to do. Most settings will ask parents to communicate new achievements with them – for example, if a child has learned to swim or has done some cooking at home. These are also good opportunities for the child to develop their communication skills by talking about what they have done. Other professionals will also share information with the setting about their own assessments of children, which should feed in to the EYFS and also support practitioners in their work with individual children.
- **Standardised testing:** Standardised testing is a type of summative assessment that allows us to look at a child's level at the end of a year or scheme of work.

> See also Section 8.2 on summative assessment.

In practice

- What types of opportunity do children in your setting have for carrying out group activities?
- How often do these take place and how do adults assess what they are doing?

Case study

Jasmine has just started working with Emil, who is three. He has a stammer and his parents have discussed this with Jasmine and outlined ways in which they manage this at home. Emil's speech and language assessment shows that he lacks confidence and needs to be given opportunities to speak without pressure in a calm environment. Jasmine has also just received a written report from the health visitor and speech and language therapist, which gives her details of what she can do to support Emil.

- Why is it important that Jasmine uses the information from Emil's parents and other professionals and continues to work with them?
- How will this information feed in to Jasmine's assessment of Emil's communication and language skills?

Different approaches to planning

Below, we look at some of the different approaches to planning and how they are used in practice.

The planning cycle – plan, do, review process

You must remember the importance of using formative assessment and regular observation as part of the planning and reviewing process and know that this is part of a cycle. All those who work with children and young people and assess their learning must continuously look at the different ways in which they show us what they understand and have learned. In this way, we can amend our plans if necessary to continue to move them forward in their learning.

> For more on this, see Section 8.3.

Long-, medium- and short-term planning

Early years settings will usually create different types of plan to be used at different stages during the academic year; this is known as long-, medium- and short-term planning. Settings and individual practitioners will devise their own formats so that they use the one that works best for them. There may be some overlap in terms of which heading different types of plan come under – for example, a plan for the week may come under medium- or short-term planning; however, individual settings will all have their own systems for this.

Long-term plans and **schemes of work** will usually be compiled well in advance and may even be reused, with some amendments, year on year. Depending on the size of the setting, they are also likely to be created by more than one person as part of a team. Long-term plans may be created as far as a year ahead so that it is clear what is going to be covered and to ensure a broad range of activities for children. This also helps staff to plan well in advance for the resources and equipment that will be needed, particularly if there is a large team who may need to use them. Plans will usually be stored on computer systems so that staff can refer to them, and printed out for those who need them to be more accessible.

Medium-term plans may include those for the term or half-term, as well as for the week. Termly or half-termly plans will be broken down into weeks and will show progression over time. They will have more details about individual learning activities and should include space for notes or amendments about assessment. Again, these plans are likely to be stored on computer systems and placed in class or subject planning folders.

> **Research**
>
> If you have not seen them, ask to look at copies of long-, medium- and short-term plans for the children you support.
> - How do they feed in to one another?
> - What key information can you find in each?

Short-term plans will be for the week or day. They will be detailed, and will include timings, objectives, assessment information and details about additional resources and support. You may be involved with these if you are invited to planning meetings with other staff. These may be formal, with time set aside each week to plan together, or in the form of informal discussions and conversations both before and after the activities take place. You will need to know about the way in which planning takes place so that you can contribute to this and make your own suggestions.

In the moment planning/child-led planning

In early years settings, your planning may also be guided by individual children's interests and learning, as the EYFS states that 'Practitioners must consider the individual needs, interests and stage of development of each child.' For example, a child may bring in a bird's nest and this may shape their learning for the day if they want to find out more about it, create a model or paint a picture. It is important to allow children to lead their learning in this situation and to be flexible enough to change plans if needed.

> **Practice points**
>
> - Always plan with others if possible or ask to see short-term plans in advance if not.
> - Find out where long- and medium-term plans are kept so that you have an idea of context.
> - Check planning and your role before the learning activity so that you can prepare more effectively.
> - Don't be afraid to put forward your own suggestions at the planning stage.
> - Be flexible, able to change plans and to be led by children's interests.

8.3 The purpose of accurately observing, recording and reporting on children's and young people's participation, conceptual understanding and progress

As we have already mentioned, observations are a way of gathering information on children and young people. We make observations of children and young people all the time, as we work with them and get to know their personalities and their likes and abilities. However, more formal observations and assessments of children and young people help us to find out more about their learning and progress. These in turn give us a way of meeting individual needs and planning for next steps. These are all very important parts of the **planning, learning and assessment cycle**. It is known as a cycle because as educators it is something that we are doing all the time and because each aspect is reliant on the others. It is also important to record this information accurately and in a timely way so that it can be shared with colleagues and parents.

> **Key term**
>
> **Planning, learning and assessment cycle:** the process through which children's needs and abilities are identified, which enables teachers to plan for next steps.

CORE Chapter 8: Observation and Assessment

Plan – Using this information, practitioners plan resources, activities and ways of working to support children's and young people's interests, and their learning and development.

START HERE
Observation – Looking at what children and young people can already do in a variety of situations. Noticing when they need more support, but also if they are not showing expected learning and development.

The child or young person

Assessment/Next steps – Looking at what the observations are telling us about the child's or young person's learning and developmental needs, but also any interests or areas where they need additional support so that it can lead into the next steps.

▲ The planning cycle

Observations can take different forms and you may be asked to complete and record them in a range of formats. It is helpful to know about why we refer to different forms of observation as they will be suitable to use in different situations. Your setting may provide a template for some of these, but others, such as free description, will be noted down as they happen.

Common formats for observations

- **Checklists:** These are simply observations that check off what a child or young person is able to do; the focus in this situation will be on whether or not they are able to do it rather than on the process. For example, checklists may be used as part of the RBA to say that a child is able to count to ten.
- **Snapshots:** These are often used in early years settings through quickly writing down or taking a photograph to capture something a child has done. They will usually have a short description to put them in context.

> For more on snapshots, see Section 8.4.

- **Free descriptions:** These allow us to write down everything that a child or group is doing, usually during a timed period. They will provide more information than a snapshot, and will be detailed, which means they will usually last only five to ten minutes. They can be tricky to carry out as it can be difficult to write everything down quickly.

- **Event/time samples:** These are used to check on how regularly a child or young person carries out a particular activity or behaviour over a period of time. The observer needs to stand away from the child so that they do not interrupt or influence their behaviour. This type of observation is sometimes used for children and young people who have special educational needs as it helps us to identify specific areas for development.

Practice points

Observations

- Make sure you are clear on what you have been asked to observe.
- Always ensure that your observations are as accurate as possible.
- Sit back from the child or young person so that you are not a distraction.
- Become involved with what is happening only if the teacher has asked you to do so.
- Include only the level of detail that is needed.

Identifying developmental progress

Our records and regular observations of children and young people will also help us to monitor their developmental progress. We need to have a good understanding of child development to be able to do this. (Refer to Core Chapter 7 for more on this.) It is particularly useful with younger children, as their development progresses relatively quickly during the early years, which is why observation is a key part of the EYFS.

The **EYFS *Development Matters*** document also helps us to look at children's progress against expected age-related milestones by setting them out in detail. We should also look at the way in which children and young people approach different activities, their level of confidence and how they work with others, as this forms part of their social and emotional development. Through watching them and recording what we have seen, we are able to document different stages of development.

Key term

EYFS Development Matters: non-statutory guidance to support early years practitioners with observation, assessment and planning.

145

Informing planning, feedback and next steps

Observing children's and young people's learning and development, and feeding back to colleagues, is a key aspect of your role, whether in early years settings or schools. Feedback from individual learning activities will need to include information about children's and young people's participation and what happened during the session. It may also include what they said, their approach to learning and how they worked with others. Feedback may be recorded on the lesson plan, or on an evaluation or feedback sheet. In this way, we will be able to monitor children's and young people's progress and will have evidence of how they have responded in different situations and when working in groups or individually.

When working with children and young people it helps to write things down as they happen as it is difficult to remember everything afterwards, particularly if you are working with a group. Observations also allow us to identify whether children and young people are responding positively to particular topics or learning activities, which helps us to review our approach to teaching.

In the early years in particular, observations should be linked to children's next steps for learning. They should, therefore, lead very closely into planning for individual children's needs, and early years practitioners should show how they are doing this.

> **Research**
>
> Look up the EYFS *Development Matters* document.
> https://assets.publishing.service.gov.uk/government/uploads/system/uploads/attachment_data/file/971620/Development_Matters.pdf
>
> How do you think this will support assessment in the early years?

Snapshot or anecdotal observation

Jack identified the first letter of his name today and tried to form the shape of 'J' starting at the top. Next steps: continue work on identifying and writing own name.

▲ Example of a snapshot observation with next steps

▲ How do you feed back to colleagues after carrying out learning activities with children?

Adhering to policies and procedures relevant to recording information, maintaining validity and reliability

Information about children's and young people's learning may be recorded through formal observation sheets, in photographs, on feedback sheets to colleagues or through lesson evaluations. It may then be transferred to digital spreadsheets or other

CORE Chapter 8: Observation and Assessment

commercially available computer assessment programs. When recording and reporting information, it is important that all educational practitioners use the methods set out in their school's or early years setting's assessment, recording and reporting policy. Another important aspect of recording is to ensure that it is done accurately and that the information that is recorded is necessary. You should also make sure that you only record what is seen at the time, to ensure that the observation is **valid** and **reliable**.

When recording and reporting information about children and young people, you should also be aware of legal requirements regarding confidentiality and the storage of records, whether these are paper-based or on a computer or tablet. Information and data on children and young people should be held in line with GDPR (General Data Protection Regulation) legislation and data protection laws. Remember that, for safeguarding reasons, photographic records of children and young people should be taken only using equipment that belongs to the setting.

Key terms

Valid: worth consideration; should be recorded.

Reliable: able to be trusted.

Practice points

Recording and reporting information

- Ensure information is valid and reliable.
- Remember confidentiality and keep records secure.
- Store any passwords securely.
- Ensure that pupil records are updated regularly.

In practice

Ask if you can see a copy of your school or early years assessment, recording and reporting policy. What does it say about the following?
- The types of assessment used in your setting
- How assessment outcomes are recorded
- Confidentiality
- Reporting to parents

Enabling interventions

Observing will help us to gather evidence about a child's or young person's current level of learning or development in a particular area. This will in turn enable us to plan for the right type of **intervention** from adults where required. For example, children and young people who over time show that they are having problems with literacy or mathematical concepts may need to have extra support through targeted interventions. Interventions may also be introduced for other areas, such as speech and language, problem solving, social skills or behaviour. They will provide individual or small-group support for areas that children and young people find more challenging, and should enable them to develop confidence and make progress.

Key term

Intervention: an activity or strategy which is used in addition to those which have already been carried out in the classroom, designed to support children who are working below national expectations but who should reach them with the right support.

Sharing information with relevant colleagues, the family and other agencies

Keeping accurate observations and records on children's and young people's participation and progress will also ensure that we have evidence we can share with parents and colleagues. At any time, we should have access to up-to-date information about their progress in different areas. This is important so that we can write reports and give information to parents and other agencies if needed.

Test yourself

As part of its RBA, a primary school carries out assessments of children's communication and language development. The teaching assistant who is trained in delivering the assessment feeds back to the teacher about all of the children so that specific interventions can be put in place for those who need it.
- How does this process support teaching and learning?
- Why is this area of development important?

8.4 The different roles that practitioners play in assessment processes and requirements

Depending on your role, the age of the children and young people you work with, and the setting in which you work, your involvement is likely to be slightly different. However, all practitioners will be involved in assessment and should understand its importance.

Early years practitioners

All staff in early years settings will work closely to assess and monitor young children in line with the requirements of the EYFS curriculum:

> 'Ongoing assessment (also known as formative assessment) is an integral part of the learning and development process. It involves practitioners knowing children's level of achievement and interests, and then to shape teaching and learning experiences for each child reflecting that knowledge.'
>
> (Source: Statutory Framework for the Early Years Foundation Stage, 2021)

Observe, record and review children's progress

The EYFS requires that practitioners carry out regular observations throughout this stage. Practitioners in both early years settings and school reception classes will be doing this all the time. Key persons in particular will need to ensure that they monitor the learning and development of their key children closely, and work with parents to encourage them to share developments at home.

Observations may take the form of photographs of children with a brief sentence to explain what the child was doing or saying, and should include the area of learning and development; this is why such observations are sometimes known as snapshots (see page 145). In some settings, they may be stored on tablets or computers, while in others they are printed out and put in a child's learning journey document or journal, which should be accessible to all relevant adults in the setting.

Other observations may be noted down without photos as notes, particularly in the case of something significant that has happened quickly, so that it is not missed – for example, 'Tania was able to put on and zip up her coat independently.'

▲ Which area of development and caption do you think you might find on this photo?

It is also important that the child's learning journal contains observations from all of these areas, so it is helpful to check regularly for gaps. If a child is particularly able in one area, or regularly goes to work on activities that interest them, there may be lots of observations and photographs of this, but it is important to ensure that all areas of a child's learning and development are being monitored and covered through observations.

Assess children's individual needs

Throughout the EYFS, early years practitioners will be using observations every day to look at children's learning and development. This also helps to assess their individual needs going forward. For example, observations may highlight that they have a particular interest that regularly engages them, or when their behaviour is different from usual. Knowing about children's individual needs will help us to plan activities that will interest them and be enjoyable as well as providing challenges.

> **Case study**
>
> Tamara works in a large early years setting. She is the key person for a number of children and regularly observes them to monitor and assess their learning and development. She has noticed that Sohail, who is almost four, is making very limited progress in his communication and language development compared to others the same age. He seems to be saying individual words or names of objects but is not trying to link them together – for example, pointing and saying 'drink' or 'book'.
> ▶ How can Tamara find out if this is a cause for concern?
> ▶ What else could she do?

Plan activities and support statutory assessments

Based on what they know about children through observation and assessment, early years practitioners will then plan next steps and future learning for children. This should be based on their 'individual needs, interests and stage of development', according to the EYFS statutory framework, which includes the different ways in which children learn. Practitioners will need to show that they are planning activities that challenge children and take their learning forward. These should be a mix of adult-led and child-initiated activities.

In the case of statutory assessments such as the RBA and the EYFS Profile, the role of early years practitioners will be to ensure that they are assessing and monitoring children's progress regularly so that they have an up-to-date picture of their level of development when it comes to the statutory assessment.

Practice points

The role of early years practitioners in observations
- Make sure you regularly observe your key children.
- Check that all areas of learning and development are assessed regularly.
- Remember to plan activities that support children's individual needs.

Teachers, lecturers and teaching assistants

Teachers, lecturers and teaching assistants work in the following ways to assess and monitor children's and young people's progress.

Monitor children's and young people's understanding and progress

Schools and colleges need to have assessment procedures that allow them to monitor the way in which children and young people are progressing. While the role of both teachers and lecturers is to ensure that they are constantly monitoring individual pupil progress and levels, teaching assistants are more likely to take a supporting role in the process. This means that they will feed back to teachers or lecturers on lessons they have carried out with pupils so that this information can be recorded centrally. Alternatively, they may be asked to enter the results of summative assessments on to computer systems.

As the monitoring of pupil progress is likely to be done through online records, teaching staff may need specific training in the use of computer software. In addition to being a template for assessment, most commercially available computer programs will work out specific data – for example, checking on the achievements of boys and girls, or looking at pupil achievement year on year and subject by subject. This helps management teams to look at strengths and weaknesses, and provides a wider picture of achievement.

Provide targeted feedback to enable children and young people to improve

Through ongoing assessment, teaching staff are able to provide targeted feedback to children and young people. This means that they will use assessment to be specific about what aspects of their learning should be targeted through teaching in order to help pupils to make progress. Teachers and lecturers will set learning targets for pupils – usually once every few weeks – so that they have something to work towards. Teaching assistants working with specific pupils should be aware of these targets and pupils should be reminded of them regularly while they carry out learning activities.

Case study

Brian is working in a Year 3 class and regularly takes out a small group of children to support them with their writing. They have three literacy targets, which are stuck on to the inside covers of their literacy books. While working with the group, Brian notices that two of his group need to go back over their work to check their spelling and punctuation, and this happens to be one of their targets.
- Why is it important for Brian to say something about this?
- How will this targeted approach enable the children to improve?

Prepare children and young people for national assessments

Teachers, lecturers and teaching assistants will all need to be able to prepare pupils for national assessments such as the SATs at the end of Key Stage 2. They will need to ensure that the curriculum requirements of the assessments have been covered through teaching and learning, and that they have prepared the pupils as to

Education and Early Years T Level: Early Years Educator

what to expect. Through careful regular assessment and monitoring, they will be able to tell which pupils may need more support as they work towards the requirements of the test.

Assessors

Assessors will usually work with older students in sixth form and FE colleges. Some of their roles in relation to assessment are described below.

Assess individuals' performance/relevant knowledge

The role of an assessor is to regularly check students' progress against a set of knowledge and skills in a technical qualification, such as an apprenticeship. As a result, they will need to have experience, or what is known as occupational competence, in carrying out the role themselves. Assessors will need to regularly visit students in their workplace to observe them, assess what they are able to do, provide them with feedback and make plans for next steps towards their qualification. They will also mark assignments and look at students' portfolios of work, which may be paper-based or online.

> **Research**
>
> Research some of the occupations an assessor might assess in the workplace.
>
> What kinds of qualifications might someone need in order to become an assessor?

Ensure that the standards and requirements of the specification are met

Technical qualifications will set out exactly what students need to know and be able to do in order to meet the requirements of the specification. Assessors will need to check students' progress against the knowledge and skills that are set out in their chosen subject. If the requirements are not yet met, this will be fed back to the student and reassessed at a later date. If students are unable to meet the criteria, they will not pass the qualification.

▲ Why is it important for work-based learners to be observed in the workplace?

Coaches and mentors

The roles of coaches and mentors are slightly different in that a mentor's role is more long term and informal, whereas that of a coach has a structure and is more likely to focus on individual goals. A key aspect of the role of a coach or mentor is to support another person's learning and development, and to provide pastoral advice and guidance. However, each of them aims to help and support pupils to achieve their full potential.

Set and review key performance indicators

Key performance indicators are a way of showing that something is on target to be achieved or met. **Mentors** help pupils to make changes in their thinking or learning so that they can progress. They should be a role model for the mentee (the person they are mentoring) and able to advise them about what they need to do next. A **coach** supports learning and development, and helps pupils to review and improve their work through challenging their ideas and encouraging them to reflect on what they are doing.

In each case, coaches and mentors will need to set targets and assess individuals' progress towards these. They will then look at ways in which pupils can continue to move forward with their learning.

Provide support that is relevant to individual needs and advise on how to improve individual performance

Coaches and mentors will get to know pupils so that they are in the best position to work with them and identify barriers to their progress and achievement, which may be connected to special educational needs, self-esteem, issues in their personal life or motivation. They may need specific support or special considerations – for example, in exam situations, particularly if they have had any issues that affect their learning, such as a family bereavement or an illness.

Coaches and mentors may be able to advise children and young people as to how they can improve their individual performance – for example, through discussing their mind-set or looking at other aspects of their learning. Coaches and mentors may also need to share information with colleagues, particularly if there are any safeguarding issues.

> **Assessment practice**
>
> 1. What is the purpose of assessment?
> 2. What is the difference between formative and summative assessment?
> 3. Give **one** example of a national assessment used in England.
> 4. Explain why it is important to monitor the progress of children and young people.
> 5. Explain what is meant by assessment for learning.
> 6. What is the planning, learning and assessment cycle?
> 7. Identify **three** reasons why observations are important.
> 8. Explain the roles of mentor and coach, and the differences between them.

CORE Chapter 9:
Reflective Practice

Whatever your role, whether you work in a school or an early years setting, you will need to be able to engage in reflective practice. This calls for you to regularly step back and think about your own practice and evaluate what you are doing. The process is called continuing professional development (CPD), and you will be supported in doing this with your line manager. In this chapter, we will look at why reflective practice is important and how it will help you to develop in your role when working with children and young people.

Learning outcomes

This chapter covers the following knowledge outcomes for Core Element 9:
- 9.1 The key concepts of specific models of reflection and how they can be applied in practice
- 9.2 The current priorities and debates in education
- 9.3 Why practitioners must engage in feedback and continuous professional development
- 9.4 How practitioners can meet their own developmental needs

9.1 The key concepts of specific models of reflection

Models of reflection give us as individuals the tools to think about and act on our practice. Management teams in schools and early years settings are also encouraged to reflect and self-evaluate on a regular basis, as it helps them to set annual targets for the organisation, and to see the best way forward for the setting and the children and young people within it.

Several theorists have outlined what they consider to be important aspects of learning and reflecting on experience. These models are designed to help those who use them by giving the exercise of reflection a structure. They encourage the individual to step back and look at the past so that they can learn from their experiences and plan for the future. You need to know the key concepts of each of them so that you can consider how they can be applied in practice, and use the aspects that are helpful to you.

Kolb's experiential learning cycle

David A. Kolb, an American theorist, published his **experiential learning theory (ELT)** in 1984. Experiential learning means learning from experience, and is based on the learner having some form of reflection in the process. In his model (shown in the diagram), Kolb assumes that learning involves four different stages, and that we learn effectively only when we have passed through each of these. The cycle can be started at any point, however, the sequence of passing through it should remain the same.

> **Key terms**
>
> **Experiential learning theory (ELT):** the theory that knowledge is created through experience.
>
> **Abstract conceptualisation (AC):** this is when the learner has a new idea or has changed their thinking due to their experience.
>
> **Active experimentation (AE):** the learner applies their new way of thinking to a future experience.
>
> **Concrete experience (CE):** this is when the learner encounters an activity or experience for themselves.
>
> **Reflective observation of a new experience (RO):** this stage is when the learner thinks back, or reflects, on their experience.

At each stage in the cycle, it is very important for the learner to be supported effectively, whether by a teacher, trainer or mentor. This is because they need to be shown how to think critically as they pass through the different stages.

Gibbs' reflective cycle

Another model of reflection is known as **Gibbs' reflective cycle** and was developed in 1988 by Graham Gibbs. This model is said to be **iterative**, which means you learn through repetition and improve each time.

Gibbs states that there are six stages of reflecting on experience, under the following headings:

1. **Description:** What happened? This should include all details about who was there, what happened, and what you and others did. What was the result?
2. **Feelings:** What were you and others thinking or feeling before/during/after the situation? How do you and others feel now?
3. **Evaluation:** What was good or bad about the situation? What did you or others do that made these positives or negatives happen?
4. **Analysis:** What sense can you make of the situation?
5. **Conclusion:** What could you have done differently? What did you learn?
6. **Action plan:** Do you need to develop new skills so that you could handle this type of situation better in the future? Can you plan to make some changes? Make sure you include a date for review.

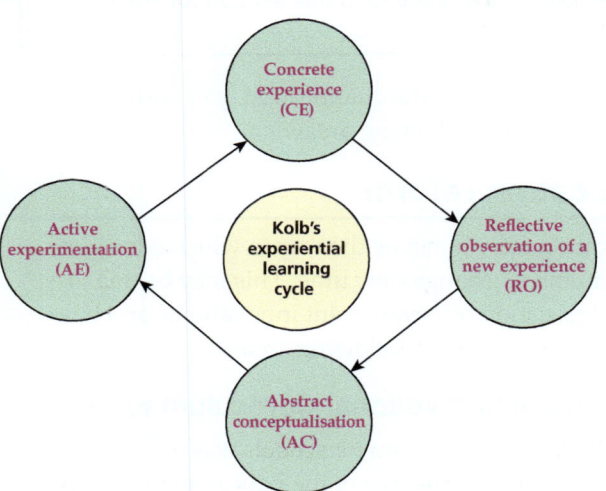

▲ Kolb's experiential learning cycle

> **In practice**
>
> Carry out a reflective exercise using Gibbs' reflective cycle. This can relate to something you have had to do as part of your course, or could be a way of looking at another aspect of your life.
> ▶ What parts of the model do you find useful?
> ▶ How might it help you going forward?

Boud, Keogh and Walker's model

David Boud, Rosemary Keogh and David Walker's model was developed in 1985 and contains three stages of reflecting on practice. This model has a focus on feelings and emotions, and encourages the individual to separate them into those that are positive and those that are negative.

The three stages are as follows.
1. **Experience:** In the first stage, the experience takes place, and the learner will have feelings, ideas and behaviour related to this.
2. **Reflective process:** The second stage involves thinking about what has happened, using positive feelings and removing those that might be obstructive (get in the way), then re-evaluating.
3. **Outcomes:** The third stage is about looking at the experience again in light of what has been learned and using this new perspective to change behaviour.

As part of this chapter, you will need to be able to consider how reflective models can be applied in practice. In each of these theories, the learner needs to revisit an experience or learning activity, think carefully about what happened, and then consider how they might change or develop from the experience. If we think about our job role, or activities carried out within it, this process can be very helpful.

> **Reflect**
>
> Find out more about each of the three models of reflection. You can use the internet, publications or books.
> ▶ Do you find any of them more helpful than the others?
> ▶ Why do you think this is the case?

> **Case study**
>
> Janice is working as a nursery assistant at a local day nursery. She is timetabled to split her time between the baby room and the toddler room. However, she finds that on most days this does not work well as the handover time is in the middle of a session and she does not have time to speak with colleagues about the children's needs. After thinking about it, she has worked out a plan to resolve this and asks to speak to her line manager about it.
> ▶ How does this show that Janice is using reflection in her practice?
> ▶ What other advantages are there to what she is doing?

9.2 Current priorities and debates in education

When you are working in education, you will need to have some idea of the kinds of current discussions, priorities and debates that are going on in this area. You can keep up to date with these through making sure that you are aware of current news stories, looking at websites and magazines aimed at the teaching and childcare sectors, and making sure that you know about any current news stories and debates that are taking place. Distance and online self-directed learning have also become more accessible to those who are unable to attend college or university, and it is now possible to undertake qualifications in your own time.

> See page 158 at the end of this section for some useful resources.

For the purpose of this qualification, you will need to know about the following areas.

Education reform

Education reform means the way in which education requirements change over time. This may be due to new legislation or government innovations, and has changed many of the following areas.

The impact of National Curriculum reforms

The National Curriculum for schools was first introduced in 1988 as part of the Education Reform Act. Up until that time, schools were able to decide what was taught and when. From 1988 onwards, the curriculum for pupils aged five to sixteen was divided into twelve subject areas, each of which was prescribed in detail through programmes of study. In 2014, however, new National Curriculum reforms considerably 'slimmed down' the National Curriculum in many areas. This has meant that schools have more freedom in making decisions about what and how to teach, although **core subjects** in primary school remain prescriptive – in other words, much of what must be taught is outlined.

> **Key term**
>
> **Core subjects:** English, maths and science.

The pros and cons of selective education

A selective, or grammar, school is one that allows children to enter only on the basis of an examination – that is, the child will sit the exam and the school will then decide whether or not they should be admitted. These schools usually provide secondary education. The idea of selective education is very **divisive**, which means that some people are strongly for or against it.

Those who are in favour of selective schools say that they encourage **social mobility**, meaning that children of less **affluent** parents can have access to an education with those of a similar ability, which is not based on social background.

> **Key terms**
>
> **Social mobility:** movement of individuals or groups between different social classes or levels.
>
> **Affluent:** being wealthy, having a relatively large amount of money and/or material possessions.

Those who are against selective education say that children whose parents can afford to have tutors and additional support may be more likely to pass the tests. In addition, selective schools are likely to contain more children from affluent and/or professional backgrounds than children from disadvantaged families.

High-stakes accountability, via Ofsted, and its effect on staff and children

Ofsted, the Office for Standards in Education, is a body that regularly inspects schools, colleges and early years settings with the aim of ensuring that standards in education are consistent. It will then publish a report on its website that is accessible to anyone. The inspection process can cause anxiety and stress among staff in schools, colleges and early years settings because Ofsted is looking at outcomes for children and young people, and making a formal judgement about how well settings are managed and run. Ofsted will also inform settings about what they do well and what they need to do better. Ofsted is important, however, as it looks independently at different aspects of what organisations do and holds them to account by reporting to parents and the government.

> **Key term**
>
> **Ofsted:** stands for the Office for Standards in Education, Children's Services and Skills. Ofsted inspects and regulates services providing education and skills for learners of all ages, including those that care for babies, children and young people.

> **Research**
>
> Find the most recent Ofsted report of a school or college that you know here: www.gov.uk/government/organisations/ofsted

> **Reflect**
>
> What do you think about Ofsted and the process of inspection?
>
> Do you think that it is necessary? Give reasons for your answer.

How education is funded in England: schools, further education (FE) and higher education (HE)

As mentioned in Core Chapter 1, the following types of school, FE and HE setting are currently funded in the ways described in the following table.

Type of setting	Funding
State or 'maintained' schools	Funded by government and run by local authorities
	There are different types of maintained school, including community schools, foundation schools, voluntary aided or controlled schools, and special schools
Academies and free schools	Entirely government funded but not run by local authorities
	Academies and free schools have control over their budgeting, and greater flexibility over their curriculum, finances and teachers' pay
Independent/private schools	Paid for by fees from parents/carers
	No government or state funding, although some places may be funded by local authority if pupils are placed there for a specific reason, such as SEND
	Some specialist independent schools may be funded through donations if they have charitable status, for example, those run by the National Autistic Society or Royal National Institute of Blind People
Further education Sixth form colleges	Funding is provided through the Education and Skills Funding Agency (ESFA)
Higher education	Universities provide higher education in England
	They are funded in different ways: • through tuition fees paid by students • through government funding • through endowments from (money donated by) previous students

▲ How different settings are funded

National assessments

National assessments are those which take place at different stages during a pupil's schooling. Their purpose is to provide a picture of pupils' levels at specific stages. This can be helpful when looking at the national picture.

The arguments for and against National Curriculum tests

There have been many discussions for and against the use of National Curriculum tests (SATs). These have always taken place at the end of Years 2 and 6 in England, and are used to monitor and measure progress during the primary years. However, this changed in 2022/23 when the Key Stage 1 tests were removed. A formal baseline assessment (the RBA) now takes place at the start of reception in England. Critics say that children and young people have too many tests and assessments, and that this encourages teachers to 'teach to the test' rather than offer a broad and balanced curriculum.

For more on national assessments, see Core Chapter 8.

> **Good to know**
>
> In Wales, pupils are also assessed in reception in the first six weeks of school. This is known as the Compact Profile. Pupils in Wales also sit assessment tests in reading and numeracy at the end of each school year from Year 2 to Year 9.

The advantages and disadvantages of GCSEs versus iGCSEs

GCSE (General Certificate of Secondary Education) exams have been taken at age 16 in England, Wales and Northern Ireland since 1988. Some students choose to take **International GCSEs**, sometimes known as **iGCSEs**, which are qualifications for English speakers overseas (GCSEs are designed for students in the UK). International GCSEs are recognised by many other countries and many of them are accredited, which means that they are regulated by Ofqual.

> **Key term**
>
> *International GCSE (sometimes iGCSE):* International General Certificate for Secondary Education. The iGCSE is available internationally.

International GCSEs are at the same level (Level 2) as GCSEs, although there may be some differences in course content and the amount of coursework required for different subjects. Apart from practical subjects such as art and drama, both GCSEs and iGCSEs now tend to be tested mainly through exams at the end of two years of study, although until recently GCSEs included more coursework. Some iGCSEs are still graded A–E, whereas others are awarded using the GCSE 9–1 grading scale. iGCSEs tend to be offered by private and international schools, as UK state schools do not offer them, and those studying them may go on to study the **International Baccalaureate** between the ages of 16 and 18. Some say that iGCSEs are easier than GCSEs, even though both are accepted by universities and held in similar esteem.

> **Key term**
>
> *International Baccalaureate:* two-year international programme leading to an internationally recognised diploma, which prepares students for higher education.

> **Case study**
>
> Luke, who lives in Prague and studies at an international school, will be taking iGCSEs next summer. His mother is Czech and his father English, and he is bilingual. Luke's school offers iGCSEs, so that he will have a recognised qualification in the UK if he chooses to go to university there.
> ▶ Why are iGCSEs a good way of measuring attainment for English speakers at international schools?
> ▶ Would iGCSEs still be a good option if Luke decided to stay in the Czech Republic for university?

Technology and education

Twenty years ago, technology in the classroom was usually limited to one PC in the corner of the room. Nowadays, most classrooms have interactive whiteboards and laptops, and teachers and pupils use a range of technology to support teaching and learning. As technology has been developed and improved, its impact has been widely felt, particularly when supporting pupils with SEND.

The pros and cons of technology

Many people feel that the use of information and communications technology (ICT) in the classroom is part of the teaching and learning process, as children and young people need to be able to use it and it is part of the National Curriculum's computing aims. It can also be used very creatively across different subject and curriculum areas. Others, however, say that it can limit social interactions, and that many children and young people already spend enough time looking at screens. Technology can also quickly become outdated, has a tendency to cause issues and is an expensive outlay for educational settings.

> For more on the use of technology, see Core Chapter 2, Section 2.6.

▲ What types of ICT do you use with children and young people in your setting?

The opportunities offered by blended learning

Blended learning offers students a combination of classroom-based and online learning. It gives students the opportunity to access teaching and learning materials online at any time, as well as supporting each individual's needs. On the negative side, it may add to the workload of teachers and relies on the technology working successfully.

> **Key term**
>
> *Blended learning:* a style of teaching that uses a blend of online and face-to-face teaching.

Children's and young people's health and wellbeing

Children's and young people's health and wellbeing can be affected by several factors in the classroom.

The impact of exam stress on children's and young people's health and wellbeing

Children's and young people's health and wellbeing can be affected by exam stress, in particular their mental health. It can be difficult for adults to pick up on signs of stress when it is more prolonged and is affecting children's and young people's health and wellbeing. Mental health is a priority and all adults in educational settings should be mindful of the additional stress on children and young people at exam times, and should look out for any signs of stress such as mood changes, lack of appetite or health problems.

> For more on the importance of children's and young people's emotional health and wellbeing, see Core Chapter 3, Section 3.3.

The quality of support for children and young people with SEND

There are often discussions in the media about the quality of support for children and young people with special educational needs and disabilities. Funding and provision may vary depending on locality, and accessing appropriate provision can be challenging for some pupils, depending on the funding that is available. A report from the National Audit Office in September 2019 stated that 'whilst some children with special educational needs and disabilities are receiving high quality support, many others are not getting the help they should'. It also made a series of recommendations, including an investigation into the reasons for local variations.

> For more on SEND, see Core Chapter 11.

You may find some of the websites listed in the 'Research' box helpful for keeping up to date with aspects of education. Teaching and public services unions are also a helpful source of information, and there are online blogs and social media pages specific to your role.

> **Research**
>
> Using the websites listed below, or others, find out more about a current aspect of education that interests you.
> - Times Educational Supplement (TES): www.tes.com
> - Nursery World: www.nurseryworld.co.uk
> - Professional Association for Childcare and Early Years (PACEY): www.pacey.org.uk
> - Early Years Educator (EYE): www.earlyyearseducator.co.uk
> - Education Today: www.education-today.co.uk
> - BBC: www.bbc.co.uk
> - Teach Primary: www.teachprimary.com
>
> It is also worth finding out about different trade unions and whether you might join one when you start your employment with a school or early years setting. Unions offer support, advice and legal representation if you have any issues in your role. Members also have access to training, and unions may **lobby** parliament on a range of topics on behalf of their members.
>
> The first three listed below are public service and education specific.
> - Unison: www.unison.org.uk
> - National Education Union (NEU): www.neu.org.uk
> - Voice: www.voicetheunion.org.uk
> - GMB: www.gmb.org.uk
> - Unite: www.unitetheunion.org

> **Key term**
>
> *Lobby:* when an individual or organisation sets out to influence governmental decisions.

9.3 The importance of receiving ongoing developmental feedback

As part of your role in a school or early years setting, you are likely to receive some kind of ongoing developmental feedback, or **continuing professional development (CPD)** with your line manager. This may also be known as performance management or appraisal, and may involve being observed in your practice. It is important because it encourages you to reflect on what has happened, and to proactively and regularly examine your role and how it relates to the role of others in your team. CPD usually takes place on a yearly cycle, and you will be asked to review what you have done and think about what you would like to achieve in your role in the future.

> **Key term**
>
> **Continuing professional development (CPD):** ongoing professional training and development to keep up to date.

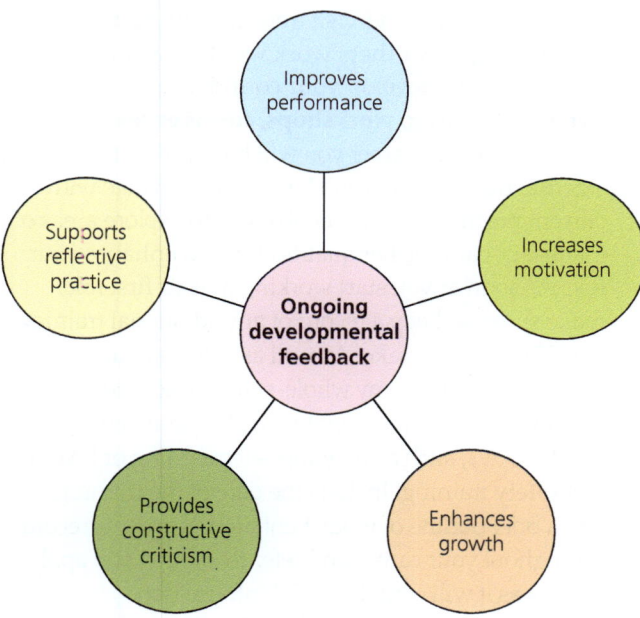

▲ Have you been able to meet with your line manager to set professional targets?

It is important to receive ongoing developmental feedback for the following reasons.

▶ **Improves performance:** Ongoing feedback will help you to reflect on your performance and think about how you can develop. If you are observed working with children or young people, your feedback may suggest the use of strategies or teaching points that can be used to improve your work with them and better support their learning and development.

▶ **Increases motivation:** Talking to another person about your role and setting targets that are time limited should help to develop your motivation and give you renewed enthusiasm for your role.

▶ **Enhances both personal and professional growth:** Feedback enhances our personal and professional growth as it allows us to see our situation from another point of view. A change of perspective can often help draw our attention to things that we may not have seen before.

▶ **Provides constructive criticism:** We often say that the person giving feedback is acting as 'a critical friend'. This means that they are showing us how we might improve our practice by working with us to develop positive steps forward.

▶ **Supports reflective practice to identify developmental needs:** Ongoing feedback is designed to encourage you to reflect on your practice and enable you to start to think about developmental needs through a structured process.

Before a CPD or performance management meeting with your line manager, you are likely to be asked to complete a self-evaluation or self-assessment of your role, which might include questions such as these:

▶ Is my job description still accurate? Are there any changes that need to be made, and if so what are they?
▶ What do I think are my greatest strengths and which are the areas I need to improve?
▶ What areas of my job satisfy me the most?
▶ Do I have gaps in my knowledge? What skills or training would help me improve my performance?
▶ What goals or targets would I like to work towards over the next 12 months?

These questions are helpful to consider as they will encourage you to reflect on what you have done in your role and what you would like to do going forward. They will also focus you on your experiences and give you some ideas to take with you to the meeting.

> **Case study**
>
> Becca is working as an early years assistant in a nursery and has been asked to prepare for her first appraisal with her line manager. She has been given a list of questions to think about, including any additional training she feels she might need. However, she has a busy week before the meeting and runs out of time to prepare for it.
> ▶ Should Becca still go to the meeting?
> ▶ What should she say to her line manager?

In addition, working with others to have a more active role in your own professional development has other advantages, which include:

▶ **Maintaining up-to-date knowledge and skills:** Taking time to reflect on your role with others may draw attention to additional training needs and enable you to develop your knowledge and skills.
▶ **Improving provision and outcomes for children and young people:** staying alert to changes and improvements that can affect your practice is likely to improve educational outcomes.
▶ **Adhering to regulatory requirements and keeping up to date with legislative changes:** Working with others will help you to keep up to date and implement any new statutory requirements as they come in, as schools and early years settings will be required to do this.
▶ **Ensuring understanding of current priorities, debates and approaches in education:** Ongoing CPD will help to draw your attention to these and make sure you have appropriate training.

> See Section 9.2 for more on keeping up to date with current issues through websites and journals.

▶ **Making meaningful contributions to a team:** All those who work in educational settings will be working as part of a team. It is important to think regularly about how what you do impacts on others, and how you can best support them. In doing this you will be supporting the aims of the team as a whole, as well as the children and young people in the setting.
▶ **Improving opportunities for progression and promotion in own role:** Ongoing CPD will mean that you have a record of how you have been proactive in reflecting on your role and moving forwards. It will improve opportunities as it will bring your hopes and expectations to the attention of managers, while also enabling them to be aware of your strengths and interests.

9.4 How practitioners can meet their own developmental needs

Your own professional development should be ongoing, and personal reflection should help you to regularly think about ways in which you can change and improve your practice. You should also be able to meet your professional development needs and keep up to date in other ways, through:

▶ **Self-directed learning, reading and research.**

> For details of this, see Section 9.2.

▶ **Shadowing and visits to other settings:** An easy way of accessing information, gaining ideas and thinking about your own practice is through watching or shadowing others. You may be able to observe an experienced practitioner working with the same age group in your setting. If not, ask if you can go and visit another setting to do this. Seeing how others work will be invaluable in helping you to develop your confidence.
▶ **External training, workshops, conferences:** Throughout your career you will have access to external training. This will keep you up to date with current practice, and will enable you to explore areas of interest or gain further qualifications to enhance your role. As soon as you start working in your first role, make sure you keep a record of any additional training or CPD you undertake. As well as external training, this should include any whole-staff development training sessions that might take place at meetings or **INSET days**, such as ongoing safeguarding or health and safety training. Include the date of the training and a brief outline of what it entailed. Keep this record throughout your career and refer to it when you apply for jobs as it will contain useful information.
▶ **Appraisal, peer observation, feedback, and setting and reviewing professional goals:** Although you will set and review goals as part of your ongoing performance management with your line manager, you can also think independently about your practice and should regularly reassess goals. Peer observation also enables you and a colleague to observe each other's practice and give feedback. This process also helps you to reflect on and examine what you do as part of your role.

CORE Chapter 9: Reflective Practice

Key term

INSET day: in-service training day, or day when teaching staff meet in term time, without pupils, for additional training.

In practice

Find out whether you can go in to another setting to observe other professionals at work. This may be for whatever length of time is convenient, whether this is an hour or a whole morning. Before you go, think about one or two things that you are going to look at (e.g. behaviour management, displays, staff relationships with children and young people, organisation and routines), but don't try to pack in too much.
- Write down anything that is helpful to you in your chosen area.
- See if you can implement in your own practice some of what you have seen.
- Reflect on what has happened.

Assessment practice

1. What does reflective practice mean?
2. Why are theories of reflection helpful in practice?
3. Give **two** examples of current debates and priorities in education.
4. What are some of the pros and cons of using technology when working with children and young people?
5. What do we mean by blended learning?
6. In addition to having regular feedback, how else can you keep up to date with different aspects of educational practice?
7. Explain the importance of receiving professional feedback from others.
8. How can you work independently in meeting your own development needs?

CORE Chapter 10:
Equality and Diversity

As part of their role in any school or early years setting, adults will need to promote equality, diversity and inclusion. This is important so that all children and young people are involved, respected and given full access to the curriculum as well as the wider life of the school, college or early years setting, and they learn these values for life. Promoting equality and diversity means that the differences between individuals are recognised and respected. Your organisation will have policies on equal opportunities and inclusion for all, and these will set out its aims for ensuring that these practices are part of the life of the setting and the wider community.

Learning outcomes

This chapter covers the following knowledge outcomes for Core Element 10:

- **10.1** The basic principles of laws, regulations and codes of practice that underpin equality, diversity and human rights
- **10.2** The links between legal requirements and organisational policies and procedures relating to equality, diversity, discrimination, confidentiality and the rights of children and young people
- **10.3** Why it is important to promote equality, diversity and inclusion
- **10.4** The consequences of labelling children and young people, and the importance of having high and realistic expectations
- **10.5** The possible barriers to children's and young people's participation, and how practitioners can use strategies to overcome these

CORE Chapter 10: Equality and Diversity

10.1 The basic principles of laws, regulations and codes of practice in relation to equality, diversity and human rights

United Nations Convention on the Rights of the Child 1989

UNICEF (the United Nations charity supporting children worldwide) describes the United Nations Convention on the Rights of the Child, or UNCRC, as 'the most complete statement of children's rights ever produced'. The United Kingdom, along with 195 other states, signed and **ratified** this legally binding agreement in 1989. It states that all children and young people – whatever their ethnicity, gender, religion, language or ability – should be treated equally and without discrimination. The UNCRC acknowledges the rights and freedoms that all children and young people under the age of 18 should be given through a series of 54 articles or entitlements. All of these rights are linked and there is none that is more important than the others. The nations that have ratified the treaty must fulfil it by international law and it is the most widely ratified human rights treaty in the world.

The UNCRC has four general principles (as described in the table). These help us to interpret the other remaining articles and are key to ensuring the rights for all children.

> **Research**
> - Read through the summary of these articles, which you can find on the UNICEF UK website: www.unicef.org.uk
> - As well as those listed above, what other articles should you know about if you are working in a school or early years setting?

> **Key terms**
>
> **Ratify:** to vote on or sign a written agreement to make it official.
>
> **Equality:** being equal in status, rights and opportunities.
>
> **Diversity:** recognising our individual differences.
>
> **Discrimination:** unfair treatment of a group of people due to **prejudice**.
>
> **Prejudice:** a set of preconceived negative ideas about a particular group of people.

The Equality Act 2010

The Equality Act 2010 is the key legislation for **equality** and **diversity** in the UK. It replaced and updated nine previous equality laws in England, Scotland and Wales in order to protect the rights of individuals and ensure that they are protected from unfair treatment. Under the terms of the Equality Act 2010, all individuals should be given the same rights and opportunities so that they are able to reach their full potential. There are nine 'protected characteristics' under the act that everyone in the UK is protected against **discrimination** on the grounds of (see the next page).

It is important to understand that discrimination can be categorised as either direct or indirect.

- **Direct discrimination** means treating an individual worse than another owing to a protected characteristic. This can be easy to identify – for example, not allowing a child with diabetes to come to the setting as there is no one trained to support them.

Article 2: Non-discrimination	The UNCRC applies to every child without discrimination, whatever their ethnicity, sex, religion, language, abilities or any other status, whatever they think or say, whatever their family background
Article 3: Best interest of the child	The best interests of the child must be a top priority in all decisions and actions that affect children
Article 6: Right to life, survival and development	Every child has the right to life; governments must do all they can to ensure that children survive and develop to their full potential
Article 12: Right to be heard	Every child has the right to express their views, feelings and wishes in all matters affecting them, and to have their views considered and taken seriously; this right applies at all times – for example, during immigration proceedings, housing decisions or the child's day-to-day home life

▲ The four general principles of the UN Convention on the Rights of the Child

- **Indirect discrimination** is discrimination in which a rule is applied to all and affects some in a more negative way than others. It can be less easy to identify but still amounts to the same thing – for example, a building that has been chosen for an event that is not accessible to those with a disability.

Protected characteristics

There are nine protected characteristics under the Equality Act. This means that everyone in the UK is protected against discrimination on the grounds of any of these. For example, pregnancy and maternity are a protected characteristic, which means it is illegal for someone to lose their job because they are pregnant or have a child.

▲ Why is it important that individuals are not discriminated against on the basis of these characteristics?

Special Educational Needs and Disability Code of Practice: 0 to 25 years 2015

The SEND Code of Practice 2015 sets out the statutory guidance for early education providers, schools, colleges, health and social services professionals, and local authorities for children and young people from birth up to 25 years of age. Its basic principles are that children and young people with all areas of need should have access to a family-centred system for their care and education so that they can achieve the best possible outcomes, thus ensuring they are treated equally.

There should be collaboration between different services, which should work together with families, who should be able to participate in any decisions that are made and to express their views. Where children and young people are not making adequate progress in their early years setting, school or college, the setting should be able to request an education, health and care (EHC) needs assessment from the local authority so that they can develop an **Education, health and care plan (EHCP)**. This can then lead to additional funding for the setting to provide more support for the child or young person.

> See page 179 for more on EHCPs.

> **Key term**
>
> *Education, health and care plan (EHCP):* an EHCP is for children and young people aged up to 25 who need more support than is available through special educational needs support; it is drawn up to outline provision for a child or young person following an assessment of special educational needs. EHCPs identify educational, health and social needs, and set out the additional support to meet those needs. Find out more here: www.gov.uk/children-with-special-educational-needs/extra-SEN-help

> For more on assessment of special educational needs, see Core Chapter 11, page 172.

Under the SEND Code of Practice there are four broad areas of need. However, a child or young person may be affected by more than one of these needs.

1. **Communication and interaction:** This means that the child or young person has difficulties in the area of speech, language and communication. This may make it harder for them to be able to understand or make sense of what others are saying, or to be able to express what they want to say in the appropriate way. An example of this might be a child or young person who is on the autism spectrum, as they are likely to have difficulties in this area.
2. **Cognition and learning:** This means that the child or young person may find learning more of a challenge than others of the same age. This may mean that they have a specific learning difficulty, such as dyslexia, which affects a particular aspect of their learning, or have difficulty in understanding some or all aspects of the curriculum. Learning

difficulties may be wide ranging, and in some cases are categorised as either moderate, severe or profound and multiple. They may also affect organisation and memory.

3 **Social, emotional and mental health:** This means that the child or young person may have difficulty managing their relationships and emotions. This is also likely to affect their behaviour and learning, and can affect others' learning. An example of this might be a child or young person who has a condition such as ADHD, but it could also be unwanted behaviour due to the child's or young person's experiences. Children with social and emotional difficulties may also be affected by mental health conditions that are likely to affect their wellbeing.

4 **Sensory and/or physical:** This means that the child or young person may have a physical need, condition or disability, or a sensory impairment that may affect their vision or hearing. This includes sensory processing difficulties, which can also relate to behaviour. In these situations, they may need to have additional support, resources or materials in order to access the curriculum.

> For more on the SEND Code of Practice, see Core Chapter 11.

The SEND Code of Practice sets out that support for children and young people with SEND should take the form of a four-part cycle:
1 **Assess** the child or young person's special educational needs
2 **Plan** to provide a child or young person with support
3 **Do** make sure appropriate intervention and support is in place
4 **Review** the effectiveness of the support put in place.

This is known as the **graduated approach**. Any earlier decisions and actions are revisited, refined and revised as understanding of a child or young person's needs grows and it is clear what supports them to make good progress.

UK General Data Protection Regulation (UK GDPR)

All adults working in early years settings and schools need to be aware of legislation surrounding confidentiality, particularly the UK General Data Protection Regulation legislation, or UK GDPR. This EU legislation replaced much of the previous data protection legislation. As schools and early years settings will collect and store data on both staff and children and young people, they should ensure that this is kept and disposed of securely. Your setting's confidentiality policy will set out your responsibilities under this legislation, which has six key privacy principles:
1 Data must only be collected for a valid reason and be processed fairly and transparently.
2 Data must only be used for the purpose for which it was originally obtained.
3 Only the necessary amount of data should be collected.
4 Data should be kept up to date and accurate.
5 Data should not be stored for any longer than is needed.
6 Data should be protected and secure – for example, using passwords or locked away.

In addition, data may be shared where this is necessary, such as in cases of safeguarding or children's and young people's welfare. Where possible, data should be shared with consent; however, where safeguarding is an issue it can be shared with relevant authorities without consent.

10.2 The links between legal requirements and organisational policies and procedures relating to equality, diversity, discrimination, confidentiality and the rights of children and young people

In order to comply with legal requirements, your school or early years setting should have a range of policies and procedures in place around equality, diversity, discrimination and confidentiality. This is to ensure that children and young people, parents, staff, visitors and all those who have contact with the organisation are aware of the way in which it operates and the agreed way of working. It also ensures that staff have a reference point so that they know how to respond in different situations and are proactive in ensuring that all children and young people have equal opportunities. Equality and diversity policies should ensure that all staff and children and young people know how to:
- treat others
- challenge negative attitudes in others
- ensure that facilities and activities are accessible and inclusive for all
- plan for and promote multiculturalism and diversity in lessons
- ensure learning resources are inclusive and do not discriminate
- ensure that teaching is inclusive and uses a variety of methods.

Inclusion policy

This may be a standalone policy but could also be part of the SEND or equality and diversity policy. It should set out how the school or early years setting will value, respect and celebrate individuality, and enable all children and young people to achieve their best outcomes through breaking down barriers to learning. The following articles of the UNCRC are also relevant here:

▶ Article 24: Every child has the right to the best possible health, including healthcare, water and food, and a clean environment and education on health and wellbeing.
▶ Article 28: Every child has the right to an education.
▶ Article 30: Every child has the right to learn and use the language, customs and religion of their family.

Confidentiality policy

This policy will outline how the setting will keep to its obligations under GDPR, and protect and store the personal information of children and young people and staff. It should also include details of how the setting will share information, where needed, with other professionals when this is in the best interests of the child or young person.

Accessibility policy

> See Core Chapter 11, Section 11.1.

Partnership working – sharing information

Safe partnership working may form part of the confidentiality policy and explain the need to share information with others only on a need-to-know basis. Partnership working is also linked to the SEND Code of Practice, as this highlights the importance of parents, children and young people and professionals working together to share information safely and improve outcomes.

Admissions policy

Schools and early years settings should have an admissions policy, which should set out their criteria for allowing entry. Under the SEN Code of Practice, in cases of children and young people who already have an EHCP, parents are able to name and gain a place for their child at their preferred school.

Special educational needs policy

> All schools and early years settings are required to have a policy for SEND under the 2015 SEND Code of Practice (see Core Chapter 11, Section 11.1).

Safeguarding policy

> This policy will need to refer to various DfE guidance documents. See Core Chapter 3 for details.

Research

▶ Find out the location of policies and procedures in your setting.
▶ Make sure you know who is responsible for equality and inclusion.
▶ Check your responsibilities under your confidentiality policy.

10.3 Why it is important to promote equality, diversity and inclusion

As well as knowing about legislation and policies, all adults in the setting will need to promote equality, diversity and inclusion when working with children and young people. It is important for you to be a good **role model** and to demonstrate this through your actions, what you say and how you treat others, so that everyone feels valued and welcome. Schools and early years settings should also use other methods to promote positive images and messages around diversity, and use teaching and learning experiences that reflect the wider community, so that all children, young people and adults feel included and differences are celebrated.

You should remember that it is also possible to unintentionally discriminate against some pupils. One example is reward systems, although these may be a useful way of recognising achievement.

Key term

Role model: someone who is looked to by others as an example.

Some common ways to do this include the following:
▶ A range of books and stories should be available in schools and early years settings, which reflect different countries, cultures, languages and backgrounds, as well as images and stories about children and young people of all races, so that everyone is represented.

CORE Chapter 10: Equality and Diversity

- Resources that are used by the school or early years setting should reflect cultural diversity – for example, in early years role-play areas or in subject areas such as history or geography.
- The setting should show, through learning experiences and events, that it is inclusive and promotes inclusion and diversity. These kinds of opportunities may include activities such as themed weeks, celebrations of different festivals, crafts, cooking, dancing or listening to music from different cultures and backgrounds.
- Your school or early years setting should promote equality, multiculturalism and diversity through the way in which lessons are taught.
- Your setting should have a range of displays and information boards that reflect different cultures, age groups, languages and religions.
- Older children and young people should be given opportunities to talk about prejudice and stereotyping so that they can recognise what is meant by these and explore their own views.
- All families should be welcomed and events that are held at the setting should reflect different cultures.

> **Good to know**
>
> Always check and make a note of the correct pronunciation and spelling of children and young people's and parents' names, and ensure that you remember them correctly.

> **Reflect**
>
> Look at the following scenarios and, for each one, consider whether it is an example of discrimination. If so, is it direct or indirect?
> - A pupil with a physical disability, who is a talented musician, cannot gain access to the main part of the school's music department as it is upstairs.
> - A parent has to come in to school every lunchtime to administer medication to her five year old who has diabetes as there are no members of staff who are trained or prepared to do this.
> - A refugee family who don't speak English are not able to access an open morning for new parents.
> - A three-year-old partially sighted child has been refused access to a local nursery.

Responsibility of adults	Why this is important
Complying with legal responsibilities (Equality Act 2010)	All those working in schools and early years settings are obliged by law to comply with their legal responsibilities under the Equality Act 2010 See Section 10.1.
Preventing discrimination	There should be clear policies and guidelines for equality and diversity in the setting, and if discrimination occurs it should be challenged and/or reported. You should remember that discrimination may also be unintentional, for example, giving rewards for attendance to pupils, some of whom may never be able to achieve this.
Ensuring equality of opportunity	All individuals are entitled to the same opportunities regarding participation, and access to activities and experiences
Meeting individual needs/ensuring accessibility	Each child or young person has unique needs and aspirations, and should be given support by adults to meet those needs so that they can access the curriculum and wider life of the school. Adults should also look carefully at the ways in which achievements and behaviour are recognised, so that all pupils' needs and preferences are taken into account.
Appreciating and celebrating differences/valuing diversity	Schools and early years settings should show how they celebrate and appreciate differences and value diversity in different ways, so that all children and young people develop a positive sense of identity
Recognising and valuing different family circumstances and cultures	Schools and early years settings should have an awareness of the different backgrounds and circumstances of children and young people so that they can acknowledge and value these differences See Core Chapter 5 for more on different family structures.
Ensuring dignity and respect for all	All children and young people and their families are entitled to respect from the setting so that they also learn to respect others

▲ Promoting equality, diversity and inclusion in early years settings

▲ How does your setting ensure that it is a welcoming and inclusive environment?

10.4 The consequences of labelling children and young people

When we work with children and young people, we may hear about the term **labelling**. Labels are sometimes used by adults to categorise children's and young people's circumstances or needs – for example, medical needs, areas of SEND, looked after children, Traveller children, those with mental health issues, or those who are 'at risk' of offending.

Although in some cases, the purpose of labelling allows professionals to successfully apply strategies to support children with additional needs, for example, it can also have negative connotations and it is important to get to know each individual rather than make assumptions.

We should always think about and challenge our own perceptions of others and try to avoid labelling where possible as this can lead to negative and discriminatory attitudes. Using labels may also have a direct impact on children and young people, particularly if we have low expectations of their abilities as a result. Remember that there is no one word to describe any person, and nobody should be defined by a label.

Causing the individual to feel stigmatised, which can lead to social, emotional and mental health issues

Labelling may cause the child or young person to feel **stigmatised**, which means that they may feel labelled with a sense of disapproval by others. This in turn can cause the person not to feel valued, and to have low self-esteem or feel that others are not interested in them.

Changing how others view the individual, particularly if they have a negative or limited understanding of a need or disability

If a child or young person has been given a label, or it has been applied in a negative way, this may cause others to see them differently. It is important that we meet and get to know each person on an individual basis and base our views on this. We can also try to change others' perceptions of a child or young person by highlighting their strengths or sharing their positive achievements.

Establishing a set of limits associated with that label, which may lead to practitioners offering the individual limited opportunities

Labelling can also cause some people to see the label rather than the person, and to think that they are restricted in their abilities. This may mean that they are not given equal opportunities or a chance to access the same activities as others.

Placing a burden of guilt or 'blame' on the individual's parents

Parents may feel that they have failed or that they are inadequate due to negative labels. For example, labelling may highlight any guilt they may feel because of the circumstances that have had an impact on their child. This will also increase any negativity they feel around their child and make it harder for them to be positive themselves.

CORE Chapter 10: Equality and Diversity

> **Case study**
>
> Jeanette works as a teaching assistant and has just been told that Aidan, who is a looked after child, will be starting at her primary school on Monday in the Year 4 class she supports. She knows nothing else about him as they have no other information at present. Jeanette says to the class teacher, 'Oh, it looks like we are going to have another one working on my table.'
> ▶ Why are Jeanette's comments unacceptable?
> ▶ What should her attitude be towards Aidan?

It is important to have high and realistic expectations for children and young people. This is because a 'can do' attitude and mind-set will encourage them to feel motivated, and so aim higher and achieve more. This will empower them, raise their self-esteem and encourage their development. If expectations are low, or they and others feel that something is missing or they won't be able to achieve, it will be harder for the child or young person to motivate themselves and as a result their achievements may be lower.

Positive expectations	Result
Encouraging independence	If adults encourage children and young people to do things for themselves rather than doing things for them, this will develop their confidence and belief in themselves and their own abilities
Increasing motivation and confidence	A positive outlook and belief in their own ability will improve children's and young people's motivation and help to develop their confidence in their work
	We can support them by giving plenty of positive praise, as well as by the use of rewards, house points and other age-appropriate motivational tools, depending on the setting's policies
Improving academic outcomes	Having high yet realistic expectations encourages children and young people to develop and improve learning
Creating a culture of achievement	Schools and early years settings should create and celebrate a culture of achievement so that children and young people feel that they can set their own personal best and feel rewarded for effort, regardless of ability

▲ The importance of having positive expectations for children and young people

10.5 The possible barriers to children's and young people's participation, and how practitioners can use strategies to overcome these

As we have seen, barriers to children's and young people's participation may not just be physical. They can be due to a range of issues, attitudes and expectations from those around them, which may all affect their self-esteem and influence how they can access the curriculum and the wider life of the setting. The impact of these barriers will be that the child or young person who is affected will not feel included or part of the group, and this in turn can have wider and longer-ranging effects.

Physical accessibility

Physical barriers to participation may occur if the learning environment has not been designed to suit the ages of the children and young people who are using it, or if provision has not been made for pupils who have SEND, where this is needed. This needs to be addressed so that they are not excluded from any aspect of the learning environment.

Mental health issues

Mental health issues may prevent children and young people from participating if they feel unable to do so, or are depressed, withdrawn or anxious. If adults are not aware, and appropriate support and treatment is not sought, this may have long-term effects on their learning and participation in education.

Attitudes and expectations

See Section 10.4.

Curriculum

The early years setting or school should ensure that it has an inclusive curriculum that meets the needs of all individuals. This means learning experiences that take in to account all abilities, needs, backgrounds and ethnic backgrounds, and that teach children and young people about different religions and cultures. Diversity should be shown to be valued, and differences should be recognised and celebrated.

Family background

Children and young people will come from a range of family backgrounds, which may or may not be supportive and take an interest in and support what they are doing at the setting. They may also have challenging personal circumstances, such as being a young carer, or come from a background of abuse or neglect. All of these factors will affect how they feel about themselves and whether they are motivated and feel able to participate in teaching and learning activities.

> See Core Chapter 2, Section 2.7, for more about family backgrounds.

Socio-economic barriers

This means the circumstances of different groups of people. If the child's or young person's background means that they have poor living conditions or limited resources, this may affect how much they are able to engage with learning activities. For example, those from lower-income families will find it more difficult to pay towards educational visits or extracurricular activities.

How practitioners can use strategies to overcome barriers to children's and young people's participation

Strategies for overcoming barriers to participation, and how they can be used, are given in the table below.

Strategies to overcome barriers to participation	How to do this
Training to understand inclusion	All members of staff should be aware of the setting's policies for equality and inclusion
	If they are working with an individual, they should have training where necessary, and as much information as possible about the individual's needs, condition or disability
Partnership working, including supporting children's and young people's psychological wellbeing	Working closely with parents and other professionals will enable practitioners to find out as much as possible about the child or young person and share professional knowledge about their background; it will also give them opportunities to ask for ways in which they can best support them, as well as to find out about available resources
	For more on psychological wellbeing, see Core 5 and 6 and EYE 5.
Adaptations to the physical environment	Adaptations may need to be made to the environment, particularly if a child or young person has sensory needs or a disability
	There should also be additional resources where these are needed; this may mean installing a hearing loop, for example, or making sure there is enough space for wheelchairs
Providing accessible curriculum and assessment	The curriculum should be accessible to all children and young people so that they have the resources they need to fully participate in teaching and learning activities in line with their needs
	They should also be given appropriate assessment and feedback so that they can make progress and understand their future learning needs
Reviewing equality, diversity and inclusion policies	All equality and inclusion policies should be reviewed on a regular basis to ensure that they are up to date and that staff have read and understood their responsibilities
Providing information about financial support	In cases where children and young people and their families need financial support and help, schools and early years settings should be able to give them further information about how to access this – for example, through local education authorities or Citizens Advice
Supporting children and young people through transitions	See Core Chapter 7, Section 7.6

▲ Strategies to overcome barriers to participation, and how to use them in your practice

CORE Chapter 10: Equality and Diversity

▲ How does your setting ensure that there are no barriers to participation for children and young people?

> **Research**
>
> In 1963, Jane Elliott, a teacher in Iowa, USA, carried out an exercise with her class to explore the effects of racial discrimination. A very powerful documentary about this, A Class Divided, showed the effects of treating people differently according to their physical characteristics. The recording is available on video-streaming sites. Watch the first 16 minutes of the documentary and answer the following questions.
>
> ▶ What do you think about this lesson and how it affected the children?
> ▶ What barriers were created by treating the class in this way?
> ▶ What would be the long-term effects on the group if this were permanent?

> **Assessment practice**
>
> 1 What is the purpose of the Equality Act 2010?
> 2 Name **five** of the protected characteristics identified in the Equality Act 2010.
> 3 Why is it important to know about the UK GDPR when working in schools and early years settings?
> 4 Give **four** reasons why it is important to promote equality, diversity and inclusion.
> 5 Outline the consequences of labelling children and young people.
> 6 How does having high and realistic expectations support the development of children and young people?
> 7 What kinds of barriers to learning might exist in an educational setting?
> 8 Explain **three** ways in which practitioners can use strategies to support children's and young people's participation. Include reasons why each is effective.

CORE Chapter 11: Special Educational Needs and Disability

Part of your role, whether you are working in a school or early years setting, will be to support children and young people who have special educational needs and disabilities (SEND). The number of children with SEND is increasing: in January 2019, 14.9 per cent of all those in schools in England had special educational needs (source: School Census, DfE). In this chapter, we will look at the legislation that is in place to support them, and consider how their overall development can be affected, and the kinds of strategies you might use as an early years practitioner or teaching assistant.

Learning outcomes

This chapter covers the following knowledge outcomes for Core Element 11:

- **11.1** The laws, codes of practice and policies affecting provision for children and young people with disabilities and those with special educational needs and disabilities
- **11.2** How professionals and organisations support children and young people with special educational needs and disabilities
- **11.3** The principles of integration, equity and inclusion, and the differences between them
- **11.4** Why practitioners must use appropriate terminology when discussing the needs of children and young people with SEND
- **11.5** The differences between the medical and social models of disability
- **11.6** How a primary disability might affect children's and young people's social, emotional and physical development
- **11.7** A range of cognitive skills necessary for effective educational development, and how single or multiple disabilities might affect these
- **11.8** How cognitive difficulties may impact upon language, communication and educational development
- **11.9** How a chronic condition may affect children's and young people's emotions, education, behaviour and quality of life
- **11.10** How adults remove barriers in order to empower and value individuals, depending on their specific learning difficulty, medical condition or disability
- **11.11** When and how speech can be supplemented or replaced by augmentative and alternative communication

CORE Chapter 11: Special Educational Needs and Disability

11.1 The laws, codes of practice and policies affecting provision for children and young people with special educational needs and disabilities (SEND)

As an early years practitioner or teaching assistant, you will need to be aware of your own statutory duties and responsibilities when working with children and young people who have **SEND (sometimes called SEN)**. Although the main statutory document is the Special Educational Needs and Disability Code of Practice 2015, there are also three separate guidance documents that break down the statutory duties and responsibilities of practitioners within each age range. These are set out in broadly the same way but focus on relevant areas.

> **Key term**
>
> **SEND (sometimes called SEN):** 'A child or young person has SEN if they have a learning difficulty or disability which calls for special educational provision to be made for him or her' (SEND Code of Practice, 2015).

▲ Special Educational Needs and Disability Code of Practice: 0 to 25 years

Each of the three documents starts with the same headings, with a short explanation in each of these areas.
- **The context:** The Children and Families Act 2014 and its new statutory obligations (see page 44).
- **Principles underlying the code:** These are the seven principles that must be observed by all professionals who work with children and young people who have SEND – for example, enabling children and young people and their parents to participate in decision making.
- **Working together across education, health and care for joint outcomes:** Under this part of the Children and Families Act 2014, local authorities have a duty to ensure that services work together to improve the quality of provision for children and young people with SEND.
- **The Local Offer:** All local authorities must publish a Local Offer, which outlines in a clear way what is available in the local area for children and young people who have SEND.

> **Research**
>
> Using the document that is most relevant to your occupational specialism, look up the four headings above, which start around page 5.
> - What are the seven principles underlying the code?
> - Where can you find out more information about each of these four headings?

Early years: guide to the SEND Code of Practice: 0 to 25 years

According to the Early Years Foundation Stage (EYFS) Statutory Guidance, all maintained nurseries and other providers who have funding from local authorities in England must have regard to the SEND Code of Practice 2015, to meet the needs of children with SEND in schools and early years settings. The guide to the SEND Code of Practice for early years settings was published in September 2014 and highlights the main duties and responsibilities for early years providers. As practitioners working with this age group will see them at the earliest stages, they are also well placed to notice and act upon any concerns around their development.

> See page 178 of this chapter for details of the support available for those working with children from birth to five years.

The focus of the guide is on a number of areas, some of which are outlined below:

▶ **Improving outcomes for children with SEND through high aspirations and expectations, including the EYFS statutory requirements:** All providers must follow this framework, in particular with regard to the safeguarding and welfare requirements. They must ensure that they follow their duty under the Equality Act 2010 and prevent those who have SEND from being placed at a disadvantage.

▶ **Progress check at age two:** All children should have a progress check between the ages of two and three, and parents should be provided with a short report on their child's learning and development. This should identify strengths and also any areas of concern, so that plans can be put in place to provide additional support.

> See also page 178, under the heading 'The support available in childcare, schools and colleges for young people with special educational needs and disabilities'.

▶ **SEND in the early years:** Identifying and supporting. Providers must have systems in place in order to identify and support children with SEND. The document states that children's progress can be assessed using the Early Years Outcomes document; from 2021 the non-statutory *Development Matters* can be used. Where there is a cause for concern it is important that this is acted upon without delay. Where needs are identified providers must work with parents to act upon the four stages of action, also known as the **graduated approach**: assess, plan, do and review. This should involve parents as well as specialists where needed.

▶ **The role of the SENDCo (sometimes known as the SENCo) and area SENDCo in early years provision:** There must be a qualified teacher who acts as the SENDCo in a maintained nursery; other early years providers may be part of a network of settings that share a SENDCo – for example, childminders who are part of an agency. Local authorities may also provide area SENDCos to give advice and guidance to early years providers in the area. The SENDCo must ensure that everyone in the setting understands their role with regard to supporting children with SEND, works closely with parents and professionals, and provides advice and support to colleagues.

▶ **Requesting an EHC (education, health and care) needs assessment:** If a child has not made expected progress, despite steps towards assessing and meeting their needs by the early years provider, the setting may need to request an EHC needs assessment through the local authority. Parents can also request one, as can young people over the age of 16.

> For more on education, health and care plans (EHCPs), see page 179 of this chapter.

▲ What should you do if you are asked to support a child with SEND?

Schools: guide to the SEND Code of Practice: 0 to 25 years

Schools and **alternative provision settings** also have statutory duties and responsibilities under the Children and Families Act 2014 and the SEND Code of Practice 2015. The schools guide to the SEND Code of Practice: 0 to 25 years was published in September 2014 and highlights the main duties and responsibilities for schools.

> See page 179 for details of the support available for those working with children and young people from five to fifteen years.

> **Key term**
>
> *Alternative provision settings:* education providers for pupils who are unable to go to a mainstream school. This may be, for example, due to exclusion or illness.

The guide's focus is on a number of areas, some of which are outlined below.

▶ **Improving outcomes for children with SEND through high aspirations and expectations:** As with early years children, pupils with SEND in schools as well as those with medical conditions are entitled to the best possible provision. Mainstream schools must provide support and an inclusive environment to enable them to receive this alongside their peers.

▶ **Identifying SEND in schools:** A school should have a SEND policy that outlines its approach to identifying and responding to SEND at the earliest point. This should be done with the full knowledge and involvement of parents, so that they can reinforce this at home.

▶ **Deciding whether to make special educational provision and defining desired outcomes:** Where a pupil does not make expected progress despite intervention by the school, specialists may be involved, with parental approval, to continue to support the pupil's needs using appropriate strategies and interventions.

▶ **Requesting an EHC needs assessment:** If a child has not made expected progress, despite steps towards assessing and meeting their needs by the school, the setting may need to request an EHC needs assessment through the local authority.

> For more on education, health and care plans (EHCPs), see page 179.

Research

Choose one of the following to research:
▶ Early years: guide to the SEND Code of Practice: 0 to 25 years
▶ Schools: guide to the SEND Code of Practice: 0 to 25 years
▶ Further education: guide to the SEND Code of Practice: 0 to 25 years.
1 What can you find out about your own responsibilities through the guidance?
2 How would you ensure that you were able to access any training needs?

Further education: guide to the SEND Code of Practice: 0 to 25 years

This guidance is for further education colleges, sixth-form colleges, 16 to 19 academies and independent colleges. These institutions all have statutory duties and responsibilities under the Children and Families Act 2014 and the SEND Code of Practice 2015. The further education guide to the SEND Code of Practice: 0 to 25 years was published in September 2014 and highlights the main duties and responsibilities for colleges. Its focus is on a number of areas, some of which are outlined below.

▶ **Statutory duties of post-16 institutions:** Colleges must work with the local authority on arrangements for children and young people with SEND. They must admit a young person if they are named on an EHCP, and fulfil their duties to those who have SEND and who may not have an EHCP. They must not discriminate in any way against young people with a disability and must make reasonable adjustments to ensure that they have what they need to prevent disadvantage.

▶ **Identifying and supporting children and young people in college:** The college must put in place whatever is needed to support children and young people who have SEND, and keep this under review. They should work with students and their parents to assess, plan, do and review, and ensure that all staff are trained where needed. Colleges need to have a named person on-site to oversee SEND provision, similar to the role of the SENDCo in schools and early years settings.

▶ **Preparing for adulthood:** All those who work with children and young people with SEND should encourage and support them as they prepare for adult life, and support them to achieve the best outcomes in employment, health, independence and community participation.

▶ **Young people's right to make their own decisions:** After the end of the academic year in which they turn 16, young people can make requests and decisions under the Children and Families Act 2014, although their parents can still support them in doing this.

▶ **Planning the transition into post-16 education, and training and careers advice:** Young people with SEND may need specialist provision post-16, and schools and colleges should work in partnership to allow them to attend taster days. They should also ensure that students have access to careers advice that allows them to consider the widest range of career options, through activities such as work experience and taster sessions.

▶ **Pathways to employment:** Children and young people with SEND should have the support they need to achieve the skills, experience and qualifications they require. Colleges should provide courses that offer pathways to employment and prepare students with SEND for work. They should do this through helping them to develop the skills employers need and value, often through work-based training such as apprenticeships and internships.

The link between these guidance documents, the Children and Families Act 2014 and the Special Educational Needs and Disability Code of Practice: 0 to 25 years 2015

These guidance documents link to the SEND Code of Practice 2015 as they are specific to the age groups concerned. The SEND Code of Practice 2015 is a long document and so this guidance enables providers to look at those aspects that are relevant to them. The Code of Practice sets out the duties, policies and procedures that all organisations working with children and young people from birth to the age of 25 must take into account in relation to their care and education. This is a statutory requirement.

The Children and Families Act 2014 influenced the SEND Code of Practice as it brought in wide-ranging reforms in the areas of special educational needs, adoption, family courts and social care. These reforms highlighted a need for better cooperation between professionals when working with SEND children and young people, and these were incorporated into the code. For example:
- the requirement for a Local Offer (see page 173)
- joined-up services across education, health and care
- the requirement for education, health and care plans (EHCPs)
- statutory rights for young people in further education
- a focus on preparing for adulthood and planning for the transition to paid employment.

Test yourself
1 What is the purpose of the three documents?
2 What are the responsibilities of a SENDCo?
3 What is meant by a Local Offer?
4 What legislation do the guidance documents bring together?

▲ Local Offer

The purpose of a range of organisational policies and procedures that support children and young people with SEND

A number of policies and procedures will be in place in your setting to support children and young people with SEND. In many cases, these policies link to legal requirements and should be read alongside the SEND policy. All staff will need to be aware of them to ensure both consistency and transparency when working with these pupils.

SEND policy

All schools and early years settings will need to have a SEND policy to show how they support children and young people who have special educational needs and disabilities. The policy should set out the setting's aims and objectives, and outline the procedures that should be followed when identifying, assessing and providing for those with SEND. The policy should provide clear guidance to parents, staff and children and young people, particularly around the following:

- **Identification:** Schools and early years settings must have a clear policy for the way in which they identify and respond to SEND. The SEND Code of Practice highlights the importance of early identification so that effective provision can be made to support the child or young person.
- **Assessment:** If a child or young person is identified as having SEND, schools and early years settings will have carried out an initial assessment, working alongside parents. This should be reviewed on a regular basis so that progress or any lack of improvement can be monitored. Where the child or young person is making little or no progress over time, the policy is likely to ask for more specialist assessment from other agencies outside the setting through the SENDCo.
- **Provision:** When SEND support has been agreed alongside parents, the policy should outline how agreed interventions and targets will be put in place, and the success criteria for meeting these outcomes, as well as a review date. The views of the child or young person must also be taken into account, as well as input from teachers, the SENDCo and other professionals. This cycle is known as the **graduated approach** (assess, plan, do, review).

Equality policy

An equality or equal opportunities policy should set out the commitment of schools and early years settings to equality and anti-discriminatory practice, and meet the requirements of the Equality Act 2010. It should state how **inclusion** is a key part of the environment, curriculum and community.

> **Key term**
>
> *Inclusion:* the process of identifying, understanding and breaking down barriers to participation and belonging.

Accessibility or access policy/plan

It is a legal requirement of the Equality Act 2010 that schools should have an accessibility or access policy or plan. This should complement the SEND and equality policies of the setting, and should set out access arrangements for children with disabilities, staff and visitors. As well as physical access to buildings and facilities, the access policy should state how the setting makes provision for equal access to the curriculum and wider context of the school for all pupils.

Alternative provision policy

The policy for alternative provision sets out what a mainstream (usually secondary) school will do in cases where pupils cannot attend due to emotional, behaviour or health reasons. This may be linked to SEND where pupils have these specific needs but are unable to attend school. It does not apply to early years settings.

Anti-bullying policy

In schools and early years settings, this may form part of the behaviour policy. It will set out what the provider has in place to prevent all types of bullying among children and young people, and the roles of staff and parents in acting on any incidents that may occur.

Behaviour policy

All schools and early years settings will have a policy for behaviour that gives clear guidelines on the general expectations of the setting. Staff and children and young people should be aware of sanctions that will be put in place if the rules are broken, as well as the kinds of positive reinforcement that can be put in place when expectations are met, so that pupils are clear on expectations. However, it should be remembered that behaviour is a complex issue and in some cases can be a key indicator of an underlying or unmet need. If there are continuous issues with behaviour, assessments should take place to find any learning or communication difficulties which may cause the pupil to respond in a particular way. In this situation, the behaviour policy should be considered alongside the SEND policy, as these pupils' needs may be complex. Where a pupil has additional needs relating to behaviour, for example, if it is anxiety-driven, generic sanctions for behaviour may drive the behaviour as rewards may be unattainable. Behaviour policies need to outline the kinds of adaptations which should be made for SEND pupils so that achievable targets for behaviour are drawn up for and with them alongside parents or carers. In all cases, the graduated approach should be used so that targets are reviewed after a set period to determine their effectiveness.

Medical needs policy

This policy may also be part of a first aid or health and safety policy. It will set out the setting's requirements for children and young people with health and medical needs and conditions – for example, procedures for administering medicines and who is able to do this.

In the case of early years children, the EYFS states that settings should have a policy for administering medicines, which should be read alongside the EYFS guidance.

Teaching and learning policy

This policy sets out the way in which a school or early years setting provides activities and opportunities that meet the individual learning needs of each child and young person through a differentiated curriculum. This should encourage independence and creativity, and enable them to work collaboratively when needed.

Complaints policy

All educational provision should have a complaints policy so that parents are able to raise concerns and make complaints. It should set out a clear procedure to be followed and show the different stages complaints will go through. There should also be information on what the complainant should do if they are not satisfied with the way in which a complaint has been dealt with.

> **Research**
>
> Using your setting's SEND policy, and looking in particular at the areas of identification, assessment and provision, outline the steps which are taken when a pupil is a cause for concern and may have an area of special educational need.

The support available in early years provision, schools and colleges for young people with special educational needs and disabilities

The SEND Code of Practice sets out what early years settings, schools, colleges and other educational institutions should do to support SEND children and young people. It is a framework to help all educational professionals as well as those from health and care settings and youth offending teams.

> For more on the SEND Code of Practice and the four areas of need, see Core Chapter 10, Section 10.1.

In addition to what is set out in the Code of Practice, children and young people who have SEND will also be entitled to the following support.

0–5 years

- **A written progress check when a child is two years old:** Between the ages of two and three, all early years practitioners must carry out a progress review and provide a written summary to parents of the three prime areas of children's development: communication and language, physical development, and personal, social and emotional development. This review must outline the areas in which the child is making good progress, and also those in which they may need some additional support or a further assessment. If there is any cause for concern – for example, that they may have a developmental delay – this must be highlighted so that action can be taken.
- **A child's health visitor carrying out a health check for a child when they are aged two to three:** This check looks at a child's physical development milestones, as well as their health and wellbeing, to ensure that they are making expected progress. It also enables intervention where progress is not as expected, so that appropriate steps can be put in place to support the child.
- **Reception Baseline Assessment (RBA) (from autumn 2021):** This is an on-entry assessment of mathematics and language, communication and literacy in the first few weeks of primary school. Its purpose is to measure each child's progress to the end of Key Stage 2 when they leave primary school. It is not intended as a diagnostic assessment (see page 142) although it can be used to inform teaching in the first term.

> See also pages 16 and 141.

- **A written assessment in the summer term of a child's first year of primary school:** This assessment takes place at the end of reception, and should form part of the Early Years Profile, which takes place at the end of the Foundation Stage.

> For more on this, see Core Chapter 8, page 141.

- **Reasonable adjustments for children with disabilities:** A reasonable adjustment is something that settings must do under the Equality Act 2010 to ensure that a person with disabilities is not placed at a disadvantage when compared to those without disabilities. This, therefore, applies to staff and visitors as well as children and young people. Reasonable adjustments may be, for example, providing training for staff where needed, ensuring there is enough equipment for children with disabilities, and promoting inclusion in all areas of learning and development.

CORE Chapter 11: Special Educational Needs and Disability

> **Case study**
>
> You are working in a secondary school and are employed as a learning support assistant for Fabiola, who has disabilities and learning difficulties. She has an EHCP and works with you on academic targets, much of the time out of class. At a review meeting after half a term in Year 7, her parents comment on the fact that although Fabiola is out of the class receiving interventions and one-to-one work with you, this is not helping her to be included with her peers, and she feels isolated.
> ▸ Has the school made a reasonable adjustment in Fabiola's case?
> ▸ Can you suggest any ways in which Fabiola could feel more part of the class?

5–15 years

▸ **A special learning programme:** Where schools identify that additional support is needed they should, after discussion with parents, put into practice a programme of support that targets the pupil's area of weakness. This will then be monitored so that progress can be checked regularly.

▸ **Extra help from a teacher, teaching assistant or mental health lead:** This support programme means that the pupil will receive regular support from a school-based professional in line with their needs.

▸ **Opportunities to work in smaller groups or other areas of the school:** The additional support may be provided in small groups or individually, within the class or in other areas in the school.

▸ **Observation in class or at break:** School staff may carry out observations of pupils in class or at break time to help them assess their level of need.

▸ **Help taking part in class activities:** Pupils with SEND may need extra help during class activities to help them to access the curriculum.

▸ **Extra encouragement in their learning – for example, to ask questions or to try something they find difficult:** Pupils may need encouragement or specific questioning techniques, such as scaffolding their learning and giving effective feedback, to enable them to manage their own learning.

> See also Core Chapter 2, Section 2.2.

▸ **Help communicating with other children or young people:** If children and young people have communication needs, they may need help when speaking to their peers or to adults using **augmentative and alternative communication (AAC)**.

> See also Section 11.11.

▸ **Support with physical or personal care difficulties, such as eating, getting around school safely or using the toilet:** Specially trained staff may need to support pupils with physical or personal care needs, according to school policies.

▸ **Early Help Assessment (EHA):** EHA is a tool which helps to identify the support needed by a child or young person and in some cases the whole family. It is carried out in partnership with different professionals as well as the child's or young person's parents or carers so that information does not need to be duplicated. Providing help at the earliest stage possible is important, as it helps professionals to work together and plan the right kind of support as soon as possible. An EHA can be used from early years right through a child's or young person's school years, and the voice of the child or young person is important so that their wishes can be taken into account.

> **Research**
>
> Look at the Early Help Assessment form on the Achieving for Children website. What do you notice about the information which is requested? How will this help professionals to make an assessment together about the support which is needed by the child or young person and their family? Could this form be used for a child or young person of any age?
>
> www.achievingforchildren.org.uk/early-help-assessment/

The education, health and care plan (EHCP)

Where early years settings, schools and colleges cannot meet the needs of children and young people through normal provision, they may put them forward for an assessment for an EHCP. EHCPs are intended to support children and young people from birth to 25 years with needs that fall outside of the SEND provision offered by early years provision, schools or colleges. This can take place only after schools or early years settings have taken steps to meet the needs of children and young people, but they have not made expected progress. These steps would need to be evidenced through using and recording the graduated approach (assess, do, plan, review) so that it is clear what measures have been taken so far.

An EHC assessment will take place when requested by the school or early years setting, a parent if they feel it is appropriate, or it can be requested by the young person themselves if they are between the ages of 16 and 25.

After the child or young person has been assessed by the local authority, the EHCP will be drawn up. It will need to specify their needs and the support that is required for their SEND, health or social care. It should set out the anticipated outcomes as a result of the support, and include the reports that have been provided by all professionals who work with them. Once in place, it should be reviewed at least once each year. It will stay in place until the child or young person leaves education, or they no longer need it.

> **In practice**
>
> Ask in your setting if you can see an example of an EHCP for a child or young person.
> ▶ How does it set out the responsibilities of the setting for supporting them?
> ▶ What does it say about how the plan will be reviewed?

11.2 How professionals and organisations support children and young people with special educational needs and disabilities

A range of professionals and organisations support children and young people with special educational needs and disabilities, as described below.

Teachers

Teachers and early years practitioners will support the individual needs of all children and young people for whom they are responsible. Each child is unique and, although children and young people will be of broadly a similar age, they may be at different stages in their development. This means that there will be children and young people with a range of needs in each class or age group, some of whom will need to have additional support to access the curriculum. There are two aspects to this strategy:

1. If a child or young person has an identified special educational need, they will have specific targets and provision in place that will need to be coordinated by the teacher, along with the special educational needs and disabilities coordinator (SENDCo) or early years SENDCo. The child's or young person's parents and other healthcare or education professionals may also be involved. There should be regular reviews so that their progress can be checked and targets reviewed to ensure that the measures that have been put in place are effective.
2. If a child or young person does not have an identified special educational need, but parents and practitioners have a cause for concern, they will need to ensure that they are documenting what this is, speaking to parents, and differentiating work and educational experiences appropriately to allow for this. They will also need to raise the awareness of the SENDCo or early years SENDCo and involve them in setting up assessments with other professionals if necessary.

Educational psychologists

An educational psychologist is a professional who is trained in psychology and child development. Educational psychologists can assess the educational needs of children and young people, and provide support and advice to parents, teachers and early years practitioners. They may also provide curriculum materials, teaching approaches or behavioural strategies to help support the child's or young person's needs more effectively.

Medical practitioners

Medical practitioners such as doctors and nurses may be involved in supporting children and young people where they have health and medical needs. For example, a child with spina bifida who is in a mainstream school is likely to have an EHCP and medical practitioners will meet regularly with and advise the school on how to support their medical care needs. They may also be asked to provide reports for annual reviews of the child's or young person's progress so that all those working with the child or young person have up-to-date knowledge of their condition.

The role of a multi-agency team in providing integrated support for children and young people with special educational needs and disabilities

There are many benefits to working in a multi-agency team to support children and young people with SEND, particularly where they have serious health issues, safeguarding issues or severe needs. Different agencies may include health professionals, youth workers, social workers and mental health services, as well as teachers or early years workers.

The role of the multi-agency team is to ensure that children and young people who have multiple needs can receive coordinated support more quickly. Information sharing is of key importance, and is required by legislation so that provision for children and young people with SEND is more effective.

The views of the child or young person and their parents should also be sought regarding issues that concern them, and these should be included in meetings and annual reviews.

11.3 The principles of integration, equity and inclusion, and the differences between them

Over the years, there have been many developments in the way in which children and young people with SEND have been educated. The principles of integration, equity and inclusion differ in the way that this should be approached. The principle of integration looks at meeting the needs of SEND pupils in a way that still thinks of them as being separate or apart from others. The principle of inclusion encompasses the needs of all children and young people, including those who have SEND, in a way which anticipates and allows for their needs. The principle of equity asks us to think about what pupils need to make sure they have the same opportunities as others and to reduce educational disadvantage. The differences between these principles are explained in the text that follows.

Examples of reasonable adjustments for children and young people with SEND

- A child has a congenital heart condition and is just starting nursery. The nursery, along with the child's parents, gives training to all staff on how to monitor and manage the condition and how they will manage any periods of absence due to hospital stays.
- A pupil who has sensory processing difficulties may be given ear defenders to keep out the noise rather than be taken away from his peers to a quiet area to work.
- A pupil who has come back to school with hearing loss following meningitis is provided with a hearing induction loop and sits at the front in all lessons.
- A pupil who has severe dyslexia is provided with a scribe (amanuensis) during some lessons.
- A pupil who is temporarily in a wheelchair due to a broken leg is given a peer 'buddy' to ensure they are able to move around the school and to use the lift with them when needed.

How the principles of integration, equity and inclusion differ

Principles of integration

- Children and young people with SEND require separate support and extra resources to access the curriculum.
- The success of children and young people depends on their ability to adapt to the learning environment.
- Extra adaptations and support within the learning environment should benefit only those with SEND.

Principles of inclusion

- A curriculum should offer all students equal rights, access and choices.
- The learning environment should be adapted to support the success of each child and young person.
- Extra adaptations and support within the learning environment should benefit everyone.

Principles of equity

- The curriculum is fair, and children's holistic development needs are well planned for (including health, and social and emotional development).
- Social cohesion is promoted and children learn to connect with one another.
- Partnerships with parents should be strong, with shared aspirations for children and young people.
- The educator should understand their own culture, personal views and biases.

> **Reflect**
>
> Looking at the following examples, consider how the setting can approach each situation in an inclusive way.
> - A Year 2 pupil who has Asperger's Syndrome who is socially isolated from his peers and wants to use the computer whenever he finishes his work.
> - A child in nursery who has food allergies so is excluded from cooking activities.
> - A Year 9 pupil whose behaviour has recently become a cause for concern.
> - A disabled pupil in Year 11 who would like to audition for the school play.
> - A diabetic pupil in reception whose mother has to come into school each day to test his blood sugar and administer insulin.

11.4 Appropriate terminology to use when discussing the needs of children and young people with special educational needs and disabilities

All those working with children and young people who have special educational needs and disabilities should use appropriate language when working with them and describing their needs. In the past, negative terminology has been used, which can be offensive and highlight the **disability** or need rather than the individual. This can in turn be hurtful and damaging to the confidence and self-esteem of the child or young person, and can also be hurtful to their family. We should try to avoid labelling people or emphasising their needs. For example:

- You should refer to 'a person with a disability', rather than 'a disabled person'. This places the emphasis on the individual, rather than on the disability.
- It is important to avoid phrases such as 'suffers from', which implies discomfort, pain or despair. This type of language makes the assumption that a person who has SEND has something wrong with them or is to be pitied.
- You should also avoid language which implies that individuals are victims – for example, 'confined to a wheelchair' should be 'wheelchair user'. Many people who use a wheelchair view them as liberating rather than something that is confining.
- Avoid colloquial language to describe a disability or medical condition – 'fits' or 'spells' should be 'seizures'. Medical terms should be used in each case.

It is important that you use the correct terminology when discussing the needs of children and young people who have SEND, particularly as your setting is likely to have policies and requirements in place to do this. These requirements are summarised in the table below.

> **Key term**
>
> **Disability:** 'A physical or mental impairment which has a substantial or long-term negative effect on your ability to do normal activities' (DfE, 2010).

Requirement	Why this is important
Complying with organisational policies	All staff in your setting will need to use appropriate terminology when referring to children and young people with SEND. This will be in line with the requirements of the organisation's policies, such as the SEND policy.
Avoiding stereotyping or labelling	When working with or talking about children and young people with SEND, practitioners should avoid making assumptions about what they can or can't do. Stereotyping and labelling are damaging and can be barriers to the achievements of children and young people who have special educational needs and disabilities.
Valuing and respecting individuals	Using appropriate language is an important part of valuing and respecting others and protecting their rights. In the same way, we should not use any other discriminatory language – for example, racist, sexist or homophobic – to describe other people.
Maintaining professionalism	Practitioners should use the correct terms so that they maintain professionalism when working with pupils with SEND and their families.

▲ When and why it is important to use the correct terminology

> **Case study**
>
> Alix is about to bring her daughter, Sasha, to the nursery for the first time. Sasha is two and has epilepsy, which is mainly controlled but she has to wear a padded helmet to stop her from hurting her head if she has a seizure. You have a meeting with Alix and her husband to discuss Sasha's needs and what to do in the case of a seizure, but the staff team have not talked about this in advance. One member of staff repeatedly refers to her seizures as 'fits' during the meeting.
>
> ▶ How might this make Sasha's parents feel?
> ▶ Why is it important to be well prepared for this type of meeting?

11.5 The differences between the medical and social models of disability

Historically, children and young people with disabilities were segregated and educated away from other pupils, in separate environments. This was primarily because a disability was seen as a problem that belonged to the individual. In the 1980s, the **social model of disability** was developed and this highlighted how disability was caused by society and how it was organised, rather than the person's impairment. The social model is inclusive and encourages society to think about how people with disabilities can participate with others rather than being segregated.

The table describes the medical and social models of disability. The differences are similar to those between the principles of integration and inclusion, in that the child or young person with SEND should not be the one who needs to make changes.

Along with the Disability Discrimination Act in 1995 and later the Equality Act 2010, the social model of disability has changed access and participation for people with disabilities as it has challenged society to remove barriers. Barriers may occur owing to negative attitudes, such as assuming that people with disabilities will be unable to do things, or that there is something 'wrong' with them. Barriers may also be physical, such as inaccessible buildings or a lack of equipment.

Medical model	Social model
Child is faulty	Child is valued
Diagnosis	Strengths and needs defined by self and others
Labelling	Identifies barriers and develops solutions
Impairment becomes focus of attention	Outcome-based programme designed
Assessment, monitoring, programmes of therapy imposed	Resources are made available to ordinary services
Segregation and alternative services	Training for parents and professionals
Ordinary needs put on hold	Relationships nurtured
Re-entry if 'normal' enough or permanent exclusion	Diversity welcomed, child is included
Society remains unchanged	Society evolves

(Source: Mason, M. and Rieser, R. (1994) *Altogether Better (From 'Special Needs' to Equality in Education)*. Charity Projects/Comic Relief)

▲ The medical and social models of disability

11.6 How a primary disability may affect children's and young people's development

According to the Disabled Living Foundation (Family Resources Survey, 2015/2016), there are around 13.3 million people in the UK with a disability and, of these, 800,000 are children under 16.

A **primary disability** refers to the disability that affects the person the most, and may be related to physical mobility or impairments, learning or cognitive impairments, or social or behavioural impairments. The impact of these may be different in different children, even if they have the same condition or disability.

Disabilities may also be caused by long- or short-term health conditions, and can be permanent or temporary – for example, in the case of accidents or illness. Some people with disabilities may have more than one impairment or restriction on their daily life.

> For more on cognitive difficulties, including explanations, refer to Section 11.8.

If a child or young person has a disability it is likely that this will also affect their development in other ways. This is because they are still growing and developing, and also because development is **holistic** and a disability in one area of development will impact on others. You should also remember that a primary disability may not always be visible to other people – for example, in the case of ADHD (attention deficit hyperactivity disorder) or dyslexia.

The tables below and on the next page describe how a primary disability may affect both social and emotional development, and physical development.

> **Key terms**
>
> *Primary disability:* a physical or mental impairment that has a negative effect on a person's ability to carry out normal activities.
>
> *Holistic:* overall or all round; the idea that the parts of something are interconnected so looking at the whole rather than each individual part. Here, it means all-round care needs, with an appreciation of the contribution of each care need to overall wellbeing.

Area of effect	Result
Impulse control	Some disabilities – for example, Tourette's syndrome – will affect a person's ability to control their impulses. This may mean that they have 'tics' or difficulty controlling their behaviour or physical movements. In some cases, this can be controlled with medication, although this is not always the case. A primary disability may also affect impulse control if a child or young person has social and emotional needs and is unable to control their emotions.
Language development	A primary disability may affect social, emotional and language development if a child or young person becomes easily frustrated and finds it hard to communicate. They may be unable to express their emotions if they have less developed language skills than others, or if their emotions due to their condition affect the way in which they come across.
Mood and emotions	Depending on their type or level of disability, a child or young person may find it overwhelming at times and need support in managing their emotions. Younger children may not understand why they are not able to do some of the same things as other children. There may also be frustration or anxiety that comes out as anger.

▲ How a primary disability may affect social and emotional development

CORE Chapter 11: Special Educational Needs and Disability

Area of effect	Result
Attention, concentration and memory	A primary disability can affect physical development if it causes a child or young person physical pain or discomfort. They may, therefore, find it harder to concentrate and keep their attention on a task for as long as others. They may also be on medication to control pain or other symptoms of their condition, which could lead to tiredness and distraction. A cognitive or learning disability is likely to affect memory as it may take longer for a child or young person to learn new skills and to consolidate them. See also Section 11.7.
Sensory processing	Sensory processing refers to difficulties that children and young people have with receiving and processing information which is received through the senses. Sensory processing systems absorb and filter information around the five senses of sight, taste, smell, hearing and touch, but also around proprioception, or spatial awareness, and vestibular, which is our balance and how we move against gravity. We all need to be able to process this sensory information and filter out things we should either respond to or ignore. Difficulties in sensory processing are often a feature of children and young people on the autistic spectrum, for example, they may be hypersensitive (sensory avoiding) or hyposensitive (sensory seeking). Difficulties with sensory processing may have a significant impact on the way in which a child or young person experiences and interacts with their environment if they are unable to use these filters. For example, they may become overloaded by what they can see or hear in the learning environment, which may cause them to react in a specific way.
Motor control	Motor control is the ability to control and coordinate physical movement. If the disability or condition is in the area of physical development, this may affect how the person controls their movements or speech, for example, in the case of cerebral palsy. Motor control may also be affected if the child or young person has a cognitive difficulty that impacts on their processing skills. It may take longer for them to send the information to various parts of the body and, therefore, to practise these skills.

▲ How a primary disability may affect physical development

> **Research**
>
> What can you find out about sensory processing and the types of behaviour which may indicate that a child or young person has sensory processing needs? How might this need affect them in the classroom?

11.7 The range of cognitive skills necessary for effective educational development, and how single or multiple disabilities might affect these

Cognitive skills enable a person to focus their attention, remember information and process it, and to apply what they have learned in different situations. They are, therefore, a key aspect of educational development. The development of cognitive skills may be particularly challenging for children and young people who have **neurological** **and neurodevelopmental** disabilities and disorders. Although all individuals are different and their level of cognitive skills may vary, children and young people who have single or multiple disabilities may be affected in the areas described below, depending on their type and level of need.

> **Key terms**
>
> **Neurological:** relating to or affecting the brain and nervous system.
>
> **Neurodevelopmental:** relating to the development of the central nervous system – for example, in the case of autistic spectrum disorder or ADHD.

Attention

When we are learning something new, we need to be able to concentrate on what we are doing or listening to over time. Depending on their type and level of disability, children and young people may not be able to sustain their attention on what they are doing for as long as others of the same age.

Short- and long-term memory

Our memories are important when learning, as they enable us to remember language, information and experiences, whether these occurred a short or long time ago. Often when we are teaching, we start by asking children what they already know about a subject, or what they remember from last time. Children and young people who have single or multiple disabilities may find this challenging and need to have support to help them to remember.

Perception

Perception is the ability to work something out using a range of information that is presented to us. This may not always be obvious to others and can be more abstract – for example, when interpreting why a character in a book has behaved in a particular way. Those with certain disabilities may find this more difficult to work out.

Logic and reasoning

Logic and reasoning, or being able to make connections, will help us when learning as they enable us to process and interpret information. Logic and reasoning are important for being able to solve problems and think about why things happen, which is a key part of learning. Children and young people who have single or multiple disabilities may find it harder to make these types of connection.

Auditory and visual processing

Auditory and visual processing or perception skills involve the interpretation of information through sounds and images. When we are learning, we use all of our senses, including vision and hearing, and then process this information. Children and young people who have auditory and visual processing disorders will not have an auditory or visual impairment but will have problems making sense of the information they receive. Children and young people with auditory processing disorders (APD) may find it difficult to understand speech and respond appropriately, particularly if it takes place in a noisy environment. Those with visual processing disorders (VPDs) may have a range of difficulties, including having trouble judging distances, spatial processing, or the way in which they see shapes and symbols. They may also have difficulties with fine and gross motor skills. These can all have an effect on their confidence and the way in which they respond in the classroom.

11.8 How cognitive difficulties may have an impact on language, communication and educational development

Depending on their nature and severity, cognitive difficulties are likely to impact in some way on the development of language and communication, and, therefore, educational development in other areas. This is because a child or young person will need to have a good developing memory in order to remember language and vocabulary, as well as having the processing skills needed for understanding and using language and organising their thoughts. The process of learning is also dependent on language and the two skills support each other, so cognitive difficulties will make it harder for these children and young people to develop their communication and language skills; the effects of this may be wide ranging.

> See Core Chapter 7 for more on language and cognitive development, and receptive and expressive language.

Area of skill	Area and impact of cognitive difficulty
Language and communication	Children who have cognitive difficulties may also find it difficult to use both receptive and expressive language, and take longer to process information. Language may be slower to develop, as may the specific vocabulary they need to access the curriculum. As discussed in Section 11.6, it may be harder for them to express their feelings, which can lead to frustration and misunderstanding or upset. As language and communication are so crucial to our relationships with friends, family and others, these are also likely to be affected unless we are able to take the children's needs into consideration.
Reading, writing and comprehension skills	Children and young people who are having difficulties with their cognitive skills may also find language skills such as reading, writing and comprehension more challenging. They may find more difficult comprehension questions even harder as they will have problems picking up inferences or looking beyond the obvious. They may take longer to learn and refine skills in this area.

Area of skill	Area and impact of cognitive difficulty
Mathematical skills and concepts	Children and young people with cognitive difficulties may also find mathematical skills and concepts challenging, as they are built on logical and abstract thought. The individual needs to be able to think carefully in steps and apply their knowledge in different situations. Children and young people may need support in talking through what they are being asked to do and how they can apply their existing knowledge. This includes children or young people with dyscalculia, a cognitive difficulty with understanding numbers and making calculations.
Vocabulary and communication skills	A child or young person will need to have a good developing memory in order to remember language and vocabulary, and to organise their thoughts. Cognitive difficulties are likely to affect this and make it more difficult for them. They will have less ability to process their thoughts and articulate them to others. This is difficult not only in learning situations, but children's and young people's communication with their peers may also be affected.
Attention span	Children and young people with cognitive difficulties may find it harder to concentrate and hold their attention than others. They may find it hard to focus on what they are doing and to apply new knowledge in different situations, so it will be harder for them to be motivated, organise their learning and access the curriculum. This includes children or young people with ADHD, a behavioural disorder that includes symptoms such as inattentiveness, hyperactivity and impulsiveness.
Coordination skills	A cognitive difficulty may also impact on a child's or young person's coordination skills. Problems with coordination will also impact on their fine and gross motor development, so handwriting, tying laces and games may all be difficult for these children and young people. This includes dyspraxia, a neurological condition that affects physical coordination, making children and young people seem clumsy, as well as affecting their organisational skills and ability to organise their thoughts.
Logical reasoning	See Section 11.7.
Memory and building on prior knowledge	See Section 11.7.

▲ The impact of cognitive difficulties on different aspects of learning

11.9 How a chronic condition may affect children's or young people's emotions, education, behaviour and quality of life

Chronic health conditions are those that are long-standing, often lifelong, and will, therefore, have both physical and psychological effects on a person. At different times they are likely to cause a child or young person anxiety, pain and often fatigue, so are likely to affect their behaviour and emotions. As some of these conditions may be controlled with medication, the child or young person may also have to deal with side effects, including feeling more tired or depressed. All those who work with children and young people who have chronic conditions should be aware of who they are and what their conditions involve, so that they are prepared for what to do if support is needed. This kind of information will be held by the SENDCo and there should be regular contact with parents and families as well as healthcare workers to keep up to date with each child's or young person's needs.

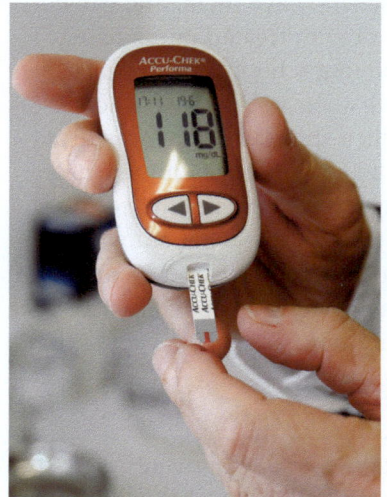

▲ You may need additional training if you are working with a child or young person who has a chronic health condition

187

Muscular dystrophy

Muscular dystrophy is a progressive muscle-wasting condition that can take different forms. It can mean that a child's or young person's life expectancy is significantly reduced. An awareness of this, alongside the fact that they are finding it more and more difficult to control their movements, the side effects of medication and anxiety about the future may well have an effect on their emotions and quality of life. They may also find it difficult to concentrate on day-to-day tasks.

Epilepsy

Epilepsy is a neurological condition; it can usually be controlled with medication, although this can cause side effects in some people. Epilepsy causes seizures, which can be severe, but equally you may be unaware that a child or young person has a diagnosis if the epilepsy is controlled. Its effects can, therefore, vary depending on how severe it is. The child or young person may have anxiety about having seizures or be wary about taking part in some activities. If you know that a child or young person you work with has epilepsy, you should be clear on what you should do if they have a seizure, and this information should be on their EHCP or in their records.

Severe allergies

These may be worse at different times of year (e.g. in the case of hay fever) or they may be triggered by specific foods such as nuts. Severe allergies can be very dangerous to those who have them, and can be life-threatening if they are not treated immediately. A child or young person in a school or early years setting who has a severe allergy should have access to specific medication, which should be kept on-site at all times so that it can be administered immediately by trained staff. Having a severe allergy may cause a child or young person to have anxiety about what can happen if they have an episode. We can reassure them by ensuring that we have plans in place so that all staff know what to do in the event of this happening.

Cystic fibrosis

This is a genetic condition, and one in twenty-five people in the UK carry the faulty gene, often without knowing. If both parents carry it, there is a chance that their baby may be born with the condition (source: Cystic Fibrosis Trust). It is usually diagnosed as part of newborn screening using the **heel prick test**. Cystic fibrosis affects how salt and water move both into and out of cells in the body, and affects the lungs and digestive system even though the individual may look healthy. They are likely to need a range of different treatments, including medication, physiotherapy and being careful about their diet. People with cystic fibrosis may also have organ transplants if their symptoms are severe.

If you are working with a child or young person who has this condition, they may find it overwhelming to deal with and need emotional support from their family and adults in school, as well as from their peers. They may get tired very quickly and it may be hard for them to focus on the life of the setting.

> **Key term**
>
> **Heel prick test:** this is a blood test that is carried out on all babies when they are a few days old to test for serious conditions.

Depression

Depression and mental health issues are now at the forefront of public awareness, and occur in around 1–3 per cent of children and young people (source: Royal College of Psychiatrists). Although these issues clearly affect the emotions, they may also cause problems in behaviour and relationships as well as academic work. Depression can also cause eating disorders, self-harm, drug or alcohol misuse, and withdrawal from others. Adults may not be aware of any of these issues, and it is important to have positive relationships with children and young people so that it is easier to detect when something is wrong, and so that they are more likely to trust and confide in you.

Fragile X syndrome

Fragile X is an inherited genetic condition that causes learning disabilities. It can cause a range of problems with learning and behaviour, which can be mild to severe, and is detected only through a genetic test. As well as having learning disabilities, children and young people with Fragile X may have a short attention span and be overactive and impulsive, as well as having social, emotional and communication problems. They may share features of autism, such as social anxiety and difficulties relating to others, a preference for routines, as well as repetitive body movements such as spinning or flapping. The condition may affect quality of life in some more than others, depending on its severity.

Sickle cell disease

This is the name given to a group of inherited disorders that affect the shape of red blood cells and cause painful episodes called sickle cell crises, as well as tiredness, shortness of breath and **anaemia**. Sickle cell disease predominantly affects people who are from an African or Caribbean background, and can also cause a delay in growth and a greater risk of serious infections.

Those who have sickle cell disease will need ongoing and lifelong specialist treatment. If they have an episode, they may be absent from the setting for several days at a time on a regular basis. They will need support from their family as well as the setting, and although symptoms may not always be obvious, those with this condition are likely to need help in managing their feelings.

> **Key term**
>
> *Anaemia:* a health condition in which there are not enough red blood cells in your body, which means that your body may not get enough oxygen.

Diabetes

Diabetes is a chronic condition in which sugar levels build up in the blood and become too high because the body is unable to make insulin. There are two main types of diabetes: Type 1 and Type 2. Type 1 may be genetic, which means that it often runs in families and is a lifelong condition; it can be present from birth or can arise later It is the type most likely to be seen in children. Type 2 can come on later in life and be caused by poor diet and lack of exercise. In each case, they are managed by injecting insulin with meals so that glucose can be kept at a safe level, although with Type 2 oral medication may be used initially.

Diabetes may cause a child or young person to feel unwell, or to be anxious about managing their levels. They may sometimes find it hard to focus on schoolwork, and it can cause problems with memory and processing skills if it is not managed effectively. They may also have more time off due to hospital appointments.

> **Research**
>
> Find out more about two of the chronic conditions above and prepare a presentation or factsheet to share the information with others.

11.10 How adults can remove barriers in order to empower and value children and young people

Adults must support children and young people with SEND by promoting their independence and removing any **barriers to their learning**. This is because we need to ensure that they have full access to the curriculum and wider aspects of learning in the school or early years setting. We also need to encourage them to do as much as they can for themselves so that they do not become reliant on adults doing things for them – this is very important.

The way that adults do this will depend on the specific needs of the child or young person and will vary between them, but may include the actions listed in the table on the next page.

> **Key term**
>
> *Barrier to learning:* anything that prevents a child or young person from taking part fully in the activities or experiences that are offered by the school or early years setting.

What adults can do	How they can do this
Create an accessible and secure environment	The learning environment must be accessible to all those with SEND in the setting. In other words, they should have access to any specific materials or resources they may need. Staff should also have access to equipment to support them (e.g. if a hearing loop is needed) and training to ensure that they are supported effectively. The environment should be adapted if necessary, and there should be an inclusive ethos which ensures that there are equal opportunities for everyone. In addition, the environment should be secure and safe, in line with health and safety requirements, and checked for any hazards that may be specific to children and young people with SEND.
Promote value and respect	Your school or early years setting should have an ethos of promoting value and respect for all. This should be part of the equality policy, and means that everyone who comes in to the setting should be treated fairly and with respect. When you are working with children and young people with SEND, ensure that you model this behaviour as children and young people will take their lead from the adults around them.
Involve the individual in planning their own learning and healthcare needs	From an early age, children and young people of all abilities should be involved in making self-assessments of their learning and thinking about next steps. For those with SEND who are involved with meetings and discussions with adults about their learning targets and/or healthcare needs, this is particularly important and will help them to develop their independence and confidence. See also Core Chapter 8.
Provide context and relevance to learning	Any adult working with children and young people will need to be able to do this. It is much harder to take on new knowledge and skills, particularly those that are more challenging, if we are unable to see their relevance to our lives. In some cases, children and young people with SEND may find it harder to make these types of connections, and so we may need to make sure that they have understood the relevance of what they are doing.
Use enabling language	Adults must ensure that they use enabling language at all times when speaking to children and young people, particularly those who have SEND. This means ensuring that the way in which they speak to them is positive and inclusive. This is because they may feel that they are unable to carry out tasks and activities, or have low self-esteem.
Work with the family and other professionals	All educators will need to work with parents and families, and with other professionals when supporting children and young people who have SEND. This is because it is the best way to gain knowledge and understanding of the needs of each individual. By sharing background information, both formally and informally, and meeting regularly with others to discuss the child's or young person's progress, you will ensure that channels of communication are kept open and relationships are positive.
Implement the setting's policies and procedures	All adults must ensure that they comply with the policies and procedures of the setting, as these will be dictated by government legislation and guidance. You should have read and understood the policies listed in Section 11.1 that are relevant to SEND so that you can support all children and young people effectively and know about how the school or early years setting aims to remove barriers.

▲ How adults can support children and young people with SEND

CORE Chapter 11: Special Educational Needs and Disability

> **Case study**
>
> You are working as a teaching assistant in a primary school and have just been told that a boy called Thusan will be joining Year 2 in your class from September. Thusan has a visual impairment called nystagmus and his vision is very poor, so some adaptations will need to be made in the classroom and around the school. The SENDCo has told you and the teacher that Thusan does not need to have a learning support assistant, but that for the first few weeks he may need some extra support to get settled. You have been told that he takes some medication and has involuntary head movements, but you know little else about his needs or condition. His parents are coming to school for a meeting with you, the class teacher and the SENDCo to discuss his needs, but he will be unable to come for a transition visit himself before starting as he has recently had an operation.
>
> ▶ What should you do before the meeting?
> ▶ Why is it important for as many people as possible to be involved in supporting Thusan's first few weeks at your school?

11.11 When and how speech can be supplemented or replaced by augmentative and alternative communication (AAC)

We all use many ways of communicating, and it is something many of us do without thinking. Communication enables us to share information with other people and to interpret what they are saying to us. For those who have special educational needs and who cannot communicate without support, the following systems will enable them to develop their independence and participate more fully in all areas of their life. They will give them the opportunity to develop their relationships with others, express themselves more easily and live more independently as they grow older.

Augmentative and alternative communication (AAC) may be used to support children and young people who have a condition or impairment that makes it difficult for them to communicate effectively with others. This may be due to a learning difficulty, a speech or physical difficulty, a brain injury or autism spectrum condition. The term AAC covers all types of communication and strategies that support the creation of speech and communication, and may be used as a temporary measure (e.g. in the case of an accident or illness) or a permanent one. These measures may or may not involve technology, but all are designed to help those who face challenges with spoken communication and those who are communicating with them. Children and young people who need support in this area will need adults in schools and early years settings to work together with speech therapists to help them to find the type of AAC that works best for them.

No-tech communication

No-tech, or unaided, communication involves the use of gestures and body language, pointing, signing and facial expression to support communication. Children and young people who have limited vocalisations or no speech may find it easier to use these forms of communication, as well as talk partners, in order to ensure that their intended meaning is passed to another person.

▲ How does AAC support children and young people in schools and early years settings?

191

Low-tech communication systems

Low-tech, or aided, communication usually involves AAC that does not need any form of power such as a battery. It may involve pen and paper, **picture exchange communication systems (PECS)**, photographs or symbols to support communication. These will give the child or young person a starting point when communicating and also when receiving information so that it is easier to process and understand.

> **Key term**
>
> **Picture exchange communication systems (PECS):** a method of communication that uses simple pictures.

High-tech communication systems

These may include mobile devices, laptops, tablets, speech synthesis or eye-tracking devices. High-tech communication systems will usually need batteries or mains power. They may be recommended after an assessment by a speech therapist or AAC specialist. High-tech communication systems should be used to fit the needs and requirements of each individual and what suits them best, using the physical movements they are able to control – for example, their head or eyes. High-tech systems may also involve the use of voice output communication aids (VOCAs), which produce the sound of a voice.

For more information on communication aids and examples of their use, visit the website of The Communication Trust: www.thecommunicationtrust.org.uk

 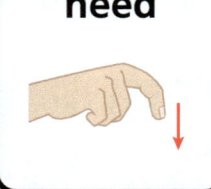   

▲ How can alternative methods of communication enhance our work with children who have speech, communication and language needs?

Assessment practice

1. What is the main legislation affecting SEND in England?
2. Explain the purpose of the progress check at age two.
3. How is the SEND Code of Practice linked to the Children and Families Act 2014?
4. Name **four** policies or procedures in your school or early years setting that support the needs of children and young people with SEND.
5. What support is available for children with SEND between the ages of five and fifteen years?
6. What is the purpose of an EHCP and when is it used?
7. Explain the importance of a multi-agency team when working with children and young people who have SEND.
8. Give **three** reasons why it is important to use the right terminology when talking about the needs of children and young people with SEND.
9. Name four ways in which adults can support children and young people by removing barriers to participation.
10. Discuss the link between cognitive ability and the development of language. Your response should give three examples of the different skills it may impact and how you might support the child or young person in each case.

CORE Chapter 12:
English as an Additional Language

Increasing numbers of children and young people in education settings are able to use more than one language. While this may seem a new development for some parts of England, the reality is that the use of more than one language is normal in other countries, such as Wales. This chapter looks at the process by which a new language is learned, the factors affecting how easily children and young people can pick up a new language and also how practitioners can support children. We also look at the social and emotional needs of children and young people who are learning to use more than one language.

Learning outcomes

This chapter covers the following knowledge outcomes for Core Element 12:

- **12.1** The characteristics of the five stages of acquiring an additional language
- **12.2** How a range of factors might affect language acquisition
- **12.3** How a child's or young person's home language affects their education and development
- **12.4** The communication, social and emotional needs of children and young people being taught English as an additional language
- **12.5** How practitioners can use a range of strategies to support children and young people being taught English as an additional language

12.1 The characteristics of the five stages of acquiring an additional language

The term **English as an additional language** is sometimes abbreviated to **EAL**. While this term is applied to everyone who speaks a language other than English at home, children and young people with EAL may acquire English in two broad ways and so have slightly different needs.

1 **Simultaneous language learning**: Some children and young people come in to settings already knowing English as they have been exposed to it since early childhood. Simultaneous language learning occurs when, for example, a child has one parent that uses English and another that speaks Urdu, or they may have spent time playing with English-speaking children. In some cases, adults may not even realise that the children and young people use another language or languages at home.
2 **Sequential language learning**: This occurs when children and young people learn English after they have already developed their home language. They may come in to settings and not be able to understand or communicate in English.

> **Key terms**
>
> **Simultaneous language learning:** where children are exposed to two or more languages in their first three years.
>
> **Sequential language learning:** where a language is learned after a home language has been established.

The five stages of acquiring an additional language

Sequential language learners who are new to English when they first arrive in a setting usually develop English following a broad pattern that has five stages.

1 Silent/receptive stage

Children and young people attempt at first to use their home language. When this does not work as a strategy, they move into a silent or receptive stage. While the term 'silent' stage is sometimes used, it is important to remember that children and young people can still communicate. They may, for example, point to objects or find ways of attracting adults' attention. The main feature of this stage is that they are not yet attempting to try out English. Instead, they are learning to tune in or listen to the sounds of the new language. Over time, children and young people start to recognise frequently used words and their meaning. The first words that children and young people understand are often linked to routines such as 'snack time' or 'line up', as well as things that have particular importance for them. It is important that pressure is not put on children and young people to talk in this period.

2 Early production

Once children and young people have begun to understand more of what is being said, they may start to use the odd phrase or word spontaneously. They may, for example, copy other children by saying 'thank you' or defend their possessions by saying 'that's mine!' This is known as **early production**.

Some first words are also said during group or whole-class routines such as 'good morning everyone' or in early years settings during songs and rhymes.

> **Key term**
>
> **Early production:** being able to say or repeat some words.

3 Speech emergence

In this stage, children and young people are no longer using 'set phrases' but instead are having a go at talking. Sentences are often quite short and limited (e.g. 'that's blue', 'I don't like it'). This is, however, a great breakthrough. For some children and young people early production and speech emergence happen at about the same time.

> **Practice points**
>
> **Supporting the early stages of language acquisition**
> - Children and young people will need a lot of reassurance and one-to-one support.
> - Use visual timetables and photos to prepare children and young people for transitions, e.g. moving to the canteen for lunch or going to the hall for PE.
> - Expect that children and young people may lose concentration easily until they have intermediate fluency.
> - Use routines as a way of helping children and young people recognise key words and phrases.

4 Intermediate fluency

In this stage, children and young people are increasingly able to express themselves. They may not always be able to talk in long sentences or use language to explain fully what they know or are feeling. Younger children are more likely in this stage to use a word from their home language if they do not know it in English. This is sometimes known as **code switching**. It does not mean that the child has become confused or is mixing up their languages. It just means that they do not yet have the equivalent word or phrase in English. Older children and young people in this stage might point to an object or picture and ask how to say it in English.

5 Continued language development/ advanced fluency

In this stage, children and young people increase their knowledge of and **fluency** in English. They increase their vocabulary, and this helps them to express more complex ideas and thoughts. Children and young people of school age may still need additional support to develop skill and confidence in literacy.

> **Key terms**
>
> **Code switching:** using a word or phrase from one language when speaking another.
>
> **Fluency:** being able to use a language easily and to an advanced level.

12.2 Factors affecting language acquisition

How long will it take for a child or young person who is new to English to pick it up? This is one of the questions most frequently asked by both parents and adults working with children and young people. Unfortunately, the answer is complex as there are many factors at work.

Age and stage of development

The age of a child or young person is one of the most important factors. Older children and young people usually acquire the language more quickly than children aged under four. They have an advantage in that their brains have already mastered a language and so connections in the brain have been made. Older teenagers can also use other strategies, such as online tools, and know how to ask questions in order to make progress.

Personality

The level of children's extroversion and openness to new experiences can make a difference to their progress. Children who are sociable and not afraid of trying out new things will find it easier to pick up another language.

Cognition

Children's and young people's brains have to process and learn a new language. Some children and young people are able to remember the sounds and meanings of new words and phrases faster than others. They may also be able to quickly understand and remember the grammatical rules of the new language they are learning.

Bilingualism

Children and young people who have already mastered two languages (**bilingualism**) may be quicker to pick up a third than those who have not.

> **Key term**
>
> **Bilingualism:** the ability to use two languages.

Cultural background

The support that children and young people have at home, and also whether their parents have some English, can make a difference to language acquisition. Where education and learning English are seen as being positive, there may be better progress.

Special educational needs or disabilities

While not all children and young people with special educational needs or disabilities (SEND) will have difficulty in acquiring English, social and communication difficulties may cause their progress to be slower. Some children and young people who have medical conditions may have fewer opportunities and less exposure to English because of repeated absence from the setting and so need longer. We have seen that language learning also requires processing of information, and children who have learning difficulties may need additional support with this.

Learning environment and available support

How much support children and young people have from adults and their peers has a significant impact on language learning. At first, children and young people need a lot of adult help, both practically but also emotionally. Where this is provided in combination with opportunities to listen to and eventually practise English, progress tends to be much faster. Slower progress is made when children and young people are left to 'naturally' (passively) pick up English, and where no attempt is made to help them link sounds and phrases to meanings of words.

12.3 How home language affects education and development

The impact of having a home language alongside English is quite complex. The research on this shows that for many children and young people there are positive benefits.

Understanding of language overall

One of the main factors in acquiring and using English is the strength of the home language. Children and young people who have not fully mastered the language used at home, or who are exposed to a mixture of incomplete or ungrammatical languages, find it hard to make good progress in their education unless they have more support. This is one reason why parents of young children who have a home language are encouraged to use it rather than switch to English.

Their family connections and their support network

It is important to recognise how a child's or young person's home language connects them to family members including those who they do not live with. A strong home language is important in helping family members to bond and to support one another. In the same way, children and young people's home language may be important in their relationships with their peers and their immediate community. This means that when looking at the language needs of children and young people, it is important to find out which languages are used at home and how they are used.

How children and young people learn a curriculum

When children and young people learn about a subject in one language, they are likely to acquire the concepts and vocabulary in that language. For children and young people who started their education in their home language, this can mean that they may not be able to show the equivalent competence in English. A good example of this is mathematics. Most bilingual adults, even if they are fluent in the other language, will do calculations in the language in which they were taught.

Acquisition of additional languages

Languages are effectively codes. Children and young people who have mastered their home language and English, either simultaneously or sequentially, are likely to find learning new languages easier as their brains have developed to handle using more than one code.

12.4 Understanding communication and social/emotional needs

In order to support children and young people, it is important to understand both their communication and their social and emotional needs.

Communication needs

Some common challenges connected with communication include the following.

Unequal proficiency

It is quite common for children and young people to have areas of strength as well as weakness in English. They may be able to talk and understand quite well, but not be able to read or write, or in the case of young children, know that books in English are read from left to right and from top to bottom. Similarly, some children and young people who started their education in their home language may have had English lessons that focused only on listening and reading. It is, therefore, important not to make any assumptions about children's and young people's competence until you have worked with them for a while.

Difficulty understanding the curriculum

Some children and young people may not have the vocabulary or technical words that allow them to understand or fully take part in activities or lessons. They may not have come across the term 'times', as in 'two times four', or 'sentence' when asked to read a sentence out loud. Where children and young people have started their education in their home language, they are likely to have followed a different curriculum and so may have gained knowledge in some areas, but not others. It is particularly important to think about this when helping children and young people with subjects such as mathematics and science.

Children and young people may have difficulty accessing resources in English

Both sequential and simultaneous language learners typically have some missing vocabulary. This means that when trying to read English they may not know the meanings of certain words or may be mistaken about their meaning. This can make studying frustrating or difficult for them. It is, therefore, important when supporting children and young people to check whether they understand the meanings of words and also to think about the vocabulary they will need in order to access the activity. For instance, if a child is about to complete an activity about shapes, it will be important to teach the names of shapes first.

Difficulty responding to questions in English

Until children and young people have mastered English, they may need more time to respond to questions. This is because their brains will take longer to process a question and then to retrieve and formulate an answer. When questions are asked to a group of children or young people, they may not be able to respond quickly and so may appear not to have understood or to know the answer. Repeated experience of not being able to answer quickly may stop them from trying to contribute.

> **Practice points**
> - Consider asking a question to an individual child rather than to the group.
> - Prevent other children or young people from interrupting or shouting out.
> - Allow plenty of time for a response and show that you are happy to wait.

Social and emotional needs

As well as communication needs, children's and young people's progress can be affected by how they are feeling.

Negative attitudes towards their culture, language, ethnicity or religion

While there are many benefits to being able to speak more than one language, including higher levels of cognition, these benefits disappear if children and young people are faced with discrimination or simply negative attitudes. Unfortunately, sometimes when children and young people have arrived in settings not speaking English, they have been considered to be a 'problem'. As language is linked to culture, ethnicity and in some cases religion, where there are negative attitudes, children and young people can feel that their own identity is being rejected in some way. Negative attitudes are conveyed through gesture, facial expression and overall body language. Children and young people can see very quickly whether or not adults and their peers are welcoming.

Isolation from their peers

It can be hard for children and young people to start out in a setting and realise that they cannot communicate easily with others. For children and young people who have always had friends, the early period of language learning can be very tough. Some children and young people can become withdrawn and even depressed in this period. This is one reason why, in the silent/receptive period, it is important to encourage non-verbal interactions and to find some activities that do not rely on language that they can do with their peers. A good example of this for older children and young people is sport, and for younger children playing with sensory materials.

> **Practice points**
>
> Always acknowledge non-verbal ways of communication that a child or young person uses.
> - Find practical tasks or play activities that require little or no language, which children and young people can join in with.
> - Make sure that in breaks and at mealtimes, children and young people have a friendly, kind peer who can sit or play with them.
> - Observe carefully signs that a child or young person may be becoming withdrawn or depressed. Talk to parents about the child's or young person's mood at home.

▲ Reflect on how this activity is meeting these children's social and emotional needs

Children/young people may not have support available at home to develop English as an additional language

Think about how it might feel to be the only one in a class not to have learned your spellings or not to have been able to complete a homework project because your parent can't help you. Sometimes, there is a mismatch between tasks that are set for home and the English language skills of parents to support them. In some cases, children and young people may not have the resources in English at home to support them. This can lead to children and young people feeling that they are missing out in some way. Best practice in this situation is to make sure that children and young people have additional support in settings to complete tasks or to select tasks that can be done without home language support.

12.5 Strategies to support children and young people being taught EAL

There are many strategies that can be used to help children and young people as they are learning English. Different strategies work with different ages and also at different stages of learning a language.

Using EAL specialist support

It is important to get as much specialist EAL support as possible. Support can vary between settings and also local authorities or cities. Here are some examples of specialist support:

- **EAL teachers or tutors:** These may work directly with the child or young person, or they may provide advice or resources.
- **Translators and interpreters:** Some settings have access to people who can translate documents into a home language or interpret. These services are very important when working with parents in order to share information. They may also be needed to assess children or young people.
- **Bilingual support:** Some settings help children and young people when they first join by using an adult who has the language, if available, to help them settle and to ensure that they can access the curriculum.

Peer and group support

For the first few days in a setting, children and young people benefit from having a friend or mentor who can play with them, show them things and prevent them from feeling isolated. It is also important to create a welcoming atmosphere where the culture is to help one another. Any unkind comments, unfriendly actions or bullying need to be dealt with firmly. The culture of the group is significantly influenced by adults. Competitive environments that focus more on individual achievement rather than on group effort or group achievement tend to make it harder for children and young people to get group support.

Making the verbal curriculum more visual

During the silent/receptive period (see page 194), it is important for children and young people to make connections between what they can see and the words that are being used. This means also using props, posters, photos and visual timetables. It also means using body language or facial expressions to communicate. Children and young people also find it helpful to have books that have plenty of pictures or diagrams in them. This strategy also benefits other children and young people who may have language difficulties.

▲ Explain how this game will help these children learn about body parts

Providing opportunities to talk before writing

For older children and young people, research has shown that talking before writing can be very helpful. Words or phrases that children or young people want to use can be written down for them. This is a strategy that often improves the written work of the whole group.

Using drama and role play

Drama and role play can be outlets for children's and young people's feelings. While young children will often use their home language in role play, older children and young people can use drama and role play as a way of learning the language of emotions, and also vocabulary and phrases linked to context. Drama and role play is also visual, which may mean that children and young people can understand more of what is happening.

Scaffolding learning

The term scaffolding is discussed in Core Chapter 2.

> Revisit Core Chapter 2 if you need to remind yourself about this.

In terms of language learning, it means thinking step by step about what a child or young person already knows and what they need to learn next. This might mean making a list of vocabulary that a young person will need to know before a lesson takes place or choosing a simpler text that introduces the young person to the concept. For young children, scaffolding learning is linked closely to planning play and activities. Adults, for example, may join children as they play or during activities and draw their attention to English words to describe what they are doing or what they are using – for example, if a child is digging in the sand tray with a spoon, the adult may point to the spoon and say 'Spoon. You have a spoon.' Look again at scaffolding learning in Core Chapter 2.

Creating language-rich environments

There are many ways of creating a language-rich environment, depending on the age and stage of development of children and young people. The key is to focus on the following questions.

Will there be opportunities to listen to language at the right level?

This means thinking about background noise, how activities are planned and the vocabulary level being used.

How will links be made between words and the meanings of words?

This is about using visual cues and props, as well as thinking about showing and demonstrating to aid understanding.

Will there be opportunities for verbal and non-verbal interactions?

This is about making sure that children and young people can express themselves without any pressure.

Are there appropriate opportunities for literacy?

This is about helping children and young people learn to read and write. For young children, this might mean sharing very simple picture books. For older children and young people, this might mean that adults help them to write words or check that they understand what they are reading.

Providing bilingual resources

Thanks to technological advances, a wide range of bilingual resources are now available. These are very useful for older children and young people, who can, for instance, use online dictionaries, which often include features that allow them to hear how words in English are pronounced. It is worth noting that online translation of sentences or whole texts can be very unreliable, so should be used with caution. In addition, older children and young people may be helped to acquire mathematical and scientific concepts and vocabulary in their home language through the use of online lessons and materials.

For younger children, a range of bilingual picture books are available, some accompanied by audio. These often come with a 'pen' that when put on to the text or the picture allows the child to hear the text either in their home language or in English. This feature is important as it allows children to hear a book in English as well as in their home language. A text-only bilingual book is of limited use for pre-school children unless an adult who is fluent in the home language is available to read it.

Working in partnership with parents/carers

A shared understanding between families and settings is important.

> This is discussed in Core Chapter 5.

We need to know about how the child or young person is feeling, and also whether the family has any questions or concerns. We also need to find out more about children's and young people's previous experiences. By working in partnership, we can provide more targeted support and also reduce the emotional impact. To achieve this we need to make sure that families feel welcome and also that barriers to communication are removed. We might need, for example, to find an interpreter to make this easier. Where this is not possible, you may need to ask an adult to help, although you will need to explain the importance of confidentiality. When sharing information about progress and concerns, it is not good practice to involve children and young people in interpreting for their own families.

> **Practice points**
>
> **Partnership with parents**
> - Find out about the language(s) that are used at home. Who speaks what and when?
> - Ask about whether the child or young person has had any exposure to English.
> - Find out about what the child's or young person's level of home language is and, if they have attended school, how they were getting along.
> - Talk to parents about their child's personality.
> - Find out about the interests and hobbies of the child or young person.
> - Share with parents information about the setting and also details of how they can contact you.

Celebrating an individual's culture

We have seen that language and culture go together. We have also looked at the way that children and young people make better progress where their culture is valued and respected. In settings, this means creating an environment and activities where many cultures, religions and ways of family life are celebrated. This might mean playing a range of music, showing and using fabrics and artefacts from different cultures, and providing a wide range of foods. It also means helping children and young people to realise that every family is unique and we all have different traditions, festivals that are celebrated and priorities.

Creating an environment that celebrates the rich differences that exist even when people share the same language and culture makes it easier to show that we celebrate individual children's and young people's culture. It is worth noting that some older children and young people may not always want attention drawn to them, because they are trying to fit in. This means that, before asking a direct question that puts them on the spot or singling them out, you should check beforehand if they are happy about this.

Positive outcomes of multi-lingualism

It is important that adults working with children and young people understand there are many positive outcomes associated with being able to use more than one language. Providing children and young people are in a supportive environment, they are likely to do well and also benefit from having more than one language.

Emotional and social positive outcomes

Children and young people who are able to use more than one language are more likely to remain connected to their family members and culture. This in turn can lead to a stronger self-identity and therefore confidence.

Cognitive positive outcomes

Research shows that children and young people who are using more than one language are able to think flexibly as the brain is able to switch into different modes of thought.

Case study

Ahmed is an outgoing, confident eight-year-old boy. However, he is new to English. Before he started at school, his teacher found out from Ahmed's family that he had a favourite football team. He paired Ahmed with a kind, friendly child who also supported the same club. The teacher used a visual timetable and lots of photos to help Ahmed understand what was about to happen next. The teacher also used Ahmed's interest in sport as a starting point for teaching some simple English words. Ahmed now has some single words such as 'goal', 'ball' and 'striker' that he can say when he sees photos. His teacher is planning to build his vocabulary further using this interest. The teacher has also given Ahmed some practical responsibility in the classroom to maintain his confidence. This week, Ahmed has started spontaneously to use some phrases such as 'No, it's my turn!' and has also joined in with a few of the words of a class poem.
▶ What stage of language acquisition is Ahmed showing?
▶ What strategies has the teacher used to support Ahmed's progress?
▶ How have Ahmed's social and emotional needs been met?

Assessment practice

1. What are the features of the silent/receptive stage of language acquisition?
2. Explain how age might be a factor in the acquisition of language.
3. Give **two** other factors that might influence the language acquisition of English.
4. How might having a strong home language support the acquisition of English?
5. Give an example of one communication need and one social and emotional need when a child or young person is acquiring English.
6. Explain how specialist EAL support can be used to support children and young people.
7. How can peer or group support be used to help children and young people?
8. Give an example of a bilingual resource that might help a young person to learn some new English words.

CORE Skills

As part of the Employer-set Project, you will be assessed on the following four Core Skills. This chapter looks at the skills themselves, and gives guidance as to what they mean and how they can be demonstrated.

Core Skills

Core Skill 1 Communicate information clearly to engage children and young people, for example, to stimulate discussion and to secure understanding

Core Skill 2 Work with others to plan and provide activities to meet children and young people's needs

Core Skill 3 Use formative and summative assessment to monitor children and students' progress to plan and shape educational opportunities

Core Skill 4 How to assess and manage risks to your own and others' safety when planning activities

Core Skill 1: Communicate information clearly to engage children and young people

> You should read this section alongside Core Chapter 2 around communication and providing effective feedback, as well as Core Chapter 4 on the use of positive language and motivation.

To pass the Employer-set Project and gain this qualification, you must demonstrate that you are able to communicate information clearly to engage children and young people.

Below we look at some ways to do this.

Ensure that communication is age-appropriate

This means that you should use language and communicate information that is appropriate for the age and stage of development of the children and young people you are working with.

Young children

You may need to use more simple language and vocabulary with young children and check on their understanding, particularly when giving instructions. They will also enjoy rhymes, songs and repetition, which can help them to remember key information, particularly if these are part of a daily routine. An example of this might be a particular song that they sing at lunchtime or home time, or a lullaby at nap time.

Older children and young people

Older children may need adults to provide them with concrete examples when communicating with them. At times, they may respond well to humour as this will gain their attention. They will need illustrative stories to demonstrate meaning, and examples that encourage them to test their own values and critical thinking skills. An example of this might be a fictional story or play with a moral, such as a fable.

Explaining technical information to a non-technical audience

You may need to explain vocabulary and information that is new to the topic or area you are learning about, to ensure that all children and young people are clear on what it means.

Using verbal and non-verbal cues

Verbal and **non-verbal cues** are important when communicating with children and young people. This includes the body language you show them while communicating. For example, with very young children it is important that you get down to their level when speaking to them, as standing over them is intimidating and may not encourage them to respond. Verbal cues are prompts that are given through speech, such as direct questions or instructions. However, they may also be more indirect through the clues given by our tone of voice, whether we speak slowly or place emphasis on particular words.

> **Key terms**
>
> **Verbal cues:** prompts that help the listener to answer, e.g. speaking more slowly or emphasising particular words.
>
> **Non-verbal cues:** prompts using body language, e.g. facial expression, eye contact or gestures.

Encouraging and modelling interaction

Communication and interaction are key elements of teaching and learning, and all those who work with children and young people will need to be able to model and encourage good communication skills through demonstrating these themselves. You may also need to adapt the way you do this depending on the needs of the person you are communicating with.

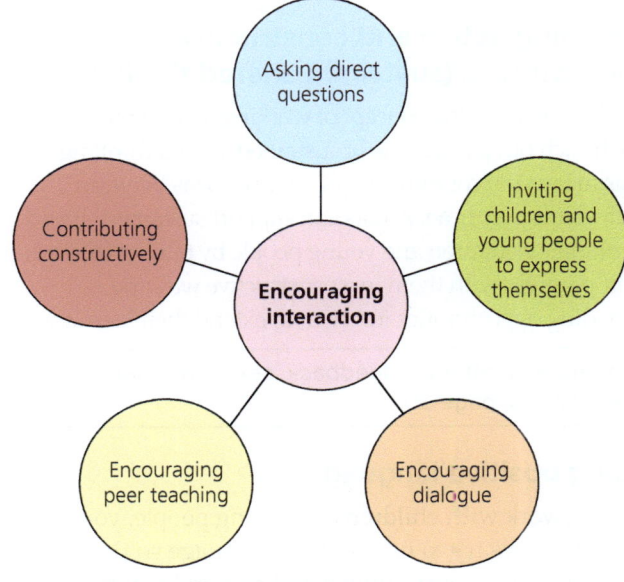

▲ Ways of encouraging interaction

Asking direct questions

You should make sure that you are clear when questioning children and young people, so that you know they understand what you are asking. Make sure that you ask only what you need to know, and ensure that you give them time to think and respond. You should also show that you value what they say by acknowledging their responses, particularly if they are finding the subject matter difficult. For example, 'Yes, that's a good answer, Matt, can you think of any other reasons?'

Inviting children and young people to express their own ideas through discussion, interactive activities or creative tasks

Make sure you involve all children and young people in discussions or activities, particularly if they are not confident in putting forward their ideas. Sometimes, it may also help to use creative or interactive tasks to enhance or encourage communication where children and young people have difficulty in expressing themselves verbally.

Encouraging a dialogue through oral and written formative feedback

> See Core Chapter 2, Section 2.5, page 35.

Encouraging children and young people to teach one another

Encouraging children and young people to work together on projects and group activities will give them opportunities to share ideas and listen to one another, rather than just put forward their own ideas.

Providing active and constructive contributions (sustained shared thinking)

Leading on from the concept of working together to teach each other is the use of sustained shared thinking. This means the continuation of sharing ideas between individuals over time. Adults can support sustained shared thinking for children and young people by talking through their progress with them in a constructive way and providing opportunities for them to extend their learning.

> For more on effective feedback, see Core Chapter 2, Section 2.5, page 35.

Using positive language

In your work with children and young people, you should always try to use positive language so that you recognise their contributions and respond to what they say in a way that values them. This will help to build their confidence and self-esteem so that they feel able to progress in their learning.

> For more on this, see Core Chapters 2 and 4.

▲ What makes effective communication an important part of your work with children and young people?

Helping children and young people to focus on strengths, rather than disadvantages

Make sure you build on what children and young people know and are able to do, so that they start from a place of knowledge. This will develop their confidence rather than focus on what they don't know or are unfamiliar with.

Using praise and constructive feedback to build confidence as well as competence

You should praise children and young people for their contributions and show that you are listening to them by giving effective feedback.

Modelling language that celebrates diversity

You should make sure that you use language that is inclusive and that celebrates the differences and individuality of children and young people.

> See Core Chapter 10 for more on this.

Adapting contributions to meet the needs of the children and young people

Think about the communication needs of the children and young people you are working with – for example, their age, whether they have special educational needs, or if they speak English as an additional language.

These may all impact on the way in which you communicate with them.

> See Core Chapter 12 for more on English as an additional language.

> **Research**
>
> Read through the UNICEF document 'Communicating with Children: Principles and Practices to Nurture, Inspire, Excite, Educate and Heal', which is available on the UNICEF website: www.unicef.org
>
> Find out more about communicating with the age group you work with. What key points do you find useful? How might they influence the way in which you communicate with children and young people?

> **Practice points**
>
> **Effective communication**
> - Use body language that shows you are open and approachable.
> - Be positive in your communication with children and young people – smile and be interested in what they have to say.
> - Remember you are a role model for the way in which they communicate with others.
> - Speak clearly and give eye contact.
> - Do not interrupt children or young people, or say things for them; give them an opportunity to speak.
> - Give children and young people 'thinking time' when you ask them a question.

Core Skill 2: Work with others to plan and provide activities to meet children's and young people's needs

> You should read this section alongside Core Chapter 5: Parents, Families and Carers, and Core Chapter 6: Working with Others, as well as Core Chapter 11: Special Educational Needs and Disability, and the Occupational Specialism unit on planning: Early Years Educator Performance Outcome 3.

This Core Skill involves the following aspects.

Communicating openly and effectively with other professionals, speaking clearly and confidently

> Establishing professional relationships with relevant colleagues and parents/carers – see Core Chapters 5 and 6.
>
> Determining a child's or young person's specific needs – see Core Chapter 11.
>
> Passing on information that could impact on other teams/professionals – see Core Chapters 6 and 11.
>
> Sharing ideas and best practice – see Core Chapter 6.

Planning collaboratively

> Liaising with colleagues to plan appropriate activities for children and young people – see Core Chapter 6.
>
> Discussing how best to support children and young people in meeting objectives, taking into account their individual needs or learning targets. This may or may not be related to an area of SEND – for example, a child or young person who needs support with staying focused, or someone who works best with a partner – see Core Chapter 11.
>
> Contributing to long-, medium- and short-term planning – see Core Chapter 8 and Early Years Educator Performance Outcome 3.
>
> Sharing resources – see Early Years Educator Performance Outcome 1.
>
> Presenting information in an organised and logical way – see Core Chapter 8 and Early Years Educator Performance Outcome 3.

Supporting education in the setting

> Using high expectations and encouragement to create a positive learning environment – see Core Chapter 4.
>
> Managing behaviour effectively and in line with the setting's policies and procedures – see Core Chapter 4.
>
> Monitoring education activities through observation and assessment – see Core Chapter 8.

Education and Early Years T Level: Early Years Educator

> Contributing to effective record keeping, using precise terminology, and correct grammar, spelling and punctuation – see Core Chapter 3 and Early Years Educator Performance Outcome 4, Assisting Teaching Performance Outcome 3.

> **Good to know**
>
> As part of Task 2 in the Employer-set Project, you will be required to make a presentation to your peers. When doing this, you should take into account the requirements of Core Skill 1 around effective communication and clear language, and Core Skill 2 around presenting information. You will also need to listen to the presentations of others, and show that you can listen actively to them and make constructive contributions to discussions.

Core Skill 3: Use formative and summative assessment to monitor children's and young people's progress to plan and shape educational opportunities

> You should read this section alongside Core Chapter 8: Observation and Assessment.

You must be able to use formative and summative assessment to monitor children's and young people's progress to plan and shape educational opportunities. This includes but is not limited to:

- establishing learning goals for and with the child or young person
- observing the child or young person and recording data on their progress, as appropriate
- using questions and answers or formal tasks to check the child's or young person's understanding
- analysing assessment data to determine the next steps in supporting the child or young person to meet their goals.

As part of Core Skill 3, you will need to know how to use formative and summative assessment in order to monitor children's progress in the early years.

> For more about the purpose of assessment and for definitions of formative and summative assessment, see Core Chapter 8, Section 8.2.

Establishing learning goals for/with the child or young person

Early years practitioners regularly use observations and assessments to help them to establish learning goals for children through next steps for learning. As the children you work with are very young, you may or may not be able to draw their attention to these when you are working with them – for example, a two year old will not be aware, but a four year old may know that they have a target around being able to count to ten.

Observing the child or young person and recording data on their progress, as appropriate

> For more on this, see Core Chapter 8, Section 8.3.

Using questions and answers or formal tests to check the child's or young person's understanding

> For more on this, see Core Chapter 8, Section 8.2, on summative assessment and questioning.

Analysing assessment data to determine the next steps in supporting the child or young person to meet their goals

You are likely to work alongside colleagues to analyse data from national assessments so that you can work out the child's next steps for learning. In the EYFS, as you are regularly observing and assessing pupils' progress, you will use this information alongside what you know about children's development. You can use the current *Development Matters* statements to help you with this process.

CORE Skills

In practice

Pupil A and pupil B have just been assessed as part of the EYFS Profile. They will be assessed against the Early Learning Goals as 'Emerging' or 'Expected'.

Consider the data presented below for these two pupils.

	Communication and language	Physical development	Personal, social and emotional development
Pupil A	L/A = Emerging U = Emerging S = Emerging	M = Expected H = Emerging	SC/SA = Emerging MFB = Emerging MR = Emerging
Pupil B	L/A = Expected U = Expected S = Expected	M = Emerging H = Expected	SC/SA = Expected MFB = Expected MR = Expected

Notes: L/A = listening and attention, U = understanding, S = speaking, M = moving and handling, H = health and self-care, SC/SA = self-confidence and self-awareness, MFB = managing feelings and behaviour, MR = making relationships

▶ How will this assessment in the prime areas help Year 1 teachers?
▶ Will this data enable teachers to set targets for these pupils?

Core Skill 4: How to assess and manage risks to your own and others' safety when planning activities

As part of Core Skill 4, you will need to know how to assess and manage **risk** to your own and others' safety. This means both in the learning environment and when you are outside the school or early years setting on trips.

Assess and manage risks to your own and others' safety when planning activities, using the Health and Safety Executive's 'Five steps to risk assessment'

You should know about and understand the different kinds of risks that may occur when planning learning activities. The **Health and Safety Executive (HSE)** has published a list of five steps to support this.

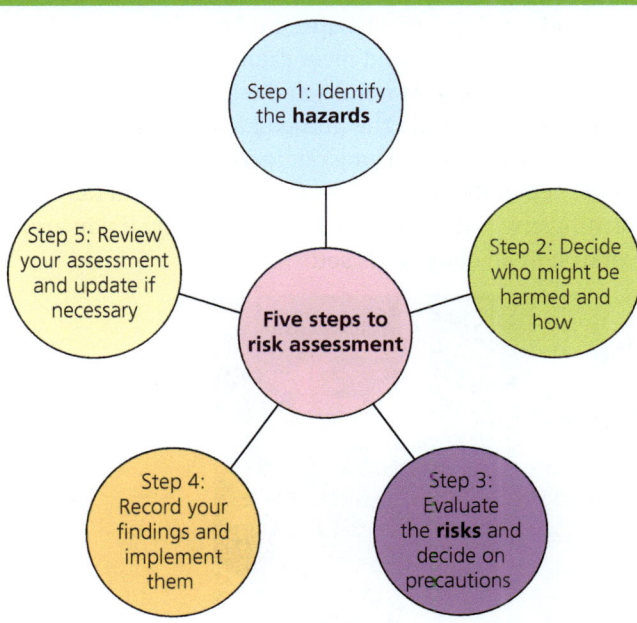

▲ The Health and Safety Executive's 'Five steps to risk assessment'

Key terms

Risk: the chance, whether high or low, that someone could be harmed by a hazard.

Health and Safety Executive (HSE): an independent regulator for the prevention of work-related death, injury and ill health.

Education and Early Years T Level: Early Years Educator

> **Key terms**
>
> **Risk assessment:** a check for potential risks so that measures may be put in place to control them.
>
> **Hazard:** something in the environment that could cause harm.

The HSE's 'Five steps to risk assessment' are as follows:

Step 1: Identify the hazards

According to the HSE, you should look at the whole activity you are going to carry out, from beginning to end, so that you can identify each hazard. When you are doing this, take in to consideration the fact that these are likely to include different types of hazard:
- physical
- security
- fire
- food safety
- personal safety.

Physical hazards

These will be the ones you might come across in the general environment, such as coats being left on the floor and causing a trip hazard, broken glass around a litter bin, or damage and mess caused in outdoor areas overnight by foxes. Materials and equipment should be checked, as should the immediate area you will be working in, before carrying out learning activities. You should remember to check both the indoor and outdoor learning environment regularly, particularly if you are working in an early years setting.

▲ Identifying a physical hazard

Security hazards

These may occur when unidentified people gain access to the site or young children or older pupils are able to leave it without permission. If you are working outside, gates should be checked to ensure they are not left open, and hedges to ensure there are no gaps. Security hazards may also occur with younger pupils if a different adult arrives to collect them at the end of the day or session without being given permission by parents. You should ensure that you know the school's policy for collection and for ensuring that children are kept safe and secure at all times.

> For more on this, see the information on safeguarding in Core Chapter 3.

Fire hazards

In the case of cooking or science activities, safety equipment such as fire blankets should be available for use if needed during the activity. Fire extinguishers and electrical items will need to be checked regularly to ensure that they are not faulty, and the dates of these checks should be displayed on the equipment.

> See Early Years Educator Performance Outcome 4, K4.11, for more on fire safety.

Food safety

Adults should be good role models when cooking and working in kitchens, pointing out hazards to children and young people where they occur and making sure that equipment is used correctly. Hazards may include hot surfaces and flames, and sharp knives. Food preparation should always be carried out hygienically and in line with food handling and safety requirements. All children and young people should inform the setting of any allergies or specific dietary requirements.

> See Early Years Educator Performance Outcome 4, K4.10 for more on food safety.

Personal safety

Safety equipment and **PPE** should always be used where needed, and staff should be aware of the correct procedures when carrying out activities that have a higher level of risk. If you are to be using any specialised equipment with children and young people, such as glue guns or sewing machines, always ensure that they have been given clear instructions and are supervised at all times.

CORE Skills

> **Key term**
>
> **PPE:** personal protective equipment – equipment to protect the user from risk. Examples of PPE might be helmets, eye protection, gloves or gowns, and high-visibility (hi-vis) jackets.

> **In practice**
>
> Ask your school or early years setting if you can look at a risk assessment for an off-site visit. There is likely to be a member of staff who manages this – for example, a school may have an **educational visits coordinator (EVC)** whose role is to go through risk assessments with the staff members who are managing the trip.

Step 2: Decide who might be harmed and how

When carrying out a risk assessment, you will need to think about who has the potential to be harmed so that you can record this. When working with children and young people, you should consider whether they are more at risk, and the kinds of steps you can put in place to reduce the risk. If children or young people have special educational needs or a disability, or other specific requirements, how will this affect the level of risk? How might they be harmed?

> See Early Years Educator Performance Outcome 4, K4.11 for more on risk assessments.

Step 3: Evaluate the risks and decide on precautions

If a hazard has been identified, the next stage is to consider the level of risk and how likely it is to happen (high, medium or low risk of occurrence). The kind of precaution or action you take should take this into account. For example, if you are working outside in an early years setting on a hot day, the children should wear sun hats and sun cream, or stay in the shade if possible.

When going on off-site visits, risk assessments will need to be carried out by the member of staff who is organising the trip. This should take account of issues such as:
- adult/child ratio
- transport (e.g. insurance, seat belts, or check the route if walking)
- child allergies, medical needs or SEND of children and young people so that any medication can be taken
- first aid requirements
- on-site risk assessment at the location.

Step 4: Record your findings and implement them

You should record your findings on a risk assessment form so that you can refer to it if needed. If further action needs to be taken following the assessment, you should ensure that this happens. You may need to also share this with other staff.

Step 5: Review your risk assessment and update if necessary

A risk assessment should be reviewed annually and updated as necessary if circumstances are different or anything changes. This may need to happen sooner if there is an incident or a significant change at the setting.

Education and Early Years T Level: Early Years Educator

> **In practice**
>
> Carry out a risk assessment in an area of your setting, taking into account the five steps outlined on the previous two pages. You may be able to use a template that is used regularly by your setting. If not, there are others available, such as the HSE risk assessment template provided below.

Risk assessment template

Company name: Assessment carried out by:

Date of next review: Date assessment was carried out:

What are the hazards?	Who might be harmed and how?	What are you already doing to control the risks?	What further action do you need to take to control the risks?	Who needs to carry out the action?	When is the action needed by?	Done

More information on managing risk: www.hse.gov.uk/simple-health-safety/risk/index.htm

Published by the Health and Safety Executive   09/20

▲ A risk assessment template from the HSE

For more information on managing risk, visit **www.hse.gov.uk/simple-health-safety/risk/**

Reproduced by kind permission of HSE. HSE would like to make it clear it has not reviewed this product and does not endorse the business activity of Hodder Education.

Performance Outcome 1:
Support and Promote Children's Play, Development and Early Education

If you work with babies and young children, you need to be able to support their development and early education. The starting point for this is to recognise individual children's stage of development and then use this information to find opportunities for learning and to plan for play.

In this unit, we look at the expected patterns of development, the importance of recognising where development is atypical, and specific activities that can support early language, mathematics and literacy. We also look at how different types of play can support children's development, and the types of resources and activities that can be used.

Learning outcomes

This chapter covers the following knowledge outcomes for Performance Outcome 1:

- **K1.1** The expected patterns of children's development from birth to 7 years
- **K1.2** How a range of biological and environmental factors may impact on children's learning and development
- **K1.3** How the following areas of development can impact on children's holistic development within play and early education:
  - speech, language and communication
  - personal, social and emotional development
  - physical development
  - cognitive development
- **K1.4** How children develop speech and language and the differences between the two
- **K1.5** The expected stages of language acquisition and how a range of biological and environmental factors can affect the speed of acquisition
- **K1.6** How daily exposure to stories and rhymes supports development of communication and vocabulary
- **K1.7** The potential effects and long-term impact on a child's holistic development if atypical development is not recognised and why practitioners must recognise atypical development as early as possible
- **K1.8** The current statutory requirements for the Early Years Foundation Stage and Key Stage 1 National Curriculum requirements
- **K1.9** The links between the Early Years Foundation Stage and Key Stage 1 National Curriculum including what information is shared with Key Stage 1 teachers
- **K1.10** The purpose of a range of pedagogical strategies to support children's development of early literacy and the purpose of systematic synthetic phonics to support the teaching of reading
- **K1.11** The purpose of a range of strategies to support children's early writing skills
- **K1.12** How daily routines, games, rhymes and stories can be used to support children's development, learning and mathematical understanding
- **K1.13** The purpose of a range of strategies to promote mathematical thinking and approaches that encourage early reasoning
- **K1.14** How number enables children to develop mathematical skills
- **K1.15** Stages and types of play, activities associated with different types of play and how they promote children's development and sense of agency
- **K1.16** The resources and equipment needed to support children's play and education, both indoors and outdoors
- **K1.17** The difference between adult-led and child-initiated play and how adults can lead and promote play
- **K1.18** The benefits of adult-led and child-initiated play and how to offer an appropriate balance
- **K1.19** How learning outside of the setting positively enhances children's education and development and where this may take place
- **K1.20** The distinctive qualities offered by the outdoors as an educational environment compared to traditional classroom environments

K1.1 The expected patterns of children's development from birth to 7 years

This area of development is about:
- how babies and children take and store information that they gather from their five senses: sight, touch, taste, hearing and smelling
- how children process and store this information, using their memory
- how they learn to make links to what they already know, and use this to solve problems.

For example:
- A toddler has learned how to climb onto a chair. He likes the taste of biscuits. He remembers where the biscuits are kept. He remembers how his parent often uses a chair to get things down from the top of the cupboards. He pushes a chair in front of the cupboard where the biscuits are kept. He climbs on the chair and then gets the biscuits.

Brain development

The brain is the control centre of the body, and is in charge of all areas of development. Understanding something about it is, therefore, very useful.
- Babies are born with billions of **neurons**, the cells of the brain. Together they can come together to allow electrical signals to move like lightning across the brain.
- At first, signals pass through simple networks in the brain. These allow the baby to breathe and swallow, and show other simple **reflexes** that are important for survival.
- The brain develops rapidly over the first couple of years. This is as a result of stimulation.
- The five senses bring new sensations and so the neurons form new and more complex connections.
- For language, attachment and some other areas of development, it is thought that we are born with a template for these connections. This explains why patterns of development are similar between babies.
- These connections can only fully develop if enough stimulation is provided, such as: talking to and touching babies, responding to their cries and providing them with opportunities to communicate.

▲ How is this baby learning about communication?

> **Key term**
>
> **Reflexes:** instinctive movements usually linked to survival.

Shaping the brain

One of the interesting things about the brain is that it keeps on changing. This is because every experience and skill that we learn will create new pathways.

In their first few years, children's brains are also growing, and making new connections and pathways. What children do, hear, touch and taste in their early years will all have an influence on their later development.

The more often a movement, action or experience occurs, the stronger the pathways that are laid down. We can see the need for repetition when babies and toddlers are learning. They will often enjoy and want to do the same action or experience several times.

When children regularly do an activity, it will shape the connections and pathways in the brain. A good example of this is music. Children who have the opportunities to hear and use musical instruments will develop pathways that will help them to become musical.

Studies show that the brains of children who are neglected may not develop complex pathways.

Performance Outcome 1: Support and Promote Children's Play, Development and Early Education

Learning new skills and keeping active throughout our lives are important ways of preventing brains from ageing.

> **Case study**
>
> Oliver is four years old. His parents have spent a lot of time talking with him, and also taking him to different places such as the park, the beach and the woods. He knows the names of different animals and plants.
>
> Oliver is learning to play the piano, and his parents encourage him to practise every day. He can play some simple tunes.
>
> His parents also play board games with him, so he has learned to roll a dice and move a counter on the board.
> ▶ Think about how the experiences that Oliver has had may influence his development.
> ▶ Why is it important that his activities and experiences are repeated often?

Pruning

At first, the brain makes plenty of networks and connections. At around 18 months, the brain starts to remove or 'prune' networks that are not being used or that are weak.
▶ In a healthy brain, this is actually a good thing. It allows the remaining pathways to be stronger and for signals to move across the brain more quickly.
▶ Pruning can cause problems for older adults who are not active, not learning new skills or not having new experiences.

The developing brain

As well as making new connections in early childhood, there are also changes to the structure of the brain. It is thought that it takes at least 25 years before the brain is fully mature.

One of the key areas of the brain to develop is known as the **frontal cortex**, just behind your forehead. This part of the brain is responsible for reasoning, predicting and being logical. It also affects how we make decisions.

Children and young people are likely to make decisions based on the 'here and now'. They might decide not to work hard in a subject because they don't like the teacher. An adult might not like the teacher but might work hard anyway, because they know that passing this subject will get them a better job.

Myelinisation

As well as the structure of the brain changing, the speed of our reactions and thinking also changes during childhood. This is partly because the networks of pathways become faster, but also because the pathways become coated with a substance called myelin.

The table below shows the expected patterns of cognitive, neurological and brain development. Note that the text in this table might not be recognised in other contexts.

Age	Cognitive and neurological developments in children at this stage
0–12 months	• Able to focus on close objects • Becoming aware of physical sensations such as hunger and thirst • Increasing interest in the environment and playing with objects • By the age of 12 months, an average child's brain is already at least 70% of adult volume
1–2 years	• Can understand and respond to simple instructions from others • Can identify familiar objects in books • Able to remember and repeat past events • connections are rapidly forming in the child's brain, roughly twice as fast as in adult
2–3 years	• Can categorise objects. e.g. can pick out a toy from a box of books • Able to name familiar objects in books • Can sort blocks from the smallest to largest
3–5 years	• Able to organise objects by size, shape and colour • Increasingly curious and asking questions to gather information • Understanding the concept of past and present • From 3, a child's brain enters a phase of 'synaptic pruning', where networks in the brain are refined
5–7 years	• Understanding the concepts of space, time and dimensions • Can carry out simple addition and subtraction • Beginning to reason and debate with others

Speech, language and communication development

Speech, language and communication development is an important area and links closely to children's cognitive development.

We have looked in detail at the expected pattern of this area of development in Core Chapter 7 on pages 120 and 124.

213

Literacy development

The development of literacy is closely tied to children's language development. It is also affected by the opportunity that children have to experience books and stories and to see text.

Children's development is also affected by the way that adults draw children's attention to print and provide them with experiences with early writing. For writing, children also need to develop fine motor skills, as pencils are used when children first learn to write.

The differences in early literacy levels between children of the same age can be very significant, and this is why it is hard to find accurate age–stage milestones for the first four years.

- For children aged between four and five years, the Department for Education has set goals in reading and writing for children at the end of the reception year (see page 16), although some children, especially those born in the summer, do not achieve them.
- The Department for Education has also provided non-statutory guidance to support practitioners in developing the literacy skills of children from birth to five years. This document is called *Development Matters*, and is widely used in early years settings as a way of recognising young children's development.

Early literacy skills

In order for children to become literate, they need to develop some early literacy skills. These include the ability to hear rhymes or to recognise and create letter shapes. Many of these skills develop alongside one another rather than sequentially and depend on a range of factors, not simply on a child's age. Children need to have opportunities at home and in early years settings to develop the skills as well as being interested in them. Other areas of children's development, such as language and physical development, also play a part in how quickly children can gain these early literacy skills. For many children these skills will develop slowly over time and they will need significant amounts of practice.

> **Research**
>
> Find a copy of *Development Matters*.
>
> What type of activities does it suggest to encourage literacy with children from birth to three years?

Mathematical development

There are many components to mathematics. While there is often a focus on number, mathematics also includes time, shape, measuring, recognising patterns and problem solving.

Children's mathematical development is very variable. Some children may be able to complete a jigsaw puzzle, but not be able to count five objects accurately. This is because mathematical development depends on:

- children's cognitive (thinking) and language development
- how adults interact and provide opportunities for children to experience mathematical concepts.

Later on in this unit, we look at how you can support children's mathematics.

- For children between four and five years, the Department for Education has set goals known as Early Learning Goals for children at the end of the reception year. These goals focus only on number, although settings are required to provide opportunities for children to experience a range of mathematical opportunities.
- *Development Matters* also supports practitioners to plan and assess mathematics for children from birth to five years. The table on page 213 shows what most children will be learning to do at different ages. *Development Matters* also provides ideas and strategies to support children's learning and so is worth reading.

> **Research**
>
> Referring to *Development Matters*, list three ways in which a practitioner might support the number skills of a child aged between three and four years.

Physical development

Physical development is an important area as it allows children to explore, become independent and join other children in play.

We looked at expected patterns of physical development on pages 108–9 in Core Chapter 7.

Performance Outcome 1: Support and Promote Children's Play, Development and Early Education

> **Test yourself**
>
> Look back at pages 108–9 and see if you can answer these three questions.
> 1. At what age would you expect a baby to be able to roll over?
> 2. At what age would you expect a child to be able to run and stop?
> 3. At what age can children colour within the lines of a picture or shape?

Personal, social and emotional development

This area of development looks at the skills that children need in order to manage their emotions and also be with other children and adults.

We looked at the importance of this area and also patterns of expected development in Core Chapter 7 on pages 109–11.

> **Test yourself**
>
> Look back at pages 109–11 and see if you can answer these three questions.
> 1. At what age do babies start to show distress if they cannot be with their parents?
> 2. At what age can children start to play cooperatively?
> 3. At what age can children play games with rules?

K1.2 How a range of biological and environmental factors may impact on children's learning and development

This knowledge outcome is covered in Core Chapter 7 on page 112.

> **Test yourself**
>
> Can you name:
> 1. two biological factors
> 2. two environmental factors that could impact on children's learning and development?

K1.3 How areas of children's development can impact on holistic development within play and early education

This knowledge outcome is covered in Core Chapter 7 on page 104.

> **Test yourself**
>
> 1. Explain how communication and language are linked to other areas of development.
> 2. Give an example of how a child with lower levels of communication and language might be disadvantaged.

K1.4 How children develop speech and language and the differences between the two

We looked at the importance of language in Core Chapter 7. We also looked at how babies and young children develop language skills as well as the theories of language. It might be useful for you to revisit that chapter as you study this topic.

In this section, we look at some of the ways in which most children develop speech and language. It is important to understand the difference between the two.

1. Speech refers to:
   - accurately forming and saying sounds
   - putting the correct sounds in the correct place within a word.
2. Language refers to:
   - communicating meaning through words
   - joining words together in the correct order to build sentences and have conversations
   - understanding how words are made and changed to convey plurals/past tenses.

How children develop speech

Speech sounds and confidence in talking develops over time.
▶ The first sounds that are made are coos and then babbles.
▶ Toddlers' speech is often difficult to understand, as they are not able to make all of the sounds.

▶ Most children cannot say all of the speech sounds used in English until they are around six or seven, although by the age of three, most of what children say can be understood.

As well as being able to produce speech sounds, children also need to develop confidence in talking. The table shows typical patterns in speech development.

Age	Patterns in speech development
6 months–2 years	• Babbling, using vowels and consonants, e.g. ma, da, pa. • Babbling becomes longer and more tuneful, e.g. bababababa from 9 months. • From 12 months, babbling and occasional words used such as 'te-te' for teddy. • From 18 months, increasing numbers of words are used, although they may not be clear. There is less babbling now.
18 months–3 years	m, p, t, d, n, w – speech is difficult to understand, even for familiar adults.
3–4 years	m, p, b, t, d, n, w, f, s, y, h, ng, k, g, l, s, z, v • Speech is becoming easier to understand. • By 3 years, children's speech can be mostly understood. • Words with blends such as sp+oon in '**sp**oon' may be difficult for younger children to say. • May have difficulties with these sounds: ch, sh, th, r and j.
4–5 years	• Speech should be clear and easily understood. • Children may still have difficulties with 'th' and longer words with several components, e.g. 'scaffolding'.

Helping children develop speech

Learning to speak requires confidence as well as practice.

Children can gain confidence and practise speech when you listen carefully to them and allow them enough time.

It is also important that you speak clearly to them and keep background noise to a minimum. This can help babies and toddlers to hear the sounds in words.

For this qualification, you need to know the ways to encourage speech, shown in the table below. (Not all of these strategies would be recognised in other contexts or by other professionals.)

Strategy	Explanation
Leading conversations	Children can gain confidence by leading conversations and being carefully listened to. This makes them think that what they have to say is important.
Speaking about ideas and feelings	• Once children are around 3 years old, they often have more vocabulary and so can express their ideas and feelings. • It can take young children a little while to find the words they need to talk about their ideas and feelings. This means that we need to give them time and show interest, even if it seems to be taking a long time.
Taking part in group conversations	• Group conversations can help children learn to listen, but also talk in front of others. • This works best when children are in small groups and also are nearly fluent in their language. This is typically at 3.5 years.
Participating in role play with others	• Most children at around three years will enjoy role or pretend play. • Role play is recognised as helping children's language and as children become more fluent, they start to enjoy playing alongside each other and taking parts.
Speaking confidently	As children develop their language, they need opportunities to talk in front of others in order that they can speak clearly and confidently and, over time, grammatically. The ability to do this is known as '**oracy**'.

> **Key term**
>
> **Oracy:** the ability to speak clearly and grammatically to others

Performance Outcome 1: Support and Promote Children's Play, Development and Early Education

Your role in helping children's speech

As well as practising these strategies, there are some things that you should *not* do.

1 Correcting children's speech: children who are frequently corrected tend to lose confidence in talking. If a child mispronounces a word or is ungrammatical, you should repeat back their words to them as a continued part of the conversation. For example:

Child: We <u>wented</u> swimming. <u>I</u> <u>swimmed</u> very fast.

You: Wow, you <u>went</u> swimming. And you <u>swam</u> fast. That sounds fun.

2 Interrupting children: you should avoid interrupting or letting other children interrupt when one child is talking. This can be tricky, but if a child is frequently interrupted, they can lose confidence.

> ### Good to know
>
> #### Stammering
>
> Stammering or stuttering affects children's speech. They may hesitate or repeat a word several times or a sound at the start of a word. It is almost as if a child is stuck on that word.
>
> Stammering is part of normal speech development between around two and a half and three and a half years, as children's language becomes more complex. You can help children by slowing down your own speech and showing that there is no rush by, for example, sitting down.
>
> Children are likely to stammer more when they feel under pressure. You can help by reducing the number of questions and, in group situations, not expecting children to talk in front of others. There are also some things that you must *not* do:
>
> - rush children or finish their sentence
> - tell children to slow down
> - let other children interrupt them.
>
> For most children, stammering will reduce and disappear, but for some children, they will need to be referred for a speech and language assessment. You should seek a referral if any of the following are observed:
>
> - Most of their speech is very unclear because of stammering.
> - They are nearly or over four years old.
> - They show signs of frustration, e.g. clenched fists.
> - They have developed strategies to make the sounds, e.g. screwing up eyes or throwing back the head.
> - They start to talk less or refuse to talk in front of others.

How children develop language

In Core Chapter 7, we looked at the typical patterns for how children develop language. Here are some specific features of language and typical ages at which children may show these features.

Listening to and understanding instructions

There are many factors that affect how well children can listen to and understand instructions.

The number of words in an instruction matters, and also how many parts there are to a question. For example:

- 'Go out!' is a simple instruction with few words.
- 'Find your book, take it to the black bookcase and then bring me your coat' is a long instruction. The child would need to carry out three different steps and also get them in the right order. This requires the child to have a good memory and be paying attention carefully.

In general:

- most babies and toddlers can follow a simple instruction with few words
- most two- and three-year-olds can follow an instruction with two actions
- four- and five-year-olds can usually follow three-step instructions.

Asking 'how' and 'why' questions

These questions are useful because they open up areas of discussion and also knowledge. Most children learn to use these questions from around three years onwards. When they start using 'why', it is normal for them to use it repeatedly as a way of keeping an adult's attention! But remember that it is important for you to answer 'why' and 'how' questions, whenever possible.

Using pronouns appropriately

Pronouns are words such as 'I', 'me', 'they' and 'it'. Most children start to use 'I' and 'me' instead of their own name at around three years, as well as other pronouns.

Education and Early Years T Level: Early Years Educator

Using joining words telling stories

By four years, most children are starting to create longer sentences by using words such as 'and', 'but' and 'because'.

Joining words are often referred to as 'conjunctions'. You can help children learn conjunctions by using them as you talk to children.

K1.5 The expected stages of language acquisition and how a range of biological and environmental factors can affect the speed of acquisition

This knowledge outcome is covered in Core Chapter 7 on page 124.

K1.6 How daily exposure to stories and rhymes supports development of communication and vocabulary

Babies and young children need regular opportunities to share books, and also learn and practise new rhymes. Most early years settings are encouraged to do this every day. It is thought that books, stories and rhymes are helpful in supporting early language, but also developing later literacy skills.

The table shows some specific ways in which they can help.

How stories and rhymes support language and literacy	Explanation
Introducing sounds	• Nursery rhymes, along with books that use rhyme, can help babies and young children hear and then use speech sounds as well as the patterns in words. • When children know a wide range of rhymes, it makes it easier for them to learn to read. • Children can also hear syllables in words such as 'Ch-ap-ter'.
Introducing words and expanding vocabulary	• Books, stories and rhymes can also help children learn new vocabulary. Children who may not live by the seaside, but hear a story about a family going to a beach, might pick up words such as 'shore', 'waves' and 'sand'. • Babies respond well to books, and if children have an early love of books, they are more likely to become keen readers.
Allowing opportunities for recall	Rhymes, books and stories can all help children to remember words and their sounds. We can help children do this by giving them opportunities to: • sing or say their favourite rhymes • talk about the plot of a book • join in where a book has a repeated phrase.

▲ Why might this child remember words from this book?

> ### Practice points
>
> #### Choosing nursery rhymes
> ▶ Make sure children experience different types of rhymes: counting, action, singing and finger rhymes.
> ▶ Learn rhymes before you use them. Look out for books or lists of rhymes on the internet.
> ▶ Speak clearly and slowly when introducing a rhyme.
> ▶ Repeat a new rhyme several times.
> ▶ Make sure that babies and children have the physical skills needed for action rhymes.

Performance Outcome 1: Support and Promote Children's Play, Development and Early Education

K1.7 The potential effects and long-term impact on a child's holistic development if atypical development is not recognised

We know that children develop at different rates, but we have also seen that there are patterns to children's development. Early years practitioners need to notice when children's development is not following the typical age–stage patterns.
- Sometimes, the child might just need a little more time and support.
- In other cases, the child might need to be seen by a professional, such as a speech and language therapist or a paediatrician.

Where there is a delay in noticing that a child might need additional support or a referral, there can be long-term consequences to their holistic or overall development. This is because, as we saw in Core Chapter 7, the different areas of development are interconnected.

Impact on different areas of development

Cognitive development

As we saw in Core Chapter 7, cognitive development includes memory, reasoning and also learning abstract concepts. Where children have delay in this area and are not getting sufficient support, they might:
- have difficulty in following instructions and participating in group tasks
- lack the ability to group and categorise objects. This is a skill that is required for reading and writing
- need more time to process information
- miss out on learning, if more time is not given.

Speech, language and communication development

We have seen that language development impacts on children's cognition, but also their ability to manage their feelings and express emotions appropriately. This means that children whose needs are not recognised may:
- find it hard to concentrate and listen
- show feelings and expressions of frustration.

Personal, social and emotional development

Children's personal, social and emotional development is linked to relationships and cooperation with others. Emotional development also affects how easily children can control strong emotions and persevere.

Children who have difficulties with this area of development which are not identified might:
- have lower levels of self-regulation (see page 74 in Core Chapter 4) and not be able to persevere or control their strong feelings. This can affect their ability to engage in educational activities
- show a lack of social cooperation and find it hard to make and maintain friendships or cope in group situations. This is required for engagement in play opportunities.

Physical development

We have seen that physical development is linked to children's ability to move, develop self-care skills, and also explore and use materials and objects. Children who have difficulties with physical development and who are not identified might:
- not be able to access educational opportunities, such as going on a nature walk, or keep up with other children if they have mobility needs
- have lower levels of confidence and self-image if their development is faster or slower than others. This is because they might start to compare themselves to other children.

Why practitioners must recognise atypical development as early as possible

The Early Years Foundation Stage (EYFS) requires practitioners to:
- identify children whose development might be concerning
- tell parents and take actions to support the child.

Education and Early Years T Level: Early Years Educator

The table shows three reasons why early identification of atypical development is important.

Why identify early?	Explanation
Support the best outcomes for children	We have seen how difficulties in one area of development can affect other areas of a child's development. Early identification makes a difference to children's overall development and so improves their outcomes.
Support a child's individual needs	The child can be supported and so be helped to make progress. This might happen through: • early intervention – a specific skill is focused on as part of a programme • tailored planning – with specific activities that will support skills and knowledge • **differentiation** – extra time, support or equipment is provided so that the child can join in an activity alongside other children.
Involve relevant external agencies	Sometimes, it will be important for the child to be seen by other professionals, when: • the child is not showing progress despite extra support in the setting and at home • the child's development is significantly delayed or there is a feature of their development that is unusual. An example would be a toddler who is still not walking at 19 months, or a 5-year-old who has frequent outbursts.

▲ Why might some children need additional support?

Performance Outcome 1: Support and Promote Children's Play, Development and Early Education

K1.8 The current statutory requirements for the EYFS and Key Stage 1 National Curriculum

In Core Chapter 2 we looked at the scope and purpose of the statutory framework for the EYFS. You may wish to read that chapter alongside this one.

The EYFS is divided into two main parts:
1. Learning and development requirements
2. Safeguarding and promoting welfare.

Learning and development requirements

The EYFS has four overarching principles, shown in the diagram. They should shape practice in early years settings.

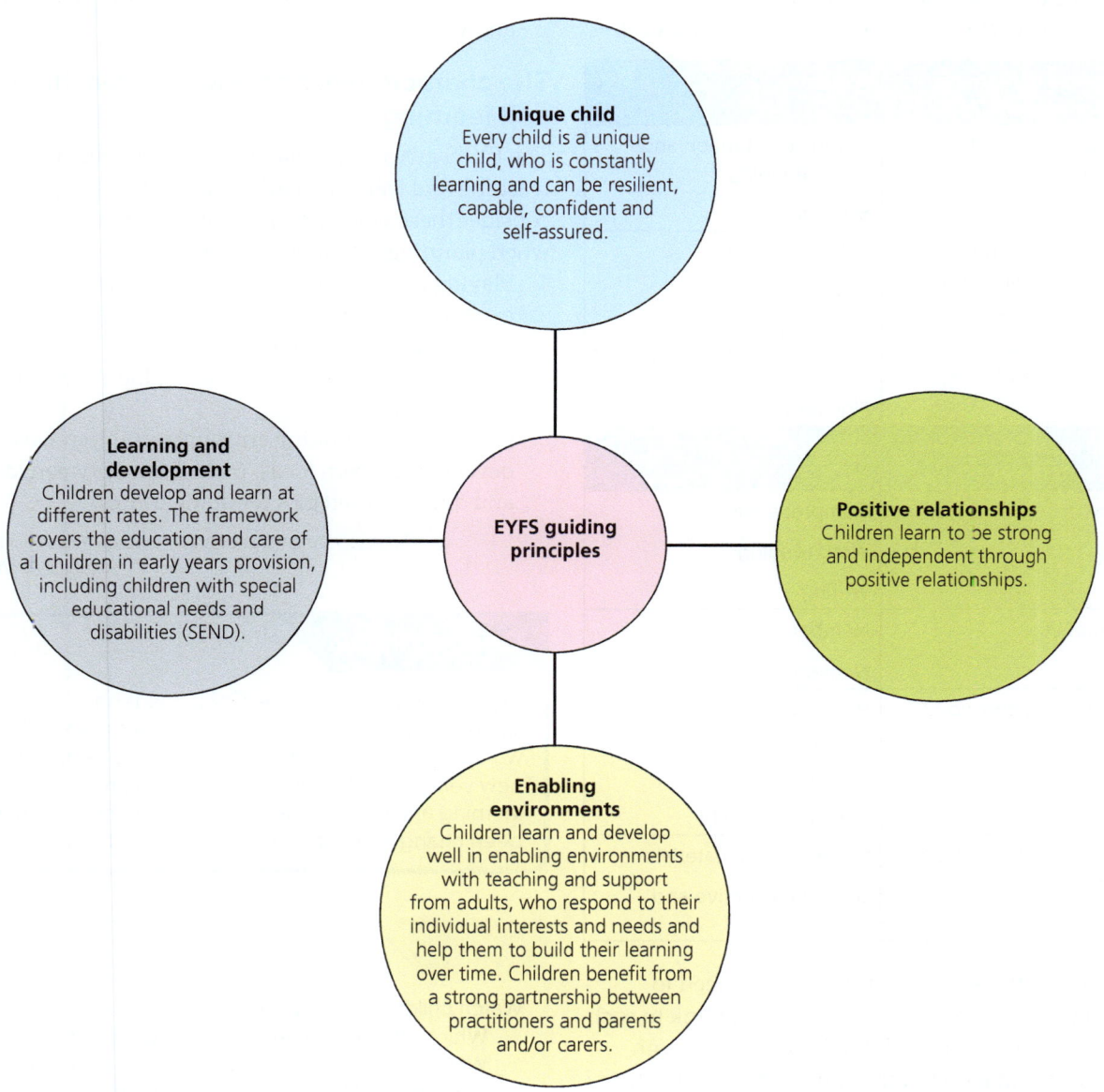

▲ The EYFS guiding principles

Source: Statutory framework for the Early Years Foundation Stage, July 2020

> **Reflect**
>
> The latest version of the framework gives more emphasis to the role of the adult in children's development than in previous versions. Read through the guiding principles: do you think the principles reflect this approach?

Areas of learning and developing

There are seven areas of learning and development – three prime and four specific. Within each area of learning and development, there are various aspects.

Prime areas of learning and development	Aspects
Communication and language	Listening, attention and understanding
	Speaking
Personal, social and emotional development	Self-regulation
	Managing self
	Building relationships
Physical development	Gross motor skills
	Fine motor skills

Specific areas of learning and development	Aspects
Literacy	Comprehension
	Word reading
	Writing
Mathematics	Number
	Numerical patterns
Understanding the world	Past and present
	People, culture and communities
	The natural world
Expressive arts and design	Creating with materials
	Being imaginative and expressive

Early years settings and reception classes need to provide opportunities and experiences that link to each of the areas of learning and development, although settings working with toddlers and babies are likely to focus mainly on the prime areas.

Remember that the areas of learning and development are much broader than in the Early Learning Goals (we will look at these later).

The difference between the prime and specific areas of learning

The seven areas of learning and development are divided into prime and specific as is shown in the table.

The prime areas are more important as they provide the foundations for future learning in the specific areas of learning. For example:
- Communication and language development: children who have not developed language will struggle to learn with literacy. This is because language is the starting point for learning to read and write.

The characteristics of effective teaching and learning

The EYFS gives three characteristics of effective teaching and learning. Early years settings should consider these when observing children, and also when planning activities and experiences:
1. Playing and exploring – children investigate and experience things, and 'have a go'.
2. Active learning – children concentrate and keep on trying if they encounter difficulties, and enjoy achievements.
3. Creating and thinking critically – children have and develop their own ideas, make links between ideas, and develop strategies for doing things.

Source: Statutory framework for the Early Years Foundation Stage, July 2020, DfE

> **Good to know**
>
> In previous versions of the EYFS, the term 'characteristics of effective learning' was used. As we mentioned above, there is more emphasis in the new version on the role of the adult in promoting learning and development. This is why this term has been changed to 'effective teaching and learning'.

> **Reflect**
>
> Watch children as they are playing.
> - Which children are immersed in their play?
> - Which of the three characteristics of effective teaching and learning can you observe?

Performance Outcome 1: Support and Promote Children's Play, Development and Early Education

The Early Learning Goals

The Early Learning Goals are the skills and knowledge that children are expected to have before they start in Year 1. There are Early Learning Goals for each of the seven areas of learning. The Early Learning Goals are assessed by teachers at the end of the reception year (see page 16).

Early Learning Goals are sometimes revised. From 2021 there are 17 Early Learning Goals.

Some key points of the goals at the time of writing are explained further in the box below.

> **Research**
>
> Look up the current Early Learning Goals and read through them.

▲ How might early dressing skills help children towards the Early Learning Goals for managing self?

Physical development

Gross motor skills
- Negotiate space and obstacles safely, with consideration for themselves and others.
- Demonstrate strength, balance and coordination when playing.
- Move energetically, such as running, jumping, dancing, hopping, skipping and climbing.

Fine motor skills
- Hold a pencil effectively in preparation for fluent writing – using the tripod grip in almost all cases.
- Use a range of small tools, including scissors, paint brushes and cutlery.
- Begin to show accuracy and care when drawing.

Literacy: Word reading

Children at the expected level of development will:
- say a sound for each letter in the alphabet and at least ten **digraphs**
- read words consistent with their phonic knowledge by **sound blending**
- read aloud simple sentences and books that are consistent with their phonic knowledge, including some common exception words.

Mathematics: Number

Children at the expected level of development will:
- have a deep understanding of number to 10, including the composition of each number
- **subitise** (recognise quantities without counting) up to 5
- automatically recall (without reference to rhymes, counting or other aids) **number bonds** up to 5 (including subtraction facts) and some number bonds to 10, including **double facts**.

> **Key terms**
>
> **Gross motor skills:** movements that require whole limb movement such as walking or throwing.
>
> **Fine motor skills:** movements that require hand and finger movements.
>
> **Digraph:** two sounds that when put together make a single sound, such as 'c-h' to make **'ch'** as in **ch**at.
>
> **Sound blending:** building words from individual sounds, e.g. s-t-o-p for stop.
>
> **Subitise:** recognise quantities without counting.
>
> **Number bond:** a pair of numbers that add to a total, e.g. 1+4=5.
>
> **Double facts:** two numbers that are the same added together, e.g. 2+2.

> **Good to know**
>
> To reduce the amount of assessment for teachers in the reception year, the Early Learning Goals do not cover everything that is outlined in the seven areas of learning.
>
> For example, in mathematics, children are expected to have developed some knowledge about shape, size and measures, but the Early Learning Goals only look at their number skills.

Assessment requirements

All early years settings monitor and assess children's ongoing progress. This information helps with planning and also meeting individual children's needs.

Parents have to be informed if there is any cause for concern about children's progress. In addition, additional checks take place.

The progress check at two years

Early years settings are required to assess children's progress in the prime areas when children turn two years old. If children go to more than one setting, practitioners from each setting need to liaise with each other.

The results of the EYFS progress check are explained to parents and if there are concerns, the child might need more support or a referral to other professionals.

This progress check is meant to link to the check that health visitors carry out:
- In some areas, health visitors and early years staff work together to provide a combined assessment.
- In other areas, the EYFS and the health visitor checks are carried out separately and some months apart.

> **Research**
>
> Find out about whether your work placement carries out a two-year-old progress check.
> - How is it carried out and shared with parents?
> - Is it integrated with the health visitor check?

EYFS Profile

In the final term of the reception year and before the end of June, children are assessed to see whether they have reached the Early Learning Goals set out in the EYFS.

This assessment is based on teachers' judgements. Teachers are expected to make the decisions based on:
- what children do during their play
- teacher-led activities such as mathematical games.

The results of the profile must be shared with the local authority and parents. A copy of the profile must also be passed to the Year 1 teacher.

Legal requirements for safeguarding and welfare

To keep children safe and healthy, all early years settings have to follow the legal requirements, and these are set out in the EYFS. The table shows the areas that are covered at the time of writing.

Area	Requirements
Child protection	Settings need to meet these requirements for child protection.
	The setting must provide a policy and training for all staff.
Suitable people	This looks at who can work with children.
	Early years providers must: • register staff with Ofsted • make sure that staff have been vetted by the Disclosure and Barring Service (DBS).
	Staff must be medically fit enough to carry out their role.
Staff qualifications, training, support and skills	This section outlines the requirements for settings to provide training for their staff, and also the minimum level of training for staff to work in different types of settings.
	It also includes the requirement for first aid qualifications.
Key person	This looks at the legal requirement for each child to be allocated a key person and the role of the key person.
Staff-to-child ratios	This looks at how many adults are required to work with different ages of children and in different situations (see also K4.11).

Performance Outcome 1: Support and Promote Children's Play, Development and Early Education

Area	Requirements
Health	This looks at the requirements to keep children healthy. It includes requirements for administering medicine and reporting diseases.
Managing behaviour	This sets out: • the requirement that no corporal punishment such as smacking is used by practitioners • a duty to report if corporal punishment is used by anyone else who cares for the child. The section also forbids the threat of corporal punishment or other punishment that could affect a child's wellbeing.
Safety and suitability of premises, environment and equipment	This section covers a wide range of requirements, including: • outings • the amount of space required • risk assessment • forbidding smoking.
Special educational needs and disability (SEND)	This sets out the requirements for arrangements for children who have SEND. It includes the requirement for: • settings to have a SENDCo • childminders to identify a SENDCo.

▲ Why must staff and regular volunteers hold a valid, up-to-date enhanced DBS certificate?

The statutory requirements for assessment

We looked at the structure and scope of the National Curriculum in Core Chapter 2. You will find it on page 18.

To check that children and young people are making expected progress, there are assessments at different stages. These are required by the Department for Education and the results of the assessments are given to parents. Most data from the assessments is made public.

Phonics screening

In Year 1, there is a phonics assessment for all pupils. This is to check that children have learned the sounds or phonics that they will need in order to read. (See also synthetic phonics on page 229.)

> **Research**
>
> You can find out more about the phonics test and look at a sample provided by the government: www.gov.uk/government/publications/phonics-screening-check-sample-materials-and-training-video

End of Key Stage 1 assessment and Teacher Assessment frameworks

At the end of Key Stage 1 (KS1), when children are in Year 2, statutory assessment tests (SATs) in the core subjects of English (reading and writing), maths and science take place. Some schools also choose to do tests in punctuation, spelling and grammar, but this is not compulsory.

Education and Early Years T Level: Early Years Educator

Teachers also assess children's progress using Teacher Assessment frameworks. Parents are given the results of teacher assessments in a report. For mathematics, reading and writing, and science, the following judgements are given:
- working towards the expected standard
- working at the expected standard
- working at greater depth within the expected standard.

Why practitioners promote diversity, equality and inclusion in early education

In Core Chapter 10, we looked at why it is essential to promote diversity, equality and inclusion. Look again at pages 166–7 and remind yourself that practitioners do this in order to:
- support and include every child to ensure equal opportunities and inclusion
- recognise diversity
- fulfil legal responsibilities under the Equality Act 2010 (for example, the provisions on reasonable adjustments).

▲ Why is it important that all parents feel that they and their family are valued?

The table below shows further reasons why it is important to promote diversity, equality and inclusion in early education.

Why promote diversity?	Explanation
Fulfil professional responsibilities	Early years practitioners have a professional responsibility to support all children, to ensure that they can achieve their potential. This means: • supporting children with SEND • valuing and encouraging children from all backgrounds.
Protect the reputation of the early years setting	The way that early years settings work with all children affects their reputation with parents and other professionals such as local authority advisors and health teams.
	This is important for an early years setting's survival if there are funding cuts. Settings that have a good reputation are more likely to be kept open and retain funding.
Develop trust and effective partnerships with parents and carers	In order to work effectively, it is important that parents and carers feel confident that settings are doing everything possible to support their child's learning and also their wellbeing. In Core Chapter 5 and Performance Outcome 5, we look at the importance of working with parents and carers.

K1.9 The links between the EYFS and KS1 National Curriculum

The transition from the EYFS reception class into KS1 is meant to be smooth. The idea is that children should have gained the skills and knowledge in reception that they will need to cope with more formal teaching.

Some children do find the transition difficult, however. Because of this, some schools begin Year 1 with opportunities for children to learn through play as well as take part in structured teacher-led activity.

How the areas of learning and development feed into KS1 subjects

The areas of the EYFS are meant to provide a foundation for subjects that are taught in KS1. We

Performance Outcome 1: Support and Promote Children's Play, Development and Early Education

can see the link between the areas of learning and development and those taught in KS1 in the following table.

EYFS Areas of learning and development	KS1 subjects
Personal, social and emotional development	Personal, social and health education
Communication and language	(throughout)
Physical development	PE
Literacy	English
Mathematics	Mathematics
Understanding the world	History
	Geography
	Science
	Religious education
Expressive arts and design	Art and design
	Music

Play-based learning in KS1

Many parents and teachers have found that the children find the transition into Year 1 difficult as a result of its more formal approach to teaching. There have been many different approaches over a number of years, to make this transition easier:
▶ At one time, it was recommended that KS1 should be more play-based, and at the very least at the start of the first term.
▶ Some schools have continued with this approach, but many have not.

The approach to play-based learning in KS1 is, therefore, quite variable.

Characteristics of learning

Approaches to expectations and the curriculum change quickly. The term 'characteristics of learning' which was a key feature of the EYFS in 2008 has now been changed to 'characteristics of effective teaching and learning'. While some schools consciously focus on these in Years 1 and 2, many do not.

Creative curriculum

The term 'creative curriculum' has been used to draw schools' attention to the importance of giving children wider experiences and making the curriculum seem more relevant.

At the time of writing, this term is not often used in schools now, but schools are increasingly taking this approach as a result of changes to the Ofsted inspection framework.

> **Research**
>
> When you are on placement in a school:
> ▶ Find out whether they continue play-based learning into KS1.
> ▶ Ask a Year 1 or 2 teacher about the characteristics of effective learning, and whether they influence their teaching practice.

Sharing information with KS1 teachers

To make sure that the transition to KS1 is smooth, most schools have systems in place to pass on information about children who are about to complete this transition.

We have seen already that there is a requirement for the EYFS Profile to be passed on. Most schools also share information about a child's:
▶ strengths and weaknesses
▶ emotional or learning needs
▶ progress in literacy and mathematics.

It is also good practice for children to spend some time with their new class teacher, so that they can build a relationship before they start in the class.

K1.10 The purpose of a range of pedagogical strategies to support children's development of early literacy

There are many ways in which early years settings and reception classes can support children's early literacy.

Ways to support literacy	How to do this in practice
Role play	Role play can encourage early literacy in both early years settings and reception classes. You could: • draw children's attention to print using props such as menu cards and diaries • encourage children to try some early writing, using props such as notepads and pens, chalk boards or white boards. Young children might just make marks and 'pretend' to write, but reception-aged children can practise the writing skills that they have been taught without feeling under pressure.
Quiet areas with books	All age groups within early years need to create areas where children can share and use books. • These areas can be inside and outside. • Children can look again at books that they have shared with adults, while older children can pick out books and have a go at reading them independently. • Children of all ages including babies also need time to share books with adults.
Writing resources	All age groups need opportunities to try out early writing. • Babies and toddlers: this might be a sensory activity where they can smear and experiment with their hands. • Children from around three years: a mixture of sensory activities, such as using soapy water with brushes, or using more traditional materials such as whiteboards and markers, chalks, pencils and paper. • Pre-school children are likely to recognise their name and experiment with some letter shapes. • Children in the reception class might try to link sounds with letter shapes as they learn to read.
Songs and nursery rhymes	Songs and nursery rhymes are important to support both language and literacy. • It is good practice for adults to plan songs and rhymes with all ages of children in early years. • In the reception class, songs and nursery rhymes can help reinforce the letter sounds that are being taught; e.g. '5 little peas in a pea pod pressed' to draw children's attention to the 'p' sound.
Story writing	Pre-school children and reception-aged children will probably not be able to write their own story, but they can be involved in creating a story if you: • help them to put their story in sequence • write it down for them. When adults write for children, this is known as 'scribing.'
Guided reading	This is a strategy used in schools to support children's reading: • Children are put into small groups. • With an adult, they explore a book or a text. For guided reading to work well, children's reading levels have to be similar. Most guided reading activities are planned for around half an hour.
Developing a love of books at home	Children need to develop a love of books in the setting but also at home. Research shows that children who share books with their family are more likely to enjoy reading and have higher literacy skills. Many settings provide books for parents to take home and encourage parents to share books at bedtime.

Performance Outcome 1: Support and Promote Children's Play, Development and Early Education

> **Research**
>
> If you are in a school, ask if you can watch a guided reading session.
> - Observe how the session is structured.
> - Watch children's reactions during the session.

> **Research**
>
> Find out about these other approaches to teaching reading:
> - 'Look say' or whole word
> - Analytical phonics.

> **Good to know**
>
> Reading journals work well with parents who know how to help their child's reading and are confident to write in the journal. It can be harder for parents who have their own difficulties with reading and writing, or who do not have English as a fluent language.

The purpose of systematic synthetic phonics to support the teaching of reading

There are many strategies to teach children how to read. Currently, all schools in England are encouraged to use an approach known as **synthetic phonics**.

- This is a letter-sound approach. It is highly structured, which is why the term 'systematic' is often used.
- Most programmes begin with children learning the following letters and their corresponding sounds: S-A-T-P-I-N. Using these letter sounds, children can begin to write and read simple words.
- Children are encouraged to break words down into the smallest units of sound. For example, 'brown' will be broken down into 'b-r-ow-n' before building it up again.
- This approach to teaching reading is thought to be helpful for children who find it difficult to read and spell.

K1.11 The purpose of a range of strategies to support children's development of early writing skills

Early writing is sometimes referred to as mark making. This is because very young children begin the process of writing by scribbling or making marks with a variety of resources.

There are many ways in which early years settings and reception classes support children with their writing.

Providing equipment and opportunities to encourage early mark making

To encourage enjoyment of mark making and early writing, early years settings provide a wide range of opportunities for children, including sensory materials that we look at later on. The table below shows some examples of equipment and opportunities that are common in early years settings.

Activities and equipment to develop fine motor skills

In order to hold a pencil effectively, a child needs to develop a dynamic tripod grasp. The drawings on the next page show how children usually develop this grasp.

Equipment for mark making	Examples and how to use them
Commercial resources	You could buy some resources for young children, such as magnetic drawing boards and water doodling mats.
Real-life props	Many settings create a mark making or early writing table. You could use a range of real-life resources such as: envelopes, markers, clipboards, stickers and diaries.
Role play	Role play can often incorporate opportunities for writing. It is particularly useful for children over three years. Children can use real props as part of their play.
Blackboards, whiteboards and painting areas	Young children enjoy making large-scale movements when they make marks.

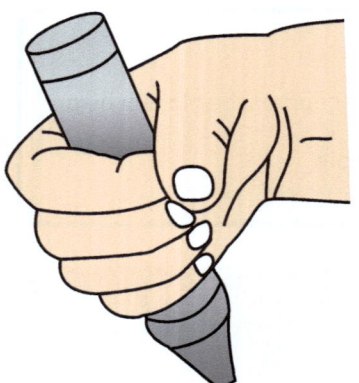 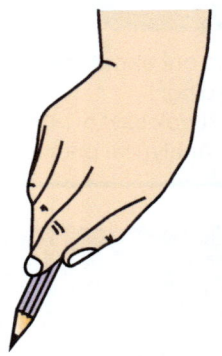  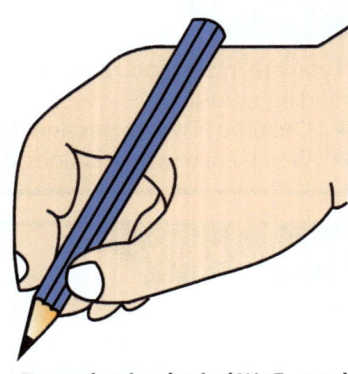

Palmar grip (1–1½ years)   Digital grip (2–3 years)   Static tripod grip (3½–4 years)   Dynamic tripod grip (4½–5 years)

▲ Observe a child on your work placement. How are they holding their pencil?

Children also need to be able to control the pencil to make the small movements involved in writing. These are **fine motor skills**. In early years settings, activities and equipment are put out to encourage children to develop the fine motor movements needed. Here are some examples of activities and equipment that will encourage fine motor movements:
- picking out sequins from a bowl of chickpeas
- threading beads
- lacing cards
- peeling bananas, satsumas
- filling bottles in the water or sand tray using spoons
- using tongs to move chickpeas from one bowl to another.

Involving parents/carers in approaches to support early writing skills

Parents have an important role in supporting children's early writing. Early years settings can:
- plan information for parents
- explain the stages of how children learn to write
- suggest practical ways in which parents might support writing skills.

This is important, because many parents have unrealistic expectations of their pre-school children. They might not realise that the 'scribbles' that children are making are actually helping them to learn some of the skills of writing.

Research also shows that children who see their parents write at home are more likely to be interested in trying to write. It is particularly important for boys to see their fathers or close male relations writing.

Modelling and demonstrating writing

One of the key strategies that is used to motivate young children to write is for adults to role-model writing.
- By jotting down a note or writing a child's name next to something that they have made, children can become interested in writing.
- Older children can also benefit if you explain how they are forming letter shapes, or what they are about to write.
- When writing is being modelled, it is useful for children to repeat what they have just seen.

This links to the social cognitive theory that we looked at in Core Chapter 7.

Incorporating a range of media

In the early stages of early writing, the focus is to encourage young children to have a go at making marks. Sensory materials are often provided from babies onwards.

Here are some examples of materials that early years settings may put out for children to make marks using their hands or with objects:
- coloured water
- gloop – cornflour and water
- damp sand
- shaving foam
- chalks
- finger paints
- sponge painting.

Planning opportunities for shared writing

Shared writing is a process where children are helped by adults to write.

Performance Outcome 1: Support and Promote Children's Play, Development and Early Education

- You can help children to think about what they would like to say, and then support them in their writing.
- For children who are not reading, you might scribe for them.
- For children who are just starting to read and write, you might help them to spell certain words, or remind them about how to produce letter shapes.

Shared writing can help children's confidence while they learn writing skills.

Valuing children's personal/spontaneous attempts at early writing

To encourage children to write, you have to be very positive when they try to do it. If you are positive, children are more likely to enjoy writing and so keep practising. This helps them to make progress and develop some of the skills that will be needed.

In the early stages of writing, when children are making marks, it might not be clear what they have written – but it is still important to value it.

> **Practice points**
>
> **Encouraging early writing**
> - Make sure that the resources are interesting for children.
> - Look out for real-life props such as diaries, notepads and envelopes.
> - Put out letter shapes, words and name cards alongside writing resources.
> - Show interest in what children are doing, but do not criticise or correct.
> - Ask children if they have enjoyed their writing.

K1.12 How daily routines, games and stories can be used to support children's development, learning and mathematical understanding

There are many mathematical concepts that children need to develop.

The process of developing these concepts begins early in life. It is thought that humans are born with the ability to think mathematically. Research has shown that babies and toddlers notice if two objects are shown to them and then one is taken away.

It is now recognised that adults can play an important role in helping young children develop mathematical understanding. Your role is to:
- draw children's attention to mathematical concepts
- help to develop mathematical language such as 'bigger, matching and less'.

Daily routines

Daily routines such as getting dressed, mealtimes and washing hands can be a good way for children to learn some mathematical skills and language:
- During routines, children can learn about time as they start to recognise when events take place.
- They can also learn about sequencing, as most routines follow a certain pattern or order.
- Routines such as putting on shoes involve matching.
- Collecting the plates after meal time involves grouping.
- Routines can also help children learn about prediction, as they work out what comes next.

Specific opportunities for counting and size and shape can also take place. The table shows some of the ways in which daily routines can support early mathematics.

Routine	Examples of mathematical opportunities
Getting dressed	Counting the buttons
	Talking about the position of zips – up, down or halfway
	Finding front and back
Putting on/removing shoes	Matching shoes
	Counting up and down as they go on or off, one by one
	Talk about different sizes of shoes
Snack and mealtimes	Counting out plates and beakers
	One-to-one correspondence – one plate for each child, one cup for each child
	Talk about quantities – more, less, one more, a lot, a little
	Cutting circular foods to talk about fractions – half, quarter
	Learning about volume if children pour their own drinks
Washing hands	Comparing adult's and child's size of hands
	Counting fingers

Games

This table gives examples of games that can help young children learn some mathematical concepts.

Game	Examples of mathematical opportunities
Number and counting	Roll-a-dice games with sensory materials or board games with children over four years
	Beetle drive – or games where children have to collect items according to the number on the dice
	What's the time, Mr Wolf?
	Hopscotch
Shape, size and pattern	Picture lotto using shapes
	Guessing games – 'Guess what object I am looking for … It's large, it's square and it's yellow!'
	Short straws game in the sand tray – find the longest straw
Positional language	Hunt the thimble, using clues with positional language
	Treasure hunts using clues with positional language such as 'on top of' or 'next to'
Weight, volume and capacity	Choose a bottle or a bucket. Which one will contain the most water?
Matching and sorting	Snap – to help children with matching
	Dominos
	Picture lotto
	Magnetic fishing game with a card for children to match their catch against

Practice points

Making up games
- Simple games work best.
- Choose only one concept to focus on, such as numbers or size.
- Match the game to the children's current level of mathematics.
- Try using sensory materials such as sand or dough. For example, roll the dice to tell you how many spoonfuls of sand to put into your beaker.
- Be ready to stop if children are starting to look bored or frustrated.

Stories and rhymes

We know that stories and rhymes can support children's language and early literacy development, but they can also support children's early mathematics.
- Some rhymes such as 'Five Little Ducks went swimming one day' help with counting, numerical order and subtraction.
- There are also many stories that look at counting and mathematical concepts including size, e.g. Goldilocks and the Three Bears, as well as spatial awareness and capacity.

Research

Visit your local library or look at the children's books in your work placement.

Find three books that you could use to help children aged between three and five years to learn some mathematical language or concepts.

K1.13 The purpose of a range of strategies to promote mathematical thinking and approaches that encourage early reasoning

Adults have an important role in developing children's early mathematics. We have already seen the importance of daily routines, games, stories and rhymes. Here we look at some other important strategies.

Using real world examples and incidental learning

You can often draw children's attention to mathematical concepts and thinking spontaneously. You might notice that:
- a button has fallen off a coat
- a child has odd socks.

Through every session, there will be many opportunities to draw children's attention to changes in quantity, shape, size or patterns. Children can make significant progress in this way.

Using practical everyday tasks to reinforce concepts

We have seen that daily routines can be used to support mathematical concepts. In the same way,

Performance Outcome 1: Support and Promote Children's Play, Development and Early Education

some everyday tasks such as tidying up can help to reinforce concepts such as size, shape and number. We can:

- match items
- count them as they are put away
- talk about the size of items.

Young children need a lot of repetition to learn skills such as counting, which is why everyday tasks and routines support their learning.

Having a language-rich environment that includes mathematical vocabulary

Language is very important in the development of mathematics. Children need adults to model mathematical vocabulary such as:

- the names of shapes
- words to describe size such as 'large', 'medium' and 'small'
- terms such as 'divide', 'share', 'equal' and 'subtract'.

A language-rich environment means that you look for opportunities to develop mathematical vocabulary during children's play and also during activities.

Involving parents and carers in mathematical learning

When parents are able to draw children's attention to mathematical concepts and language at home, children make significant progress. Many early years settings provide information for parents about how they can help at home.

Research has shown that meaningful practical activities – such as counting steps or counting out money – are more helpful than parents using worksheets to teach their children.

Providing appropriate resources and equipment

The resources and equipment that we put out and also how we put them out can affect the opportunities for mathematics. The table below shows an example of a concept, a resource that could be used and also how it might be put out.

Using a scaffolded approach to the use of mathematical learning

As well as drawing children's attention to mathematical concepts, children also need adults to guide them in their thinking.

In Core Chapter 2, we looked at Jerome Bruner's and Lev Vygotsky's approach to learning. We saw that through careful observation, modelling and questioning, children's thinking can be developed further.

For mathematical concepts, this means identifying children's current level of mathematical knowledge and building on this.

Concept	Resource/equipment	Ideas for setting out
Size	Small, medium and large bottles for the sand/water tray	The three different-sized bottles are put in a line.
Number	Several farm animals, with some of the same animal	Match farm animals in groups of three.
Volume	Measuring jugs, water and bottles	Bottles are marked with lines – half full, quarter full. Can children fill them to the line?
Shape	A jigsaw	Jigsaw is nearly completed, but three spaces are left to complete. The three pieces are placed apart.
Pattern	Lacing threads and beads	A completed lace with beads of alternative colours.

Case study

Barnaby is three and a half years old. He enjoys counting. He can accurately count to three but he cannot yet look at three objects and know that there are three.

His key person has spoken to his parents, and together they have decided to point out when there are three things. His key person is grouping objects that Barnaby might play with in threes. She has also organised a treasure hunt where toy cars will either be grouped in threes or twos. Cars are Barnaby's favourite resource. As Barnaby finds the groups of cars, his key person asks him to guess whether there are three or two cars.

- Why is it important that Barnaby's stage of development was recognised?
- Explain why using cars for an activity may help Barnaby's learning.
- Why is it important for parents to be involved in Barnaby's mathematical learning?

K1.14 How number enables children to develop mathematical skills

The latest approach to supporting children's mathematical development is to focus on number. Having a strong sense of number can make a difference to children's later ability to measure, weigh and to carry out other tasks. Children will need many everyday opportunities to do some counting that is meaningful for them, e.g. counting out spoonfuls of yoghurt, counting out as they take cars from a box to play with. They will also need adults to draw their attention to number in activities such as tidying away or cooking. Having a strong sense of the value of numbers, i.e. three bricks is one fewer than four bricks, gained through practical experience means that later on children are more likely to cope with numbers when presented abstractly.

The aim is that children towards the end of their reception year are:
- counting confidently
- developing a deep understanding of the numbers up to 10
- verbally counting beyond 20, recognising the pattern of the counting system
- recognising relationships and patterns between numbers.

> **Research**
>
> Find out more about the early skills in mathematical development by visiting the Early Childhood Maths group and looking at their guide to building firm foundations in mathematics: https://earlymaths.org/building-firm-foundations-in-mathematics/

Ages and stages of mathematical development

How quickly young children develop numeracy and the concepts associated with it is variable. This is because it depends on the following:
- children's cognitive and language development
- how frequently adults draw children's attention to number as they play and in everyday activities in meaningful and enjoyable ways
- the opportunities children have to count and explore quantities
- how interested and motivated children are in number and quantities.

In addition, children do not always pick up skills and concepts in a neat order. This means that a child might be able to point to the numeral 8, but not be able to count eight objects accurately.

Reliable age/stage milestones for young children's development aged from birth to four years in mathematics are, therefore, hard to find. A good source of information about the broad sequences of mathematical development that are linked to the EYFS can be found in *Development Matters*.

For children at the end of reception, the Department for Education has also set Early Learning Goals for number. These are considered to be very stretching, especially for children born in the summer months.

K1.15 Stages of play and types of play

One of the interesting things about working with children is watching the way that they play. Play is developmentally significant for young children, but it is also a source of pleasure and enjoyment.

One of the interesting features of all types of play is the way that it can develop children's sense of self-agency. Self-agency is an important element in the construction of self-concept. It is sometimes called self-efficacy. By choosing what and how to play, babies and children can have strong feelings of empowerment and control. This is important in the development of independence, perseverance and confidence.

It is now recognised that play is essential for children's overall wellbeing, and that children actually have a right to play. Play is a key way in which early years settings will meet their learning and development requirements in the EYFS. We will look at self-concept in more detail in Performance Outcome 2 (page 260).

Stage of play

Some stages of play have been observed in different ages of children.

The typical pattern is that play becomes increasingly social and more organised as children develop. Remember that, although older children can play cooperatively, there may be times when they choose to play alongside another child or alone.

Performance Outcome 1: Support and Promote Children's Play, Development and Early Education

Mildred Parten conducted the original study that looked at children's social stages of play. She observed children aged between two and five years engaged in free play (they were free to play with whatever or whoever they chose).

When observing children's play, you might also find that there are differences to the ages and stages given. This is because the stage of play also depends on their:
- experiences with other children
- level of language
- emotional and social development.

For the purpose of this qualification, the following stages of play along with ages and features are given.

Age	Stage of play	Examples
0–12 months	Unoccupied play	Random movements and gestures
		Remaining in one place
		Foundation for future play as babies learn to enjoy exploration and discovery
0–2 years	Solitary play	Playing alone
		Entertaining themselves during play
		Exploring the environment
18 months to 2.5 years	Onlooker play	Interested in other children's play
		Observing other children in play
		Playing closely to other children but not joining in
2–3 years	Parallel play	Choosing similar toys or activities to other children
		Playing alongside other children
		Watching and listening to other children's play
3–4 years	Associative play	Playing with other children in pairs or groups
		Choosing the same toys or activities as other children
		Beginning to engage with others
4–5 years	Cooperative play	Playing with other children in groups
		Defining rules of play
		Beginning to work together and have shared goals

Types of play

What children play with can shape their development.

To help with planning, play is put into different types. Each type of play has its own benefits. The spider diagram shows the types of play that are usually provided in most early years settings.

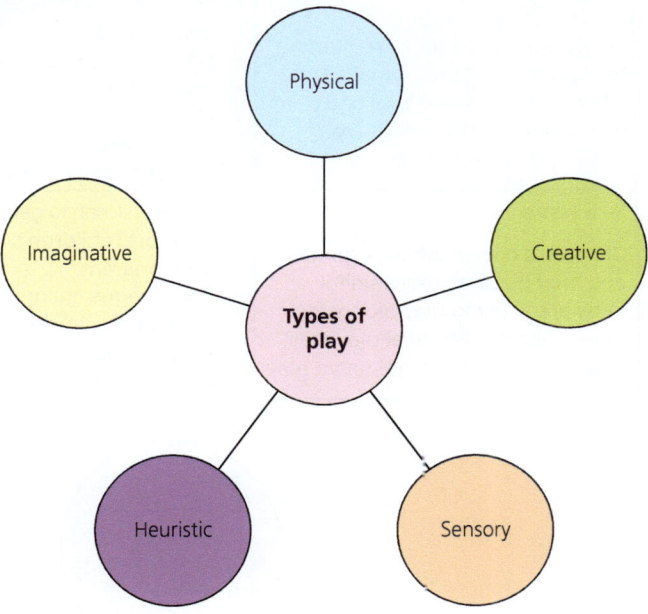

▲ Types of play

How different types of play promote children's development

Each type of play can benefit children in different ways. In this section we look at:
- the different play types
- their benefits
- how they link to the areas of learning and development in the EYFS.

Education and Early Years T Level: Early Years Educator

Physical play

This is play that involves large movements such as climbing, balancing and running. Physical play needs to be provided indoors as well as outdoors. This means early years settings might organise games and activities such as dancing indoors.

Creative play

Creative play covers many different activities, as shown in the spider diagram.

Sometimes, children combine creative play with imaginative play. They might make items to go into the home corner, or pretend to be pirates after 'building' a boat.

Age and stage of development	How it supports development	Links to EYFS areas of learning and development
0–1 year In their first year, babies are learning to become mobile and coordinate their movements	• Strengthens muscles • Motivates babies to move • Encourages balancing skills • Helps with hand–eye coordination • Builds a sense of agency and independence	• Physical development • Personal, social and emotional development • Mathematics
1–3 years In this period toddlers are starting to explore what they can do and what they can make toys and resources do. Their skills are developing quickly	• Helps toddlers become independent and grow in confidence • Encourages social skills • Supports early decision making • Develops strength, stamina and coordination • Helps toddlers to learn about height, surfaces and also problem solving	• Physical development • Personal, social and emotional development • Mathematics
3–5 years Children's coordination is good and they become more skilful. They are likely to play alongside other children. Physical play may be combined with imaginative play	• Helps children to gain confidence and independence • Supports children's understanding of the environment • Encourages children to learn to manage risks and to make decisions • Helps children to build muscle strength, coordination and also stamina	• Physical development • Personal, social and emotional development • Understanding the world • Mathematics

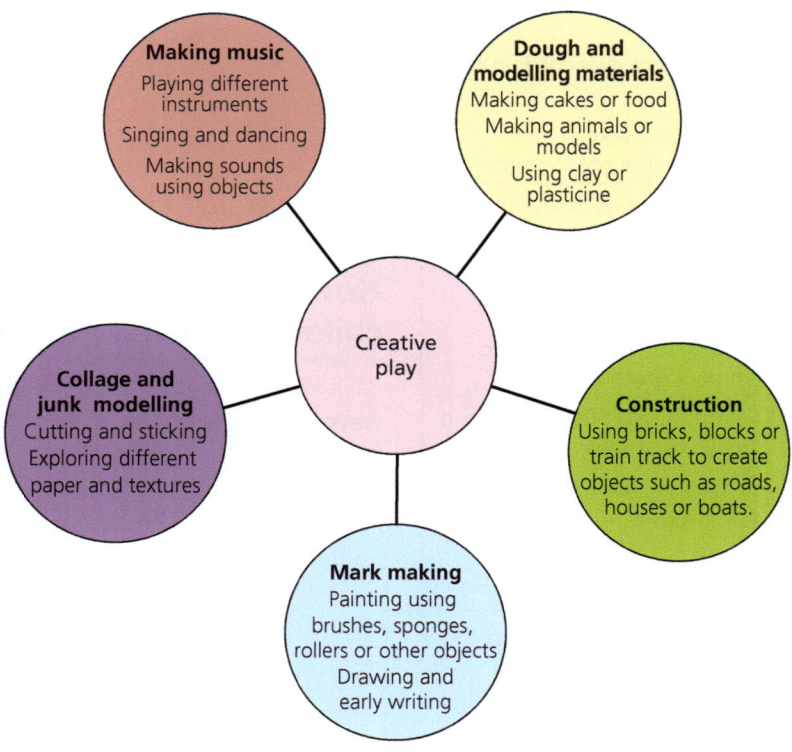

▲ Creative play

Performance Outcome 1: Support and Promote Children's Play, Development and Early Education

Development of creative play

Babies use rattles and other toys to explore, but they might not necessarily have a goal in mind. Creative play is, therefore, seen and planned for with children aged over two years.

As children develop, they might sometimes involve other children in their ideas, although some children will want to be independent.

Areas of development	Links to EYFS
Physical development Children use hand–eye coordination, manipulate objects and build strength in their hands.	**Physical development** Children use tools such as brushes, scissors and pencils.
Cognitive development Children learn about: • cause and effect • textures and materials • how to use objects to represent their thoughts. Children's imagination is promoted. As problem solving is often needed, children's memory and concentration are also supported.	**Personal, social and emotional development** Children feel competent and develop confidence. Children learn to persevere and cope with setbacks.
Language development Children use language to collaborate with other children. They might learn specific vocabulary as they use materials.	**Communication and language** Children might talk with other children or explain to adults what they are trying to do. They might learn specific words as they use materials.
Emotional development Children have to cope with setbacks and so learn to regulate their impulses and emotions. Children gain enjoyment, feel pride and so become more confident. Creative play helps children learn to feel independent and make choices.	**Literacy** When mark making or painting, children might try to form letters or create words as part of their play.
Social development Some creative play might involve working with other children. Children will learn to: • negotiate • take turns • work with others.	**Mathematics** During creative play, children have opportunities to: • use shapes and experience the concept of size • do some practical measuring • notice and use patterns. **Expressive arts and design** Children learn to use materials to model and to create things that reflect their thinking.

Imaginative play

This type of play encourages children to pretend in some way.

Imaginative play can be split into two broad areas:
1. Role play
2. Small world play.

Role play

Role play includes:
▶ dressing up
▶ home corner
▶ any play where children are actively pretending.

This might be a child putting on a cape to become superwoman, or going into the home corner and pretending to be a parent putting a baby to bed.

> **Reflect**
>
> Look at how children use role play in your work placement.
>
> What areas and props are available for them?

Small world play

Small world play includes:
- farm animals
- cuddly toys
- play people
- dinosaurs.

During small world play, children take a directing role. They pretend that these toys have come to life. They might give some toys a speaking part, or they might simply move them around.

> **Reflect**
>
> Make a list of small world resources in your setting.
>
> Which age group seems to use them most?

▲ What type of play is being shown here?

How imaginative play develops

Imaginative play begins quite early.
- Toddlers will often show some imaginative play in short bursts. They might hug a teddy or pretend to give a cuddly toy something to eat.
- From around the age of two and a half years, many children increasingly use imaginative play.
- As language develops, children often cooperate to develop very complex imaginative play. They might work out in advance what is going to happen, or who will have which part.

Benefits of imaginative play

Imaginative play can provide a wide range of developmental benefits for children, especially when children combine it with physical play.

Area of development	Benefits of imaginative play
Physical	Imaginative play often involves fine motor movement: children might dress themselves or move toys, props and resources.
	Some role play might also involve using gross motor movements: children might run away, hide or use wheeled toys as part of role play.
Cognitive	Imaginative play helps children to understand and make connections between their own experiences and the props or toys that they are using. Some elements of imaginative play might also involve problem solving.
Language	Imaginative play usually involves children talking or expressing themselves. They might put on voices to make sounds or to be characters.
	Older children might use language to negotiate with other children and talk to them during play.
Emotional	Imaginative play is enjoyable for children. They can: • express emotions • try being someone else • take on powerful roles • be in charge.
Social	Children often play together during imaginative play, especially from around 3 years. During imaginative play, children are learning to understand what it might feel like to be someone or something else, and so develop empathy and nurturing skills.

Performance Outcome 1: Support and Promote Children's Play, Development and Early Education

Links to the EYFS areas of learning and development

Imaginative play can be used to support all of the areas of the EYFS. The spider diagram below shows the links to the EYFS at the time of writing.

Sensory play

Sensory play is a term used to describe activities that stimulate children's senses, particularly touch and sight. It includes playing with:
- water
- mirrors and lighting
- sand, dough and mud.

Sensory play is used with all ages of children, including babies. Some sensory play involving light and sound might also come from toys and resources that involve technology, such as a voice-activated light.

> **Reflect**
>
> Why is it important for children's later outcomes that early years practitioners and teachers focus on children's self-regulation skills?

Benefits of sensory play

There are many benefits of sensory play. Some benefits will depend on how physically active children are during the play. The table on page 240 shows how sensory play links to the areas of development as well as the EYFS.

▲ Imaginative play and EYFS areas of learning and development

Education and Early Years T Level: Early Years Educator

Areas of development	Links to EYFS
Physical development Children might use fine motor skills to manipulate materials by moulding and scooping dough and sand. They might also develop coordination, e.g. making a light come on by jumping.	**Physical development** Children might use tools such as scoops in materials such as mud, sand and water.
Cognitive development Sensory materials encourage children to learn through cause and effect. Sensory materials stimulate babies' and children's senses. Children also explore and investigate sound, light and textures.	**Personal, social and emotional development** Sensory activities can be very enjoyable for babies and young children. Sensory activities can help children to release emotions such as anger or sadness.
Language development Children might talk or ask questions because they find sensory activities interesting. They might develop some specific vocabulary such as 'sticky' or 'runny'.	**Communication and language** Children might chat to each other as they use sensory play. Sensory activities may encourage conversation as it is a relaxing activity.
Emotional development Children might gain enjoyment and pleasure. They might also express strong emotions or find sensory activity comforting. Some children might use sensory activities as a way of having some control, e.g. splashing water or squeezing dough.	**Literacy** Some children might use gloop, water and sand to make marks. This supports early writing.
Social development Babies and children often play together or in parallel during sensory play. They might share materials and resources.	**Mathematical development** Children might use sensory activities to measure and to look at volume, e.g. filling up different-sized cups of water. **Expressive arts and design** Children will explore materials and media during creative play. This is one of the aspects within expressive arts and design.

> **Good to know**
>
> **Gloop**
>
> Gloop is a mixture of cornflour and water. When mixed together, it creates a runny mixture which can also feel solid when pressed hard. It is normally white in colour, but food colouring can be added.

Heuristic play/Discovery play

Heuristic or discovery play is about play that allows babies and children to explore objects. There are three broad types of discovery play that are linked to different ages of children:
1. treasure basket play
2. heuristic play
3. loose part play.

Treasure basket play

This type of play is for babies. The idea is that items made of only natural materials are put in a basket. Items might include:
- a wooden nail brush
- a leather purse
- a large shell.

No toys are put out. The babies reach into the basket and can touch and hold the objects. They can also put them in their mouths as this is a key way in which babies explore.

Heuristic play

While the term 'heuristic play' is used as an overall type of play for this qualification, the term is often used to describe a certain way of playing with older babies and toddlers:

Performance Outcome 1: Support and Promote Children's Play, Development and Early Education

- Heuristic play involves putting out a range of different containers alongside smaller items.
- No toys are put out, although items can be made of plastic.
- Items might include cardboard tubes, kitchen roll holders, shells, bottles, biscuit tins, wooden curtain rings, bracelets and corks.
- Children spend time seeing what they can do with the items. They might post items, move things from place to place or build with them.

Loose part play

Loose part play can be for any age, although usually it is used for children aged over three years.

- It involves putting out everyday items or unusual items in small groups for children to find.
- Loose part play often takes place outdoors.
- Children might come across a strip of fabric, some empty decorating pots and a suitcase.
- The children often explore these items before incorporating them into their play.

Benefits of discovery play

There are many benefits of heuristic play at all ages. The table shows how they link to the areas of development as well as the EYFS.

Areas of development	Links to the EYFS
Physical development Children use fine motor skills to manipulate the objects. Mobile children will also move the objects and incorporate them into other play. Movements during heuristic play support balance and coordination of motor skills.	**Physical development** Children use fine motor skills to manipulate the objects. Mobile children will also move the objects and incorporate them into other play.
Cognitive development The different type of materials stimulate babies' and children's senses. Babies, for example, will mouth objects. Children learn about the differences between objects such as colour and shape. Older children might also use the objects as symbols, e.g. using a strip of fabric to pretend it is a flying carpet. By manipulating objects, children develop an understanding of size and weight.	**Personal, social and emotional development** Children concentrate and persevere for long periods with this type of play. Older children might also cooperate with other children.
Language development Children talk or ask questions about what they have found. They might also learn specific vocabulary relating to the items.	**Communication and language** Children talk or ask questions about what they have found. They might also learn specific vocabulary relating to the items.
Emotional development Children find this activity enjoyable. It can give them confidence. Children are also proud of what they can make objects do.	**Mathematics** Children learn about shape, size and also volume. They may also count some items, e.g. dropping corks into a bottle.
Social development Older children learn to cooperate and share when they use loose part play. They might also share ideas and work together to lift or move large items.	**Understanding the world** Some children might also make connections between everyday items and their own lives. **Expressive arts and design** Some children might try to build or use the objects to create something. This links closely to creative play.

Education and Early Years T Level: Early Years Educator

A range of activities associated with different types of play in promoting children's development and sense of agency

We have seen that there are developmental benefits with each type of play. This means that we can plan activities that link to each of the play types.

When adults plan and carry out activities with children, these are known as **adult-led play**. We will look at this further on page 249.

Physical play

The role of adults is to make sure that there is sufficient challenge in children's physical play. Adults may also plan specific activities to support children's interests and needs based on individual observations and assessments. Here are some examples of activities that adults might set up.

Activity	How to support children's interests and needs during play
Hopscotch	This is a game for children aged 4 and over. It can help children with: • hopping and balance skills • recognising numerals.
Ball games	Babies and children love playing with balls. • You can simply roll a ball over to a baby who is mobile. • For toddlers and older children, you can encourage throwing and catching activities, such as aiming at some bottles filled with water positioned as skittles, and seeing how many can be knocked down.
Bean bags and hoops	Throwing bean bags onto hoops on the floor can support children's throwing skills. You could also put numbers on different hoops and ask children to throw a bean bag into the highest number.
Bead threading	Bead threading, such as making pasta necklaces or threading large wooden beads, can boost children's: • fine motor skills • ability to notice and make patterns. Typically, these activities work best for children from two years with support.
Large and small block play	Playing with blocks can help children's fine and gross motor skills. To build using blocks, children need hand–eye coordination. Playing with blocks can begin from around 8 months as babies like knocking down towers that adults have built.

Creative play

We have seen that creative play is an umbrella term for a wide range of activities and resources. Here are some examples of activities that you might plan for different ages of children. While you plan, remember that it is the children who are meant to be showing their creativity – not you!

> **Research**
>
> Find out how to play hopscotch if you are not familiar with it. You could use this website to help you: www.helpmykidlearn.ie/activities/5-7/detail/hopscotch

Activity	How to support children's interests and needs during play
Sewing	Many children are interested in simple sewing, but they might need you to support them. • The starting point for children at around 3 years might be to use lacing cards. • Older children can sew using cloth that has pre-punched holes, or binca, a type of fabric designed for easy stitching as it contains holes.
Collage	Collage means 'to stick'. • You might plan an activity for a group or an individual child where they create patterns, pictures or explore collage by sticking items on a sheet together. • It is interesting for children to have a wide range of materials to choose from. • Collage works well with children from around 2 years old, although toddlers usually want to touch rather than stick different items such as stickers, fabric and lace. • When preparing collage activities, you should make sure that there are no items that may be a choking hazard.

Performance Outcome 1: Support and Promote Children's Play, Development and Early Education

Activity	How to support children's interests and needs during play
Painting and drawing	Your role during a painting or drawing activity is often to work alongside children and role-model techniques. • You could pick up a sponge to make a pattern, and a child who is interested may also copy. • With older children, you can also plan an activity to show how different primary coloured paints can be mixed together.
Junk modelling	This means making a model out of packaging and items that would normally be recycled, such as cardboard boxes, plastic bottles and tubes. This activity usually works best with children over 3 years old. They often need to learn how to: • use staplers and masking tape • join a curved item to a flat surface.
Block play	Many early years settings have wooden blocks of different lengths, widths and shapes. These blocks can encourage children's mathematical as well as their imaginative skills. • You could suggest to children that it might be fun to build a boat using the blocks, and then play alongside them. • Planning activities using block play can be useful with children who do not normally choose to play with them, so that they can see the possibilities of this resource.

> **Research**
>
> Find out more about the benefits of block play:
> www.youtube.com/watch?v=tRlnvg7tb2k

Imaginative play

We have seen that imaginative play can be divided into different types. Here are some ways in which you could plan activities.

▲ Why is it important for children to have access to a wide range of materials?

Activity	How to support children's interests and needs during play
Role play	The EYFS suggests that role play is one way in which children may develop vocabulary. This is because you can plan a range of different scenarios such as a fruit shop, a shoe shop or an airline. • Your role is to choose appropriate props and then create the new area with children. • As some children might not have the vocabulary or experience to know how to 'act' in this area, you need to role-model this. Children could, for example, take the part of a shopkeeper or passport officer at the station.
Puppet play	Puppets can fascinate all ages of children. With babies and toddlers, you can plan to use different puppets. • Babies and toddlers enjoy 'peek-a-boo' with puppets when the puppet disappears and then returns. • As children develop skills, they can enjoy using finger puppets and sock puppets. You can model how to make and use these.
Small world play	You can plan a range of opportunities for small world play. This could include putting out shredded paper with farm animals or strips of cardboard so that children can make roads. Your role is usually to: • play alongside toddlers and be a play partner. • set out small world play in interesting ways for older children.

Education and Early Years T Level: Early Years Educator

Sensory play

Sensory play involves play with materials that mainly encourage learning through the senses. This is sometimes called messy play, as children might get their hands wet or make a mess in the setting.

The way children use sensory play changes as they develop:
- ▶ Toddlers tend to be interested in just exploring the materials.
- ▶ Older children tend to combine sensory play with imaginative play.

Activity	How to support children's interests and needs during play
Slime or foam	You can make slime or foam with children. This is a good activity as children can be part of the process. • Your role is to encourage conversations and use specific vocabulary. • Remember that some children might find these resources uncomfortable because they dislike the feeling. It is important not to force children to use them.
Dough	Dough is one area where we can see the differences in children's play. • Older children often use dough to support their imaginative play, such as making cakes as part of their role play. • You can plan activities based on dough: for example, ask two children to play a dice game where they make a number of pizzas based on the number on the dice.
Sand and water	Sand and water are in most early years settings. • You can focus children's attention on different skills such as pouring and filling by putting out bottles and funnels. • Children can also enjoy finding hidden things in sand trays.
Mud kitchen	Many early years settings now have an outdoor mud kitchen. This is a combination of a role-play kitchen with mud, sand and bark chippings used by children as they play. Your role could be to: • provide new resources for this area • role-play being a customer for a mud pizza.

▲ Why is it important for a dough table to look inviting?

Heuristic play

Heuristic play for toddlers involves using household objects and natural objects as well as general purpose and recycled objects. You need to make sure that:
- ▶ there is enough variety of resources
- ▶ the resources are safe.

Performance Outcome 1: Support and Promote Children's Play, Development and Early Education

K1.16 The resources and equipment needed to support children's play and education, both indoors and outdoors

Factors to consider when setting up for play

Factors to consider	How to implement this
Age and stage appropriate	Resources have to be appropriate for the child's age and stage of development, so that they are more likely to enjoy their play. • When resources are not sufficiently challenging, children can become bored. • On the other hand, if children cannot manage to use the resources, they can become frustrated and lose interest.
Needs and interests of individual children	Planning in early years settings reflects children's interests as well as their developmental needs. Children need to find things that they want to use and do. It is also good to put out some 'surprises' for children to inspire them. This might mean adding something new to existing resources.
Health and safety/risk assessments	When setting up and monitoring play environments, we have to check that resources are safe and also we have identified any risks and taken steps to reduce them. See also Core Chapter 3.
Manufacturers' instructions	It is important to be aware of manufacturers' instructions. • They might have a warning for equipment not to be used with children under three years. • They will explain how the product is meant to be used and also list any restrictions on the number of children or their weight. If the original instructions are not available, you can often find a copy of them on the internet.
Weather conditions	The weather can make a difference to what is safe to put outdoors. This needs to be part of the risk assessment. • In wet weather, some items might be too slippery. • In very hot conditions, items containing metal might become too hot to touch.
Opportunities for both indoor and outdoor play	It is important that the outdoors is not seen only as a place for physical play. It is best practice for you to provide similar opportunities indoors and outdoors. This might mean: • a place for sharing books outdoors • somewhere to practise balancing skills indoors. You also need to provide play opportunities for non-mobile and mobile babies.
Resources in good working order, safe and clean	As part of risk assessment, it is essential that every item and area inside and outdoors is clean and safe.
Diversity, equality and inclusion	When providing resources, it is important that you think about the messages that they send out to children. • Does the home corner feel like a place that is like their home? • Do characters in books look like them? • Are there objects around that represent their culture and language? • Settings are required to make sure that children with SEND have the same opportunities to learn and play as other children. You might need to think about making resources physically accessible and adapting them so that all children can benefit from them.

The appropriateness of resources will depend on the type of indoor or outdoor play

The resources that are available for children should reflect the different play types and also the different ages and stages of the children. The table on the next page gives some examples of resources that might be put out for different types of play.

Research

Make a list of the different outdoor play opportunities available in your work placement.

Is there a good range of different play types available?

Education and Early Years T Level: Early Years Educator

Play type	0–1 years	1–3 years	3–5 years
Physical play	Baby gym Baby walkers Ball pit Baby swing Catching bubbles	Sit and ride toys Simple trikes Slides Play tunnels Soft play areas Moving objects from place to place, e.g. filling up a bucket of water and pouring it onto a flower bed Walking with support on a low wall Walking up and down steps	Wheeled toys, e.g. trikes and scooters Hoops Climbing frame and obstacle course Dancing Ball skills, e.g. throwing, kicking, batting Jumping, e.g. on a trampoline or from a low step
Creative play	Large markers Hand painting Stacking blocks Simple jigsaws	Sponges, large brushes Jigsaws Wooden cubes and blocks Stacking bricks Lacing cards	Junk modelling – boxes of different sizes and shapes, tubes Paints, brushes, sponges, rollers Printing activities Modelling clay Collage materials, glue, fabric, haberdashery, scissors Sewing, large needles, embroidery thread, large weave fabric Block play Lego and other construction toys
Imaginary play	N/A	Play kitchen Tea set Pram, pushchair Bags	Farm animals, play people, dinosaurs Cars Shop – till, counter, bags, weighing scales, open and closed sign Home corner, kitchen, oven, tea towel, tablecloth Dressing up Clothes, shoes, accessories
Sensory play	Water Gloop Flashing and revolving lights Bubbles Fabrics and different textures for feeling	Water in buckets, trays, bins (under supervision) Sand (from two years) Bottles, scoops, tubes, watermills Gloop Catching and making bubbles	

Performance Outcome 1: Support and Promote Children's Play, Development and Early Education

Play type	0–1 years	1–3 years	3–5 years
Heuristic/discovery play	**Treasure basket** Low basket with 30–50 items all made from natural materials and safe for touching and mouthing	**Heuristic play** Wide range of everyday items set out for each child or pair of children Heuristic play can be set up indoors and outdoors Grouping of different-sized tins, cardboard boxes, brushes, metal objects, tubes and plastic bottles Small repeated items such as shells, pegs, hair curlers	**Loose part play** Places in and outdoors where children may come across items from everyday life or unusual objects, e.g. rope, balls, kitchen plunger, very large cardboard box, wide cardboard tube, polythene sheeting

K1.17 The difference between adult-led and child-initiated play

The EYFS requires early years settings to use a mixture of **adult-led** and **child-initiated play**. These are two different ways of working with children, and it is useful to understand what these terms mean.

> **Key terms**
>
> *Adult-led play:* play opportunities and activities which are planned and provided by the adult. The adult may direct children, e.g. as part of a Forest School programme, children will be asked to find sticks to make a bonfire.
>
> *Child-initiated play:* play in which children are able to make their own decisions about what and how to play, and who to play with. In some settings, it is also called 'free play'.

As well as adult-led and child-initiated play, there is also a 'middle way':

- Adults set up a play opportunity with an aim in mind, e.g. putting out birthday candles and cards with dough so that children may make birthday cakes.
- Unlike adult-led activities, the adult will not direct the play and children might choose not to follow the prompts.

How adults can lead and promote play

There are many ways in which adults can lead and promote play. Here are some examples:

1 **Creating a safe environment that stimulates imagination**: you should make sure that children feel safe in all types of play and that there are enough interesting resources available for them to use.

2 **Providing play prompts and cues**: some children benefit from the way that you might lay out a play environment. You could put out cups and saucers or a tablecloth in the home corner. This will act as a prompt for children to play in certain ways.

3 **Intervening in play when necessary**: you need to intervene in play when:
   – children are doing something unsafe and might cause harm to themselves or others
   – resources are being damaged
   – children are being aggressive or unkind.

4 **Providing time, space and resources for play**: you need to:
   – make sure that children have sufficient time to play
   – think about space when putting out resources, especially items such as wheeled toys or construction play
   – put out a variety of resources that might be combined in different ways.

5 **Encouraging children's engagement in play**: while children cannot be made to play, you can help them to enjoy their play by:
   – joining in with them
   – giving them ideas
   – providing resources that match their play interests and stage of development.

K1.18 The benefits of adult-led and child-initiated play

We have seen that the role of the adult can change how children play. There are times when children need adults to be very involved, but also times when the adult should be a spectator or facilitator.

It is important to understand the benefits of adult-led and child-initiated play and when to use them.

Adult-led play and activities

Adult-led play can allow children to learn and do things that they could not otherwise do by themselves. This table shows the importance of adult-led play and activities.

Benefits of adult-led play and activities	How adult-led play and activities can support children
Target specific areas of children's development	Learning to read or how to manage a zip are examples of skills that children can develop if they are guided by adults.
Introduce new concepts	Some adult-led play and activities provide children with new ways of thinking or ideas: • You might show children how to measure items by organising a game of short straws. This adult-led activity may encourage children to learn how to compare lengths.
Prompt conversations and encourage sustained shared thinking	Many adult-led activities encourage conversations and also lead to children and adults exploring topics together. When adults and children have sustained conversations that explore questions of interest to the child, they are engaging in sustained shared thinking. For example: • You might organise the role-play area to become a shoe shop and set it up with children. • During this activity, you might talk to a child about why we have different types of shoes and how we might be able to guess what a shoe is for. • By the end of their conversation, the child's knowledge and vocabulary about shoes will have been extended.
Create a stimulating and engaging learning environment	Adult-led play and activities should not be boring! By providing adult-led activities alongside child-initiated activities, a more stimulating and engaging learning environment occurs. It often happens that an activity begins by being adult-led, but then once children have mastered the skills or concepts, they can incorporate them into their own child-initiated play. A good example of this is cooking: • You might lead a cooking activity, but afterwards, children play it again in their home corner.
Respond to children's cues, questions, interests and ideas	For adult-led play and activities to be effective, you need to: • watch children's reactions • respond to their questions • base further activities and play on their interests and ideas.
Extend children's learning through scaffolding	During adult-led play, you can help children to develop: • their skills by breaking tasks down into small steps • their thinking through the use of careful questioning.

Child-initiated play

There are, nonetheless, many benefits when children can choose their own play and activities. This is shown in the table opposite.

> **Reflect**
>
> Observe an early years practitioner supporting children during adult-led play.
> ▶ How does the adult develop children's skills or knowledge?
> ▶ How do children respond to the activity?

Performance Outcome 1: Support and Promote Children's Play, Development and Early Education

Benefits of child-initiated play and activities	How child-initiated play and activities can support children
Promoting choice and agency	Children's personal, social and emotional development is helped when they choose their own play: • It can increase their independence and self-confidence. • They also learn about how to make choices, which is an important life skill.
Concentration and length of engagement	One of the key benefits of child-initiated play is that children tend to concentrate for longer and with greater intensity.
Allowing children to develop and explore own interests	What children want to play and how they play is often different to adults. When children can choose their own play, they can follow and explore their own interests. This might mean: • exploring a train track • trying to build the highest tower of biscuit tins in the world!
Promoting control and time management	As well as concentrating, children learn how to: • set their own challenges • persevere and control strong emotions. Older children in early years settings may also start to: • develop a sense of time management, as they learn to judge how long activities take to do.
Allowing children to practise new skills and develop new understanding	Child-initiated play is often a reflection of what children have seen or done with adults. It offers children a chance to: • explore ideas and concepts by themselves • practise the skills that they have learned.

How to offer an appropriate balance of adult-led and child-initiated play

There are no requirements as to how much time should be spent in adult-led or child-initiated play in the EYFS. It is up to the adults to decide what the balance should be. This balance should be based on the needs of children:
▶ A baby relies heavily on an adult, so a lot of time in a baby room is spent in adult-led play such as peek-a-boo or catching bubbles.
▶ Some children who have learning needs or developmental delay may need additional time and support from adults, so more adult-led activity may be offered.
▶ While two-year-old children enjoy being with adults, they tend to have their own ideas and so their play tends to be more child-initiated.

Early years settings can ensure that there are both adult-led activities and child-initiated play opportunities by:
▶ planning for adult-led and child-initiated play activities
▶ giving children access to resources and equipment to accommodate child-initiated play
▶ offering the appropriate level of support for children to apply their knowledge and skills to different situations
▶ stepping in when children ask for help, or show signs that they are becoming frustrated or losing confidence
▶ ensuring that children have access to resources and equipment that provoke their interest in and accommodate child-initiated play.

Research

Write down a list of activities and play over the course of a session, and the time which they will take.
▶ Which activities are adult-led, e.g. rhyme time, laying the table for lunch?
▶ Which activities are child-initiated?
▶ What proportion of time is adult-led?

K1.19 How learning outside the setting positively enhances children's education and development

Babies and young children love being outdoors or going to see new places. It is a significant way of supporting their overall learning and education. Being outdoors or going to a new place can be stimulating and so support children's cognitive development. It is especially important where children are at risk of education disadvantage.

The table on the next page shows some of the ways in which learning outside links to the areas of learning within the EYFS.

EYFS area of learning	How this is boosted by learning outside
Physical development	Children who spend time outdoors are likely to have opportunities to: • walk or run around • develop new physical skills, such as gently holding a seedling when planting it. When early years settings plan visits within easy walking distance, children are having some physical exercise. Being outdoors, walking, running and seeing interesting things can help children's overall physical and mental wellbeing.
Understanding the world	Some of the places that children visit might help them to: • learn more about their local community, plant and animal life • recognise changing weather patterns.
Personal, social and emotional development	Children often feel proud and confident after going on trips or spending time outdoors, especially doing 'adult' tasks such as planting or tidying. This helps children to: • become independent • develop an awareness of safety, hazards and risks.
Communication and language	One of the most important aspects of children being outdoors is the contribution it makes to their language development, especially their vocabulary. This is because every new experience is an opportunity for a child to learn the words associated with it.

Where learning outside the setting may take place

There are many places where early years settings may take children. Some early years settings have a plan in place as part of their curriculum. This links to the Understanding the World area of learning and development.

> **Reflect**
>
> Imagine you were visiting a farm with a small group of young children.
>
> Try to think of a hundred words to do with the farm and the activities that take place there that would be interesting to children. For example: tractor, cow, lamb, hay.

Outdoor places	How these can benefit children's development
Grounds and immediate surroundings	• Practitioners at early years settings might take children to the local shops, library or to post a letter. • Non-mobile babies and toddlers may also be taken for a walk in the pushchair.
Creative spaces	Many art galleries, theatres, cinemas and museums welcome young children. Some early years settings organise regular trips to these types of places.
The built environment	Where early years settings are in towns or cities, practitioners might go for walks with children to: • point out different features such as bridges and tower blocks • use public transport.
Heritage sites	Some early years settings organise trips to places of interest such as castles or palaces. These trips are normally organised for the oldest children within the group, as they are more likely to be developmentally ready.
The natural environment	Practitioners might take children to a countryside park, woods, parks and gardens. This provides children with opportunities to see plants and animals.
Farms, zoos and animal sanctuaries	Most young children love animals, so many early years settings will arrange visits to farms, zoos or animal sanctuaries.
Sacred spaces	Churches, mosques and synagogues are sometimes visited by early years settings, particularly when these are familiar places to some of the children within the setting. • Visiting sacred spaces has to be carefully considered, as some families may object to this type of outing. • Visits are normally planned for the older children in the group.

Performance Outcome 1: Support and Promote Children's Play, Development and Early Education

> **Good to know**
>
> Farm visits pose specific health and safety risks to visitors. Pregnant women should not touch lambs to prevent the risk of infection to their unborn babies.
>
> All children and adults should wash their hands immediately after touching animals on farms to avoid infections such as e-coli, which causes serious vomiting and diarrhoea.

> **Research**
>
> Look at the EYFS regulations in respect of outings.
>
> What are the requirements if a childminder or a pre-school wanted to take a small group out to the local shops?

K1.20 The distinctive qualities offered by the outdoors as an educational environment compared to traditional classroom environments

There is something special for babies and young children about being outdoors. It is often a place where children will choose to go even when it is cold and wet. The table shows some of the benefits of being outside and how these support children's learning.

Special qualities of the outdoors	How these contribute to children's learning
Greater opportunity for risk and challenge	Outdoor environments are usually more challenging for children. They learn to: • move on different surfaces • judge heights when climbing • negotiate with others on wheeled toys. Ideally, outdoor spaces need to have slopes and areas which are not flat, to encourage children to learn how to judge risk.
Space	Babies and children have more space outdoors. This allows them to: • move more freely • be noisier • learn about their size in relation to other objects. Seeing far into the distance has also been shown to positively affect young children's eyesight.
Animals, plants and lifecycles	Being outdoors allows children to see animals and plants. Adults can draw their attention to lifecycles such as: • the way that spiders catch flies for food • how garden birds create nests in the spring.
Changing seasons	When the seasons change, so too does the light and what is happening in nature. Drawing children's attention to falling leaves or buds on trees can help them understand lifecycles and the systems within nature.
Changing weather	Changing weather means that children learn about weather systems, clouds and maybe frost and snow. Being out in different weathers helps children to: • connect to the natural world • link clothing to weather.

Skills practice

You are working in a day care unit that takes children from birth to five years. The unit is divided into three main rooms, for 0–2 years, 2–3 years and 3–5 years, respectively. The day care unit has a wide range of resources and equipment to support age-appropriate learning and ensures that as well as meeting children's individual needs, there is a good balance of child-initiated and adult-led activities. The latest Ofsted report judges the nursery to be Good with Outstanding features.

While relationships with parents are strong, some parents have expressed concern that while their children are happy, there are not enough opportunities for mathematics and literacy. They are concerned that there is too much play and that their children are not really benefiting.

The manager of the unit has decided that an information session is needed to help parents understand how play and learning are integrated and also to explain to parents how everyday activities and routines are supporting mathematics and literacy.

The manager has asked you to prepare some materials that can be used for the information session. While many of the parents who have expressed concerns have children in the 3–5 year room, the manager wants the session to look at learning across the age range. She would also like parents to understand how they can help their children with mathematics and literacy at home.

You will need to prepare the following:
- A digital slideshow presentation of 10 slides that includes:
  - the different play types and how they benefit children at different ages
  - how daily routines in each of the rooms may support mathematics
  - the benefits of child-initiated and adult-led play and activities.
- Practical examples of games and activities that can be used to support mathematics and literacy for babies and children of different ages.
- An outline of the current Early Learning Goals and an explanation of how play and activities in the day care unit may create the foundations for children to achieve them.
- An information booklet that parents can take away with them to support home learning in mathematics and literacy. The information booklet should include:
  - an explanation of how sharing books and rhymes supports early literacy
  - examples of books and rhymes for different ages that parents may want to try at home
  - an explanation of how daily routines can support early mathematics in the home, with examples.

Performance Outcome 2:
Develop Relationships with Children to Facilitate their Development

The relationships that children have with their parents, family, early years practitioners and also other children can shape their learning and development. In this unit, we will look at:
▶ the importance of attachment and relationships
▶ other aspects of emotional development, including behaviour, self-concept, self-regulation and self-efficacy.

Some parts of this unit, especially the outcomes about behaviour and attachment, closely link to Core Chapters 4 and 7. Page numbers are provided for outcomes already covered in the core chapters.

Learning outcomes

This chapter covers the following knowledge outcomes for Performance Outcome 2:

K2.1   Different forms of attachment that children develop and analyse, and evaluating key aspects of attachment theories related to current practice and the key person
K2.2   The features of secure attachment and how it impacts positively on children's development and behaviour
K2.3   The potential positive and negative effects of transitions and significant events on children's relationships and holistic development
K2.4   Typical behaviours for age and stage of development
K2.5   Implications of a range of behavioural signs and approaches to their management
K2.6   The concept of self-regulation in children, the stages of self-regulation and how self-regulation supports children's development
K2.7   Factors affecting children's behaviour
K2.8   How children's effective and ineffective communication skills may impact on relationships with others, and how a range of biological and environmental factors can affect the development of communication and speech
K2.9   How a range of factors can affect children's self-concept
K2.10 Effective practice to develop self-efficacy in children

K2.1 Different forms of attachment that children develop and analyse, and evaluating key aspects of attachment theories related to current practice and the key person

We looked at attachment and theories of attachment in Core Chapter 7. You will need to reread pages 113–17 to check that you understand the importance of attachment, and page 118 for the role of the key person.

Test yourself

1. What did Bowlby notice about children in later life who had experienced maternal deprivation?
2. At what age do children typically show discriminate attachments?
3. What is the role of the key person in an early years setting?

Good to know

The role of the key person is considered essential in early years.

It is a statutory requirement in the Early Years Foundation Stage (EYFS) for settings to allocate a key person to each child.

The Ofsted inspection for early years also checks that settings have an effective key person system.

K2.2 The features of secure attachment and how it impacts positively on children's development and behaviour

As well as looking at theories and stages of attachment, we also looked at the importance and features of secure attachment in Core Chapter 7. Read page 119 and then see if you can answer the following questions in the case study.

Case study

Olivia is two years old. She is due to start with a childminder next week. As part of the settling in process, the childminder and the parent assess whether she has formed a sufficiently strong attachment with the childminder.

Olivia's father tells her he is going to tidy up in the kitchen and leaves Olivia with the childminder in the play area. Olivia looks at the door, but carries on playing with the childminder. When another child accidentally bumps into her, she puts her arms around the childminder for a cuddle.

After 15 minutes, Olivia's father comes back. She notices him and smiles, but carries on playing. The next day when Olivia's dad brings her to the childminder to start, she runs to hug the childminder and happily says goodbye.

- Identify the signs that Olivia has formed an attachment with the childminder.
- What are the signs that Olivia also has a secure attachment to her father?
- Explain why secure attachments are important for children's overall development.

▲ What are the signs of a secure attachment?

K2.3 The potential positive and negative effects of transitions and significant events on children's relationships and holistic development

In Core Chapter 7, we looked at how transitions can affect children and young people of different ages. Reread pages 131–3 to see how young children can be affected by different types of transitions.

Performance Outcome 2: Develop Relationships with Children to Facilitate their Development

> **Practice points**
>
> **Supporting transitions**
>
> When children are new to a setting or situation, they may show signs of distress or anxiety. There are several ways that we can help children, including:
> - responding to their feelings by talking to them or offering them physical comfort if appropriate
> - using distraction techniques, such as getting out a puppet or inviting them to try out a play activity
> - staying calm and relaxed
> - recognising that the child might not want to move out of a room or do a new activity
> - predicting situations that might cause further anxiety, such as the arrival of other children in the room ready for lunch, and taking steps to reduce anxiety
> - using the information gained from parents to reassure the child.

K2.4 Typical behaviours for age and stage of development

One of the day-to-day roles for adults working with children is to help them learn how to be with others and show appropriate behaviour. By understanding typical behaviours for children at different ages and stages we can adjust our practice, which can help us to build more effective relationships. It is also important to recognise when children may need additional support because their behaviours are not age typical. If our expectations for children's behaviour are not in line with their stage of development, there is a danger that we may not always handle situations appropriately. This can harm relationships with children.

Typical behaviours for age and stage of development are covered in Core Chapter 4. You will need to revisit pages 60–1, because the topic of behaviour is part of this performance outcome. After you have looked again at typical behaviours for young children, use these Test yourself questions to see how much you can remember.

> **Test yourself**
>
> 1. At what age are children likely to have tantrums?
> 2. Outline typical behaviours for a child aged between two and three years.
> 3. At what age might you expect children to understand the need for rules?

K2.5 Implications of a range of behavioural signs and approaches to their management

There are signs that young children might need support with their behaviour. We looked at these signs and ways of managing behaviour in Core Chapter 4. You will need to revisit pages 77–8 to check your knowledge and understanding.

> **Practice points**
>
> **Managing unwanted behaviour**
>
> 1. Stay calm and be positive.
> 2. Make sure that the child and others around are safe.
> 3. Work out the reason why the child is showing the behaviour. It could be:
>   - tiredness or hunger
>   - frustration
>   - boredom
>   - the child retaliating to something another child has done or said
>   - behaviour linked to development, such as throwing or climbing
>   - attention-seeking.
> 4. Act appropriately:
>   - For hunger or tiredness – meet these needs immediately.
>   - For boredom, frustration or developmental behaviours – try refocusing the child on another activity or distraction.
>   - For squabbles and retaliation – talk to all the children, and encourage them to find a solution or suggest another activity.
>   - For attention-seeking behaviours – ignore the behaviour, but aim to do something positive instead; e.g. 'I am going to get a puzzle. Does anyone want to help me?'

K2.6 The concept of self-regulation in children, the stages of self-regulation and how self-regulation supports children's development

Self-regulation is our ability to:
- control our own emotions, thoughts and behaviour
- adjust to changing situations and cope with unexpected stress.

Stages of self-regulation

Self-regulation develops gradually in childhood, although as we see later, there are many factors that might affect its development. The table shows the stages of self-regulation in babies and children.

Age group	Stage of self-regulation
Babies	Babies might suck a dummy or their fingers to self-soothe. They will pick up on an adult's reactions and adapt their own reactions; e.g.: • baby tumbles, but is not hurt • adult smiles • baby chuckles.
Toddlers	Toddlers find it hard to wait and share. With adult help they can start to understand that they might have to wait to have certain needs met.
Pre-school children	With support and explanation, they begin to: • recognise what behaviour is required in certain situations, such as whispering in a library • use strategies to manage their emotions, such as asking an adult for help when a task is difficult.
School-aged children	At school, children become more able to: • control their own wants • understand other people's needs.
Older school-aged children	As they get older, children are able to express their emotions and feelings related to situations.

Long-term factors affecting self-regulation

The development of self-regulation is dependent on a range of factors:

- Brain development – as children's brains mature, they are able to think and process information differently.
- How the brain has processed previous experiences of being stressed or unhappy – children's quality of relationships, how they are parented and nurtured by other adults, plays an important factor in self-regulation. Children who have been consistently soothed and guided by adults when they have been unhappy or in stressful situations learn how to manage stress.
- Communication abilities – children who have language delay or difficulties in communication might find self-regulation difficult. This is because some self-regulation involves talking about feelings, or coaching and talking to ourselves.

The range of factors affecting self-regulation explains why two children of the same age might show very different reactions when disappointed.

▲ What is the link between self-regulation and being able to cope when you are losing a game?

Short-term factors affecting self-regulation

On a day-to-day basis, children's self-regulation can fluctuate as a result of:
- tiredness
- hunger
- over-stimulation.

Performance Outcome 2: Develop Relationships with Children to Facilitate their Development

Children who usually show expected or strong levels of self-regulation might suddenly have a sudden outburst or become over-emotional.
- When working with children, it is important for you to notice when they are looking tired or might be hungry.
- When planning special days and events such as birthdays or a big outing, remember to plan in some quiet moments, to avoid children from becoming over-stimulated.

How self-regulation supports children's holistic development

Children whose self-regulation skills are typical for their age are more likely to find it easier to cope with day-to-day life. Here are some of examples of how self-regulation skills can help children.

Behaviour

Children who are developing self-regulation skills are more able to control their immediate impulses. This allows them to apply and respond to reasoning and so helps them to appreciate rules and boundaries. This in turn allows them to participate in games and activities.

The development of self-regulation helps children to persevere and cope with set-backs. This is important in developing a sense of self-worth and confidence.

Relationships with others

Children who can self-regulate are more likely to have friends, as they can share, cooperate and enjoy being in small groups.
- As friendships can be fluid in the early years, children are more likely to cope when they are not always included in games, or if a friend wants to play with someone else.
- When they are older and in school, they can benefit from large group activities.

Education

Children with self-regulation skills are also likely to have stronger education outcomes. This is because they manage the stress of transitioning into an early years setting or reception class.

Self-regulation also helps them to:
- concentrate and listen during learning experiences and activities
- avoid being distracted
- persevere if they find a task or skill difficult
- remember information in order to carry out instructions and complete a task.

Supporting self-regulation

Research has shown that there are several ways in which practitioners and parents can help children to develop self-regulation skills.

Area for boosting self-regulation	How this can support children's self-regulation
Routines	Early routines seem to help babies and young children feel secure and so lessen anxiety. This in turn helps them to stay calm.
Appropriate boundaries	Fair and appropriate boundaries on behaviour can help young children. Boundaries reduce children's stress because they know what they can and cannot do.
Consistent adult responses	Children who are used to having predictable, consistent adult responses are more likely to develop better self-regulation skills. Consistent responses include: • the way that adults interact with children • how they support their behaviour. A child who is with an unpredictable adult suffering from mood swings is more likely to feel under stress. This will interfere with the child's ability to manage their emotions.
Calm environments	For children who find self-regulation difficult, it can be helpful to be in environments that are calm, with few distractions. This means: • lower levels of noise • a tidy environment.
Articulating emotions	Being able to put words to feelings can help children to self-regulate. Adults can help children by: • drawing children's attention to words about emotions, for example, by sharing stories • providing activities that help children to talk about their feelings.

K2.7 Factors affecting children's behaviour

In Core Chapter 4, we looked at children's and young people's behaviour. We also considered the factors that might affect young children's behaviour.

In order to complete this unit, you will need to revisit pages 63–4. Then see if you can answer the questions for this case study.

> **Case study**
>
> Kyle is three years old. His parents have just separated and his mother reports that he is refusing to go to bed. She has to wake him to bring him to nursery.
>
> His key person is currently on holiday, and another member of staff is working with him. Kyle is usually happy, but recently he has become aggressive and is easily frustrated. Staff at the nursery are having to supervise him closely as in the past week, Kyle has hit one child and bit another.
>
> Kyle is due to be assessed by a speech and language therapist, as he has only started to use words in the past few months.
> - Explain how the separation of his parents is affecting Kyle's behaviour.
> - How might the absence of his key person contribute to his behaviour?
> - What other factors might be influencing Kyle's behaviour?

K2.8 How children's effective and ineffective communication skills may impact on relationships with others

How well children can talk and communicate can affect many other areas of their development, especially social development. Remember that communication includes language but also facial expressions. How often a child smiles affects other people's responses and feelings towards them.

A child who communicates effectively can:
- express their own needs, interests and opinions
- feel heard and understood by others
- develop a relationship with adults and other children
- know what is expected of them
- cooperate with others.

This means that a child who can communicate well for their age is more likely to feel happy and confident, and be invited to join in play by other children.

They may also find it easier to manage their behaviour, as we have already seen that language, self-regulation and behaviour are linked.

A child who has delayed or difficulties with communication skills might:
- feel unheard or misunderstood
- experience frustration with self and others
- have difficulty bonding with peers and adults
- display behaviour which could be interpreted as inappropriate.

In addition, a child who has delayed, or difficulties with, communication skills, such as autistic spectrum condition, might not always understand the facial expression, actions and intentions of others. This can lead to them showing aggression or laughing inappropriately.

Children who have delayed, or difficulties with, communication might feel isolated, and miss out on learning social skills through play and interactions with others.

How a range of biological and environmental factors can affect the development of communication and speech

We saw in Core Chapter 7 that it is now widely recognised that babies are born ready to learn language.

However, this does not explain why children learn language at different speeds. There are a range of factors that can influence language learning.

Biological factors

The table opposite shows biological factors that influence language learning.

Performance Outcome 2: Develop Relationships with Children to Facilitate their Development

Biological factor	How this affects language learning
Health	A common cause of communication and language difficulties is temporary hearing loss, as a result of the ears being partially blocked by a sticky substance. Other health issues can also make a difference – if children are feeling poorly or tired, they are less likely to want to communicate.
Personality traits	While children's personalities are not fully formed, researchers have seen that certain character traits can be seen early in life. These include: • how sociable babies are • how they respond to new situations and materials. The way babies respond influences how parents respond back to them: • Some babies and toddlers are more motivated to communicate than others. • Happy, smiley babies are likely to get more attention and opportunities to develop language. • They might also receive more positive facial expressions from their parents. This can increase their communication and language skills.
Special educational needs and disabilities	There are a range of special educational needs and disabilities (SEND), such as autistic spectrum conditions that might either delay communication and language or make it harder for children to communicate. Disabilities which affect sight and hearing can also make it harder for babies and children to communicate, unless they are recognised and responded to quickly.

Environmental factors

As well as biological factors, there are also environmental factors. Here are some examples:

Environmental factor	How this affects language learning
Parental engagement	Babies and young children who have parents who spend time talking and playing with them are more likely to be faster to learn the skills of communication and language. The level of parental engagement can depend on: • the strength of attachment (see Core Chapter 7) • the energy levels and knowledge of parents. Some parents do not realise the importance of talking to their baby. Others might be in busy family situations and working several jobs, so that they are too exhausted to spend much time talking to their baby or toddler.
Stimulation	Toys, activities and resources are all ways of providing stimulation for communication and language. • Adults find it easier to interact and play with babies and toddlers when there is something to do or to look at. • Toddlers and young children are also more likely to begin a conversation if they have seen or are doing something that is interesting to them.
Language-rich environment	This term is used to describe situations where there are plenty of opportunities for babies, toddlers and children to talk and listen. A language-rich environment is likely to have these following features: • quiet spaces, as these encourage babies and children to talk more • adults who listen carefully and allow time for babies and children to respond • resources that encourage talking, such as toy telephones or pop-up toys for babies • books and stories that are frequently shared with babies and children • a layout which encourages interaction, e.g. babies facing each other at mealtimes • activities such as daily rhymes, peek-a-boo and puppets that encourage interaction.
Cognitive ability – development of early speech	Cognitive ability is linked to biological factors (see above) and is a factor in language development. Early speech, however, is focused on producing sounds – see K1.3 within Performance Outcome 1 on pages 215 and 104, and 7.3 within Core Chapter 7 on page 120.
Bilingualism	As we saw in Core Chapter 12, some babies and toddlers will be learning more than one language at the same time. • For most children, learning two languages at the same time works well and there is no delay. This is because they associate each language with a different person or situation. • Where the languages are not sufficiently separated for babies and toddlers to realise that they are two separate codes, children can take longer to speak.

K2.9 How a range of factors can affect children's self-concept

In Core Chapter 4, we looked at the development of the self-concept, and how it consisted of several parts. Reread pages 65–6, then see if you can answer these Test yourself questions.

> **Test yourself**
>
> 1 Name the different components of self-concept.
> 2 Explain how self-concept might affect a child's behaviour.
> 3 Give an example of how an adult might support a child's self-concept.

Throughout childhood, children are learning about themselves. The construction of self-concept is gradual and depends on a number of factors, which are explored below:

- age
- gender
- education
- relation to adults
- abuse
- media
- culture
- socio-economic background.

Age

How children develop a sense of themselves changes according to age.

In Core Chapter 4, we looked at the way that, over time, children's and young people's self-concept develops. This is partly linked to cognitive development, but also as a result of experiencing comments and reactions from others.

Younger children define themselves in concrete terms, such as:

> 'My name is Jasmine. I like dolls. I can ride a tricycle and a scooter.'

This changes once children become more aware of what others are doing and also what has been said about them. Five- and six-year-olds are more likely to say things such as:

> 'My name is Tia. I am quite a good reader, but my friend Sara is on the green shelf. She is allowed to read any book.'

Gender

As part of developing a self-concept, children also have to learn about:

- gender
- expectations of different genders (including stereotypes)
- what it might mean to be a boy or a girl.

As part of this process, children subconsciously pick up on the cues in their everyday life as well as the behaviours and reactions of adults. The clothes, toys and books that children are given can also influence their understanding of what gender means, and how people see boys and girls.

> **Case study**
>
> Amel is four years old. Both of his parents drive, but when both parents are in the car, his father always drives. When his parents discuss where to go or what to buy, his father's ideas are normally followed. His mother works shifts as a GP. This means that Amel's father often gives him his dinner and puts him to bed.
>
> Amel goes to nursery. In the outdoor area, there are wheeled toys. Amel often makes comments such as 'I'll drive us to the shops', and does not like it if a girl says that she does not want to. In the role-play area, Amel enjoys setting the table and then putting a baby doll to bed.
>
> ▸ How is Amel's play influenced by what he has seen at home?

Stages in the development of gender concept

There are clear stages in the way that children develop a sense of what it means to be a boy or a girl.

Age	How children develop their sense of gender
9–12 months	Babies react differently to male and female faces.
18–24 months	Toddlers are starting to show preferences for gender-stereotyped toys.
2 years	Children can point to a picture of a child of the same gender.
2.5–3 years	Children are identifying the differences between genders by using clues such as hair length and style, and dress.
3–4 years	Children are beginning to associate tasks and objects with gender – i.e. some roles are determined by gender.
5–6 years	Children have acquired the concept of **gender stability**. They know that gender is not dependent on type of clothes or haircut.

Performance Outcome 2: Develop Relationships with Children to Facilitate their Development

▲ How might the choice of clothing affect how children perceive themselves?

Education

Education can make a significant difference to children's self-concept.
- Children who feel encouraged and supported through learning to read and write and develop abstract mathematical concepts are likely to feel positive about themselves. High quality teaching and encouragement are very important.
- On the other hand, if children's educational experiences make them feel uncomfortable, stressed or inadequate, they are more likely to develop a negative view of themselves.

Relation to adults

How others, particularly adults, react to children is one of the most important factors in the development of self-concept in early childhood. Parents, close family members and early years practitioners have a huge influence on children's feelings about themselves, both positively and negatively. Here are some of the ways in which this occurs:

Body gesture and facial expression

- When adults or other children frequently greet babies and children with warmth and smiles, they are more likely to see themselves as being likeable.
- When adults constantly look disappointed, angry or just bored, babies and children might start to think that they do not matter.

Expectations and comments from others

Children and young people often pick up what is said to them or about them. They might hear things such as, 'You are so kind', or 'I hear that he's good at sport'.
- While the occasional comment is not likely to make much of an impact, repeated comments like this will influence what a child or young person thinks about themselves.

Similarly, what adults say and how they react also send out messages about what they expect of children:
- An adult who does not wait to see if a child can manage to do something for themselves communicates that the child is not competent.
- On the other hand, an adult who says something such as 'Sofia can lay the table. She is good at it now,' helps a child to feel that they *are* competent.

Comparison to others

As children become older, they are likely to notice how they are doing or being treated compared to others. From this comparison, they subconsciously draw conclusions.
- A child who repeatedly comes bottom in a spelling test may decide that they are 'no good' at spelling and will stop trying.
- On the other hand, a child who sees that they are better at something compared to their friends might practise the skill more.

Abuse

Sadly, children who have experienced abuse are more likely to develop a low self-esteem as a result of the actions and/or words of adults. Abuse experienced in childhood can have a significant impact on long-term mental health as a result of lowered self-esteem. The trauma of abuse can cause depression and anxiety as well as creating difficulties in forming healthy relationships with others. In some cases, abused children go on to become abusers themselves. In others, being abused in childhood results in the adult forming relationships with an abusive partner. The long-term effects of abuse are one reason why child protection and safeguarding procedures are so important in all settings. We look at the indicators of abuse in EYE Performance Outcome 4.

The media

- The effects of media in early childhood are limited, but can impact on young children's understanding of gender roles.
- Later on, media such as films and also social media can affect older children's development of the ideal self. Older children and young people might start to feel that they should be good looking, successful and popular. If this does not correspond with how they are feeling about themselves, they are likely to develop a lower self-esteem and self-concept.
- Parents with babies and young children are also highly likely to be influenced by the media. This can affect their expectations as a parent and their parenting style. For example, they might see on social media that their friend's child is already swimming, and so might organise swimming lessons and put pressure on their child to do well.

Culture

How children value and see themselves can be linked to the culture in which they are being raised.

- In some cultures or households, boys are valued more than girls, and so might have a more positive self-concept.
- A girl with a brother in this kind of culture might repeatedly see that she is not as valued or allowed to do the same things. This could negatively affect her self-concept.

Socio-economic background

Being from a poor background can lower self-concept, especially for older children who are aware that they do not have the same clothes as others or that they receive free school meals. They may also realise that they cannot go on holidays or join in with activities and hobbies.

As comparison to others is a key way in which self-concept is formed, not being the same as others can be problematic.

K2.10 Effective practice to develop self-efficacy in children

Self-efficacy (see page 105) is considered to play an important role in self-concept. It is about how children view themselves, either
- capable of being competent and independent, or
- helpless.

Self-efficacy is important, as it affects whether children will try out new things as they grow older, and persevere with them knowing that eventually they will be able to master them. Children with low self-efficacy are likely to assume that they cannot do things, and will either not try or quickly give up.

It is thought that children's self-concept in relation to self-efficacy is formed in the first few years of life. It is linked to children's direct experiences and how adults respond to their efforts. Here are some of the ways that can help babies' and children's self-efficacy:

Providing opportunities for choice

Activities and environments that provide babies and children with choice are important in self-efficacy.
- For babies, you can provide choice during treasure basket play, where they can select the items they find interesting.
- For older children, you can offer choices about what to get out and play with.

It is important that you respect children's choices: when a baby turns away to indicate that no more food is needed, do not keep pressing them to eat.

Remember that while it is important to give children opportunities for choice, these choices should be age/stage-appropriate.

Providing opportunities for exploration

Children need opportunities to explore and see for themselves what they can do, and also how things around them work. This links to one of the reasons why child-initiated play (discussed in Performance Outcome 1) is so important.

It is good practice for adults sometimes to stand back and not interfere when children are trying to make things work or do things for themselves as part of their exploration. Too much help from adults can prevent children from developing a sense of self-efficacy.

Encouraging perseverance and praising effort

For children to develop self-efficacy, they need encouragement and permission from adults to have a go at being independent. They also need adults to show through their actions and words that persevering, practice and effort are highly valued.

Performance Outcome 2: Develop Relationships with Children to Facilitate their Development

▲ How might this activity affect this child's sense of self-efficacy?

Setting realistic and attainable goals

When encouraging self-efficacy, you have to help children set realistic and attainable goals for themselves. This is because young children need to experience a level of success from their efforts.

In some cases, you can help children to set a goal of doing just a small part of a larger task. A good example of this is learning dressing skills. Young children might not be able to get themselves completely dressed, but adults can encourage them to do as much as they can.

Practice points

Self-efficacy
- Allow children plenty of time if they are trying to do something for themselves.
- Avoid standing over or hovering too close, as this can put pressure on children.
- Don't expect children to talk or respond to you if they are concentrating on a task.
- If children are frustrated, give them practical tips to encourage them to persevere.
- When help is needed, talk to children about what they have already achieved by themselves.
- When a task is clearly too difficult for a child, talk them through the elements so that with effort they will be able to do it by themselves.

Case study

Ava is two and a half years old. She is keen to put her coat on for herself. Her parents are unsure that she has the skills yet to manage it, but as she seems keen, they stand back and give her some space and time.

She manages to get her arms in and tries to do up the zip. She starts to look frustrated, but her mother says, 'Zips are tricky. You may need a little help this time, but with practice you will be able to do it.' Her mother shows her how the ends of the zip need to be put together. She encourages Ava to pull up the zip herself.

Over the next few days, Ava becomes faster at putting on her coat, and is able to find the two ends of the zip, although her mother puts them together to start her off. Ava's mother never rushes her and accepts that it will take about ten minutes longer for Ava to get ready to go out. Ava's parents are very encouraging and praise her effort even when she needs help.

An aunt comes to visit and watches Ava struggle, suggesting that it would be better for her to be given a coat with Velcro to make it easier. Ava's mother says, 'No, she'll be able to do it.' Two months later, Ava can do her own zip up most of the time. As most children are four years old before they can manage this, it is a significant achievement.

- Outline the important role that Ava's mother played in this process.
- Why was it important that Ava's mother provided a little practical help but still encouraged Ava to be independent?
- Explain what the process of learning to put a coat on has taught Ava about herself.

Skills practice

As part of this qualification, you will need to show that you can apply the knowledge that you have gained. Here are some questions that link to the knowledge we have considered, but also the skills that you will need to show.

1. Give two ways in which adults can support a three-year-old child's independence. (2.18)
2. What behaviours might an adult model to support children's positive behaviour? (2.19)
3. Outline ways in which an adult might support a child's positive self-concept. (2.21)

Performance Outcome 3:
Plan, Provide and Review Care, Play and Educational Opportunities to Enable Children to Progress

When you visit an early years setting, you will see that children are engaged in varying play opportunities or are doing activities guided by adults. You will also see a range of resources and equipment. The environment and the activities are a result of careful planning.

Plans are based on several factors that include the early years curriculum, the interests of children, but also assessments of children's stage of development and needs. In this unit, we look at the importance of planning and ways in which early years settings may plan as well as the role of observation and assessment in planning. We also consider the ways in which practitioners may continue to develop their own professional skills.

Learning outcomes

This chapter covers the following knowledge outcomes for Performance Outcome 3:

- **K3.1** How well-considered planning and provision supports children's educational and developmental progress
- **K3.2** The purpose of observation, assessment and planning and different approaches towards the assessment of children and planning
- **K3.3** A range of developmental indicators that may suggest a child is in need of additional support
- **K3.4** Different types of assessment and their purpose
- **K3.5** Practitioner responsibilities to undertake continuing professional development and ways to meet own developmental needs.

Performance Outcome 3: Plan, Provide and Review Care, Play and Educational Opportunities

K3.1 How well-considered planning and provision supports children's educational and developmental progress

Early years settings spend time planning their activities, equipment and play opportunities carefully. This helps to ensure that children's time in the setting meets:
- their needs
- the requirements of the early years curriculum.

Here are some of the ways in which careful planning can support children's progress.

Type of planning	How it supports children's progress
Meeting the individual needs and circumstances of children	By planning carefully, early years settings can make sure that individual children's needs are met. For example: • A child who is new to a setting might need to spend some time with their key person to help them feel secure. • A child who is moving home might enjoy a role-play area that is about letting or estate agents.
Targeting specific support that children require	Some children might need specific activities or resources to help their development. For example, you might plan: • an activity that requires sharing for a child who finds this difficult • an obstacle course for a child who needs to build up their confidence in physical activity.
Increasing participation through incorporating children's interests	Babies and children concentrate for longer when they are doing something that they enjoy and find interesting. This means that when you are planning to teach a new skill to a child or group of children, you could base it on something that they are already interested in. For example: • If you identify a group of children who enjoy playing with dinosaurs in the sand tray, you could plan a counting activity that involves using toy dinosaurs.
Including ongoing assessment to support the learning and development process	Observing children's reactions and responses is an important part of working with children. • You might notice that a child likes to hold onto a rail when climbing stairs. You could use this information to plan more climbing activities to build the child's confidence. Some activities and experiences can also be planned to help you learn more about children's knowledge and skills. For example: • You could plan a game of picture lotto to see how well children can take turns and understand simple rules.
Including opportunities for stretch and challenge	Young children's brains are developing and need stimulation. Planning can ensure that children have a wide range of different opportunities that can help them make progress and develop their skills. Challenging yet enjoyable opportunities also prevent children from becoming bored and showing unwanted behaviours.
Adapting activities to ensure differentiation	When planning group activities, it is important that all children can join in and have opportunities to learn and develop. The term **differentiation** is used to describe the way that a single activity can be adapted to make sure that children at different ages and stages of development can take part.

Case study

Making fish cakes

Melissa is a childminder. In the school holidays, she looks after two children aged seven and nine years, as well as two children aged two and three years. The wide difference in abilities as a result of the age gap means that Melissa has to choose activities that can be differentiated.

All of the children enjoy cooking. Today the children are making fish cakes:
- Melissa shows the older children how to peel a potato, and asks the younger ones to get out the bowls and spoons to do some stirring.
- Once the potatoes are cooked and cooled, the younger ones mash them with some milk.
- The older children, with supervision, open a tin of tuna and a tin of sweetcorn. They put these into bowls.
- Each child then creates their own mixture using the mashed potatoes, sweetcorn and tuna.
- Melissa helps the younger ones while guiding the older children. She finishes off the fishcakes while all the children set the table.

Afterwards they all sit down for lunch.
- Explain how Melissa has differentiated this activity.
- Why is this an example of a challenging and stretching activity?
- Can you link this activity to areas of the Early Years Foundation Stage (EYFS)?

K3.2 The purpose of observation, assessment and planning to support children's progress

In Core Chapter 8 we looked in general at the role of observation and assessment. You might find it helpful to revisit that chapter.

In this section, we look specifically at how observation, assessment and planning are used in early years settings. A good starting point is to understand the difference between the terms 'observation', 'assessment' and 'planning'.

- **Observation** is about gathering information about a child or group of children. This can be done by simply watching them or recording what they are doing. Observations can be carried out while directly working with children or from a distance.
- **Assessment** means using the information that has been gained from observations to identify and record a child's needs and interests. Assessment can also include checking that children's progress is in line with developmental or curriculum expectations.
- **Planning** is about using the information collected from the observation and assessments to plan appropriate provision and activities, and so support children's development.

Planning process

The three elements of observation, assessment and planning work together as a process. This is sometimes shown in diagram form as a circle (as shown at the top of page 267). In early years, we are continually observing, assessing and planning. This is partly because young children develop quickly, so an assessment carried out three months ago would be quickly out of date.

▲ How can these dinosaurs be used to support counting for children who enjoy playing in the sand?

Performance Outcome 3: Plan, Provide and Review Care, Play and Educational Opportunities

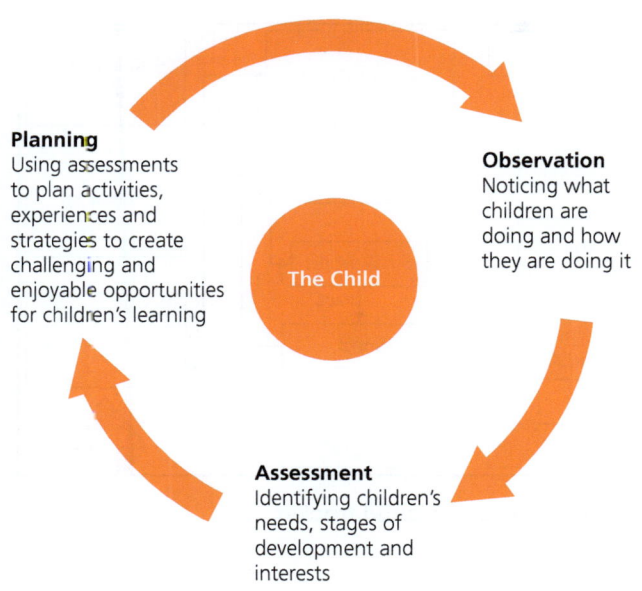

▲ The Observation, Assessment and Planning cycle

Evaluating plans

An additional but essential element of the observation and planning process is evaluation. This is because in some cases the outcomes of the plans are affected by factors such as the child's health, the quality of our practice and whether the observations and assessments leading to the plan were sufficient or accurate.

Different ways of observing children

There are a variety of ways for gathering information about children's learning and development. Here are some of the common methods that you might come across.

Narrative observations

These are also called **running/written records**.

For this type of approach, you observe a child continuously for a period of time. You write down what you can see happening without making any judgements – almost as if you were commentating on a sport.

While you can find out quite a lot about a child using this method, it needs plenty of practice. You need to be able to convert what you see into words and write down things very quickly.

	Narrative observations
Advantage	• You can gain plenty of information about a child's overall development.
Disadvantages	• It is hard to quickly write down everything a child says and does. • You cannot work with children while using this method.

Name of child: Olive Date: 22/06/2021
Age: 11 months Recorded by: Jenny Smith
10.29 Babyroom

Olive crawls over to the windowsill. She kneels. She pulls herself up to the windowsill using her hands. She picks up a felt toy. She puts it in her mouth. She drops it and then looks down to find it. She holds onto the windowsill with her right hand, bends her knees and reaches to pick it up. She smiles at me and puts toy back in her mouth. She moves one hand and one foot at a time along the windowsill. She is looking out at the other children. One child comes to the window. Olive smiles. The child waves. Olives taps the window with one hand. Olive turns her head and smiles at me. She vocalises loudly. The child smiles again. Olive flexes her knees and bounces up and down while holding on with one hand to the windowsill. Olive bends knees and lets go of windowsill. She sits down on the floor in a controlled way. She crawls over to me with the toy in her right hand.

End of observation: 10.35

▲ An example of a running record

Practice points

Using a narrative, running/written recording

▶ Make sure you have paper and pen to hand.
▶ Write the date and time when you start recording.
▶ At the start of the recording, note down what the child is doing and who they are with.
▶ Considering using codes such as 'C' for child or 'A' for adult to speed you up.
▶ Keep sentences very short.
▶ Write down the time when the recording ends.

Snapshot observations

Using notepads or sticky notes, practitioners write:
▶ a line or two to help them remember a skill or something significant that a child has done
▶ the time of the note
▶ the name of the child.

This provides a 'snapshot' of what the child is doing or has done. At the end of the session, the notes should be written up more fully.

Education and Early Years T Level: Early Years Educator

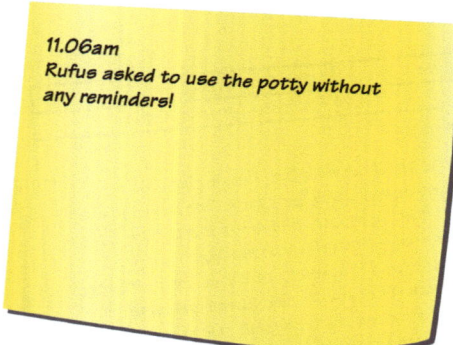

▲ An example of a sticky note used for a snapshot observation

	Snapshot observations
Advantages	• It is quick and easy to do. • This can be useful in group settings where children move between adults.
Disadvantages	• Notes might not provide sufficient information. • If not written up more fully, the notes might not be helpful.

Child tracker

This observation method is used to see which play activities children choose and how long they stay there for. It is useful when settings want to:
- check whether a child is able to concentrate on one activity for a while
- see which play opportunities children are using.

To carry out a child tracker, a plan of the indoor or outdoor space and play opportunities is created, e.g. sand, water and trains. As the child moves from one area to another, an arrow is drawn along between the two points. The time the child spent in each area is noted.

This method can be used at the same time as a narrative observation.

	Child tracker
Advantages	• This provides information about children's movements and interest in play opportunities. • It is easy to do.
Disadvantages	• It does not provide information about children's skills or development. • You cannot work with children while using this method.

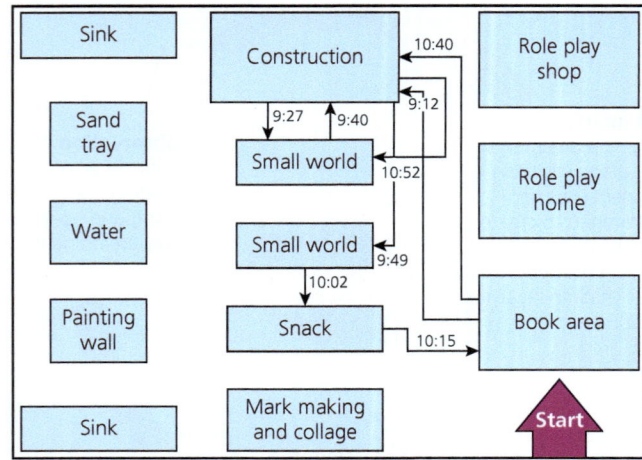

▲ An example of a child tracker

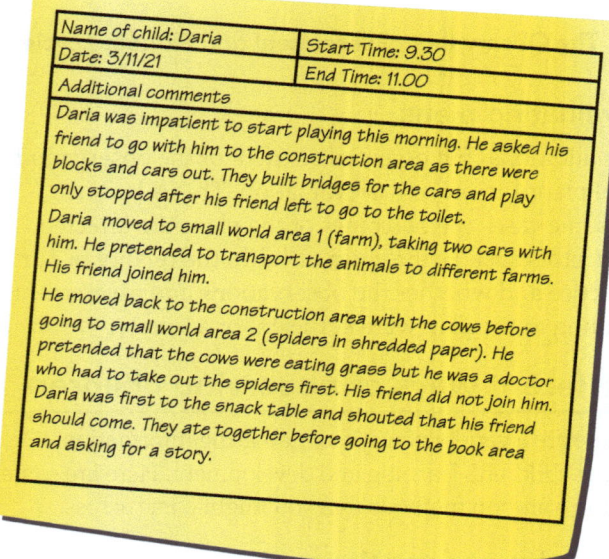

▲ An example of additional notes to accompany a child tracker

Learning stories/journals

Learning stories or journals record special moments in a child's play and development. They can be:
- online, using commercial software
- paper-based, almost like a scrapbook.

They usually include photographs or film clips, with comments about what has been recorded. Some settings working with babies and toddlers write as if the child was speaking, e.g. 'I popped my first bubble today. I laughed and laughed'. Some settings ask older children to comment and record down what they say.

Learning stories and journals can combine assessment and planning as part of their format.

Performance Outcome 3: Plan, Provide and Review Care, Play and Educational Opportunities

	Learning stories/journals
Advantage	• Learning stories and journals are very popular with parents.
Disadvantages	• The quality of 'stories' can be variable, and might not capture all aspects of a child's development. • This method can be time-consuming when paper-based, and takes adults away from being with children. • Online assessment using commercial software might not always be precise.

Checklist

Checklists can sometimes be referred to as tick charts.
▶ They contain a list of statements that link to age-related milestones.
▶ The adult then considers whether or not a child is able to demonstrate the skill.

Checklists and tick charts can be used alongside narrative observations or learning journals to help the practitioner think about whether the child is showing expected development.

Checklist: Dressing Skills		
Name of Child	Date	Comment
Hats, bonnets and sunhats		
Takes off hat		
Puts on hat		
Footwear		
Takes off socks		
Takes off shoes		
Attempts to put shoes and boots on		
Can put socks on with support		
Can put socks on unaided		
Can put shoes and boots on correct feet (excluding buckles or laces)		
T shirts, jumpers and coats etc.		
Pushes arms through tops		
Takes off T shirts, jumpers, etc. once started off		
Pulls head or arms through tops and can remove cardigans and coats		
Can put on top without fastenings unaided (although may be back to front)		
Can take off tops with easy fastenings		
Can put on tops with simple fastenings		
Trousers, shorts and pants		
Pulls down trousers, pants, etc. but does not step out of them		
Pulls up pants/trousers once legs are in		
Pulls down and steps out of shorts, trousers and pants		
Can put on pants and shorts unaided (although may be back to front)		

▲ An example of a checklist

A checklist can be carried out when an adult is working with a child or group of children. They can tick off the skills as they see them.

	Checklist
Advantages	• It provides information about whether a child is showing expected development linked to age milestones. • Atypical aspects of development can be quickly identified. • This method can be used while working with a child or group of children. • It is quick and easy to use, with minimal writing.
Disadvantage	• A child might not always show the skill on the checklist while they are playing or carrying out an activity.

Film clips

An increasing number of early years settings and also parents film children as they play or take part in activities. A film clip can be repeated to focus on different areas of development, e.g. physical coordination or social skills.

▶ Film clips can be sent in by parents as a way of sharing information about their child at home.
▶ Depending on the age and the activity, some filming can be done alongside working with children.

	Film clips
Advantages	• Film clips can be replayed. • They can provide a more accurate picture of the child's activity than written records.
Disadvantage	• Film clips must be stored securely as part of the GDPR (see page 46). As part of GDPR regulations, early years settings must ask parents for their consent.

Good to know

It is now recognised that simply recording observations without analysing them is not useful.

In the past, some early years settings spent a lot of time writing down comments or observations, but not using them to assess children or plan for their needs. This meant that some children whose development was atypical were not identified, because practitioners were not thinking about how their development compared to the expected age/stage milestones. A lot of practitioner time which could have been used to work with children was instead spent observing them.

In the latest EYFS and also the Ofsted inspection, early years settings are expected to have effective systems of observation and assessment. They are warned against spending time away from working with children.

Performance Outcome 3: Plan, Provide and Review Care, Play and Educational Opportunities

> **Practice points**
>
> **Writing informative observations**
>
> Your observation should provide you with as much detailed information as possible. If you are using an observation method that does not generate detailed information, such as the child tracker, write comments separately.
>
> ▶ Refer to expected developmental milestones before starting an observation – this will help draw your attention to when a child shows expected progress, but also atypical development.
> ▶ Make sure that you focus on *how* a child is doing things – the skills as well as what they are doing; e.g. 'he is colouring and staying within the lines' rather than 'he is enjoying colouring'.
> ▶ Notice a child's body language. Do they seem confident in what they are doing? Do they make eye contact when communicating with adults?
> ▶ Notice how well a child is concentrating and for how long. Are they easily distracted?
> ▶ Look at how a child copes when difficulties are experienced. Does the child persevere or immediately seek help?
> ▶ How much interaction and communication is taking place?
> ▶ For language, note down: the sentence length, use of vocabulary and the child's understanding.

Different approaches towards the assessment of children

Later in this unit, we will look at systems that early years settings might use to assess children. In this section, we look at how information is gathered to help with assessment. There are several ways in which this might occur.

Assessment approach	How information is gathered
Observations	We have already explained different methods of observations and how they help to gather information.
Question and answer	By asking simple questions, you can often find out about children's: • level of language • ability to sequence events • knowledge. It is good practice for this approach to be used as part of activities, play or daily routines. For example, you might ask a child: • what is going to happen next in a story • if they can lay out four places on a table for a snack.
Group activities	Noting children's reactions and responses during group activities can help you find out about their emotional and social skills, e.g. whether they can: • take turns • play cooperatively with others. Using group activities as a way of assessing knowledge can be less reliable as some children may know an answer, but might not say it while others are around.
Partnerships with parents and carers	It is important to receive information from parents and carers about how their child is at home. This is because children are often more relaxed at home and so may respond differently. For example: • Children who are quiet in a setting can be very chatty at home. • At home they might have opportunities to do different things, such as helping to look after pets or creating playlists for music events. They might be learning skills and knowledge that are not available in the setting. Parents and carers can talk to you about their child at home, or can send in photos or film clips.

Education and Early Years T Level: Early Years Educator

Assessment approach	How information is gathered
Partnerships with other professionals	Other professionals can also provide information to help your assessment. This might include speech and language therapists or educational psychologists, who carry out their own specialised assessments. This information can draw together a picture of the child's overall needs, which can also support planning.
Children's products	Sometimes, what children produce – such as drawings or models – can tell us about their understanding and level of development. You might not always see how the child has produced items, but the product itself may be used for assessment. For example, in the role-play area: • a child might write their name spontaneously on a note pad without an adult being present • two children might work together to build a complex road system for their cars.
Standardised testing	There is no standardised testing in the early years. However: • in Year 1 there is a standardised phonics check • in Year 2 SATs (Statutory Assessment Tests) take place. We looked at these in Core Chapter 2.

▲ What does this early mark making tell you about this child's understanding of writing?

Different approaches towards planning

Every early years setting has their own way of planning. This is often linked to the numbers of children and practitioners, and also the pedagogy (educational approach) of the setting. This means that you will need to find out the approach taken in the setting in which you work or are on placement.

We have already discussed the importance of plans in meeting children's needs and covering the areas of learning and development within the EYFS. They are also practical and useful, letting practitioners know:
▶ what resources need to be put out
▶ what activities will be on offer
▶ who is going to do the activities.

It is good practice for plans to be shared with parents – they might be very interested to know what type of activities, outings and experiences will be on offer.

Plans with different timescales

Typically, early years settings will produce more than one plan.
▶ Many settings have a long-term plan that covers a term or often a year.
▶ They might use this plan to create a medium-term plan, covering a month or so.
▶ They are also likely to have short-term plans, either daily or weekly.
▶ Settings might also have individual plans for some children who may have individual developmental needs: this is covered in Core Chapter 11.

Long-term planning

In the last few years, more settings have started to create long-term curriculum plans or education programmes. This is because the inspection framework looks more closely at the quality of education and whether settings have a long-term view of what experiences, knowledge and skills children will have when they leave the setting.

In settings where children stay for several years, there might be a long-term plan for each year or group. For example:
▶ A day care setting where children attend for four to five years might plan cooking opportunities. They might look at age-appropriate cooking skills such as washing, stirring and cutting and choose different recipes for each age group. By the time the children

leave, they will have cooked and prepared a range of different foods and meals.

Features of long-term planning

- ▶ It provides an outline of the skills, knowledge and experiences that the setting expects to provide.
- ▶ It may be amended according to changes in circumstances, such as the EYFS curriculum.
- ▶ It will be reviewed frequently.
- ▶ It will show how the EYFS curriculum areas of learning and development are to be covered.

> **Research**
>
> Find out whether your work placement has a long-term plan.
> ▶ How many months does it cover?
> ▶ How detailed is it?
> ▶ When is the long-term plan drawn up?

Medium-term planning

Medium-term planning can be for a half term, a month or a couple of weeks at a time. Often medium-term planning will include some of the main adult-led activities such as outings, cooking or visitors. Many settings will then show how these adult-led activities link to different areas of the curriculum. This is to ensure that each area of the curriculum is sufficiently covered.

Where settings use themes, for instance 'ourselves', or 'growing', as a basis for their work with children, the medium-term plan might show the type of activities and resources that will be on offer. Some early settings base their themes on children's interests.

Features of medium-term planning

- ▶ It might cover half a term, a month or a fortnight.
- ▶ It is likely to show adult-led or guided activities that are linked to the curriculum.
- ▶ The plan might be based on themes, and influenced by children's interests.
- ▶ It can be amended as a result of observations and feedback from short-term planning.

Short-term planning

Most settings have some form of short-term planning, and many have more than one type. Short-term plans have practical importance and are most referred to. Here are some examples of approaches to short-term planning that settings might use.

Type of short-term plan	How settings use this plan
Daily or weekly plans	Daily or weekly plans help adults know: • what activities, experiences and play opportunities will be offered • which adults will be responsible for organising them. In some cases, short-term planning will also show groupings of children or activities for individual children.
Continuous provision plans	Some settings have daily or sometimes weekly **continuous provision plans**. These plans are usually for the indoors and outdoors. • They show what play equipment and opportunities will be available. • To make sure there is enough variety of opportunity, some settings also divide the continuous provision plans into mornings and afternoons. • These plans are usually influenced by what individual children have shown interest in while being observed. • Some continuous plans also indicate to adults how they should develop children's learning.
In the moment planning/ child-led planning	Some settings create short-term plans based on what they have observed individual or groups of children doing. They use the observations to create further learning opportunities.
Plan, do, review planning	This planning model is based on the **HighScope approach**. • It encourages children to plan ahead what they are going to do in the session or the next day. • Children come together and discuss what they did and what they learned, and then, together with adults, plan for the next session. The HighScope approach was first developed in America in the 1960s to improve outcomes for children at risk of education disadvantage. It has been widely adopted as it improves children's thinking and language skills.

Features of short-term planning
- It identifies the adult-led activities and play opportunities on offer.
- The plan will incorporate children's interests and individual needs.
- It might indicate which staff are responsible for an activity or area.
- It might also show which children need to be a focus for certain activities or strategies.
- It shows how activities, experiences and play opportunities link to aspects of the EYFS.

> **Research**
>
> Find out how your work placement uses short-term planning.
> - Do they use more than one type of short-term plan?
> - How do they plan for the individual needs of children?

> **Good to know**
>
> Some settings use activity or detailed plans. These are quite time-consuming to produce, but students or volunteers can find them helpful.
>
> As a student, you may be asked to create an activity plan. These are useful as a way of making sure that an activity goes smoothly, but also that it meets children's needs. After an activity, you may be asked to reflect on how well it worked and the responses of individual children.
>
> Here are examples of the type of information that is recorded in an activity plan:
> - name of activity
> - objective, learning outcome or reason for this activity
> - child or children to take part and their ages
> - how the activity links to the EYFS curriculum
> - resources needed for the activity
> - safety issues to be considered
> - timing of the activity
> - the role of the adult during the activity
> - target language to be used by the adult
> - how the activity is to be introduced to children and then carried out.

K3.3 A range of developmental indicators that may suggest a child is in need of additional support

One of the purposes of assessment is to identify children who might need additional support. As we saw in Core Chapter 11, this is important because if early identification does not take place, children's overall development may be affected. We also know that early support can often make a positive difference to children's learning and their emotional wellbeing.

- One of the ways to identify children who might need additional support is by comparing the child's development to developmental milestones for each of the areas of development.
- Some parents notice things about their child that might be significant. When parents have concerns, it is worth following them up.

Cognitive development

Here are some broad indicators that a child might need additional support.
- The child is not showing the developmental skills, problem solving, concentration and memory expected for their age.
- The child needs significantly more time to learn a new skill than other children of the same age.
- The child shows limited understanding.
- The child has a limited attention span.

Examples of atypical cognitive development
- Anna is 14 months old. She is playing with a toy car and it slips to the ground. She does not look down at it or try and work out where it has gone. This is **atypical** (out of the ordinary), because most babies do this by 12 months.
- Ahmed is three years old. He is very easily distracted even when he wants to play with toys and resources. He finds it difficult to follow a single instruction such as 'get your coat'.
- Jake is four and a half years old. His group is learning a new action rhyme this week. By the end of the week, the other children have remembered the words and the simple actions. Jake cannot say the words with the actions.

Performance Outcome 3: Plan, Provide and Review Care, Play and Educational Opportunities

> **Good to know**
>
> **Sources for developmental milestones**
>
> The areas of learning and development in the EYFS are not the same as the developmental areas used by other health professionals. Therefore, you might need to find sources for developmental milestones. There are several places where you can find them, including those given in this book. You might find that they can differ slightly.
>
> If you are searching online, look out for the NHS logo on websites, as these are likely to be ones that health visitors and doctors refer to. Some specialist organisations, such as the ICAN charity for communication, give information relating to age/stage expectations.

Speech, language and communication development

As well as delay when compared to the milestones, here are some other indicators that might mean a child needs additional support:

- There is a lack of eye contact or lack of interest in communicating with familiar adults or children, e.g. not smiling, lack of vocalisations and talking.
- Levels of understanding are atypical for age, e.g. a three-year-old child cannot point to a picture of a 'big' dog, or does not seem to understand words that link to routines such as snack time.
- The speech sounds in words are not being used consistently, e.g. a child might point to a dog and say 'bog', but a moment later say 'day'.
- A child over three years old stammers, or a two-year-old shows signs of frustration or 'blocking' on a sound, e.g. 'bbbbbb … bag'.
- Speech cannot be understood by familiar adults after two and half years old, or by other adults when a child is over three.
- The number of words and sentence length is atypical compared to milestones.

Physical development

There are many indicators that a child may need additional support. They include ones that can be linked to safeguarding issues, such as:

- failure to thrive where a baby or toddler is below weight and height for their age – this might occur when a child is malnourished or not able to absorb the nutrients in food, and can affect their energy levels
- ongoing health problems, both those which are known and those which have not been diagnosed, may affect a child's attendance or ability to concentrate.

It is also important to look out for:

- atypical fine and gross motor skills, including difficulty in exploring and manipulating objects
- frequently falling, tripping or bumping into objects
- floppy and poor muscle tone
- difficulty balancing compared to children of same age
- difficulties with self-care skills such as feeding and drinking from a cup
- lack of energy and interest in moving or doing things.

Examples of atypical physical development

- Ayse is one year old. She cannot sit up even when supported. This is atypical as most children are sitting independently by this age.
- Jayden is three years old. He is always falling over and is covered in bruises. Staff have to watch out that he does not walk into other children or objects.
- Pamina is four years old. She gets frustrated when trying to use the collage table. She cannot hold a pencil or stick small pieces of fabric onto a piece of paper.

Personal, social and emotional development

It is important to look out for:

- atypical development for the age of the child, although there can be many influences on this area of development (such as transition, which we looked at in Core Chapter 7)
- changes to how children respond and behave. Significant changes might include lacking in confidence, withdrawing or isolating themselves, **regression** and clinginess to adults.

> **Key term**
>
> **Regression:** where children revert to behaviours associated with younger children, as a result of trauma or emotional upheaval.

K3.4 Different types of assessment and their purpose

Assessment is considered to be essential in early years settings. When a setting is inspected, the way practitioners assess children and then act on this information is looked at closely.

In Core Chapter 8, we saw that there are two broad types of assessment:
1. formative assessment
2. summative assessment.

Formative assessment (assessment for learning and development)

This is ongoing assessment which is based on observations and other information. It is used to help plan activities and review progress in the short term. It is also used to identify any gaps in learning and development.

- In the early years, many settings keep notes of what they have seen children do and then plan for the child's next steps.
- Learning journals are a good example of how observation, formative assessment and planning come together.
- It is good practice to share the significant moments of development or special moments for the child with parents. This can happen at the end of a session when parents collect their children or by using online platforms such as WhatsApp (although this must be set up securely to guarantee confidentiality).

> **Reflect**
>
> Look at the narrative observation of Olive on page 267.
> - Use this observation to make comments about Olive's stage of development in relation to physical development, emotional and social development and language development.
> - Give examples of resources, activities and the role of the adult that might promote Olive's development.

Summative assessment (assessment of learning and development)

This is a 'summing up' of what we know about a child. Some summative assessments form part of the statutory requirements of the EYFS, e.g. the progress check at aged two (see page 17). Summative assessments are very important for:
- checking that a child is making expected progress
- informing planning for children/young people's next steps

- providing information when children change early years settings, such as when they move to a reception class.

It is good practice for early years settings to write summative assessments regularly and to share them with parents. In addition, there are two statutory summative assessments in the EYFS:
- the progress check at two (see page 224)
- the EYFS Profile (see page 224).

SUMMATIVE ASSESSMENT
Date: 24/1/21
Name of child: Leo XXX
Age: 2 years 1 month

Communication and language	Physical development
Leo is talking well and is using more than fifty words. He has started to join words together. He is starting to use language to express his feelings and needs, e.g. 'no sleep!' or 'more train'. His language is within expected development for his age.	Leo can feed himself using a spoon. He can remove some items of clothing such as socks, hats and tries to put on his shoes. He is starting to indicate when his nappy needs changing. He can walk up and down steps when holding an adult's hand, one foot to each step. He is very active and enjoys climbing, throwing and is attempting to pedal. He uses his left hand for tasks such as feeding, painting and reaching out for objects. All aspects of his physical development are within expected range of development.
Personal, social and emotional development	**Next steps to support development**
Leo is very settled and happy. Transitions in the morning and afternoon are smooth, although he can be wary of other parents that he is not familiar with. Leo plays alongside other children and sometimes passes toys to them – an early social skill. Leo follows routines such as tidying up. He is starting to understand that he must wait, e.g. he has to have a bib on before eating. He sometimes shows signs of frustration especially when tired. Leo's development in this area is typical of his age and stage of development.	Introduce a fork with a spoon at mealtimes. Provide opportunities for Leo to kick a ball, throw and catch. Involve Leo in daily routines, e.g. collect coat and shoes, lay table. Share books every day and introduce new rhymes. Observe whether Leo has bladder maturation with the view to starting toilet training. Reassure Leo when he meets unfamiliar adults.

▲ Example of a summative assessment

Regular summative assessments

Early years settings regularly carry out summative assessments to check that children's development links to typical patterns of development. How often this takes place will often depend on the ages of the children:
- Practitioners working with babies might carry out a summative assessment of their development every month.
- Reception classes might carry out a summative assessment each term.

Performance Outcome 3: Plan, Provide and Review Care, Play and Educational Opportunities

Writing a summative assessment

A summative assessment should contain the following information for each of the developmental areas or EYFS areas of learning and development:
- What development is the child currently showing?
- What progress has been made since the last summative assessment?
- How does the child's level of development, knowledge or skills compare to children of a similar age?
- General comments about the child.
- What might be the next steps for supporting this child's development? (This feeds into the medium-term or short-term planning.)

A summative assessment is based on the information from a range of sources which we looked at earlier in this chapter, including observations and information from parents and professionals.

Some settings write the summative assessment with the parents, or ask for their ideas about what they would like the child to be able to do next.

K3.5 Practitioner responsibilities to undertake continuing professional development

When you have finished taking this qualification, you might be tempted to think that you have finished learning about how to care for and promote children's development. But this will not be the case. As part of being a professional, you will need to keep up to date and develop your skills and knowledge further. This process is known as continuing professional development, or CPD (see page 159).

CPD can be organised by early years settings, local authorities and also professional bodies such as PACEY or the Early Years Alliance. Here are some of the reasons why CPD is so important.

Reason for CPD	Why this is important
Maintaining up-to-date early years knowledge and practice	Approaches to working with children change over time. This is sometimes because research shows some approaches are more useful than others. A good example of this is sleep positions for babies: • A few years ago, it was thought that putting babies to sleep on their front was the safest. • Now it is recognised that babies need to be placed on their backs.
Adhering to framework/ curriculum requirements	From time to time, the early years curriculum changes. When this happens, Ofsted will also change its framework for inspection. For example: • The latest change to the EYFS focused on promoting communication, language and in particular children's language. This change occurred because research showed that children from disadvantaged backgrounds were starting in school with lower levels of language. The statutory requirements to safeguarding and welfare can also change. For example: • There is a new requirement for early years settings to promote children's oral health, by adding tooth brushing in their routines. This requirement changed because a large number of children need to have their teeth extracted due to dental decay. As settings are required to follow the EYFS, it is essential that everyone knows about any changes. • Information about changes could be a focus for staff meetings or training days. • Leaders of early years settings might ask practitioners to read articles that explain changes.
Supporting curriculum development	There can be new ideas and practice in relation to areas of the curriculum. For example: • Research into mathematics showed that young children can learn about number through everyday activities when adults draw their attention to it.
Supporting reflective practice for assessment, planning and provision	We have seen that assessment, planning and our provision for children can have a significant impact on their development and wellbeing. By focusing and reflecting on your practice in these areas, you can improve your effectiveness. Approaches to planning, assessment and provision do change over time and it is important to stay up-to-date and then reflect on any changes that you need to make.
Promoting best outcomes for children and families	Some children that you work with might be at risk of educational disadvantage. Changing outcomes for this group of children has been a focus for the UK government policy in England for some time.

Education and Early Years T Level: Early Years Educator

Reason for CPD	Why this is important
	As part of the Ofsted inspection, all early years settings need to show that they are helping disadvantaged children to make progress. You might need to learn about how best to support these children and their families.
Keeping up to date with legislation changes to inform policies and procedures	As part of the safeguarding and welfare requirements, settings have to comply with a range of legislation including food handling, first aid and health and safety. You might be asked to attend training or research, so that you can feedback to the team or understand how to implement changes in policies and procedures.
Unifying and making a meaningful contribution to the team	In early years settings that have many team members, it is helpful if everyone is taking the same approach. This means that teams will often come together for CPD. When teams come together for group CPD, it is often called 'Inset'. • As part of inset training, you might be encouraged to voice your opinions or provide some ideas. • If you have stayed up to date with the latest developments, you will find it easier to contribute to team discussions.
Improving your own skills and quality of practice	If you work as part of a team, you and your manager might identify areas where you could improve your knowledge or skills. This could occur as part of an appraisal or performance review. You might also realise that you need additional skills and knowledge when you work with particular groups of children, such as two-year-olds.
Improving opportunities for progression and promotion in your own role	In order to progress and gain promotion, you will need to show the ways in which you are skilled and knowledgeable. You might also need to develop some specialist knowledge, such as: • working with children who are bereaved • supporting children who have English as an additional language.

How to meet your own developmental needs

There are many ways in which you can develop your skills and knowledge. We considered many of these in Core Chapter 9, and it might help if you revisit that chapter.

The spider diagram shows the range of ways in which you can meet your professional development needs.

▲ Some ways to meet your own needs for professional development

Performance Outcome 3: Plan, Provide and Review Care, Play and Educational Opportunities

Feedback from others

Listening carefully to what other professionals and parents tell you about your practice can make a huge difference to your skills and knowledge. To benefit from feedback you need to avoid being defensive and instead, pick up on the key messages for your practice.

This might not always be a comfortable process, but if you can deal with constructive criticism, your work with children and their families can improve.

Self-directed learning, and reading and researching

It can be worthwhile for you to choose an area of child development, psychology or practice and then do some of your own research to find out more.
- This might involve reading books and early years journals such as *Nursery World*, or going online and looking at reputable websites such as for the NHS or Ofsted.
- You can also approach other professionals to learn more.

This self-directed learning is very important, especially as you develop confidence and competence.

Shadowing or observing other professionals

Your practice can develop if you learn by:
- watching others at work
- finding out more about how and why they do things.

This process is known as **shadowing**. The aim is to watch, listen and learn.

If you are allowed to shadow professionals such as speech and language therapists or occupational therapists as they work with children in your setting, this can help you to develop additional knowledge and skills.

Internal and external training courses

There are a wide range of training courses available, organised locally or online. Some might be free, others are paid for. Going on external courses (outside your setting) can help you meet people from other settings and develop your understanding of practice in the setting.

Most early years settings organise internal training ('INSET' training – see page 160).

To benefit from training, it is helpful to:
- take notes
- join in discussions
- listen carefully.

After online or external training, many early years settings expect staff to share key points with the rest of the team.

Focused reflection

Focused reflection is about thinking about your own practice. It can be in the form of thinking through how an activity has gone or how better to communicate and support an individual child.

It is helpful to ask others to contribute when carrying out focused reflection, as it can be hard to work out your own strengths and weaknesses.

A good way of reflecting on your practice is asking another person to film you as you work. Remember that if you do this, it is essential that you follow regulations and your setting's policy surrounding the filming of children, including GDPR, for which you must have consent from parents and carers. (See pages 46 and 270.)

Visits to other settings

One of the best ways to develop your practice is to visit other early years settings. Every setting, even chains of nurseries, will feel different. This will be due to a combination of factors, including layout, the group of children that attend and the vision of the team.
- By visiting other settings, you can reflect on what your setting is doing well, but also how things can be done differently.
- If you are also able to shadow individual staff as they work, this might help you to reflect on your own practice.

> **Skills practice**
>
> The pre-school where you work is due to have an Ofsted inspection in the next few months. In the last Ofsted inspection, it was noted that the planning, observation and assessment systems in place were not supporting all children to make progress. You have been asked to lead a session for other staff members about planning, observation and assessment.
>
> 1. To understand the current requirements for observation, assessment and planning, your manager has suggested that you should:
>   - research the requirements of the EYFS in relation to observation, assessment and planning
>   - read the Ofsted Early Years Inspection Handbook to understand what Ofsted will be looking for
>   - research short- and long-term planning models that are used in a range of settings.
> 2. In addition, your pre-school manager thinks that it would be helpful to read some recent Ofsted reports that have been carried out on pre-schools who also take children from two to five years.
> 3. As the quality of observations and assessments were criticised in the last inspection, your manager wants you to carry out three observation methods on children of different ages and talk to the team about how they can be used for formative assessments. He also wants you to provide an example of a summative assessment on a two-year-old child that could be used to meet the requirements of the progress check at this age.
> 4. Some of the team find it difficult to use assessment to develop children's learning and development. Your manager has asked you to plan four appropriate activities that link to the EYFS, based on the information from the summative assessment.

Performance Outcome 4: Safeguard and Promote the Health, Safety and Wellbeing of Children

One of the roles of all settings working with children is to keep them healthy and safe. In early years, this role is more complex because of the age and stages of development of children. The importance of keeping children healthy and safe is reflected in the statutory framework for the EYFS. In this section, we look at several aspects of how to keep children healthy and safe, including safeguarding, sleep, physical activity and nutrition as well as infection control. We also look at emergencies and accidents.

Learning outcomes

This chapter covers the following knowledge outcomes for Performance Outcome 4.

- **K4.1** The key principles of safeguarding
- **K4.2** The different types of abuse and the associated signs of abuse
- **K4.3** How health and wellbeing supports babies' and children's resilience, curiosity and independence, brain development, play and learning experiences and holistic development
- **K4.4** Factors that contribute to children's wellbeing and the signs that indicate a child needs support
- **K4.5** How meeting basic care needs impacts on children's self-actualisation and how practitioners provide physical care
- **K4.6** How a range of strategies support children to develop self-care skills and the impact of self-care skills on children's health, safety and wellbeing
- **K4.7** How sleep and rest enhances babies' and children's holistic development and current guidance for sleep requirements and safe sleeping procedures
- **K4.8** Balanced diets for babies and children and how oral health can be promoted
- **K4.9** The signs and symptoms of a range of common illnesses/infections including the signs that require immediate medical attention
- **K4.10** How illnesses and infections are spread and effective practice to prevent and control infection
- **K4.11** The difference between an accident and an emergency situation, preventions and precautions and limitations of own role

K4.1 The key principles of safeguarding

Everyone who works with children and young people under the age of 18 has a responsibility to keep them safe and free from harm. Make sure you are:
- familiar with your setting's safeguarding and child protection policy
- up to date with training through the setting.

The key principles of safeguarding are:
1. The **paramountcy** principle – the welfare of the child comes first.
2. Early intervention is crucial to protect children.
3. Safeguarding is the responsibility of all practitioners in a setting.
4. The four guiding principles from the Early Years Foundation Stage (EYFS) that shape practice.

Paramountcy principle

This is a key principle in family law and is a component of the Children Act 1989. It means that:
- the child's welfare should always be the main consideration when decisions are being made about them
- adults should, as far as possible, consider and meet the wishes of the child.

Early intervention is crucial

As soon as there are concerns about a child, these should be raised in line with legal requirements and the setting's safeguarding policy.

The document 'Working Together to Safeguard Children 2018' published by the Department for Education stresses the importance of an early help assessment as soon as possible, whatever the age of the child.
- Local authorities are required by law to provide services for the safeguarding and welfare of children.
- Early years settings will need to work with them through your setting's Designated Safeguarding Lead (DSL).

> **Research**
>
> Look at your local authority's safeguarding page. What information does it give you about the following:
> - how early years settings should refer a child if they are concerned
> - early help assessment
> - what to do if you have any concerns about an adult's actions, behaviour or suitability for working with children.

Safeguarding is the responsibility of all

All those who work with children and young people are responsible for keeping them safe. If there are any safeguarding concerns, these should be acted upon: doing nothing might mean putting a child at further risk.

> **In practice**
>
> Make sure you know where to find your setting's safeguarding policy. A hard copy may be stored in the office, and it should be accessible on the setting's website. Once you have done so, use this to do the following:
> - Outline your responsibilities under the policy.
> - Identify your DSL.
> - Describe how you would report any concerns while maintaining confidentiality.

The guiding principles from the EYFS

These principles are covered in the diagram on page 221 of Performance Outcome 1.

> **Research**
>
> Read through Section 3 of the EYFS Statutory Framework on safeguarding and welfare requirements. Write down what it tells you about:
> - suitable people and the importance of having appropriate checks
> - the responsibilities of the DSL
> - staff training for safeguarding.

Performance Outcome 4: Safeguard and Promote the Health, Safety and Wellbeing of Children

K4.2 The different types of abuse and the associated signs of abuse

Sadly, there are a number of different types of abuse, and all adults who work with children have a responsibility to be aware of and look out for signs of these in order to protect them and keep them safe.

According to the NSPCC, some children and young people might also be more at risk, for example:
- those in care
- those who are suffering neglect
- those with disabilities.

Abuse is likely to be very traumatic. It can cause outward signs in children, such as physical marks and changes in behaviour, and can have long-term effects on them.

You should also know the steps to take according to your setting's safeguarding or child protection policy if you have any concerns about a child.

This diagram shows the different types of abuse.

- bruising, bites, burns and non-accidental injuries, particularly if you notice them on a regular basis, or regular fractures or broken bones
- reluctance to remove clothes or change in case marks are seen
- flinching or cowering when adults make a sudden movement.

> **Practice points**
>
> ### What to do if you spot a suspicious injury
> - When the child is not with the parent, ask them about how the injury happened
> - Mention the injury to the parent, and note their reaction and explanation.
> - Keep a note of the injury and explanation, in case the setting is accused of having caused the injuries.
> - Report the injuries to the DSL in your setting.

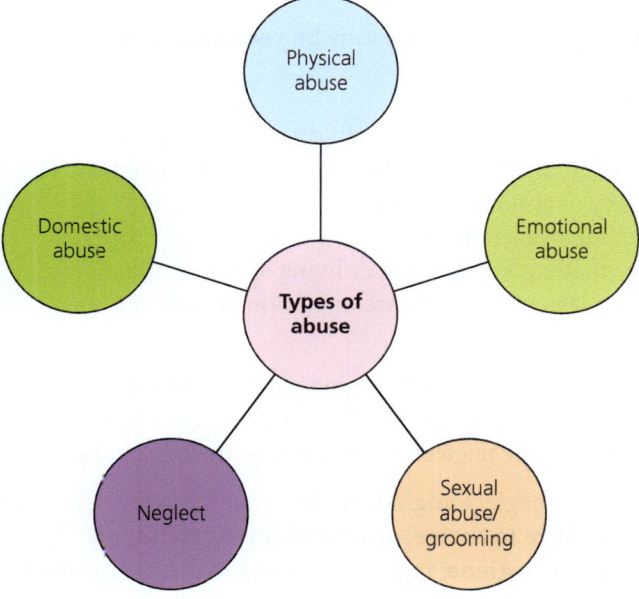

▲ Types of abuse

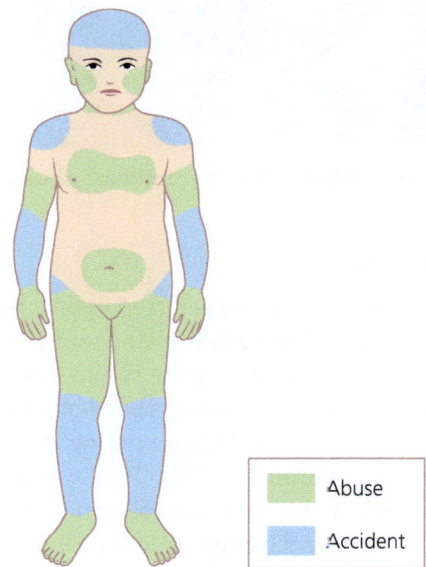

▲ Diagram showing areas of accidental and non-accidental injury

Associated signs of abuse

Physical abuse

This is when a baby or child is physically hurt or harmed by the actions of an adult. It can be tricky to detect this, as young children often have bumps and bruises. There are some things, however, that you should look out for:
- repeated illnesses and/or medical investigations, particularly if a child is regularly absent from an early years setting

Emotional abuse

This is when a baby or child is continually emotionally mistreated over time, affecting their emotional development. Emotional abuse occurs when a child is regularly and repeatedly made to feel worthless, unloved or frightened. It might be the only form of abuse a child suffers, but it can be alongside other forms of abuse.

Emotional abuse is harder to detect than other forms, as there are no outward or obvious signs. However, signs may include:
- withdrawal: the child is quieter and backs away from involvement in activities or being with friends
- changes in behaviour: for example, behaviour associated with comfort-seeking such as thumb sucking
- toileting problems: the child forgets to go and has regular 'accidents', when they didn't before
- developmental regression: for example, behaving in a way normally associated with a younger child
- poor concentration and cannot stay focused on tasks and activities
- difficulty in relating to others and making friends
- being affectionate to lots of different people, and needing more adult attention.

▲ Can you identify signs of emotional abuse in children?

Sexual abuse

This is when sexual activity is forced upon a baby or child. It includes both physical and non-physical contact, which may be forcing the victim to look at pornographic material or taking sexual photographs. 'Sexual abuse can also include grooming, or exploitation of children by adults. This is sometimes known as CSE, or child sexual exploitation (see Core Element 3.7 on page 53). Signs might include:
- sexualised behaviour or language: children may display signs of knowing more than is appropriate for their age, for example, simulating a sexual act in their play or talking in a way which is not expected
- sexually transmitted diseases (STDs – sometimes known as STIs, sexually transmitted infections), urinary infections, swelling, soreness, discharge: sometimes young children might be reluctant to use the toilet or say that it hurts. They may also have increased toileting accidents
- the child being easily upset, clingy or seeming more anxious than usual.

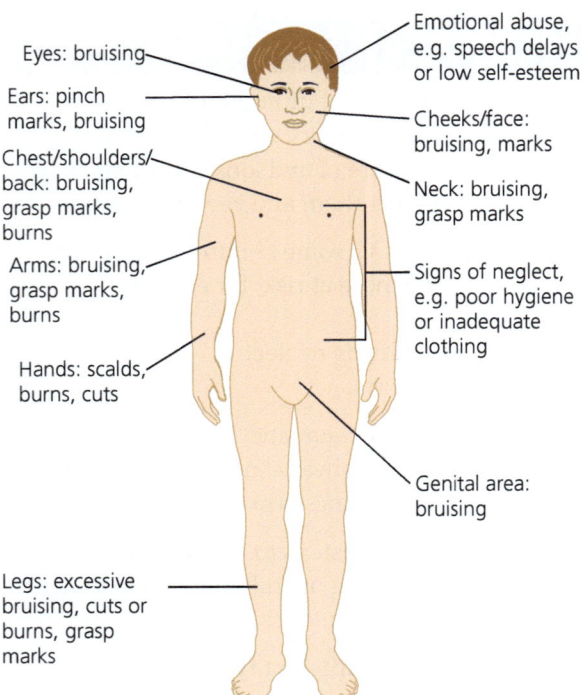

▲ Areas where abuse may be seen or detected

Neglect

This is when a baby's or child's needs are persistently not met by those who have parental responsibility. The baby or child might have:
- insufficient food
- inadequate clothing or living space
- a lack of medical care or emotional support when needed.

This can impact on their physical and emotional development and, depending on their age and the extent of the neglect, their ability to make friends.

Signs of neglect might include:
- **failure to thrive**, grow and develop normally
- **poor hygiene**: regularly coming to the setting with a dirty appearance, such as dirty clothes
- **inadequate clothing**: regularly coming to the setting without appropriate clothing, for example, no coat in rainy weather
- **untreated health problems**: the child is regularly unwell, and health issues seem to be neglected
- **hungry/thirsty**: the child is always hungry or thirsty, or is regularly asking for food from adults or other children
- **failure to attend setting**: the child is often absent, possibly with no explanation given
- **housing issues**: the child is regularly moved around, often without informing the setting, or is living in cramped or inadequate accommodation.

Performance Outcome 4: Safeguard and Promote the Health, Safety and Wellbeing of Children

Domestic abuse (Domestic Abuse Act 2021)

This is when there is violent behaviour within a relationship or family: a child or young person who sees or hears or experiences the effects of the abuse is also a victim of abuse. Domestic abuse also includes 'honour'-based violence within a family. Signs might include:

- aggression in the child and possibly witnessed in the parent or carer: young children may also, when they role play, show the aggression that they have seen at home
- anti-social behaviour: the child acts in ways that are not linked to expected development for behaviours
- depression or anxiety: the child appears withdrawn and unhappy
- problems in the setting: they might have problems in their relationships with others within the setting, or other issues such as problems forming friendships or responding to staff.

Remember that this list is not exhaustive, and that there might be other signs of abuse.

> **Test yourself**
>
> 1. Who is responsible for safeguarding in your early years placement?
> 2. Name the five different types of abuse.
> 3. What type of abuse might you suspect if a baby or young child was dirty and constantly hungry?
> 4. Why is emotional abuse difficult to detect?

K4.3 The importance of health and wellbeing to aspects of babies' and children's development

Feeling well, happy and settled can make a huge difference to some aspects of babies' and children's development.

- When children are feeling poorly or are not emotionally secure, they are less likely to have the energy and confidence to play, concentrate or join in activities.
- This can affect their overall development.

The table below shows some specific reasons why it is important that we ensure that babies and children are healthy and that we consider their wellbeing.

Aspect of health and wellbeing	Why this is important for children's development
Resilience	The term **resilience** describes the ability to cope with setbacks or physical difficulties. • In the case of babies and young children, their health and wellbeing can help them to cope emotionally if they have setbacks. • Health and wellbeing also plays a part in how easily the body can fight potential infection. Children who are unwell or unhappy are more likely to have frequent illnesses.
Curiosity and independence	Being alert, curious and keen to do things without help makes a significant difference to babies' and children's ability to learn. • Children who are not well are not likely to have the energy to be curious and independent. • In the same way, children who are unhappy or insecure might not be confident enough to explore.
Brain development	In the early years, babies' and children's brains are rapidly developing. This development is linked to having a healthy diet, sufficient sleep and opportunities for stimulation. Children's brain development is affected when: • they are unwell • there are problems that affect their wellbeing • they are not playing, interacting or exploring. This is because development is linked to stimulation.
Play opportunities and learning experiences	We know that play is important for children's development, as well as opportunities to take part in activities with adults. • Where there are problems with health or wellbeing, babies and children might not be able to engage with play and learning. They might be too tired or unconfident. • This can reduce their opportunities for stimulation and interaction.
Holistic development	Children's overall or holistic development is affected by their health and wellbeing. For example: • A child might not feel like playing with other children. This in turn will affect their social and language development. • If a child is feeling too tired to concentrate or explore, they might miss out on physical skills.

▲ How might health and wellbeing affect children's curiosity?

K4.4 Factors that contribute to children's wellbeing and the signs that indicate a child needs support

Factors contributing to health and wellbeing

A number of factors are important when looking at children's health and wellbeing. These factors form the basis of good practice in early years settings, and many are also covered by statutory requirements in the EYFS.

Sleep and rest

Babies and young children need significantly more sleep than adults. This is because their brains are growing and processing information. Their bodies are also physically growing and this growth takes place during sleep.

Babies and young children also need times to rest.
- They are not able to take part in constant activity and concentration. This is linked to the size of their hearts and lungs.
- Rest is also needed for their brains to catch up on everything they have seen, touched and done.

On page 301 (Section K4.7) we look in more detail at the importance of sleep.

Physical activity

Babies and young children need opportunities to move.
- For babies, movement is important as a way of developing the skills and muscles that they will need to stand and walk.
- For young children, physical activity is important to strengthen bones, develop coordination, and develop heart and lung capacity.

While these are some of the physical benefits, there are emotional ones too:
- During physical activity, we release feel good hormones known as endorphins. They contribute to positive feelings.
- Physical activity also helps babies and children to develop confidence and a sense of self-efficacy (see page 262).

Health and nutrition

Alongside sleep and physical activity, nutrition plays a significant part in children's health and wellbeing. This is because food and drink:
- give the body energy
- provide the nutrients needed to fight infection and grow.

Performance Outcome 4: Safeguard and Promote the Health, Safety and Wellbeing of Children

Later in this chapter, we look at what makes a healthy diet for babies and children.

Stability and safe environments

Babies and children benefit from routines and also consistent responses from adults. This helps them to feel relaxed, which is essential in order for them to learn and develop.

Babies and children must also be kept physically safe. We look at ways in which we can prevent accidents and emergencies at the end of this unit.

Adult care

Babies and children rely on adults to provide personal care for them. This includes nappy changes, help with toileting and feeding.

- ▶ The care that adults provide for babies and young children can prevent illness and infections.
- ▶ The way that this care takes place can make a significant difference to whether children feel safe and comfortable, so it is good practice for the child's key person to carry out many care activities.

▲ How is this adult supporting this baby's health and wellbeing?

Secure attachments

Babies and young children flourish when they have secure attachments to their parents, but also the practitioners who work with them. We looked at the importance of attachment in Core Chapter 7.

Secure attachments in early years settings:
- ▶ help prevent separation anxiety
- ▶ form the basis of the key person system (see page 118).

> **Research**
>
> The statutory framework for the EYFS requires all early years settings to have a key person system. Find out how your work placement's system helps children to develop secure attachment.

Opportunities for indoor/outdoor play

As we saw in Performance Outcome 1, play is important for children's overall health and wellbeing. Children need opportunities to play both in and out of doors.

- ▶ Time outdoors is seen as so important that it is a requirement in the EYFS for all children to be outdoors at least once a day.
- ▶ Children also need variety in their play and so early years settings will put out a range of different play opportunities. In Performance Outcome 1, we saw how the different play types can impact on children's development.

Friendships

Being with other children becomes increasingly important.

While many two-year-olds are not yet playing cooperatively, they start to enjoy watching and being with other children.

By around three years, children start to develop friendships. These are important for children's emotional and social development, as they help children to:
- ▶ learn the skills that they need to be with others
- ▶ feel good about themselves and so support their emotional wellbeing.

Signs that may indicate a child needs support

The table on page 288 shows signs that may indicate that a child or their family needs support. It is also important to understand that in some cases, these may indicate that there is a safeguarding issue.

Education and Early Years T Level: Early Years Educator

Signs indicating the child needs support	How to interpret these signs
Lack of personal hygiene	Babies and young children need adults to help them stay clean. This covers everything from nappy changes to keeping hair clean. Where there is a lack of personal hygiene, it might be a sign: • of neglect • that a parent is not coping.
Recurring health problems	There are many reasons why babies and children have recurring health problems. In some cases, this might be because: • the child's nutrition or sleep requirements are not being met • the child is stressed – which can be the result of separation anxiety, transitions or inconsistent care.
Not meeting developmental milestones	We saw in Core Chapter 7 and Performance Outcome 1 that there are a range of developmental milestones. They help us to assess whether a child is showing typical development. • Where babies or children are not showing expected development for their age, a child might need additional support. • There are many reasons why this may be the case, including poor nutrition, sleep, medical conditions or learning difficulties. We have seen in Performance Outcome 2 why it is important for atypical development to be identified.
Being isolated from friendship groups	While typically children start to have friends from around three years, these friendships are not necessarily stable ones until children are around five years old. It is, however, worth recognising when young children do not show an interest in other children or when older children are isolated from friendship groups. It may indicate that a child has difficulty with social communication or that their withdrawal is linked to a child protection issue.

K4.5 How meeting basic care needs impacts on children's self-actualisation

In Core Chapter 2, we looked at Maslow's theory of self-actualisation. In this theory, he suggested that unless a person's basic needs are met, they cannot fulfil their potential.

We can link this theory to our practice of working with babies and young children. Look back at page 33, and see how the pyramid diagram links to babies' and young children's needs.

Here we can see some practical ways that Maslow's ideas link to policies and practice in the early years.
▶ When babies' and children's basic needs are met, we can see that they are more likely to be ready to learn, play and develop.
▶ Without meeting these basic needs, there is a danger that children will be too distracted and distressed to benefit from early years education.

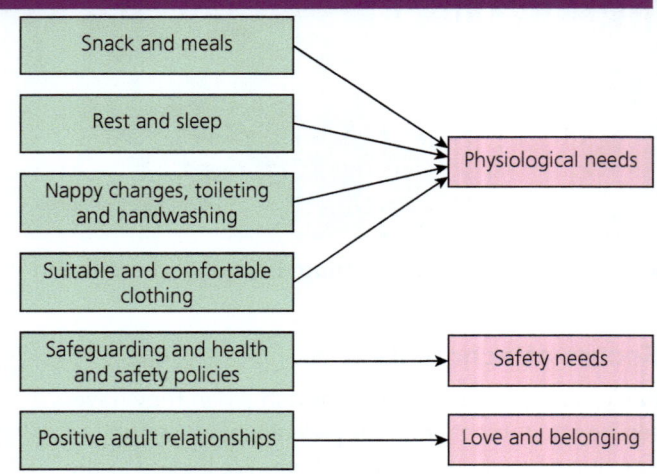

▲ How Maslow's theory of self-actualisation links to policy and practice in early years

Performance Outcome 4: Safeguard and Promote the Health, Safety and Wellbeing of Children

How practitioners provide physical care for babies and young children

Nutrition and hydration

The EYFS requires that:
- early years settings have water on offer at all times for babies and children
- any meals or snacks provided by the setting meet babies' and children's nutritional needs.

We look in more detail about the nutritional requirements of children later in this chapter (see page 303).

Nutrition and hydration for babies from birth to six months

When working with babies, early years settings usually follow the feeding routines that parents are using with their children. This is usually linked to a baby's sleep pattern.
- Some parents will be using formula milk, which they give to their babies using a bottle. Formula milk is specially made so that babies can easily digest it.
- Other mothers might breastfeed their babies. They might either come into the setting to breastfeed or provide bottles of **expressed** milk – which they have pumped out of the breast for feeding later.
- Some parents choose to breastfeed and also use formula milk at other times. This is known as 'mixed' feeding.

Apart from formula milk and breast milk, under no circumstances should any other type of milk be given to babies.

The role of the practitioner with regards to breastfeeding

If a baby is being breastfed in the setting, your role is to help the mother feel at ease.
- Ask her where she would prefer to sit and feed.
- Offer her a drink, as breastfeeding can make women thirsty.

Wherever possible, we should encourage breastfeeding as it has many benefits for babies.

The role of the practitioner with regards to bottle feeding

On pages 319–20 we look at how to:
- sterilise a bottle
- make up a formula feed
- prepare breast milk that has been expressed.

The role of the adult during a bottle feed is to make the baby feel comfortable and emotionally secure. Ideally, the baby's key person should do as many of the feeds as possible.

Practice points

Do:	Don't:
• Check which milk is for which baby. • Wash your hands before feeding. • Check the temperature of the bottle by putting some of the liquid onto your wrist. • Hold the baby in the crook of your arm, so they can look into your eyes. • Talk or even sing to the baby. • As the bottle empties, tilt it so that the liquid always covers the teat. • Throw away any leftover milk straight away.	• Give or prepare any milk unless you are sure that it is the milk for the baby you are feeding. • Lie the baby down flat – this may cause them to choke. • Rush feeding. Babies might need to take a short break and then carry on. • Make a baby finish the bottle. If babies are overfed, they might be sick afterwards.

Keeping records

It is important to keep a record of:
- when a baby has been fed
- how much they have taken.

This information needs to be shared with parents at the end of the session.

Complementary feeding or weaning: six months to a year

At around six months, babies are usually weaned. This is sometimes called **complementary feeding**. The idea is that the baby gets some food other than milk. This is important because as babies grow, they need a wider range of nutrients.

Education and Early Years T Level: Early Years Educator

Some babies may be weaned earlier on the advice of health professionals. Early weaning is not recommended, as babies' stomachs are not ready for it.

- At first babies are given a few teaspoons of pureed fruit or vegetables alongside a formula or breast milk feed.
- New foods are introduced little by little, but by nine months babies are likely to be having three small meals a day.
- From 12 months, babies can be given cow's milk to drink (see pages 304–5 for more information on how to wean).

Baby-led weaning

Traditionally, the weaning process involved babies being given spoonfuls of pureed food and only a few months later being encouraged to feed themselves.

Baby-led weaning is different:
- Babies are encouraged to pick up foods and feed themselves from the start.
- The adult does not feed the baby.

It is thought that by touching, playing and exploring food, babies are more likely to try out new foods. However, it can be very messy and take the baby longer to eat.

It is always important to find out about the approach that is used by parents. Some parents do a mixture of baby-led and traditional weaning.

The role of the adult

There are several things that you need to think about when babies are being weaned.

▲ Why is it important that this baby is having foods other than milk?

What to do	Explanation
Be prepared	Anyone working with babies knows that you need to be prepared. The baby's food has to be ready, as hungry babies can be loud! • As weaning can be messy, babies are usually put in a bib. • Have everything that you might need to hand, as you cannot leave a baby alone with food. • In group settings where there is more than one baby, it is important to check that the right food is given to the right baby. Some babies might have identified food allergies.
Safety	You have to think about keeping babies safe. • If you are using a highchair, strap the baby in with a harness. • Make sure you know how to undo a harness quickly. This is important, because in the first few weeks of weaning, babies can gag or choke on food. • You should also know the first aid procedure in case a baby chokes. • Never leave a baby alone in a highchair or with food, even for a moment.
Watching for allergic reaction	During feeding and for a while afterwards, it is important to look out for any allergic reactions. • Foods are usually introduced one at a time at first, just in case the baby has an allergic reaction to it. • Some foods are not given until babies are much older, in case of allergic reactions. A reaction might occur immediately, and although this is rare, it can be dangerous because the baby might struggle to breathe. For more information on first aid, see page 316.

Performance Outcome 4: Safeguard and Promote the Health, Safety and Wellbeing of Children

Make the experience enjoyable	Babies need to enjoy mealtimes. Follow these tips to make it an enjoyable experience: • Sit at the same level as the baby. • Talk to the baby and offer the food. • If you are spoon feeding, do not put too much on the spoon. • Wait for the baby to finish before offering more. • Babies often want to play with food. This is fine and is not a problem. • Sometimes, babies throw food on the floor. If a baby repeats this action, it is likely to be a sign that they have had enough of that food.
Follow the babies' lead	Babies know when they are full. They will try to tell you this by turning their heads or even pushing food away. • It can be a good idea to offer a drink of water and then see if they want any more, but you should never keep insisting. This can cause problems with weight gain later on. • There will be some days when babies want to eat more than on others. This is usually linked to a growth spurt. • Babies may also show that they do not like the taste of a food. If this happens, you should not insist on the food. Instead, offer something else as long as it is healthy. The food that they did not like can be given another day.

▲ The role of the adult in baby-led weaning

Offering drink

When babies are being weaned, it is important that they are regularly offered water.

You might need to help the baby learn to sip at first.
▶ To avoid water going into the baby's airways: gently tip the cup, watch for a gulp and then bring it back down again.
▶ Never keep the beaker tipped up as this can prevent the baby from breathing properly.

Good to know

Different types of beakers

There are different types of beakers for babies.
▶ Health professionals often recommend 'free flow' beakers: if you turn them upside down, the water comes out easily.
▶ Other types of beakers encourage babies to suck rather than to sip. These can delay babies' progress in learning to drink from a cup.

Cleaning up

Babies will need to have their hands and faces washed after mealtimes.
▶ Make this as fun as possible – you can sing a song, or make it into a game.
▶ Never wipe a baby's face from behind them.

Once the baby is out of the highchair and is safe, you will need to clean the highchair.

Practice points

When cleaning a baby's face, avoid covering the mouth and nose at the same time. If this happens, babies will turn their head away and might use their hands to push you away. This is instinctive, and nature's way of making sure that babies can breathe.

Sharing information with parents

During the weaning process, practitioners must work closely with parents. Parents might want to use certain types of baby food such as organic, or might want to use baby-led weaning.

Share information about:
▶ what a baby has eaten
▶ how much of it they ate
▶ their response to it.

Meal and snack times

Later in this chapter, we will see the importance of nutrition in babies' and children's development. We will also look at what is meant by the term 'balanced diet'.

Meal and snack times are an important part of the routine in early years settings. If children become hungry, this can affect their mood and ability to concentrate.

Creating a happy atmosphere

Babies and children are more likely to try out new foods and eat well if they are happy. This means that snack and mealtimes need to be calm and happy. It is good practice for you to:
- sit with children as they eat
- help children learn that snacks and meals are social occasions.

▲ Why is it important that mealtimes are happy?

Role model

Adults are significant role models for children. When it comes to food, children need to see adults who enjoy their food.

Comments about dieting or being fussy about food are not helpful, because children can start to pick up adults' concerns about food and start to refuse foods.

Changing appetites

Providing that the food on offer is balanced and healthy, children are able to self-regulate their food intake. This means that they will eat more on some days than on others.
- It is important not to restrict food intake or force children to eat more than they want.
- There are many factors affecting how much a child will eat. Children will often eat more just before and during a growth spurt.

Variety matters

A healthy diet is one where there is plenty of variety.

Children will often say that they have had enough of one food, but are happy to eat something else. If the food is nutritious and healthy, this is not a problem.

Presenting food

Too much food on a plate can cause problems for children. There is a danger of over-eating to please an adult. The way we present food is, therefore, important.

- Ideally, we should encourage children to self-serve and try several different things.
- Presenting food in fun ways can help children relax and so try something new.

> **Good to know**
>
> **Puddings**
>
> In some families, children were not allowed to have a pudding unless they finished their main course. Nutritionists now view this as unhelpful, as children learn a hidden message that vegetables are boring but anything sweet is a reward.
>
> Today, it is recommended that children learn to enjoy all their foods, provided that they are nutritious and do not contain added sugar. The order does not matter if a variety of foods are on offer.

Hydration

Babies and children should have access to water at all times. There is no need to ask them to keep drinking, apart from in hot weather or if they have been vigorous in physical activity. This is because the body makes us feel thirsty when we are starting to become dehydrated.
- Babies might need milk feeds, but the main drink for children should be just water unless they have milk at snack times (see page 305 for requirements for dairy foods).
- As with meal and snack times, adults need to act as a good role model and drink water in front of children. You can make the experience of drinking plain water more fun by adding in ice cubes and watching them melt.

> **Practice points**
>
> **Mealtimes**
> - Encourage children to try new tastes.
> - Encourage children to serve themselves.
> - Provide children with bowls, beakers and cutlery that will help them to feed themselves.
> - Encourage children to use cutlery and to feed themselves.
> - Supervise children in case of a reaction to food or choking.
> - Cut some foods into smaller sizes in order to allow children to manage.

Performance Outcome 4: Safeguard and Promote the Health, Safety and Wellbeing of Children

Rest/sleep

Later in this unit, we look at why sleep is important and how much sleep babies and children need. In this section we look at ways in which practitioners help children to rest and sleep.

Rest

Rest and sleep are two different things:
- Rest is when the body can relax and stay fairly still, but the brain remains active and continues to concentrate on what is happening.
- Sleep allows the body to rest and the brain to change its pattern of activity.

Restful activities include sharing books quietly and doing activities that require minimum physical effort.

You will need to spot when children need a little rest. If they do, you could:
- change the pace of the activity, or
- suggest a more restful activity, such as listening to a story.

Naps

Most babies and young children need a nap each day. Sleep is linked to routines, and this is one reason why it is good practice to keep to a routine wherever possible.

Most practitioners will help prepare children for their nap by having a quiet period of rest first. This can help children to relax before sleep.

Many children will find it easier to nap if the room is darkened and there is a sleep routine in place. This might include:
- a certain story or song
- having a cuddly toy (only for children over 12 months)
- being 'tucked in'.

> **In practice**
>
> Find out how your work placement helps babies and children rest and sleep.
> - Is there a routine in place for naps?
> - Where do children sleep?

> **Good to know**
>
> You might be surprised to know that when children are overtired, they find it harder to fall asleep. This is because their bodies are unable to relax. Relaxation is needed for sleep.
>
> If children are prevented from napping or are woken too early from a nap, there is a danger that they will struggle to sleep at bedtime. This can lead parents to think that the nap was the problem.
>
> The timing of naps, though, is important. A late nap in the afternoon can mean that children are not tired enough at bedtime.

Nappy changing

Nappy changing is essential in order to prevent babies and toddlers from developing skin infections.
- You need to do this in a hygienic way so as to prevent the spread of bacteria and viruses. All early years settings should provide disposable aprons and gloves, which should always be worn.
- Nappies should always be placed in a designated bin, and you should always wash your hands before and afterwards.
- As many settings change babies and toddlers on a raised surface, always make sure that children are not left unattended in case they fall.

You also have to make the experience as pleasant for children as possible. You can do this by:
- talking to the child
- giving them something to play with or look at
- involving them before and afterwards.

For example, you could give a baby a rattle to hold, and encourage a toddler to hold the clean nappy.

Nappy changing is a skill that is best learned by watching someone else before attempting it yourself. One of the hardest parts is remembering to talk to the baby or child at the same time.

Here are some of the key steps in the nappy changing process:
1. Clean the changing mat.
2. Check that everything is to hand and that you know which products are suitable for the child.
3. Talk to the child and either carry or lead them to the changing table.
4. Wash your hands and put on disposable gloves and apron.
5. Remove/undo the child's clothing and move them so that they will be away from the soiled nappy.

6 Remove the soiled nappy and fold it in on itself. If the bin is in reach, put it in the bin immediately; if not, put the nappy out of reach of the baby.

7 Clean the genital area thoroughly by using either baby wipes or cotton wool dipped in water. Make sure that wiping takes place from front to back when changing a girl.

8 When the area is dry, put on barrier cream if parents have requested it, or otherwise continue by putting on the clean nappy.

9 Put the clothes back on the child, and take them from the changing mat to a place of safety.

10 Clean the changing mat thoroughly. Remove and dispose of the gloves and apron.

11 Wash your hands, and if appropriate make a record of the time of the nappy change along with any comments, e.g. early signs of nappy rash.

> ### Practice points
>
> #### Nappy changing
>
> Some babies and toddlers are very wriggly. This can make nappy changing very tricky. Where possible, ask colleagues or parents about the strategies they use for changing particular babies or toddlers.
> - Have everything to hand as you will need to be quick.
> - Take off outer layers of clothing while the baby is sitting or the toddler is standing.
> - Invite the baby or toddler to lie down – this can work better than insisting that they should be still even if it means waiting for a moment.
> - Give the baby or toddler something to hold or focus on while laying down.
> - Encourage older toddlers to be involved by, for example, holding the packet of wipes.
> - Work quickly and if necessary finish dressing later on.
> - Remember to wash your hands.

Toileting

You will also need to support the move out of nappies and into using the toilet. The move out of nappies is often referred to as toilet training.

Toilet training

There is no exact age when children will be ready to move from nappies and use a potty. Some children will be ready at 15 months, although many will be over two years old. Each child will be different, although most children are clean and dry by three years.

As a practitioner, you need to work with parents to recognise when the child is ready:
- The signs of a child being ready are mainly physical, as the bladder has to be sufficiently mature.
- If children are trained before they are ready, there is a danger that they will become frustrated and upset and overall the process will take longer.

The spider diagram below shows the signs that children are ready to move out of nappies.

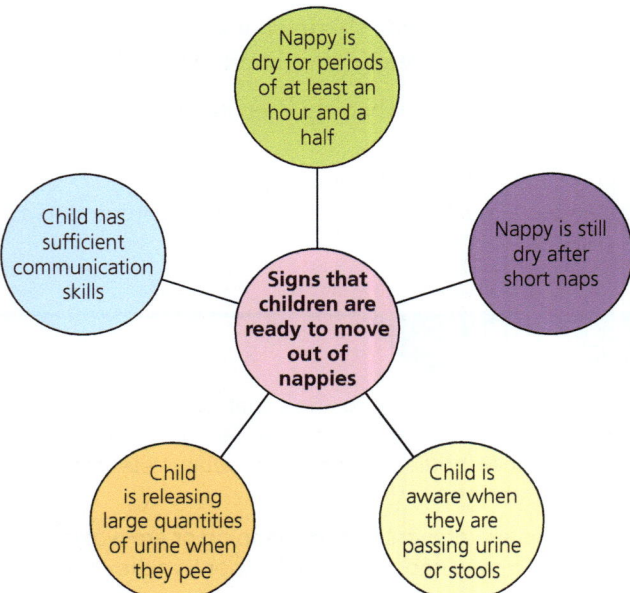

▲ Signs that children are ready to move out of nappies

Your role is to show the child where the potty or toilet is and then let the child use it independently. You might need to remind children to go, but only after at least an hour has passed. This is important:
- If you ask too often, children might become frustrated because there is not sufficient urine to pass.
- There is also a danger that they do not pick up on the signals that their bladder sends when it is full. This can result in more accidents.

It is also important for you to stay calm, as there are likely to be a few accidents in the first few days.

You will need to work with parents too. They need to agree whether the child is ready to be toilet trained and talk to you about how well the child is coping.

Performance Outcome 4: Safeguard and Promote the Health, Safety and Wellbeing of Children

> **Good to know**
>
> For some children, passing stools can be a source of anxiety. This is sometimes because adults talk about 'dirty' when nappy changing. This means that it is not uncommon for children to want to have their nappy back on if they feel that they need to pass a stool. It is better for children to be given a nappy, or they might not go and this can result in constipation.
>
> If children become constipated, the pain of passing a stool can then make them even more fearful, and the constipation increases. In this situation:
> - Put a nappy on loosely, or use it to line the potty.
> - Once the child has passed the stool, the child can wear pants again.
>
> Some children prefer to pass stools where no one is watching, while others like an adult to be there.

Supporting toileting

When children are out of nappies, your role is to support their toileting. This means:
- helping children to remember to go before a nap or before going outdoors
- reminding children who are showing signs that they need the toilet. These include fidgeting when sitting or touching genital areas.

Some children know that they need to go, but worry about missing out on what is happening or that another child may take a toy they are using.

Making toileting a pleasant experience

It is important that we help make going to the toilet a pleasant experience. This means checking that the toilets are clean and also finding ways of making them attractive while maintaining hygiene.

It is important to recognise how much support children will need. Children might:
- need to be helped up onto the toilet seat, or prefer to use a potty
- need a little help with undressing or manage undressing by themselves
- like to have the door partially open or closed.

When children have finished using the toilet, you should check that they have wiped themselves and remind girls to wipe from front to back. Also make sure that they wash their hands and that you also wash yours.

> **Practice points**
>
> **Safeguarding**
> - Always tell other staff when you are taking children to the toilet.
> - Ask children if they need help and only do what is required.
> - Encourage children to be as independent as possible.
> - Monitor whether children appear to be fearful or have any bruising/pain when they use the toilet.

Dealing with toileting accidents

Toileting accidents are common, especially in the early days of moving into nappies. When an accident happens:
1. Start by reassuring the child and asking other children in the area to move away.
2. Where possible, move the child into the toilet or a private space to remove soiled clothing.
3. Put on gloves and a disposable apron.
4. While removing clothes, remember to keep reassuring the child.
5. Make sure that the child is clean before encouraging them to put on fresh clothing.
6. Wherever possible, try to involve the child as much as possible, for example, getting dressed.
7. Afterwards, disinfect the area where the accident happened.

Personal hygiene, including oral health

Part of your role will be to support children's personal hygiene. This includes regular handwashing, but may also include other activities such as skin care, brushing hair and teeth brushing. We look at oral health later in this chapter, on page 311.

As skin and hair care needs can vary between children, it is essential to gain additional information from parents.
- A child might need a particular moisturiser or soap because of eczema.
- Parents might also have views about when and how personal hygiene tasks are carried out.

Typically, it is the role of the key person to support children's personal hygiene.

Handwashing

To prevent the spread of infection, it is essential that children wash their hands. In early years settings, this becomes part of the daily routine. Children should always wash their hands:

- before eating or touching food
- after blowing their nose
- after using the toilet
- after playing outdoors
- after playing with sensory materials such as gloop or dough
- after touching animals or animal feeding bowls or food.

Your role is to encourage children to enjoy handwashing and to make it part of the routine. You can help children to enjoy handwashing by:

- singing songs or rhymes
- chatting to them as they wash.

> **Research**
>
> There are some concerns that children are now lacking in vitamin D because of their lack of exposure to sunlight. Find out what the NHS's current recommendations are for exposure to sunlight.

▲ Why is it important for children to enjoy handwashing?

Care of skin

Caring for children's skin is important as it acts as an important barrier to prevent infection from entering the body. We also need to protect skin from the sun as this can cause long-term damage.

According to guidance at the time of writing, babies and young children should have limited exposure to sunlight, of around 10 minutes. For the rest of the time, they need to be kept out of strong sunshine, so:

- their skin should be kept covered, or
- they should have suncream applied on them.

As with all skin care, parents need to agree to the application of suncream. In most early years settings, they will be responsible for supplying it.

Care of hair

Most early years settings will not have responsibility for the care of children's hair unless they offer home-based care, for example, childminders or nannies.

Although most early years settings will not be responsible for combing and styling children's hair, practitioners will probably keep an eye out for head lice. Head lice are parasites that live on the scalp and draw blood from the scalp. They are very common in early years settings – they spread very easily because children are often in close contact with each other.

As head lice can move onto adults' hair, it is important for you to check your own hair regularly and tie back long hair.

Signs of a head lice infestation include:

- an itchy scalp
- white flecks on strands of hair which do not move if touched – these are the empty egg cases, often called 'nits'
- scabs or blood spots on the scalp where the head lice have bitten
- sight of a head lice.

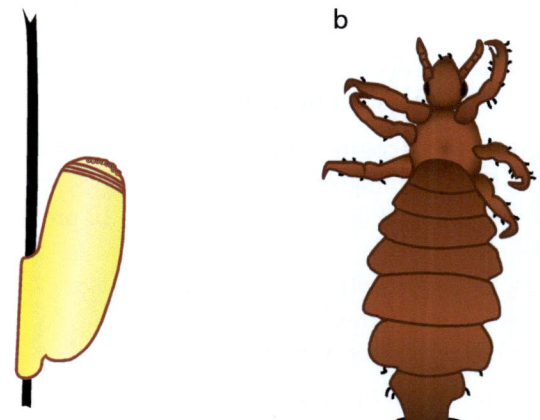

▲ a) a nit (egg case) and b) a head louse

The nits in hair are often easier to spot than the head lice.

If you suspect that a child has a case of head lice, you should inform the parents. There are several ways of

Performance Outcome 4: Safeguard and Promote the Health, Safety and Wellbeing of Children

treating head lice and it will be parents' responsibility to do this.

Early years settings will also put up a sign, warning parents to look out for signs of head lice in their children.

Physical activity, including access to the outdoors

We have seen in Performance Outcome 1 that physical activity both indoors and outside is essential to children's overall development and health. It is a requirement of the EYFS that children should spend time outdoors every day. Most early years settings try to provide outdoor play and activities as part of their overall provision.

> **Research**
> - How easy is it for children in your work placement setting to go outdoors?
> - What is the balance of time between outdoor and indoor play?

Suitable clothing for activities

While parents are usually responsible for providing the majority of clothing, early years settings will often provide guidance as to what is needed. This is important as some parents may not realise that during play, children need clothing that they can easily move in and can be washed.

Some items of more specialist clothing – such as aprons and all-in-ones for wet weather – are usually provided by the setting.

> **Practice points**
>
> **Suitable clothing**
> - Check that footwear is suitable for the weather conditions and activity.
> - Monitor children to check that they are not becoming too hot or cold.
> - Encourage children to see the link between the clothes they need and the weather.
> - Allow enough time to put on and take off clothes when changing from indoors to outdoors.

Safety needs

Preventing accidents and keeping children safe is a key role for the practitioner. You can find the information on how to do this and the main causes of accidents later in this chapter, on pages 324–5.

Consideration for medical conditions

It is important to know which children have medical conditions and how these might affect them. In some cases, practitioners will also administer or supervise the taking of medicines such as inhalers or insulin injections.

Legal requirements about medicines are covered in the EYFS. At the time of writing, the following requirements are in place:
- Early years settings should have a policy and procedures for the administering of medicines.
- Information about children's medication must be kept up to date.
- Prescription medicines can only be administered if they have been prescribed for the child by a doctor, dentist, nurse or pharmacist.
- Written permission for each medicine has to be obtained from the child's parent/carer.
- Early years settings must keep a written record every time a medicine is administered, and inform parents that this has taken place.

Common medical conditions

There are a few common medical conditions that can affect children's physical care needs. It is important to understand how they affect children, including any triggers and the signs that medication or urgent medical help is needed.

> **Practice points**
>
> **Administering medicines**
> - Make sure the medicine is in date.
> - Make sure the medicine has been correctly stored.
> - Read the instructions about how and when to administer the medicine.
> - Check that the right medicine is being given to the right child.
> - Record the date, time and dosage given.
> - Store the medicine correctly and securely to avoid children accessing it.

Medical conditions	Symptoms	What you should do
Asthma	Causes shortness of breath During an asthma attack, airways narrow, which can be fatal	Find out about how to use the salbutamol reliever inhaler correctly. The reliever inhaler is usually blue. (Note that some parents and older children may refer to the reliever inhaler as Ventolin as this is one of the leading brands.) Observe children during physical activity for signs of breathlessness. Always have a reliever inhaler nearby. Find out what individual children's triggers may be, e.g. dust, cold air, certain smells. If a child says they are struggling to breathe, always offer the inhaler.
Diabetes	Causes fluctuations in glucose levels and can be dangerous if a child loses consciousness (hypo glycaemia) Diabetes Type 1 is a genetic condition, usually controlled by injection Diabetes Type 2 can be controlled by diet alone. It is rare in young children.	Find out which type of diabetes a child has. Find out what dietary needs the child has and in the case of Type 1, the timing of snacks and meals. Talk to parents if higher than usual physical activity levels are planned when children have Type 1. Observe children during physical activity and look for signs that the child is becoming unwell.
Eczema	Skin condition causing a rash, itchiness and dry skin	Find out what may cause eczema to flare up, e.g. certain foods, soap or suncreams. Find out when to apply creams.
Epilepsy	Affects brain activity and can cause seizures	Find out about any triggers, e.g. tiredness, dehydration, flashing lights. Find out about any warning signs before a seizure takes place. Find out about the type of seizures that are typical for a child and when to get emergency help.
Sickle cell disease	Abnormally shaped red blood cells affect the circulation Blockages affecting blood flow occur. These are known as crises and cause significant pain	Find out about how sickle cell disease affects the child and the signs that the child is having a crisis. Find out when to get emergency help. Help prevent crises by offering plenty of fluids and making sure that the child does not become cold.

K4.6 How practitioners use a range of strategies to support children to develop self-care skills

It is good practice to help young children develop the self-care skills they need to become independent. By being able to feed, dress and manage toileting, children develop confidence as well as fine motor skills.

The importance of self-care skills is reflected in the EYFS. Self-care is part of the personal, social and emotional area of learning and development leading to the following Early Learning Goal: 'Manage their own basic hygiene and personal needs, including dressing, going to the toilet and understanding the importance of healthy food choices'.

Supporting children's self-care

The table on page 299 shows some of the strategies that we can use to support children's self-care as well as ways to make self-care into learning opportunities.

Performance Outcome 4: Safeguard and Promote the Health, Safety and Wellbeing of Children

Care routine	Ways of supporting children's self-care skills	Learning opportunities
Nappy changing	Encourage children to make movements while undressing and dressing. Put up mobiles so that children have something to look at during nappy changing. Encourage toddlers to find their clean nappy and bring it to the changing area.	Interact with babies and toddlers. Sing rhymes to them during nappy change. Talk to toddlers about clean and dirty.
Toileting	Encourage children to do as much undressing by themselves. Give children privacy, e.g. partially closing a door. Encourage children to wash their own hands when they have finished.	Talk about how washing hands prevents germs.
Handwashing	Encourage children to wash their own hands. Model handwashing. Encourage children to dry their own hands.	Talk about when it is important to wash hands and why. Look at how water goes down the plughole.
Bath or shower time	Encourage children to dress and undress according to their skill level. Help children to do as much washing as possible. Encourage children to dry themselves but 'finish' off to ensure that they are fully dry.	Provide a range of water toys so children can explore scooping and pouring.
Skin	Encourage children to put on suncream according to their skills level. Encourage children to dress to go outdoors. Allow children to choose the order in which they get dressed, e.g. sunhats before shoes.	Talk to children about the weather and link this to the clothes we wear or the use of suncream.
Hair	Look for ways of helping children to be involved, e.g. they watch their hair being brushed in a mirror. Encourage children to do as much as they can according to their skill level. With children who have long hair, encourage them to choose different styles.	Encourage children to count how many strokes of the comb or hair brush will be needed. Talk to children about how people have different types and colours of hair.
Teeth	Encourage children to put toothpaste onto the toothbrush. Use a mirror so that children can see when you are cleaning their teeth. Allow children to spend a little time cleaning their own teeth as well.	Talk to children about what we use our teeth for. Count children's teeth with them in front of the mirror.
Mealtimes	Encourage children to self-feed wherever possible. Allow children to serve themselves food by providing healthy food options. Encourage children to choose where they wish to sit.	Use this time for children to talk together. Point out the colours and textures of the food.
Rest/sleep	Encourage children to reflect on how being tired makes them feel. Allow children to choose the stories that you will share with them before bedtime. Allow children enough time to self-settle. Give children a choice of 'rest' activities including sharing stories with them.	Talk to children about why sleep and rest is important.

Making self-care tasks enjoyable

It is important that children do not come to see self-care tasks such as tidying away, dressing or washing hands as being boring. One of your roles is to find ways of making these tasks interesting and fun. You could try:
- putting on music
- chatting to children as they are carrying out the task
- having specific songs.

Giving children time and plenty of opportunities

Children are often slow at first to do things for themselves. This is because they have to develop the fine motor skills and sequence to do things such as dressing. To support children, you need to:
- build in extra time
- give children plenty of opportunities to practise these skills.

Encouraging care of belongings and facilities

Learning to tidy up and look after their own belongings is an important skill for children. You can help children by:
- building routines that encourage tidying away and caring for resources
- supporting children to recognise their name
- keeping their items, such as coats, in particular places.

Scaffolding tasks to support children's progression

In Core Chapter 2, we looked at the role of scaffolding in supporting children's learning. In terms of self-care, this means:
- breaking tasks into smaller steps
- encouraging children through modelling and giving practical support to do as much as they can.

> **Practice points**
>
> **Dressing skills**
> - Start by encouraging children to take off shoes, hats and coats. Undressing is easier than dressing.
> - Encourage children to sit down when putting on socks, shoes, jumpers and trousers.
> - Show children how to tell the front from the back of clothes, e.g. using labels and cues such as fastenings.
> - Make sure that children have plenty of time and space around them.
> - Plan activities to help children learn how buttons and zips work so they can use this knowledge to help them.

Providing size-appropriate facilities

One of the reasons why children find some self-care tasks difficult is because the resources or equipment is not quite at the right height or size for them. A good example of this is mealtimes. Children might find it hard to:
- pour water into a cup if the jug is too large
- sit properly on a chair that is too high.

One of your roles is to observe children during self-care tasks and consider whether adjustments need to be made to the environment or the resources.

How self-care skills impact on children's health, safety and wellbeing

Self-care skills are essential for children's health, safety and wellbeing for many reasons.

Privacy and dignity

When children have mastered tasks such as going to the toilet or washing their own hands and faces, they have more privacy and potentially dignity. This becomes particularly important as children start to become more self-aware and also develop a sense of embarrassment.

Independence, self-efficacy, confidence and resilience

Once babies and children start to do things for themselves, however small, it changes how they think about themselves. Babies and children can start to see themselves as being competent. This, as we saw in Performance Outcome 2, is known as self-efficacy. This in turn helps children gain confidence and also

▲ How can independence help children's confidence?

Performance Outcome 4: Safeguard and Promote the Health, Safety and Wellbeing of Children

Personal hygiene and prevention of infection

As well as the personal, social and emotional benefits, children who learn good personal hygiene routines and habits are more likely to stay healthy. This is because they reduce opportunities for infection to spread. In light of the COVID-19 pandemic, teaching good respiratory hygiene (coughs, sneezes and face touching) is especially crucial. See K4.10 and the artwork on page 318 for more on handwashing and preventing the spread of infection.

K4.7 How sleep and rest enhances babies' and children's holistic development

Over the past few years, it has been widely recognised that many children are not getting enough sleep. This has serious implications for their long-term health and learning, as shown in this table.

Aspect of development	How this is affected by lack of sleep
Brain function	The brain is the control centre of the human body. Signals in the brain are responsible for turning on and off various activities within the brain, but also within the cells of the body. When children don't have enough sleep, the brain cannot function properly. This causes a range of short- and long-term difficulties.
Mental health and mood levels	Lack of sleep affects children's mental health. They are likely to: • have mood swings • find it hard to control their impulses • show unwanted behaviour, which affects how adults and other children respond to them.
Concentration, memory and learning	The ability to concentrate and focus plays an important part in learning. • When children lack sleep, they have difficulty in concentrating and focusing properly. • This affects the brain's ability to take in new information, and so learning becomes difficult. • Long-term memories might also be affected. This is because during sleep, the brain reviews the information that has been taken in. Some is stored while other information is deleted. Children who sleep well are, therefore, more likely to have better memories of what they have experienced and learned.
Energy levels	Overall, children who are tired show lower levels of physical activity. • They may not feel like trying out something new or going for a walk. • They might show signs of hyperactivity – their energy levels might seem high, but they might lack attention and concentration. The high levels of energy can sometimes lead parents and carers to mistakenly believe that their child is not tired. • The opposite is true: when children show high energy levels and overexcited behaviours, they might find it hard to rest and relax ready for sleep.
Bodily growth and repair	During sleep, the brain releases signals to stimulate growth and appetite hormones. • When children lack sleep over a long term, this can interfere with the hormonal signals. • It is now recognised that lack of sleep is linked to children becoming overweight and obese. • Lack of sleep can also affect children's immune systems. This is because sleep allows the body to repair cells and fight infection. When children are not sleeping enough, they are more likely to have frequent infections.

Current NHS guidance regarding sleep requirements for babies and children

While the amount of sleep that babies and children need can vary slightly, it is important for parents and practitioners to know how much sleep is typically needed at each age.

Most babies and toddlers will need naps alongside night-time sleeps. The amount of sleep that a child has should be calculated over a 24-hour period. The table on page 302 shows how much sleep children need, based on current NHS guidance.

Age	Amount of sleep required	
	Daytime	Night-time
Newborn, 1 week	8 hours	8.5 hours
4 weeks	6–7 hours	8–9 hours
3 months	4–5 hours	10–11 hours
6 months	3 hours	11 hours
9 months	2.5 hours	11 hours
12 months	2.5 hours	11 hours
2 years	1.5 hours	11.5 hours
3 years	Up to 45 minutes	11.5–12 hours
4 years		11.5 hours
5 years		11 hours

Reflect

Can you see how the amount of sleep children need gradually decreases over time?

Plot a graph showing how much sleep children are likely to need at night between the ages of one and five years.

Practice points

Signs of tiredness

It is useful to spot when babies or children are starting to become tired. Delaying sleep can result in children becoming overtired, making it harder for them to sleep. Signs of needing sleep include:
- rubbing eyes and/or yawning
- circles under eyes
- lack of concentration and hyperactivity
- tantrums and mood swings
- not cooperating with simple requests.

Safe sleeping procedures for babies

Sadly in the first year of life, some babies die while they are asleep. Research into cot death or sudden infant death syndrome (SIDS) has resulted in changes in the way that babies sleep.

It is essential for anyone working with babies to check the latest guidance from the NHS or the organisation that specialises in SIDS, the Lullaby Trust: www.lullabytrust.org.uk

Safety aspect	What to do
Sleeping position	• Babies should be placed on their backs to sleep. • Babies' feet should touch the end of the cot or Moses basket.
Cots and Moses baskets	• Babies should sleep in Moses baskets or cots. • Cot mattresses should be flat, firm and waterproof. They should be regularly cleaned. • Cot bumpers, pillows and cuddly toys should not be used. • Cots should meet latest safety standards. • Blankets and sheets (if needed) should only come up to shoulder level and be tucked in. • Specially designed 'gro bags' can be used. These are a type of sleeping bag that are designed to prevent babies from overheating.
Room temperature and preventing overheating	• Babies must not become overheated by, for example, wearing too many clothes. • Room temperature should be kept between 16°C and 20°C.

Good to know

Smoking is a big risk factor for cot death. Your setting will be smoke-free, but if you smoke during your breaks, you might put babies at risk. This is because when you hold a baby, they breathe in some of the air from your lungs. This will contain dangerous chemicals. You should not pick up a baby for at least 20 minutes if you have smoked.

Performance Outcome 4: Safeguard and Promote the Health, Safety and Wellbeing of Children

K4.8 The concept of a balanced diet for babies and children aged 0–7 years

What is a balanced diet?

The term 'balanced diet' is often used, so it is important to understand what it means.

A balanced diet provides the body with what it needs to keep healthy, including energy:
- The human body is a machine that needs a range of nutrients to keep it going.
- The nutrients are found in food and drink.
- A balanced diet means that we take in just the right amount of nutrients for our age and activity level.

> **Key terms**
>
> *Malnourished:* the body is not getting all of the required nutrients.
>
> *Undernourished:* the body is getting the nutrients, but not in the required quantities.

The terms **malnourished** and **undernourished** are used to describe people who do not have a balanced diet.

Children who are overweight and obese can still be malnourished – they might have too many of some nutrients but are missing others.

Nutrients can be divided into macronutrients and micronutrients.

Macronutrients

Macronutrients are needed in large quantities. The three main macronutrients are carbohydrates, protein and fat. (Some organisations also list water as a macronutrient.)

Many foods contain more than one macronutrient, such as cheese, which contains protein as well as energy.

Macronutrient	Role in the body	Foods containing this macronutrient
Carbohydrate (also called starchy foods)	Provides some energy	Bread, pasta, rice, potatoes, noodles, plantain, porridge, breakfast cereal
Protein	Provides some energy, but is particularly needed for the repair and growth of cells	Meat, fish, eggs, milk, cheese, yoghurt, nuts, beans, lentils
Fat	Provides significant amounts of energy	Healthy foods containing fat also contain protein, such as fish, meat and cheese

Micronutrients

Micronutrients are required in very small quantities but are still essential. They include vitamins and minerals.
- Micronutrients are needed in very small amounts.
- There are four types of micronutrients – as shown in the table on page 304.
- When children have a balanced diet, they are likely to absorb the micronutrients that they need.
- Where children do not have a balanced diet, they are likely to be missing out on some micronutrients.
- Micronutrients are needed for the immune system, blood cells and for healthy growth.

Most foods contain macronutrients and also micronutrients. Some micronutrients require the presence of other micronutrients and/or macronutrients in order to be absorbed. For example:
- Iron is more easily absorbed in foods that contain vitamin C.

The table shows some of the key micronutrients and why they are needed in the body.

Type of micronutrient	Examples	Foods containing these micronutrients
Water-soluble vitamins (which dissolve in water)	Vitamin B group including B12 Vitamin C	Vitamin B group found in some starchy foods Vitamin C found in many fruit and vegetables
Fat-soluble vitamins	Vitamins A, D, E and K	Vitamin A found in dairy products and yellow-coloured fruit, spinach, carrots, sweet potatoes and red peppers Vitamin D from sunlight in spring and summer, and also found in meat, oily fish and egg yolks Vitamin E found in plant oils, rapeseed, olive oil and sunflower oils and also nuts and seeds Vitamin K found in green leafy vegetables, cereal grains
Microminerals	Potassium, calcium, phosphorus, magnesium, sodium	Usually absorbed as part of a balanced diet
Trace minerals	Iron, manganese, copper, zinc and selenium	Needed in tiny quantities but essential Usually found as a part of a balanced diet Good sources of iron include red meat, beans, nuts and dried fruit such as apricots

> **Good to know**
>
> **Fat-free diets**
>
> A fat-free diet can be harmful for children and adults. This is because some vitamins can only be absorbed alongside fat.

A balanced diet for babies aged six months to one year

There are three stages in weaning. Each stage is important as it helps babies to learn the skills of eating and also introduces new tastes and foods.

Creating a balanced diet for babies depends on the stage of weaning that they have reached. Early years settings also have to work in partnership with parents when drawing up a weaning programme. As discussed on pages 307–9, this is because some babies may have special dietary needs or their parents may have dietary preferences.

The table below shows the stages of weaning and examples of the types of foods that might be given to babies.

Stage and age	Description	Suitable foods
Puree and mashed foods From 6 months	At first, foods are pureed so that the baby can learn to swallow them, but then foods are mashed. Babies learn to take food from a spoon. Foods are introduced one by one so you can identify any foods that might cause an allergic reaction. Baby rice or fruit and vegetables are the first food groups to be introduced. Babies are introduced to drinking from a cup. Babies should not be given cow's milk to drink but it can be used in cooking. Babies still need breast milk or formula feeds at this stage.	Mashed or soft fruit and vegetables Or Baby rice or cereal mixed with breast or bottled milk Cooked meat that is soft, e.g. chicken or fish Pasta, rice and noodles Dairy products such as yoghurt and cheese

Performance Outcome 4: Safeguard and Promote the Health, Safety and Wellbeing of Children

Soft finger foods, mashed and chopped foods From 8–9 months	Babies are given foods that they need to chew slightly. This action helps develop the tongue and mouth movements. They are given a wider range of foods with different textures. They are moving to having three meals a day and having fewer milk feeds.	Foods can be mixed so that babies are having mini-meals. Babies need a wide range of foods from all of the different food groups.
Finger foods 12 months	Babies learn to chew in this stage, which helps to further develop the tongue and mouth movements. Babies also learn to feed themselves by picking finger foods. This encourages their fine motor coordination. Cow's milk can be used as a drink.	Babies should be gaining their food intake from solid food and so will not need milk feeds. Babies should be encouraged to drink water or cow's milk with meals from a cup.

Foods to avoid giving to babies

The NHS advises that the following foods should not be given to babies:

- salt and salty foods such as bacon or ham
- honey
- raw or lightly cooked eggs
- rice drinks
- uncooked soft and unpasteurised cheese, as it could contain bacteria
- liver
- swordfish
- whole nuts such as peanuts, as they can be a choking hazard
- whole jelly cubes, as they can be a choking hazard.

> **Research**
>
> Find out more about weaning by visiting the NHS webpage, Start4life: www.nhs.uk/start4life/weaning/

A balanced diet for children aged one to four years

A balanced diet for children is different from one for adults. Children need more foods high in protein, especially dairy foods. This is because their stomachs are smaller than adults and they are growing quickly.

The British Nutrition Foundation has produced an easy way for adults to create a balanced diet for children aged one to four years. The table below shows different food types and also how many portions per day are needed.

Food type	How many portions needed a day	Why it is good for children's diet
Fruits and vegetables	5	Contains vitamins and minerals. Fruit and vegetables are thought to be important for overall health. They also help digestion as they contain fibre. Some fibre is important in children's diet in order to prevent constipation. Some fruits and vegetables such as potatoes, plantains and bananas contain high levels of carbohydrates and so are a source of energy.
Starchy foods Bread, pasta, rice, potatoes, couscous	5	Contains carbohydrates, which are important for slow burning energy. Also contains vitamin B and some minerals.
Milk and dairy foods Cheese, yoghurt	3	Contains protein needed for growth and repair of cells. Also provides fat that is needed for energy as well as vitamins and calcium. Calcium is important for healthy teeth and bones.
Protein Meat, eggs, fish, poultry, beans, pulses and nuts	2	Contains protein needed for growth and repair of cells as well as some fat that provides energy. They also contain important minerals. Beans, pulses and nuts also contain carbohydrates.

> **Research**
>
> For exact portion sizes for different types of food, download the leaflet '5532-a-day' from:
> **www.nutrition.org.uk**

Hydration

As well as food, the human body also needs water or foods that contain water. How much children need to drink depends on their activity level, but also how much water is contained in their food. For example:

▶ A child who has toast for breakfast is likely to become thirstier more quickly than a child who had porridge.

It is a requirement of the EYFS that water is always available for children.

Salt, sugar and fat intake

Malnourished children are more likely to have high levels of salt and sugar in their diet. Both salty and sugary foods should be avoided.

> **Good to know**
>
> **Drinks**
>
> Bear these points in mind when you plan a balanced diet for a child:
> ▶ Drinks other than water are likely to contain energy or calories as well as other nutrients.
> ▶ Giving drinks such as milk just before a mealtime might fill a child up, so cause the child not to be hungry. The best option is to give them plain water in between meals and snacks.

▲ Why is it important that children enjoy fruit and vegetables?

Food	Effect on children's health
Salt	Too much salt can damage the kidneys. Later in life, it can affect blood pressure. For this reason, the law states that commercial baby food is salt-free. The recommended salt intakes for babies and children are: • up to 12 months – less than 1g of salt a day • one to three years – 2g of salt a day • four to six years – 3g of salt a day
Sugar	Foods that contain sugar contain significant amounts of calories, which is how energy is measured. Most sugary foods such as biscuits, sweets and sugary drinks are high in calories, but low in micronutrients and protein. • These types of foods are known as 'empty calories'. • They fill children up, but do not help to achieve a balanced diet. As young children have small stomachs, they need foods that contain enough macronutrients and micronutrients. • Sugary foods, even those that have artificial sugars, can prevent children from enjoying the taste of less sweet foods, such as vegetables. • Foods containing high levels of sugar can contribute to children becoming overweight and developing tooth decay.
Fat	Children do need fat in their diet, but this needs to come from foods that contain other macronutrients and/or micronutrients, such as cheese or nuts. Many foods that are unhealthy for children contain: • high levels of salt and fat, e.g. crisps • high levels of sugar and fat, e.g. cakes and ice cream.

Performance Outcome 4: Safeguard and Promote the Health, Safety and Wellbeing of Children

> **Good to know**
>
> **Fruit and sugar**
>
> Whole, unprocessed fruits such as oranges, apples and pears contain naturally occurring sugars.
> ▶ When children eat these fruits whole, the naturally occurring sugars are not a problem. This is because the amount of sugar is relatively low compared to the size of the fruit.
> ▶ On the other hand, fruit juices or smoothies are proportionally high in calories. A small glass of orange juice might contain the juice of two or three oranges. While children can easily drink a small glass and still be hungry for other foods, they would be unable to eat two or three oranges as the fibre in the oranges would make them feel full.

> **Research**
>
> Look at the back of a packet of crisps and a carton of orange juice.
> ▶ How many calories do they contain?
> ▶ Which vitamins or protein are listed for crisps and orange squash?
>
> Using this information, explain why these foods are not recommended for young children.

> **Good to know**
>
> **Vitamins**
>
> Advice from NHS England:
> ▶ Breastfed babies need a daily vitamin D drop from birth onwards.
> ▶ Formula-fed babies do not need vitamin D as it is included in the formula milk.
> ▶ From six months to five years, all children should be given daily vitamin A, C and D supplements.

A range of special diets that children might have, and how to meet those needs

Food intolerances

Food intolerances are not life-threatening but can be very uncomfortable.

▶ Reactions often come a few hours after eating the food.
▶ Common food intolerances include milk and wheat.
▶ Common symptoms include skin reactions or digestive problems including stomach pains or diarrhoea.

It can sometimes be hard to know that a food has caused an intolerance, as the symptoms could be caused by something else.

NHS England does not recommend that foods should be excluded from children's diets without consulting a dietitian or GP.

Food allergies

Food allergies, on the other hand, can be life-threatening.
▶ With an allergy, a protein in the food causes the body's immune system to overreact.
▶ The allergic reaction happens quickly and might include a rash or swelling of the face and lips.
▶ Swelling can also happen in the airways, causing breathing difficulties.
▶ An allergic reaction can happen even if a very small amount of food is drunk or eaten.
▶ In some severe allergies, a reaction occurs when the food is touched by the child or is being eaten by another child.
▶ Common food allergies in children include nuts and milk.

Children with a severe food allergy may be prescribed an **adrenaline autoinjector**, often referred to as an **EpiPen®**. This should be used at the first sign of an allergic reaction.

> **Key term**
>
> **Adrenaline autoinjector/EpiPen®:** A device which administers adrenaline to decrease swelling in the case of an acute allergic reaction.

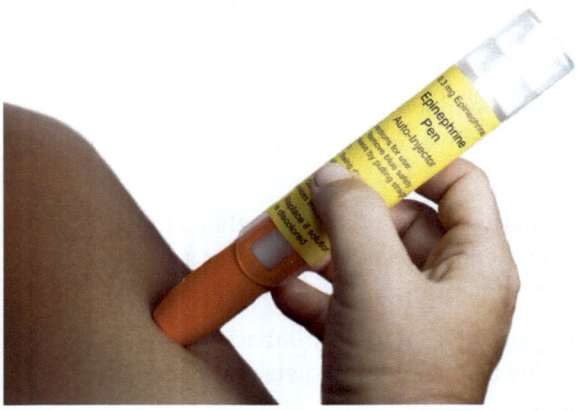

▲ An EpiPen®

Medical conditions

Some children may have medical conditions that affect their diet. As with food allergies, medical conditions must be taken very seriously. Two common medical conditions are diabetes and coeliac disease.

Diabetes

Diabetes is a disease caused by the body not being able to produce enough of a hormone called insulin.
- Insulin is important because it controls the level of glucose, a type of sugar, in the blood.
- When food is digested, it is turned into glucose.
- Insulin helps to convert the glucose into energy that can be used by the cells.
- If there is not enough insulin, the body starts to shut down.
- If there is too much insulin, organs in the body can become damaged.

It is, therefore, a serious medical condition. There are two types of diabetes and it is important not to confuse them.
1. Type 1 diabetes is an inherited condition, and is the one that you are more likely to come across in very young children. People with Type 1 diabetes cannot produce insulin, so injections of insulin are given usually before mealtimes.
2. Type 2 diabetes is not seen in young children although has been increasingly diagnosed in teenagers. Type 2 diabetes is different to Type 1. It can usually be managed by diet alone but later on may require oral medication and eventually insulin injections.

When a child has been diagnosed with Type 1 diabetes, you should make sure that you know about their diet and also the timings of their meals. It is important that children with Type 1 diabetes have regular meals and snacks.

> **Research**
>
> Find out more about diabetes by visiting this website: www.diabetes.org.uk
>
> Download a copy of 'Supporting children with Type 1 diabetes in school and early years setting'.

Coeliac disease

Coeliac disease is a condition where the body attacks itself if it comes into contact with gluten.
- Gluten is found in wheat, barley and rye.
- Foods with wheat include bread and pasta.

Coeliac disease can be serious because it affects the body's ability to absorb other nutrients from food, and it can also damage the intestine.
- Children with coeliac disease must not be given any foods that contain gluten.
- You also need to check that sensory play activities such as dough are gluten-free.

Religious requirements

Some families practise religions that have dietary restrictions. In some religions, pork cannot be eaten (Judaism and Islam) while in others, beef is prohibited (Hinduism).

Religions such as Judaism and Islam also specify how meat including beef and chicken must be prepared:
- Foods that meet Jewish food laws are called **kosher**.
- Foods that meet Islamic requirements are called **halal**.

It is important to find out from families about their religious food requirements and avoid making any assumptions. This is because families vary in how strictly they follow religious teachings.

Social and cultural requirements

Some families have dietary requirements that are based on social and cultural requirements. For example:
- They may be vegetarians, so do not eat any meat or fish.

Performance Outcome 4: Safeguard and Promote the Health, Safety and Wellbeing of Children

- Increasingly, some adults choose a vegan diet where no animal products are eaten such as eggs and cheese.
- Some families might want food to be sourced locally, or meat, eggs and poultry to be free-range.
- An increasing number of families are keen for their children to have a healthy diet and so do not want their children to have any foods that contain **added sugar** (i.e. apart from those sugars that naturally occur within the food).

The potential consequences of not meeting special dietary needs

There are a range of consequences if a child's dietary needs are not met.

- Some dietary needs are linked to medical conditions and allergies. Not meeting these needs can be life-threatening.
- Failure to meet other dietary needs such as religious or cultural ones can damage the trust that parents have in us. This can lead to a breakdown in the relationship and might result in parents taking their children away from the setting.

A range of short- and long-term impacts of an unbalanced diet

Short-term impacts

Below are some examples of short-term effects on an unbalanced diet. Many of these are linked to children becoming hungry. In some cases, a diet might be balanced, but the timing of the meals or snacks needs to be altered.

Short-term impact of an unbalanced diet	Explanation
Lack of concentration and energy	When children are hungry, their brains find it harder to concentrate and have energy to do things.
Anxiety and behavioural problems	Unwanted behaviour and anxiety can be caused by hunger.
	This is because when a child is hungry or thirsty, parts of the brain that affect mood and self-regulation cannot function properly.
Headaches	Headaches can be caused by lack of hydration. This is why water needs to be available for children at all times.
	Some children might also have headaches if their energy levels are too low and they need to eat.
Tiredness	Food provides energy for children. When children are hungry, they have less energy and seem tired.
Problems sleeping	Children who are hungry might not sleep well.
Stomach pains	Children who are hungry might have stomach pains or complain of feeling sick.
	In some cases, stomach pains might also be an early sign of constipation.
Mood and tantrums	There is a link between mood changes and hunger.

Long-term impact of an unbalanced diet

When babies do not have the nutrients they need in the right quantities, there can be some very serious long-term effects on children's health and cognition.

Long-term impact of an unbalanced diet	Explanation
Dental health problems	Tooth decay can be caused by: • too much sugar in the diet • eating and drinking too often (see Good to know feature on page 312). Children's teeth need the right amount of calcium and vitamin D to become strong.
Obesity and diabetes	Children who have too many calories in their diet retain it as fat and will put on weight. This causes children to become overweight or obese. Being overweight or obese puts children at increased risk of developing Type 2 diabetes (see above).
Chronic diseases and high blood pressure	When children become overweight or obese, they are at risk of developing a range of health conditions and **chronic diseases**. These include: • heart disease • cancers • high blood pressure which can lead to strokes.
Anaemia	Iron is a very important mineral in our diets: • It is needed to make red blood cells which carry oxygen around the body. • Lack of iron causes a medical condition called **anaemia**, which can become very serious if it is not treated. The signs of anaemia include severe tiredness and lack of energy. Babies who are anaemic may not, for example, have the strength to learn to crawl or walk. Iron is found in: • meat, poultry, some fish, beans and brown rice • some green leafy vegetables such as water cress. Meals that have iron-rich foods should also include foods that contain vitamin C, such as fruit and vegetables. This is because the body absorbs iron more easily when vitamin C is present.
Bone and teeth growth	A diet lacking in calcium and vitamin D can cause long-term problems with bones and teeth that can continue into adulthood. A lack of calcium can cause weakness in the teeth and bones. • In childhood this can cause a disease called **rickets**. • In later life, a disease called **osteoporosis** can cause older people's bones to fracture more easily.
Negative impacts on cognitive development	During childhood, children's brains are developing. A very poor diet can: • affect this brain development • lower children's academic attainment if they continue to be malnourished.

Key terms

Chronic disease: a long-term health condition.

Anaemia: a health condition in which there are not enough red blood cells in your body, which means that your body may not get enough oxygen.

Osteoporosis and rickets: diseases that affect the bones.

Performance Outcome 4: Safeguard and Promote the Health, Safety and Wellbeing of Children

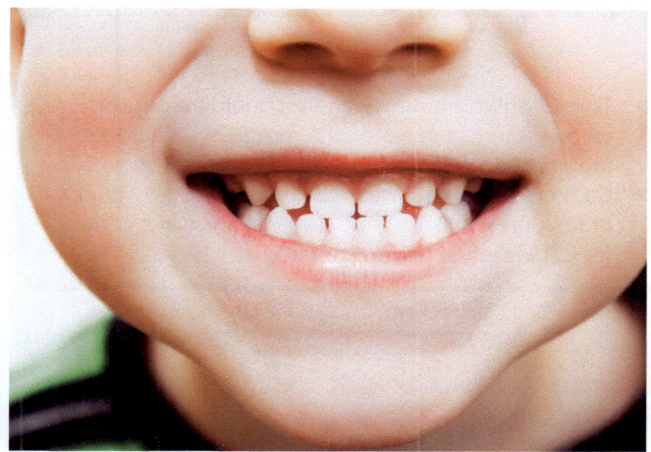

▲ How does a healthy diet help a child to have healthy teeth and gums?

How oral health can be promoted in the setting

Over the past few years, hospital admissions for children as a result of dental decay have increased. This has led to many children needing teeth extractions.

From 2021, the EYFS includes requirements about oral health in the safeguarding and wellbeing section.

There are many ways that practitioners can help children to develop oral health.

Incorporating oral health into care routines

As part of care routines, you might need to clean babies' and children's teeth.
- The current recommendations are that young children should not clean their teeth independently, because they do not have the skills to do so effectively.
- This means that while young children might have a go at being independent, parents or practitioners need to be responsible for cleaning teeth.

It is important to follow the current guidelines relating to cleaning teeth. This table gives NHS guidance at the time of writing.

Age	Guidelines for cleaning teeth
6 months–6 years	• Brush teeth twice daily for about 2 minutes. • Brush last thing at night before bed and on one other occasion. • Use children's fluoride toothpaste containing no less than 1,000ppm of fluoride (check label) or family toothpaste containing between 1,350ppm and 1,500ppm fluoride.

Age	Guidelines for cleaning teeth
6 months–3 years	• Start brushing the baby's teeth as soon as the first milk tooth breaks through (usually at around 6 months, but it can be earlier or later). • Parents or carers should brush or supervise toothbrushing. • Use only a smear of toothpaste. • Make sure children don't eat or lick toothpaste from the tube.
3–6 years	• Brushing should be supervised by a parent or carer. • Use only a pea-sized amount of toothpaste. • Spit out after brushing and don't rinse – if you rinse, the fluoride won't work as well.

> **Practice points**
>
> **Tooth brushing**
> ▶ Encourage children to be involved, e.g. by holding the toothpaste.
> ▶ Use a mirror so children can see what is happening.
> ▶ Let children have a little go and then follow up.
> ▶ Make up a story, e.g. 'We are going upstairs to clean the bedrooms ... now the windows.'

Communications on oral health promotion in the setting

To promote oral health in the setting, practitioners can:
- plan activities for children to help them realise the importance of their teeth and how best to look after them
- invite dental practitioners into the setting to talk to children about their work and how to look after their teeth
- create posters or books with children about how to care for teeth
- share books about going to the dentist and how to keep teeth clean.

Providing information to parents and carers about good oral health

- Many parents might not know which foods and drinks are harmful to children's teeth. Dental decay can be caused by sugary foods and drinks, and also by snacking too much on healthy foods and drinks that are acidic, such as orange juice.
- Some parents might not realise that the adult teeth can be affected if the milk teeth become decayed.

Education and Early Years T Level: Early Years Educator

> **Good to know**
>
> Frequent snacking can cause tooth decay, even when the foods are 'healthy'. This is because when eating or drinking, the teeth are coated with the food and the acidity in the mouth is changed. This encourages the harmful bacteria to grow.
>
> ▶ To prevent tooth decay, there should be periods where, apart from water, the mouth is kept free of food and drinks.
> ▶ Beakers or bottles with orange juice, sugary drinks or flavoured milk for repeatedly sipping are harmful for babies' and children's teeth.

K4.9 The signs and symptoms of common illnesses and infections

It is important to recognise:
▶ signs that children are becoming unwell
▶ when an infection might be more serious.

Whenever children look as if they are becoming unwell, they should always be removed from other children to avoid the spread of infection.

The table below shows some of the more common illnesses and infections, and notes which ones are **notifiable diseases**.

▲ Signs that a child might be unwell

> **Research**
>
> You can find a list of notifiable diseases on the government webpage, 'Notifiable diseases and causative organisms' at: www.gov.uk/guidance/notifiable-diseases-and-causative-organisms-how-to-report

> **Key term**
>
> **Notifiable disease:** illnesses which need to be reported to local authorities so that these can be monitored in case of local or national outbreaks.

Infection	Incubation time	Signs and symptoms	Treatment
Chicken pox (varicella)	2–3 weeks Infectious until spots have become scabs	Red or pink spots that turn to blisters, usually start on head and behind ears Spots come in crops and are very itchy Slight fever and headache Children feel unwell	No specific treatment Paracetamol to relieve fever Calamine lotion and cooling gels to ease itching
Common cold virus	1–5 days	Raised temperature in young children Sneezing and runny nose Sore throat, headache and achy muscles Sometimes, ears are affected Infectious until symptoms have finished	No specific treatment Offer plenty of drinks

Performance Outcome 4: Safeguard and Promote the Health, Safety and Wellbeing of Children

Infection	Incubation time	Signs and symptoms	Treatment
Conjunctivitis	Highly contagious if caused by an infection	Red, itchy and watery eyes May be burning or bloodshot May be caused by an infection or an allergy such as hay fever	Clean off any pus using a cold flannel or pad Use eye drops or antihistamines for hay fever
Diarrhoea and vomiting (food poisoning, gastroenteritis, norovirus)	Food poisoning: variable, from hours to days Gastroenteritis and norovirus: 18–72 hours	Diarrhoea Vomiting Fever	Hygiene measures need to be in place to avoid it spreading to other children Offer plenty of drinks, but not fizzy or fruit juices Introduce food once vomiting has stopped Foods high in carbohydrates such as pasta, bread and rice are recommended Seek medical attention if: • persistent vomiting without diarrhoea • blood or mucus in stools • diarrhoea symptoms have not improved after 7 days
Ear infection		Temperature Child feels unwell and may report ear pain Difficulties hearing Babies and toddlers may rub or pull at their ear Younger children may suffer from inner ear infections, caused by a virus	Antibiotics may be prescribed if infection appears severe Rest and plenty of fluids Paracetamol may be given to reduce pain
Hand, foot and mouth	3–5 days	High fever Loss of appetite Cough Sore throat Mouth ulcers Blisters that develop from a rash on hands and feet	No specific treatment Offer plenty of fluids and soft foods to make eating easier Painkillers may be taken and gels for mouth ulcers Children should be kept away from pregnant women
Head lice (see also page 296)	Spread by head to head contact	Itchy scalp Nits – egg cases on shaft of hair Lice	Over-the-counter treatments, e.g. medicated lotions and/or wet combing with a head lice comb to treat lice and eggs Children do not need to stay away from school but parents should be informed so they can check for signs
Impetigo bullous	4–10 days	Fluid-filled blisters appear on the chest Blisters spread quickly but are not painful or itchy	Antibiotic cream or tablets

Infection	Incubation time	Signs and symptoms	Treatment
Impetigo non-bullous		Red sore around the nose and mouth Sores burst, leaving yellow-brown crusts	Antibiotic cream or tablets
Influenza		Sudden onset, unlike a cold which is more gradual Fever Headache Children feel very unwell, e.g. tiredness, aching muscles, sore throat, dry chesty cough	No specific treatment Paracetamol can be given to reduce fever Offer plenty of drinks
Measles	10–14 days Highly infectious *Notifiable disease*	Child feels unwell Cold-like symptoms: runny nose, cough, watery eyes, sneezing Fever Tiny greyish spots in mouth and throat after a few days Blotchy red rash starts behind ears and on face Sensitivity to light	Paracetamol to reduce fever Children may prefer to be in a darkened room Offer plenty of drinks
Meningitis (bacterial and viral)	Viral 3–6 days Bacterial 2–10 days *Notifiable disease*	This can be a fatal disease involving infection of the membranes surrounding the brain and spinal cord Very rapid onset Early symptoms include: • severe headache and stiff neck • fever and confusion • muscle pain • cold hands and feet, shivering Later symptoms: • nausea and vomiting • drowsiness and unresponsiveness • unusual crying • rapid breathing rate • unable to tolerate bright light • blotchy, pale skin with red rash that does not fade under pressure or colour when a glass is pressed against it	Hospitalisation and treatment with antibiotics (for bacterial meningitis) and fluids Viral meningitis may be treated at home with rest, fluids and painkillers Long-term problems can sometimes result, including loss of hearing or sight
Mumps (virus)	14–25 days (often 17) Highly contagious *Notifiable disease*	Early symptoms: • headache • joint pain • fever Later symptoms: • swelling of salivary glands (underneath ears) • discomfort when chewing	No specific treatment Paracetamol to reduce pain or fever Offer plenty of drinks Offer soft foods as children will have difficulty in swallowing

Performance Outcome 4: Safeguard and Promote the Health, Safety and Wellbeing of Children

Infection	Incubation time	Signs and symptoms	Treatment
Rubella (German measles)	2–3 weeks *Notifiable disease*	Slight fever and mild cold symptoms Rash of tiny red-pink flat spots – not very itchy Rash starts on face and neck and spreads to body Swollen glands behind the ear	No specific treatment but plenty of rest Paracetamol can be given to reduce temperature and treat symptoms Children must be kept away from pregnant women – if this disease is caught in early pregnancy, it can cause birth defects
Scabies	30–45 days *Contagious*	Tiny rash caused by a parasite burrowing into the skin Very itchy rash Babies may develop blisters on their feet	Cream to be applied to child and all household members All bedding and clothing to be washed at 50°C or sealed in a bag for 3 days
Scarlet fever	2–5 days *Notifiable disease*	Begins with sore throat, headache and fever Rash begins with red blotches, turns into a fine pink-red rash that feels like sandpaper	Antibiotics Paracetamol to relieve fever
Slapped cheek syndrome (virus)	4–14 days	Rose red rash that usually appears on cheeks and on body Slight fever, headache Some nasal discharge	Painkillers and antihistamines if skin is very itchy
Tonsillitis		Sore throat High temperature White pus-filled spots on tonsils Headache	No specific treatment but paracetamol may be given to reduce fever Offer soft foods and plenty of drinks
Viral infections (unspecified)		Some viral infections are hard to identify. Signs of a viral infection affecting the intestine might include: • diarrhoea • constipation • stomach pain • sickness • loss of appetite	Treat as for diarrhoea and vomiting Monitor child in case further symptoms appear
Whooping cough	6–20 days *Notifiable disease*	Symptoms mild at first and are cold-like, e.g. sneezing, runny nose but a dry irritating cough Child might feel unwell and have a slight temperature Later symptoms are more serious: • bouts of intense coughing which bring up thick phlegm • a 'whooping' sound might occur when breathing in • vomiting after coughing • choking noises, difficulty breathing • tiredness and exhaustion as a result of the coughing	Antibiotics given as soon as possible, within first three weeks Rest and plenty of fluids Babies under 12 months might be hospitalised

> **Good to know**
>
> Outbreaks of food poisoning also have to be notified to the health protection team.
>
> You can find out more about when to report infections by downloading a copy of 'Health protection in schools and other childcare facilities' at: www.gov.uk

Signs that a child needs immediate medical attention

Children might show some signs and symptoms which mean that immediate medical attention is needed. If you are ever concerned, it is important that you err on the side of caution and act quickly. This is because babies' and young children's immune systems are still developing, so an infection can quickly take hold. In the case of diseases such as meningitis, these can be fatal.

The table indicates when you should seek medical help.

Signs	Symptoms
Temperature	Raised temperature of 38°C if the child is under 3 months
	Raised temperature of 39°C if the child is 3–6 months
	High temperature with quietness and lack of responsiveness
	Convulsions
Breathing	Difficulty in breathing
	Fast breathing
	Grunting when breathing
	Lips and face turning blue
Skin colour and rash	Spotty, purple-red rash
	A rash that does not fade
	Turning blue
	Skin mottled colour
	Very pale
Responsiveness	Lack of response
	Floppiness
	Hard to wake up
	Difficulty in staying awake
Other	High pitched cry
	Continuous cry
	Neck stiffness
	Not drinking for more than 8 hours
	Repeated vomiting
	Bile stained vomiting (green)
	In babies, bulging fontanelle (soft part at top of skull)

> **Good to know**
>
> **Making a 999 or 112 call**
>
> Stay calm. The call handler will ask questions. Listen carefully to them.
>
> You can expect to be asked the following:
> - whether the child is breathing, bleeding or unconscious
> - what happened and the injuries or symptoms
> - your name and exact location (including postcode if you know it)
> - the age of the child.
>
> You might be asked to follow some instructions. If necessary, put your phone on speaker so that your hands are free.

K4.10 How illnesses and infections are spread and effective practice to prevent and control infection

How illnesses and infection spread

We have seen that there are a number of infections that can affect babies and children. Infections are more likely to spread when:
- children or adults are in close contact with someone who is already infected
- hygiene processes or procedures are not being followed.

Outbreaks of infections of disease such as measles and rubella might also occur when children have not been fully immunised.

Performance Outcome 4: Safeguard and Promote the Health, Safety and Wellbeing of Children

A good starting point is to understand how most bacteria and viruses enter the body.
- **Ingestion** – bacteria and viruses are swallowed or taken into the body. This is a common route for infection in young children:
  - They often touch things that have bacteria and virus on them.
  - They then put their fingers in their mouths or touch their eyes and noses, and ingest the germs.
  - They could eat food or drink that has bacteria on it, causing food poisoning.
- **Inhalation** – bacteria and viruses can be breathed in.
- **Puncture wounds** – bacteria, viruses and some fungal infections enter the body through grazes, bites and wounds.

> **Research**
>
> Find out about:
> - how the recent COVID-19 infection was spread
> - the measures that were taken to reduce it.

Effective practice to prevent the spread of infection

The table shows some of the everyday ways in which the risk of infection through these routes can be reduced. As well as following these general approaches, there may be times when more specific measures will need to be put in place, e.g. for COVID-19. In such cases, you should seek further advice from the NHS website or your local health protection team.

Following hygiene processes and procedures

Hygiene processes and procedures are part of infection control. In early years settings, many hygiene processes and procedures take place. It is essential that you find out about these and follow them carefully.

Handwashing

Handwashing is a key way in which infection can be prevented from spreading, among both children and adults. Many bacteria, germs and fungi thrive on our hands, and are also passed across onto toys, surfaces, food and others' hands.

There are many situations when you should wash and dry your hands (even if you are in a hurry or if they look clean), such as:
- after changing nappies
- before handling food
- during the food preparation process.

The step-by-step diagram on the following page shows you how to wash your hands thoroughly using hot water and soap.

How bacteria/virus enter the body	How to reduce the risk of infection
Ingestion	Cleaning routines.
	Handwashing for adults and children (see below).
	Wash your hands after blowing your nose.
	Replace sensory materials such as water or dough regularly.
	Wipe toys and resources that have been mouthed by babies.
	Follow food hygiene procedures.
Inhalation	Good ventilation allows the air to be changed.
	Cover your mouth when coughing.
	Sneeze into a tissue.
	Spend time outdoors.
	Isolate or remove children who are showing signs of being unwell.
Puncture wounds	Wash and cover cuts and grazes.
	Keep children away from wasps and bees.

Education and Early Years T Level: Early Years Educator

▲ It is important to know how to wash your hands thoroughly when working with children

Using correct personal protective equipment (PPE)

Early years settings use a range of items to protect children and adults from disease and infections. Under the Health and Safety Act of 1974, you have a duty to use them if they are provided.

The two items that you are most likely to use are disposable gloves and aprons.
- These should be used every time you change a nappy or come into contact with blood, e.g. from a cut or vomit.
- You should also use these items to clean toilets and any spillages involving urine, faeces or vomit.
- Afterwards, you should always remove the gloves and the aprons immediately – do not walk around with them.
- You should also wash your hands, as this will give you added protection.

Dealing with spillages safely

Any spillages, including toileting accidents or where a child has been sick, must be dealt with hygienically to prevent the spread of germs.

- The first step is to remove any children from the area.
- The next step is always to put on disposable gloves and an apron.
- You should then get the correct cleaning products which will disinfect the area, some paper towels and a plastic bag.
- Use the paper towels to mop up any liquid or to scoop any solids. Put the soiled paper towels into the plastic bag as you go.
- Once the floor has been partially cleaned, put some disinfectant onto the paper towel or disposable cloth to wipe up the area. Put the clothes or paper towels in the plastic bag. Dry the area with the paper towels.
- Throw away the plastic bag in the appropriate waste bin. Remove your apron and gloves and throw these away.
- Afterwards, wash hands thoroughly.

Safe disposal of waste

Early years settings other than childminders and nannies are required to dispose of bodily waste

Performance Outcome 4: Safeguard and Promote the Health, Safety and Wellbeing of Children

separately. This means that there are separate bins both indoors and outdoors for items such as:
- nappies
- soiled paper towels
- anything that has been in contact with blood, faeces, vomit or urine.

These bins are often yellow or are distinguished from ordinary waste paper bins. They will have lids on them, again to prevent spread of infection. If you work in a setting where waste is disposed of in this way, you must use them as this will be part of the setting's health and safety policy.

In home-based settings, it is good practice to have separate bins for items of bodily waste which should:
- have lids on them
- be regularly emptied and the contents moved to an outdoor bin in a secure area.

You should never let children play with bins, although they might be interested in them.

Modelling and encouraging effective hygiene practice

Point out and talk about the steps you are taking which show that you are using effective hygiene practice.
- When talking to younger children, ask them why it is important; for example, 'Why do we need to wash our hands before we have lunch?'
- Always model good practice in your day-to-day behaviour so that children can see you using it.

> **Research**
>
> Find out the system in your setting to dispose of waste.

Cleaning

Keeping resources and areas clean is a key part of infection control. Who does the general cleaning depends very much on the setting.
- In large group care settings, a caretaker or cleaner will come and clean at the end of the day.
- In other settings, including nannies and in smaller group care, it may be the responsibility of the practitioners.

In addition to general cleaning, which includes mopping floors, vacuuming and cleaning toilets, most practitioners also need to maintain the cleanliness of areas during the session, including toilets, kitchen and tables where children eat. The table below shows what is usually cleaned in early years settings.

Items to be cleaned	Frequency and method of cleaning
Basins and taps	Daily and when needed
Toilets	Clean thoroughly each day and immediately after any accident. Use disinfectant
Nappy changing mats	Wipe down with disinfectant each time after use
Bins	Empty bins daily and wash them out
	Bins should be lined to prevent spread of infection
Carpets	Daily
Floors	Daily with hot water and detergent
	Use disinfectant if there has been a toileting accident or sickness
Tables and chairs	Daily with disposable cloths
Bedding	Every few days or immediately if soiled
	Machine wash at a minimum of 60°C
Soft toys	Weekly
	Wash in the machine at 60°C
Plastic toys	Clean weekly with a weak solution of bleach
	Sterilise if used by young babies
Water trays/containers	Change the water after use
	Dry the tray to prevent mould if not in use
Water toys	Wash with a weak solution of bleach from time to time
	Always dry toys when not in use to prevent mould
Sand tray indoors	Change regularly
	Wash and dry the tray when sand is changed
Sand outdoors	Rake daily
	Keep covered when not in use
Playdough	Change frequently
	Children should wash hands before and after using it

Sterilisation

Sterilisation is a process by which bacteria, viruses and germs are removed from items. There are two main methods of sterilising:
1. exposing objects to high temperatures
2. soaking them in a chemical mixture.

Items that babies use for feeding or play with require sterilising. The spider diagram gives examples of these items.

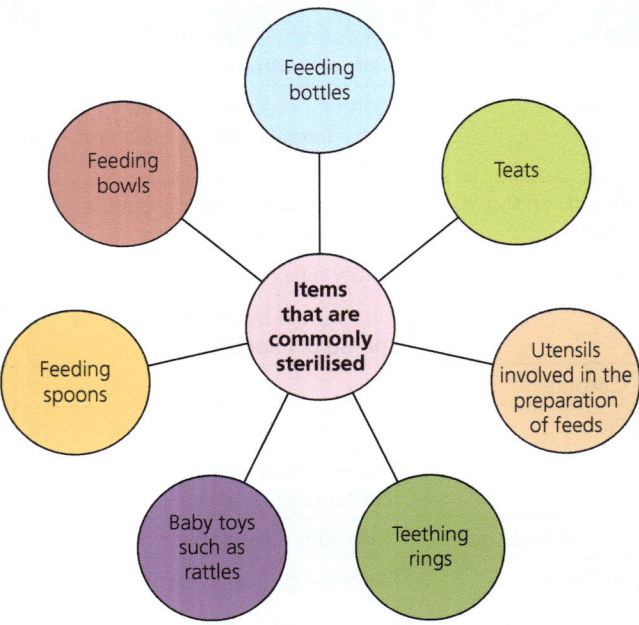

▲ Items that are commonly sterilised in early years settings

Food hygiene

Good food hygiene can reduce the possibility of food poisoning. Food poisoning can be very dangerous for babies and young children. If you are preparing or serving food, your employer should:
- show you how to do it correctly, or
- send you on a food hygiene course.

Here are some key points about food hygiene:
1. Always wash your hands:
   – at the start of the preparation and serving of food
   – after you have touched any raw meat, poultry or fish during the cooking process
   – when your hands become dirty.
2. Wear an apron when cooking, tie back long hair and keep nails short to prevent infection.
3. If you have any cuts on your hands, these have to be covered up with a plaster. Blue plasters are usually used in kitchens that prepare food for children.
4. Throughout the food preparation process, keep the surfaces clean.
5. Use separate chopping boards and dishes for raw meat, poultry and fish.

Storage of food

Always store food according to manufacturer's instructions. Instructions will include when food should be thrown away after being opened as well as best before dates. For food that needs refrigerating or freezing:
- Check the temperatures of the fridge or freezer.
- Make sure that food that has already been cooked or will be eaten uncooked is kept away from raw meat, poultry and fish, because these foods carry bacteria.
- Wrap or cover foods to prevent them from becoming contaminated with raw foods.

Reheating food and keeping food warm

Most early years settings do not reheat food because there is a higher danger of food poisoning unless they are using ready meals.

If food is reheated:
- Only reheat it once.
- Reheat it to a temperature until it is clearly piping hot and actually cooked.
- Do not keep food warm because it can cause bacteria to grow.

Washing fruit and vegetables

Fruit and vegetables should always be washed and in some cases peeled before being given to children.

Cooking meat, fish, poultry and eggs thoroughly

Meat, fish, poultry (especially chicken) and eggs are naturally high in bacteria, so make sure that they are always cooked very thoroughly.

Preparing feeds safely

Formula feed is milk that is given to babies instead of breast milk. There are different types of formula feed:
- powdered milk made up with boiling water
- formula feed that comes ready-made.

It is important that formula feed is prepared hygienically. If the milk, the bottle or the teat are contaminated, the bacteria will be swallowed by the baby. As babies' immune systems are still developing, this can mean that they can become very ill.

To prevent the risk of food poisoning, there has been a significant change in the approach used to make up powdered formula feed.
- Whereas it used to be normal practice to make up several bottles in advance, today it is recommended that no formula feed made from powdered milk should be made up ahead of time.

You should always follow the manufacturer's instructions:
- Wash hands thoroughly at the start of the process.
- Make sure that all equipment including teats and bottles have been sterilised.

Performance Outcome 4: Safeguard and Promote the Health, Safety and Wellbeing of Children

> **Research**
>
> Find out the latest guidelines in relation to preparing powdered formula feed by visiting: www.nhs.uk/Conditions/pregnancy-and-baby/pages/making-up-infant-formula.aspx#close

The role of immunisations in reducing disease

For many years, babies and children have been protected from some serious diseases by being vaccinated against them. This process is called **immunisation**, although many parents will talk about their child 'having jabs'.

Some of these illnesses and infections are still spread because:
- babies and children have not been vaccinated, or
- they have not had a complete vaccination where two doses were required.

The immunisation schedule

The number of diseases that children can be vaccinated against has increased in the past few years. It is also recognised that the sooner babies can be immunised, the safer they can be kept.

The table below shows the current immunisation schedule at the time of writing. The timing or the type of vaccinations may change, so you should always refer to the NHS for the latest vaccination schedule.

> **Good to know**
>
> ### How vaccines work
>
> A vaccine contains a tiny amount of live or dead cells from viruses and bacteria.
> - When these cells enter the body, the immune system is tricked into working.
> - New cells and **antibodies** (cells which fight infection) are made.
> - These antibodies are ready to fight if you ever come into contact with the disease.
>
> When vaccine uptake is high, the disease can, in theory, die out. This has happened in the case of smallpox and polio in many parts of the world.
>
> High levels of vaccination can help those children who cannot be vaccinated for medical reasons.

Age	Immunisations	Purpose
8 weeks	'6 in 1': diphtheria, tetanus, whooping cough, polio, haemophilus influenzae type b (Hib) and hepatitis B	Often known as the '6 in 1' because a single jab is given for six diseases Each of these diseases can be life-threatening in babies
	MenB	To prevent meningitis B strain
	Rotavirus	To prevent a strain of diarrhoea and sickness
12 weeks	2nd dose of the 6 in 1	
	PCV	To prevent infections that may cause pneumonia
	2nd dose of rotavirus	
16 weeks	3rd dose of the 6 in 1	
	2nd dose of the MenB	
1 year	MenC at the same time as booster dose of Hib	MenC is to prevent the C strain of meningitis
	Measles, mumps and rubella (MMR)	Mumps and measles diseases can make children very ill and can cause life-long disability Rubella poses a risk to pregnant women and their unborn baby
	2nd dose of the PCV	
	3rd dose of MenB	
2 years–9 years	Dose of flu vaccine to be taken every year	
3 years 4 months	2nd dose of MMR	
	4th dose of diphtheria, tetanus, whooping cough (pertussis) and polio	Known as the '4 in 1' pre-school booster, as it is a single jab

> **Good to know**
>
> **Why some vaccinations are repeated**
>
> Some vaccinations need to be repeated. This helps to make sure that they are effective.
>
> Vaccinations such as the flu jab happen every year. This is because the flu virus keeps changing. A common mistake is for parents to believe that their children will be safe after having just one set of injections.

Why some children are not immunised

There are two main reasons why some children are not immunised.

1. Medical reasons: a very tiny number of children cannot be immunised for all or some types of diseases because they have medical conditions which do not make it safe. A good example is:
   - the measles vaccine – children who are having cancer treatment are not given this injection because it is one of the only vaccines that contains a live virus.

   Even though the amount of virus is tiny, it can be fatal for children who are on drugs that affect their immunity.
2. Parental choice: some parents choose not to have their children vaccinated. They might be concerned about the safety of the vaccine or have other personal reasons. While it is important to respect parents' views, health professionals are keen to point out that:
   - Millions of children have been vaccinated.
   - The safety record of all current vaccinations is excellent.
   - These diseases can be extremely serious.

Removing unwell children or staff members from the setting

One way to prevent the spread of infection is by removing children or adults who have an infection. The amount of time that children or staff need to stay at home depends on the disease.

The table shows the current recommendations for exclusion for some common infections.

Infection	Exclusion period
Chicken pox	5 days from onset of rash and all the lesions have crusted over
Diarrhoea and vomiting	48 hours after last symptoms
Flu	Until recovered
Impetigo	Until lesions are crusted/healed or 48 hours after starting antibiotic treatment
Measles	4 days from onset of rash and recovered
Mumps	5 days after onset of swelling
Rubella	5 days from onset of rash
Scarlet fever	Exclude until 24 hours of antibiotic treatment is completed
Scabies	Once treatment is completed
Whooping cough	2 days from starting antibiotic treatment, or 21 days from onset of symptoms if not treated with antibiotics

Referring on where medical intervention is necessary

As part of the prevention and control of infections, there may be times when we need to seek the advice of professionals or refer parents on for medical intervention.

Notification and seeking advice

We have seen that where there are outbreaks of some infections, early years settings are required to notify the relevant health authorities. A good example of this is where there is an outbreak of food poisoning. As a result of notification, advice will be given to settings about procedures that need to take place. In addition, parents are also likely to be given advice about how to reduce the risk of infection.

Signposting parents

There are times when we may need to advise parents that their children need further medical support. It may be that the symptoms that a child is showing needs to be investigated further. A good example of this is where a child has a temperature and a headache. A visit to a pharmacist or a GP may be needed. It is worth noting that unless there is a medical emergency, early years practitioners are not able to refer children to medical services unless there is specific consent in place. A nanny, for example, may have this consent and so can seek advice while they have charge of a child.

Performance Outcome 4: Safeguard and Promote the Health, Safety and Wellbeing of Children

> **Research**
>
> Find the full list by downloading 'Health protection in schools and other childcare facilities' at: www.gov.uk

> **Test yourself**
>
> 1. What might cause you to think a baby or child is unwell?
> 2. What are the main ways in which illnesses and infections are spread?
> 3. What illnesses might cause a rash?
> 4. When should you call for immediate medical attention?

K4.11 The difference between an accident and an emergency situation, preventions and precautions, and limitations of own role

From time to time in early years settings, there will be an accident, incident or emergency. A good starting point is to understand what these terms mean.

- An **accident** is an unintended incident which might cause physical injury to a child or member of staff; for example, falls, scalds, poisoning and choking.
- An **incident** is where an event takes place that might cause an injury or develop into an emergency, such as a child going missing.
- An **emergency** is a life-threatening situation or one that poses immediate risk.

Accidents become emergencies when:

- a child is unconscious and/or has no pulse
- a child is not breathing or has difficulty in doing so
- a child's lips and face swell, e.g. following a bee sting
- there is severe bleeding
- a child's leg or arm is sticking out at an unnatural angle
- a child has severe burns
- a child has had a blow to the head and is drowsy, has difficulty seeing, is sick or feeling nauseous.

In such cases, immediate medical attention is needed – you should make a 112 or 999 call.

Other emergencies

The table below shows some of the usual responses to different types of emergency situations, although you should always find out the setting's own procedures.

Situation	Likely actions to take
Missing child	Follow procedures: • report to line manager immediately • systematically search the premises • alert police and parents if necessary.
Gas leak, fire or bomb threat	Phone 999 or 112 if you are the first on scene and it is safe to do so. Follow evacuation procedure, e.g. take register with you. Use the closest exit available, providing that it is away from the incident.
Breaches of security involving intruders	Stay calm but tell children to move away if you are the first on the scene and the intruder appears aggressive.
Criminal activity	Move and talk slowly to defuse the situation. Encourage the intruder to move into the office or away from children, and to leave the premises. Assess the situation as to whether it is safe or you need to call 999 or 112. In serious situations, evacuate the building or move children to a room or cupboard that can be locked.

Situation	Likely actions to take
Extreme weather including floods	Phone 999 or 112 if you are first on scene and it is safe to do so. Call for help. Consider evacuation if it is still safe to do so. In the case of flooding, move children to higher ground or upstairs.
Hazardous substance release	Remove children away from the area. Do not touch the substance. If the substance is in the air, take children indoors and seal the room. Encourage children to cover their faces. Call 999 or 112.

▲ Would you know what to do if this child went missing?

Effective practice to prevent accidents

Practitioners need to prevent children from having accidents.

Babies and children are significantly at risk of having a serious accident, because they are curious, impulsive and unable to evaluate risk for themselves.

While the majority of accidents occur in children's own homes, each year serious and preventable accidents occur in early years settings. Some result in children's deaths. The table below and on the next page shows the five main causes of accidents and how they can be prevented.

Cause of accident	Examples	Role of the practitioner
Choking, strangulation or suffocation	Choking on food Choking on toys or resources Putting a cord around a neck, e.g. while pretending to take a dog for a walk Putting plastic bags over head	Supervise snack and mealtimes. Cut up fruit such as grapes. Do not give young children whole nuts. Make sure that toys and resources are suitable for babies and toddlers who are mouthing. Identify children who regularly put things in their mouths. Remove cords or ropes. Check that any blind cords are safely attached in line with advice. Remove plastic bags. Remove toys from cots.

Performance Outcome 4: Safeguard and Promote the Health, Safety and Wellbeing of Children

Cause of accident	Examples	Role of the practitioner
Falls	Falls down stairs Falls from climbing frames or on trampolines Falls while climbing furniture Unstable furniture falling onto children Running into furniture	Use safety gates for babies and toddlers. Put corner protectors on furniture if babies are starting to walk. Teach children how to use stairs properly. Make sure children are concentrating and not rushing during climbing activities. Make sure items are not left on stairs for children to trip over. Make sure that climbing frames and other resources are supervised or fenced off when not in use. Make sure that furniture such as cupboards are attached to walls. Create safe climbing areas for babies and toddlers.
Poisoning	Swallowing lithium batteries Drinking cleaning products and medicines Eating poisonous leaves and flowers Eating uncooked beans, pulses and lentils	Identify which babies and children are mouthing as part of their stage of development. Make sure that any toys with lithium batteries are supervised. Make sure compartments where batteries are kept are sealed. Keep cleaning products and medicines locked away from children. Risk-assess plants that might be poisonous in outdoor spaces. If using uncooked beans, pulses and lentils as sensory activities, make sure children do not eat them.
Burns and scalds	Scalds caused by hot drinks or food Scalds caused by hot water in taps Burns caused by children playing with matches or lighters Accidents while cooking	Do not prepare or have hot drinks when working with children. Check the temperature of food and dishes before serving or allowing children to self-serve. Check temperature of hot taps. Do not smoke near children. Keep matches and lighters locked up or tidied away out of reach. Risk-assess cooking activities carried out with children, e.g. how many children are safe to be in the kitchen.
Drowning	Drowning while playing with water, e.g. water tray, paddling pool, builders' tray Drowning in the natural environment, e.g. rivers, seaside, canals Drowning at the swimming pool	Recognise that children can drown in 15 cm of water. Supervise any type of water play, including in shallow trays. On outings, supervise children very carefully and adjust the group size to reflect risk level.

> **Good to know**
>
> **Lithium batteries**
>
> The small lithium batteries found in watches, torches and some toys are very dangerous if swallowed. Children are often attracted to them because they are shiny and look like tablets or sweets.
> ▶ Avoid using resources with lithium batteries where possible.
> ▶ If this is not possible, check that the battery compartment is sealed and that a child cannot open it or a battery can't fall out.
> ▶ If you suspect a child might have swallowed a battery, call 999 or take the child immediately to A&E.

Observations and supervision of children, including staff-to-child ratios

Many accidents at home and also in early years settings occur when adults are not properly supervising children. Accidents can happen very quickly and so one of the key roles of the practitioner is to supervise children at all times.

There are different levels of supervision depending on the age and stage of development, but remember that the EYFS requires children to be always in sight and/or in hearing of an adult.
▶ Very close supervision is always needed for babies and toddlers, as their awareness of danger is very limited.
▶ It is also needed for young children during more hazardous activities such as outings, cooking or playing with water.
▶ Older children can often play at a distance from an adult, for example, in a school playground.

Observing children

While supervising children, it is important to keep observing what they are doing and what they are playing with. Play can quickly change and become unsafe. For example:
▶ A child who is standing near a fence might start to see if they can climb it.
▶ A bucket that has been used for transporting sand might be put over a child's head as a helmet.

The following signs indicate that you should investigate more closely what children are doing:
▶ loud, excited voices
▶ sudden squabbling
▶ silence, with children looking secretive.

If you notice a sudden change in how a child or children are playing and these signs are present, it is likely that they have found something interesting to do. In some cases, what they are doing may be safe, but you should always investigate.

Behaviour changes

Tiredness affects babies' and young children's risk of having an accident.
▶ When we are tired, we might not be able to judge distances accurately or control our movements. This is important when climbing or reaching out for an object.
▶ Tiredness affects children's ability to control their immediate impulses and emotions.

As part of observing children, we should also pick up on any signs of tiredness.

Staff-to-child ratios

The EYFS sets the staff-to-child ratios for each age group in different early years settings. These are the minimum legal ratios.

In some situations, more adults will be needed because of:
▶ the developmental needs of the children or
▶ the activity that is taking place, such as an outing.

Health and safety procedures

Every early years setting has a health and safety policy and procedures that should be followed.
▶ The health and safety policy will look at different areas and activities within the setting, and outline the procedures for working safely and keeping children safe.
▶ The procedures will be based on risk assessments. These assessments will vary from setting to setting, because the physical layout and equipment in early years settings can vary. A good example of this is toilets:
  – Some settings use community buildings so adults always have to accompany children to the toilet.
  – In other settings, the toilet might be adjacent to the main play area and older children can access them within earshot of the adult.

Knowing when and how to carry out risk assessments

The process of carrying out a risk assessment is relatively simple. We looked at this as part of Core Skill 4 on page 207.

Performance Outcome 4: Safeguard and Promote the Health, Safety and Wellbeing of Children

Most early years settings carry out written risk assessments every year or when something has changed, such as an extension being built or when planning an outing. These risk assessments are used when reviewing the health and safety policy and procedures.

> **Case study**
>
> Little Stars regularly takes children to visit the local library. A risk assessment has been done which covers taking children out in the rain and sun, and also according to the ages of children being taken out. The outing requires children to cross the road at a pelican crossing. Today roadworks have started and the pelican crossing is out of action.
> ▶ Why is a new risk assessment needed?
> ▶ Identify the potential hazard now the pelican crossing is closed.
> ▶ What might be the result of the risk assessment?

Informal risk assessments are not written down. Adults working with children should be constantly assessing risk as they plan and supervise children.

In this section, we look more closely at the risks that are associated with the age and developmental stage of children as well as common resources and activities in the setting.

Risks associated with different ages/stage of children

One of the most important things to consider when carrying out a risk assessment is to be aware of the ages/stage of children involved in the activity. This is because they will not only have different needs, but they will also play and explore in different ways. For example:

▶ Until around 18 months, most babies and toddlers automatically put objects into their mouths. This means that in planning the environment, only toys and resources that are not choking hazards can be put out.

The table below shows the potential risks associated with children's ages and how the risks might be managed.

Age/stage	Needs	Managing the risk
Babies, non-mobile	Might start to wriggle or roll so could fall off surfaces, e.g. during nappy changing Takes all objects to the mouth to explore Very vulnerable immune system so food poisoning can be fatal	Close supervision is required. Put out only objects and toys safe to go into the mouth. Frequently clean toys and resources. Food hygiene must be a priority.
Babies, mobile	Mouthing objects Will pick up small objects left on the floor using pincer grasp Holds onto furniture to pull to standing position Very vulnerable immune system so food poisoning can be fatal	Closely supervise and tidy away small toys or objects that older children might have left. Furniture has to be stable. Objects left on furniture have to be safe. Toys and resources must be frequently cleaned after use. Food hygiene must be a priority.
Toddlers	Extremely active Loves to climb, throw and explore Moves fast May not understand or remember instructions/warnings Tries to imitate older children Is impulsive and has limited understanding of danger	Close supervision is required. Offer opportunities for physical activity. Keep unsuitable resources or substances out of reach or locked.
3–5 years	May copy adults' actions and is physically more capable now May become engaged in superhero play or copy actions from films Excited by challenges and trying new things	Good supervision is required. Adults to act as role models. Provide exciting but safe activities.

Bear in mind that some children have additional needs that will affect how we keep them safe. For example:
- A child who has limited sight needs areas where they walk to be kept free of objects.
- A child who has hearing difficulties needs adults to remember that they may not hear instructions or warnings.

Indoor activities	Hazards/Risks
Water play	Drowning
	Slipping on wet floor
	Danger of water being contaminated if not regularly changed
Sand play	Sand might go in eyes
	Slipping on sandy floors
Play dough	Dough being eaten which might not be hygienic/contain too much salt
	Infection might be spread if children do not wash their hands
Art and craft, e.g. pens, pencils, paintbrushes/mark making, scissors	Poking in eye
	Cuts from scissors
Dressing up clothes – belts and similar items	Strangulation as children pretend to take a dog for a walk
	Belt striking eyes and face
Cooking activities	Danger of knives, hot hobs and ovens

> **Reflect**
>
> For each of the hazards identified in the above table, research and make a suggestion as to how you can minimise the risk.

There are some outdoor activities and resources that can cause hazards for children.

It is always important to think about the age/stage of children that will be involved in any activity or using a resource, because this will affect the potential hazards. For example:
- Babies explore by putting objects in their mouths, but four-years-olds use their hands instead.

Outdoor activities	Hazards/Risks
Slides/climbing frames	Falls caused by children pushing each other, or children losing balance
Swings	Falls as a result of a child losing balance
	Children walking in the path of a swing may be kicked
Wheeled toys such as tricycles	Falls as a result of a child losing control
	Collisions with other children
Fencing/gates	Children leaving the premises unnoticed
	Strangers entering
Water activities	Drowning
	Slipping on wet floor
	Danger of water being contaminated if not regularly changed
Sand	As for indoors, plus possibility of contamination from animal faeces
Plants	Poisoning
	Poke in eye from sticks

Removing hazards and reporting these to a supervisor

As part of an informal risk assessment, always watch out for hazards and then report these to the supervisor. Hazards might include:
- a slippery patch of ice in winter
- animal faeces in the sand tray.

Using age- and stage-appropriate equipment and following manufacturer's instructions

In Performance Outcome 1 on page 245, we looked at the importance of age–stage equipment, as well as following manufacturers' instructions.

Carrying out safety checks on equipment

It is essential to check:
- equipment before using it with children, especially anything that has moving parts such as wheeled toys or resources that enable children to climb
- restraints in pushchairs and highchairs, that they have been fastened correctly
- safety gates, that they are working properly.

Performance Outcome 4: Safeguard and Promote the Health, Safety and Wellbeing of Children

The responsibilities and limitations of the EYE role when responding to accidents and emergencies

Following the policies and procedures of the setting

It is essential that you know the policies and procedures of your setting in relation to accidents and emergencies. You cannot predict when an accident or emergency is about to happen, and time can be wasted when people do not know where things are kept or what they should do. For example, you should always know what to do if:
- the fire alarm sounds
- a child is choking.

Reporting the accident/emergency

As part of the policies and procedures, you should know who to contact if there is an accident or emergency.

In large settings, someone will be responsible for overall health and safety, and another person might be responsible for fire safety and organising evacuations (designated fire warden).
- Always contact a first aider immediately in the case of any accident or medical emergency.
- You should also know who to tell if you spot a potential hazard.
- In the case of child protection and safeguarding, you should know who to talk to if you have any concerns – the DSL.

Remaining calm and professional

Time is critical during any accident or emergency. Staying calm, thinking clearly and following the procedures saves time.
- Staying calm also helps children to feel reassured.
- If you remember to be calm and speak slowly, children are more likely to follow instructions.

Maintaining accurate and coherent records and reports, sharing information only when required and maintaining confidentiality

All accidents, incidents and emergencies have to be recorded accurately. This is important because serious accidents and incidents also have to be reported to inspectorates and agencies such as Ofsted or the Health and Safety Executive, who will investigate further.

In the case of accidents, parents also need to know what has happened and so early years settings will report any injury, however minor, to parents. Most forms require the following information:
- time and date
- details about the accident/incident/emergency including its cause and the names of the injured
- how the accident/incident/emergency was responded to
- who responded to it
- name and signature of the person reporting the accident/incident/emergency.

Remember that information about a child should only be shared as necessary in accordance with data protection legislation (see page 46) with authorised persons.

> **Research**
>
> Find out what forms have to be filled in at your setting for:
> - accidents
> - incidents
> - emergencies.

A range of fire safety precautions

Fires are a danger in both homes and in early years settings. It is essential that all early years settings:
- take steps to avoid fires starting
- ensure quick evacuation in the case of a fire.

If you are working in an early years setting, find out what you should do in the case of a fire. There are a range of measures that early years settings are required to take to prevent fires, reduce the spread of fires and plan for evacuation.

Preventing fires	
Measures to take	**What you should know**
Fire risk assessments and fire safety officers	As part of a setting's health and safety policy, a fire risk assessment must be carried out.
	Many early years settings will appoint one person to be their 'responsible person' who takes on the role of a fire safety officer/warden within the setting.
	In childminding settings, this is not required, but a general risk assessment is needed which should consider fire risk.
No smoking	The EYFS bans smoking on the premises of early years settings.
Electrical appliances	Electrical appliances and sockets can be responsible for fires. These should always be risk-assessed regularly.
	Do not overload sockets with additional plugs.
	Turn off appliances that are not being used, to reduce the risk of fire.
Smoke detectors	Smoke detectors can alert adults to the early signs of a fire before it spreads.
	Begin evacuation procedures immediately if the detector sounds the alarm.
Reducing the spread of a fire	
Fire extinguishers and fire blankets	You can use fire extinguishers and fire blankets to prevent a fire from spreading, although your priority is always to evacuate children first and call for help.
	Do not use fire extinguishers to tackle a large fire.
	Fire extinguishers must be serviced every year. They should not be moved or used for any other purpose (such as holding doors open!).
Fire doors	Fire doors can prevent a fire from spreading. They must be kept closed at all times.
Evacuation	
Evacuation procedure displays	Every adult must know the procedure in the event of a fire. This includes: • who is responsible for the registers • where to go • where to meet.
	Signs should be placed to help adults know about the evacuation procedure. Visitors and volunteers should be shown these signs.
Fire exits	Use these doors in the case of a fire.
	In early years settings, these should be signed with a 'running man' symbol.
	Fire exits must be kept clear – furniture and activities should not be put in front of them.
Clear assembly points	Adults need to know where to take children so that they will be safe in the event of a fire.
	It is important to keep children calm and check against the register that all the children you have been working with are present.
Fire evacuation practices	To help children and adults know what to do in the event of a fire, early years settings should hold fire evacuation practices.

Performance Outcome 4: Safeguard and Promote the Health, Safety and Wellbeing of Children

▲ Have you seen this symbol in your placement setting?

> **Research**
>
> Do you know what the fire procedures are in your placement setting?
>
> If you do not:
> ▶ find out what they are
> ▶ make sure you know what action you would need to take.

Skills practice

A new nursery has been opened near to your college. The nursery takes children from two to five years at present, but they are hoping to open a baby unit in the near future.

The nursery has a large garden next to a park.
▶ The children visit the park every day. The nursery has a fence around it and two gates.
▶ The garden has wheeled toys, a large slide and a climbing frame.
▶ There is a sand pit and a mud kitchen. The children have access to water from a water butt.
▶ The nursery has some chickens, guinea pigs and a couple of rabbits that the children can feed.

Indoors, there are two interconnected rooms for the children aged two to five years.
▶ Both rooms have access to the outdoor space.
▶ The children can move between the rooms and the outdoors.
▶ One room contains sensory materials, construction and opportunities for art and design.
▶ There are large sinks for the children.
▶ There are toilets off each room and a room that is used for lunch and naps. There is also a kitchen and office.

The manager is keen to develop a partnership with the college and support the training of childcare students. Working with the placement coordinator at the college, it has been decided that students on placement will take part in the following activities:
▶ supervising children as they play indoors and outdoors, including visiting the pets
▶ preparing snacks and helping children at snack and mealtimes
▶ supporting children at nap time
▶ planning activities for the sensory play/creative room.

While the manager wants to develop training placements, she must ensure that any students who come to the setting understand the importance of health and safety and safeguarding, so that the requirements of the EYFS can be met at all times.

The manager has decided that a simple induction pack would be useful. She has asked you to help with the preparation of the induction pack, which should include the following information:
▶ the importance of following the policies and procedures of the setting in relation to health and safety
▶ the requirements of the EYFS in relation to health and safety and safeguarding
▶ how to carry out a risk assessment in different areas of the nursery
▶ how to supervise children effectively
▶ health and safety considerations for every activity that the students might carry out while on placement.

Performance Outcome 5: Work in Partnership with Colleagues, Parents, Carers and Other Professionals to Support Children's Development

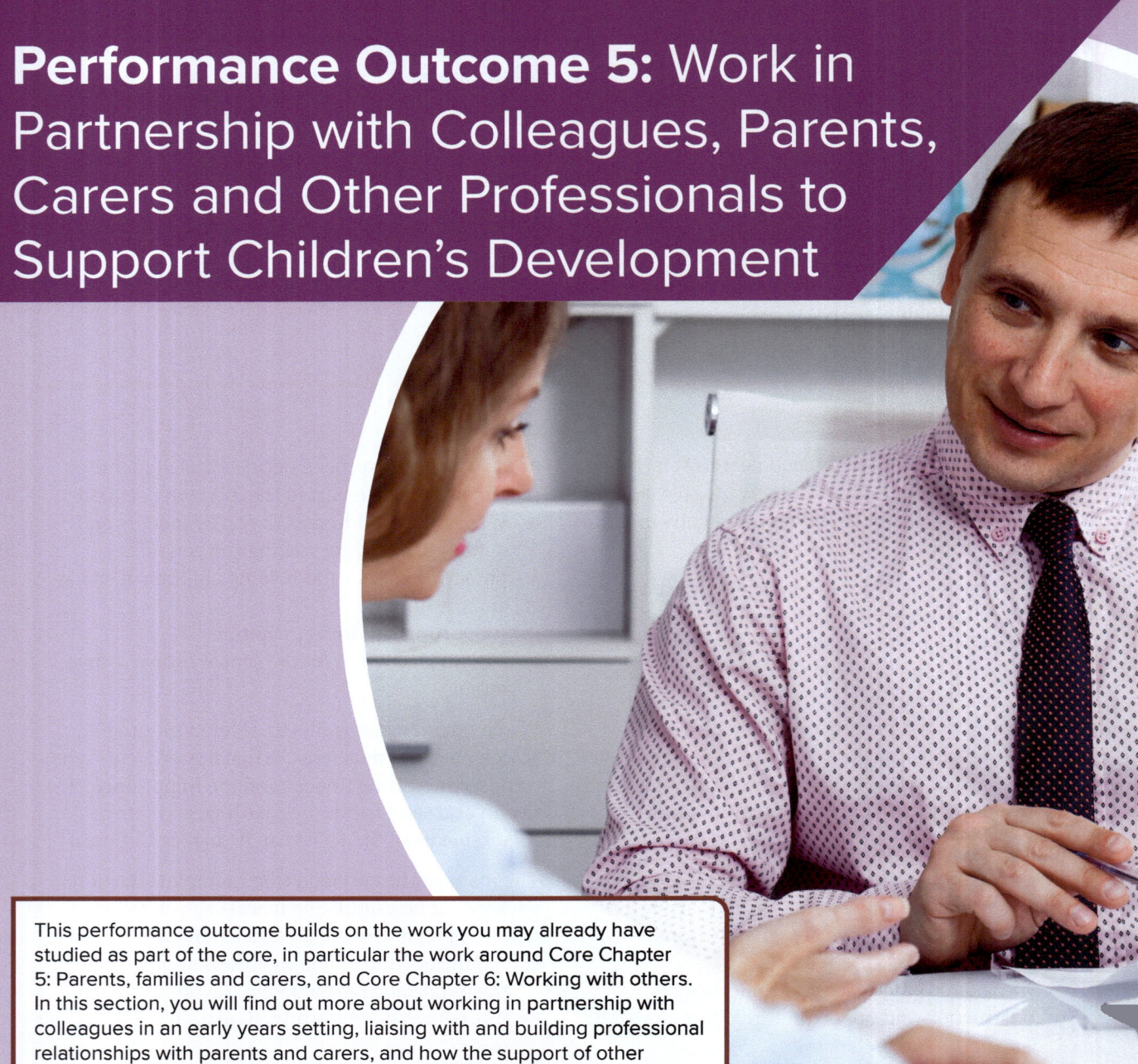

This performance outcome builds on the work you may already have studied as part of the core, in particular the work around Core Chapter 5: Parents, families and carers, and Core Chapter 6: Working with others. In this section, you will find out more about working in partnership with colleagues in an early years setting, liaising with and building professional relationships with parents and carers, and how the support of other professionals can help you support babies, young children and families throughout their early years and beyond.

Learning outcomes

This chapter covers the following knowledge outcomes for Performance Outcome 5.

- **K5.1** The legal rights and responsibilities of parents and carers
- **K5.2** How a range of family contexts may impact on parenting
- **K5.3** The roles and responsibilities of external agencies involved in early years settings
- **K5.4** The purpose and benefits of working with other professionals and the circumstances in which this would be appropriate and relevant

Skills-based outcomes will need to be considered in your work placement, and your assessor will support you to meet these.

Performance Outcome 5: Work in Partnership with Colleagues, Parents, Carers and Other Professionals

K5.1 The legal rights and responsibilities of parents and carers

The first thing to establish about parents' and carers' rights and responsibilities is the legal definition of a parent in the UK. Under the Education Act 1996, this includes:
- all biological parents, whether they are married, living together or neither
- any person who, although not a biological parent, has parental responsibility for a child or young person (including adoptive parent, foster parent, step-parent, grandparent, guardian or other relative).

The Children Act 1989

Parental rights

This legislation states that parents and carers have the legal right to:
- receive information about their child
- participate in statutory activities – such as voting in elections for parent governors, e.g. in maintained nurseries
- be asked to give consent – such as agreeing to the child taking part in school trips
- be informed about meetings involving the child – plus any assessments and the outcomes of such experiences.

Parental responsibilities

Adults with parental responsibility have a duty to:
- provide a home for the child
- protect and care for the child
- discipline the child
- make choices about the child's education
- agree to medical treatment for the child
- look after the child's property.

Amendments to the Children Act 1989

This act has been updated twice.

The Children Act 2004

This legislation:
- introduced the Children's Commissioner
- significantly reviewed how Children's Services work together to safeguard children and families (see page 12 for more on their roles).
- introduced guiding principles through the *Every Child Matters* programme.

The Childcare Act 2006

This provided the Early Years Foundation Stage (EYFS) learning, development, safeguarding, health and welfare framework. It was developed to ensure that the child remains central to all aspects of practice.

> **Good to know**
>
> Creating a Team around a Child, and/or Team around a Family promotes the voice of the child and engages in child-centred education and healthcare planning when professionals work together to ensure best practice. Partnership collaboration and improved communication was central to the Every Child Matters policy initiative of 2003, which recommended collaboration of Children's Services in order to support the needs of children, young people and their families. Partnership working and effective communication are key features of early years settings so, while this programme is not a legal requirement, its principles are still relevant to the early years practitioners and their work with children.

The United Nations Convention on the Rights of the Child

The United Nations Convention on the Rights of the Child (UNCRC) was also introduced in 1989. It includes 54 Articles.

Article 3 is particularly relevant to the Children Act 1989 (since amended in 2004 and 2006): it states that the child's best interests must be the priority when decisions are made which will affect them.

The welfare and safeguarding of children is at the centre of this legislation. The UNCRC:
- recognises the voice of the child in matters concerning them and their future outcomes
- gives children and young people a right to have their views taken into consideration as appropriate.

See Core Chapter 10 for more details on the UNCRC.

Building positive partnerships with parents and carers

The basis of positive partnership working includes:
- respecting a child's family as the primary caregivers
- recognising the rights and responsibilities that parents, carers and families have in a child's life.

Always remember that the great majority of parents and carers want what is best for their child. The trust that can exist between practitioners and parents and carers blossoms through effective communication, as we form professional partnerships with them in the best interests of the child.

Parents and carers should be involved in discussions around their children's progress, educational attainment and mental health, including concerns and intervention strategies as appropriate.
- ▶ There are many ways of communicating with parents and carers, including face-to-face meetings, newsletters and reporting procedures.
- ▶ You must be aware of the significance of confidentiality, data protection and safeguarding when working with parents/carers in the early years sector.

K5.2 How a range of family contexts may impact on parenting

The responsibilities of parenting are significant and can be overwhelming at times. You will need to be aware of factors that influence children and families so that you can understand different parenting styles and can meet the families' needs effectively.

Family structures

This table shows the many different types of family structure.

Type of family structure	Who is included in this family structure?
Nuclear family	Two parents share the care of their children living as a family unit. • Parents are not necessarily male and female, and include those who identify as LGBT. • There may be some contact with extended family but this will be limited.
Extended family	Grandparents and/or other relatives, parents and children live either in one household or very near to each other. They support each other in all aspects of care.
Blended families, also known as reconstituted families	One parent and one step-parent live in the same household. There might be children from both parents living together or visiting often.
Lone-parent family	One parent cares for their child/children.

The structure of a family unit can influence parenting styles, opportunities and choices. For example, an extended family might share the care and education of the children, and this can lead to:
- ▶ more time to talk about and encourage children's educational development
- ▶ conflicting views on parenting.

Parenting styles

There are three main types of parenting style:
1. **Authoritarian**: Parents apply strict boundaries, give instructions, remind children of the 'rules' and generally have high expectations of their children.
2. **Permissive**: Parents do not apply boundaries. Children make their own decisions, and are responsible for them.
3. **Authoritative**: This style is somewhere between the authoritarian and the permissive. For example:
   – There will be boundaries and expectations but these are explained.
   – Parents will give guidance but discuss different options.

> **Case study**
>
> Kaitlin is four years old and is starting her primary school induction days soon. She is very anxious about starting school and has started to become quite clingy to her mother. When Kaitlin is dropped off at the early years setting each morning, she is often tearful and has lost some confidence.
> ▶ How might Kaitlin's mother respond to her in this situation, from each of the different parenting style perspectives?
> ▶ How do you think Kaitlin might be affected by each parenting style?

Factors that influence parenting

Parenting is not easy or straightforward. Everyone is influenced, both positively and negatively, by their experiences, culture, lifestyle, values and principles, and their circumstances. Let's explore some of these factors in a little more detail.

Income

Financial circumstances can cause stress for families and limit opportunities for children. Parents' socio-economic situation may have a direct impact on how they feel, on their wellbeing and stress levels.

Performance Outcome 5: Work in Partnership with Colleagues, Parents, Carers and Other Professionals

- If income is sufficient, this will have a positive impact on their lives, including lifestyle choices, food and nutrition, housing and leisure activities, and educational opportunities for the family.
- When income is low, the quality of food and nutrition might be lower, housing and accommodation may be inadequate and even pose a risk to health. In extreme circumstances, the family might not have enough money to buy food or proper clothes for their children.

Education

Not all families value education highly. Our own experiences and culture influence how we feel about education and any aspiration parents/carers may have for their children.

If parents have low expectations of their child's education, the child's ambitions are also likely to be low. For example:

- A parent who does not value education might not expect their child to go to college or university to train towards a career.

On the other hand, a parent/carer might have unrealistically high expectations of their child, causing pressure. For example:

- A parent/carer might expect their child to train to be a doctor because that is what they want, even when reaching this goal might not be realistic for the child in question.

Parents/carers should be encouraged to be active in their child's educational development. Home or family learning is very valuable and parental involvement certainly contributes to educational outcomes.

- You need to make parents/carers feel welcomed and valued in the early years setting. This relationship is nurtured by the key person and can really make a difference to parental engagement.
- Parents/carers who have a positive relationship will help the child to feel safe and secure. This will create healthy attitudes towards learning as well as enabling and empowering parents/carers.

There are many different ways of encouraging a positive relationship with parents/carers.

Culture

Culture influences all aspects of life, from values and beliefs to lifestyle choice and expectations. It is important to recognise and appreciate cultural norms and expectations, including their influences of education, traditions, religion, diet and behaviour.

Being sensitive to cultural norms is essential when building meaningful relationships with families:

- You are not expected to know everything in relation to the child's culture.
- However, always bear in mind the significance of culture for parental values, and keep the child's needs at the centre of everything that you do.
- Don't be afraid to ask your colleagues at the early years setting for advice on this when working with babies, children and their families.

Practice points

- Always think of ways to involve parents/carers with the early years setting.
- Working with parents/carers helps to build trust.
- Trust encourages professional relationships and builds confidence in parents and carers.
- Children feel safe and secure when they see parents/carers chatting happily.
- Parents/carers who are involved in the early years setting are more likely to engage in activities and experiences at home.

This practice point supports preparation for the following skills-based outcomes:

S5.6 Work in partnership with parents and carers to help them to recognise and value the significant contributions they make to the child's health, wellbeing, education and development

S5.7 Encourage parents and carers to take an active role in the child's play, education and development

Stress and mental health

When it is challenging to meet even the most basic of needs for their children, parents will soon begin to feel the pressure. When pressure becomes difficult to manage, it can lead to stress.

Stress impacts family interactions inside and outside the home. We all feel stress from time to time. It can act as a motivator, giving us the energy we need to focus or prepare for significant events, but often parents/carers feel too much pressure all at the same time and are unable to cope.

This is when stress can begin to affect physical as well as mental health and wellbeing. Stress impacting family life may grow from one or more of the following situations:

- work pressures or unemployment
- caring for another family member
- change in family structure
- death of a loved one.

Often the family's support network can make a big difference to how they manage the situation, in both the short and long term.

Being able to recognise stress in yourself and others is important for the role of the practitioner.

According to the NHS, common physical indicators of stress include headaches, dizziness, muscle tension/pain, stomach problems and a racing heartbeat.

Common mental ill-health indicators and behavioural traits include difficulty in concentrating and paying attention, forgetfulness, difficulty in reaching a decision, feeling worried/overwhelmed and irritable and disruption to sleep or diet. Of course, an individual may not experience all of these indicators to be suffering from the impact of stress or mental ill-health. Professionals working in education and childcare must be mindful of the unique needs of children and their families, as well as recognising their own stress triggers and those of colleagues.

Source: www.nhs.uk/oneyou/every-mind-matters/stress

Stress and mental health impacts on family life, both inside and outside of the home environment. Parents and carers are often exposed to stressful situations and may be resilient in how they react to such situations, successfully managing their own stress levels. However, in extreme or long-term situations stress and mental health can worsen, and they may feel unable to cope with the high levels of stress they are experiencing. When parents/carers feel stressed this often effects how children feel. For example, if a parent is upset children will pick up on their feelings, which may affect how they play and express themselves and their willingness to contribute or participate in social activities and experiences, as they struggle with their own feelings.

Professionals in education and childcare use observation and knowledge of child development to recognise changes in children and to support them through sensitive, nurturing strategies. Changes to children's wellbeing may also be noticeable in the home environment. Children affected by family stress and poor mental health may become less interested in activities, less cooperative and willing to help, and may even begin to regress in their development. For example, a child who is worrying about things may begin to bed wet even if they have been dry at night for a while, or insist on being close to mum and become untypically clingy.

As an early years practitioner, it is important to be sensitive to the needs of the family and understand how such pressures might affect family life. This is one of the reasons why it is essential to build strong professional relationships with parents/carers:
- They might turn to you to share information.
- It is important to show empathy and be able to signpost families to services that can support them.

> **Case study**
>
> Miriam is a lone parent. She lives with her two young boys, aged 18 months and 4 years, in a rural area. Her oldest son has cystic fibrosis (a genetic condition affecting the lungs and digestive system). Miriam does not live close to her extended family and often feels isolated and lonely.
>
> Miriam brings her two boys to the local early years day nursery twice a week, but does not stay for the 'meet and chat' sessions available for parents and run by early years practitioners. Miriam is a qualified engineer and loves her work, but has not worked since moving to the area six months ago.
> - Think about the pressures and challenges that Miriam is facing: how might these affect how she is feeling?
> - How can the early years practitioner help?
> - Can you think of any services that might be able to support Miriam?
>
> This case study supports preparation for the following skills-based outcome: S5.8 Signpost appropriate resources and sources of support to parents/carers

K5.3 The roles and responsibilities of external agencies involved in early years settings

We looked at the roles and responsibilities of external agencies on pages 97–8 in Core Chapter 6.

Performance Outcome 5: Work in Partnership with Colleagues, Parents, Carers and Other Professionals

K5.4 The purpose and benefits of working with other professionals and the circumstances in which this would be appropriate and relevant

▲ Can you think of any benefits from professional partnership working?

From time to time, parents and carers might need expert advice and intervention from professionals in specialist health, development or child protection occupations.

Working with other professionals is particularly relevant and appropriate when:
- abuse is suspected or disclosed
- a child is at risk from harm
- a child has a special educational need or disability (SEND)
- the child requires an education, health and care plan (EHCP) (see Core Chapter 11)
- the progress of the child requires discussion in order to plan next stages in their education
- the child is a 'looked after' child in the care of the local authority
- the child has experienced trauma.

The table below explains how other professionals may be involved in these situations, how they will be involved and why. Note that this is only a general guide and not every case will be the same. You should always follow the policy and procedures of the setting when dealing with these situations.

Situation requiring action/intervention from a professional	Professional(s) who may be involved and their role
Abuse is suspected or disclosed	Health visitors may be involved, who will be able to offer advice to the family.
	Social workers: reports from disclosures may be shared with social workers. They will refer to these reports and records when considering next steps and support available for the child and their family, and to monitor the child's situation. This may involve access to early years provision, education and training for parents/carers and respite to offer breaks away from the family as appropriate.
	The GP may signpost to other services, such as support from a domestic refuge if domestic violence is disclosed.
	Meetings with other professionals, such as early years class teachers, managers, SENDCos, health visitors and/or social workers, may be arranged as a Team around a Child (TAC). If EHCPs are developed as a result of these meetings, local authority staff and SENDCos may be involved.
A child is at risk from harm	The line manager at the setting must follow the policy and procedures of the setting and involve Children's Services in order to protect the child straight away. Other services, including the police, may also be involved. The police have a legal responsibility to safeguard children and some officers will have received specialist training to support them in their role and subsequent investigation work.
A child has a special educational need or disability (SEND)	Where children have a recognised special educational need, they will be supported by specialist professionals appropriate to their needs. EHCPs are developed and reviewed through the Graduated Approach (see page 95). Parents/carers, early years educators and specialist professionals will work together in partnership to monitor and review the EHCP to make sure it remains effective in meeting the child's needs. (See below.)

Situation requiring action/intervention from a professional	Professional(s) who may be involved and their role
The child requires an education, health and care plan (EHCP) (see Core Chapter 11)	Various circumstances may require a child to have an EHCP. They typically support differentiated learning in response to SEND but may be instigated when a child's wellbeing is also a cause for concern, for example, if neglect is suspected.
The progress of the child requires discussion in order to plan next stages in their education	The SENDCo may offer strategies, identify resources and monitor progress to contribute to discussions around the next stages for children. Assessment checks of children aged two years is generally undertaken by the child's key person. Childminders who are involved in the assessment process will find help and support in preparing the progress check, or making referrals for children, from their early years and childcare advisor, who will be able to explain the requirements and expectations.
The child is a 'looked after' child in the care of the local authority	Children in the care of the local authority may be placed in temporary foster care. Social workers will work alongside staff in their childcare or educational setting to make sure children are settled and making good progress. They will support the transition and ensure that services involved work collaboratively in the best interest of the child and family. Social workers will provide training and ongoing advice and support to foster parents.
The child has experienced trauma	A child that has experienced trauma, such as domestic abuse, will require specialist support. Early years educators may work in partnership with a social worker and are likely to liaise with Children and Young People's Mental Health Services (CYPMHS) to ensure that support is maintained and effective. CYPMHS social workers will work with children, families and settings across education and childcare to ensure children are safeguarded and protected.

Specialist advice can make a positive difference to the outcomes for babies and young children. Below we have some examples of how collaboration can promote children's development, wellbeing and educational achievement.

The advantages of working with other professionals

- By working with other professionals, children and families have greater access to a range of services. This increases the opportunity for support and gives children, families and staff in education and childcare the chance to benefit from new strategies and techniques.
- Early identification and intervention becomes more skilled, consistent and accurate through collaboration with specialised professionals.
- When professionals work together to offer specialised advice, they can target support to meet the specific needs of parents/carers and their children.
- Working in partnership improves communication between professionals and services, so that children can be better safeguarded. If everyone knows their roles and responsibilities, and the situation is carefully monitored and evaluated, there will be a consistent approach, providing evidence for reporting purposes and guaranteeing that a child's progress is reviewed regularly.
- Effective partnerships are built on effective communication with parents and carers. When sound relationships are established, parents and carers are much more likely to volunteer for helping with outings and activities.
- Including parents in decisions about their child's learning and development becomes much more likely when partnership working is in place. It is also easier to share advice and signpost to resources and sources of support.
- Consulting parents about the child's needs and interests comes naturally when parents and carers have professional relationships with staff in education and childcare.

Performance Outcome 5: Work in Partnership with Colleagues, Parents, Carers and Other Professionals

Respecting and valuing the parent/carer as primary educator and nurturer

You will find it very difficult to build a professional relationship with a parent/carer without having respect for them and valuing their role and significant contributions to their child's holistic health and learning.

While safeguarding the child is crucial, remember that in most cases parents/carers are the people who:
- know their children best
- care the most about them
- want the best for them.

Significance of professional relationships

Establishing a positive partnership with parents and carers is key to:
- getting to know the child
- building trust
- supporting children to feel safe and secure in the early years setting.

Confidentiality

As a member of staff working in education and childcare, you will be exchanging personal and sensitive data.

You must:
- understand the limits and boundaries of your role here (see Core Chapter 6)
- be aware of how information is shared, recorded and stored securely at your setting in line with policy and procedures
- never share information except with the parent/carer who is authorised to know this.

There might be occasions when confidential information is shared with other professionals, for example, when protecting children and young people from harm.

> **Skills practice**
>
> A team meeting has been arranged to discuss the needs of one of the children at your setting. The meeting will involve a range of professionals and the child's parents. A summary of what will be discussed at the meeting is included on the right.
>
> Read through the summary and think about how working collaboratively with colleagues, other professionals and parents will help to meet the child's needs.
>
> **Summary of what will be discussed at the team meeting:**
>
> Charlie's key person, Eli, is concerned about his speech, language and communication. Charlie is three and a half years old, and although his receptive language skills appear to be progressing as expected, Eli is concerned about Charlie's limited expressive communication.

> **Test yourself**
>
> 1 Identify three benefits of actively involving parents and carers in the care and education of their children. For each benefit, explain how effective partnerships contribute to improved outcomes for children and their families.
> 2 Describe a range of family structures, and explain how each structure might impact on parenting.
> 3 Explain why it is beneficial to work with other professionals.
> 4 Identify one professional who might contribute to the education and care of young children. Describe their role, including how they may support children and their families in different situations.

ASSESSMENT

Types of assessment

This qualification is assessed in several ways.
- Core Component:
  - Papers A and B
  - Employer-set Project (specific to your occupational specialism)
- Occupational Specialism Component:
  - synoptic assessment

Core Component assessment: Papers A and B

In order to complete the Core Component assessment, you will have to sit two question papers made up of multiple-choice, short-answer and extended-response questions. These are called Paper A and Paper B, and are directly linked to the Core Elements covered by Chapters 1–12 of this book. Each paper is worth 35 per cent of your grade for the Core Component. Paper A covers knowledge from Core Elements 1–6, and Paper B covers knowledge from Core Elements 7–12. The 'Assessment practice' or 'Skills practice' feature at the end of each chapter will help you revise for these papers. In addition, your tutor may give you some practice papers to help build your confidence in completing them. There are two opportunities each year to sit these papers. Visit the NCFE website for more details and an up-to-date assessment timetable.

Question types

There are three types of question in Papers A and B. It is a good idea for you to become familiar with each type of question and also to practise answering them.

Multiple-choice questions

Some questions in the exam will be multiple choice, requiring you to select the correct answer from four options. For example:

> Which of these describes the **function** of Ofsted?
> a) to regulate and maintain standards in examinations
> b) to regulate the higher education system in England
> c) to inspect services providing education for children and young people in England
> d) to provide data and information for parents

When answering multiple-choice questions, start by reading the question carefully. In the example we have given, you are required to focus on the function of Ofsted. Read through each of the answers carefully before making a decision. You need to start by ruling out answers that you know not to be correct. These questions are designed to have answers that look plausible, but one will always be the best fit.

Short-answer questions

Short-answer questions always have at least one command verb, such as 'describe' or 'identify', in them. You need to look carefully at these before writing an answer as the length and depth of your answer will depend on the command. 'Identify', for example, could be a single word, whereas 'describe' requires you to provide more detail.

Here is an example:

> Identify and describe one piece of health and safety legislation. (2 marks)

Read the question carefully and underline each of the command words. In the example given above, you need to do two things: identify and also describe.

Extended-response questions

Both Paper A and Paper B will have a small number of questions that require a longer answer, with more marks available for these questions. As with the short-answer questions, you should note the command words and read each question carefully. Extended-response questions usually require you to show that you can analyse and evaluate, not just that you know something. This is a different skill to simply describing or explaining.

Assessment

For example:

> Evaluate how a setting's approach to supporting children with EAL may affect their overall development and learning. (12 marks, plus 3 marks for QWC)
>
> Your response should demonstrate:
> - how children develop English as an additional language
> - specific practice that would support the development of English as an additional language
> - the range of factors that might influence an individual child's acquisition of English as an additional language.

Take a moment to read through the question and plan your answer. This may help you to structure your answer more effectively and will allow you to gain additional marks for QWC (Quality of Written Communication).

Here is a sample answer:

> The way that a setting's approaches support a child with EAL can make a significant impact on how language can affect academic as well as emotional and social development. This is because people's fluency and level of vocabulary can affect their levels of literacy, as well as the development of new concepts. Being able to communicate and articulate emotions also affects social development and how easily friendships are formed and maintained. Children who are not supported to develop English effectively may withdraw socially and also from their learning.
>
> In order to support a child, a setting would need to assess how much English has already been acquired. While some children may already be nearly fluent, others may be new to a language. It is important for a setting to use strategies that are appropriate to the individual. A four year old who is new to English may need to stay near, and interact mainly with, one adult when they start in a nursery. There are many strategies that settings can use, including the use of technology, specialist staff, as well as encouraging children's peers to support them. These strategies as part of an overall approach are only effective if the individual needs of the child are met. This is because a range of factors can affect language acquisition. These factors include age, but also personality and motivation. A child who is outgoing may try harder to make friends and be more confident to use their language, while a child who prefers playing or studying alone may not make as much progress. By adjusting their approach and using a range of strategies, settings can be more effective.

Comments on the sample

The question required that the learner should demonstrate 'how children develop English as an additional language'. The learner did not cover this in their answer, although they did mention that the setting should assess children's levels. More marks would be awarded if the learner had clearly demonstrated that they understood the stages of EAL language development.

The learner gained marks by showing that they understood the link between language and development and learning. They also showed that they understood the impact if support was not provided by settings.

The learner showed, with relevant examples, that they understood a range of strategies that settings could use, as well as some of the factors that affect how children acquire language.

The learner's level of language was good and the answer showed that they recognised the importance of meeting individuals' needs.

Core Component assessment: Employer-set Project

As well as Paper A and Paper B, you will need to complete an Employer-set project (ESP). This is worth 30 per cent of your grade for the Core Component of this qualification and relates to the four Core Skills.

> The four Core Skills are discussed in the Core Skills chapter (pages 202–10).

The ESP is split into several parts. In this section, we look at the structure of the project and how you can prepare for each part of it.

Pre-release activity

You will be given a pre-release activity to look at. Using the information provided, you then need to carry out some research that you can then use to help you in the actual task.

Here is an example of a pre-release activity:

> As part of a scheme to ensure that all children in the local area will be able to make a smooth transition into school, meetings are held with early years settings to find out which children may benefit from an early intervention programme. You work in a pre-school and have been asked to liaise with a local childminder. She has raised concerns about the development of a child who is two years and five months old, and you will be working with her to support this child.
>
> You are required to carry out some research. You should particularly focus on the following:
> - developmental norms and strategies that would be appropriate to support development
> - the early years curriculum and selection of suitable resources
> - the role of observation, reflection, assessment and planning
> - partnership working with parents, practitioners and other professionals
> - safe working practices and risk assessment
> - education theories, concepts and pedagogies.

Analysing the pre-release activity

It is a good idea when looking at the pre-release activity to note down the age of the child or children as they will be the focus of the next tasks. In this example, the child is two years and five months old. You should also look at the type of setting that the child or children are in. In this example, the child is in a pre-school. You should also note what information is provided about the child at this point. In this example, the pre-release activity tells you that the child is not making expected progress. The pre-release activity also indicates that you will be required to plan some activities for this child. Finally, the pre-release activity suggests areas where you might focus your research.

Planning research

You will use the notes from your research as a basis for answering the two next tasks. You are only allowed to have four pages of research. (Your tutor will provide you with information about how they should be presented.) This means that you need to plan your research carefully. Here are some things that you should focus on.

Developmental norms

You will need to research the developmental norms for the age of the child mentioned in the pre-release activity. In this example, the child is two years and five months. We also know that the child is showing some developmental delay. It will be important to know what development is typical for a child of this age in each of the developmental areas, but also what development might be shown by a child who is at an earlier stage.

Role of the adult and strategies

Bearing in mind the age of the child or children mentioned in the pre-release activity, you should also look at some strategies that promote different aspects of development. Consider some key areas such as communication and language, personal, social and emotional development, and also physical development.

Early Years Foundation Stage (EYFS) curriculum

It is likely that you will need to link your planning to the EYFS.

> We looked at the structure of the EYFS in Core Chapter 2, but it might also be worth examining how the areas of development and learning break down into different aspects. You can find this information in Core Chapter 7.

Most activities cover more than one aspect of the EYFS. You may need to demonstrate that you can link activities to many aspects of the EYFS. Throwing and catching, for example, may be planned to support gross motor movement, but it is also linked to positive relationships, as children need to throw and catch with an adult or other child. In addition, throwing and catching as an activity is also linked to self-regulation as children have to cope with their feelings when they miss or drop a ball.

Assessment

Resources and activities for children within this age range

It is likely that you will need to plan an activity for the child or children mentioned in the pre-release activity as part of the actual assessment. It is helpful to have identified resources and activities in advance that can be used with the age range mentioned. If the pre-release activity suggests that the child has some developmental needs, you should also research resources and activities typically used for children at earlier stages of development.

Observation and assessment

It is likely that, for the next task, you will be given examples of a summative and formative assessment on the child or children mentioned in the pre-release activity. This will provide you with more detailed information about the child. Make sure that you are confident in analysing information from a range of summative and formative assessments.

> We look at observation and assessment in Core Chapter 8 and also in Early Years Educator Performance Outcome 3.

Examples of planning formats

It is likely that you will need to show that you can plan for children's development and also for specific activities. It will be worth looking at different ways in which early years settings plan for individual children. Ideally, you should practise filling them in. You should also look at plenty of other examples from your work placement and on the internet.

As planning formats take up a lot of space, you could, in your notes, just write some of the key headings, e.g. name of child, age, aim of plan, and so on.

Safe working practices and risk assessment

As your next tasks are likely to involve planning, you will need to look at some of the potential hazards and safe working practices to consider when working with the age range mentioned in the pre-release activity.

> We look at risk assessment in Core Skills chapter 4.

In addition, you can talk to your work placement about how, when planning and providing activities, practitioners consider safety. You may not need to take detailed notes about this, but you might want to write a reminder to yourself in your notes to mention it when writing the plans.

Approaches to how children learn, and how best to support them

As part of the project, you need to show that you have understood some theories relating to how young children learn and also different approaches to providing early education.

> We look at theories of learning in Core Chapter 7 and also consider different ways of providing early education in Early Years Educator Performance Outcome 1.

To help you prepare for the tasks, it will be worth identifying two or three theories of learning. You will need to know what they are and how they apply to working with children. A good example is social learning theory. This is the idea that children can learn some skills and behaviours by watching adults.

Completing the Employer-set Project

- In exam conditions, you will be given a more detailed scenario about the child or children mentioned in the pre-release activity.
- You are also likely to be given details of assessments and reports about the child or children.
- You will then have two tasks to complete by yourself, and two other tasks involving others.
- The tasks are likely to ask you to plan for one or more aspects of the child's or children's development.

Here is an example of the type of information that you may be given:

> You are working as part of a project team that supports early years settings to provide early interventions to children. The project has been set up in an area of economic deprivation. Academic attainment in this area has been low. The aim of this project is to improve outcomes for children before they start school, as research shows that early intervention is very effective.
>
> As part of this project, Tulsa, a girl aged two years and five months, has been identified. She has been attending a local childminder's setting for three months. She attends for 15 hours a week and has two-year-old funding, which means her place is free. The childminder is experienced and keen to work with the project. She has identified that Tulsa's communication and language is delayed but believes that more progress could be made if Tulsa's parents were given strategies and ideas for activities.

Education and Early Years T Level: Early Years Educator

Task 1

You are required to produce a plan that contains strategies and examples of activities that will help improve Tulsa's home learning environment. The plan will eventually be discussed with the childminder and a rationale justifying it should be included.

In addition, you are required to produce a detailed plan of one activity that can be done in the early years setting and also in the home. You should link this plan to the wider early years curriculum, and also explain any safeguarding or safety issues.

In order to better understand Tulsa's development and to get further background information, you have been provided with Tulsa's two-year-old check and also a request for support that was sent in by the childminder, which explains the family situation.

Name of child: Tulsa Fry	Age: 2 years 5 months
Date of assessment: 23-5-2020	Carried out by: A. Carr
Personal, social and emotional development	Tulsa has settled in very quickly and is happy to wave goodbye to Mum. She is very affectionate and is mostly a happy child.
	She can be jealous when I am talking to other children and sometimes snatches things from them. This is not unusual for her age and she can be distracted.
	She often shows signs of frustration and has frequent tantrums.
	She enjoys watching the older children play and has moments of copying their play.
	She can feed herself using a spoon and is just starting to drink from an open cup although there are spills. If she is tired, Tulsa asks to be fed by an adult.
Physical development	Tulsa enjoys running and climbing, and is confident to try out new physical activities.
	Her fine motor skills are less developed and she finds some play activities, such as jigsaws or building with blocks, very challenging and, if she is tired, she gives up very easily.
Communication and language	Tulsa communicates mainly through a combination of pointing and babbling, but in the last four weeks, she is starting to use around six or seven words.
	Tulsa can follow simple instructions.

General comments

Tulsa often needs two or three hour-long naps in the day. She indicates that she is tired by finding her comforter. Her concentration and ability to self-regulate improve after these naps.

We have been working on her communication and language, and she is starting to make progress. Tulsa is starting to look at books and is increasingly trying to communicate. Her language is lower than expected for her age and we have spoken to the parents about a possible referral next month.

Parental comments

Tulsa loves coming to you. She is starting to talk more at home. We are going to try to spend more time talking to her and cut down on television watching. We are still trying to get her down to sleep and also to stay in her bed at night. Thank you for having her.

Request for early intervention	
Name of early years setting	Martha's Place
Name of child	Tulsa Fry
Age of child	2 years 5 months
Developmental concerns	

Expressive language level is low. Tulsa is using 12–15 words.

Receptive language is higher, but Tulsa has difficulty in concentrating, probably due to lack of sleep.

Self-regulation is lower than might be expected. Tulsa often has tantrums and is hard to reassure and calm down.

Assessment

> **Other information**
>
> Tulsa has been attending my setting for three months. In this time, she has made significant progress in all areas of development, but her communication and language is delayed. Her family's circumstances are not ideal. There are two other children and, at present, they live in a two-bedroomed flat. They are waiting to be rehoused. The father has bouts of depression and the eldest child, aged six years, has learning difficulties. The parents are keen for all their children to do well, but find it hard to be organised and to establish routines. They are often late to drop off and pick up, and sometimes Tulsa has not had breakfast in the morning. They try to take on board my suggestions, but they may benefit from further suggestions as to how to support Tulsa's development. Tulsa's parents may also need support in establishing routines, including bedtime, and also managing her behaviour.

Preparing for the tasks

Read through the two parts of the task carefully. Underline key phrases and, as you work, keep referring back to the information you have been given, as well as the requirements of the task.

You may find that you are asked in at least one of the tasks to refer directly to your research findings. You may also find that, for at least one of the plans, you have to show that you can link it to educational theories as well as the wider curriculum. There are many ways that you can make these references as part of your planning. Here are some suggestions that you might like to consider.

- **Add in a rationale section:** You could create a rationale section. In this section you would explain the reasons behind your choice of strategies, activities or resources. For example: 'According to Vygotsky's theory of learning, adults need to understand a child's current capabilities and then look for ways of slightly challenging them. Based on the assessments provided, I believe that the activity I have chosen will extend Tulsa's knowledge, but it will be achievable.'
- **Add in a commentary section:** You may wish to create a section titled 'Commentary'. This will contain your comments about your decisions. You might write comments such as 'As Tulsa is not confident in talking to adults, I have suggested that most activities will take place with the same adult. This will build Tulsa's confidence and help to support her self-concept.'
- **Links to the early years curriculum:** If the planning requires that you show how an activity or a series of activities links to the wider curriculum, you could put this type of title as a separate section. It will be important to explain how an activity links to aspects of the EYFS.
- **Add in a hygiene, safety and safeguarding section:** Depending on the actual tasks, it might be helpful to add in a safety and safeguarding section. For example, if you were planning an activity involving water, you might draw attention to the need for the water to be clean and also for the adult to supervise at all times. In the same way, if the activity was an outing, you might point out that there would need to be a risk assessment that included protecting children from strangers.

Task 2

This task requires you to share your responses to Task 1 with other students. You will need to talk to them about your ideas and justify them. You will also be looking at their work and making comments and suggestions. Task 2 is split into different parts.

Preparation

To prepare for Task 2, your tutor will give you back the work you did for Task 1. You will also be given other students' work and a form to help you prepare. You will have plenty of time to carry out this preparation. During this time you need to:

- think about the key points you need to say about your plan
- practise speaking aloud
- take time to analyse the other students' plans, and jot down your ideas and comments
- practise phrasing questions and comments in ways that appear fair and thoughtful.

2a Peer discussion

Your tutor will put you into a group with other students. You will be given back Task 1 as well as your preparation form. You will also be given a form to write down the feedback you are given from the other students. You will then take it in turns to talk about, listen to and give feedback on one another's plans.

- Do not take the suggestions and comments of others personally.
- Take careful notes about everything that is said.
- If you are not sure what point someone is trying to make, you can ask questions to clarify.

2b Amending your plan, with justifications

After the peer discussion, you will be given an opportunity to revise your plan using the feedback you have been given. Your revised plan should show what changes you have made, and you will need to explain why you have made them. You must reference the notes you wrote on the peer discussion feedback form. If there were points raised that you have chosen not to act on, you should explain what these were and why you decided not to act on them. If you have a 'Rationale' section in your plan, you could use this heading to include this information. For example, 'According to the notes I took, one of my peers suggested that the activity could work better outdoors. I have not made this change to the plan as there is a danger that the child might be distracted and it might be easier to focus the child's attention in a smaller space.'

Task 3

Task 3 is completed with your tutor. It is divided into two sections: a presentation of your plans followed by a discussion with your tutor.

3a Presentation

The idea of this task is to show that you know how to present information to another professional. During your presentation, you will need to explain your planning and the reasoning behind it. Some learners find it easier to do this by preparing a slide show. It is important to remember that a presentation is not a conversation or a chat. You will need to be ready to talk without interruption for around 10 minutes. It is important that you do not simply read out what is on the plan. Instead, imagine that you are explaining something to someone who does not know about early years and planning. To prepare for the presentation, you might like to write a list of points that you could talk about. Here are some examples:

▶ your identification of the child's needs, and how you arrived at these judgements
▶ factors that you took into account when drawing up the different plans, such as resources and educational theories
▶ the amendments you made following the peer discussion, and why these were made.

Practising your presentation

You will have two hours to prepare for your presentation. This means that you will have time to practise your presentation, prepare a slide show if you wish, and also to check that you have enough to say for 10 minutes – it is worth remembering that most people, when they are nervous, speed up. It can be useful to divide your presentation into three parts: introduction, middle and conclusion. Make sure you have a clear introduction and practise saying this aloud. This is important, as you have to get used to hearing your own voice.

Carrying out the presentation

Giving a presentation can make some people nervous. Here are a few tips.
▶ Remember that your tutor is on your side.
▶ Take a deep breath and smile as you start.
▶ Make a definite start by saying something like 'Good morning/afternoon. My name is _____. Today I am going to present my _____.'
▶ Try to make some eye contact while you are talking – even if briefly.
▶ Write simple notes to remind you of what you want to say and the order you want to say it in – you can put these on cards.
▶ Avoid reading from a script.
▶ Don't worry if your tutor is writing things down. This is not a bad sign.
▶ Wear a watch so you can keep an eye on the time.
▶ End your presentation by saying something like 'I hope that you have found this useful' or 'Thank you for taking the time to listen to me.'

3b Discussion with your tutor

For this task, you need to show that you can communicate well with another adult. Your tutor may take the part of a professional such as a key person, health visitor or parent. To help you prepare for this, you will be given a form that you can use to help you prepare for the discussion. You should expect your tutor to ask questions or ask you to justify what you have said. As part of this discussion, you will talk about how you reviewed your plans as a result of the peer discussion.

Task 4

The final task for the Employer-set Project is to write a reflective account. Your tutor will give you a form to complete and you will have two hours to complete the activity.

Your account should include the following sections:

Analysis
- Did each of the tasks meet the required outcomes?
- How do you know?

Evaluation
- What went well and not so well with each of the tasks?
- Why do you think this was the case?

Reflection
- What have you learned from completing the project?
- How might you approach the project differently if you were to do it again?

Occupational Specialism Component: Synoptic assessment

As part of the assignments for your occupational specialism, you will also need to complete a synoptic assessment at the end of the year, in the form of two written assignments. The purpose of the synoptic assessment is to draw together the knowledge from the different performance outcomes and relate it to practical situations or scenarios. It will also give you the opportunity to apply your knowledge and skills in greater depth.

Synoptic assessments will take the form of actual workplace scenarios or longer case studies, which are linked to your area of specialism. These question papers will be longer and you will need to consider all of the material you have been given, and ensure that you have answered each part of the instructions.

During your time in placement, even when you are in your first year, try to relate what you are seeing and doing to the knowledge that has been covered in the units you have studied. For example, when children are playing outdoors can you relate their activity to the different areas of the EYFS? Thinking like this will help you to practise for the assessment.

Glossary

Abstract conceptualisation (AC) This is when the learner has a new idea or has changed their thinking due to their experience.

Accountable Required or expected to justify actions or decisions.

Active experimentation (AE) The learner applies their new way of thinking to a future experience.

Adrenaline autoinjector/EpiPen® A device which administers adrenaline to decrease swelling in the case of an acute allergic reaction.

Adult-led play Play opportunities and activities which are planned and provided by the adult. The adult may direct children, e.g. as part of a Forest School programme, children will be asked to find sticks to make a bonfire.

Affluent Being wealthy, having a relatively large amount of money and/or material possessions.

Alternative provision settings Education providers for pupils who are unable to go to a mainstream school. This may be, for example, due to exclusion or illness.

Anaemia A health condition in which there are not enough red blood cells in your body, which means that your body may not get enough oxygen.

Animism Ascribing feelings and personality to inanimate objects, e.g. 'my car is happy'.

Barrier to learning Anything that prevents a child or young person from taking part fully in the activities or experiences that are offered by the school or early years setting.

Benchmark A point of reference for checking standards.

Bilingualism The ability to use two languages.

Blended learning A style of teaching that uses a blend of online and face-to-face teaching.

Child-initiated play Play in which children are able to make their own decisions about what and how to play, and who to play with. In some settings, it is also called 'free play'.

Chronic disease A long-term health condition.

Code switching Using a word or phrase from one language when speaking another.

Concrete experience (CE) This is when the learner encounters an activity or experience for themselves.

Continuing professional development (CPD) Ongoing professional training and development to keep up to date.

Core subjects English, maths and science.

DBS Stands for Disclosure and Barring Service, part of the suitability checks that must be made on individuals in the UK involved in the care of children and young people under 18 years of age. These specifically look at any criminal convictions recorded against an individual and are an important feature of safeguarding (see Core Chapter 3). You will find out more about DBS processes as you prepare for placement, as it is likely you will be required to undertake a DBS check yourself.

Designated safeguarding lead (DSL) Person in a school or early years setting who is responsible for all safeguarding issues.

Digraph Two sounds that when put together make a single sound, such as 'c-h' to make 'ch' as in chat.

Disability 'A physical or mental impairment which has a substantial or long term negative effect on your ability to do normal activities' (DfE, 2010).

Discrimination Unfair treatment of a group of people due to prejudice.

Diversity Recognising our individual differences.

Double facts Two numbers that are the same added together, e.g. 2+2.

Early identification Quickly recognising that a child or young person may need additional support.

Early production Being able to say or repeat some words.

Education, health and care plan (EHCP) An EHCP is for children and young people aged up to 25 who need more support than is available through special educational needs support; it is drawn up to outline provision for a child or young person following an assessment of special educational needs (see Core Chapter 11, page 179). EHCPs identify educational, health and social needs, and set out the additional support to meet those needs. Find out more here: www.gov.uk/children-with-special-educational-needs/extra-SEN-help

Emotional intelligence The ability to recognise emotions and the intentions of others, and to respond appropriately.

Equality Being equal in status, rights and opportunities.

Experiential learning theory (ELT) The theory that knowledge is created through experience.

EYFS *Development Matters* Non-statutory guidance to support early years practitioners with observation, assessment and planning.

Fine motor skills Movements that require hand and finger movements.

Fluency Being able to use a language easily and to an advanced level.

Formal observations Structured observations taking place within a set time in which the observer has specific criteria to look for.

Formative assessment Frequent, often informal, assessment that is designed to generate ongoing evidence of children's and young people's progress and attainment, and is used to inform the next steps.

Formative feedback Verbal or written information that helps children or young people to work out how they can improve.

Further education colleges Include general FE and tertiary colleges, sixth-form colleges and specialist colleges, as well as adult education provision. You can find out more on the government's website.

Gender transition When a child or young person wants to change from their biological gender to the one that they identify with.

Gestures Actions involving fingers, hands or feet, used when communicating.

Gross motor skills Movements that require whole limb movement such as walking or throwing.

Hazard Something in the environment that could cause harm.

Health and Safety Executive (HSE) An independent regulator for the prevention of work-related death, injury and ill health.

Heel prick test This is a blood test that is carried out on all babies when they are a few days old to test for serious conditions.

Holistic Overall or all round; the idea that the parts of something are interconnected so looking at the whole rather than each individual part. Here, it means all-round care needs, with an appreciation of the contribution of each care need to overall wellbeing.

Inclusion The process of identifying, understanding and breaking down barriers to participation and belonging.

Inclusive practice Developing an approach that recognises the diversity of children and young people, and promotes positive attitudes, differentiation and respect.

Informal observations Simple observations that take place during the course of the day, which may look at behaviour, relationships or confidence.

INSET day In-service training day, or day when teaching staff meet in term time, without pupils, for additional training.

International Baccalaureate Two-year international programme leading to an internationally recognised diploma, which prepares students for higher education.

International GCSE (sometimes iGCSE) International General Certificate for Secondary Education. The iGCSE is available internationally.

Intervention A programme of activities designed to support children who are working below national expectations but who should reach them with the right support.

Key person A member of staff in an early years setting who works closely with a designated group of children and their parents, carers and family (see Core Chapter 5 for more information).

Learning journal In the EYFS, individual learning journals may be used as a record of a child's progress and achievements during the year. They may include observations, photos and quotes from the child.

Lobby When an individual or organisation sets out to influence governmental decisions.

Looked after child (LAC) A child who has been in the care of their local authority for more than 24 hours, sometimes also referred to as children in care. This can include children living with foster parents, in a residential children's home, hostel or secure accommodation.

Malnourished The body is not getting all of the required nutrients.

Mindfulness A technique of reducing stress that involves acknowledging emotions and sensations.

Multidisciplinary team A team that consists of professionals working together from across the sector who have different roles. For example, a health visitor and a social worker may work together with an early years practitioner to bring together their specialist expertise in order to support a child and their family at a particular time.

Neurodevelopmental Relating to the development of the central nervous system – for example in the case of autistic spectrum disorder or ADHD.

Neurological Relating to or affecting the brain and nervous system.

Non-verbal Communication that takes place without words being said.

Non-verbal cues Prompts using body language, e.g. facial expression, eye contact or gestures.

Notifiable disease Illnesses which need to be reported to local authorities so that these can be monitored in case of local or national outbreaks.

Number bond A pair of numbers that add to a total, e.g. 1+4=5.

Ofsted Stands for the Office for Standards in Education, Children's Services and Skills. Ofsted inspects and regulates services providing education and skills for learners of all ages, including those that care for babies, children and young people.

Open question A question that cannot be answered with a yes or no response.

Oracy the ability to speak clearly and grammatically to others

Osteoporosis and rickets Diseases that affect the bones.

Parallel play Two or more children engaged in their own individual play but in close proximity to each other.

Picture exchange communication systems (PECS) A method of communication that uses simple pictures.

Planning, learning and assessment cycle The process through which children's needs and abilities are identified, which enables teachers to plan for next steps.

PPE Personal protective equipment – equipment to protect the user from risk. Examples of PPE might be helmets, eye protection, gloves or gowns, and high-visibility (hi-vis) jackets.

Prejudice A set of preconceived negative ideas about a particular group of people.

Primary disability A physical or mental impairment that has a negative effect on a person's ability to carry out normal activities.

Proximity The distance between the child or young person and the adult.

Ratify To vote on or sign a written agreement to make it official.

Receptive language The ability to understand what is being said through language.

Reflective observation of a new experience (RO) This stage is when the learner thinks back, or reflects, on their experience.

Reflexes Instinctive movements usually linked to survival.

Regression Where children revert to behaviours associated with younger children, as a result of trauma or emotional upheaval.

Regulation Control of a process by a set of rules.

Reliable Able to be trusted.

Risk The chance, whether high or low, that someone could be harmed by a hazard.

Risk assessment A check for potential risks so that measures may be put in place to control them.

Role model Someone who is looked to by others as an example.

Safeguarding Action taken to promote the welfare of children and protect them from harm (as defined by the NSPCC, 2018).

Scaffolding The way an adult supports children's and young people's learning through questions and comments.

Schema A pattern of thought or behaviour.

School readiness A collection of skills and experiences that help children to be ready for school.

Self-efficacy The feeling of being a capable person.

Self-regulation An individual's ability to control their own emotions, thoughts and behaviour and to adapt to changing situations and cope with unexpected stress.

SEND (sometimes called SEN) 'A child or young person has SEN if they have a learning difficulty or disability which calls for special educational provision to be made for him or her' (SEND Code of Practice, 2015).

Sequential language learning Where a language is learned after a home language has been established.

Simultaneous language learning Where children are exposed to two or more languages in their first three years.

Social mobility Movement of individuals or groups between different social classes or levels.

Social referencing How babies and young children look at adults' responses as a guide to how they should themselves react.

Sound blending Building words from individual sounds, e.g. s-t-o-p for stop.

Spiral curriculum The concept that a subject may be repeatedly taught but in increasing depth.

State funded Money that the government provides for something.

Statutory Something that is required by law.

Subitise Recognise quantities without counting.

Summative assessment A final assessment, usually occurring at the end of a period of study, which is used to sum up children's and young people's overall level of attainment, and to provide data for stakeholders.

Tailored intervention Designing support to help a child or young person pick up a specific skill or piece of knowledge.

Tertiary college An institution that provides general and vocational FE for students aged 16–19. Such colleges provide the next stage of education, after primary and secondary. They are distinct from general FE colleges in that they cater for a specific age group, and offer a less extensive and varied curriculum.

Undernourished The body is getting the nutrients, but not in the required quantities.

Valid Worth consideration; should be recorded.

Verbal The use of words as well as how the words are said.

Verbal cues Prompts that help the listener to answer, e.g. speaking more slowly or emphasising particular words.

Index

A

absent parents 115
abstract conceptualisation 27, 153
abuse
  bullying 52
  categories of 51–2, 283–5
  domestic 52, 285, 337–8
  emotional 51, 283–4
  female genital mutilation (FGM) 43–4, 46
  grooming 53–5
  impacts of 56–7
  interfamilial 54
  neglect 51, 284
  physical 51, 283
  of position 55–6
  reporting requirements 50–1, 56, 283
  at risk children 49–52, 283, 337
  and self-esteem 261
  sexual 51, 54, 284
  signs of 283–5
  see also safeguarding
academy schools 6, 156
accessibility 88, 169, 177, 190
accidents 324–6, 329
  see also risk assessment
accommodation (constructivism) 26
Action for Children 93
action-orientated feedback 36
active experimentation 153
ADHD (attention deficit hyperactivity disorder) 165, 184, 185, 187
admissions policy 166
adoptive families 86
adrenaline auto injector 307
adult role
  in language development 127–8
  in learning 29–30, 190, 232–3
  legal responsibilities 167
  limits and boundaries 100
  in play 247–8
  position of trust 53
  positive relationships 63, 68, 73, 257
  professional behaviour 22–3
  as role model 29, 53, 68, 74–5, 126, 166, 203–4, 292
  self-care skills 299
  self-concept 261
  see also parents
advocacy 85, 88
age-appropriate communication 203
age-appropriate play 245
agency 32
aggressive behaviour 68
Ainsworth, S. 115, 118
A-levels 7, 9
allergies 188, 290, 307
alternative provision 174, 177
amanuensis 181
anaemia 189, 310
animism 26, 123
anti-bullying policy 177
antisocial behaviour 78
anxiety 78, 132, 135
appetite 292
Applied General Qualifications 7
Apprenticeship, Skills, Children and Learning Act 2009 137
apprenticeships 7–8, 19
approachability 22
art and design
  activities 243
  Early Years Foundation Stage (EYFS) 17
  National Curriculum 18
assessment
  benchmarks 137
  debates 156
  diagnostic 142
  formative 138–40, 178, 206, 276
  group activities 143, 271
  information gathering 271
  monitoring and recording 137, 149
  observation 21, 139, 142, 145–6, 148, 267–71
  peer assessment 140
  and planning 142, 143–5
  practitioner roles 148–50
  preparation for 149–51
  of produced items 272
  questioning 139, 143, 271
  self-assessment 21, 140
  statutory requirements 225
  strategies 35
  summative 138, 141–2, 143, 206, 276–7
assessment for learning (AfL) 138
  see also formative assessment
assessors 150
assimilation 26
associative play 235
asthma 298
attachment 64, 113–19, 126–7, 254, 287
attachment disorders 57
attention 185, 187, 274
attention-seeking 76, 77
auditory processing 186
auditory processing disorders (APD) 186
augmentative and alternative communication (AAC) 179, 191–2
authoritarian parenting style 86, 334
authoritative parenting style 86, 334
autistic spectrum conditions 185, 259

B

ball games 242
bath time 299
batteries 325–6
bead threading 242
behaviour
  adapting 66
  aggression 68
  antisocial 78
  boundaries 73–4, 78, 257
  changes in 78, 135, 284, 326
  expectations 73–4, 76, 78, 169, 261
  factors affecting 62–4, 258
  managing 21, 60, 67–74, 76–81, 255
  modelling 74–5
  policy 67, 74, 76, 80, 177
  professional 22–3
  as reaction to abuse 57
  reinforcement 74
  reward systems 71–2, 76, 79
  self-damaging 78
  and self-esteem 64–5
  and stage of development 61, 104, 120, 255
  triggers 80
behaviourism 23–5
benchmarks 137
bereavement 132–3
Bergman, J. 29

Index

bilingualism 39, 127, 195, 200, 259
  see also English as an additional language (EAL)
blended families 86, 334
blended learning 157
block play 242, 243
blood pressure 310
Bloom's taxonomy 25, 28
body language 20, 71
bomb threat 323
books 228
  see also stories
bottle feeding 288–9
Boud, D. 154
boundaries 73, 78, 257
Bowlby, J. 114, 118
brain development 212–13, 285
breastfeeding 288–9
Bronfenbrenner, U. 32–3
Bruner, J. 27–8, 29, 123, 233
buddy systems 133, 181
built environment 250
bullying 52, 57, 63, 64, 177
burns 325

C

carbohydrates 304
careers advisor 13–14
categorical self 65
cerebral palsy 185
charities 89, 93
checklists 145, 269–70
chicken pox 312, 322
childcare
  holistic 2, 4
  provision 2–5
  settings 2
Childcare Act 2006 333
Childcare Register 3
child-centred learning *see* student-led learning
child criminal exploitation 52
childminders 2–3, 11
Children Act 1989 43, 50, 282, 333
Children and Families Act 2014 6, 44, 173–6
Children and Young People's Mental Health Services (CYPMHS) 13, 94, 98
Children's Commissioner 43
children's services 89, 95, 97
child sexual exploitation 284
child tracker observation 268
choking 324
Chomsky, N. 122
chronic health conditions 187–9, 297–8

Citizens Advice 89
citizenship 18
classical conditioning 23
cleaning 319
clinginess 61
  see also attachment
clinical commissioning groups (CCGs) 94
clothing 297
coaches 150–1
coeliac disease 308
Cognitive Abilities Tests (CATs) 142
cognitive constructivism 25–8
cognitive development 26–7, 38, 105–7, 123, 185–7, 219, 274
collaborative working 98–102, 205
collage 242
commentary 28
common cold 312
communication
  age-appropriate 203
  body language 20, 71
  enabling language 190
  encouragement 203–4
  facial expression 20, 261
  factors affecting 258
  feedback 21, 35–6, 73
  gestures 71, 261
  giving instructions 70
  language level 20, 70, 190
  non-verbal 69–71, 203
  positive attention 73
  positive language 204
  posture and proximity 20
  questioning 204
  terminology 182
  using technology 88
  verbal 69–70, 203
  see also language development
community centres 89
comparison 261
complaints policy 178
compulsory education 8–9
computing 18, 157
concentration 185, 301
concrete experience 153
concrete operations stage of development 27, 123
conditioning 23–4
confidence 22, 39, 104, 130–1, 135, 300
confidentiality 46, 99, 101, 166, 339
conflict 100
conjunctivitis 313
connectivism 30–1
consent 99, 133, 165, 270
conservation 27

constructivism 25–30
continuing professional development (CPD) 3, 158–9, 277–9
continuous provision plans 273
cooperative play 235
coordination skills 187
  see also motor skills
coping skills 75
co-regulation 21
cot death 302
counselling 49, 96, 98
counsellor 13
Counter-Terrorism and Security Act 2015 44, 46
county lines 00
creative curriculum 227
creative play 236–7, 242–3, 246
crèche 2
criminal activity 323
critical thinking 32
culture 68, 167, 197, 200, 262, 308–9, 335
curiosity 105, 285
currency of knowledge 31
curriculum *see* National Curriculum
cyberbullying 52
cystic fibrosis 188

D

data protection 44, 99, 147, 165
Data Protection Act 2018 44, 46
Department for Education (DfE) 9, 18
depression 47, 78, 188
design and technology 18
designated safeguarding lead (DSL) 12–13, 50–1, 55, 282
development
  atypical 219–20, 274–5
  and behaviour 61, 104
  biological factors 112, 126, 258–9
  brain 212–13, 285
  cognitive 26–7, 38, 105–7, 123, 185–7, 219, 274
  delay in 87, 219–20
  emotional 60, 66, 104, 109–11, 184, 219, 275
  environmental factors 113, 126–7, 259
  factors affecting 38–9, 112–13, 126–7, 184–5, 258–9, 285
  holistic 104, 184, 219, 285
  language 29, 38, 104–5, 120–8, 184, 186–7, 213–14, 217–18, 259, 275
  milestones 275, 287

physical 17, 60, 105, 108–9, 185, 219, 223, 250, 275
 and play 236–41
 progress 145
 social 59, 66, 75, 104, 109–11, 184, 219, 275
 speech 215–17
Development Matters 145, 174, 206, 214, 234
diabetes 189, 298, 308, 310
diagnostic assessment 142
diarrhoea 313, 322
diet
 balanced 303–6
 specialist 307–9
 unbalanced 309–10
 see also mealtimes
differentiation 11, 21, 265
digital grip 230
dignity 167
digraphs 223
direct discrimination 163–4
disability
 and development 112, 184–5
 models of 183
 neurodevelopmental 185
 neurological 185
 terminology 182
 see also special educational needs and disabilities (SEND)
Disability Discrimination Act 1995 183
Disclosure and Barring Service (DBS) 3, 44, 45, 225
discovery learning 29
discrimination 63, 163–4, 167, 183
diversity 48, 163–7, 204, 226, 245
doctors see general practitioner (GP)
domestic abuse 52, 285, 337–8
double facts 223
dough play 244
Dowling, M. 29
Downes, S. 31
Down's syndrome 112
drama 199
drawing 243
drowning 325
dummies 126
dynamic tripod grip 230
dyslexia 6, 112, 164, 181, 184

E

ear infection 313
Early Help Assessment (EHA) 49, 179–80
early intervention 21

Early Learning Goals 16, 139, 141, 214, 223
early years educator 10–11
Early Years Foundation Stage (EYFS)
 background 16
 communication and language 17, 250
 Early Learning Goals 16, 139, 141, 214, 223–4
 effective learning and teaching 17–18, 222
 expressive arts and design 17
 goals and assessment 16–17, 139, 141, 148–9, 223–5
 guiding principles 221
 individual needs of child 144, 148, 167, 221
 key person 14, 45, 64, 87, 114, 118, 148
 learning journal 139, 148
 links to National Curriculum 226–7
 literacy 17, 223, 228–31
 mathematics 17, 223, 231–4
 parental involvement 113
 personal, social and emotional development (PSED) 17, 48, 250
 physical development 17, 223, 250
 prime areas 17, 222
 progress check (age two) 17, 174, 178, 224
 Safeguarding and Welfare Requirements 45
 scope of 16
 specific areas 17, 222
 understanding the world 17, 250
Early Years Foundation Stage Profile (EYFSP) 16, 141, 224
early years practitioner 10, 148–9
Early Years Register 3
eating disorders 188
ecological systems theory 32–3
eczema 298
education
 compulsory 8–9
 funding 155–6
 legislation and regulation 2, 8–10
 occupational roles 10–14
 pedagogical approaches 23–34
 post-16 provision 7, 19, 175–6
 selective 155
 see also Early Years Foundation Stage (EYFS); National Curriculum; school
education, health and care plan (EHCP) 6, 44, 95, 98, 174–5, 179–80, 338
Education Act 1944 8

Education Act 1996 2
educational psychologist 13, 95, 180
educational reform 154–5
educational visits coordinator (EVC) 209
Education and Skills Act 2008 9
education mental health practitioner 95
Education Reform Act 1988 9, 154–5
egocentric speech 123
egocentrism 26
Elementary Education Act 1870 8
emergencies 316, 323–4, 329
 see also accidents
Emerson, P. 116–17
emotional abuse 51, 283–4
emotional development 60, 66, 104, 109–11, 184, 219, 275
emotional health 47–8, 74
emotional intelligence 106
empathy 22, 59
employer-set project 343–7
enabling language 190
encouragement 203–4
energy levels 301
engaging children 20–3
English, National Curriculum 18
English as an additional language (EAL) 39, 87–8, 194–200
English Baccalaureate (EBacc) 19
enquiry-based learning 28
environment
 and behaviour 62–4, 69, 76
 and development 113, 126–7, 259
 at home 84
 language-rich 199–200, 233, 259
 and learning 40
 for outdoor learning 250–1
 and risk of abuse 52
epilepsy 182, 188, 298
equality 163–7, 177, 226, 245
Equality Act 2010 99, 163, 167, 177, 183, 226
equity 181
esteem see self-esteem
event/time samples 145
exam stress 157–8
exercise 75
existential self 65
experiential learning 34
experiential learning theory (ELT) 28, 153
expressive language 120–2
extended families 85, 334
eye contact 70

F

facial expression 20, 261
falls 325
families
  breakdown 134
  circumstances 62, 68, 132, 167, 170
  culture 68, 167, 197, 200, 262, 308–9, 335
  home communication 88
  home visits 88
  peer relationships 63
  rights of 93, 163, 333
  support for 68, 88–9, 93–7
  support from 40, 49, 79, 84
  types of 85–6, 334
  see also parents
Family Action 93
family hubs 97
Family Rights Group 93
farm visits 250–1
fats 304, 306–7
favouritism 55
feedback 21, 35–6, 73, 146, 158–9
female genital mutilation (FGM) 43–4, 46
Female Genital Mutilation Act 2003 43
film clip observations 270
fine motor skills 60, 105, 108–9, 186, 223, 229–30
fire hazards 208
fire safety 323, 329–30
first aid 316
flipped learning 28, 29
floods 324
flu 314, 322
foam play 244
focused reflection 279
food see diet; mealtimes; nutrition
food allergies 307
food hygiene 320
food intolerances 307–8
food poisoning 313, 316
food safety 208
formal operations stage of development 27, 123
formative assessment 138–40, 178, 206, 276
formative feedback 35, 73
foster families 86
foundation schools 5
Fragile X syndrome 188–9
free schools 156
Freire, P 32

friendships 66, 83, 129–31, 257, 287
further education (FE) colleges 7, 155–6

G

games 232, 242
  and impulse control 74
gamification 31
gastroenteritis 313
GCSEs (General Certificate of Secondary Education) 9, 19, 142, 156–7
gender 260–1
gender transition 131
General Data Protection Regulations (GDPR) 2018 44, 46, 99, 147, 165
general practitioner (GP) 96, 180, 337
geography 17, 18
German measles 315
gestures 71, 261
Gibbs, G. 153
Gibbs' reflective cycle 153
gluten 308
goal setting 263
graduated approach 174
grammar schools 155
grooming 53–5
gross motor skills 60, 105, 108–9, 186, 223
group assessments 143, 271
guided reading 228

H

hair care 296–7, 299
hand, foot and mouth disease 313
handwashing 296, 299, 317–18
Hart, B. 29
hazardous substances 324
hazards 208–9, 327–8
head lice 296–7, 313
head teacher 12
Health and Safety at Work Act 1974 43
Health and Safety Executive 207
health and safety policy 44–5, 326
health and wellbeing 38, 95–7, 285–8
  anxiety 78, 132, 135
  emotional health 47–8, 74, 100
  exam stress 157–8
  mental health 47, 57, 96, 130, 168, 169, 188, 300, 335–6
  in need children 49, 287
  recurring problems 287
  supporting 48–9, 287

healthcare centres 89
health visitor 17, 96, 98, 178, 224, 337
hearing induction loop 181, 190
heel prick test 188
helicopter parenting style 86
heuristic play 240–1, 244, 247
hierarchy of needs 33–4
high blood pressure 310
higher education institutions (HEIs) 7–8, 10, 155–6
higher level teaching assistant (HLTA) 11
HighScope approach 27, 273
history, National Curriculum 18
holistic
  care 2, 4, 96
  development 104, 184, 219, 285
  learning 31–2
holophrases 125
home environment 84
homeschooling 2
home visits 88
hopscotch 242
house points 72
humanism 31–4
hunger 63, 80, 309
hydration 288–90, 292, 306

I

ideal self 65
illness 132, 187–9, 297–8, 312–22
imaginative play 237–9, 243, 246
immersive learning 31
immunisation 321–2
impetigo 313–14, 322
impulse control 66, 74, 184
incentive and recognition systems 71–2
inclusion policy 165–6
inclusive practice 166–8, 169–71, 177, 181, 226, 245
independence 285, 300
  see also self-care skills
independent schools 2, 6, 156
indirect discrimination 164
influenza 314, 322
informal learning 31
information
  recording 146–7
  sharing 36–7, 68, 85, 133, 147, 165–6, 181, 291
  storing 44
information and communications technology (ICT) 157

in-group/out-group 129–30
inspections 16
  see also Ofsted (Office for Standards in Education)
instinctive parenting style 86
Institute for Apprenticeships and Technical Education 7
integration 181
interfamilial abuse 54
internal working model 114
International Baccalaureate 7, 157
International GCSEs (iGCSEs) 142, 156–7
interventions 21, 48–9, 147

J

job roles 10–14
junk modelling 243

K

Keeping Children Safe in Education 2019 50
Keogh, R. 154
key instant recall facts (KIRF) approach 25
key person 14, 45, 64, 87, 114, 118, 148
Kolb, D.A. 28, 153
Kolb's experiential learning cycle 28, 153

L

labelling 168, 182
language, definition 215
language acquisition device (LAD) 122
language acquisition support system (LASS) 123
language development 29, 38, 104–5, 120–8, 184, 186–7, 213–14, 217–18, 259, 275
  see also speech development
language-rich environments 199–200, 233, 259
languages, National Curriculum 18
Lave, J. 31
leadership 49
learning
  barriers to 189–90
  blended 157
  characteristics of 227
  environment 40
  factors affecting 38–9
  holistic 31–2
  home environment 84

informal 31
metacognition 34–5
from mistakes 35, 79
online 37–8
outdoors 249–51
and play 29, 227, 232–3
policy 178
role of adult 29–30, 190, 232–3
student-centred 32
see also teaching
learning journal 139, 148, 268–9
lecturer 12
lesson planning 21, 37
LGBT (lesbian, gay, bisexual or transgender) 85
literacy 214
  Early Years Foundation Stage (EYFS) 17, 223, 228–31
  reading 39
  synthetic phonics 40
  writing 39–40
Little Albert 23, 25
local authority designated officer (LADO) 00
local education authorities (LEAs) 95
Local Safeguarding Partnerships 43
logic 186
lone-parent families see single-parent families
looked after children 49–50, 95, 338
loose part play 241, 247

M

macronutrients 303
maintained settings 2, 4–6, 156
Malaguzzi, L. 32
malnourishment 303
manufacturers' instructions 245
marbles in a jar 72
mark making 229–30, 272
  see also writing
Maslow, A. 33–4, 288
massively open online courses (MOOCS) 31
mastery learning 25
maternal deprivation 114
mathematics 39–40, 187
  Early Years Foundation Stage (EYFS) 17, 223, 231–4
  mathematical development 214, 234
  National Curriculum 18
  resources 233
maturity 60
mealtimes 288–92, 299
measles 314–15, 322

media, and self-concept 262
medical model of disability 183
medical needs 177–8, 297–8, 308
  see also illness
medicines 297–8
memory 185–6, 301
meningitis 314
mental health 47–8, 57, 96, 130, 168, 169, 188, 300, 335–6
Mental Health Foundation Association 13
mental health lead 13
mentors 13, 150–1
metacognition 34–5
micronutrients 304
mindfulness 75
minerals 304
missing child 323
mistakes, learning from 35, 79
modelling 28
  see also role model
monotropy 114
mood 184
motivation 24, 39, 105, 135
motor control 185
motor skills 60, 105, 108–9, 186, 223, 229–30
moving house 132
mud kitchen 244
multi-academy trusts (MATs) 6
multi-agency teams 180–1
multi-lingualism 00
multidisciplinary teams 94
mumps 314, 322
muscular dystrophy 188
music, National Curriculum 18

N

nannies 3–4, 11
nappy changing 293–4, 299
naps 293
  see also sleep
narrative observation 267
National Curriculum 9, 16, 18, 48
  core subjects 18–19, 155
  English Baccalaureate (EBacc) 19
  foundation subjects 18
  inclusive 169–70
  Key Stage 1 18–19, 141, 156, 225–7
  Key Stage 2 18–19, 141–2
  Key Stage 3 18–19, 142
  Key Stage 4 18–19, 142
  reforms 154–5
  SATs (Statutory Assessment Tests) 18, 141–2, 156, 225

Index

see also assessment
negative reinforcement 24
neglect 284
neurodevelopmental disabilities 185
neurological disabilities 185
new baby, arrival of 77, 132, 134
NHS (National Health Service) 89, 94
nodes 30
noise 63–4, 181
non-verbal communication 69–71, 203
norovirus 313
notifiable diseases 312, 322
NSPCC (National Society for the Prevention of Cruelty to Children) 93
nuclear families 85, 334
number bonds 223
numeracy 234
  see also mathematics
nursery provision 4
nursery rhymes 218, 228
nurses 96, 98, 180
Nutbrown, C. 29
nutrition 288–92, 303–6

O

obesity 310
object permanence 26
observation 21, 139, 142, 145–6, 148, 206, 267–71
observation, assessment and planning cycle 267
occupational roles 10–14
occupational therapist 96–7, 98
Ofqual (Office of Qualifications and Examinations Regulation) 9, 137
Ofsted (Office for Standards in Education) 2, 9, 16, 155
online learning 37–8
onlooker play 235
open days/evenings 88
open-door policy 87
open questions 139
operant conditioning 23–4
oracy 216
oral health *see* teeth
outdoor learning 249–51
outdoor play 113, 245, 297
overheating 302

P

painting 243
palmar grip 230
parallel play 110, 235
paramountcy principle 282
parent governors 85
parents
  absent 115
  education of parent 335
  expectations of 68, 82
  factors influencing 334–5
  guilt and blame 168
  home communication 88
  involving 84–5
  and language development 126–7
  parenting styles 86, 334
  responsibilities of 333
  rights of 93, 163, 333
  support for 68, 88–9, 93–7
  support from 40, 49, 79, 84, 113, 230, 233, 259
  volunteering 84–5
  working with 82–5, 86–9, 118, 133, 143, 190, 200, 271, 333–9
  see also families
parent teacher associations (PTAs) 85
Parten, M. 129, 235
participation, barriers to 169–71, 189–90
partnership working 98–102, 166, 271–2, 333–9
pastoral support 13
patience 22
Pavlov, I. 23, 25
peer assessment 140
peer relationships 63
perception 186
permissive parenting style 86, 334
personal, social and emotional development (PSED) 17, 48, 250
Personal, Social and Health Education (PSHE) 48
personal hygiene 294–6, 298–301, 317–19
personality 112, 195, 259
personal protective equipment (PPE) 208–9, 318
personal safety 208
phonics screening 225
physical abuse 51, 283
physical activity and nutrition coordinator (PANCo) 13
physical development 17, 60, 105, 108–9, 185, 219, 223, 250, 275
physical education (PE) 18
physical exercise 75
physical play 236, 246
physiotherapist 98
Piaget, J. 25–7, 123
picture exchange communication systems (PECS) 191–2
planning 265–7, 272–4
  child-led 144, 273
  cycle 143–5, 267
  feedback 146
  lessons 21, 37
  long-term 144, 272–3
  medium-term 143–4, 273
  plan, do, review 273
  schemes of work 144
  short-term 143–4, 273–4
planning, learning and assessment cycle 143–5
play
  activities 242–4
  adult-led 247–9
  age-appropriate 245
  child-initiated 247–9
  creative 236–7, 242–3, 246
  and development 236–41
  heuristic 240, 244, 247
  imaginative 237–9, 243, 246
  importance of 234
  and impulse control 74
  and learning 29, 227, 232–3
  outdoor 113, 245, 297
  parallel 110, 235
  physical 236, 246
  resources and equipment 245–7
  sensory 239, 244, 246
  sharing toys 61
  and stage of development 61
  stages of 234–5
  types of 235
pointing 71
poisoning 325
  see also food poisoning
pornography 54
position of trust 53
positive reinforcement 24, 74
positivity 22
post-16 provision 7, 19, 175–6
posture 20
power, of adult 53
praise 73, 79, 204, 262
prejudice 163
preoperational stage of development 26, 123
pre-release activity 342–3
pre-schools 4–5
Prevent Duty Guidance 2015 44, 46
primary carers 82
  see also families; parents
primary disability 184–5
privacy 100, 300
private settings 2, 4, 6, 156
privation 116

problem solving 75, 78, 105
professional behaviour 22–3
progress check (age two) 17, 174, 178, 224
  see also assessment
project-based learning 27
protected characteristics 164
protein 304
proximity 20, 70
puberty 60, 109, 131
puddings 292
punctuality 21
punishment 24
puppet play 243

Q

qualifications
  GCSEs 9, 19, 142
  International Baccalaureate 7
  legislation and regulation 9–10
  A-levels 7, 9
  vocational 19
qualified teacher status (QTS) 12
questioning 139, 143, 204

R

reading 39, 186, 228–9
  synthetic phonics 40
reading journals 228–9
reasonable adjustments 178–9, 181
reasoning 186
Reception Baseline Assessment (RBA) 16, 141, 149, 156, 178
receptive language 102, 120–2
referrals 49, 99–100, 133
reflection 22, 28, 79, 279
  models of 153–4
reflective observation 153
Reggio Emilia 32
regression 77, 135, 275
reinforcement 24, 74, 79
relationships and sex education (RSE) 19
religion, and diet 308
religious education 19, 250
research 342
resilience 47–8, 76, 130, 285, 300
resourcefulness 22
respect 22, 48, 86, 100, 167, 182, 190
responsibility, and self-concept 79
rest 286, 293, 299, 300–2
reward systems 79
rhymes 232
  see also nursery rhymes

rights
  of children 163–9, 181, 333
  of families 93, 163, 333
risk 207
  and resilience 76
risk assessment 45, 80, 207–10, 245, 326–8
Risley, T. 29
rocking 78
Rogers, C. 34
role model 28, 53, 68, 74–5, 126, 166, 203–4, 292
role play 199, 228, 237, 243
room leader 11
routine 63, 73, 231, 257
rubella 315, 322
running recording 267
Rutter, M. 116

S

safeguarding
  actions to take 56, 283
  definition 43
  early intervention 282
  EYFS Safeguarding and Welfare Requirements 45
  grooming 53–5
  guidance 46–7
  inappropriate relationships 55–6
  legislation and regulation 43–4, 224–5
  in need children 49–50, 287
  paramountcy principle 282
  policy 50–1
  reporting requirements 50–1, 56, 283
  at risk children 49–52, 283, 337
  see also abuse
safeguarding officer 50
Safeguarding Vulnerable Groups Act 2006 44
safety needs 287
  see also safeguarding
salt 306–7
Sams, A. 29
sand play 244
SATs (Statutory Assessment Tests) 18, 141–2, 156, 225
Save the Children 93
scabies 315, 322
scaffolding 28, 199, 233
scalds 325
scarlet fever 315, 322
Schaffer, R. 116–17
schemas 26, 29
schemes of work 144

school
  alternative provision 174, 177
  homeschooling 2, 6
  inspections 16
  maintained 5–6
  non-maintained 6
  pre-schools 4–5
  private 6
  provision 5–6, 8–9
  readiness for 104–5, 133
  sixth forms 7
  starting 83, 131, 134
  see also education
school nurse 96, 98
science, National Curriculum 18
scribe 181
seasons 251
secure attachment 119, 254
security hazards 46, 208, 323
seizures 182, 188, 298
selective education 155
self-actualisation 32, 34, 288
self-agency 234
self-assessment 21, 140
self-awareness 65
self-care skills 105, 179, 263, 298–300
self-concept 64–6, 76, 79, 130, 234, 260–2
self-definition 65
self-efficacy 105, 234, 262–3, 300
self-esteem 57, 62, 64–5, 104, 130–1, 182
self-harm 78
self-reflection 79
self-regulation 63, 66, 74–5, 78, 256–7
self-soothing 78
Selman, R. 129
SEND see special educational needs and disabilities (SEND)
SENDCo see special educational needs and disabilities coordinator (SENDCo)
SENDIASS 89
sensorimotor stage of development 26, 123
sensory perception 106
sensory play 239, 244, 246
sensory processing 181, 185–6
separation anxiety 78, 114, 118
settings 5–6
  see also individual setting type by name
settling-in policies 133
sewing 242
sexual abuse 51, 54, 284
sexually transmitted diseases (STDs) 284

Index

Sexual Offences (Amendment) Act 2000 53
shadowing 279
sharing information 36–7, 68, 85, 133, 147, 165–6, 180, 291
sharing toys 61
siblings, and language development 127
sickle cell disease 189, 298
Siemens, G. 30–1
single-parent families 85, 334, 336
sixth form 7
skin care 296, 299
Skinner, B.F. 23–4, 25, 124
slapped cheek syndrome 315
sleep 286, 293, 299, 300–2
  safety 302
slime play 244
small world play 238, 243
smoking 302
snapshot observations 145–6, 267–8
social constructivism 25, 28, 30
social development 59, 66, 75, 104, 109–11, 184, 219, 275
social identity theory 129–30
socialisation 75
social media 37, 101
social mobility 155
social model of disability 183
social networking 31
social norms 59, 66
social referencing 117
social skills 130
social worker 13, 337–8
socio-economic factors 39, 57, 113, 170, 262, 334–5
sociograms 270
solitary play 235
songs 228
sound blending 223
special educational needs and disabilities (SEND)
  accessibility 88, 169, 177, 190
  aids and adaptations 40
  chronic health conditions 187–9
  Code of Practice 44, 95, 164–5, 173–9
  and development 112
  differentiation 11
  emotional development 60
  friendships 131
  graduated approach 174
  impact of 38
  inclusion 181
  integration 181
  labelling 168, 182

Local Offer 173, 176
  models of disability 183
  multi-agency teams 180, 190, 337
  policy 176–7
  quality of support 158
  reasonable adjustments 178–9, 181
  social development 59
  statutory duties 174–6
  supporting 158, 180
  technology 37
  terminology 182
  working with families 87
  see also education, health and care plan (EHCP)
special educational needs and disabilities coordinator (SENDCo) 12, 96, 174, 338
special educational provision (SEP) 6
speech and language therapist 97, 98, 100
speech development 215–17
  see also augmentative and alternative communication (AAC); language development
spillages 318
spiral curriculum 29
stability 68
staff development 48
staff-to-child ratios 45, 326
stammering 217
star charts 71–2
static tripod grip 230
statutory settings see maintained settings
stepfamilies 86
stereotyping 182
sterilisation 319–20
stigma 168
stimulus 23
Stirling Children's Wellbeing Scale 48–9
stories 218, 228, 232
'Strange Situation' experiment 115
strangulation 324
stress 63, 135, 157–8, 335–6
student-centred learning 32
sudden infant death syndrome (SIDS) 302
suffocation 324
sugar 306–7
summative assessment 138, 141–2, 143, 206, 276–7
sustained shared thinking 28, 204
synoptic assessment 347
synthetic phonics 40, 229

T

tailored intervention 21
Tajfel, H. 129–30
teacher, role of 12, 180
  see also adult role
teaching
  effective 17–18, 222
  policy 178
  quality of 39
  scaffolding 28, 199, 233
  see also assessment; education; learning
teaching assistant 11
Team Around the Child (TAC) 97, 333, 337
technology 30, 37–8, 157, 191
teeth 299, 310–12
temperament 112
terminology 182
tertiary colleges 7
thinking
  Bruner's modes of 27–8
  in children 25–6, 27–8
  critical 32
  see also cognitive development
thumb sucking 78
time management 21
tiredness 63, 80, 286, 293, 301, 309, 326
toileting 294–5, 299
tonsillitis 315
Tourette's syndrome 184
toys 245
traineeships 19
transitions 64, 69, 82–4, 131–5, 254–5
translators 88
trauma 338
traveller children 168
treasure basket play 240, 247
trust schools 5
Turner, J. 129–30

U

undernourishment 303
uninvolved parenting style 86
United Nations Convention on the Rights of the Child (UNCRC) 1989 33, 163, 165–6, 333
universities 7–8
unoccupied play 235

V

vaccines 321–2

verbal communication 69–70, 203
viral infections 315
virtual reality (VR) 27
visual processing 186
visual processing disorders (VPDs) 186
vitamins 304, 307
vocational qualifications 19
voice output communication aids (VOCAs) 192
voluntary aided schools 5
voluntary controlled schools 5
voluntary organisations 93
voluntary settings 2
vomiting 313, 322
Vygotsky, L. 30, 123–4, 233

W

Walker, D. 154
Warwick-Edinburgh Mental Wellbeing Scale 49
waste disposal 318–19
water play 244
Watson, J.B. 23, 25
weaning 289–91
weather 245, 251, 324
Wenger, E. 31
whistleblowing 51
whooping cough 315, 322
withdrawal 77
writing 39–40, 104, 186, 228, 230–1

Y

youth worker 96

Z

zone of proximal development 30